In the Arena

Arena

AN AUTOBIOGRAPHY

Charlton Heston

In the Arena

AN AUTOBIOGRAPHY

BOULEVARD BOOKS
NEW YORK

IN THE ARENA: AN AUTOBIOGRAPHY

A Boulevard Book / published by arrangement with Simon & Schuster, Inc.

PRINTING HISTORY
Simon & Schuster edition published 1995
Boulevard trade paperback edition / June 1997

The Putnam Berkley World Wide Web site address is
http://www.berkley.com

ISBN: 1-57297-267-X

BOULEVARD
Boulevard Books are published by The Berkley Publishing Group,
200 Madison Avenue, New York, New York 10016.
BOULEVARD and its logo are trademarks
belonging to Berkley Publishing Corporation.

PRINTED IN THE UNITED STATES OF AMERICA

10   9   8   7   6   5   4   3   2   1

I offer this book to those at the center of my life: Lydia, Holly and Carlton, Fraser and Marilyn . . . and my grandson Jack, who perhaps will read it for himself in a few years.

Jack Alexander Clarke Heston, looking ahead.

Contents

Acknowledgments

HOW MANY PEOPLE make a book? Michael Korda planted the seed when he published my last one: "Then we get first crack when you decide to write your autobiography." Chuck Adams, whose benign editorial hand urged me on, and Virginia Clark, who saved me from egregious errors of spelling and syntax. I think most crucial of all, though, was my assistant, Carol Lanning, who, in addition to all the faxing, FedEx and phone calls, encapsulated my writing time in the midst of my acting . . . in essence, running my working life.

In addition, of course, there are the friends, blood kin, and colleagues who have shared it all. Thanks . . . every one of you.

It is not the critic who counts, not the man who points out where the strong stumbled, or how the doer could have done better. The credit belongs to the man who is in the arena, his face marred by dust and sweat and blood, who strives valiantly, who errs and falls short again and again: there is no effort without error.

But he who tries, who knows the great enthusiasms, the great devotions, who spends himself in a worthy cause, at best knows the triumph of achievement, and at the worst, fails while daring. His place shall never be with those cold and timid souls who know neither victory nor defeat.

—Theodore Roosevelt

1

In the Beginning

In the beginning . . . the earth was without form, and void.
The darkness was over all.

— Genesis 1:1–2

NO, WE'RE NOT GOING BACK *that* far. I just mean *my* beginning.
That's how it starts for all of us, isn't it?

My first recollection is digging in the sandy Michigan earth
with a red toy shovel. It must've been early spring, because only a
few inches down the ground was still frozen. My first frustration. I
was three . . . perhaps only two? I also remember picking up kindling for the kitchen stove from the backyard, and feeling the sharp
edges of the split quarters of pine against my arms, though I was
surely too young then to have chopped them, as I did later. I can
remember my mother's large mirror, which she'd sometimes take
off the wall and lay on her bed, so I could roll marbles around
on it. My true pleasure in that game, though, was the reflection of
the room in the mirror, upside down and mysterious, like Lewis
Carroll's *Through the Looking Glass*.

I wasn't born in Michigan, but in No Man's Land. No, I don't
intend a metaphysical profundity. That was the real name of an
unincorporated bit of Chicago's northern suburbs where my parents, Russell Whitford Carter and Lilla Charlton, were living in a tiny
house on the shore of Lake Michigan on land that's doubtless now
worth forty or fifty thousand dollars a front foot.

13

Please understand, I don't remember this part of my life; my mother told me about it when we left Michigan after she and my father were divorced and we moved back to Chicago's North Shore. The house, really a cottage, was still there then. It's long since been replaced by a twelve-story condominium.

Like all of us, I'm an inadequate witness to my own infancy. My father having died a generation ago, the only qualified informant available is my mother. She's not far from a hundred years old now, she being the only one alive who knows how far. As she's been all the years of my life, my mother's a woman of indomitable courage and wide interests, with very firm opinions on many, many subjects.

A couple of years ago, she phoned me. "Charlton," she began. (My mother has always called me Charlton.) "I need to see you."

"Wonderful, Mother," I said. "Let me get you a plane reservation; come for a visit." No, that wouldn't do, she said firmly. She needed to talk to me in person, as soon as possible. This began to sound ominous. Was she perhaps seriously ill? Had she decided to sell her house? What could she not discuss on the phone?

As it happened, Lydia and I were due to overnight in New York the next week, where I was speaking at a banquet. I was due back on the Coast the next day, but we could easily stop for a couple of hours in Chicago on the way. That suited my mother best, she said.

The car met us at O'Hare and delivered us to her Wilmette home. She greeted us warmly, served us tea, and then said to me, "It has come to my attention that you have signed a contract with a publisher to write your autobiography. Since you have not discussed this with me, I can only conclude that you think I will not like it."

"On the contrary, Mother," I said. "I hope you *will* like it. I hope everyone will. I'm sorry you've decided you won't before I've written a word." That was all I said for the next hour.

In civilized but impassioned tones, my mother outlined in vivid detail the failure of her marriage to my father, her contempt for him and his father, and her heartfelt gratitude and love for my stepfather, who, she said, had rescued us all from a life of exile in the Michigan woods.

Over the half century since my parents had divorced, I'd already heard a good deal of what she told me that afternoon. Still, I didn't argue with her, or even try to stem the flow of her words, though given my own memories of my father, they were painful. I simply sat, listening. (Lydia said afterward I never moved a muscle the whole time.)

When she'd at last finished, I said, "Mother, what you've told me is part of *your* life. The only life I have even a chance of capturing on paper is my own. That's what I have to try to do. You surely know I have no thought of hurting you." That did not content her, I think, but she let it stand. We've not discussed this book since.

My mother has now lived through almost all of what's surely a significant century for America. It includes a technological revolution unimaginable at her birth; the Great Depression; two major wars and several small ones, often attended by one or another of her male relatives, a couple of them killed in the process. Both of her husbands died relatively young, as did two of her three children, both younger than I. Her only sister's gone now, too. For four-score years and more, they shared ocean-deep, almost telepathic ties. Of my mother's womb blood, only I survive—and she.

I think of my mother as a heroine from a Brontë novel— *Wuthering Heights* or *Jane Eyre*. I cherish a photograph of her holding me when I was about five months old. We're in a bleak, wintery woodland—there's no snow, but the trees are bare. She's wearing a full, heavy cloak with a deep cape collar. She holds me close against her cheek, an amorphous baby face in a wool cap. Her hair is black and full, in slight disarray, her eyes glowing with fierce defiance, unafraid. I'd know her anywhere.

While I have no early memories of Chicago, my mother's heart is rooted in that city. She was born there, of Scots/English stock who came to America through Canada. The Scots line is Clan Fraser of Inverness. The title and the lands were the gift of William the Conqueror as part of the spoils of his conquest of England in 1066 to one of his Norman captains, making him a baron in the bargain. The Normans were of course Norsemen, like the Vikings who had been raiding and raping along the Scottish coast for some centuries, thus accounting for the preponderance of tall, blond, blue-eyed males in our family—a blood strain I'm very proud of.

The clan motto is in ancient Norman French: *Je suis prest*—"I am ready"—a good motto for an actor (or a medieval Scots chieftain, for that matter).

(Scots tend to thrive in any climate, century, or circumstance, but the Fraser best known to history was Simon, the Twelfth Baron. After the bloody Scottish defeat supporting Bonnie Prince Charlie at the battle of Culloden in 1745, he avoided capture by the English so cleverly and so often that he earned the nickname "Simon the Fox." Snared at last, he was thrown in the Tower of London and condemned to death as a traitor. On his way to the block, a woman in the jeering crowd taunted him, "They'll cut yer ugly head off now, ye filthy Scots dog!"

"Aye, so they wull, ye bluddy English bitch," he retorted equably. And so they did. He was the last nobleman executed in Britain, and the last man beheaded in that country. Dubious distinctions, but there they are. We take our family memories where we find them.)

My mother seldom speaks of her father, who was a professional gambler. He divorced (or was divorced by) her mother and seems to have disappeared from family annals, at which point my grandmother took her two little girls home to her father. His name was James Charlton; I think he was the strongest male influence in my mother's life.

His photographs show a powerful, impressively bearded face that had the look of a man who understood his own life. He was a senior railway executive, more than moderately affluent. I guess he had to be. He lived in a large house, with a library of considerable distinction, where he maintained a household composed entirely of women.

As well as my grandmother and her two daughters, who were small girls at the time, and several servants, there were my great-grandmother and at least two of her other daughters, who were unmarried. Oddly, my great-grandfather also became my grandfather, many years before my birth. He adopted my mother and my aunt when he took them into his home, perhaps simply to give them a father. (These things counted then.)

Though he undertook responsibility for all of his female blood kin, it's clear that the center of his own life was his wife, an invalid who spent most of her day in her rooms, in the company of a female companion—which made nine women in the house.

When James Charlton came home from his office each evening, he'd hold the tip of his stick against the doorbell until someone answered it, then go directly upstairs to see his wife. He'd visit with her for an hour, consuming two ounces of single-malt scotch and water, then, if she was feeling well, he'd bring her down to dinner with the rest of his extended family. On such occasions, my mother often had the pleasant chore of carrying her grandmother's train.

Almost a century later, it's hard to flesh out the image of James Charlton beyond the easy take of him as a turn-of-the-century patriarch. Modern political correctness would demand that his generosity to the women who lived on his bounty be dismissed as the largess of a sexist tyrant, though there's no evidence of this. My mother has often pointed out that, though her grandfather supervised every detail of his household affairs with the same close attention he gave to his railroad, whatever his wife wanted done in the house was carried out without question or delay.

James Charlton spent only an hour or two a day in his wife's company. When she died, he supervised every detail of her funeral, presiding in sober courtesy at the reception in his home afterward, which was attended by many guests. When they'd left, he went upstairs to his own bedroom, got into bed, and was dead three days later. Clearly, his wife meant a great deal more to him than we might have imagined.

James Charlton left the many women dependent on him well provided for, though his considerable fortune was much diminished within a generation. My grandmother's elder sister seems to have become the head of the family. My grandmother married again, and produced a son, killed in the Anzio landing in World War II. My mother and her sister, May, went to good schools, traveled to Europe, and, at some point, my mother met my father.

Their marriage, which can't have lasted more than a dozen years or so, is to this day such a source of pain and bitter regret to my mother that it's difficult for her to discuss it with any degree of calm, though it produced her two eldest children. It's painful to me to distress her, so we avoid the subject.

It's possible that they met while my father, Russell, was going through boot training at the Great Lakes Naval Training Center north of Chicago before serving in the Mediterranean in World War I. I doubt this, though. My mother would still have been a teenager; her background makes it unlikely that she'd meet a sailor on liberty. I think they met a year or two earlier in Michigan, in the hamlet of St. Helen. Certainly my mother and her sister, May, spent some summers there, probably before America entered the war. I believe that's where my parents met.

My father was a good-looking man of immense charm, with a rich bass voice. (The latter was perhaps his most useful bequest to me—it's gotten me a lot of parts.) He was the second son of John Carter, who'd been a pit boy in a Yorkshire coal mine at the age of seven, then somehow made his way to America and a measure of success. Like most men who've succeeded on their own, he was a firm conservative. But at the height of World War II, when President Roosevelt threatened to jail John L. Lewis, the radical leader of the United Mine Workers Union, for striking the miners in wartime, my grandfather said in an interview, "You can't pay a man too much money to dig coal."

I remember him only as a somewhat portly man with a house on top of a hill and a gold chiming watch he'd let me listen to. I'd like to have known him as a young man, when he seems to have roamed around the country, starting a family in San Diego, where my father was born, and a magazine in St. Louis, *Carter's Weekly,* which later became *Redbook.*

What brought him to Michigan around the turn of the century was opportunity, though how he perceived it I can't imagine. He had somehow discovered that the County of Roscommon was about to dissolve as a governing entity of the state because the Stevens Lumber Company, having logged the northern half of Michigan, had no further use for the land and planned to abandon it to avoid further tax liability. John Carter offered to put the county back on the tax rolls in return for title to half its land. I gather he was often hard-pressed to meet this obligation (perhaps that was why he sold his magazine), but he managed to bring it off, nonetheless.

All my early memories, to my mother's intense annoyance, are of the Michigan woods. There were still a few groves of virgin timber untouched by the loggers—great mossy cathedrals of

hundred-foot pines blocking the sun, denying any undergrowth on
the flat forest floor. In the decades since the timber operations had
shut down, the second-growth trees had proliferated, too; not only
the dominant white pine but a range of smaller evergreen, birches,
maples, some oak, as well as all sorts of wild fruit trees, berries,
and ferns that have no chance of sustenance in a virgin forest. It
was wonderful country for a boy.

Wild game was plentiful, of course, as it still is, though the
larger predators had disappeared by then, migrated north over the
Mackinac Straits to Canada. I never saw a moose there, or a timber
wolf, though there were a few black bear, and occasional wolver-
ines. It was the edible game that concerned people who lived in St.
Helen—white-tailed deer, principally; also partridge and duck
when they flew south in the fall along the great flyway from Canada.
Rabbit was always available, and perfectly tasty. Deer was the most
desirable game, of course; if hung properly, venison is delicious,
and a good-sized buck will provide a lot of meat.

Aside from my mother, just about all the adults in the settle-
ment hunted, and all the boys over nine or so. There were generous
limits on most game except deer. The yearly license allowed the
taking of one buck per hunter, a limit generally respected, though
certainly no one in the county ever went hungry for want of venison.

There was no hunting in the summer, but there were three
lakes within a mile or so of my house, with plenty of good pan fish
—bullheads, bluegills, sunfish, northern pike, a few bass.

You could fish in the winter, too, which I enjoyed a lot more.
By the end of November, usually, the ice on the lakes was thick
enough to drive a truck on, towing a fishing shanty behind on
runners. They were sturdy little structures, about six feet by six,
with room inside for a stove and plain benches around a square
hole cut in the floor. Under that, a hole was cut in the ice. With the
stove going and the door shut, it was comfortable even at ten and
twenty below zero, as it often is in Michigan in the winter.

We fished with a spear, some six feet long, with three sharp
tines—like Neptune's trident. The bait was a handmade wooden
fish about eight inches long, weighted with lead and suspended
from fish line fixed to the roof over the hole.

Like most fishing, it was a very sedentary sport, but there

was a certain cozy, contemplative comfort, especially for small boys, sitting there in the warm dark with the men, the wind hissing over the ice outside. The water beneath your knees was green, translucent. You swam your little wooden fish in lazy eights till the dark shape of a pike drifted into range to inspect your bait. Then you speared him (more easily than you might imagine), yanked him up, and tossed him out the door on the ice, where he froze in a minute or two.

Hunting is a solitary occupation, unless you count the crowds of city guys who crash around in the woods together in deer season, drinking beer and scaring off all the game. When I was a boy, we hunted for the pot, usually alone. Partridge was the most reliable game, plentiful in the Michigan woods. They're not much smaller than a chicken, though a good deal harder to hit. In fact, I found them all but impossible. A covey of partridge exploding out of the brush five yards ahead of you is a startling experience. The first few times I tried it, in my dad's company, I was seriously over-gunned, using a borrowed .20 gauge with a stock too long for me. To this day, I am an inadequate wing shot. (In vast areas of this country, that's a serious character flaw. The appropriate, modest appraisal of a neighbor is "Yeah, he can shoot a little.")

I did contribute my deer to our table before we left Michigan, but most of my hunting was with a .22 rifle, after rabbits. If you know anything about guns, rabbits, or boys, you know the rabbits were not in much danger, though eventually I managed to bring home a meager bag for the pot.

In addition to marksmanship and the ability to read cover and move through it quietly, hunting requires patience and concentration. Life has lent me these qualities since, but I lacked them as a boy. It's then that the firm hunter's discipline wavers a bit. Often I found it more interesting to stop being a little kid with a cold hunting rabbits with a single-shot .22 and become Davy Crockett hunting renegade Comanche with a long rifle. I did that a lot.

Pretending to be other people. All kids play such games, of course, but I did it more than most, I think. The books my parents read to me, later those I read myself, gave me wonderful people to be: Tom Sawyer and Injun Joe and Jim Hawkins and Long John Silver, Huck Finn and Nigger Jim, plus all the larger animals in

Ernest Thompson Seton's *Lives of the Hunted*. I crowded the woods with them all, mostly by myself.

I went to school too, of course. It was a one-room frame building with a bell in a squat steeple, just over a mile through the woods to the crossroads (a graveled two-lane and a dirt-trail road) that, along with the railroad tracks, defined St. Helen. There were thirteen pupils in eight grades, three of whom were my cousins. The teacher was a strong young man with his hands full. In addition to keeping the school clean, the stove going, and the students in order, he had to teach us reading, penmanship, history, geography, and arithmetic at every grade level. Well, almost every level. There were a couple of grades with no pupils; mine had only me.

I learned a lot in that school—most importantly, how to read. True, at first I really did miss the basic concept. My parents read to me all the time at home. When they'd gone over my reading assignment with me once or twice, I was able to get through it in school the next day with only an occasional stumble. I was quite proud of my progress, until one day, I suddenly got the idea: you were supposed to be able to read things you'd never heard before. I've always had a quick memory; I was simply memorizing each lesson in turn. I can still remember my surge of delight at realizing I could learn to read anything. I've never gotten over the infinite wonder of that.

I have no idea how good our teacher was, though he was clearly industrious, juggling his whole curriculum at several grade levels every day. However taxing this may have been for him, it had advantages for us. We sat at individual desks with hinged tops covering book storage space, with inkwells in the upper right-hand corner (I remember on winter mornings before the stove had heated the room, the ink would be frozen; you'd dip your pen and get only a dull click). There was a wide bench at the front of the room where the two or three pupils reciting would sit while the rest of us worked on other assignments.

I was able to listen to the lessons at the front of the room, however peripherally; I also got one-thirteenth of the teacher's time. Not many school children today are so fortunate.

I had no close friends, really. True, there were my three cousins, but one was older than I, one younger, and one a girl.

Besides, they lived several miles away over a rutted one-lane trail winding through the woods behind our house, so little used that the birch branches slashed across the windshield as you drove. We did go to each other's birthday parties. I don't remember feeling lonely, though, or ever afraid in the woods, as I might be in parts of any big city. I wasn't "being brave," it was just that I knew there was nothing there to hurt me.

I did get lost once, wandering in the deeper woods on the other side of the state road, where there were no houses. After an hour or so of looking for trees with moss on what I'd been told would be their north sides, and taking a bearing from the sun, which kept disappearing behind the clouds, I got a little anxious. (Half a lifetime later I made a film, *The Mountain Men,* about the fur trappers in the Rockies in the 1830s in which my character insists, "Ain't never been lost. Been fearsome confused once or twice, mebbe." That was me, thirty years earlier.)

About then, I stumbled on the railway tracks. While I was trying to decide which way to follow them, a handcar came along and gave me a ride back to St. Helen. I even got to help pump. It was a great day.

More often, I roamed the woods nearer my house. We acquired a dog, a very large, dark-coated shepherd named Lobo. Of course I loved him, cherishing my understanding that he was part wolf. (I doubt now that this was true.) He was the first of three great dogs among the many in my life. In winter, he could easily pull me on my sled (when he felt like it), allowing me to play out *The Call of the Wild.* The autumn I was nine Lobo was shot by an angry neighbor whose dog he'd mauled in a fight. It was the first loss of my life. I still think of him.

Living in the woods, we had no sidewalk to shovel nor lawn to mow, and there was no point in raking leaves. I did learn to split kindling for the kitchen stove, using a single-bit ax as my father taught me. My younger cousin, wandering behind his older brother while he was chopping wood with a double-bitted ax, was badly cut in the head on the backswing. "A boy can't handle a double-bit" was my father's pronouncement. "That's a lumberman's tool."

Actually, I liked chopping wood (as did Abraham Lincoln, Kaiser Wilhelm, and Ronald Reagan, though I adduce no trickle-down virtue from this). It gave me a feeling of useful work, reducing small logs to stacks of sweet-smelling kindling so my mother could cook dinner. The genes are involved here, too, I think. Man's dominance over the other territorial carnivores was earned in part with the edged flint ax.

It wasn't frontier life, though. We had running water and central heating, with a furnace burning larger logs than the ones I split for the kitchen range. We also had electricity, generated by a two-cycle diesel engine. Every so often, it came up to speed in a tonal range that would snap the stems on a couple of dozen cut-crystal glasses my mother kept in a glass cabinet. When the glasses started to jitter on their shelves, Mother would call for me and we'd race to lift them to safety. Unlike her, they were too fragile to survive their time in the North Woods.

Even so, I think my mother may have felt a little like those crystal glasses, marooned in the wilderness. If that's true, she never told me, nor so far as I know, my father. If they quarreled, I never heard them. I think she was determined to play out the hand she'd been dealt.

However mismatched they may have been for each other, my parents were wonderful for me. This didn't change when my sister, Lilla Ann, was born, when I was six. When I was in the house, reading or refighting The Great War on the carpet with my toy soldiers, my mother was there, pointing me toward books, talking about the theater in Chicago, or playing Caruso records on the wind-up Victrola. She used to take me out sometimes to pick blue-berries (in Michigan, we call them huckleberries) in the woods around the house, with my little sister. It was easy to get enough for the table, even with Lilla eating most of what she picked. I remember my mother most vividly in soft summer dresses, very beautiful.

My dad gave me time, too. He often took me with him, usually in a truck, sometimes with Lobo standing on the running board, with his front paws braced on the fender. He loved it. We'd rattle over new-cut roads to inspect the various building projects the Carters had under way. They were building an earth dam I found fascinating, though I have no idea what it was for. It involved a lot of very loud explosions of dynamite, diverting streams, and draining swamps, which was enough for me.

In memory, my father is dressed for the field, in khaki shirt, open collar, and rolled-up sleeves, wide brass-buckled belt and britches, with tall boots. Indeed, the word "father" still triggers an image of those boots for me, perhaps because they were a symbol of male stability.

I have a picture of him standing beside me in those clothes. I'm perhaps eight years old, formally dressed for running away from home. I have on a white shirt and a black bow tie, certainly not my normal attire, with my knickers sliding down over my hips. I'm carrying a miniature classic hobo's bindle, which my budding performance instincts must have told me was an essential prop for my odyssey.

Unfortunately, I can no longer recall what boyhood trauma impelled my decision—maybe it was just an early career choice. I recall announcing to my father that I was running away, leaving it to him to pass the tragic news to my mother. He took it very calmly, which disappointed me. "Do you want me to drive you to West Branch?" he said. "You could catch a train there, if you plan to go south to the city."

"No, no," I said. I could manage. Well, maybe just as far as the state road. That was fine with him, though I'd better put a peanut butter sandwich in my bindle, just in case. Yes, he would explain it to my mother. So he drove me half a mile to the road and left me there, with a cheery wave. The photo was taken an hour later, when I'd come back home, as dramatically as possible under the circumstances. I look relieved, my father looks happy, but un-surprised.

Actually, thinking back, I did wear knickers mostly, though certainly not a bow tie. Though my mother made most of my baby sister's clothes, we, along with just about everyone in the village and in tens of thousands of towns throughout the country, did much of our shopping through the Sears Roebuck and Montgomery Ward mail-order houses. They were wondrous horns of postal plenty, announced in seasonal catalogues the size of phone books, the Spring/Summer version in March, Fall/Winter in September. They sold everything from anemometers to ant farms, barbed wire to brassieres, and on through the alphabet. My first pubescent juices stirred while staring transfixed at the underwear models. (They were in the first part of the catalogue, just after housedresses.) I don't think I could've handled ads for a thong bikini.

My own clothing needs were simple. One pair of corduroy knickers a year, which I grew out of before they wore out, as I did the high laced boots boys wore in the winter. They came with a pocket on one side, containing a fairly good knife. In summer you wore shorts and sneakers. As far as I know, the only brand then was Keds, costing two dollars, not two hundred.

My boyhood memories are thick with trees—Midwestern oak, poplar, and maple, but mostly the birch and pine of the Michigan peninsulas. Even in summer, they dominated the other trees. In the fall, the fierce, bright colors of the maples flame through the woods as the partridge flush out of the brush ahead of the hunters. But in winter, the days shorten early; the snow comes soon. As the afternoon light fades, the pines darken against the white drifts, looming close to the narrow trail roads.

Walking through the woods in December, I felt no menace, only promise. It meant Christmas and finding the Tree. There was passionate local argument as to which kind of pine made the best Christmas tree. Blue spruce and balsam were the favorites; our family was firmly loyal to the blue spruce. It's dense, short-needled, and dark blue-green, and lasts the longest if it's cut and handled properly.

I feel sorry for people who buy their trees from city tree lots, packed with stubby fledglings grown for the trade each year. A proper Christmas tree is cut from the top ten feet or so of a mature, forty-foot pine, the top being the newest growth, full of sap that holds the needles longer. Felling such a tree is not boy's work, though my father let me come along. When the tree toppled in an explosion of snow, I helped trim the branches from the fallen trunk. When this was cut into short logs for burning in the furnace that heated our house, I helped load them on the truck, too. The Tree was loaded last, clotted with packed snow from its fall. Trucked back to the house, it was stuck in a snowdrift against the front steps. Then came a dreary hour of boy's work, throwing the heavy logs from the sawed-up trunk through the cellar window to feed the furnace.

We never put our tree up until Christmas Eve. For a few years I knew this was Santa's work, then I joined in the sweet deception for my little sister. Everyone knows the pleasure of transforming a tree into a Christmas wonder, the arguments about how many ornaments, which kind of icicles, the frustration of stringing lights. Then, we used candles the size of your finger, clipped to the branches in tiny tin cups to catch the wax. These were very dangerous, of course. (So were fireworks, but we all had those, too, on the Fourth.) By God's grace and my parents' care, we never had a fire. The candles were incomparably beautiful, glistening and glimmering among the branches as light bulbs never have since.

I don't need to describe a tree on Christmas morning—we all know that delight. In California now, our Tree still comes from the woods of my boyhood, trucked two thousand miles—not two thousand yards. It's taller, because our ceiling's higher. But I don't get to go out in the dark, snowy woods on a winter afternoon and watch it fall, crashing in a cloud of snow for Christmas. I can't sit through Christmas afternoon behind the Tree in a window seat hidden from the house, devouring my Christmas books. My first copies of *Treasure Island* and *Tom Sawyer* still have some blue-spruce needles scattered in the pages. They smell of Christmas still.

The outside world intruded rarely into my personal boy-space of home, pine woods, and books. Once, though, as I was walking on the edge of a cleared cow pasture by the state road, I heard what sounded like an outboard motor overhead. I looked up and stood dumbstruck to see an actual airplane come stuttering down to a landing—just as in the movie *Wings.* The pilot climbed out, yes, boots and a leather jacket with a white silk scarf—I felt as if we were in a movie, somehow. He pulled off his helmet and goggles and tossed them into the cockpit. "Hey, sport," he said (no one had ever called me "sport" before. It sounded very grown-up). "Y'know where I can get some gas—maybe a sandwich?" I directed him to the most impressive building in St. Helen, which belonged to my grandfather and lay a few hundred yards across the railway tracks, at the foot of my grandfather's hill—a cobblestone store which was also the post office. In front of it was the only gasoline pump in fifteen miles.

The pilot was blond and curly-haired (could it be *Lindbergh??!!*). He started across the field with a couple of gas cans. "Don't steal my airplane now, sport," he called back. I didn't dare go near the plane, fragile and wondrous as a great bird, but stood staring for a time, then bolted off to find my dad, anybody, to bear witness to this miracle. Of course I found no one; as I ran panting

back to the pasture, I heard the motor start. The plane was bumping
over the rough ground, lifting clear and banking south as I climbed
the fence. I don't think he saw me wave.

There was also an Indian when I was a boy. He lived, for a
time, in a small cabin on the Au Sable River, a mile or so north of
the schoolhouse. He was probably a Chippewa ("Michigan" is a
Chippewa word), though I didn't know that then, nor anything else
about him. I have no idea whether he built the cabin, owned it, or
was squatting there. Wandering along the river bank one afternoon,
in search of whatever it is boys look for, I came upon him sitting in
his doorway repairing some beaver traps.

Beaver were prevalent in northern Michigan then, as they
are still, busily cutting down a lot of poplar, building dams, and
flooding trail roads. I had two rusty traps myself, though I'd barely
learned how to set them, and had no clue how to bait or place
them. The beaver were safe from me, though visions of beaver pelts
danced in my head—at twenty-some dollars apiece, they positively
leapt. This man clearly knew about trapping beaver.

Besides, he was an honest-to-God *Indian!* No, he didn't have
a bear-claw necklace or braided hair, but his flat, obsidian eyes and
iron focus on the work he was doing defined him. I stood transfixed
at the edge of the clearing, thirty feet away, for some minutes. Then
he stood and strode off into the woods with his traps, turning a
casual eye to me as he passed, neither accepting nor rejecting, just
marking my presence.

I went back several times over the next weeks. Often there
was no sign of him, no smoke from the chimney (but it was still a
real Indian *camp*)! Even when I saw him, he never spoke or more
than flicked a glance at me, till one day when he was splitting
kindling by his woodpile. He stopped and leaned on his ax. "What
you want here, kid?" he asked. "Work?"

"Uhhh—yeah," I managed. "Sure. Yes." This was the least of
what I wanted, but I knew it was the right answer.

"You know how to chop wood?"

"Sure I do. Yes, sir." I did, too. Outside of school, or at
home, adults didn't often ask me questions for which I had good
answers.

"This here's all cut." He sank the ax deep in the chopping
block, with a one-handed swing. "Come back next week. Maybe I'll

give you some work." I did go back, every day the next week, but there was no sign of life around the cabin, and the ax was gone from the chopping block. I don't know the meaning, or the ending of that story. I remember it, though.

I didn't speak to a full-blood American Indian again until many years later, when I was made a blood member of the Minicon-jou Sioux in the Black Hills of South Dakota, while I was making a film about them, *The Savage.* In Texas, on another film, *Arrowhead,* I worked with some Chiricahua Apache, including a very old chief who, tribal lore held, had fought against the Long Knives (that's what the Apache called the saber-armed U.S. Cavalry). But no Indian I've ever met burns as vividly in my memory as that solitary, proud Chippewa I met on the banks of the Au Sable when I was a boy.

2

In a Strange Land

For, lo, I was a stranger in a strange land.

— Exodus 18:3

IN 1933, WHEN I WAS TEN and in the midst of what I recall as an idyllically happy boyhood, my life changed, drastically and forever. Perhaps there were dark times that I've blocked out, but nothing of that survives for me. One week I was a kid knocking around in the woods, the next I was on a Pullman car heading south with my mother and my kid sister, Lilla, and a new baby brother. His name was Alan.

We were bound for Columbus, Georgia, where my mother's sister, May, lived in what struck me as palatial affluence with her husband, Dr. Will Jenkins, a pioneering radiologist (of considerable reputation, I found out much later). Their home had black-and-white marble floors. It was set in the middle of an acre or so of rose garden, certainly the grandest house I'd ever seen. There seemed to be plenty of room for my mother and three children; we fell readily into the ease of a well-off Southern household.

Columbus is not a large city even now; back then it was much smaller. The country was in the midst of the Depression, but I doubt it affected Dr. Will. He sometimes took me out shooting at Midland, his large farm outside the city.

My Aunt May was a striking woman, a sort of Noël Coward character set down in southern Georgia in the thirties. She lacked my mother's inner strength, but she was a spectacular lady. She was also very kind to me, letting me ride her horses (I remember being thrown several times by a fractious sorrel gelding named Stormcloud), and swim in the pool at the country club.

On Sundays, we sometimes went out to Fort Benning, the Army post nearby, to watch the officers play polo. I also used a telephone for the first time in my life. I called up the local drugstore, under my aunt's direction, and asked them to deliver a copy of *Wild West Weekly*. They did, too.

I even made a friend, which I'd not really been able to do in St. Helen. He was a black boy named Joshua, a son of the extended black family that worked for the Jenkins. (The polite usage then was "colored people," but I just called him Josh.)

We had a fine time that summer, he leading me through the good small-boy stuff to be found in the Georgia piney woods (yellow pine, not white; no birch, but some interesting swamp, very different from the Michigan woods and the cold black lakes). I remember Josh's house, weathered gray and full of family, smelling of soap and wood smoke.

I have no idea what he or his family thought of me; it never occurred to me to think in any special way about him. He was just my friend. I've often thought since, through the decades when American opinion on race and religion changed, how lucky I was to have been a boy in a place where the question didn't come up.

In St. Helen, there were certainly no blacks. As far as I know, there were no Jews, no Italians or Poles either—only Anglo-Saxons, each on his acre or so of cleared woodland. I thus grew almost to adolescence innocent of the possibility of prejudice, until I was old enough to sort those things out for myself. Lucky for me.

I missed my dad desperately, and the woods I knew best, but Georgia was kind to a Yankee kid. My aunt and uncle couldn't have been nicer, with the horses, the farm, and the pool. As far as I can remember, I was having a fine time . . . until the day my mother told me she and my father were being divorced.

This was then and still remains the most traumatic experience of my life, including World War II. "Divorce" was a word I'd never even heard before. I had no idea what it meant, until my mother explained to me that she and my father were not going to be married anymore. I couldn't even comprehend this idea, let

alone accept it. My memory is that I cried for two days, but this can't
be true.

Children are resilient; I came to accept the new reality, even
if I couldn't understand it. Until my parents' divorce became final,
we would all live with my aunt and uncle in Georgia; I would go to
school. I don't remember any word on what would happen after
that. In my heart of hearts, I was convinced that it was somehow,
shamefully, all my fault.

I have no more memories of Georgia then, nor any at all of
our return to Michigan. I think my mother must've taken the three
of us north on the train, as we'd come down. I know we were back
in St. Helen in the late winter; I must've gone to school for a few
weeks. It was a bleak spring.

I remember my mother and her new husband coming back
from their wedding, fifteen miles away in a town only a little larger
than St. Helen. My stepfather brought me a toy dirigible, but I lost
it in the woods.

Chet Heston, dark-haired, lean, laconic, was a friend of the
family. He'd lived in St. Helen for a year or so. I knew him well;
he'd been around the house a lot. He was a good man. Not many
days after he married my mother, we left St. Helen, with a trailer
full of belongings towed behind the car. We drove away in the chill
dark before dawn, very cold. I caught a last glimpse of our house
before the pines hid it, but I had no chance to say good-bye to my
father.

There were no motels, then. Owners of private homes who
were strapped for cash and had a spare bedroom or two would put
up a sign: TOURIST ROOMS. We stayed at one the first night driving
south, somewhere near Detroit. My .22 rifle was stolen from under
the tarp on the trailer. It was just one more bad thing, but I was
stunned. Nobody ever stole anything in St. Helen. Aside from my
books and some clothes, it was all I had. I suppose it took two days,
maybe three, to get to Alliance, Chet's hometown in Ohio, where
he had friends and family. He needed to find work, if he was to
support his new family. Looking back, I've always respected him for
standing fast. In the depths of the Depression, the bleakest time in
this century for a man to find work, he gutted it out.

First, he found us a place to live: all five of us in a rented
room in an old house on a brick-paved street with a cherry tree in

the backyard. We could use the one bathroom in the house and the kitchen to cook our meals, but the owner, a rather fierce old woman named Mrs. Beatty, was very firm about our not using any other part of her house, except the kitchen door.

Oddly, she allowed me to sit in the fork of the cherry tree. I liked that. I used to climb up there and read...or sometimes just sit.

I attended the last weeks of the spring semester in the local public school, making three schools in one year (I never did get the Civil War; I missed it in Georgia, Michigan, and Ohio). I don't recall much about the school, except that somehow I caught head lice. Even after they were exterminated with a very strong and noxious shampoo, I had to hang my cap and coat in the hall at school, apart from the other kids'. I was very embarrassed, though I could hardly have felt more apart from them as it was.

It was a tough time, toughest of all, surely, for Chet. My lonely misery didn't count against his desperate search for a way to make a living. No, I never heard it discussed, but it surely had to be the center of our life there.

He must've found some work, probably day labor, because our rent was always paid and we had food on the table. On the Fourth of July, Chet gave me a cap pistol, which delighted me, but it only came with one roll of caps. With the pistol, it cost twenty-five cents. Extra caps were a nickel a roll. My stepfather decided to invest another dime, to celebrate the Fourth. I was grateful for that.

I think we were only in Alliance a few weeks, until Chet discovered how threadbare the local labor market was. I remember going downtown one day with two sons of Chet's brother, Claude, to collect some food for their family from a relief office. We filled a red wagon with some sacks of flour, sugar, beans, and a bag of apples. It weighed enough to need all three of us to get it to their little house.

When I got back to our room, I told the story as a small adventure. Chet stood up, white-faced. "I'm not taking any relief handout, ever! You hear me?" he said, and walked out of the house. At the time, I had no idea why he was so angry.

By midsummer, we were back where I was born, in Wilmette, stopping briefly at a rambling frame house with a floating population of mostly young people who were trying to find their

various ways through the Depression. My mother's younger half-
brother, Jimmy, was among them. He was the one who was killed
not many years later in the Anzio landing, but that summer he was
fresh out of college, married to the daughter of the dour old widower who owned the house. I think this tenuous connection gained
the five of us a temporary roost.

Almost at once, we drove north to Wisconsin, chasing the
rumored "plenty of jobs there." As in Ohio, Chet found nothing
more than casual day labor; we lived in a green tent, sustained by
pancakes and the fish we caught in the lakes where we camped.
"We've always wanted to go on a camping trip," my mother said.
Indeed, I was having a pretty good time, but I knew it was no
camping trip. Kids figure out things like that.

By the end of summer, we were back in Wilmette, in the big
frame house on Maple Avenue. At last, Chet somehow found a
permanent job that would support us all. He lied to get it, assuring
the foreman at Bell and Gossett, the steel plant that hired him, that
he was a skilled welder, which he then taught himself to be on the
job, because he had to.

I admire Chet Heston more for his desperate odyssey that
summer than for anything else I know about him; he never quit.
Some of the college boys who lounged on the long veranda on
Maple did little else for the few summers left until World War II
would call them to their destinies. Chet was no college boy. But he
didn't cut and run.

At first we only rented three of the seven bedrooms on the
second and third floors at Maple Avenue. I imagine old Mr. Moore
was glad to oust some of the freeloaders he was carrying, and get
some rental income. At some point, Chet undertook to buy the
house on a long-term mortgage. As he rose gradually through the
ranks to an executive position in what became a defense plant
during the war, he finally made secure the family he had undertaken to support, in the worst of all times. When he dropped dead
of a mercifully quick heart attack twenty years later, I was proud to
pay off the last of the mortgage and give my mother the deed to the
house he'd worked so hard to provide.

The house on Maple was a lifesaver for us, maybe especially
for me; I got my own room. It was on the third floor, with steep
angled ceilings converted from an attic, but there were two win-

dows and the other rooms were empty. I had the whole floor to myself. That meant a lot to me.

At some point, I think in 1934, about the first year we were living in Wilmette, my father came to see me. Perhaps he'd written my mother beforehand, planning the visit, perhaps he was in Chicago on business. Neither of them ever mentioned it afterward. I was playing softball in a field near the house when a car stopped at the curb. I recognized my dad behind the wheel and walked over, trembling. I hadn't seen him since we'd left Michigan. "Hello, son," he said.

"Hi . . . Daddy," I answered, my mouth dry. I was desperately glad to see him, but still I felt somehow guilty, caught in a criminal act, with the other boys watching behind me on the field. We talked for a few minutes, but he never got out of the car and I can't remember what he said. Perhaps he'd planned to take me to the drugstore for ice cream, so we could talk, but sensed my confusion and distress, compounded by his own.

His car window was down, but there still seemed to be a pane of glass between us (or so it seems now; then I had no such metaphors available). As he said good-bye and drove away, I felt the tears on my cheeks (perhaps he did, too). I turned and hurled the ball back on the field and ran home to my room on the third floor. I didn't see him again for ten years.

Though I've long since learned to be a public person whom I can step inside instantly, I retain a certain shyness I've known all my life. Maybe it was my backwoods Michigan boyhood, or my parents' divorce, a dark and terrible secret I told no one—until my wife, Lydia, the night we married. As we sat at supper, I said, "You know, darling, I . . . uh . . . should tell you. Chet Heston is . . . uh . . . not my father. My parents were divorced."

"Oh?" she said, her eyes widening. A small silence, then, "Charlie . . . what's your name?"

It's also possible that I'm a loner because I'm an actor. Or is it the other way around? Whichever, an actor at work is giving you somebody else. He's not performing *to* you; you're watching him be another man—a *character*. With many actors, it may be someone very like them, even the same guy every time, but they're pretending to *be* that guy. In my case, it's often a real historical figure, a far better man than I am myself. But even when I play a fictional

character, it's not me—it's a cardinal, or a cowboy or a quarterback.
I get to *be* him, not me.

As a boy, I was whisked out of the woods for reasons I didn't
begin to comprehend and plunked down in a new life I wasn't
really equipped for. I wasn't very happy with myself. Of course very
few teenage boys *are* happy, but I didn't know that. I thought I was
the only one. I retreated even further into the pretend games I'd
entertained myself with all my life, finding better guys to be than I
was.

Wilmette truly was a "strange land" for me. It was an affluent
suburb; I don't think many of the men who lived there had the
desperate worries about feeding their families that Chet faced.
There were country clubs and beach clubs and wide, shaded streets.
There were also, to my eternal good fortune, good schools. This
was of course before our school system had collapsed, when
America still had the best public education in the world.

Indeed New Trier, the high school serving the town, three
miles north of our new home, was named the best high school in
the nation, according to *Life* magazine. (How did we manage to
ruin such a priceless national resource as the schools that teach our
children?)

In fact I wasn't really equipped to take advantage of half of
what New Trier offered. Scholastically, I could handle it; I came
from a family of book-lovers. But I was still a green kid, nervous
about crossing a paved street with moving cars. I didn't know how
to drive a car (when we got there, I'd never even been on a bicycle),
or how to dance. I'd never played any kind of team sport (with
thirteen pupils in eight grades, half of them girls?) or been on a
date with a girl. The only extracurricular activities I qualified for at
New Trier were the rifle team and the chess club. That does not
make for a brilliant career at a high-profile high school.

On top of all this, I was a nerd, before the word had even
been invented—shy, skinny, short, pimply, and ill-dressed. When I
was fifteen, I began to grow about half an inch a month, so I was
constantly too big for my clothes. Girls? I didn't have a clue, a car,
any place to take them or any money to spend. My hormones were
constantly aboil with erotic fantasies about girls, of course, but that
was it.

Still, there was the school itself. Now sunk in the mire of

American public education, we've forgotten how a good school can ignite a kid. I was in an accelerated program, which meant I had a lot of options to choose from. I took mechanical drawing (I still love the cool precision of an ordered plan, profile, and end-view working drawing of a doorway or cabinet in hard pencil on glazed heavy stock; I can produce one for the contractor I've hired to build it for me). I took woodworking; I like the feel of wood, changing under the shaping steel edge of good tools.

I was already reveling in the glories of the English language (its intricate rules of syntax and grammar were a larger problem I've still not solved). At New Trier we not only began to find our way into Shakespeare, but I discovered Wolfe and Hemingway and Frost as well.

Freshman Latin was required. How many public schools even offer it now? I'm afraid I blew that one, squeaking through with a C −.

Algebra was another near miss for me: I barely got through. Geometry, on the other hand, I enjoyed. There were actual shapes there I could understand visually; its lucid logic made sense. I loved history, partly because I had a great teacher, Mr. Carpenter, God bless him. He introduced me to a subject that would guide me crucially in preparing for many roles.

Our accelerated group could also choose extra electives in art or music. Since I can't sing (no, I don't want to talk about it), I picked art; I'd been drawing ever since I did those cowboys in my geography book up in Michigan. Actually, like a lot of actors, I can draw; acting's also a visual art. I signed up for every art elective I could; Art History took us to the Art Institute of Chicago, the first time I ever stood face to face with a great painting.

By my junior year I was still at it. One day I stayed after school to explore the laws of perspective (one of the few areas of art that has laws as immutable as any in mathematics). While explaining the function of the vanishing point, my teacher put his hand on my knee (I was taller by then, and not quite so nerdy). My knee-jerk reflex kicked over a still-life display. Never mind; he still made the verities of perspective clear to me. I'm grateful for that. We never discussed his stray hand.

But New Trier gave me far more than the foundation of a

decent education (better, I suspect, than the average college can do
today). They gave me the center of my life: my work. The school
had a very sophisticated drama program. I stumbled into it by accident, going along with a boy named Warren Mackenzie, about my
only friend in the school, who wanted to read for a role in the
Freshman Play. I had no idea what an audition was, but I took a
shot at it anyway and got a part. So did he, going on to become an
artist. I began my life.

I dived into New Trier's theater program like a thirsty frog
in a pond. From a one-eyed pirate in that first play through every
part I could get in every production till I graduated, I soaked up
different people to be, and some idea of what acting was. When I
was fourteen I even got to play Macbeth in a radio adaptation of the
play broadcast to the English classes. (I think I got the part because
even as a kid my voice had a bass range. In Michigan they used to
call me "Moose.") I can't have been good, or even remotely plausible, but that was the kind of challenge they offered kids at that
school.

My social life was still essentially nonexistent, but as long as
I could be imaginary people in plays, I didn't mind. Well, I minded,
but there was nothing I could do about it. Real girls expected to be
taken out and bought hamburgers and Cokes and taken home in
cars; I had to settle for the women in the plays we did. In one of
them, *Death Takes a Holiday,* I had a scene with the prettiest girl
I'd ever been within five feet of.

I had no idea even of how to talk to her during rehearsals,
except on stage, but there was a scene where she fainted in my
arms and I carried her over to a couch. (This is an opportunity that
doesn't come up on your average adolescent pizza/Coke date; you
can sort of scout out the ground.)

I'd done that, clumsily, for several weeks during rehearsals.
I was still pretty pimply, but carrying her across the stage was no
problem (Scots blood has good strength genes) until opening
night. She wore a satin evening gown; I wore, God help me, the
first dinner jacket I'd ever seen, let alone had on my back. She was
not a heavy girl, but as soon as I'd swept her into my arms I felt her
satin bottom sliding down my satin lapels. Three feet short of the
couch, I dropped her on the floor, falling on top of her in a desper-

ate effort to save the scene. It got a huge laugh and permanently soured any chance I might have had with the girl. Marianne, her name was.

Back on Maple Avenue, things were going well. As always, my mother was firmly supportive; I think she saw that New Trier was working for me. She had old friends nearby, and had made new ones. This was a happy time for her, or so I saw it.

I think Chet relaxed a little, too, once he saw that his extended family would survive, even thrive. He was always impeccably fair to me, if never close. He never adopted me; I took his name to hide what still seemed to me the unspeakable secret of my parents' divorce.

Chet saw raising me as his rightful responsibility. He questioned me closely on each report card—why a B-minus was not a B, a B not an A, what happened with this C?

He saw that I did my chores, shoveling the walks in winter, stoking the coal furnace and carrying out the ashes, mowing the lawn in summer, raking and burning the leaves in the fall.

In my freshman summer I caddied at a local country club, not very well. I found the game boring and my shyness didn't help either. I got the standard dollar-and-a-half a round, but few tips; I suspect the golfers I carried for thought me either stupid or sullen. I don't think I was sullen . . . maybe a little detached. I also failed at selling the *Saturday Evening Post,* being then incapable of presenting the modestly engaging persona a salesman needs.

The summer of my junior year, when I'd gotten strong enough, I worked in Chet's steel mill on Chicago's South Side, on the labor gang. It was hot, exhausting, head-down-and-gut-out-the-day *work.* Eighty-five cents an hour for eight hours, which by God you earned. I think it did me some good, just to know I could do it, but that summer, I really hated it.

I think that was the year after Chet caught his hand in a steel-rolling press at work and lost his right forefinger. As always, he showed best in adversity. He was back at work in two weeks and began teaching himself to fire both his rifles and shotguns with his middle finger. He was hunting again the next fall, and soon took up hunting deer with a bow, a more difficult challenge—particularly with a maimed right hand.

I remember one Sunday, when he'd been working at ar-

chery for some time, he took me with him to the archery range
where he practiced, and let me try his hunting bow. He never did
take me with him on a hunting trip, though, and fishing only once.
I was aware of it at the time, though I'm not sure I understood it.

I do now, surely. Chet was shy, too. Besides, as an adolescent, I wasn't Prince Charming: try a pimply Prince Hamlet, brooding. We were both doing our best at a relationship each of us was
uneasy with. We did sometimes play chess. He could beat me . . .
but not always.

My last two years at New Trier were focused more and more
on the theater program. I dropped off the rifle team and the chess
club, and gave up on football. From one of the shortest kids in my
class, I'd shot up to about the tallest, but I was a gangly Ichabod
Crane, with neither the weight nor the understanding of the game
to be useful.

I found another stage, as well. The Winnetka Community
Theatre was a vigorous amateur group where I seized a foothold
and some valuable experience. I did minor parts in three or four
plays, including *Family Portrait,* an interesting drama about Christ's
family in which He never appears. As I recall, I played a young
nephew. Considering I was later to play John the Baptist, Moses,
and God, I suppose the casting's not surprising. Come to think of
it, I also had a small part in a play about Jesse James called *Missouri
Legend.* I've since, God knows, done more than my share of Westerns. (You perhaps believe in predestination?)

In any event, in the spring of my senior year, the Winnetka
Community Theatre awarded me a scholarship to the School of
Speech at Northwestern University, then as now regarded as one of
the outstanding drama schools in the country. I've never adequately
thanked the Winnetka group for giving me a crucial leg up on my
life. Their scholarship was for three hundred dollars, the annual
tuition at Northwestern then, which Chet couldn't have afforded. I
was stunned. I hadn't realized such a scholarship existed; I don't
know whether it was even given every year. I'd never played a
major role for them at that point, but I suppose likely high school
candidates were not thick on the ground in the area. The scholarship focused my plans wonderfully. Now I could go to NU and find
out if I could *really* be an actor.

Of course, by 1941, every high school boy in the country

understood the shadow looming over all of us. American opinion still opposed involvement in the war that had by then engulfed Europe (in August, the extension of the draft would only pass in Congress by fifteen votes) but it seemed likely we'd be in it before long. College would take second place to saving the world for democracy. Fair enough. That you might get killed was surely a downside, but we all accepted the clear reality.

Meantime, I had a more immediate problem. Mr. Edwards, my chemistry teacher, told me I was about to flunk his course. If this happened, I couldn't graduate even though I was getting A's and B's in all my other subjects. I had one semester to complete a year's worth of lab experiments and pass the final exam. Otherwise, no diploma, no scholarship, no Northwestern.

Chet was not pleased by this news, but he helped me deal with it. I quit my paper route and the grocery store job, though not the house chores. I spent an hour after school every day in the lab catching up on my chemistry experiments and did my best to bone up on the basics of a subject that remains a mystery to me.

In the midst of all this, I was offered the lead in the Senior Play, the first but God knows not the last time the lure of a good part would complicate my life. *The American Way* would be the most challenging production the school had ever undertaken, mounting a play that had just closed on Broadway starring Fredric March. It was the story of a young German immigrant's experience finding success in America, only to be entangled in the rising conflicts Hitler had unleashed on the world. As I recall, I was killed in the end—a fate my roles have often brought me.

I did the play, I didn't flunk chemistry. In fact *The American Way* taught me a couple of useful things about what would become my life. Midway through rehearsals, a letter came for me in the mail at Maple Avenue. I think it was the first letter I ever received; what's more, it was anonymous, signed "a friend" and *it contained ten dollars!* There was a paragraph about what a good actor I was, how the writer had seen everything I'd done, both at school and the Winnetka Community Theatre, and how I seemed most effective when paired with a young actress who was with me again in *American Way.* (No, this was not the girl I'd dropped on stage a year or so earlier.) The enclosed money was to help me take her out. Even as a teenager, I realized this letter could only be from her mother.

This embarrassed me enormously, as did many events in my life then. (Woody Allen fans will understand this.) I still had absolutely no experience with girls offstage, and all my time outside classes was committed to doing the play and passing chemistry. On the other hand, what about the ten dollars? In the end, unable to return it or cope with the intricacies of going out on a date with a real girl, I confess I spent it.

The play was a great success. After the first performance, I was confronted backstage by a large and vehement young man, a few years older than I, who told me I had to star in a film he was planning. David Bradley was an independent filmmaker. Today, with some five hundred film departments attached to the nation's colleges and universities, a couple of independent filmmakers are likely to run out of any bush you brush against. In the 1940s, David was probably one of no more than twenty or so across the entire country.

He'd been making films since he was ten, on 16mm black-and-white, ranging from Dickens to short stories by Saki. I didn't know enough then to judge those I saw, but to make them at all was an extraordinary achievement.

His next and by far his most ambitious project was to be a film of Ibsen's *Peer Gynt.* It would be silent, like all his films to that point, with subtitled dialogue enhanced by Grieg's *Peer Gynt Suite.* I'd never read the play, was only peripherally aware of Ibsen, and had never made a movie. David nevertheless made it clear, shouting for emphasis, that I *had* to do the film.

Actually, I was a pretty easy sell, especially when you consider there was no money involved. I said to David, "Well, I'll be working in a steel mill all summer; I guess you can shoot on weekends, right?"

"No, no!" he shouted. "I'll need you every day, all week, all summer." OK, I thought. Playing Peer Gynt in a movie, free, still looked better than handling hot steel for eighty-five cents an hour. Oddly, I don't recall a major confrontation with Chet on the issue, though he'd certainly expected me to work all summer again in the mill. He accepted my announcement that I'd be making a movie with hardly a word. Maybe he felt he'd fulfilled his responsibility. I had my scholarship; once I graduated, I'd be on my own.

At New Trier, having flirted with disaster in chemistry, I did

OK on the test and, penalized for lateness, scraped through with a flat D. Even with this handicap, I finished well in the class. If I'd had the sense to take advantage of it, New Trier could've given me the kind of education that'll earn you a degree in most colleges now.

The graduation ceremony, however, was a problem. We were supposed to wear what was then called "summer formal." For the boys, that meant evening trousers and white formal jackets. Many though certainly not all of the seniors actually owned formal wear. Both the junior and the senior classes celebrated Christmas with elaborate private parties in Chicago's Loop hotels, dancing to the music of Benny Goodman, Artie Shaw, and so on. Black-tie, of course. I wasn't usually invited to these affairs for any number of good reasons. But one or two of the wealthier families, acting out of a sense of egality and good fellowship, would insist that all members of the class be included in their children's guest lists. Both years, I'd gotten a couple of engraved invitations.

I'd never considered actually attending; I wasn't in any way equipped for that kind of event, I didn't even show the invitations to Chet or my mother, though I kept them for a while, admiring the embossed lettering on the thick, creamy paper: "the pleasure of your company . . ."

But Commencement was something altogether different. Of course I would take part, of course the proper outfit would be rented. I think the whole rig, including a carnation made out of red feathers, rented for five dollars. It didn't fit me very well, but then nothing off a rack really did, by that time. I'd gotten a lot taller, and my arms and shoulders were excessive.

Still, for graduation, I looked OK, even pretty good. I marched down the aisle to "Pomp and Circumstance," and took my diploma with my family watching . . . Mother, Chet, my sister, Lilla, and my brother, Alan. Chet shook my hand; my mother hugged me and said, "Well, we'll be going home, now. I know you have the Senior Ball. Try not to be too late."

I can't imagine why I hadn't sorted out a solution to the Senior Ball. Like going to it, for God's sake. It wasn't downtown in the Drake Hotel like the Christmas parties, it was right there in the gym. I didn't need a car or a date, or even any money . . . I could've stood around on the sidelines; who knew I couldn't dance?

Instead, I slid out a side door, walked the half mile over to the shores of Lake Michigan, and spent the next three hours wandering slowly south to Wilmette, watching the waves slide up the sand in the moonlight and feeling disgustingly sorry for myself. I eased through the front door on Maple about 2 A.M., having loosened my tie to suggest celebration in case anyone was still up. No one was.

SO THERE I WAS, acting in the movies. I'd never done it before, so I didn't know it was hard to do. I really didn't know how to act on the stage, so I didn't find it difficult to switch to film. Don't misunderstand me: it wasn't that I was quick, or gifted; I just didn't understand the myriad ways in which the work can be daunting . . . so it wasn't. Fools rush in, as someone said. And kids.

David Bradley was young, but he was no kid. He may have been something like a genius. His *Peer Gynt,* which remains the only film ever made of Ibsen's most complex work, had many good things in it. His vision of the piece, executed with a bunch of high school kids and amateurs, was remarkable. To marry his silent film to records of Grieg's music, which could only be synchronized when David was sitting beside the projector, was even more complicated.

My performance as Peer has only physical virtues. David somehow perceived what other directors have also found: my face is useful to the camera. I had no concept of performing the part; I'm not sure David did either. As well as being the only actor to play Peer Gynt on film, I'm certainly the only one who ever played the part totally unaware that it's a satiric role. Come to think of it, that may be the way to do it. Innocently.

Peer Gynt shot through most of the summer. As I was struggling with the end of my adolescence, David was struggling with his film. Especially in view of the fact that it was essentially a one-man project, it's a remarkable achievement. It was also an incomparable learning experience for me.

Then there was Northwestern. Aside from having one of the best theater departments in the country, Northwestern's Speech School offered many advantages. Not only was my tuition paid by the Winnetka scholarship, the campus wasn't three miles from the house on Maple, where I still lived on Chet's largess. I could (and I'm afraid often did) run a block from home, hop a fence, and clamber on the back end of the El platform, thus avoiding the ten-cent fare and riding free two stops to the campus station. It didn't work in the opposite direction, but it was an easy walk home.

Somehow I left behind the nerd I'd been in high school. Now I was at NU, on a scholarship I'd earned, with an actual movie under my belt and a whole banquet spread of theater courses to feast on. I was in fact still a kind of jerky, oddball kid, but I now believed in myself. Almost overnight, I managed to find the confidence that has never left me since. Understand, nothing had really happened, except inside my head. From that day on to the time when I no longer had to audition, I was always sure I'd get any part I read for. I didn't, of course. The point is that I was positive I would. You have no idea how crucial this is.

I even lucked out in the job I was required to take to pay back my scholarship. Instead of KP in one of the dining halls, I was to design and produce the posters required for each of the Speech School's major productions . . . six of them, each needing a couple of hundred silk-screened posters. I'd never heard of silk screen before, but it's an easy process to learn. It was a fair amount of work, but I enjoyed it.

Beyond the usual liberal arts courses, there were the Speech School's freshman requirements: History of the Theater, Voice and Diction, Acting, and Fundamentals of Theater Practice. Like a starving man, I tried to gulp them all down whole, without chewing. I was where I wanted to be, doing what I wanted to do.

Theater Practice was the most important. History of costume; makeup; how to build sets, light them, move them on stage; all these were things I really knew nothing about. I had to learn them; this course taught me. It also provided me with the lodestone of my life, the girl who married me.

LYDIA CLARKE came from a family deeply rooted in the foundations of the American experience. Her ancestor, Margaret Huntington, landed in Boston in 1633, her husband having died at sea, leaving her with four children and not a single soul to turn to in the New World. Demonstrating the right stuff that would mold the new American woman, she thrived, as did her progeny, producing more than a century later a signer of the Declaration of Independence,

Samuel Huntington, and a century after that any family's full share of the gravestones of the Civil War.

Lydia's father spent eighteen months in the trenches of World War I and came home intact to become the youngest principal ever in the high school in Two Rivers, Wisconsin, where his children were born. At the time, his credentials as a Greek and Latin scholar weighed as much in his favor as his war record (now, of course, he'd have to take a course in Sensitivity I just to have a chance at the job). When he retired, they named a new school after him. I knew him. He was a superior man. I wish to God my grandson could study under his ilk.

When I first saw Lydia, I knew none of this. Indeed, for the first two or three days I sat behind her in the Theater Practice class, I didn't really see her at all . . . only her tumbling mane of black Irish hair, which made me tremble. She sat bent over her notebook, taking notes on the complex technicalities of the lectures. Bemused, I sat taking note only of her. I don't think I even wanted to see her face, at first. I had all I could handle with her hair.

In the end, I did handle it . . . stroked it a little, unable to resist, a bit like Lennie in *Of Mice and Men*. Lydia insists I pulled it, but I don't think that's true. It was certainly not a classic movie "cute meet" . . . not at all the way Cary Grant or Gary Cooper would've handled it. Today, of course, even touching the hair of a girl I'd never met would get me dragged up before the Campus Thought Police for sexual harassment.

I don't think Lydia was interested in bringing charges; indeed, she was perhaps slightly interested in me, though I can't think why—I was still a pretty weird sort of guy. I couldn't figure out how to advance the relationship anyway, other than tense, offhand remarks between classes—"Hi, there. How ya doin'?" I didn't even know how to ask her to go out with me, for God's sake.

Fate, as they say, then took a hand (perhaps slightly nudged by Lydia). We were both cast in the same bill of one-acts, though in different plays. I was in *Francesca da Rimini* playing one of a pair of Renaissance lovers condemned by Dante to the nastier circles of Hell, all tights and tunics and curled hair and daggers at the belt, and everyone so beautiful you want to puke . . . exactly the kind of part at which I've made a large part of my living.

Lydia was cast in a moody 1920s English piece called *Madras House,* playing a plain sister, a character description they tried to fulfill by pulling her hair back in a knot . . . a futile effort. We rehearsed our plays separately, so it wasn't till dress rehearsal that Lydia asked me (could it have been on purpose?!) how to read her opening line. She was to enter, distraught, and say, "Minnie, my frog is dead!"

Well, of *course* I knew how that should be read . . . several ways it might be read, indeed. I also had firm ideas about all the other performances, and the costumes, and the plays themselves. This was the kind of conversation I knew how to undertake, though I'm afraid I had no idea how to stop.

Still, there we were, talking like real people. I did the opening night in a state of besotted euphoria. My Renaissance bit was on first, then *Madras House.* I decided I had been terrible as the Renaissance lover (as in fact I probably was). As I sat brooding in my tiny corner of the dressing room, Lydia came down the stairs from the stage to say, "I thought you were marvelous!"

Well, again, Cooper or Grant would've thought of twenty ways to say something funny, or rueful, or engaging. I stuck out my tongue. In the infinity of her female wisdom, she neither walked out nor hit me with anything, until I said in a strangled voice, "What I mean is . . . I, ah, would like to talk to you about it. Could we go and . . . ah, have some coffee? Please?"

Yes, she would like that (this to the music of the spheres). Of course, as we walked off-campus to the Coffee Shop, I realized I had no money. Not a nickel. I certainly couldn't mention this to the celestial beauty actually walking beside me (from the front, she looked even better than when I was sitting behind her).

All I could do was silently pray that there would be a pal in the Coffee Shop I could hit on for a loan. There was—a student I'd just done a play with named Bill Sweeney. He lent me a quarter, may his name be written in the Golden Book, and Lydia and I had tea, which lasts longer, because you can get more hot water free.

I sat there for some two hours, talking about . . . *everything,* to this breathtakingly beautiful, enchantingly intelligent, real *girl,* who seemed to want to talk to me, too. I finally left her at her dormitory and ran the three miles home along the dark streets, beside the canal and across the golf course, saying over and over, "I love her, I love her." I did, too.

Never doubt that this can happen. I'd barely spoken to her before that night, but I knew absolutely, as the door closed behind her. I'd never even had a *date* with a girl, for Pete's sake, but I *knew*. What are the odds on this . . . one in a hundred, a thousand? It happened to me.

I can't tell you much about the next months, my recollection obscured by the golden mist I moved through, my feet only touching the ground occasionally. (I know, this bit here is a little soppy, but it's true. I gave you the misfit misery of my adolescence, now you have to put up with my wonder at having lucked into a superb girl my first time at bat.)

While my falling in love with Lydia almost instantly makes complete sense to me, I've never understood what drew her to me. Her generosity of spirit, is my guess, though Lydia has never been very forthcoming on the question. When I pressed her on this subject once, she smiled and said, "Words, Charlie . . . words. I loved the way you talked about things—paintings, horses, trees." (Let's be clear, here, in case any of us might meet. Everyone who knows me well calls me "Chuck." I *hate* the nickname "Charlie." No one ever calls me that more than once—except Lydia. When she says it, my heart shivers. To this day.)

The next months passed in a hazy mix of work and love. There were very few nights when I wasn't acting, rehearsing, or building sets. Lydia was nearly as busy, which vastly restricted our time together, though we were sometimes in the same production. Somewhere in there, we even squeezed in a couple of plays at the Winnetka Community Theatre, to which I felt some obligation.

During the day, of course, we had our regular schedule of classes, in my case including English at 8 A.M. Since I was thrashing around in the theater one way or another every night till midnight, and mooning over Lydia whenever we had a spare half hour, this cut down on my sleep time markedly. I remember one Sunday morning when I was due at the Children's Theatre to put up the sets for *Treasure Island;* as I walked up the front steps of the building, I literally fell asleep in midstride and walked into a glass door. At least the bloody nose woke me up.

In the middle of all this, on December 7, 1941, the Japanese attacked Pearl Harbor. I was lovesick and work-besotted, but everyone in the country then over seven remembers exactly what he was doing that grim Sunday morning. (I was sitting in my room on Maple, writing a paper on *Macbeth*.) Every healthy male over seventeen and under forty also knew where he'd be before long: in uniform.

We all shared the national outrage at the attack with a unanimity of public opinion rarely seen since. I enlisted in the Army Air Corps (there was no independent Air Force then). I suppose I picked it because it seemed gallant, though I hadn't been near an airplane since my first breathtaking glimpse of a fabric biplane in that Michigan pasture. It also meant I'd probably get to finish the semester; the Air Corps call-up rate was slower than some of the other services, since most of the assignments involved technical training.

In fact, I got another six months. I spent it acting and studying acting, which is in fact a very slippery subject to learn. I had the advantage of a great teacher, Alvina Krause, who imposed a fierce discipline on an art generally regarded as having all the structure of a dish of Jell-O.

Her reputation was formidable, so was her manner. She cared deeply about acting and was unforgiving with those pupils who fell short of her standards. She wasn't interested in teaching self-esteem. It was from her that I learned to be suspicious of directorial praise. Never mind telling me it's good... how can it be better?

Outside of her class, I only worked for her in one play, Ibsen's *Hedda Gabler*. This is the most popular of his plays, but they're all difficult pieces, certainly for student actors. I played Judge Brack, the most interesting of the male roles, and enjoyed a small success, though I doubt I can really have been very good in it. I wore the first of many beards, false and real, I've used pursuing my trade, but made little further creative contribution, I suspect. It's possible I brought a degree of physical presence to the part, though Miss Krause was firmly noncommittal. Many years later I was in Chicago doing a play and was invited to do a seminar at Northwestern's Speech School. It was all very ego-rewarding of course; I had a fine, expansive time. I even summoned the courage to say to A.K.

(we never called her that to her face) "Miss Krause, when I was in
school, I don't remember your ever saying anything encouraging
to me. Did you feel then I had no chance as an actor?"

She sniffed in mild disdain. "People who have to be encouraged to act have no business doing it."

Through all this, of course, the only thing that could possibly
distract me from acting (and reading and talking and thinking about
it) was Lydia. "In love" was an inadequate phrase, at least for me.
Try "obsessed." We shared several classes, acted and worked in
stage crews together. Since I had no money, we seldom went out
on actual dates, but we were working most of the time anyway.

Please understand, I'm talking about this from my end. Lydia
wasn't obsessed. I don't think she was even in love, at that point.
Intrigued, sure, maybe even attracted, but I was the one charging
around the campus whistling Grieg under her window every morning. She kept me at a careful arm's length, perhaps waiting to see if
I might ripen into an actual human being.

(I have a theory about that, developed over many years. I
think a man tends to fall in love the way he might fall off a bridge:
"My God . . . what is this? This fabulous girl . . . I love her . . . I must
make her mine!" whereas women consider these things more carefully, "Mmmm . . . I wonder. There's something there, if I can just
polish him up a little.")

But she did go out with me, whenever we had coinciding
free time. She must have been drawn to me a little, because I never
had much money to spend on her. We walked along the lakefront
a lot. I remember it was snowing one time, and she had actually
taken my arm . . . on her own. I never moved my elbow the whole
forty minutes we walked, with the flakes whirling down. When we
got back to her dorm, her glove and the sleeve of my jacket were
coated over with snow.

In the spring, we often stood beside a lilac bush near the
Speech School embracing for ten minutes at a time. I still send her
lilacs on her birthday every year.

The last months I had as a civilian, I got a great part-time
job, running the elevator at a very posh apartment building on Lake
Michigan, about fifteen minutes from home on the El. I was pretty
posh myself, in a stiff shirt, bow tie, blue uniform, and white gloves,
replacing the regular operators on their days off, working two shifts

from Friday midnight till 4 P.M. Saturday, then Sunday from four to midnight. This allowed me to work in the theater, either performing or rehearsing, or on crew every weekday till midnight.

It sounds tough, but it wasn't, really. The building was only twelve stories high, with two apartments on each floor, each so expensive that most of the people who lived in them were neither very young nor very social. The night shifts were a cinch; the day man I relieved would say, "The Reillys are out to dinner, old Mr. Cohen's walking his dog, and the Thorntons have guests tonight. Everyone else is buttoned up." I kept a typewriter in the boiler room where I had time to work on class assignments. I even rehearsed scenes in the lobby once everyone was tucked in. Then I'd get a few hours sleep till the garage man woke me to bring down the early birds. Also, I was seventeen and in love. That gives you a lot of energy. It was a great job; I got to play the perfect elevator man, a role I worked very hard on; perfect posture, clear diction, level the car exactly at each floor, remember all the names. It was useful training. It's a shame elevators are automated now. It would be a nice fall-back job.

A week or so before Christmas, I was absolutely thunderstruck when the tenants began pressing envelopes into my hand as I let them off at their floors. I had no idea elevator operators were tipped. I received more than two hundred dollars in all, more money than I'd ever seen at one time in my life.

I spent most of it on Christmas presents for Lydia, of course, including tickets for the opening of the Ballet Theater at the Chicago Civic Opera. It was white-tie. I'd never even seen such an outfit, except in the movies, but I knew you could rent them. I did. Lydia wore a long dress and was beautiful in anything she put on, anyway. (She still is.) It never occurred to me to call a cab or rent a limo to take us downtown. No, we rode down on the elevated commuter train, for thirteen cents. Each. The ballet was my first, and awesome: Nora Kaye danced *Firebird*.

I did have the brains to make a reservation at the Pump Room in the Ambassador East Hotel for supper afterward. It was then, and may well still be, the most famous restaurant in Chicago.

We'd never been there, of course, but they were very nice to us, giving us one of the front banquettes. Lydia did look fabulous

and I suppose I made a useful dress extra in my rented white tie
and tails. We had a marvelous time. As we were ending our meal, a
voice from the next banquette said, "Chuck! My word. How are
you?" It was the man who lived in the largest apartment in the
building where I worked.

"Mr. Paget!" I said, feeling somehow undaunted. "Happy
New Year to you, sir." I lifted my glass to him, as well I might. His
twenty-dollar tip had paid for much of our evening.

My last weeks on campus were a little pressed. I went to all
my classes, though obviously grades were not significant by then.
Whenever I got back, if I got back, I surely wasn't going back to
school. I did act in one more play, with Lydia this time. A Restoration piece, *The Beaux' Stratagem*—knee breeches, white dress
wigs, snuff boxes, and silver buckles. I was very arch, but I don't
think very good.

For one thing, I was preoccupied with getting Lydia into bed
and married to me. In either order. She rejected both options with
adamantine resolve. Even though by this time her commitment to
me was at least perceptible, she had no intention of getting pregnant or wed, either condition being cause for expulsion from her
dorm. She was going to get her degree.

Lord knows I did my desperate best, unable to bear even
the idea of going off and leaving her for some 4F jerk. I fell back
on the ploy soldiers have used for centuries: "You realize you may
never see me again. We must have something to carry in our hearts!
It may be years, it may be never." And so on. I gave a heartbreaking
performance, not least because I meant it, but it never dented her
resolve by a millimeter. She was not going to marry anybody, and
she was not going to bed with me. (Well, of course we had no bed
anyway, though we explored a number of erotic elaborations this
side of the final ecstasy at great length in odd corners here and
there.)

So there we were, locked in a scoreless tie late in the fourth
quarter with no time-outs remaining. Down in the basement of the
Speech School late one afternoon, Lydia was helping me silk-screen
the last set of posters I would do for the school.

"I got a letter from this boy I knew in high school. He's at
Harvard, but he's coming to town for a few days. Pete."

"Pete?"

"We never dated, but I thought I might see him. He's going in the Navy."

"The *Navy?*"

"We might even have dinner . . . with other people, of course, at that place on Ridge Road. Not a date."

"No! I mean, of course, no, not a date. Sure. I guess . . . sure."

Noël Coward would've handled it better, and funnier. So would Cary Grant. I'd blown it, but all was not lost. She might not be willing to marry me, yet, but I was not going to lose this girl five days before I checked in for World War II.

I needed a car. The family car was out of the question, but I did have a friend with one. I bullied him into letting me take it. "For one hour, for God's sake, Bob. Of course I have a license!" (I didn't, nor did I know how to drive. I could start a car, point it, and stop it. What else do you need? Traffic was lighter then.)

On the way to the Ridge Road restaurant where the nefarious Pete was plotting to steal my girl, I composed and rehearsed a very good speech, designed to win her heart. I avoided disaster, both driving and parking the car, and strode confidently into the restaurant, where I saw three or four couples, including Lydia, dining sedately around a large table. They all turned and looked at me . . . and I forgot my speech. Every word.

As the silence lengthened, I stepped to the table, took Lydia's hand, and said "Come with me." *And she did.* I can't think what would have happened had she not, but I believe with all my heart that the rest of my life began with that moment. That boyish, quixotic disruption of a simple dinner is therefore the most important single action I've ever taken. I remain proud of it, and eternally grateful to my girl, as she surely became, irreversibly, when she stood and walked out of the restaurant, holding my hand.

So THEN I attended World War II, along with, in the end, some thirteen million other Americans. We all understood we had to win it, but we all felt strongly about surviving it as well. With that in mind, I redoubled my efforts to get Lydia to marry me before I went overseas.

"Just think, darling," I wrote, "if we're married and I get killed, you get ten thousand dollars, free and clear." This appeal, though eminently rational to my Scots soul, failed to move her. She was going to stay in school and get her degree; she was not going to get married before then, if at all. But yes, she loved me.

After some weeks, I gave up even mentioning marriage in my letters, because I was exhausted by the grind of basic training. There must've been scores of these temporary camps cut into spare corners around the country to run millions of men through, strain out the dregs, and get the rest of us in reasonable shape to serve. Mine was in the piney woods outside Greensboro, North Carolina.

Toward the end of this rite of military passage, I shambled back to my barracks after a fun day on the rifle range and the obstacle course to find a yellow envelope on my bunk. The wire said, "HAVE DECIDED TO ACCEPT YOUR PROPOSAL. LOVE, LYDIA."

So she came down to Greensboro over a weekend and married me. A two-day pass was the most I could wangle, after a dramatic plea to the first sergeant. The first day I raced into town, where I got us a room at a tourist bed-and-breakfast and bought a wedding ring for twelve dollars. (Look, it was the best I could do on a private's pay. It's held up very well, still serviceable. Amortized over our marriage, that works out to less than twenty-five cents a year. One of the best buys I ever made.)

Then I met my girl's train; even after a day and a half in coach, she was shining when she stepped down into my arms. We dropped off her bag, picked up the license, and began looking for a church. Greensboro was smaller then, but a busy Army town, all the same. Southerners have always treated soldiers well; my uniform and the beautiful girl beside me earned us smiles as we wandered the neighborhoods, searching for an appropriate altar.

Spring comes early in the Carolinas. In March, the dogwood was already blooming; the streets were rich with blossoms. When we saw the classic white Colonial lines through the trees, we knew we'd found the right place. "Grace Methodist" was printed neatly on the sign in front. We went up the steps and through the open door, to find the church empty, though still exactly what we wanted.

I heard voices from the basement, where we found two pleasant ladies preparing a church supper. "Excuse me, ma'am," I said. "We'd like to get married. I wonder if I could talk to the minister?" Well, of course I could. The ladies even dialed the number for me. The minister was equally accommodating. Yes, he would be happy to marry us; certainly, two hours from now would suit him very well.

That gave us time to walk back six blocks or so to our tourist room so Lydia could change into her bridal suit, a marvelous violet outfit with a hat covered with violet flowers. She looked . . . well, I don't have to tell you. She was a vision that still shimmers in my mind. As we walked back to the church, a shower opened over us. Who cared? We ran laughing up the steps and inside to the altar, where the minister was waiting, with our two friendly ladies as witnesses and wedding party combined. No, the minister wouldn't accept any money. "Not from a soldier."

The rain had stopped, but we still hurried, going back to our tourist room, where, at long last, we consummated our marriage with wildly conjugal enthusiasm. We napped a bit, went out to dinner, and saw about twenty minutes of a movie, then went back to the room and conjugaled some more. I have to say, it was worth the wait.

The next day, I don't remember what we did (well, I do, of course, but I told you that already). At last I took my girl . . . my *wife* to the station and put her on the night train north, drawing a heart in the grime on the outside of her window with my finger, to keep her company going back to school, where they threw her out of the dormitory, a married woman being inappropriate company for the other girls. I had thirty-six dollars a month stopped from my pay and sent directly to Lydia, giving her a pretty fair stipend to use for rent. She managed.

I almost didn't, checking back on base. I was over half an hour late and had the bad luck to sign in while the first sergeant was going over some rosters. He quickly warmed to his work, reaming me out before ordering company punishment when I managed an edgewise word. "I just got married, Sergeant." This transparent lie outraged him even more, till I showed him our marriage license.

He examined it closely and snorted, "Ahh, you goddamn college boys always got a smart answer, don'cha?" He crumpled it into a ball and threw it back to me. "Awright, Heston . . . get the hell outta here. But I don' wanna see you back here again with any more o' these fuckin' valid excuses!"

Lydia stayed in school. I went to school, first radio, then aerial gunnery, for neither of which I was particularly well qualified. Morse code was easy enough to learn ... for an actor, like learning any part, though I was never more than acceptably good at it. The same was true for aerial gunnery. I'd shot birds in Michigan when I was a kid, with indifferent success; that experience, reasonably enough, was supposed to equip you automatically to run a .50-caliber machine gun. I can't say it did, in my case. But I was very good at enemy aircraft identification ... again, easy for an actor, though it is amazing that you can learn to name any one of thirty or forty different airplanes by seeing a silhouette flashed on a screen for a tenth of a second.

Over three or four months, I was shuttled more or less randomly through several air bases: Scott Field, Illinois; Shepherd Field, Texas; Selfridge Field, Michigan. In retrospect, I suppose the whole command structure was sorting out how to win two wars at once, only barely having time to tool up for that daunting task.

I had a marvelous stroke of luck in what I sensed would be my last state-side posting, Selfridge Field, outside Detroit. I was a sergeant by then, and could wangle a three-day pass. For Lydia, it was an easy train ride from Chicago; I met her and we checked into the Book Cadillac, Detroit's classiest hotel.

I was late getting off base, and Lydia had already checked into the room when I got there. After some vigorous conjugaling, I wanted to confirm the tickets I'd reserved for the next night's performance of Paul Robeson's *Othello* at the Cass Theatre. Thumbing through the phone book looking up "Cass," my finger stopped at "Carter, Russell W." I sat for almost a minute, while my tongue dried on the roof of my mouth.

"Darling ..." I said finally. "Look ... I think this is my father."

I still didn't move, till Lydia touched my cheek and said, "Charlie ... don't you want to call him?"

So I did, though I don't remember dialing the number. Lydia hates telephones, but I think she did it for me. A man's voice answered. I said, "Is this the Russell Carter of St. Helen?" Yes, it was.

"Hello," I said. "I'm ... Charlton." There was a pause.

"Where are you?" he said. I told him. "Wait! I'll be there in twenty minutes." He was, too. He took us out to his house in Grosse

Pointe; we met his wife, Velda, whom I'd known in St. Helen when I was a boy, and my new half-sister, Kay, a beautiful blond six-year-old.

He was as I remembered him, though older and not as tall, somehow—all fathers are tall to their young sons. For ten years Chet had tried his best, I think, in the hard role of surrogate father. In the end, though, I'd missed my dad terribly; to find him again just before shipping out was a wonderful stroke of fortune.

He insisted we stay in his home that last weekend. (I'm afraid we broke the bed in his guest room, but it might have been our last time together.) He and Velda, with Kay, made a little more family for Lydia while I was off at the war. We wrote while I was overseas and had a lot of good times together after I came home. That we came together again was a gift of God.

My war looked as if it would be medium-nasty at first. We were clearly prepping for the CBI—the China/Burma/India theater. At least we wouldn't be facing the Luftwaffe, then still as formidable as any air force in the world. Nevertheless, while you'd rather fight the Japanese, you wouldn't like to be captured by them. We knew about the Bataan death march. Never mind—we were in the pipeline. We got all the appropriate shots, tropical issue uniforms, training films on troop ship discipline over long voyages.

I couldn't tell Lydia any of this, of course, but I had invented a simple plan to tell her where I was, whenever I got there. I bought two identical world maps and marked them exactly alike into grids, with each square numbered in the sequence of Shakespeare's plays. Each square was quartered to represent the acts, and quartering one corner again would give you the scene. I think the CBI, where we surely were bound, fell in *Othello*'s square. I could write Lydia when we got there and say, "I was thinking of when we saw *Othello*. That marvelous bit in Act II, Scene 3, I think. Remember?"

In mid-1944, we were on hold in Seattle, waiting for transport and orders. One rainy night well after lights out we were rousted up, at least twenty crews, plus support personnel, loaded into trucks, and driven through the wet midnight streets to the docks.

Of course it was still raining when we stopped on the pier and jumped down out of the trucks, just as MGM would've filmed it. It got a little goofy then. We picked up our barracks bags and moved up the gangways of what was certainly not a troop ship. It was gleaming white, with polished brass railings, and still manned by civilians in neat white uniforms. Our officers assigned the berthing—staff sergeants and up got private cabins; the bar was open, complete with stewards. We couldn't believe our eyes.

After the war, I found out what had happened. Army Intelligence had reported renewed Japanese activity in the Aleutians. They had successfully invaded and occupied Adak and Attu in 1942, in the darkest days of the Pacific war, and only been driven out a few months earlier. If they were coming back, a few medium bombers would come in handy, tropical uniforms or not.

There were still passenger ships cruising between the U.S. West Coast ports and Canada, up the sheltered inward passage to Alaska. The Army had simply commandeered one of these liners, evacuated the civilian passengers, loaded us aboard, and sent us north. It's the nicest thing the Army ever did for me.

By the time they'd delivered us to the Eleventh Air Force in Alaska and sorted us out along the Aleutian Chain, it was clear the Japs had no intention of re-invading the Aleutians. For the remainder of the war, that was more or less that. The Navy had a large base on Kodiak and another at Dutch Harbor; the Eleventh had bases strung all along the fifteen hundred miles of the Aleutian Chain, hooking across the North Pacific almost to the Japanese Kurils.

The Eleventh had mounted some air strikes out of Attu against Paramushiru, the northernmost Japanese target, but they'd been ineffective and largely abandoned. By 1944 the B-29s were coming on line out of Guam and Okinawa, a vastly superior aircraft that finally ended the war. We rarely flew and were seldom in harm's way, unless you take the weather into account. The average wind velocity in the Aleutians is 32 MPH; if you go down in the Northern Pacific, your survival time in the water is six minutes.

So, for the rest of the war, there we were. The islands are completely treeless, covered with arctic tundra (at Christmas, one guy's wife sent him a one-foot plastic tree. He stuck it in the snow outside his hut, with a fence around it and a hand-carved sign: ALEUTIAN NATIONAL FOREST.) There's one active volcano, Aniakchak, whose crater, surprisingly, contains orchids. A few of us tried to climb its slope once, floundering in failure waist deep in snow a few hours out.

Our offensive role abandoned, we awaited the return of the Japanese, an increasingly unlikely event. The absence of women raised the level of tension, though God knows their presence would've brought it to explosive levels. I got into the last fistfight of my life (so far) over a chess game. When one of the great caribou herds drifted near an airbase, we took a few head to vary our diet. (Unlike the city guys, those of us who were actual hunters knew we were simply harvesting meat.) The animals had never been hunted; it was like shooting cows. True, bringing them down with Garand rifles and hard-nosed military loads required accurate shooting. Fresh meat was surely welcome, though.

My Aleutian service was terminated when one of our planes crashed, trying to land with a forty-mile crosswind. Running to help, I slipped on the ice and slid under an ambulance racing to the wreck. They picked me up with the survivors. I woke up in plaster on a plane bound for the mainland hospital. When I got out, I was grounded and running the control tower at Elmendorf Air Base, in Anchorage, Alaska.

So far, I'd had an easy war. But we were still facing at least another year, maybe more, invading the main islands of Japan. I've researched this since. Operation Downfall was to be a two-pronged assault: Operation Olympic, scheduled for November 1945, aimed at Kyushu, followed by Operation Coronet, in March 1946, landing on Hokkaido, targeting Tokyo and the Emperor. The Eleventh Air Force, including our B-25s, would move to Okinawa, with an infinity of targets—on both sides. The Japanese were fierce defensive fighters; they would surely defend their home islands savagely, foot by blood-soaked foot. The Pentagon estimated half a million American casualties, a million and a half Japanese. The estimates may have been low.

We all knew what was coming; ignorant of the plans, we still sensed their gruesome statistics and faced the awful implications as best we could. Lydia had graduated by then; she had her degree, but when—or would—she have her husband back? Then, suddenly, it was over. They dropped two bombs, and the dreary, endless,

bloody mess was finished at last. In two days the Japanese surrendered.

Yeah, I know. Indeed I know. The politically correct view is
that the atomic bombs were inhumane, even a shameful atrocity.
Never say that to any of us who were facing Operation Downfall.
The two bombs on Hiroshima and Nagasaki killed 125,000. Invading
Japan would've cost millions of lives, most of them Japanese.

Far beyond that, our dread *coup de grâce,* with the strategic
defense we then developed, kept the Soviets at bay for forty years,
saving unmeasured millions more, till their empire finally collapsed. It was an exemplar for the world; God knows it was for me.
It meant I would come home alive, intact, with my life ahead of me.

I finally got my orders home in March 1946 (just when we'd
have been jumping off on Operation Coronet, aimed at the Imperial
Palace). I infinitely preferred going home instead, but events
seemed to conspire against me. Driving in high spirits to take off
for the States, I lost my jeep on a sharp icy turn and buried it in
four feet of snow a hundred yards from the Operations shack. I
wasn't hurt, nor was the jeep—but I didn't want to explore the
subject with higher authority as I checked out of two years in the
Eleventh.

"Ahh, Sergeant, you have a jeep assigned to you, right?"

"Yeah, that's right. It's outside; here are the keys." I boarded
the aircraft and, strapped in with my bags, did my best trying to lift
us off the airstrip with my stomach muscles.

A few hours later, somewhere over Canada, we lost an engine, then another (out of four). Son of a bitch!! I thought. If we
crash now, I am going to be goddamn mad. We didn't, landing late
but intact in Great Falls, Montana, at one of the processing centers
the Army had established to return several million men to civilian
life.

Essentially, we were treading water there for several days
while they funneled the discharge and travel orders through. After
a couple of days lying on my bunk reading paperbacks, I was glad
to get an assignment one morning, however ignominious. They
gave me a detail of ten men to clean the latrines in the area. Most
of them were privates and pfcs. One man, though, reported not in
fatigues but wearing his Class A uniform. He was older than I (most

guys were), bigger than I (most guys weren't), and he had an attitude.

He was a buck sergeant; as a staff sergeant I had one stripe on him. However, he also had the Silver Star and the Purple Heart with two clusters pinned on the left breast of his tunic. "Lemme tell you somepin', son," he said quietly. "Ah done mah time. Ah showed up f'the war; ah did whut they ast me. Now Ah'm goin' home. Ah be goddamned if I scrub shit outta toilets mah last day in this unifo'm."

I agreed with him. If you win the Silver Star, you should never have to scrub shit for anyone. Still, that didn't address my situation. "Sergeant," I said, "we have a problem. If you don't do what I order you to do, I have to report you. Then they'll bring charges against you, and both of us will be stuck here for at least a month. OK. I order you to polish the mirrors and put in fresh toilet paper where needed. Can you handle that?"

His eyes glowed for a second, then he chuckled. "Yeah . . . Ah b'lieve Ah can. You pretty slick, son. Thet's awraht." That was the only significant command decision I made in the war.

Two days later, I got my discharge and they cut my travel orders home.

3

Roads Not Taken

Two roads diverged in a wood, and I —
I took the one less traveled by,
And that has made all the difference.

— ROBERT FROST

MR. FROST HAD IT RIGHT, but it's more complicated. In a war, you don't get to pick your road. You go where they send you, do what they hand you, as well as you can. Don't screw up. Now, here I was home, intact, with my girl and the rest of my life to live.

At first I was just happy—and a little amazed. Then I found I had to remember how to make choices again. You get out of the habit—what to wear, where to eat, what to do next. Choosing. For me, that was figuring out how to make a living acting.

I could've gone back to Northwestern on the GI Bill, of course, with free housing from a grateful Uncle Sam thrown in, but it never crossed my mind. I'd given up all the years I could spare; I wanted to get at it. You can study acting, but after a certain point, that doesn't count. It's the only art you can't practice, really. You have to have a part and an honest-to-God audience, in a theater, in front of a screen in a multiplex cinema, or a TV set in somebody's bedroom.

I left my uniforms at my folks' house, dug out some of my old college civvies, and took up married life in the single room Lydia had hung on to after she got her degree. She was making a good part of a living modeling, and I had my veteran's bonus— twenty bucks a week for a year. The 52/20 Club. With all the guys coming home, housing was impossible, but we were fine. We stored the coffee pot, hot plate, toaster, and groceries in my army footlocker at the foot of the bed. No refrigerator, but we did have a record player and an awful lot of books. It was close quarters, but we were ready for some closeness.

First, I wrote some audition pieces for radio. It was still very big then, and Chicago was a major center. I made the appropriate rounds, but I never got a nibble. That surprised me. It still does, really; my voice has always been a useful asset. I suppose I was too green. Or too rusty.

Within a month, I found myself involved in something much more exciting: a chance to play Mercutio in a Broadway production of *Romeo and Juliet.* The Capulets would all be black and the Montagues white. It was the idea of a British director, Harry Wagstaff Gribble. The season before he'd taken a play about a family of Polish Jews in New York, *Anna Lucasta,* and mounted it very successfully on Broadway with an all-black cast. That company was in Chicago at the end of an equally successful road tour when he hit on his biracial concept for *Romeo.* His Juliet would be Hilda Simms, a beautiful black actress who was playing the title role in *Lucasta,* where he'd found most of the actors to play the Capulets. He was reading Chicago actors for the Montagues, and I was cast as Mercutio.

I was stunned, but not as surprised as I should've been. It's a marvelous part, with one brilliant set-piece speech, usually played as a drunk scene, and a fine quarrel ending in a fight where Mercutio's killed before the audience has a chance to get tired of him. To make your Broadway debut in such a part is the stuff of actors' dreams, especially in a production as innovative as Gribble planned. I know better now than I did then how lucky I was. True, I'd worked on the part at Northwestern (New Trier, too, for that matter), I knew how to fence, and I was right for it. However, in the end, we didn't get to do the play.

We'd been rehearsing for several weeks, waiting for *Lucasta* to close so we could all go to New York. I was spending most of my time on the duel with Brock Peters, who was very good in *Lucasta,* better as Tybalt. Suddenly Gribble's backers got cold feet, or went bankrupt, or suffered any one of the several things that can go wrong with production money.

I've often wondered what would've happened if we *had* gotten it on? A dozen years later, Leonard Bernstein had an enormous success using the same idea with the same play in *West Side Story,* but he cast his Capulets as Puerto Ricans, not nearly as challenging as our black Juliet. Just rehearsing the duel scene with Brock, who was a pal, I found the racial tension was electric.

Nineteen forty-six might have been a bit early for that casting, but it could have worked spectacularly...too. On the other hand, a blow-away hit might not have been altogether healthy for me in my first Broadway part. Blazing, overnight success can be dangerously destabilizing for an actor, especially a young one. Besides, what would I have done for a second part?

THE COLLAPSE of *Romeo and Juliet* galvanized Lydia and me both. We spent a week or so visiting our families, then I took off for New York. Our plan was for me to scout the city...a place to live first.

I went bearing an invitation from a good Army buddy, Bruce Marcus, whose family lived in Brooklyn. "Come stay at my folks' place," he'd said. Delighted at having their son home safe from the war, they put me up for a week or so without question, though a Midwestern *goy* with an acting bug must've struck them as a pretty odd bird. (It was the first time I'd eaten kosher, though a few years later I was to invent that ritual meal, as Moses.) The open-hearted kindness of the Marcus family can't be repaid, only remembered.

Another Army buddy, Bill Darrid, later a writer-producer, pointed me at permanent housing, which was even harder to find in New York than in Chicago. Bill had heard of a patriotic Polish landlord, one Edgar Pitske, who owned several cold-water tenements on the West Side in Hell's Kitchen. An old-style Tammany pol, he'd renovated one of them and limited applications to overseas veterans.

I was quick enough to get one. It was a nineteenth-century railroad flat: four flights of walk-up to two tiny rooms and an alcove for the bed, with two narrow windows in the street wall. There was no heat, but in cold weather the gas oven heated our small space pretty well (in the summer you were out of luck). More important, Mr. Pitske had added to each flat a tiny bathroom with a tile floor, new plumbing, and occasionally running hot water. It was a steal at thirty bucks a month, the cockroaches thrown in for free. (It occurs to me that our cold-water flat provided a crucial amenity lacking in the multimillion-dollar apartment blocks the welfare state would build for the poor a few years later: we had to earn the rent ourselves. That iron imperative focuses the mind wonderfully.)

I wired Lydia to join me and, while the plasterers finished up the Hell's Kitchen flat, I found us a furnished room in Sheepshead Bay, Brooklyn. It was pretty crappy: blazing hot, mosquitoes the size of grasshoppers that blew right through the citronella-soaked Kleenex we put over the holes in the rusty screens. The bed wasn't four feet wide; it made for a resourceful and sweaty sex life; I often fell out.

Meanwhile, back in Hell's Kitchen, Pitske gave us a new paint job. "Y'got yer cherce o'blue er erster." We took erster, and bought some cheap linoleum for the kitchen and second-hand carpet for the front room. I built a bed frame into two sides of the alcove, a closet in one corner of the kitchen, and bookshelves along one wall in the living room.

We got the rest of the furniture at the Salvation Army's second-hand warehouse. Their prices were paltry, but we had to pay. We weren't taking charity. The fund-raising tapes I've done for the Salvation Army ever since leave me still in their debt. They helped us set up a livable space to start off in.

Moving day was a little abrupt. I'd come up to Hell's Kitchen with a couple of suitcases and some chores to do before going back to get the rest of the luggage and Lydia. In mid-afternoon, she appeared at the flat, dead tired and furious. Our Sheepshead landlord had demanded the room back, insisting she wasn't married. When she'd struggled to the subway wearing both her winter coats (in August) and dragging three suitcases, she found she had no money in her purse. She did find a stamp which some good guy bought for the nickel she needed (yeah, that's all the subway cost then). Now, I suppose he would've taken her stamp and her suitcases, too. At least.

It was a nicer town then. We were just about broke most of the time, but so was everyone we knew. We'd trade cheap spaghetti dinners in each other's brownstone basements or tenement walk-ups. Our grocery budget was seven bucks a week. Pasta or meatloaf mostly, some fish. I remember a Kraft macaroni-and-cheese dinner for fifteen cents a box, serves two. We used to cut a couple of slices

of salami into it. Pretty good, actually. There was a good Chinese
restaurant on West Forty-fifth Street where you could fill up for a
dollar and a half. Afterward, we'd stroll across town and win-
dowshop . . . Doubleday's for both of us, Abercrombie & Fitch for
me, and Cartier's for Lydia.

A year or so ago, I was in New York doing publicity for a
film. The next city was Philadelphia, and the studio suggested I
drive down. "It takes about the same time as going all the way out
to LaGuardia and catching the shuttle. You'll be more comfortable
in the limo anyway." Driving down Ninth Avenue the next morning,
I noticed our old street. "Turn right on Forty-fifth," I told the driver.
"Stop in the middle of the block, at four-thirty-three. I want to get
out a minute." He stopped, but he didn't open the door for me.

"You don' wanna get out heah, sir," he said. "This heah's
Hell's Kitchen."

"I know," I said. "I used to live here." I got out and looked
up at the blind, boarded windows, the steel plate blocking the front
door. It was a pleasant spring morning, with no sign of hostiles
lying in ambush, but I remembered how Lydia used to walk home
alone after her evening performance. Yeah . . . a nicer town then.

WE BOTH STARTED making acting rounds and looking for in-the-
meantime work right away. Outside of acting jobs, actors can only
take casual work; if a part comes up, they must always be able to
say "Look, I won't be able to work next Wednesday, Thursday, or
Friday. I have a part in a TV show." This limits the jobs you can get
to those where you can be instantly replaced and hardly missed
when you're gone. Carwashes, grocery bag-boys, that kind of thing.
Waiting tables is good, though we never tried it.

I sometimes think the hardest thing about acting is getting
the damn part in the first place. Statistically, it's impossible. To beat
the odds, you need the guts of a burglar and skin thick enough to
turn cold steel, or at least the cold eye of a casting director. I know
one very good actor who, after a dozen years of making an in-and-
out living in some so-so parts and a couple of very good ones, just
packed it in and took a job in his cousin's carpet company, where I
have no doubt he is now giving a fine performance as an executive
vice president.

Lydia and I were lucky, as you have to be. She found modeling work almost at once. Lingerie, mostly, for the color inserts in the Sunday papers, and figure work for several good painters. I couldn't get any lingerie ads, but I did get some work posing in the life classes at the Art Students League. I made $1.25 an hour, with a five-minute break every half hour. Free tea and cookies. It was fairly tough work holding a pose, also boring. I used to run over Shakespearean soliloquies in my head. It's a good acting discipline to let those passions surge through your mind without even twitching.

There was an odd sort of sex discrimination in the life classes, though nobody seemed to make anything of it. The women models posed nude, but the men all wore some sort of loincloth. Lydia cut down a jock strap for me and covered it with gray velour. It looked kind of dashing, I thought, though none of the women in the class seemed to notice. I did get an erection once, but I wasn't thinking about either sex or Shakespeare at the time. I think it was because the studio was warmer than usual. It got pretty crowded inside that jockstrap, but I never moved a muscle . . . well, no other muscle . . . and in the end, it gave up. (Now, see? I could've embroidered that into a really exciting story. No, tell it like it is . . . or was.)

There were still certain marginal advantages to being a returned veteran. They were fading by the fall of 1946, but you'd still get the occasional free beer in a bar, and the weekly twenty bucks I told you about, as well as my first chance at our walkup on Forty-fifth Street. Later on I took fencing lessons on the GI Bill, too, but my most lasting benefit stemmed from a notice I read in a trade paper: Theatre Inc., a new production company with a couple of successes to its credit, announced they would guarantee an audition to any actor-veteran. ("Veteran" you had to prove. "Actor" they would take on faith.)

I got a wire telling me to appear at the Booth Theatre, 3:30 P.M., September 21. The Booth is a little gem of a theater just off Broadway. I've never done a play there, but I guess my professional career got started on that small stage.

Actors waiting to audition are a quirky, mixed bunch. Some seem stretched on an inner rack, pale with anxiety. Others wear party faces, joking tensely with pals. We were also cold, that afternoon in Shubert Alley. The wind under the marquee of the Booth was enough to make you keep your hands in your pockets. Across

Forty-fourth Street, a stunning girl came out of Sardi's, huddling
into her fur as the doorman handed her into a black limo. As it
pulled past us toward Times Square, you could see her kiss the
cheek of the lean, gray-mustached man beside her. One of the
actors beside me watched in envious awe. "That guy's sure got it
all."

"Just about," said an older actor, also lean and gray-
mustached, though lacking the limo. "But he can't act."

It wasn't clear whether any of us waiting there outside the
Booth could, either, but at least we were getting a chance to try.

There were four or five Theatre Inc. people sitting in the
fifth row, though they probably spelled each other through the long
chore of watching several hundred actors showing their stuff. I did
Mercutio's Queen Mab speech because I knew it well, it's a good
audition piece, and I was technically equipped for it. It's also a very
complex undertaking; I doubt I can really have been very good in
it. As a director, though, sitting on the other end of the audition
process, I've since learned you can sometimes catch something
else, maybe more important. Some kid walks on and your eye is . . .
caught, somehow. They call it "being there." Filling your space is
what they mean. Perhaps I did that.

Anyway, they asked me to stay, and the next time they took a
break, a red-headed, freckle-faced guy walked over and introduced
himself: Robert Fryer. As Theatre Inc.'s casting director, he was on
the first rung of a long and distinguished career as a producer, in
the theater and in film, from *Auntie Mame* to *Macbeth*. I've worked
for him many times since, in some marvelous parts, but his picking
me out of that audition started it all. Not incidentally, Bobby's also
a good friend. A few years ago, I ran across that first telegram he
sent me. I put it in a silver frame and gave it to him for Christmas.

All that was a long time later, though. What he had in mind
then was a production they were planning of an Elizabethan play,
The Changeling. Since it was not by Shakespeare, but Thomas Mid-
dleton, that was pretty brave of them. When Bobby told me he
wanted me to read for the male lead, the cold September dusk
turned into a brilliant May morning.

Outside, of course, it was still fall, darker and danker each
day. But my interior weather stayed warm and clear. Theatre Inc.
put back their schedule on *Changeling,* so Lydia and I kept up our

rounds of the producers and agents. That's hard to do, day after day, but crucial. You're the little ball, bouncing around the spinning roulette wheel, hoping to fall into the right slot. As a new kid with my army haircut just grown out, there weren't many of those slots for me. Skinny, six-three, broken nose, and cheekbones sticking out? Too tall for the male stars who worry about how tall the other actors are, too young for the parts I was right for, naahh, nothing today. Leave your picture, come back next month.

There was an agent named Chamberlain Brown who, it was widely understood, was most interested in young actors, but that wasn't an accommodation I was prepared to make. (Somehow, there didn't seem to be many women of influence in the corridors of power in the theater then. That kind of offer, I would've considered. Where was the women's movement when I needed them?)

I'll bet I left pictures and résumés with three-quarters of the agents and producers in town. At last, I was offered an honest-to-God part. *Harvey,* the play about the imaginary rabbit that Jimmy Stewart later immortalized both on stage and film, was still running on Broadway. They needed a replacement for the ambulance driver, who had five lines. I was reconciled to this somewhat modest Broadway debut because of the salubrious effect of a part in a long-running show, when I found out it was for a road company. There I drew the line. Another road not taken, though I can't really imagine that one leading very far. There's not a lot you can do with five lines of ambulance driver on a two-month national road tour.

Besides, the next choice that came up looked a lot better. I'd left quite a paper trail in the offices around Manhattan, but I still have no idea how Forrest Wood found us. He'd been dispatched to Manhattan from Asheville, North Carolina, to find a director for the Community Theater there. He checked various producers; one of them (may his name be written in the Golden Book) remembered me warmly enough to dig up my phone number. Forrest met Lydia and me in the bar of the Great Northern Hotel, where I persuaded him that he should hire *both* of us as codirectors.

Forrest went back to Asheville to recommend us to the board of directors. He must have been eloquent; they hired us for the princely sum of a hundred dollars a week. Each. That's a lot more than I'd have gotten on the road as the ambulance driver. In two days we'd locked up in Hell's Kitchen and boarded a Trailways bus for the Great Smokies, cushioned on two pillows I'd rented for a dollar, "T'keep y'all from gettin' quat s'tahred on the trip," as a pretty blond vendor told us in the station.

Asheville was then a very handsome town, nestled in the foothills of the Blue Ridge Mountains in the western toe of the Carolinas. (Lydia and I went back a couple of years ago to do a performance for them to raise funds; we had a fine time, raised a lot of money, and they named the theater after us. I'm happy to report that, though the town's grown, the place and the people are still the same.) Asheville's far enough south for a mild winter, and high enough for a cool summer. The mountains may lack the fierce grandeur of the Rockies, but they have an elderly, easy beauty of their own.

We got to Asheville at night. (Why are most of my memories of arrivals in new places night scenes? Smoky darks and unknown shadows, lamp-lit Caravaggio faces and swirling movement.) The theater honchos were there, and Forrest, whom we soon learned to call "For'st." They moved us into a large bedroom, with kitchen and parlour privileges, in a spacious old house belonging to an elderly German widow of means just modest enough to welcome a month's rent on a front bedroom. She had clear black eyes, perfectly dressed white hair, and flawless English. Her manner was that of a rather remote hostess rather than a landlady. It was certainly a marked improvement on Hell's Kitchen and Mr. Pitske.

The next day, we inspected the theater, which was not bad, as municipal auditoriums go, and then had a meeting to explore the theater's production plans. Aside from a secretary, Lydia and I were the theater's only employees, but they had a dedicated board, who were determined to make an honest cultural contribution.

The theater Lydia and I found ourselves running (we'd be "artistic directors" now, but that grandiloquent title hadn't been invented then) was part of the tributary theater, an accurate description. The Asheville Community Theater (ACT) was one of hundreds, maybe thousands, of similar theaters around the country providing live theater to local audiences, all sustained by in-kind contributions and loans of just about everything you might need to stage a play: furniture, props, costumes, lumber, and hardware from private companies and private people, paid for by a program credit or a simple "Thanks a lot." A local church or the community center would usually provide the auditorium, with rehearsal space, plus lights, heat, parking, and phones. The local press was usually generous with publicity and critical opinion; depending on the quality of the production and the energy and resourcefulness of the promotion, many tributary theaters generated very respectable grosses. ACT was one of these, certainly during the time we were there. Given our low overhead, consisting in large part of our salaries, this gave us a reasonable operating fund.

You understand, of course, that all the Ashevillians who worked in ACT did it free. Cast, crew, front-of-the-house staff . . . they were all amateurs. The word's too often used as a dismissive pejorative—which is snobbish, also wrong. "Amateur" comes from the Latin for love. Amateurs do it for love. (That's probably why sex is the only thing amateurs do better than pros . . . enthusiasm counts for a lot.) Indeed, most theater professionals and a lot of filmmakers, too, spent some part of their apprenticeship in the tributary theater.

Still, the level of talent, training, and experience in such a company is spotty, though some of the people we used had actually studied acting. Several more had worked in ACT for years. A lot of it depends on the play you pick. I didn't want to strain my actors beyond their capacities. Or mine, for that matter. The only thing I'd gotten paid for since my minor role in World War II was standing naked in front of a bunch of art students. I was taking money under false pretenses; the ACT board, having made the unusual decision to upgrade the quality of their productions by hiring a professional director, had ended up with me.

I did not, in fact, defraud them. ACT hired me because they were sure I could direct. I was sure of it, too. I'd only done it once in the Air Corps, and at Northwestern. This was the first time I'd been paid for it, but that filled the job description. I was a professional director. I was a trained actor, I'd studied movement, voice and diction, dramatic structure, stage lighting, set construction, costume and makeup; I had a sense of casting and performance, as well as pace and timing, which are not the same thing. Far more important than any of this, though, a director has to make you believe in him. I can do that. I was a pretty good sergeant.

Still, I had to pick the right first play. You don't do Molière

or Shaw, certainly not Shakespeare. Lydia suggested James Thurber's *The Male Animal.* It's very funny, one set, smallish cast, and it
has a little meat on its bones, too. It was a good choice, not least
because I knew the play; I'd acted in it at Northwestern. So had
Lydia, in summer stock, while I was overseas; I was tempted to use
her, but I found a local lady who could manage it, so I made what
seemed a politic concession.

It went very smoothly, especially for a green director. We
blocked the play in three nights (community theaters rehearse at
night, because people have jobs during the day). That means you
can only rehearse four hours a night, which means a longer rehearsal period overall—not a bad idea, with an amateur cast.

I'd designed the set, as I ended up doing for all the plays we
did. I wanted to get that under way properly, so I turned a couple
of rehearsals over to Lydia and spent some time in the scene shop,
where a local contractor was ACT's master carpenter. He was damn
good, too. Our sets did not fall down, our doors neither wobbled
nor stuck, all notorious pitfalls in tributary theater.

I also designed our poster, shamelessly stealing one of Thurber's immortal *New Yorker* cartoons. Stores generously displayed
them, restaurants put miniature versions I'd had printed on the
tables. The week before *The Male Animal* opened, Lydia and I
interviewed each other on the local radio station, talking about the
movies opening in Asheville and, of course, our play.

It went very well. Perhaps local curiosity about the new kids
in town helped, certainly Mr. Thurber's play itself was the main
factor. It held up wonderfully well with our amateur cast. It was
successfully revived on Broadway a few years later, as I suspect it
could be now. The only adjustment I made to my actors' limitations
was to shift the locale of the play from Ohio to Georgia. Since they
were all Southerners, switching to lines like "But Ah'm not fum
Atlanna . . . Ah'm fum *S'wickleh!*" simply tripped more likely from
the tongue.

True, one of the principals over-celebrated his good notices
and showed up for the second performance a little bruised by the
grape, and broke a record of "Who?" (this was an old 78) as he
fumbled it onto the phonograph, whereupon he said, "Aww, looky
heah. *Whooo?* . . . an' it's *broh-kin.*" He stood fumbling with the

pieces till the stage manager simply started the record offstage, but I've seen worse than that on Broadway. Hell, I've *done* worse than that on Broadway.

We sold out for the brief run ACT always scheduled (you can't expect a cast of working men and women to give free performances every night indefinitely), and set to work on another play. This time I chose a political comedy only recently closed in New York: Lindsay and Crouse's *State of the Union.* This was a slightly tougher undertaking technically—it had two sets. I remember I wrote to the Book Cadillac Hotel in Detroit, where the second act took place, and got them to lend us a full set of room-service china and napery to make our Presidential Suite look properly Northern. Also a waiter's uniform, all for a program credit.

Union also had a more serious theme than Thurber's play. I cast Lydia in the female lead (after *The Male Animal,* I was ACT's golden boy). Besides, I knew she'd be good in it, providing the deeper edge that play required. She exceeded my expectations; so did the play. We had another sell-out. Carl Sandburg, who lived in town, attended a performance and had lovely things to say. You could say we were on a roll.

This seemed a good time to take a quick look at the New York scene. Our deal with ACT left both parties free to terminate on a month's notice. We'd undertaken the Asheville adventure as a chance to save up a nest egg. We had enough put by to go back and test the water. I left Lydia to finish the run of *State of the Union* and bussed north. I was glad to be back, but it was after Easter, and Broadway was slowing down for the summer. My only hot iron in the fire was at Theatre Inc., and Bobby Fryer said they weren't doing *The Changeling* till fall. On the bird-in-the-hand principle, I went back to Asheville Community Theater.

Spring in the mountains is just as beautiful as they say, blooming dogwood and soft, lengthening days. Better than this, though, was the chance to do what I wanted to do, the way I wanted to do it. Asheville and its people began to seem more and more attractive. We were working very hard. I have few memories of that time beyond choosing, casting, and rehearsing the plays; designing and supervising the sets; advertising; and getting each play opened and through its run. There was the occasional small party, but I don't remember any sports or social expeditions. We'd go to a small

Chinese restaurant after rehearsal now and then with some of the younger people in the company, but the work was my meat and drink.

I remember one afternoon our landlady, Frau Schiller, who I was amazed to find had been an actress in Germany, read us scenes from *Othello* in Goethe's German translation. It sounded marvelous, and so did she. I tried to woo her onto our stage in the next play we had cooking, *Kind Lady,* about an old lady in a wheel-chair trapped in her own house by a clutch of nasties, but she would have none of it. "That would be very nice, but I think I must not. These people are just playing at theater. It is good for you, and you help them, but it's not the same. I have played Desdemona in Berlin. I would rather remember that."

She was right. I understood that. Everyone in ACT was wonderful to us; they worked with heart-warming enthusiasm and more than a little skill, but it wasn't meat and drink to them. It was cocktail nuts to nibble; a lot of fun, making plays. Not to me. I wanted the arena . . . sweat, sand, and blood, where it really counts. To take the test, and give your best . . . and then somehow be better. Like the Olympic motto, *Citius, Altius, Fortius.* Faster, Higher, Stronger. ("Fun." I've heard that for years. Six months in Madrid, on one film? "What fun." No, it's not. It's six months of twelve-hour days and six-day weeks, trying to get it right and falling a little short almost every day. It's supposed to be fun for you . . . not for us.)

Wendell Jeffries, ACT president, wanted us to sign a year's contract, with a nice raise. There was talk of a car, an expanded production budget, a radio talk show (with TV already stirring on the horizon), a new theater, all sorts of good things. Really good things—it would've been a wonderful life. Asheville is one of the loveliest towns I've ever seen, in Thomas Wolfe's "wooded cup of hills." Lydia and I could've built a theater, a home, and a family together there, and done it just about as we chose. The big culture frog in the Carolina pond.

But somehow it wasn't what we wanted, either of us. We talked about it, but we had no doubts. We gave our notice, feeling gratifyingly noble. We did two more plays after *Kind Lady.* For the last, I wanted something special. Tennessee Williams' *The Glass Menagerie* was still selling out in New York, the first jewel of the rich legacy he was to leave the American theater. I hadn't seen it, but Lydia had, in its Chicago tryout, just before she graduated. She said it was a deeply moving and eloquent play, and we should do it. Also, I should play the son/narrator, Tom. (There are only three other characters.) When I read it, I agreed with her. I was determined to do the play, and the part. I hadn't acted on a stage since the war.

We mounted the second production of *Menagerie* done anywhere. I'm still proud of it, not least because we brought a groundbreaking Southern play to Asheville. Maybe that's why Williams let our unknown company do it there. It explores the Southern psyche as movingly, and accurately, as Thomas Wolfe's novel *You Can't Go Home Again* had years earlier.

I wanted to use the intermittent images projected on the set that Williams indicates, but the technology was beyond us. The play was not. Its melancholy reverie, playing in Tom's memory, spoke clearly to me. I can't be sure at this distance, but I think I was good in it. It may have been the first really good work I did. It surely gave us a triumphant exit from Asheville.

When we climbed on the bus back to New York in August of 1947 with our nest egg, we were vastly more enriched by the baggage we carried inside, including some friendships, like Dick and Pat Creedy, which still flourish. We rolled into the terminal and splurged on a cab to get the suitcases back to Hell's Kitchen. While Lydia unpacked, I went straight to the Theatre Inc. offices to report myself available for *The Changeling*.

The frosted glass door was dark, though the company logo was still painted there. It was half-obscured by a rough-lettered cardboard sign: CLOSED.

4

Shakespeare and Other Fellas

And one man in his time plays many parts . . .

— W. SHAKESPEARE, *As You Like It*

THEATRE INC. *closed!?* How could they be? Nobody told me! What about *The Changeling?* What about *me?* A man can fail at anything, often predictably: a farmer can lose his wheat crop, but not to a blizzard in July. For actors, though, disaster can leap from any corner, any time, tiger-quick.

I know, such a furor over losing a part you never had in the first place. But actors, especially young ones, build castles in very thin air. Theatre Inc. had planned a play and promised me a chance to read for it. Now the play was off, and so were they. *The Changeling,* as far as I know, has still never had a professional production in this country, but I already had myself on stage in it. I'd dug out my school copy of *Elizabethan & Stuart Plays* and worked on scenes, down in Asheville. I was *going* to do it. Nuhh-uh. Not in this life.

I walked home, hurting like a kicked cat. I don't usually buckle like that, but I did then. I flopped on the bed and told Lydia my sad story. She wasn't as sympathetic as I'd expected. "Well, you ought to go make some more rounds, then. We've been away a while. Didn't Bill Darrid say Cornell-McClintic was casting?" Well, yes; there had been something in a postcard. But clear across town, *now?* Still, after she gave me a cup of coffee, I went.

Katharine Cornell and Helen Hayes were just about even in the First Lady of the American Theater contest, though both disdained the idea. When Guthrie McClintic, Miss Cornell's husband and director, announced her in Shakespeare's *Antony and Cleopatra,* it was very large news indeed. I wasn't surprised to find even the hall outside their offices in Radio City crowded. The waiting room was jammed.

I'd made rounds enough to know that the dozen or so actors seated smugly behind the railing had appointments, made by agents. They'd no doubt actually worked on Broadway, possibly even with Miss Cornell! The rest of us were mere supplicants scratching at the gate.

It occurred to me that the gate was a real one, and only three feet high. I have long legs. When the secretary escorted one of the anointed into the inner sanctum, I stepped over the railing and sank into an empty chair. That step put me on one of Mr. Frost's roads "less traveled by." Maybe it was the one that made all the difference.

As the afternoon wore on, the unruly rabble outside the gate was dispersed (funny how your attitude changes once you get inside, even illegally). I acted inconspicuous. Finally, I was the only actor left. The secretary looked at me sharply. "What is your name, please? I don't have anyone else listed."

"That's strange," I said, now acting amazed. "Maynard Morris of MCA made the appointment. I'm Charlton Heston." My name was nothing to conjure with then, of course, and I'd never met Maynard Morris, nor gotten inside the MCA offices. (They had higher gates.)

It worked, though. "Well, Mr. McClintic has a little time. Follow me." I did, acting tall. I'd heard Miss Cornell liked tall actors around her, being tall herself. Her biographer, Tad Mosel, says she was on the short side, but did indeed hire tall men. I'll tell you this: onstage she was *very* tall.

Guthrie McClintic was not. He was lean and loose-jointed, with an intense, beagle sort of face. I think I caught him at a good time. At the end of the day with his work done, he seemed inclined to indulgence with the last kid he had to see. I went on at some length about my training and experience, exaggerating my Shakespearean credentials, till he interrupted. "Care to try a cold reading?"

Maybe he was calling my bluff; a cold reading of a new text can be a daunting experience. (This is no measure of talent; a lot of fine actors aren't good at it. Paul Scofield, notoriously, doesn't even rehearse well, mumbling morose internal anxieties until opening night.) For not the last time in my life, I was lucky: I always could read cold. I'd never seen *Antony and Cleopatra,* but I'd studied it at Northwestern and recently read Granville Barker's superb preface. The speech he handed me was Octavius Caesar's elegy over the dead lovers, ending the play.

I gave him an adequate cold reading, after which he looked at me quizzically and said, "Not bad. Come back tomorrow at ten." I walked home across town fully a foot above the sidewalk. Could I possibly have a chance at Caesar? Nahh, too young again. Still, it made for a euphoric evening in Hell's Kitchen.

No, of course I didn't get Caesar; that had just been a good speech to audition with. I was cast as Proculeius, one of his officers, who mostly goes on and off in armour with the odd line or two, except for one good scene at the end when he captures Cleopatra, tearing off a couple of yards of verse in the struggle. I suppose I seemed up to the job physically; there are a fair number of parts in Shakespeare that include heavy lifting. He staged his plays with neither scenery nor intermission; all large props, prisoners, corpses, and wounded had to be cleared off for the next scene. Some of his actors were stagehands with lines, really.

Another note in our Shakespeare as Actually Staged series. A no-credit lecture, skip if you like. Almost all the plays have a surprising number of small parts, none very good, but often easily combined into larger roles that serve the same structural needs and also become significant characters instead of faceless figures. When McClintic took the company on the road at the end of the Broadway run, he cut the cast down a bit and combined some of the parts; I picked up a few new speeches and a little more money. Much later, when I filmed the play, I blended still more roles into Proculeius and made it a really good part. (No, that time I played Antony.)

Shakespeare surely understood this. I think he also had a large company to support. Crony casting, they call it now; I'm sure it was even more common then, given the low Elizabethan salaries. I can hear Dick Burbage over lunch at the Boar's Head: "And, Will

... you'll remember to write some sort of bit for old Miles, won't you?" Small-part actors have been living on those roles for four hundred years.

One of the supremely happy memories of my life is that of me walking up Sixth Avenue a few days later on a brilliant autumn morning, on the way to my first rehearsal in my first engagement in an honest-to-God Broadway play. That's pretty heady stuff when you've been pointing to it for so long.

(Decades later, I can still feel the September sun on my shoulders. A kid actor with a sixty-five-dollar-a-week bit part, I felt like God—or Laurence Olivier, which comes to about the same thing.)

The first day of rehearsal on a play is different from starting a film, where you often begin with a minor scene with one or two actors. Beginning a play is like going on a voyage into unknown waters. There's a sense of—portent, even ritual. In 1947, everyone wore jacket and tie; I recall Miss Cornell in a fur coat, which she dropped on the stage by her chair. We all gathered around a long table and, after a talk by McClintic, read the play through. Once. If you've never heard that happen, a dozen or so good professionals sitting around a table stroking through one of his greater works, you can't really imagine how much better old Will is than all the other fellas.

Then McClintic said, "All right, ladies and gentlemen, let's begin." The men took off their jackets, loosened their ties, and we started. I remember noticing that the principal actors wore French cuffs and links. "Hah!" I thought. "That's what real actors wear . . . cuff links." Ever since, so have I.

Some directors keep their casts tied to the table for days, reading and exploring the meaning of the text at length. Playwrights like this a lot. Ours was not with us, and McClintic felt he could find the play soonest with the actors on their feet, reaching for their roles, not sitting around talking about it. All actors love to talk about acting, partly because it's a lot easier than actually doing it.

McClintic was not a physically impressive man, but his rehearsals were charged with energy and purpose. "We'll have Act One blocked by tomorrow." "Get your lines, every syllable. Shakespeare requires it." "Enter these cuts." "The following actors report for fittings Thursday at eight A.M. sharp; remember rehearsal is at nine. Don't be late." "Be ready to do Acts One and Two without books by Friday."

He'd been directing his wife for twenty-something years and a lot of other people longer than that; he knew how to do it. A good captain. As for Miss Cornell herself, even in rehearsal clothes, she glowed. I remember her as always pleasant, but somehow remote . . . maybe a little daunted by the part she faced. Cleopatra, the longest and by far the best woman's role in Shakespeare, is also the most difficult woman's role in all drama. *Antony and Cleopatra* is one of his last plays, surely one of the very best. Cleopatra glistens at its center like the "orient pearl" of the poet's line. Heroine, harridan, child, bitch, lover, leopard, slut, and queen, she was (so history suggests and Shakespeare incomparably shows us) just about everything any woman ever was. All in one: "Age cannot wither her, nor custom stale/Her infinite variety . . ."

"Infinite variety" is the catch. I've never seen the actress that could really incarnate *all* those different women. A good actress will find three or four of them, a great one half a dozen, maybe, but all eight of them at random through the play, maybe more I didn't think of?

You understand I wasn't thinking this then, in the back row of Miss Cornell's supporting cast, but I imagine she was. Ten years earlier, Tallulah Bankhead had tried the part. *The New York Times* said, "Last night, Miss Bankhead barged down the Nile as Cleopatra . . . and sank." A season or two before us, Edith Evans, then and perhaps still considered the best English actress of this century, had done the part in London. Godfrey (not yet then Sir Godfrey) Tearle had been her Antony and was now Miss C's. (No, we didn't call her that. Her husband and Godfrey and one or two of the principals called her "Kit," but the rest of us stayed with "Miss Cornell.") I never heard Godfrey comment on her performance, but he said of Edith Evans, "She was marvelous in the comedy and fine as the queen, especially in the quarrels. I'm afraid slut was not really her line of country, though. And you *do* need slut for Cleopatra."

I doubt if I'm a reliable source on Miss Cornell's Cleopatra. These were, as the play puts it, "my salad days, when I was green in judgment." The whole experience was golden for me; it still gleams misty in my mind. I thought she was marvelous; so did the critics, but they're quirky on acting generally and often unsound on Shakespeare. Still, looking back from a wiser perspective on the play and how tough that part is, I suspect she found her share of the lady.

Certainly, she gave us a hit. That's never easy to do with Shakespeare, hardest of all with a play like *Antony,* with an almost unreachable leading role. We had the longest run the play has ever had, anywhere. It was a triumph for Miss Cornell; for me, the best apprenticeship a kid actor could hope for. I was really learning acting, as both art and profession.

A few weeks into the run, New York was shut down by one of the heaviest snowfalls of the century. Some of the cast slept in the theater, not sure they could get home. Our cold-water walk-up was only a block and a half from the theater and I'd been raised in Michigan, so that didn't occur to me. The next morning, though, the island was buried in snow; not a car moved. Miss Cornell, in her fifties, walked across Manhattan through thirty inches of snow that night, getting to the theater on time, as always. So did most of her audience, including a couple who'd walked through the Lincoln Tunnel from New Jersey to see her.

McClintic had assembled a fine cast, including a few green-horns like me who could only grow in that fertile ground. Godfrey Tearle even let us drop into his dressing room in the act breaks to listen to his stories. Having since learned firsthand the bone-tired weariness that sucks your energy playing these Shakespearean monsters, I wonder he tolerated us for a minute. With those parts, you're wise to lie down with your feet up every minute you're offstage.

I was taking in a great deal more than I was expected to put out. It was an ideal Broadway debut, especially after the freedom I'd had in Asheville, more or less running my own company. Cornell-McClintic was one of the best managements in the American theater, superbly qualified to produce Shakespeare and train green kids at the same time. Quite a few of us remember the springboard we got there.

I don't mean there were any master classes in Shakespeare on matinee mornings; you absorbed that every performance from the guy who wrote it, doing it and seeing it done. Being there. The clear instruction was in the old, iron rules: Don't be late, don't be sick, don't screw up.

Godfrey Tearle demonstrated this when we were in Philadelphia, tuning the play up before Broadway. He got the flu. At sixty-something, with one of old Will's mankillers to carry, the week before opening, he got the flu. His solution was simple: he played Antony *through* the flu. He'd rage into those wrenching, soaring scenes, exit, and collapse on a cot in the wings, vomiting into the bucket beside it. I remember that every time I think I have a cold coming on, or may have pulled a muscle, working out.

There was a girl in the company, later famous, who, changing one night, felt a mouse run over her foot just as she stepped out of her panties. She sprang to safety on the sink, which promptly pulled out of the wall, flooding her dressing cubicle and dumping her on the floor. Her screams brought all of us on that side of the theater running, along with the old Irish stage doorman, who panted up four flights of stairs to find her sprawled stark naked and weeping in two inches of water and broken plumbing. He was unmoved. "How many times do I have to tell you actresses?" he said. "Don't pee in the goddamn sink!" You can't learn that in acting school.

I had no problems with promptness or staying healthy, but I was worried about screwing up my capture of Cleopatra, which McClintic had staged very effectively. I appeared at the barred entrance to the tomb where she was hidden, broke in, and seized her before she could stab herself, leaping down a flight of twenty-one steps to do it.

I'm not sure McClintic realized how risky it was. Not to me, really, but if I'd ever slipped on that jump, two hundred pounds of actor in armor would've knocked Miss Cornell right into the orchestra pit. That's why I checked my footing on those steps every night during intermission.

Whenever we moved to a new city, I took particular pains to check the step unit. It was late winter in Pittsburgh when we got there; I went straight to the theater. The stage was empty, but the work light was bright enough for me to make sure of the stairs again. As I turned to go, I heard weeping from the star dressing room. The door, with Miss Cornell's brass nameplate already on it, was half open. As I came cautiously closer, I could see in the mirrored wall inside the huddled figure of Lenore Ulric.

She'd been a blazing star for Belasco a generation earlier, but had fallen on leaner times. McClintic, perhaps in compassion, had miscast her as Charmian, Cleopatra's handmaiden. Her performance had never risen to adequacy, but there'd been no thought of replacing her; she'd soldiered on, doing her best. I've no idea what drew her to the theater that dark winter day: to visit the scene of past triumphs, or maybe just to pick up her mail. I took a step closer and saw she was kneeling in front of a life-size painting of herself as Kiki, one of her greatest successes, crying like a lost child. I slipped quietly out the stage door.

One night toward the end of our New York run, I got to the theater five minutes before half hour was called, as I'd learned early to do. Jimmy Neilsen, McClintic's superb but steel-eyed stage manager, was checking the cast in, a job he usually left to his assistant. "Heston!" he said. "Miss Cornell wants to see you in her dressing room. Now!" He jerked his thumb down the carpeted hall, though I knew where it was. I'd even been inside, on opening night, when she poured champagne for the cast after the curtain and the cheers.

I didn't feel like cheering. I'm fired, I thought, despairing. No, wait. McClintic would do that, or Jimmy Neilsen...they wouldn't have her fire me. I stopped in my tracks. What...what if she wants to go to bed with me? What if she...*now?!* My cooler, rational self took his cue. That's ridiculous...she's in the first scene. Use your head. Don't panic. Just think it through, so you don't look like an idiot.

I was moving again, toward her door. If she sees me in the sitting room and the maid is there, it's something else. If she sees me in her dressing room, be alert for anything. Especially if she's wearing a dressing gown. I didn't get any further than that; I was knocking on the door. Evelyn, her dresser/maid, let me in. Miss Cornell was not there, only her dachshund, who gave me a disdainful look.

"She says to go right on in," Evelyn said, pointing to the inner room. My throat dried as I crossed to the door, which was slightly ajar. It swung open under my knuckles. There stood the lady, luminous and vulnerable, in a red silk robe, loosely tied. Blood began to beat behind my temples.

"You wanted to see me, Miss Cornell?" My tone, I hoped, was cool, debonair, yet respectful.

"Yes, I did, Chuck. Come in. I want to show you something."
My mouth was dry now. I stepped forward, closing the door carefully behind me. "You know the scene where you capture me?"

I nodded dumbly; I was having a little trouble breathing.
Don't screw up, my cool inner self said to me, as a series of riotous
images rolled through my mind. Her smile was small, but incandescent. She ... parted ... the robe, revealing an ivory-smooth thigh,
marred by a blue-green bruise the size of my hand. "When you
throw me across your leg to take my dagger away, I always land on
your sword. Do you suppose you could wear it on your other hip,
just for that scene?"

I was suddenly voluble. "Oh, no . . . I mean, *yes,* Miss Cornell.
I can wear it . . . I don't need to wear it at *all,* you see. In that scene.
In the whole play, really. I never—ah, *use* it, do I? In the play, that
is." And so on, till she opened the door to let me escape. The
dachshund was more disdainful than ever.

It was not my finest hour. On top of which, I never did figure
out what I would've done if she'd wanted to go to bed with me. But
I wouldn't have changed my time in that company, not even for the
chance to understudy Olivier. Well, maybe for that.

THE RECORD-BREAKING RUN of *Antony* ended in Chicago, my
mother in happy attendance. Lydia and I went directly to Mt. Gretna,
Pennsylvania, where we'd been hired for the summer at one of the
oldest stock theaters in the country. Again, we were in luck. A
season in stock is a useful experience for an actor, and there
weren't that many theaters left then that still provided it. Summer
stock now consists of star packages of a core group of actors touring
from theater to theater with the same play, picking up bit players in
each venue. Lydia and I took a couple of plays around that way a
few years later.

Resident stock is different. You have a company of six or
eight actors hired for the summer to do all the parts in all the plays
in your season, changing the bill every week, rehearsing the next
one in the daytime, playing the current offering at night. There's no
room for matinees, because of rehearsal. You close Saturday night,
tear down that set through the night, and put up the next one on
Sunday. Tech rehearsal in the afternoon, dress rehearsal that night,

open Monday night, having had a read-through on the following week's play that morning. No days off, obviously.

This was the first acting job I ever got without looking for it, off my brief performance in *Antony*. Not true, really; I was hired because McClintic had hired me, the theory being if you did a small part with Cornell you could play leads anywhere else. Which is what I did: ten plays in eleven weeks, the lead in all but a couple where the comedy juvenile took that chore, giving me the blessed ease of a small part for a week.

It was hell, but it was heaven for a kid with acting ants in his pants. I remember the director pitching the job in my *Antony* dressing room, the experience we'd gain, the good parts I'd have. "I should tell you one thing, though," he said. "This is a very old theater, and it doesn't depend on the tourists. The local community supports it . . . mostly good Dutch farmers. They love the plays, but they don't want to mingle with the actors. There's a street in the town you're not supposed to cross and a separate beach on the lake you swim from. If this bothers you, you'd better tell me now."

"Hell, I don't care," I said. "What are the parts?"

Actors are the oldest minority group in the world, largely unperturbed by the scorn of real people. Maybe we cherish our difference. When blacks were isolated in innocence in the African rain forests and Jews inviolate in Mosaic dignity, actors were getting kicked in the streets of Athens, fighting with stable dogs for their share of rich men's leftovers. It doesn't seem to have outraged them. When the London theaters were shut down in the seventeenth century, the actors took it philosophically, retreating to Italy to teach fencing and seduce girls. When I first filmed in Madrid, actors couldn't stay at the Ritz Hotel, but I didn't really care. I doubt I could join the Los Angeles Country Club even now, though Victor Mature was pretty upset when they turned him down because he was an actor. "I'm no actor!" he protested. "I've got nineteen pictures to prove it." I doubt, though, that the Mt. Gretna Playhouse still maintains an actors' ghetto.

I worked like a hungry dog that summer, which is good, and learned a lot as well, also good. What you learn is facility and flexibility, which are key skills. They can also trap you in slick glibness, which is why you probably shouldn't do stock for more than a season.

WHEN WE GOT BACK, New York was suffering through a searingly hot September. It was a lot tougher in Hell's Kitchen in summer without an air conditioner than it had been in winter without central heat, but we didn't mind. Things were looking good for us. We'd saved a bit from our joint stock salaries, and Lydia acquired an agent and a part, in that order. The agent was Maynard Morris of MCA, even then a large force simply as a talent agency. She was cast as Lady Anne in an off-Broadway production of *Richard III*. Lady Anne is one of the better female roles in Shakespeare, works not overflowing with good parts for actresses. Lydia was damn good in this one. I was proud of her.

I was also grateful for her wifely concern when she got me an interview with her agent. I'd managed to get all the work I'd had till then without one, but I was glad to have a chance at an agent of Maynard's standing.

He was something of a character on Broadway, conservatively dressed, with an intense manner. He talked very rapidly, with a slight stammer, especially on the phone. He'd often hang up on himself in the middle of his last sentence. "Yes . . . yes, that's just what I t-told them. They just have to m-m-make up their m-minds. I'll g-get back when—" *Click.* He was also blessed with a genuine love of theater, something all agents should have, but many don't.

He was given to abrupt enthusiasms about performers. When Lydia introduced me, he said "How do you d-do. I'm very glad to . . . I have a part for you!"

He did, too. It was only as an understudy, but it was for the second lead. To be on Broadway so soon again seemed too good a chance to pass up. There was no guarantee I'd *be* on Broadway, of course. *Leaf and Bough* had a very small cast, with no small parts I could appear in; I was strictly a backup quarterback. Still, there was always that chance.

That's the only time I've ever understudied, and I didn't enjoy it. Understudies never rehearse till after the play's opened; till then, the director's concentrating on the original cast. The understudy has to sit and watch—very closely. I felt like a caged bear.

Theoretically, you can learn by watching, but the main thing I learned, with growing conviction, was that I could do the part better. It was a steamy play about a Midwestern family, and I was understanding the bad brother . . . the more interesting role, really. They'd cast a very good Irish actor who was doing the scenes well enough, but his strong accent was wildly out of place. He was struggling to correct this, with little success. The director, though gifted, was Hungarian, with an accent of his own. I don't think he was aware that this was a problem.

The playwright and the producer were, though I was of course not privy to any of this. I was spending all day watching, learning the lines and the blocking, trying to read the body temperature of the scenes. The out-of-town tryout was in Boston, where I found modest quarters in a rooming house.

We opened just before Christmas, to mixed notices. I spent a quiet holiday morning in my room, opening my few presents, feeling faintly bereft. I was due at the theater at ten, to watch them rehearse some changes. The author, Joe Hayes, was standing outside the stage door. "Hey, Chuck . . . let me buy you a beer," he said, pointing to the bar across the alley.

It was a little early in the day, but I thought, well, it's Christmas. I didn't get the beer anyway; we'd barely sat down when he said abruptly, "Do you think you could go on tonight?" There can only be one answer to that question: "You bet!" Half an hour later I was rehearsing. It was a grueling afternoon, but they'd let me out of the cage. I did the part that night, through the Boston and Philadelphia runs, and finally opened on Broadway with a featured part.

No, *Leaf and Bough* was not a success. (One of the critics suggested it should've been called *Bow and Leave,* which is what we did.) I got decent notices, the play got a few, too, but we barely lasted the week. It seemed to me the world had changed. So it had, but no one understood it at the time. It had barely begun, but it would alter the way almost everyone felt about almost everything. In the end, it would change the world, as it's still doing. They called it television.

TO START WITH, nobody understood television. The engineers knew how to generate the signal and transmit it, at first locally, by line of sight, then by land-lines. Live, of course; prerecorded programs on film and tape came later. Also, only in America . . . the rest of the world was still recovering from World War II. That meant it was centered in New York. The film studios, seeing their monopoly on moving, talking pictures threatened, had flatly boycotted the whole idea of television. (Good thinking, guys!)

That left this incredible new medium, its potential undreamt of, in the hands of the three big radio networks, who didn't understand it either. They were already telecasting news, sports, and a few old English movies, so they decided to have a shot at dramatic programming, too.

The film companies not only vetoed any financial involvement in television, they prohibited any of their creative people, actors, writers, directors—all of whom were under firm, exclusive contracts—from working in it. And theater people of any reputation disdained television on the grounds that it was tacky, and besides, it didn't pay much.

This meant that, more or less by default, the invention of live TV drama was left to a bunch of out-of-work twenty-three-year-olds of no reputation and minuscule professional experience, who were also totally ignorant of the new medium. I give you writers like Paddy Chayevsky and Rod Serling, directors like Frank Schaffner, George Roy Hill, and Arthur Penn, and more actors than you can shake a script at . . . Jack Lemmon and George C. Scott, Walter Matthau and James Dean, Anne Bancroft and Joanne Woodward. (Her husband, Paul Newman, had already signed with Warners; they wouldn't let him play.)

Bobby Fryer, who'd auditioned me for Theatre Inc., opened another door for me. He was working for CBS by then. They were doing *Julius Caesar* and casting it only with actors who'd done Shakespeare on Broadway. My Cornell-McClintic credit served me again. I didn't get one of the three leads, but an OK part (Cinna, I think). I also got another break. One day the actor playing Brutus got sick and they needed someone to rehearse the part for the day. Need I tell you who put his hand up first? All afternoon I filled in as Brutus so they could work through the play. When we quit, Frank Schaffner, who was directing, said, "Stick around a minute, will you?"

Ten minutes later, the producer, Tony Miner, came in, accompanied by a great stroke of luck. "Sorry," he said. "I'm running a little behind here. Frank wants me to hear you read something. Are you familiar with, uh, Antony's funeral oration?" Well, I mean

... Antony in that play is the showiest, shortest, and easiest of all the great parts. What's more, I'd won my scholarship to Northwestern doing that speech. If you're halfway right for the part and can't make an impression in a situation like that, you have no business playing Shakespeare. Don't misunderstand; I went back to my role as Cinna the next day, but the next week I got the lead in *Jane Eyre*.

It was all new, and very exciting. We were making up a new medium. I remember a little suspense story I did in which I had all the lines. Not long afterward I did another piece on the same program; I was in every scene and never spoke a word. These were little thirty-minute stories where you could try anything. CBS's "Studio One" was the classy show where we did serious drahh-ma. For them, in a few months, I went from the Brontë sisters to Turgenev to TV's first spectacle, a story about the sinking of the battleship *Bismarck*. As the credits rolled, the studio was thick with smoke and ankle deep in water, with two cameras shorted out and cast and crew wet as water rats. I loved it!

Frank Schaffner directed that one, too. Sinking the *Bismarck* must've been good preparation for his great film, *Patton,* some years later. He didn't use me in that film, but we worked together often, over the years. A lovely man and a fine director. I miss him still.

It was like Boris Becker winning Wimbledon at seventeen. When you're a kid, you can do anything because you don't know how hard it is. In live TV, we were inventing it all as we went along. Bobby Fryer came to us once and said, "Do you guys think you could do a ninety-minute version of *Macbeth?*"

"Why not?" said Frank, who tended to be short-spoken.

"Would ten days rehearsal be enough?" asked Bobby cautiously.

"Sure," I said. "I did it once in school." So we did *Macbeth,* on the first coast-to-coast telecast CBS mounted.

Actually, it wasn't bad—a lot better than the versions I've seen on TV since. That's the kind of part you have to come back to and play again and again, over the years. I did that, too.

A few months later I got another crack at the Old Gentleman from Stratford. David Bradley, for whom I'd done my teenage Peer Gynt, was planning his next feature: a 16mm *Julius Caesar,* his first sound film. (Incredibly, it was also the first film version ever made of the play.) David phoned me, insistent as ever. "You have to play Antony, Chuck! That version you were in on 'Studio One' was really crappy! Erase it from your mind. You didn't even have the right part!"

"That's fine, David. I'd like to do it. But I act for a living now. I have to have some kind of salary, even for a great part." So I got fifty bucks a week, as did the cameraman, making us the only people in the film on salary. We shot all over Chicago, using the city's remarkable selection of Roman architecture as sets; I did Antony's "Friends, Romans, countrymen!" on the steps of the Field Museum. David staged a marvelous tracking shot on top of Soldier's Field, dollying more than a hundred yards down a double colonnade of Ionic columns. We murdered Caesar in the Masonic Temple, a full-scale replica of the Roman Senate, in front of a marble replica of the statue of Pompey where the conspirators actually struck him down. We did my scenes in three weeks because I had to get back to New York for another "Studio One" production to play Petruchio in *Taming of the Shrew*.

That made five Shakespearean productions in a little over two years—on stage, screen, and television, three of them leading roles. That's the kind of experience, and exposure, a young actor doesn't get very often. David's *Caesar* turned out well; it began to surface in private screenings in Hollywood, where "Studio One" was watched regularly, too.

Live TV lasted less than ten years, then it was over. But it was a wonderful, shining time for all of us. That's what it must've been like in the beginning of Hollywood, when they were inventing the moving picture. Griffith and Chaplin and DeMille bouncing around in touring cars with the camera on the end of a board.

I'm very lucky I was there when they were inventing television. Of all the choices I made, as well as the things that just happened to me, this was the most valuable.

5

Off to See the Wizard

THE THING WAS, I didn't really plan to make movies then. By 1949, I was just about exactly where I wanted to be. I'd had a leading role on Broadway, would surely get another (this time, in a play that ran more than a week). Then, I could *really* start to choose. Already, I could do just about what I wanted to in television. None of us quite knew what television *was* yet, of course, but I'd been in it from the beginning. "Studio One" was considered the best dramatic program on the air, and I had my pick of parts on it. To top it off, Lydia was costarring on Broadway as the female lead in *Detective Story.*

True, we were still sharing our cold-water flat in Hell's Kitchen with the cockroaches, but we were happy as clams; we were honest-to-God working actors. That year on CBS, I played the leads in Emily Brontë's *Wuthering Heights,* Somerset Maugham's *Of Human Bondage,* Henry James' *Wings of the Dove,* and G. B. Shaw's *Cashel Byron's Profession.* I was learning my craft as well as earning a name and more money than I'd ever seen. (Not all that much, actually.) What more could a man want?

"The movies, dummy!" you say. "Hurrah for Hollywood . . . off on the Yellow Brick Road!" Ah, that's because you know how it all comes out. I had nothing against films. I'd been approached by

Warners and David O. Selznick. When I helped a pal, acting with him in a test he was doing for Fox, they offered me the contract. But that was the catch, you see; you had to sign an exclusive contract. Every filmmaker, actor, director, or writer was the exclusive property of one studio or another. I wanted no part of that. It would've meant that I couldn't make films for other producers, or do a play—certainly not do television. I just couldn't see tying myself down like that, so I did another "Studio One" with a striking Italian-American actress named Anne Marno, who was to have an even more striking career as Anne Bancroft.

I followed that with an off-Broadway play called *Cock-a-Doodle-Doo,* which seemed determined to imitate Samuel Beckett. How well it did this is hard to say. I played a character called AZ (A to Z, get it?), costumed solely in gold paint, from crown to toenails, save for a gold G-string. (The G-string was a reluctant concession by the director, who was told that some few inches of skin had to be left unpainted, or my body would suffocate. God knows I *felt* well-ventilated.) I'm told I made a striking impression, though the director was never able to tell me exactly what my part, let alone the play, was *about*. (Maybe that's why he fought so hard to scrap the G-string. What a career I might have had!)

Then I got an offer for Broadway, a play called *Design for a Stained-Glass Window,* set in sixteenth-century England. Martha Scott was starring; I would play her husband (fully clothed this time, and martyred for his faith). I had high hopes for it. (I always do, somehow. Why *is* that?) I began growing a full beard for the part, yet another of about forty different arrangements of facial hair, real and false, that I've undertaken in pursuit of my living. This one, though it turned out very Elizabethan, was all for naught. It took me longer to grow it than the play ran on Broadway. When the notices were read over the phone at the opening night party at Sardi's, the director, an intelligent lady at the end of a tough ten weeks, turned and threw up in an ice bucket. Martha, who'd striven with fierce energy to make the play work, looked at me and said wryly, "My sentiments, exactly."

It's always a bad feeling to close a play, especially a flop. I would have liked at least a few weeks in it, to explore the part a little, but now I had a new part. I was in the movies, after all.

A couple of weeks earlier my agents had called me in Boston

where *Window* was about to open out of town to tell me I'd had another film offer, this time from Hal Wallis, one of the very best producers in Hollywood. He was determined, they said, to sign me to a film contract. "Did you tell him I won't sign an exclusive deal?" I asked.

"He said he knows that. He doesn't care. He wants a commitment from you for five pictures. Outside of that, you can do whatever you want." This was an unheard of erosion of the basic major studio position. I was skeptical.

"Plays and television, too?"

"Absolutely. And films for other studios. He just wants his five commitments. And could you come out for a few days, so they can get some film on you?"

"Impossible," I said, a little loftily. "We open in Boston next week, and besides, I haven't finished growing my beard. Have him come see me in the play; he'll have to wait till it closes to get me anyway." (*That* was no problem. We closed before he got east to see it.) In the end, it was irrelevant; he saw me on "Studio One" in *Wuthering Heights*. He closed the deal off that performance. I felt pretty cocky when I phoned Lydia in her dressing room after a matinee and said, using the collective, "Honey, we're in the movies."

"I thought we didn't want to be," she replied equably.

"Well, maybe just for one film," I said, "to see what it's like." (Lydia still maintains this was all news to her. It seems unlikely that I would've failed to mention such a momentous possibility, but on the other hand, it's not *entirely* unlikely. I play some hands quite close to my vest. Maybe I didn't want to deal with the inevitable separation beforehand.)

Of course, Wallis didn't give me that unique deal because he thought I was the greatest thing since sliced bread. He was simply smarter than the other honchos in Hollywood. He knew the old studio system that required exclusive control of its filmmakers was on its way out; in a few years everyone would be able to get the kind of deal he gave me. (It wasn't "unique," anyway. The year before, Marlon Brando had gone out to make *The Men* under a similar pact. Marlon breached the Berlin Wall; I just kicked the next hole in it.)

•

So, ABOUT A WEEK LATER, leaving Lydia secure in her long-running play, I set off to see the Wizard, the script for my first film in my hand, riding, in Arthur Miller's lovely line, on a smile and a shoe-shine. I was met by Wallis's head of publicity, Walter Seltzer, who not long after became a successful producer of several films, including seven of mine. He was armed with a not-very-good 8 x 10 of me, which he compared carefully with the original. "If Wallis signed you off this still, he's in for a surprise," he said. "Let's get something to eat."

He took me to Romanoff's, where we sat in the next booth to Spencer Tracy, who was eating strawberries. I was awestruck, not by Romanoff's, but by Tracy, believing firmly that he was the best film actor on the planet. I still do, but unhappily I never worked with him, nor even saw him again. (A few years later, I was offered a chance to costar with him, but it was a lousy part and I turned it down, sure there would be another chance with him in something better. There was. A few years later, Stanley Kramer offered me a part in *Inherit the Wind,* but Fredric March had the only other good role besides Tracy's, so I passed again, still hoping. I never got another chance. I probably didn't deserve one.)

Walter dropped me off at the modest mansion Paramount then maintained for useful visitors with no place to sleep, a category for which I qualified. Over the next few days he showed me around the lot and the town, midwifing my birth as Hal Wallis's latest discovery. This was a process the studio system had refined over the years, and Walter was deeply versed in its arcane mysteries. He was otherwise badly cast as a movie publicist, a group usually perceived, with some accuracy, as soulless creatures with the conscience of cats. He was an intelligent, decent, and warmly witty man who, with his wife, Mickey, quickly became my first friends in Hollywood. They still are . . . first and close.

My contract with Wallis gave me what I wanted most: the chance to choose what I did. It also got me headlined in both trade papers the next day. Jack Warner, furious because I'd turned down his standard studio deal and signed with Wallis, impulsively barred my agents from his lot. Since my agents were MCA, who represented people like Bogart and Cagney, that meant they couldn't set foot inside Warners to pick up their clients' salary checks each week. Two days later, Jack drew in his horns.

He hadn't been mad at me, anyway, but at Hal Wallis. As his head of production, Hal had been the architect of Warner Bros.' glory years in the thirties and forties. Remember, this was when the man in that job really determined what pictures were made and how they made them. He was responsible for *Casablanca, Yankee Doodle Dandy,* all the early Errol Flynn films, as well as Eddie Robinson, Cagney, Bogart, and Bette Davis. Jack never forgave Hal for leaving Warners and setting up his own independent production unit at Paramount, where he made a lot of very successful films, many of them also very good, ranging from Martin & Lewis to Tennessee Williams.

"Producer." It's a much maligned and misunderstood profession. In fiction, they're often presented as megalomaniac tyrants, Machiavellian plotters, toadies, procurers, and con men. In life, there are producers like that, a lot of them with "associate," "assistant," or "executive" attached to the title. Some producer credits in that category are passed out on megabudget films like Crackerjack favors.

A real producer is a special combination, neither bird nor beast (or maybe both). He must have sound creative instincts about script, casting, design . . . about *film.* At the same time, he must have an iron-cold grasp of logistics, schedule, marketing, and costs . . . above all, costs. There really aren't a lot of guys who are good at all this. Hal was very good. Surely one of the two or three best of them all.

He was not a warm man. (I've noticed a number of producers have rather withdrawn, sharply focused natures. It's a hard job, filled with crucially difficult detail, and in the end the actors get the girls and the directors get the credit.) Never mind, Hal got the money, and the girls he wanted, including one he married, a classmate of ours at Northwestern, Martha Hyer. She brought to their marriage some money of her own, a respectable, if brief, film career, and a firm determination to be the best wife she could be to Hal. I think she succeeded in that. They spent a good part of their money on an extraordinary collection of paintings whose value multiplied many times, allowing them to build a new theater at Northwestern.

Among Hal's many talents as a filmmaker was a keen casting sense, particularly for men. Aside from all those guys at Warners, he found Burt Lancaster, Kirk Douglas, and then, fortunately, me.

(The whole question of picking people for the movies is widely
misunderstood outside the industry; inside it, too, for that matter.
Talent is a factor, so is looks. Neither is crucial. There are a number
of major stars who are not overwhelmingly attractive, many others
who couldn't conceivably act on stage. But they all have one thing
in common: the camera loves them. Never mind what *you* think . . .
how gifted, how beautiful an actress may be. If the camera doesn't
love her, forget it. You can't determine this in advance, either. That
mysterious black beast has a mind of its own, as well as the final
vote . . . indeed, a veto.)

My first film for Wallis also turned out to be my only film for
him. It's very possible that Hal never intended to make more than
one picture with me. Under the terms of our deal, he was free to
sell the other four commitments to any studio he chose, for the
best price he could get. He was investing in me as you invest in a
new stock, buying early to sell in a rising market. There was no
advantage to him in building my career for the long term, as he had
with Kirk and Burt; he didn't have me for the long term. He sold
the other commitments he had with me for far more than he'd
contracted to pay me, which seemed perfectly fair to me, though
both actors and athletes today seem to regard contracts as merely
paper to rewrite when the time is ripe.

OK . . . back to the first film. It was called *Dark City,* a film
noir, a genre that flourished in the forties. They usually involved a
cynical urban loner, often a cop or a slightly seedy private eye, who
falls among evil companions, including at least one beautiful girl,
often a treacherous bitch who does nothing to improve the hero's
sardonic view of life. Wallis had chosen stories in this vein for both
Burt's and Kirk's first films, five years before. I suppose one of the
first of them all, as well as one of the best, was *The Maltese Falcon,*
with Humphrey Bogart, whose skills and chemistry made him the
king of film noir.

Almost all of these films—maybe all—were shot in black-
and-white. They certainly should've been; it was the perfect process
for the genre. By 1950, when I came into pictures, many films were
in color, but Wallis chose black-and-white for *Dark City.* It was the
right choice, and cheaper besides.

Mind you, I didn't know any of this stuff then. I'd never

heard of film noir. *Dark City* was my first movie, that's all. I played a war veteran with a bad attitude drifting back into civilian life and a lot of trouble. My costar was Lizabeth Scott, a sultry blonde with black eyebrows, a low voice, and a challenging, bend-to-me-run-from-me chemistry. She played a nightclub singer with whom my war vet was/was not in love. Wallis had put five songs in the film for her, making *Dark City* not only among the last of the genre, but the only musical film noir ever produced.

In addition to the songs, Hal had put some very good actors in the film to help me out: Viveca Lindfors as the other woman; Dean Jagger; Jack Webb, in what was his last heavy before *Dragnet;* Don DeFore; Ed Begley (no, no, his father) and Henry Morgan, a fine and funny actor later famous in the TV series "M*A*S*H." (Just a few years ago, I worked for his son, producer Chris Morgan, and asked him to remember me to his father: "He was in my first film." The next day I asked Chris if he'd passed on my message. He grinned. "Yeah, I did. Dad said, 'Hell, I was in *everybody's* first film.'")

The director was William Dieterle, who'd done some of Wallis's best films at Warners: *A Midsummer Night's Dream, The Hunchback of Notre Dame*. He was a tallish man with a grave manner. Perhaps he was daunted by the task of initiating yet another kid fresh off the New York stage into the mysteries of acting for a camera. I don't remember finding this transition difficult. My fifteen months in live TV had already taught me the fundamental technicalities. The nuances, of course, you never stop learning. I haven't yet, but I know a lot more about it than I did when we started shooting *Dark City*.

So what are they, these mysteries? I'm asked this all the time, at seminars and parties. "What's the difference between acting for a camera and on the stage?" Focus, I guess, is the best way to put it. In the theater, a play lives on the stage; the company builds it there in rehearsals, and then the actors live in it during the performance, moving through the play each night and making it happen again, from beginning to end, as if for the first time. The shape of it can change a little—it usually does, in a long run. The actors can grow in their parts, or diminish. New actors can come in, changing it again. But the play, and the people in it, are re-created for every performance.

A film is shot in fragments, like tiles in a mosaic to be assembled later, almost never in sequence. On the first day of shooting, you may play a scene describing a murder to the victim's daughter, your wife, having just met the actress playing the part. The actor playing her father may not even have been cast; his death scene may be scheduled for next month on a mountain in a state you've never visited. Yet you first must play this revelation scene, set later in the story, as though you'd already played the murder scene.

What's more, if you mix a drink to calm her, you must toss the ice in the glass when neither of you is speaking, to avoid blurring the line for sound; you must carry it high enough to show in the bottom of the frame, and hand it to her at precisely the same moment in each take of each angle, so it doesn't leap in and out of the shot in the editing. Every move you make has to end with your toe on a precise tape mark (they'll use a sandbag instead for actors who are bad at this, but you're not supposed to be bad at it). When you embrace the actress, the moves are even more exact, to avoid blocking her chin with your shoulder, or leaning into her key light and throwing a shadow on her face. If you think this distracts from what everyone imagines to be the sensual delights of playing love scenes, you're dead right. (Not long ago, I was talking to Tom Selleck at a party when I noticed I was casting a shadow on his face. Nuts! I thought. I'm standing in his key light. I shifted my weight automatically. Maybe I've been at this too long.)

What's crucial to all this is that it has to become automatic, done with the casual ease of a veteran shortstop handling a hot grounder and making the throw to first seem routine. What you must *think* about is the scene, the man you're playing, what he's thinking, what he wants at this moment. If you do this, if the climax of the scene suddenly catches fire and you *know* you really nailed it, it's likely the script supervisor will say, "I'm sorry, but when you threw her back on the bed, your jacket came open . . . it's never done that in any of the other angles."

"Ah, Jesus!" you say. "That really worked . . . I don't know if I can give you that again. Does the damn jacket really matter here? You'll go to her close-up as she hits the bed, anyway, won't you?"

"Yeah, I think I will," says the director. "I'm printing this one; it's pure gold. But just in case it doesn't cut, could you give me one more, just for safety?" So you try it again, for safety.

Dark City was my first time at bat in film . . . you can't really count the two amateur films for David Bradley, though the *Julius Caesar* I'd done for him had been seen by a lot of people out here just before I signed with Hal; I've never been sure whether he was one of them. Certainly both films, as well as the work I'd done in live TV, gave me a useful grounding in acting for a camera. The "Studio One" roles had also given me the beginnings of a national audience before I ever stepped on a Hollywood sound stage.

I felt at home there. By the time shooting began, Walter Seltzer had found me a small furnished apartment behind Grauman's Chinese Theatre and close to Paramount. The studio was where I lived, really . . . where the work was. Some Sundays I'd go out to the Seltzers' to swim in their pool, and Walter scheduled me for some of the big industry parties, but a six-day work week and early calls don't make those affairs wildly attractive . . . not to me, anyway. (I know, I'm disappointing you. Film people live for parties, right? Not if you're getting up at six-thirty the next morning. I've been doing that for so long now that I automatically wake early, even when I'm doing a play and my whole energy is focused for the performance that night. Then, I compensate with an afternoon nap. On a film shoot, unless I have a lunch interview or a meeting on another project, or a look at a rough assembly on a scene we may have to reshoot, I skip lunch and doze in my trailer. Energy . . . it all comes down to energy and focus.)

I don't recall the *Dark City* shoot in any great detail. I hadn't started keeping my work journal yet (though that would certainly have been a good time to start), so I have no day-to-day record. I remember fragments—my very first setup for the film, which also happened to be the first shot in the film, something that almost never happens. A long tracking shot of me walking down a city street looking . . . interesting, they hoped. As for me, I was just walking.

I learned to deal cards one-handed and a couple of other card manipulations. (Did I mention my veteran was a crooked gambler?) We decided not to use them when the pro who was teaching me pointed out that you never show off such skills when you're bent on fleecing someone. I also did a scene with Liz Scott in a process car. A few years later they were obsolete: the film got faster and the equipment lighter. Now, you shoot in a real car driving down a real street. In 1950 they put you in front of a process screen with a rear projection of city traffic, and you acted in front of this in a stationary car with detachable sides and windshields, so they could photograph the actors from any angle. Magic! (You can always spot these shots: the driver hardly ever looks where he's going, and keeps moving the steering wheel.) (Historical note: some years after this, in *Touch of Evil,* I did the first dialogue scene ever shot in a moving car, and a few years after that, in *Number One* [produced by Walter Seltzer], the first such scene shot in color at night. The odds against this are pretty long when you consider I've probably only done half a dozen films where I drove cars at all. Chariots and cavalry charges are more my line.)

I also remember a scene where I had to punch Mike Mazurki, a big man. Let me qualify that. I'm a big man; Mike was *big:* six feet six and 250 pounds of muscle. Fortunately, he had a good heart as well. I wasn't used to film fights then; you do it a little differently on stage. I didn't stop my punch in time; it caught him right on the nose. He never blinked, but his eyes glowed red for a second. Then he lifted me off my feet very gently and held me, eye to eye. "At's all right, kid," he said softly. "Don' worry about it. You ain't got much of a punch anyway."

I also remember a lovely, soft scene with Viveca Lindfors, shot in the Planetarium at Griffith Observatory in L.A. It's one of the best things in the picture, or so it seemed at the time. Dieterle was a good director and I gave him a good performance, if no more than that. I haven't seen the picture in decades, but it works, as I recall.

Then, suddenly the shoot was finished. Of course I had no part in the editing (fat lot of good I'd have been there; I barely knew what editing was). I did have the brains, after the first day of shooting, to ask Wallis if I could look at the dailies. I've been doing it ever since, to my great profit. The actor who says he doesn't look at dailies is either lazy, a liar, or an idiot. It's the only time an actor can see what he's actually done in a scene. If you wait to look at the finished film, or even a rough cut, you see the best the director and the editor can *make* of what you've done. If you look at the raw printed takes of each day's work, you see what *you* did, warts and all. It's very instructive.

Dark City went into postproduction and I went back to New

York. Lydia had just closed in *Detective Story,* and we went out to Fire Island to spend a weekend with a couple we'd met only a few months earlier, Jolly and Kathryn West, now our oldest friends. In high school, Jolly had corresponded with Lydia, but never met her. Walking down West Forty-fourth Street one night, he saw Lydia's name in lights on a theater marquee and her picture in front, and said to his wife, "I know that girl." (What Hollywood used to call "a cute meet.") They went backstage and we went on from there. I've always said it's useful for actors to know some actual people.

A few weeks later we all went to a sneak of *Dark City* in Brooklyn. I was enormously impressed, but then, it was my first film and I was still learning, both how to make them and how to judge them. Wallis was very happy with it and immediately had Walter Seltzer set up a tour for me. Fourteen cities in twenty-three days, just ahead of the film's opening. It was rough, but I was learning something else crucial to a film actor—how to do interviews.

It was the same in every city: a schedule of TV and radio interviews with a press lunch in the middle and whatever else you could fit in till it was time to catch the plane to the next stop. We got a lot of good press out of it, and the picture did well when it opened.

I was off to a good start.

6

The Greatest Show on Earth

THERE ARE THREE THINGS an actor needs to succeed. The first is health, as well as peak physical form. That's why they say "By the time you're old enough to play Lear, you're not strong enough." I've driven a chariot in one role, played a dying king in the last days of his life in another. For both, I needed the same athletic condition. An actor uses his body as a pianist uses his Steinway; it has to be as close as you can get to perfect. You fall short, but you have to try. I've been lucky, and blessed. Health is a gift of God. In the theater, I've never missed a day of rehearsal, or a performance, anywhere, any time. In sixty-some films, I've never missed any part of a shooting day. This has given me the lowest insurance rate in the film industry, a more valuable asset than you might imagine.

Conversely, Elizabeth Taylor has suffered devastating health problems during her illustrious career, costing her many months of work. She's also one of the great beauties of our time, with violet eyes and a vastly underrated talent. Still, healthy is better, as I'm sure she'd agree.

The next thing an actor needs is energy. I'm not talking about the boyish bounce of a dancer auditioning for a Broadway musical . . . I mean the laser-focus on *this* close-up, *now*. *This* soliloquy in *this* performance of *Macbeth, now*.

None of us can do it always. Not many can do it at all. Think of Joe Montana on his own thirty-five, down four points with fifty-five seconds to go. Think of Olivier on the opening night of his performance-of-the-century as Othello . . . or the closing night. I can't match either man, but I understand the principle. Focus.

"Wait a minute!" you say. "What about talent!? What about looks!?" Believe me, there's a lot of that going around. I can go into any major drama school in the country and point out two or three talented people and four or five who are physically interesting—since Bogart, you don't need beautiful. A couple will also be intelligent, though I know some directors who claim this is a drawback.

No, the third thing you need to succeed as an actor is good parts. Luck plays a hand here, but there comes a point in your career when you have some control over this. Still, *how do you know which are the good parts?* You don't, of course, at least not often.

After the modest success of *Dark City,* I needed something more substantial for my second film. I was delighted to hear that William Wyler wanted to test me for the lead in his next film, *Detective Story,* based on Sidney Kingsley's hit play, in which Lydia was still playing the female lead on Broadway.

I flew to the Coast brimming with confidence. Of course I'd get the part. I always think that, about any part. I have no explanation for why I sometimes don't. On the other hand, you have to think that, or you won't get *any* of them.

I suppose I thought it was somewhere written that I would do *Detective Story.* Not in Willy Wyler's book. After sitting around the Beverly Hills Hotel for four days at Paramount's expense, I heard on Louella Parsons's radio show that he had cast Kirk Douglas. That was a very tough shot—right between the eyes.

In fact, I was a little young and possibly a little green for this role. Kirk was entering the peak period of his extraordinary career and was, in the event, very good in what turned out to be a very good film.

For me, not getting *Detective Story* turned out to be the best thing that could possibly have happened. A day or so later, I was driving off the Paramount lot to fly back to New York and do a play I liked. I was heading for the DeMille Gate, past the DeMille Building, where C. B. DeMille was standing on the steps talking to some of his people. I was driving a green Packard convertible I'd bought from my father. I'd met DeMille. Most actors working at Paramount did. You were taken to his private dining room at lunch, chatted for five minutes, and you'd met DeMille. I expect he liked to keep an eye on the kids coming up.

So, when he glanced at me as I drove past, I waved. He lifted his hand and nodded. I heard later he then turned to his secretary and said, "Who was that?" Flipping through her notebook, she replied, "It's a young Broadway actor Hal Wallis brought out. Charlton Heston. He's made one picture, *Dark City.* You ran it last week. You didn't like it."

"Ummm, I liked the way he waved just now. We'd better have him in to talk about the circus manager." So they did. DeMille talked to me for an hour and gave me the lead in *The Greatest Show on Earth,* a film that was to win the Academy Award as Best Picture of the Year and gross some $40 million (at today's ticket prices, something over $300 million).

Cecil B. DeMille directed the first feature ever made in Hollywood, *The Squaw Man,* which he'd planned to shoot in Flagstaff, Arizona. He stepped off the train there into a driving rainstorm and, deciding he didn't want to make his Western in weather like that, got back on board and rode to the end of the line: Hollywood. If it hadn't been raining that day, we'd all be living in Flagstaff, the movie capital of the world. He quickly became a dominant force in the silent era, and also the first qualified pilot in the film industry. In 1919, he established one of the first commercial airlines in the U.S., serving Los Angeles, San Diego, and San Francisco with six airplanes. He also devised the first camera boom, though his first effort was simply a twenty-foot 8 x 8 timber balanced on a fulcrum, with sandbags on one end and the camera on the other. "Still," he said, "D. W. Griffith beat me to the close-up." When the introduction of sound devastated the whole structure of filmmaking, DeMille switched smoothly to the new medium and went on to make seventy films, all but one a success. "It was called *Four Frightened People,*" I heard him say. "When it was released, there were five."

Long before I got to Hollywood, he had become the best-known director on earth. He could make anything he wanted, at just about any budget. He was the Steven Spielberg of his day. Or is Spielberg the DeMille of ours? The two men's talents differ, but they share an overwhelming advantage over other directors: an all-but-infallible gut instinct for what audiences will come to see. This has earned them a certain amount of critical disdain. But, as Bob Hope observed while presenting DeMille with the Motion Picture Academy's Irving Thalberg Award, "Mr. DeMille has brought something new to the movies. They're called customers."

Along with Hitchcock, DeMille was the only director whose name always appeared on the marquee of theaters where his films played. A year or so ago, Paramount reissued *The Ten Commandments* in 70mm in the Cinerama Dome, a huge, handsome theater on Sunset Boulevard. What name was on the marquee? Cecil B. DeMille. Of course.

In 1950, DeMille somehow knew that audiences were ready for a picture about the circus. As usual, he was absolutely right. The cast for *The Greatest Show on Earth* was impressive: James Stewart, Betty Hutton, Cornel Wilde, and so forth. My role as the circus manager was the best part, but the focus of the film was the circus itself. Even a few years earlier, this would've been impossible; movies were almost entirely shot on sound stages and studio back lots. The bulk and primitive technology of the equipment made any but fairly simple location shoots impossible. Now, all of us routinely make films entirely on location, interiors and all. Then, Errol Flynn boarded pirate ships in studio tanks, Gary Cooper gunned down bad men on studio Western streets. Many exteriors, and all interiors, from cars to cathedrals, were shot on sound stages.

We were still using the three-strip Technicolor process then, lovely, rich color, with a separate roll of film for each primary, but the camera was as big as a refrigerator, and damn near as hard to move. Everything was bigger and heavier then, the cables, the lights, the generators. The logistics of a location were awesomely complicated compared to now. Nevertheless, DeMille decided it was possible to film the real circus where it lived. We'd shoot in winter quarters in Florida, then on the road, under the big top, in the three rings, in the cages and wagons and trains that moved the whole fantastic family that a circus under canvas used to be. It's long gone now, but DeMille caught it on film. Ringling Brothers, Barnum and Bailey's circus is the star of the picture. It deserved its Best Picture Oscar.

Everyone wants to run away with the circus, even if only for ten minutes when you're twelve. I was going to do it. It looked a lot more interesting than my location shoot in Las Vegas for *Dark City*. Her play closed, Lydia came out to join me, armed with her first serious camera, instructed in its use by DeMille's still man.

Most of the principals in the cast had formidable physical preparations for their roles. Betty Hutton and Cornel Wilde had to look plausible on a trapeze, Dorothy Lamour actually learned the Iron Jaw act, a circus staple requiring pretty girls to bite down on a rubber mouthpiece hard enough so they can be spun on a rope. Gloria Grahame acquired a modest competence as an elephant rider, and Jimmy Stewart spent days perfecting his clown makeup. Every clown designs his own makeup, to which he then acquires a lifetime copyright. Jimmy was assisted in this task by Wally Westmore, the head of Paramount's makeup department, but he insisted on having the final choice. It was a good one, which was just as well, because Jimmy wore at least half the makeup, the whiteface clown base, in every scene he was in. The plot point requiring this was a little implausible, but it worked very well on screen.

My own preparation was simpler: they decided to gray my sideburns. I was a little young for the circus manager. (Over the years, I've played at least a dozen parts where I had to look older. Recently the thrust has been the other way . . . which is a lot harder.)

We also had to pick a hat, which sounds easy. It wasn't, because DeMille chose it. I was called into an anteroom in his building and found the floor covered with at least fifty fedoras. "The right hat is very important," DeMille said. "Shoes don't matter so much . . . usually, you don't even see them. But if you wear a hat, it's in every shot, and featured in every close-up." It took about an hour and a dozen more hats before we found one that clicked, but he was right. Hats count, shoes don't, especially in period films. (Now, those are the only hats you see on men, anyway, except in uniform.) Jimmy Stewart wore the same hat in every Western he made. So did I, till someone stole it. Anyway, I ended up with a good beat-up circus manager hat for *Greatest Show*.

I also acquired a brier pipe and a tobacco pouch decorated with a real tiger's claw. Pipes were very big with actors then; they made you look both determined and thoughtful at the same time. Paul Newman and I both used one, as did Clark Gable. Humphrey Bogart, Gary Cooper, and Steve McQueen used cigarettes, which make you look cool and world-weary, and killed all three of them. That makes me glad I didn't stay with the pipe. Actually, I've learned to *act* determined and thoughtful since then. I can even throw in a dollop of "anxious" on top.

This sounds as though my preparation for this part consisted mainly of deciding how my character looked. So it did. I was playing a fictional character in a contemporary setting. A historical figure from another period needs a different approach—more of that later. Much more. For my circus manager, I could begin with myself, adding the clothes, the script, and the circus. DeMille provided those.

Many actors insist that they must find the *inside* of the man first, and work outward. I'm dubious about that. I wouldn't know where to reach for the inside if I had no outside to begin with. I want to figure out what the man wears, what he uses, what he has around him. Laurence Olivier called it the "Green Umbrella" method, remembering a part he was having trouble with until he saw a green umbrella in the window of a second-hand shop, and knew instantly it was the umbrella his character would own. He bought it and worked inward from there.

Actually, my character's center was very clear. It was waiting for us in Florida: the circus itself. As winter turned toward spring, it drew its people back from wherever they'd spent the off-season to the winter quarters in Sarasota. They were coming home. As we joined them, preparing our shoot, I saw that the circus people were like my circus manager, Brad: they had sawdust in their blood. Although they had a hard life, uncomfortable and underpaid, I never heard one of them speak ill of it, or seem to yearn for anything different. There was a kind of magic, not just in the center ring, but in Clown Alley, too, and in the elephant tent at night when those great beasts stood swaying, murmuring to each other in gusty, cavernous sighs.

I wasn't in the first week's work, so I roamed the grounds, soaking up the circus, following the real manager, Art Concello, around. He wore a beat-up hat, too. I made friends with a two-year-old gorilla I'd have to carry in a scene, as well as with a twelve-foot boa constrictor. (Well, with the boa, maybe "acquaintance" is the word.) He did let me pick him up. If you've wondered, big snakes are quite heavy, and feel like cold, molten glass. The gorilla was a more amenable costar. At two, he was about the size of a four-year-old boy, weighed twice as much, and was as strong as an athletic fifteen-year-old. They told me his brain was nearly as well-developed as a human of the same age, but the process slows down from then on, and grinds to a halt around age four. Certainly his memory did. I visited the circus some five years later, looking up old friends. My pal had put on some five hundred pounds of muscle by then. His reflexes were very good, too. When I carefully approached his cage and offered him a banana, he made a lightning-quick snatch at my hand instead. He'd forgotten what pals we'd been before. Yeah, I know . . . it's elephants that never forget.

What I'll never forget is the warm friendliness of the circus people. In a sense they were an alien community, wandering over the continent six months a year, dispersing for the off-season, then gathering to put the whole thing back together and do it all over again. There were many foreigners with limited English, a number of dwarfs and midgets in Clown Alley, animal trainers and acrobats, tuba players, roustabouts, clerks, and peanut vendors. Together, they *were* the circus. They belonged to it, and so to each other. Today "family" is a label worn to cliché, but it fit the circus people perhaps more deeply than it does for other such groups, like an infantry platoon, or a movie company on location, for that matter.

Lydia, roaming the winter quarters with her camera, had the same feeling. "They're like the troupe of players in *Hamlet,* come to Elsinore to perform. But they don't live there, or anywhere, but in their wagonsful of shows."

The first scene I shot in the film had me driving with Jimmy Stewart in my jeep through the big tent, where the acrobats are rehearsing. I see Betty Hutton doing a trapeze routine and jump out of the jeep to chew her out for something or other. In the first take (the first I'd ever done for DeMille, mind you), I leaped out, tripped on the ring curb, and fell flat on my face in the center ring. As I got to my feet, chagrined, DeMille said dryly, "I believe we'll try that again. That wasn't quite the entrance I had in mind."

As we drove back to the start mark for take number two, Jimmy drawled, "Waal, Chuck's bound t'get better from here." I guess I did. We shot for several weeks in Sarasota, mostly scenes in the big top that would be difficult to film on the road during actual performances.

One of these included the only time I've ever seen an actor totally fail with a single line. Though DeMille shared Eisenstein's particular genius for moving vast masses of people on the screen, he didn't trust extras to speak lines. He always carried half a dozen actors on salary throughout the shoot, to do the odd one- and two-line bits, often unscripted, that come up in most films. We were doing a very short scene in the circus pay wagon one day. It was only three lines long; I had one, two of DeMille's standby players had the others. A farmer, waiting outside the pay window, says, "Y'gonna pay for that hay all in *silver?*" (DeMille had found that the circus used silver dollars for many transactions; it was the kind of detail he liked to weave in.)

I reply "That's the way we get paid," and shove several stacks of silver dollars off the shelf.

As the farmer struggles to catch them in his hat, a roustabout runs up shouting "Brad, Holly's spinnin' like a weathervane in a Kansas twister." The actor DeMille had given the line to never once got it right, through more than thirty takes and ten rehearsals. (It's a line I'll remember for the rest of my life, I promise you.) When someone flubs the same line more than a couple of times, the tension on a set begins to build; after nearly an hour of this, the actor was jelly and the mental energy from the whole company, *willing* him to get it, would have lit a small town, but those ten words never came out in sequence. DeMille never rebuked him, never showed the frustration boiling in all of us. Finally, he wrapped the scene and shot it with another actor the next day. All actors flub (fumble a word) or blow (go stone dry on the whole speech) now and then, but this was the worst I've ever seen. Actors' nightmares are made of such stuff.

DeMille had a reputation as a man-eater, but I never saw him devour an actor. For one thing, he knew very well that an actor angry at his director, or afraid of him, is not likely to give him a good performance. He could be rough on prop men, or assistant directors, or makeup people. If Betty Hutton was late, as she was a couple of times early in the shoot, he'd greet her politely, then turn on her hair, makeup, and wardrobe people—the wrecking crew is the trade term—in icy, public tones. "Don't you people realize that Miss Hutton has an important scene to do with us this morning? We've been waiting for twenty minutes. You had two hours to make her ready on time, and you failed. I can't tolerate that. I won't tolerate it. Believe me, ladies and gentlemen."

He never shouted, he never swore, but he always made his point. Betty's crew stood beet-red and silent, but she knew they weren't responsible; *she* was. She got the message. People weren't late on DeMille's sets often. Working for him, with an actor like Jimmy Stewart, was a marvelous basic course in professionalism. Spencer Tracy put it best: "Come on time, know your words, and don't bump into the furniture."

After tardiness, DeMille's second taboo was noise on the set, made by people who were not working. When the camera's turning, a whisper on the sidelines can ruin a take. If DeMille could identify the culprits, they were banished from the sound stage, prominent journalists, distinguished guests, even principals in the film if they weren't in the shot. Once, back in the studio after our location, during the lighting of a complex setup, DeMille had time to go back and check something in his office, where he never went while shooting. His secretary couldn't resist. "What happened, Mr. De-Mille?" she said. "Did you talk during a take?"

The last sequences we filmed in winter quarters were the circus parade moving through the streets of Sarasota, with twenty-five thousand people on the sidewalks, and then the circus train, all twenty-nine silver cars, loading its people and pulling out for the summer tour around America.

DeMille had spent the previous summer doing the whole tour with them, researching his film, but we stayed with them this time only through the weeks in Washington and Philadelphia. They filled the big top, perhaps in part because of the signs posted at every entrance, serving legal notice that anyone passing them might be photographed for the movie.

For us, the difference between the circus in winter quarters and on the road was profound. The tempo picked up, for one thing. To watch the big top go up was as exciting as anything I ever saw in the circus. With a hundred roustabouts and all the elephants lifting it, it looked like a huge flower blooming out of the earth. The circle of six strong men who drove into the ground the three-foot steel stakes holding the guy ropes that sustained the huge spread of canvas was as skilled as any act I saw in the ring. Each man swinging ten-pound sledges in turn, smashing into the stake half a second apart, no one missing his turn or his target, they'd pound the stake to its mark in thirty seconds. The tent-raising montage is one of the best scenes in the film.

Of course it was much harder to shoot scenes during actual circus performances, with our people mixed in with the real audience, but DeMille used a lot of film during the shows, striving to catch the reality around us. That's an advantage of location shooting; you can surround the fiction of your story with the real world. DeMille caught what he said was the best single shot in the film this way. He set up a masked camera near one of the exits to catch the people streaming out after the show. He exposed a thousand feet of negative, and got thirty feet of gold. A father was carrying his yawning little daughter, her eyes bright as stars with delight. Just as she passed the camera, her head fell on his shoulder, sound asleep. You can't get that with actors.

The actors did very well, but it was a tricky shoot. DeMille was giving last-minute instructions one morning before a matinee when he noticed two extra girls chattering near the back of the tent. "Young lady," he said, pointing. "No, you with the red scarf, Miss. Yes, you. I'm trying to explain to everyone what we have to do this afternoon, but you clearly feel what you're saying to your friend is more important. Please come down here and use the microphone, so we can all hear your vital message."

Very reluctantly, the girl came down, shyly took the mike, and announced, "I just said, 'I wonder when that bald-headed old son of a bitch is gonna call lunch.' "

DeMille knew when he was licked. When the laughter died, he took the mike back. "Lunch!" he said.

When we wrapped our location in Philadelphia, the circus continued on their odyssey across America, and we turned back to Hollywood, with almost half the film yet to shoot. I still didn't know much about acting in movies, and nothing at all about how much tougher it is to direct them. DeMille knew a lot, including that directors never get to sit down. Then in his seventieth year, he wore britches and puttees to support his legs when he was on location or shooting on big sets. He also had a mike boy and a stool boy who followed him closely. He could be talking to you quietly about a scene, notice an electrician on top of a scaffold two hundred feet away, and instruct him fully amplified as the mike magically ap-

peared an inch from his lips. Similarly, checking a low camera
position or the script, he'd sit down in empty air as a padded stool
caught him. Neither man was ever cued, neither ever missed. It was
a little awesome.

So was what was waiting for us at the studio. Some two
square blocks of back lot were filled with full-scale duplicates of
half a dozen cars from the circus train for the train wreck that was
the climax of the film. It seemed to me we'd brought a large part of
the circus with us. The important part was in our heads, of course.
The time with the circus was Olivier's "Green Umbrella" for me.
An actor has to know how to be almost anybody, in any life, and
make people believe him. What I learned, what I felt in Sarasota,
Washington, and Philadelphia, made me feel like a circus manager.

My contribution to the train wreck seemed simple. After
riding a capsizing club car, I was next seen unconscious, pinned
under a section of a wrecked animal cage, where I lay for much of
the sequence. Then, complications developed. They often do.

It was decided, though not by me, that as the big camera
boom swung over the devastation of the wrecked train and centered on me, a black panther would leap through the twisted bars
that pinned me and escape. "A *tame* panther, Chuck," they said.

I was dubious about that, but not well-positioned to argue,
since I was already pinned under the wreckage. The panther was
slipped in at the other end of the cage, where it settled in the
darkness. The camera turned, the partition opened to show the
panther on his way out past me, but he lay there in what struck me
as sullen silence. Two more takes. Still nothing from the panther. I
felt my best bet was to play dead, so I lay mute and motionless, till
someone said eagerly, "Poke him with a stick."

"Don't poke him with a stick!" I gritted through my teeth.

"Naah," said the trainer soothingly. "I'll just touch him in the
ass with an air hose." Personally, I'd take violent exception to being
touched in the ass with an air hose, but before I could make this
point, the hose was brought and the camera turned over. The panther agreed with me about the air hose. He leaped on my chest,
snarling, and was gone. Print. I can tell you that panthers have
horrible halitosis.

By now, the sweaty pallor the makeup man had applied was
replaced with real sweaty pallor. The scene now called for Gloria

Grahame to bring in one of her elephants to lift the broken cage off me. The elephant was Minyak, a tranquil and intelligent female who could easily do that. I certainly trusted her more than the panther. Besides, I'd recently played a scene where, as part of her elephant act, Gloria lay on the ground while Minyak held her foot an inch above Gloria's face. I could hardly object to Minyak pulling the cage off me. You know how sensitive we males are to these things.

DeMille called "Action!", Gloria led Minyak to her mark, the elephant wrapped her trunk around the cage bars—and stepped on a railroad spike. Trumpeting in pain and outrage, she stamped through the wreckage, while everyone ran for cover. Everyone but me, of course, still pinned under that damn cage. This was a lot worse than the panther. Again, I played dead. I didn't have to play terrified. Lydia, playing a small part in the scene, was paralyzed. I said Minyak was intelligent. She didn't stamp me, or even look at me reproachfully. Once her wound was treated, she rescued me in fine form. It wasn't my favorite day on *Greatest Show,* though.

We finished filming on schedule and on budget. That was expected then, even of overwhelmingly successful directors like DeMille; indeed, he expected it of himself and everyone who worked with him, from stars and extras, cameramen and coffee gofers. Today, many directors assume their reputations are passports to excess. Some of their films run tens of millions over budget, with subsequent losses many times that. Some studio heads simply surrender to this, in the desperate hope of a megahit.

The postproduction was put on a tighter schedule. Ordinarily, preproduction, filming, and postproduction take equal amounts of time. (Preproduction includes writing several drafts of the script; choosing the director, the actors, and key crew people; scouting for locations; and determining the production design, budget, and schedule. Filming is actually shooting the picture. Postproduction is editing through several cuts of the film, correcting or replacing dialogue tracks, creating sound effects, scoring the music, then finally mixing all sound tracks, marrying them to the picture itself and balancing the final version in photographic terms.) DeMille cut some weeks off his postproduction schedule to get the film in theaters for the big fall season and also to qualify for the

Academy Awards. As the Duke of Wellington said of the Battle of Waterloo, "It was a damn close-run thing," but we made it.

The Greatest Show on Earth was, in the classic phrase, a runaway smash. DeMille and the circus was a marriage made in movie heaven. He picked up his Oscar for Best Picture the following spring, and I got an enormous boost in my career. When I went into his office the next morning to congratulate him, he said, "Chuck, you've gotten some fine personal notices for this picture, but I want to read you one that may be the best review you'll ever get in your life."

He then read me a letter from a man who was enchanted with the picture. DeMille had caught not only the look but the feel of the circus perfectly. The cast was wonderful, especially Jimmy Stewart as the clown. Betty Hutton had never been better, nor had Cornel Wilde. "And I was amazed," the writer concluded, "at how well the circus manager did in there with the real actors."

7

Dancing as Fast as I Can

IN THE NEXT THREE YEARS, I made ten films, which was probably too many. (On the other hand, Hank Fonda told me he did *The Grapes of Wrath, Drums Along the Mohawk, Young Mr. Lincoln,* and a Fox musical, all in one year. None of the ten I made was *Grapes of Wrath,* though.) It was complicated. I wanted to use the freedom of my contract to work as widely as I could, and wanted to get top dollar for the films I chose, trading on my role in the Academy's Best Picture. Wallis was doing the same thing with his four commitments to me (for which *he* would get most of the top dollar, of course), so there were two sellers for the same actor. It made for a brisk market.

It's reassuring to note that the first film I did in this period also turned out to be one of the best: *Ruby Gentry,* with Jennifer Jones. Jennifer was a flawless example of the studio system to which I was a maverick exception. She'd been brought into films by David O. Selznick, under whose aegis she quickly blossomed into a major star. She was (and still is) a stunning beauty and a good actress. By this time she was married to Selznick, who managed every aspect of her career, as he did with all the players under contract to him, as well as controlling all the pictures he made.

Oddly, *Ruby* was not one of these. It was an independent

film, directed by King Vidor, one of the great directors from the silent era who'd readily made the transition to sound. He'd directed Jennifer before, in *Duel in the Sun,* with Greg Peck, a film Vidor had walked off of (literally, hoofing it four miles into town from location), furious at Selznick's determination to direct the film from the producer's chair.

This hadn't prevented King from seeking a deal with Selznick to loan Jennifer to him for *Ruby,* or Selznick from making the deal, adding three conditions to her contract: Selznick must approve her costar, the script, and all stills of Jennifer. King accepted these points, and added two of his own: Selznick could never set foot on our sound stages or locations during shooting, and could not view one foot of dailies or edited footage. Still, after King had accepted MCA's tough deal for my services, he had to send me off to Selznick so he could have a look at me, even though Selznick himself had offered me a contract two years before and presumably knew what I looked like.

Waiting in Selznick's garden, I thought of an experience a friend of mine, Milburn Stone, had had in similar circumstances a few years earlier. He'd been ushered into Selznick's office only to find him lying on a couch with his head hanging over the edge. Still prone, Selznick looked up at him for a long moment. "I'm not certain we've met," he said, "I don't recall your face." Milly, a sharp-witted fella, couldn't resist:

"How could you, you silly son of a bitch? You're looking at me upside down." He didn't get the part.

I did, though. Selznick was charming over a very pleasant lunch, talking knowledgeably about nineteenth-century painting, of which, happily, I knew something, and he told me he thought I'd be very good opposite his wife.

That excellent actor Karl Malden was cast as Jennifer's husband. Cuckolds are always difficult parts; Karl played with a strong, simple directness that hit exactly the right note. *Ruby* was a pretty steamy story for the fifties: Jennifer's Ruby was a po' white Carolina girl, I was a rich white son of a bitch who done her wrong and was paid for it with a load of buckshot in the belly. (I have unquestionably been killed in more films than any leading actor in the history of the movies. I just now counted it up: fifteen times, only once peacefully in bed. Make a note of that . . . it may appear in the test.)

The shoot went smoothly; King was a gifted director, good with actors, with a sure captain's hand. He gave me extra time, often at the end of the day, to go over the next day's scene. (That's the time for it, after the wrap, when the company's off the clock.) Sometimes I'd ask him about his silent film days, too, trying to reach back to when they were inventing it all as they went along, like kids. A whole new art form, only none of them knew it. Once he told me, "Chuck, let me sum it up for you. When I was twenty-four, I was directing at MGM, and I had a Daimler limousine with a liveried chauffeur and a footman . . . and nobody laughed."

In 1952, the ground rules required us to suggest the sex in the film, rather than anatomizing it with the camera, but the scenes worked. Jennifer's the only actress I've ever worked with who, as far as I could tell, wore no makeup for the camera. I could actually see her go pale, or flush with passion or anger. In one scene, she was supposed to hit me. Rising to a male reflex, I told her to really let go. She did, a stiff backhand to the chops that almost brought me to my knees and broke her hand. Next time you run into the film on TV, look for an elaborate set of silver Mexican bracelets suddenly appearing in several scenes on her right wrist . . . a cleverly designed brace. She never missed a day's shooting. A pro.

Lydia was in New York doing a "Studio One" on CBS, and after that finished, she came out to join me. We even spread out a little on the Hollywood social scene. Walter Seltzer assured me this exposure had a useful function, but I was always vaguely uncomfortable with it. I still am. I don't like parties with hundreds of people; I tend to wander off and read the titles on the spines of books in the library, if there is a library. Over the years I've learned well how to be a public person, a celebrity. (Christ, how I hate that word!) Walter was right, of course. If you make your living as a star (I hate that word, too), you have a responsibility to your public identity. I'm still happier relaxing with people I've known a long time.

We met some of those one Sunday, a family we still count among our dearest friends, Joe and Maggie Field. Joe was a young Marine vet, not yet the successful stockbroker he became; he'd brought his wife and two kids over to swim in the Seltzers' pool. Lydia and I dropped by on the same errand. As Maggie tells it, her son, Joe III, then four, gripped her arm and hissed, "Mother, there's

Brad!!" She'd taken him to see *The Greatest Show on Earth* not long before, and here was the circus manager live in front of him.

I'm very glad he liked that picture; his boyish enthusiasm sparked a friendship that's involved everyone in both families, on several continents and a couple of oceans. That's the sort of friends we treasure.

I do remember one party we went to then, though. It was probably one of the very last of the real Hollywood parties of the old studio era, given by Marion Davies, the longtime private lady of William Randolph Hearst (though he was not present, having recently died). What I remember best about Miss Davies' bash is a huge red granite Egyptian sarcophagus, absolutely genuine, about nine by four by four feet, full of cracked ice and a couple of dozen nebuchadnezzars of Roederer champagne. Champagne comes in splits, pints, fifths, quarts, jeroboams, methuselahs, and nebuchadnezzars, the last of which stand about three feet tall, hold several gallons of champagne, and require a strong man to pour. (How's *that* for a useful fact?) You were expecting naked girls in the swimming pool? Nah, I've seen those at a few parties, but I've never since seen an honest-to-God Egyptian sarcophagus full of nebuchadnezzars of champagne.

Around that time, Paramount offered Lydia a film. It was called *The Atomic City,* a good script about espionage in Los Alamos, just then entering the public consciousness. She was very good in what turned out to be a good film, earning a couple of Academy nominations.

I wasn't there when she shot it, of course. In the way of such things, I got a job back in New York, one I couldn't turn down, the live *Macbeth* for CBS.

It was network's first drama broadcast coast-to-coast and was watched, they told me, by more people than had seen the play performed since it was written, probably in 1606. That really seems unlikely, but we did have a huge audience, including my wife, who was watching it in her dressing room at Paramount. When my head was impaled on a spear at the end (using a life cast of the genuine article), she nearly passed out.

RUBY GENTRY was released about then and became a minor hit. This was useful for me, of course, demonstrating that I could hold up my end of a love story. Lydia has since observed it was also the first of what she calls my "hero heels."

I was already in preproduction for another film, having been away from a movie camera for all of two months, on a commitment Wallis had sold to Paramount for a handsome profit, to which he was certainly entitled. (Besides, it kicked up my market value a notch.) I'd have probably done it for nothing, for that matter—it was my first Western.

FILM HAS BEEN CALLED the American art form. That may be true; it's certainly true that Americans are the only ones who can make Westerns. (No, Sergio Leone is not the exception; Clint Eastwood and Hank Fonda lent his spaghetti Westerns what validity they had.) From the day I signed to make movies, I'd been aching to play in one.

The Savage, unhappily, was not a great Western. It had a marvelous director, George Marshall, who'd been directing films nearly as long as DeMille had, and long survived him. His daughter, Geri, and her husband, Frank Baur (he was one of DeMille's gutsier second assistant directors on *Greatest Show*), became close friends, in a town and a trade where friends are hard to find and hard to keep. (You're often close with some of the people in every company you work in, the way you are with men in the same platoon, the same air crew in wartime. But when a picture wraps, a play closes, you usually drift apart. Except for a few people.)

The Savage had an unusual story, with foreshadows of *Dances with Wolves.* Like that fine film, it explored the conflict between Indians and the U.S. Cavalry from the standpoint of the Indians (though not *all* of our cavalrymen were rotten, like Kevin Costner's). I played a white man captured as a boy and raised as a Miniconjou Sioux. There was a very good film in there. Unfortunately, we didn't quite find it.

I surely enjoyed trying, though. The Black Hills are some of the most beautiful country in America, even soaking wet. I learned a running mane mount on a bareback horse. (I came into movies a fair rider, but barebacking in wet buckskins takes a little getting used to.) I got to design my own warpaint, like all Sioux braves. I spent some time with the Miniconjou we had working in the film and learned some Sioux. When I was lanced in the chest in one scene, with a metal plate covered with balsa wood to hold the spear head, Chief American Horse (then ninety-six years old, having been born before the Battle of the Little Big Horn) christened me "Iron-breast," but I've forgotten the Sioux word for that. I haven't forgotten the Sioux, though.

I haven't forgotten George Marshall, either. I never made another picture with him, though we remained friends till he died. He taught me something very useful on *Savage*. He'd spent a morning lining up a very complex shot from a Chapman boom, with running buffalo and stuntmen doing horse falls through a long, tracking downhill move ending with me riding into the frame and speaking one line. When it was finally set, I turned to George with an intricate question about my motivation. George heard me out patiently, then said, "Look, kid. In movies, it isn't always can you act, it's can you run a horse to a mark. In this shot, that's your motivation; just hit the damn mark. OK?"

I got the message. I hit the mark. Acting is partly a question of focus.

I DID A FEW MORE Westerns then, but neither was outstanding, though they did all right at the box office. To promote one, *Pony Express,* the studio floated a plan to have me retrace the actual route of the Pony Express, from St. Joseph, Missouri, to Sacramento, California, on horseback. They finally decided there weren't any major cities on the route, so they dropped the idea. I'd have liked doing that one, though.

Arrowhead was the other Western. We shot it down on the Mexican border, in Texas, in marvelously stark country. Mil Stone, whose acquaintance I'd happily made on the *Savage* shoot, was in this one, too, and Brian Keith: I did better pictures with each of them later.

Arrowhead did have one outstanding virtue. (No, no . . . I was OK, but nothing more. I think I was coasting on chemistry there. I was working almost constantly and loving all of it, but maybe I was absorbing more than I was giving the camera.) The standout performance in *Arrowhead* was Jack Palance as a renegade Chiricahua Apache. He played the part with a deep ferocity that was mesmerizing. I've never seen an Indian role better done. In his first scene, he returns to the reservation from an education at Carlisle

Indian School. He gets off the train and stands stone-faced, a tame Apache in a black suit and a string tie, until he takes off his hat and shakes loose his mane of black hair. In that instant he became, without a word, a wild, free Chiricahua once more. It was the best moment in the picture.

(Yes, I know. I said "Indian." If you haven't already noticed: we don't do Political Correctness at this address. I find the fractioning of the American population in terms of their gender, sexual preference, and ethnic background particularly offensive. The term "Native American" really raises my hackles. *I'm* a native American, goddamnit. I was born here, so were my parents. My son, Fraser, can trace his American roots back twelve generations through his mother to 1633—by written record. *That's* a native American.)

A FAR BETTER (and far more successful) film from this period was *The Naked Jungle*. (Trivia factoid: many films have mediocre titles. We had two great ones for this. We argued to the end as to whether it should be called *The Bushmaster* instead. I'm still going to use that one someday.)

Jungle was based on a classic short story by Carl Stephenson from the thirties called "Leiningen versus the Ants," about a South American planter who battles to protect his plantation from marauding soldier ants. It would qualify as a science-fiction piece, except that there really are such creatures, and they really do devastate vast areas. *Maribunta,* they're called.

To our man-against-ant story, producer George Pal added a mail-order bride, imported from the U.S. by my planter. (We never explored why a knockout lady like Eleanor Parker would be on the mail-order market in the first place.) Anyway, when Leiningen discovers she's been married before, he marks her "damaged goods" and sends her back, interrupted by the *maribunta*.

I tried to explore Leiningen a little more deeply, helped considerably by Eleanor's cool, spunky performance as the spurned bride. Leiningen, I decided, was a virgin. No, not literally—a vigorous twenty-something male virgin is a little unlikely. Still, though, no man knows much about women; Leiningen knew nothing. He'd put most of his considerable energy and all his time into building his jungle empire; now he was going to add a bride to it like a candy decoration on a cake.

On the night of her arrival, their wedding night—the marriage had taken place in New Orleans, with a surrogate groom standing in for Leiningen—he asks her to play the piano for him. "No one has touched it till now," he tells her. She plays a bit, while fencing with him, the talk increasingly edged. Finally, she breaks off.

"You know, a piano is spoiled if it's not used. This is not a very good piano," she says and leaves the room. He follows, breaks down her door, and smashes most of the gifts he's given her, but doesn't touch her until, seizing a large bottle of perfume, he takes her by the wrists and drenches her with the contents, then slams out. The business with the perfume was not in the script, though the perfume was. It just seemed to me right for the moment, one of those happy impulses actors look for. The scene was a quarrel, but the perfume soaking down her body infused it with an irresistibly erotic quality. I called her "Madam" throughout the scene, too (that *was* in the script, just the right note). I still get letters now and then from women who've seen the film on TV. They always mention the perfume. I remember Jimmy Stewart saying to me once, "Y'know, a movie is really moments, not scenes. Half the time, they're not in the script. Someone'll come up t'me and say 'O, gosh, that movie you made with whatsername . . . that blond girl. I don't remember the title, but there was this scene where y'all of a sudden turned 'n looked at her . . . and then y'just got outta the car. I 'member that.' "

Yeah. Moments.

I DID MY FIRST biographical film then, too, a genre I was to explore often. So far, I've played thirteen different men (three of them more than once) who lived in six or eight different countries and centuries, most of them presidents or saints, geniuses or generals. That's historical figures; the numbers double if you include fictional characters in other times and places. Other actors play fictional, contemporary Americans almost all the time; I do it rarely. Why is this? What does it say, about me, or all those other guys? I have no idea.

Well, I have an idea, of course. I'm just not sure it's right. Part of it's physical equipment and chemistry. I actually do strongly resemble three of the men I've played, and I look the way you'd expect the others to look, especially if they lived so long ago there are no photographs. Perhaps more important, once I started playing biographical roles, I got an awful lot of practice; now people expect me to play those men.

French audiences accept me as a seventeenth-century French cardinal as easily as Italians buy me as a sixteenth-century Renaissance sculptor, or Spaniards as an eleventh-century Visigothic knight, or the English as a Tudor king, a Victorian general, or Long John Silver. After I'd played Moses, John the Baptist, and Judah Ben-Hur, Willy Wyler said I was the best imitation Jew in Hollywood. If they're doing a film with no Americans in the story, they still tend to want an American actor in it. My name seems to spring to mind.

My first such part was an American, though. A great one—Andrew Jackson. When he lay dead at last, Sam Houston, who'd brought his son a thousand miles by stagecoach, arriving only hours too late, led the boy to Jackson's deathbed. "Son," he said, "I want you to remember all your life that you have looked upon the face of Andrew Jackson."

"A great American." We paste on that label pretty loosely now, to a Nobel novelist or a pop singer, a pitcher or a politician. I mean something more than that. In our time, great men are an endangered species. Indeed, in the minds of many, they are less than that; they are mythic creatures who never really existed, like the unicorn. It's even been suggested that greatness in itself is somehow undemocratic. We live, after all, in the century of the common man. True enough, but I believe in the uncommon man, maybe because I've played so many of them. Great men are suspect today, perhaps because we don't happen to have any of them around. We have good men, gifted men, God knows we have plenty of *famous* men, but that's not the same thing. Andy Warhol said we live in a time when anyone can be famous—for fifteen minutes. But men like Thomas Jefferson and Andrew Jackson, Thomas More and Richelieu, Mark Antony and Michelangelo, Moses and John the Baptist, are not like everyone. They're not, believe me . . . I've played them. They're not ordinary, like the rest of us. They are *extraordinary,* and they have shaped the world.

I played Jackson twice, and still haven't reached all of him. It's very frustrating to play a man who's cut the kind of mark across history that he did. You feel small, stretching desperately in all

history that he did. You feel small, stretching desperately in all directions, trying to fill the giant figure he left looming in American memory.

The President's Lady didn't attempt a complete portrait of him; the film was based on Irving Stone's novel, which focused on Jackson's lifelong love affair with his wife, Rachel. She already had a husband when Andy met, stole, and married her. They were lovers till she died, just before he became president of the United States, but he was also tempestuously occupied all his life fighting the British, the Creeks, the United States Bank, and sundry enemies of the Republic. Our movie's most important events seemed to keep happening off-camera.

If there was an actress who could keep the audience interested in the Jacksons' domestic affairs, it was Susan Hayward. As Rachel, she gave us the tough frontier girl, the passionate wife, and the doughty companion. The trouble was, I had to keep riding off to keep Andy's various appointments with history, on the dueling ground, the floor of the Senate, the battlefield of New Orleans, and then back into her arms and our story. It seemed the only way to do Irving's novel, but it was a problem.

Indeed, as I learned later, this is a central problem in film biographies. They're made about men who are driven toward a distant, difficult goal. Whether you're painting the Sistine ceiling or freeing the Jews, driving the Moors out of Spain or just getting elected President, you have a lot on your mind and not much of a private life. However extensive the public record, the private man is hard to find.

You often have to deal with fragments. I'm six feet three, as was Jackson. Today that's just tall, useful in my profession; in Jackson's time it was freakish, like an NBA center. I read he was touchy about his height, so we used this in a couple of scenes where he knocked his head on the low Colonial door lintels. It doesn't seem like much, but it was part of the private man.

Then there was the accent. Jackson was born just before the Revolution in the Carolina Smokies, which was then the Western frontier. When I studied regional dialects at Northwestern, they taught that the closest accent in the modern world to Elizabethan English could be heard in those hills. On the other hand, both

Jackson's parents were Irish. Anyway, Old Hickory with either an Irish or an Elizabethan accent would confuse the hell out of an audience. I chose a modern Carolina accent.

I should've used the same accent in *Ruby Gentry,* for that matter. I was just too green to think of it at the time. Ever since Andy, I've undertaken the right accent for any part where my own cleaned-up Middle American isn't appropriate. I can't do it instantly, like Peter Ustinov or the late Peter Sellers could; I have to slog at it, as with so much I do. Bob Easton, the accent guru of gurus, has taught me every one, with infinite pains and a touch of genius. (I've never understood why so few American actors even try to learn the right accent for a part. Not many play foreign roles, of course, but there are at least twenty regional accents in this country, sometimes varying in different centuries. Off the top of my head, I believe only Marlon Brando and Meryl Streep, among major actors, also undertake this preparation for a part.)

Andrew Jackson was one of my American heroes before I opened the script. He still is. As always, I began with the outside. There are a lot of fine portraits of Jackson; take a look at a twenty-dollar bill and you get a good idea, though it's been handsomed up a bit. Andy was one tough cookie—they didn't call him Old Hickory for nothing. Not for the last time, I looked not unlike the man I was to play. As we developed the several makeups, I began to feel more and more comfortable underneath them.

The same thing was true of the clothes. No, not "costumes," not "wardrobe." *Clothes.* Too many designers think of them as costumes (too many actors do, too). For designers, there's no excuse. With actors, I can understand it. If you've never, or rarely, played men from other centuries, the clothes feel funny. You walk differently in chain mail than in cowboy boots and chaps. A sword rides on your hip differently from a .45 (for one thing, it's on the other side). A Roman toga does not feel like a dinner jacket. If you're not used to this, it makes you feel pretty strange, so you look strange, of course. For me, once I'm inside the clothes, I start to find my way inside the man. As Jackson, when I was inaugurated as President, it helped a lot to remember the scenes where I wore buckskins. I believe he remembered that, too.

I had the loan of a beautiful twelve-inch wax statue of Jackson that helped a lot, too. DeMille kept it in his office. He'd had it made when he was prepping *The Buccaneer,* in which Jackson appeared. He let me borrow it; I kept it in my dressing room for the entire shoot. It was a sort of token Jackson, to remind me.

The director, Henry Levin, gave me a marvelous piece of direction, which was as permanently valuable as George Marshall's remark that there are shots where your crucial contribution is to hit the mark. I was playing a key scene with Susan from the early part of the story. She was really cooking, and I felt pretty hot myself. After two or three takes on the master shot, I was positive we'd nailed it. "I don't think I can get it any better than that, Henry," I said.

"Yeah, you can," he answered. "Just remember: you don't know you're going to be President yet."

Every time I play one of these major great men, I try to remember that.

8

The Ten Commandments

I'VE SAID HOW MUCH I got out of New Trier High School. Specifically and permanently useful was my broken nose, acquired trying to play high school football. I wasn't any good, but I actually caught a pass in one game and fell on a guy's knee, significantly rearranging my nose (no face masks then). It hurt like hell at the time, but it's gotten me a lot of parts. A nose like mine on someone my size usually relegates an actor to playing second-level bad guys ("Lemme take care of him, Boss"), but it seems to work differently on my face. I've played captains and kings, cowboys, cardinals, cops, and quarterbacks, architects and astronauts, prophets, presidents, saints, geniuses, and God with this nose. I'm very grateful to the guy who gave it to me. He may well be responsible for my career.

The embodiment of the most important role I got through the nose (as it were) is on permanent display in the Chapel of San Pietro in Vincoli, in Rome. Michelangelo's marble figure of *Moses* is one of the greatest statues in the world, certainly the finest representation of the prophet. It also looks a lot like me, particularly the nose. The overall likeness is startling. Someone pointed this out to C. B. DeMille early in his deliberations on casting the part for *The Ten Commandments*. I think he never could get it out of his mind.

True, I'd worked for him in *The Greatest Show on Earth*
three years earlier. I'd picked up experience and some marquee
value since then, but DeMille never needed that. His own name on
a marquee pulled in more people than any actor could.

He'd cast me for the circus manager off a wave to him from
my car and one meeting. Moses was an infinitely more challenging
part. There was also a lot more competition; it was the role of the
year. I had to join the line.

In his autobiography, DeMille wrote, "I was never in any
doubt about who should play the part." At the time, he simply
deflected both queries and comments on the casting, for several
months. Still, he must at least have glanced at the field. I guess I
won by a nose. (OK, no more nose jokes.)

He may well have delayed announcing his choice simply to
prolong public speculation, which was rife. It wasn't The Search for
Scarlett O'Hara, but there was considerable hoo-ha in the media.
Among DeMille's talents was a sure mastery of public relations.
He released periodic announcements of other castings: Sir Cedric
Hardwicke as Sethi, the old Pharaoh, Anne Baxter as Nefretiri, John
Carradine (Keith's father, and a marvelous actor) as Aaron, and Yul
Brynner, who would resign from his still-triumphant *The King and
I* on Broadway to play Rameses, the Pharaoh of the Exodus.

Meanwhile, DeMille put me through his usual casting proce-
dure. If he was considering you for a part, he would tell your agent
only that he'd like to talk to you—no details. You went to his office,
a large room always crowded with research on his current project:
sketches and paintings (often borrowed from museums), models,
set and costume designs, props, historical artifacts, and books. It
was fascinating.

It was also informative. Film scripts are normally given a
limited advance circulation, at least to major agents, certainly to
actors who are actually offered parts. DeMille never did that; even
when he'd decided on someone, that actor saw not a page of script
till the deal was closed.

In these meetings, DeMille wouldn't even tell you that he
was considering you for a part, let alone which one. Instead, he'd
tell you the story of the movie, in some detail, from the viewpoint
of the character he had in mind for you. When I was called in, I was
pretty sure it was Moses, but he never said so. He told me the story,

showed me some sketches and models, but this left me with little I could say in response.

"Yes, I'm sure I can do that part. I see myself in it," was no good, because he'd never said he saw me in it. "Well, that surely sounds like it'll make a marvelous film" seemed about the only appropriate comment. Then, two weeks later, he asked me back and we had essentially the same meeting, except I'd had the brains to do some research on the Third Dynasty in Breasted's *History of Egypt,* as well as reading most of the King James translation of the Books of Exodus and Deuteronomy. This at least gave me something to talk to him about; he may also have decided that I understood the importance of research in historical roles.

By this time, preproduction on the film was in full swing. It was like planning an amphibious landing. A crew was already in Egypt building what was to be (and I think still remains) the largest set in the history of film, the gates and walls of the city of Per Rameses. An infinite number of costumes and props were being prepared either to be shipped to Egypt or stockpiled till we came back from the location to shoot the interiors at Paramount. In the midst of all this, DeMille finally announced that I was cast as Moses, reaping the publicity harvest he had sown. It was clearly an enormous break for me. As I observed at the time, if you can't make a career out of two leads for DeMille, you'd better turn in your suit.

My personal preproduction was extensive. Aside from the research, I had to undergo fittings for some fifteen or twenty costumes, from the intricate platelet armor I wore in my first scene as an Egyptian prince through the burlap rag of the brick pits and the Levite mantle of the Exodus. (I go firmly on record: of the many things I do preparing for a part, fitting wardrobe is the worst. It comes right before still portrait sessions. Oddly, actresses seem to enjoy both. *Vive la différence.*)

Nine distinct makeups also had to be designed, redesigned, and finally tested, from the young prince to the aged patriarch on the slope of Mt. Nebo. Then of course I had to be circumcised. What actors won't do for a good part. (Naah . . . only kidding; my parents took care of that when I was born.)

I also made a film that summer, *Lucy Gallant,* with Jane Wyman. It wasn't very good, I'm afraid, though I thought Jane was. It seemed a good modern romance to get under my belt before I

disappeared into the Old Testament, but I was maybe a little dour
for it. It was the kind of thing Rock Hudson did, often—it probably
needed that lighter weight. It shows up on TV frequently, but I
wouldn't recommend it.

In addition, I got my wife with child, in the biblical sense.
Lydia was doing a play, *The Seven Year Itch,* and had planned to
leave it and come to Egypt with me. Her doctor took a dim view of
her climbing Mt. Sinai six months pregnant, though she was all for
it. "Think of it!" she insisted. "That baby can absorb twenty-two
centuries of history in the womb. It's a very impressionable period."
Her obstetrician wasn't impressed, however, so she stayed in the
play until my yet-unborn son was entering on stage about three
inches ahead of her every night.

I did my last scene in *Lucy Gallant*—a fashion show in
which the governor of Texas appeared as himself. (I don't know
why. Everyone wants to be in a movie.) Three hours after we
wrapped, I was on a plane climbing out of L.A. for Cairo. Somewhere over the Atlantic, after refueling in Newfoundland (this was
pre-jet), we ran into my birthday. The steward produced a cake
with a pyramid on it, and a card signed by every soul on board,
which I found curiously touching. We finally landed in Cairo two
more fuel stops and thirty-some hours out of L.A. Fortunately, I
sleep in airplanes. This is because my heart is pure, as I never tire
of reminding Lydia. Actually, I suspect her heart is purer than mine,
but she feels an overriding responsibility to stay awake so she can
help the pilot in case of an impending crash.

Somehow, I often arrive for the first time in exotic places in
the dead of night. So I did in Cairo, the limo racing through the
black desert to the Mena House Hotel. Roosevelt had stayed there
for the Cairo Conference in World War II, but all I saw that night
was the bedroom of his suite, where I tucked in the mosquito
netting and dived into sleep.

I woke the next morning to find the Great Pyramid of
Cheops looming through my window behind some date palms.

The desert itself is changeless. After breakfast that first morning I rode a very handsome bay over to the vast set DeMille's people
had built some five miles deeper into the desert. I'd seen a model
of it in Hollywood, but the reality was staggering. A hundred-and-
twenty feet high, almost half a mile wide, with a double avenue of

some two dozen sphinxes, each fifteen feet high, stretching out into the desert.

I was riding through the sphinxes toward the desert when I saw a black limo approaching over the sand. It was DeMille, who'd come over by ship, seeing his set for the first time. The car stopped and DeMille opened the door and sat silent for at least two minutes, looking at the distant walls. There were maybe half a dozen key people there now, staring anxiously at DeMille, who spoke not a word. As the silence lengthened, he got out and stood on the sand, his hands on his hips, weighing what he had wrought. After perhaps five minutes, he turned to the production designer, Walt Tyler. "Paint it," he said.

"Oh, of course, Mr. DeMille. Just as I showed you on the model back home. The crews are at work now. We'll have it finished . . ."

"In three weeks," DeMille broke in. "We'll be back from the Mt. Sinai shoot then. That's when you must have this ready, for the Exodus." He turned back to the car, got in, and then leaned out the window. "That's a good job," he said, "so far," and drove away.

"Pretty tough, isn't he?" I said to Rich Richardson, who'd done the stills on DeMille's films since the silent days, and was one of about six veterans who didn't call him "Mr. DeMille."

"C.B.? Naah, he isn't so tough. All he asks for is perfection, and a good day's work." Rich paused, thinking. "A *very* good day's work."

There were several good days of work before we left for the Sinai. I had four makeups that DeMille hadn't seen that had to be tested, in the desert. Rich had been exaggerating a little. DeMille would settle, reluctantly, for the very best you could do. He preferred perfection.

I was considerably short of this, cramming in some lessons in a two-horse Third Dynasty chariot I'd have to drive for Moses' first scene in the picture when we got back from the desert. There was also that stack of research reading.

We set off for Sinai, a stripped-down company in surplus Land Rovers the British Army had left behind when they'd pulled out of Egypt. They'd built a road across the Eastern Sahara to Suez, but there were really only bits of it left. We crossed the Canal and headed more than a hundred miles down into the biblical Wilderness of Sin, the Sinai Desert. We camped for the night on the shore of the Red Sea, where DeMille and I swam in the milk-warm water. In the late light of the sinking sun, it *was* red.

The next day, we stopped at every tortured rock outcropping and forbidding billow of dune we passed, so DeMille could see how I looked moving across it, for shots he planned of Moses wandering in the wilderness when we started back to Cairo. Just before the abrupt desert night fell like a final curtain, we got to St. Catherine's Monastery, our base camp. It's the oldest Christian monastery in the world, founded in 339 on the site of the Burning Bush. When you cross the threshold for the first time, you're greeted by the monk keeping the gate with God's injunction to Moses: "Put off thy shoes from off thy feet, for the place whereon thou standest is holy ground."

They cut this ground-level gate through the wall less than a century ago; until then, visitors had to be hoisted up fifty feet in a basket. Still, during the Crusades, Christian knights rested here on their way to take Jerusalem from the Saracens, secure in the knowledge that Muslims would never attack a shrine sacred to Moses, the only religious leader in history revered by three different faiths. None of them, though, claims divinity for him. He was a man.

Very early the next morning, I stood outside the walls of the monastery, looking up at Mt. Sinai. "Gebel Musa," Muslims call it, Mountain of Moses. All the reading I'd done that summer, from the Old Testament through Freud, seemed *less*—somehow. Against the reality of that mountain, the books made a small stack. The man I looked so hard for in them kept escaping me, misted by centuries, fragmented by dogma, polemics, and scholars' squabbles. Abandoned baby, prince in Egypt, wandering exile, contented shepherd —how could all that bring him here, to climb to the "bush that burned, but was not consumed"? If Moses could find God on that mountain, I thought, I should be able to find Moses there.

It was time to start up Sinai. DeMille took only about ten of us, plus porters. We'd shoot three days at the summit, so they'd have to send up supplies for two nights. The grade was fit for camels part of the way, but I decided to walk. That's the way Moses did it. The whole party was on foot for the last, steepest mile, including DeMille, head down and panting, but never falling back from his place at the head of the column. He was a tough old bird.

The first shot planned, my first in the film, was of Moses coming down the mountain, transfigured by God to deliver the Hebrews from bondage, the only prophet of the world's religions "whom the Lord knew face to face." As I changed into wardrobe, I had an idea. "Mr. DeMille," I said. "I think I should still be barefoot in this scene. If you've just heard God tell you to free the Jews, you don't stop to put your shoes back on."

He looked at me sharply for a long beat. "I think you're right. We'll do it that way." So we did. It *was* right, too. We shot till dark, then spent a cold night in sleeping bags. I was up at four so Frank McCoy, who did my makeup, could get me ready for a dawn shot. He had to do it in the dark, by the light of a Coleman lantern, with the wind blowing sand in his spirit gum. A damn good man. We finished the sequence by dusk, broke camp the next morning, and shot our way down the mountain, getting one last sunset shot just outside the monastery. The abbot, a formidable figure in his black robe, invited DeMille and me to dinner in his chambers. It was a monastically spare meal, but the talk was good. The abbot had a lively mind and a good command of English; he spoke vividly about Moses, and the mountain. DeMille was eloquent about the footage we'd shot there: "We'll bring your mountain, not to Mohammed, but to millions who can never stand here, where God spoke to Moses, from the fire." "Mr. DeMille," I said. "When we were filming that today, I was trying to imagine God's voice." (We were to record that back in the studio.) "Surely I hear Him inside my own head, my own heart. I think it should be in my own voice, too."

The abbot sipped his wine and nodded thoughtfully. DeMille smiled. "We'll have to think about that. You already have a pretty good part, you know. It's possible, though. It might work." Some months later, that's the way we did it. I never really heard God on that mountain. But I do believe I found Moses there.

We got away before dawn the next morning, to beat the midday heat, but of course by noon we were shooting in the dunes and wadis we'd picked on our drive out. It had taken us two days to drive to Sinai, almost a week to work our way back. I was supposed to be dying of thirst, lips cracked, beard caked with sand. I surely looked the part; by the time we finished the sequence, I felt it. The last fifty miles across the Sahara we really had run out of water. That first beer in the garden of the Mena House went down as if I'd poured it in the sand. My first bath since we'd left for the Sinai felt almost as good. I spent about an hour in it, with another beer and a backlog of Lydia's letters.

I'd cut my teeth on the part with one of the most difficult scenes in the picture. Moses goes up Sinai a shepherd and comes down a prophet, the Deliverer. Whatever I reached of the truth of the scene was really rooted in the rock I stood on, barefoot. It marked my work in the entire film. I have an idea DeMille may have thought of that when he planned the shoot. He wanted me to begin on the "holy ground" of Exodus.

We shot for another month at a base near Cairo, except for a second unit in Luxor. Yul Brynner took a long weekend off from *The King and I* so he could do a day's shooting in Pharaoh's chariot at Abu Ruwash, where the dry bed of the Red Sea was created for him to lead the Egyptian host in hot pursuit of the fleeing Hebrews. The parted waters, towering on either side and then crashing down on them, were added later, back in Hollywood.

Even in that day of work, Yul gave us an early look at his Pharaoh. It was a transcendent performance of the god-king, all knowing, all powerful . . . except against the power of God. Other, smaller scenes were shot as well, but everything we did in Egypt pointed to the major reason DeMille had insisted on building the massive reproduction of the walls of the city of Per Rameses in the sands of Beni Youssef: to film the Exodus. He knew the desert would validate everything he shot there.

He believed deeply in the message of the film and the power of the man, Moses, to reach across the millennia and move people of every faith, kind, and condition. Held in special reverence by Jew, Muslim, and Christian alike, Moses has become more than an icon. Over the centuries, Moses and the Exodus he led have inspired those who search for liberty. It's no coincidence that the first tide of our Protestant forefathers in America bore the names from the Exodus: Moses and Aaron, Abraham and Joshua, Joseph and Isaac. Those same names can be read on the gravestones of the American Revolution. They've been carried by generations of black men seeking freedom, and then celebrating it. The words Moses spoke as he watched his people cross over Jordan, free at last, are cut in the rim of our Liberty Bell. They define this country: "Go, proclaim liberty throughout all the lands, unto all the inhabitants thereof."

No director since Eisenstein had DeMille's sure hand with large masses of people; here his cameras had an elegiac subject: the children of Israel, delivered from bondage by "the strong hand of the Lord." To capture this for the screen, DeMille filled that vast set with eight thousand people and five thousand head of livestock, moving them out to our desert location in a fleet of fifty trucks and buses, shuttling back and forth all night long.

They milled, murmuring, as the darkness paled to dawn: fellaheen, desert Bedouin, and Cairo's poor, some of them in clothing styles unchanged since the time of the pharaohs. Many had never seen a movie; few understood what we were doing. As Muslims, though, they all knew of Moses.

As I moved through their thousands in my Levite robe, staff in hand, I was followed by wide eyes and a soft surf of whispers: "Moussa, Moussa, Moussa." I never felt so heavily the burden that part imposed on me. "Who am I, Lord, that I should bring Israel out of bondage? When I come to the people, they will not believe me," the book of Exodus has Moses say. I knew what he meant.

By the time I reached the front of the vast column, half a mile through the wide lane of sphinxes, and stood alone, I felt somehow possessed by where I was and what was around me. This can happen sometimes in a huge film set. The *place* itself creates a reality you can't, don't *need* to, act. I went a hundred yards or so out into the desert and waited, leaning on the staff, thinking about this while they readied the shot.

When they called, I walked back and stood alone, facing that multitude. I lifted the staff of Moses and shouted, "Hear, O Israel! Remember this day, when the strong hand of the Lord bears you out of bondage!" Then I turned and said softly, "Bear us out of Egypt, Lord, as an eagle bears his young upon his wings," and stepped forward.

I never looked back, but I knew they were following me. It took more than ten minutes for that incredible mass of humanity to move past the cameras and out into the desert, and more than two hours to get everything turned around and back into position to try again. Each camera exposed a full thousand-foot reel of negative on every take. We got three complete takes that day.

Almost every film spawns an incident, usually involving a bungled line of dialogue, that becomes the catch phrase of the shoot, quoted appropriately by the company and crew till it fades from memory, funny only to those who were there. Our Egyptian location produced a story that didn't really happen, but it's the only film joke I've heard that has passed into the real world. The punch line even became the title of a play. Perhaps one of our publicity people invented it, but DeMille laughed at it, along with everyone else.

DeMille is preparing the main Exodus shot, the story goes, and has all these people and animals lined up, with three cameras covering it. DeMille calls "Action!" and everything moves past the cameras, out into the desert. He turns to the operator on the big Chapman boom. "How was it, Fred?" he calls.

"Sorry, Mr. DeMille," says Fred. "The film jammed in the first fifty feet. By the time we got reloaded, it was too late." DeMille shrugs philosophically and turns to a camera setup with a wide-angle lens, near one of the sphinxes.

"How about you, Tony?"

"Mr. DeMille, I hate to tell you this. Just as the shot was getting really good for us, one of those oxcarts broke a wheel and tipped over right in front of us. We never got another foot."

DeMille sighs. "Well, at least we have the long shot." He picks up a phone connected to a camera positioned on a sand dune a quarter of a mile away. "How about it, Phil?" Phil waves his handkerchief.

"Aaanny tiime yoou're ready, C.B.!!"

It didn't happen, but it could have. On a film set, almost anything can. As it was, we had a near-disaster that first day on the scene. After we wrapped, DeMille had climbed a hundred feet of rough stairs at the back of the city wall, then a twenty-foot ladder to the very top to check a possible camera position. He stepped off the ladder and sank to his knees, sweating. He'd had a heart attack. Harry Wilcoxon, his associate producer, turned to order up a doctor and rig pulleys to lower him to the ground, but DeMille would have none of it. "I'll climb down myself," he grated. "I'll go back to the hotel and see a doctor."

"But we have to get you to a hospital!" Wilcoxon said.

"No, you don't," said DeMille. "Tomorrow's Sunday. I'll rest.

Monday, I'll be back." He was, too—at seventy-four! I'm convinced it was sheer willpower. This was the most important film of his life. He was quite ready to die for it—but not till he'd finished shooting.

I didn't even know what had happened till we'd finished the Egyptian location and flown home. Then, while his cutters were assembling our printed footage, he permitted himself an easy week or so with his feet up, waiting to look at a rough cut before planning all he'd need to shoot in Hollywood to cut into what he already had.

I dropped into the studio to see him one day during this hiatus, hoping to get a look at some of the Exodus footage. He took me to his cutting room and had Annie Bauchens put up a rough assembly of the whole scene. (DeMille had turned Annie into an editor early in the 1920s, and she'd cut all his films since. For much of her career, she was the only woman editor in the world.) I was only beginning to learn how to view footage in that shape, loosely cut, no music, unbalanced sound mixed with silent footage, but this looked marvelous. DeMille grudgingly conceded he was not unhappy with it, but brushed aside my attempt to commiserate with him on his narrow escape. "No, no. I *had* to finish, there and then. We couldn't have made these shots anywhere else." He was surely right.

I actually made another film while *Commandments* was shut down. In the summer, before we went to Egypt, I'd run across a comedy script Paramount owned, *The Private War of Major Benson,* about a hard-nosed infantry major assigned as ROTC officer at a Catholic military school for small boys. Between the nuns and the kids, it made for a very funny script, exactly what I was looking for as a change of pace after *Commandments*. I instructed my agents to keep an eye on it for me. When I got back from Egypt, I was horrified to learn that Paramount had sold it to Universal. I phoned my agent, Herman Citron, at MCA. "Look, I *have* to do that picture."

"It's impossible, Chuck," he said. "Universal wants to go on it now, with one of their contract stars; you'll cost them too much. Besides, you won't be finished for DeMille till next summer."

"I can shoot it while he's shut down," I said. "Just get me the damn picture." He did. He made Universal an offer they couldn't refuse long before Mario Puzo wrote that line for *The Godfather*. I did *Major Benson* for no salary at all, just a percentage of the profits, which are usually almost impossible to identify, let alone collect.

It turned out very well, so well it quickly moved into profit, even by the Byzantine bookkeeping major studios employ. It's the only successful film comedy I've done. I feel a special pleasure every time Universal mails me another check for my share, which is regularly. It's also a good picture.

In addition, it gave me a chance to make a good friend a rich man. Milburn Stone had been a classic character actor before I did my first film. I think he was born to play crusty corporals and grizzled scouts (with me, one of each in *The Savage* and *Arrowhead*). He was also a lovely man. We became close friends on both films; when *Major Benson* came up, I suggested him for the general (another crusty character), in which he had a chance to display his skills at comedy. One day on the set, waiting for the next shot to be lit, Milly asked me, "Do you know anything about television?"

"Sure," I said. "I've done a lot of it, still do. It's all done live, though, back in New York. Some of it's very good."

"Yeah, but I'm talking about on *film*. They're starting to film some shows now, out here. Location and everything, just like a movie, only shorter. They've offered me a damn good part. It's a Western, which I sure Lord know how to do. They'll meet my salary and all that. I dunno, though."

"What's the problem?" I asked, puzzled.

"Well, they plan to make twenty or thirty of 'em. A series, they call it. Prob'ly take six months or so."

"*Ten Commandments* will take longer than that. There's a lot to be said for a long shoot," I pointed out.

"Yeah, but I'm worried. What if it's a big success? I might be stuck in it for another year, even two!" He frowned at this.

"Well, hell, Milly, that's simple enough," I said. "Just tell them you'll sign for one year. Then you can get out after the first batch if you want to." So he took my advice, which meant CBS had to renegotiate his contract annually for twenty-two years of "Gunsmoke." It made him a substantial fortune, but CBS still got a bargain. His creation of Doc remains one of the best performances in series television. Couldn't've happened to a better guy.

DeMille started shooting the *Ten Commandments* interiors, as well as the exteriors that required special effects, at Paramount in January, by which time his sets filled every sound stage on the lot, as well as some back-lot exterior space. I wasn't called for the first couple of weeks, while he shot several scenes with Yul, Anne Baxter, and Cedric Hardwicke. In that time, I managed to fit in still another production, though I only functioned as casting director. Lydia was the producer, and the star was our son, Fraser, who was precocious enough to secure employment at the moment of his birth.

Months before, when DeMille heard that Lydia's pregnancy would prevent her coming with us to Egypt, he asked her when the baby was due. "The end of the second week of February," she told him.

"Hmmmf," he said. "Just three months after that, we shoot the Baby Moses scenes. Exodus says he was abandoned in the Nile at the age of three months. If your baby's a boy, he could play the part." We all laughed.

By February, I was finishing up *Major Benson* on location at a military school some forty miles from Los Angeles. At the end of a long day, I drove wearily back to Universal to look at the dailies before going home. The guard stopped me at the front gate. "Your wife called with a message. She wouldn't let me phone you on the location. She said when you got here, tell you to go to the hospital. She's having your baby."

I got there before Fraser did, but not by a hell of a lot. He was showing up exactly on schedule, obviously having inherited some of his father's promptness genes. I remember sitting with Lydia in the labor room, waiting, when a woman was rolled past, on her way to Delivery. *"Wait!"* she screamed, waving her arms. "I've changed my *miiinnd!!"*

My girl smiled at me, her face sweaty. "I haven't," she said. An hour later, at 3:30 A.M., I held them both in my arms. Then I went to phone the grandparents. I said to my father, "Congratulations. You're the grandfather of a seven-pound, fourteen-and-a-half-boy ounce!"

"Oh, shucks," he said. "I was hoping for a baby." Our first word from outside came just before dawn, while Lydia was giving our son his first breakfast. It was a telegram:

CONGRATULATIONS. HE'S CAST IN THE PART.

CECIL B. DEMILLE

A great deal of the picture was still to be shot, but the film had already been validated in Egypt. Certainly for me, and I think for DeMille, its emotional underpinnings were rooted on Sinai, in the sands of Beni Youssef, and Abu Ruwash. In the classic confrontations with Pharaoh, each time I faced Yul's superb incarnation of Rameses with Moses' challenge "Let my people go!", the image that loomed in my head was that sweating, ragged host that had followed me into the desert at Beni Youssef.

Moses left a long shadow. As I stretched to fill it, I never lacked for inspiration, only capacity. I think DeMille understood the dimensions of the task; he surely did his best to help me, not so much with specific direction of the performance of each scene but by creating a kind of climate where I could find the man. He kept me insulated from the casual, jokey camaraderie of a movie company. Once I was in the makeup and wearing the Levite robe, I kept pretty much apart. Between setups, I stayed in a little trailer on the set. Even in the scenes, I only sat down in the Passover Supper. (There's the story of the old actor responding to a young man's question about which Shakespearean parts to work on. "Oh, always play the kings, my boy. They're the only ones who get to sit down." Kings, maybe—prophets, no.)

Exodus gives us a man much scarred by the stress of being the instrument of God's will, lacking Christ's serene certainty of the divinity of his mission. Moses often doubts his own capacity to cope with his people's chronic complaining. ("Kvetching," if Yiddish had been invented then?) He cries to God in despair "What shall I do with these people? They be almost ready to stone me. Did I father them, that I must carry them in my bosom?"

This conflict explodes at the foot of Mt. Sinai, where the people wait for Moses to come down from the mountain. When he does, bearing the tablets of the law, he's enraged to find them writhing in orgiastic worship of the Golden Calf his brother, Aaron, has made for them.

The scene was one of the most important scheduled for the studio shoot, but all I had to do was enter at the height of the bawdry, denounce the blasphemers in one angry speech, and hurl the tablets down at the Golden Calf. Then say, "There came a fire from the Lord; and the earth opened and swallowed them down alive. All died before the Lord."

They certainly did. I could only watch as the special effects department and the stunt coordinators took over for the harsh hand of the Lord.

The first part of the scene had been pretty awesome, too. I wasn't in that, either. The worship of the Golden Calf took several days to shoot, and attracted nearly as many visitors as the Exodus. Movies couldn't be very specific with orgies in 1955 ("playing naked before the Golden Calf" as in the book of Exodus was definitely out), but DeMille knew how to suggest a great deal.

At first the pretty extra girls and brawny muscle men he cast as the principal orgiasts threw themselves into their task with great enthusiasm, but about the fourth day of this, their energies began to . . . flag? The lion skins they were rolling around on began to rub raw places and they had honey in their navels and grape juice in their hair. All their hair. At last, one of the extra girls went over to the first assistant director. "Tell me, Eddie," she said wearily. "Who do I have to fuck to get off this picture?" (That's another DeMille story still used on any long, tough shoot, but it really did happen on *Ten Commandments.*)

WHEN WE FINALLY DID get to my entrance, I stepped out on a rocky bluff above the camp, tablets in hand, with just time for one take of my denunciatory "Who is on the Lord's side, *let him come to me!*", when they broke for lunch. As I strode through the crowd of extras, trailing clouds of Mosaic glory, one of the prettier revelers, her energies still undiminished, twitched her hip at me and said, "Party pooper." Oh, I tell you, it's not easy being the hand of the Lord God.

It wasn't easy being the father of the Baby Moses, either. It wasn't a long part, but it was crucial. ("They *talk* about you a lot, in almost every scene" is the way it's usually put.) Fraser had a distinguished cast of costars in his few scenes: Martha Scott, Nina Foch, and Judith Anderson, plus a bevy of Egyptian ladies in waiting. Since babies of three months can only work under the lights for one hour total on any given day, with no take longer than forty-five seconds, only six takes permitted in any one hour, and all this to be accomplished in not more than three hours on the lot, the shooting was scheduled very much to his convenience. Lydia had to be there, of course, as a walking dairy (meal breaks were at the option of the

actor, who was unpredictable). There were also the usual pit stops
for wardrobe change.

We'd done some long shots during the Egyptian location of
the closed basket drifting down the Nile; now they'd built a little
estuary on a sound stage, complete with genuine papyrus reeds,
and the lidded basket, which floated very seaworthily. There was
also a rather formidable nurse, hired at the behest of the California
Department of Labor. When all was ready, she plucked Fray from
his mother's arms and strode to the edge of the landing. I was
already in the water, hovering in a supervisory sort of way. I waded
over and held up my arms. "I'll take him." The nurse tightened her
grip. "Oh, no, sir," she said. *"I* have to handle him during filming."

I looked at her with only a little less candlepower than I
turned on Yul in the quarrel scenes with Pharaoh. "Give . . . me . . .
that . . . child," I said softly. She paled visibly and handed him over,
stepping back. I deposited him in the basket, where he seemed
quite content, and closed the lid as the camera turned. Nina, as the
Pharaoh's daughter, knelt and opened it, projecting wonder. I was
wondering, too: Why did the basket seem . . . lower, somehow? As
DeMille cut, I saw Fray was floating, while the basket sank under
him. I plucked him from the water, and found him still cool and
calm, as he remains to this day.

The Baby Moses was his last performance, alas. He retired
and put his salary into Paramount stock, where it has multiplied,
like the Children of Israel. Fray toils now behind the camera as a
writer-producer-director, where he often has to make bricks without straw.

Making movies is very hard work, and it's not fun. ("Nonsense!" said Lydia, reading that. "You enjoy your work more than
any man I know.") She's close. I eat my work. I drink it, and breathe
it—even dream it at night. But it's supposed to be fun for *you*—
not us. Or scary, or inspiring, or even, once in a hundred times,
profound.

There are shining times, surely—sitting a good horse at five
in the morning, waiting for the first shooting light in Montana, or
Mexico, or the Spanish Guadarramas. Struggling with a scene all
morning, and arguing through lunch about it, and then suddenly
finding the way in, like opening a locked door. Exploring Shakespeare with a camera. Yes, there are wonderful things in it, my

whole life, for instance. But it counts too much to be "fun," and if you can't understand that, I can't explain it to you.

We worked six-day weeks then (on location, we still do). The days ran nine or ten hours, often longer, with the previous day's rushes to run afterward. Paramount had given DeMille the time and the money he'd asked for, but he ran a very tight ship, on the theory that if you can photograph it so it will end up on the screen, it doesn't cost too much. Otherwise, take a damn close look at it. A lot of filmmakers have forgotten that useful maxim.

A long shoot develops a dynamic of its own. On any film, the director has to establish a working relationship with his actors, as they must with each other. Over a long schedule, this deepens; if there's friction, it intensifies.

After months of shooting, fatigue is a factor, too, for cast and crew as well. The nine different makeups I wore as Moses aged were an onerous burden. I guess I've worn more complex character and period makeups than any actor I can think of, though never as many for one part (nor am I likely to again). The simplest, as the young Egyptian prince, took half an hour; the older Moses needed up to two hours or more.

The trick I'd learned on *The President's Lady* of sleeping in the makeup chair surely helped me here. When Frank McCoy had finished, he'd tap me on the shoulder and tip the chair up. Looking back at me from the mirror would be whichever Moses I was to get inside of that day. That little stab of recognition each morning got me off on the right foot, somehow. It also gave me some extra sleep to start the day.

Then, I had no idea of the weight a director has to carry on his back. Fraser said a while ago, "When you're directing, you can always see three people out of the corner of your eye, waiting with decisions you have to make *now.*" He's right.

DeMille was older than anyone else in the company, but he seemed impervious to all this, or the fact that he was making the most costly film in history. He always appeared early, neatly dressed in a tan tweed suit, usually. If he was working outdoors, or on rough ground, he'd wear matching britches and leather puttees. By ten o'clock, the tie was loose; an hour later the jacket was off and his sleeves rolled up.

On *Greatest Show,* I'd found that, when DeMille wrapped

the company at the end of a day's shoot, he kept the cameraman,
the operator, the sound mixer, the script supervisor, and the first
assistant director on the set until he'd picked the first shot for the
next morning. If I was in it, I hung around, too, walking the setup
as it was laid out. It's useful to know what's coming up.

DeMille used a very long preproduction schedule, which is
wise. That time is comparatively cheap (not many people are on
salary, many haven't even been hired), so the mistakes you make
tend to be inside your head, where time's cheap, too. Scripts can
be rewritten, sets, costumes, locations, and even castings altered for
a fraction of what it will cost later. Circumstances can force you to
make radical changes during shooting, but it's dangerous, and very
expensive. These are among the many errors that made *Heaven's
Gate* the most disastrous failure in the history of the movies, literally
closing a studio.

DeMille prepared his shooting day just as carefully. You usually begin with a master shot of the entire scene, sometimes a
tracking shot, setting the geography for the closer angles. As he
worked through this coverage, he'd weigh each setup as they lit it
against the frame sketches or paintings he had of most scenes. He'd
rehearse enough to set the moves for camera and actors, then shoot
it, usually printing in less than six takes. Oddly, he'd often do an
entire scene without close-ups, almost unheard of now. DeMille
was making films before Griffith invented the close-up, which soon
became a useful tool, but it wasn't automatically used to climax
almost every scene until television, when they realized how crucial
it was to the small screen. Next time you see *Casablanca* on TV,
check it out. There are only three head close-ups in the whole film:
two of Bergman, one of Bogart.

Another quick *Amaze-Your-Friends* briefing on camera tech-
niques: close-ups and singles are divided into six different sizes,
ranging from an ECU (extreme close-up showing only eyes and
lips) to a full single figure. God knows how long ago, a clever
cameraman devised a system that let him tell his operator where
the bottom frame line was to be set on an actress without her being
distracted by this crucial detail. It's called the 5-T system. The two
closest sizes are 1-T, framed just below the teeth, and 2-T, which
includes the throat. If you can't figure out where the other three
sizes are framed, you flunk for the day. (If that's the rustle of femi-

nist hackles I hear rising, rest assured the system has long since been adopted unisexually.)

Actually, that cameraman was wrong. Actors need to know where the bottom frame line is, too. It defines the stage where you're acting that shot. That was the most important early lesson I learned, coming to film from the stage, where you're either on- or offstage, upstage or down. Regardless, all of you is there. On film, it depends. You may be doing something with your right hand that's crucial to what you want in the scene, and it may not even be in the shot. The guy to ask is the operator, who's the only one on the set who actually sees the shot as it's made: "Fred, what's my bottom line when I turn back to her from the door . . . four Ts?"

"Naw . . . I've got you full-figure there. We push in when you pick the gun off the table so it's just in." (Sounds like an interesting scene, doesn't it? I wonder if I shoot her? Does she deserve it?)

Finally, of course, we came to the last day. Often, the last day of a film is a gaggle of pickup shots that have been held over to be done when there's time—"phone booths," they call them. If you really have a phone booth scene, they stick the booth in the prop truck and carry it around till you have a loose half hour on the way to another location, when you put the booth on a street corner and pick up the shot.

This wasn't a phone booth. It was Pharaoh's throne room. I think DeMille had saved a good scene for the last day just so we could end the long shoot on a strong note. The only scenes Yul and I had together were confrontations. This was the last and the best of them. All the other principals had finished their parts and gone. It was just Yul and me, in the empty rows of tall lotus pillars. Yul and me—and the ringing prose of the King James Exodus:

RAMESES

Take heed you see my face no more, for on that day you shall surely die.

MOSES

Thou hast spoken truly. I will see thy face no more.

And Moses turns and goes, leaving Rameses slumped on the throne.

I've said how very fine Yul was as the obsessed, arrogant Pharaoh. I can't imagine how he could have been better, or bettered by any other actor. John Carradine was extraordinary as Aaron, the brother of Moses, as was Edward G. Robinson in a difficult composite drawn from several faint-hearted Israelites featured in the book of Exodus. Eddie's Dathan mixes them all into one wonderfully unpleasant man.

Of the women, of course Judith Anderson was marvelous as Moses' Egyptian nurse, Memnet. So was Nina Foch as Bithia, the haunted Egyptian princess who rears the babe she pulls from the Nile. As Yochabel, the real mother of Moses, Martha Scott subtly suggested a Holocaust survivor. Oddly, Martha had played my wife only a few years before on Broadway in a not-very-good play neither one of us could do much with. She was to repeat the wife-on-stage, mother-in-movies combination with me in another few years. Both plays flopped, both films were towering successes.

The value of Elmer Bernstein's score is almost impossible to measure. It's absolutely perfect for the film, guiding and shaping the emotional weight of each scene with mature mastery, though Elmer was a young composer of limited experience when DeMille chose him for this breakthrough assignment. It was a big chance for DeMille to take. As Elmer has said, "I owe him a great deal . . . indeed, everything." I could say the same.

So what do I think of my own performance as Moses? Generally impressive, often very good, and sometimes not quite what it needs to be. As a man, Moses is a towering figure, surely one of the best roles in the history of film. My chemistry is right for it; there are moments when that robed figure lives. I wish I could do it again, when I'd need less makeup and could provide a more deeply honed native gift. Never mind. I had my shot at it.

It's no news that the picture was an overwhelming, resounding, two-year smash. Converted to 1990s ticket prices, it's one of the two or three top-grossing films in history. Indeed, it's never stopped playing, which is just as well, since we can't afford to make such films now. Yes, indeed; I'm glad I was in it.

9

The Best Part

WHEN I FINISHED SHOOTING *Ten Commandments,* I'd been film-ing almost without a break for well over a year. While bringing the Jews out of bondage, however, I'd been cast in the part of my life. As with many great roles, I more or less lucked into it, being in the right place when it came along. I didn't have my usual contract approvals, either; it was a package deal. We had a firm start date, but the schedule was open-ended, with no set budget. Even tougher, we were starting without a script. I had some input on the casting of the star part, but I'd never heard of the leading man. I was definitely playing a supporting role; Lydia and I rated only feature billing. Still, I've never had a better part, and only once one as good—in the sequel. I was to be a father.

None of the three of us had any experience, and of course there was no chance to rehearse. Lydia had some coaching, and I took a class in handling babies, in which I did very well—actors are used to taking direction. I found it a little like acting class, in that bathing and diapering a doll does not fully prepare you for the real thing.

Fraser Clarke Heston took to his role as baby like a natural— he was born for the part, you could say. Lydia seemed . . . *enhanced,* somewhat. Holding your firstborn, your wife looks at you through

146

different eyes, a traveler from another country. The mothering cues
are clearly rooted very deep in the female psyche.

Come to think of it, I guess the father instincts have roots as
deeply planted. I was going to write about fatherhood as a new
part I hadn't properly prepared for—funny fumbles, strange new
priorities—but I don't really remember it that way.

From the moment I held that squirming little male cub, I
knew him for mine, felt my blood in him. (Nor did it seem odd to
me, six years later, to feel exactly the same fierce surge of love
when I held my new daughter, born to a fine pair of university
students we never met.)

Fray was born while I was shooting one of the most challenging roles of my life, searching for Moses with all that was in
me. Yet my new son became equally preoccupying. Time and my
energy seemed to expand, somehow. Lydia felt the same, I know.
From time to time we remarked on this, puzzled: "What was it we
did with all that time, before?"

All infants have the same agenda: eat, sleep, stay dry and
loved. I have no new stories to tell you about this, though it was all
wonderfully new to the three of us. I took some time off when the
Ten Commandments shoot was finished, but I had to spend a lot of
it reading scripts.

I was not overwhelmed by any of them. Obviously, a part
like Moses wouldn't come along again soon, but acting was what I
did, what I was. Besides, my Scots blood and Depression boyhood
have left me uneasy when unemployed. And I did have another
mouth to feed. I picked a Western Paramount was urging on me,
Maverick, a far better title than *Three Violent People,* which is what
they finally called it, for the inscrutable reasons that guide such
choices.

Anyway, I like doing Westerns, and the script seemed promising. (Most of the time, you judge scripts not for what they are, but
for what they might become.) Anne Baxter was available for the
female lead and Paramount was enamored of the idea of moving us
both up a few thousand years from *Commandments.*

Violent People was not a distinguished film, though there
were good people on it and good things in it. Frequent filmgoers
suspect we do it on purpose, but I promise you, nobody sets out to
make a bad movie. It's just very hard to make a good one. (Critics

and fans both have it wrong. Films are neither as good nor as bad as they think; most are . . . OK. They're judged as better or worse than what comes out the same week. It's a rare year that gives us even one honest-to-God great film, or more than a dozen real horrors. Public enthusiasm is influenced by what's currently considered culturally cool and politically correct. Societal mood is an ephemeral guide. If we're talking about film as art, we have to wait for history's judgment—and she's a tricky lady, with a long perspective and a lot of surprises.)

My most vivid memory of the shoot was my son's visit to location. We shot for several weeks in Arizona, where Lydia planned to bring Fraser once we got settled into work. When I phoned her in L.A., Fraser would listen to me on the phone, then go crawling around the apartment looking for me, even under the desk in my den. He was just over a year old by then; he couldn't really absorb the idea that I was only away for a while and that they would visit me. As he understood it, that big guy with the bony nose was gone. Well—he still had his mother.

When they flew to Phoenix, they were settled in the suite before I got back from work. As I walked in the door, I could hear Lydia giving him his bath. I walked into the bathroom and found him in the tub, playing with a rubber duck. "Hey, cowboy," I said.

He looked up at me, his eyes widening, then lowered his head and examined his duck meticulously. I picked him up and held him to me, naked and dripping, but he kept his face buried in my neck. I whispered in his ear, my heart swelling as he gripped me tightly with both arms and legs, still not making a sound. Nothing that happened to me all year was more important than that.

BY SUMMER, the *Three Violent People* shoot finished, Fray was old enough to travel. We launched on the odyssey all parents undertake, in our case, a complex journey. By the fifties, the airlines were winning the battle with the railroads, but the *Super Chief* is still one of my favorite travel memories, especially with people you love. We took a double bedroom and never left it till we got to Chicago. I spent the entire two days with my shoes off, alternately reading scripts and children's books to Fray. He had a fine time romping around on the floor with his stuffed dog, "Dog," accepting with

equanimity what he could catch of his changing world through the
train window.

My mother, of course, was enchanted with her first grand-
child. (We've been blessed with ours recently—I know just how
she felt.) My stepfather, Chet, usually a taciturn man, took to Fray as
well. He even babysat one night while the rest of us went to a film.
We came home to find Fray still awake, listening to Chet play the
banjo for him. This was Chet's very private pastime; I'd never seen
him play for anyone before.

This first round of visits was fleeting—we were due in New
York to rehearse *Detective Story* for a short tour. It would be the
first time Lydia and I had acted together since Northwestern, and at
last I'd play the part I'd coveted all the time Lydia was doing the
play in New York, Chicago, and Los Angeles. So, after a few days on
the North Shore, we entrained for Two Rivers to show Lydia's parents their grandson, where he scored another resounding hit, sending tremors across Northern Wisconsin.

Then we crossed Lake Michigan on the ferry so my father
and his family could have a look. We spent a few days in the woods,
Fray again the object of all affection. I took him to the same cold
northern lake where I'd learned to swim. Fray paddled naked in
the shallows, the same schools of minnows swirling around his
ankles that I remembered darting over the rippled white sand bottom thirty years earlier. We drove south to Detroit, to watch my
half-sister, Kay, graduate from high school, and on to New York for
rehearsals.

We didn't have to check into our old cold-water walk-up in
Hell's Kitchen this time. We'd moved across Manhattan to an awesome penthouse apartment across from the U.N., with a tiny
kitchen, a huge living room with a fireplace and a twenty-foot ceiling, two bedrooms, two terraces, and a good view of the East River.
We never got to use it much, but it gave us a good East Coast base
for eighteen years. (The rent was never more than $480 a month,
which shows how unfair New York City's archaic rent control
laws are, to the poor living in public housing surrounded by acres
of boarded-up buildings the owners can't afford to open at the
frozen rents they're allowed to charge, and to the middle class who
can't find even one room for four hundred a month.)

I hadn't done a play in two years, Lydia not since she'd left *The Seven Year Itch*. I think McLeod, an obsessive Irish detective, was a part I had to get off my chest, and of course Lydia had no problems picking up the wife's role she'd played for several hundred performances.

I considered directing the play, which I hadn't done since Asheville, but it would've been a formidable chore in the ten days of rehearsal we had, along with playing a very long role. I was also determined to spend as much time as possible with Fray. Call it laziness, cowardice, or the fathering instinct, take your pick. I didn't direct; a very good man named Mike Howard did, very well. I'm sorry I never had a chance to work with him again.

We had a company of good actors that Mike worked into a good production. Lydia was rock-solid as Mary, McLeod's tortured wife, and I was good, as best I can remember. I probably was, in fact. I've played more than my share of those harsh, driven fellas, from prophets and presidents to cops and quarterbacks. My hero-heels, by Lydia's label.

Playing the cream of the summer engagements, we had a great success with *Detective Story,* and no wonder. The advance drumbeat of publicity on *Commandments* was building week by week. DeMille was selling a lot of tickets to see me on stage, two months before the movie opened. We all had a fine time, including Fray. My mother came out for part of the tour, more to see Fray than the play, I'm sure. On matinee days, she took charge of him while we worked. He seemed fascinated with feeding the pigeons in the park, which seemed an appropriate pastime, till Mother noticed he was stealing more crackers from the birds than he gave them.

When the tour was finished, I was committed to a series of *Commandments* premieres for Paramount. The world premiere was in New York, in Times Square, to the blazing success everyone expected. It played two shows a day, with reserved seats and hardcover program. The film remained there for more than a year, as it did in most of its first-run engagements. Every actor should have a really blow-away hit every so often—it's very warming to the ego.

In the midst of all this, I had an offer to revive *Mister Roberts* on Broadway, also very ego-warming. Hank Fonda had created the title role in that play, then stayed in it for four years. I can understand why. It's an absolutely marvelous play. I don't know of another one of that genre nearly as good, and it's more than forty years old. I don't know another actor who could possibly be as good as Fonda was in it, either.

It's also true that Roberts is a part that any good actor with the right chemistry should be able to pull off. As with Hamlet, if you're right for it, the play will carry you.

I had a wonderful time with it. We had an excellent cast (though I couldn't get Mil Stone out of "Gunsmoke" long enough to play Doc). Josh Logan, who'd directed Fonda in the original production, wasn't free to direct, either, but I spent an afternoon with him talking about the part. John Forsythe, years before "Dynasty" and fresh out of the Chicago company as Roberts, directed and did a fine job. I learned a lot from him. We got good notices and excellent business through a limited run; I suppose both critics and audiences were taken with the contrast to Moses and the Old Testament, which was playing twice daily a few blocks away.

I've not had many stage roles as good as Roberts—none in a comedy like this one. For years I've been trying to persuade Tom Selleck, who's still young enough for the part, to star in a revival of the play. I'd love to direct him in it.

Mister Roberts closed in mid-December. I did a couple of new openings of *Commandments,* then we drove up into Michigan for a white Christmas. I figured Fray should have one early in his life; as a born Californian, he wouldn't get many. The woods were lovely, dark and deep, as Mr. Frost put it, but I had no promises to keep to anyone but my family.

It was a marvelous holiday. I took Fray out in the woods to watch me cut our tree. No, we didn't fell a mature, forty-foot blue spruce to get the top eight feet of new growth for the tree, sawing up the rest for the furnace, as when I was a boy. We just lopped a small four-footer, about the right size for a small, two-foot boy. It began to snow again as we dragged it to the truck. I can still remember Fray in my arms laughing with delight as he caught a snowflake on his tongue. I remember what they taste like, too, on a cold December day.

My strongest memory of that Christmas is of my son standing at the top of the stairs in red Doctor Dentons, with built-in feet and rubber buttons, with the look of wonder all parents remember in their children's eyes, seeing the Tree . . . and fairyland around it. At the same time, I remembered myself, not much older than Fray was, sitting hidden on a window seat behind our tree on Christmas afternoon, reading *Treasure Island* for the first time in the secret holiday place I'd found there, with pine needles falling on the pages.

We lingered in the winter woods. I was reading scripts, of course, but I felt no urgent need to leap in front of the cameras soon. *Ten Commandments* would be in theaters for the next year. I wanted to find something special for my next picture.

Happily, I did.

10

Orson, Willy, and the Last DeMille

THE DAY AFTER CHRISTMAS, the plumbing blocked up. It was either the septic tank or something in the lines. I didn't relish finding out, but there are no plumbers on call in the woods. There was a pick in the shed, and I chopped down through the frozen topsoil. Yep . . . something in the lines. One of my son's diapers, I figured. That meant driving fourteen miles into town to get a plumber's snake. I did, and, somewhat to my surprise, got the diaper out.

Coming home from running the snake back to West Branch —two round-trips, fifty-six miles, but the toilets were working again —I stopped for the mail. The post office in St. Helen was still in the back of the cobblestone general store. There was nothing in the box but another script, from Universal. It was called *Badge of Evil*.

I started to read it that evening, but I was so pooped from all the pick-and-snaking I fell asleep around page twenty. I finished it the next morning—an OK police story. As I'd promised I would, I phoned the studio. "It's not a bad script," I said. "But police stories are like Westerns: you guys have been making them for more than fifty years, all the great ideas are used up. It really depends on who's directing. Have you set anyone?"

"Well . . . no, actually. [pause, then brightly:] We've got Orson Welles to play the heavy, though."

Now I paused. Could they really not have thought of the obvious? "Why don't you ask him to direct, too? He's a pretty good director, you know." Well, you'd have thought I'd suggested that my mother direct the film.

"*Oh!* Ahh, yes, *Citizen Kane* and . . . umm . . . yes. Interesting. It would be, that is. To direct. For *him* . . . ah, to direct. The film. We'll, ah, get back to you. On that." Whereupon I hung up, bemused.

They did get back, a few days later. Yes, Orson would direct the film. I have no idea how intense the debate was, but I doubt anyone at Universal slapped his forehead and said, "Of *course* he should direct! How come *we* didn't think of it? What a smart guy that Chuck Heston is." More likely it was "Ahh, Christ, let Welles direct it. How bad can it be? Heston'll just get sore if we don't. Fuckin' actors."

I was delighted. It seemed to me, remembering *Kane,* that we had a chance at a great film. That's a chance you don't get very often. *Getting* the great film is even rarer. (But you sometimes get to try, pal. You get to try.)

I talked to Orson at length on the phone, before we left Michigan, then met with him after we got back to L.A. He swung open the door of the house he was renting, a looming figure in a flowing black Moorish robe from his *Othello.* I was taller, but he filled the room with his voice, his energy . . . with *himself.* His "Hello, Chuck!" rolled twice around the entry hall. He was a fascinating figure: highly intelligent, hugely gifted, genuinely witty, and funny as well (they're not the same). He gave me a very large singlemalt whiskey splashed with water, and mesmerized me for an afternoon.

He was three days into a rewrite of the entire script, which he finished a day and a half later. It was a vast improvement, most interesting to me in that he'd turned my character into a Mexican attorney. I'd played several Brits, but this was my first non-Anglo (though God knows not my last).

His name was Vargas, we decided; the very bright first son of a wealthy Mexican family, educated at USC and Harvard Law, on the fast track for high office in his country. None of this was in either the script or the picture, but, inventing his background, we could begin to invent the man. The next day I began growing a mustache, to be dyed black along with my hair. The makeup department darkened my skin to suggest Hispanic genes. Orson ordered a suit (the action in the film is almost continuous; there are no wardrobe changes) made by the best Mexican tailor in Los Angeles. A first-class Mexican tailor cuts a coat a little differently from his counterpart in London or New York.

All this gave me how Vargas looked. What about an accent? I chose the easy answer: "He's very well educated, mostly in the U.S.; he comes from a bilingual family; he speaks perfect English." That was lazy of me, and wrong. No one speaks perfect English, and no one who's not been raised speaking it is totally without an accent. Henry Higgins was right; a speech expert can tell within miles where a man was born. If I had the part to do over, I'd try for the faintest stroke of emphasis and rhythm you might hear from an internationally educated Mexican with the background we'd invented for Vargas, instead of my native Midwestern Yank. It would have been a good creative challenge, and right for the part.

I don't recall that I shared this internal debate with Orson. Had I undertaken the accent, I've no doubt he would have supported me; that I was considering it may never have crossed his mind. He was buried in the prep for his film.

It had become his film, of course, as I'd expected and Universal perhaps feared. He planned to shoot on both sides of the Mexican border, where the story was set. Universal pulled the plug on that; they wanted Orson where they could keep an eye on him. In retrospect, they were probably wise, though it did them no good in the end. Thwarted, Orson responded with his usual resourcefulness in adversity; he shot all his border-town exteriors in Venice, a beach community just south of Santa Monica, an hour from the studio. It looks marvelous, better than anything we could have found on the border, and logistically far easier.

The casting went well, and easily, though our budget of less than a million dollars for the whole film left little money for the actors. Nevertheless, they all wanted to work for Orson, in the first film he'd directed in Hollywood in ten years. Several of his old Mercury players came on board: Ray Collins, Joe Calleia, and Joe Cotten in a cameo. Marlene Dietrich played a very spooky Gypsy, wearing her old black Gypsy wig from *Golden Earrings*. I was responsible for a key casting. Dennis Weaver was just finding fame in "Gunsmoke"; I called him up and persuaded him to play a crazy motel-keeper for us. He was wonderfully loony. Janet Leigh was set as my new bride and was very good, in spite of breaking her arm a couple of weeks before shooting. She wore the lightest possible cast for filming, discarding the sling during takes. A gutsy lady.

Orson came on the picture dragging a reputation for extravagance after him like the chains clanking behind Marley's ghost. He didn't deserve it. He had his flaws as a filmmaker, but waste and inefficiency were not among them. I know directors who have wasted more money on one picture than Orson spent on the sum total of all the films he made in his career.

Still, he knew he had to make the studio believe in him. He did this very resourcefully. The Sunday before shooting started, Orson called some of the actors to his house for an undercover rehearsal of the first day's work, a sound-stage interior of a tiny apartment. The next day, Orson began laying out a master shot that covered the whole scene. It was a very complicated setup, with walls pulling out of the way as the camera moved from room to room, and four principal actors, plus three or four bit players working through the scene.

On any movie set, one of the A.D.s (assistant directors) calls the production department to report when rehearsals on the first shot begin, when the first take is made, and when the first print is recorded. Lunch came and went and we were still rehearsing the shot; no camera had yet turned. Studio executives began to gather in uneasy little knots in corners, a bit daunted about approaching Orson while he was cueing an extra's move just as the tracking camera picked him up. They were also very worried. With most of the first day gone, not a frame of film had passed through the gate yet.

About four o'clock, Orson called for a take, the first of a good many. Just after six, he said silkily, "Cut! Print the last three takes. That's a wrap on this set; we're two days ahead of schedule." He'd designed his master to include all the coverage he needed in the twelve-page scene, scheduled for three shooting days: close-ups, two-shots, over-shoulders, and inserts. All this was planned, of course, to astound Universal, which it surely did. It was also a fine way to shoot the scene.

The front-office people never came near the set again. They

kept hoping for another miraculous twelve-page day. They never
got one, but Orson had persuaded them that even if he did get into
trouble, he could get out of it. As a matter of fact, they were dead
right; he had a remarkably sure foot for tightropes.

Looking back, I think he relished it. I won't say he deliberately painted himself into corners, but he did love leaping out of them. I remember a scene where I was driving an open convertible down an alley in Venice, doing several pages of dialogue.

In 1957, they still shot moving car scenes in a breakaway car with the front off and the camera shooting past the actors at a process screen of traffic footage. Bogart and Gable and Lancaster and Douglas drove hundreds of miles in front of those screens; I'd put in some time there myself on my first film, *Dark City*. Orson decided to shoot it in a real car, driving down a real alley.

Nowadays, of course, that's a piece of cake. The film is faster, the lights are half the size, so are the mikes and cables. When Orson's cameraman, Russ Metty, had the shot rigged, the back of the car was crammed with batteries and the recording unit, with cables twisting around the seats to mikes taped to the dashboard, and the camera strapped to a wooden platform on the hood, with no room for even the camera operator and the sound mixer. Someone suggested cutting the front off the car and towing the rear half behind a truck large enough to carry a crew. Orson snorted. "Nonsense! These boys can shoot it without a crew."

And so we did. With a crash course in switching on both camera and sound, I drove down the alley half a mile to our start mark and said "Turn over."

Mort Mills, my partner in the scene, flipped the right switches, checked the appropriate dials, and said "Speed." (Technical note: nobody *ever* says "Lights, camera, action!" on a movie set.)

I gunned the car and yelled "Action!" as we tore off, acting away. We had a marvelous time. When we got down to the end of the alley, Orson said "How was it?"

"Perfect!" I said. "I'd like one more." It was my first experience of the heady bliss of directing a film. By the time I'd done three takes, I felt like D. W. Griffith. As a matter of record, this was the first time a dialogue scene was shot in a moving car.

The opening shot of the film was an even more spectacular example of Orson's alchemist's ability to transmute adversity into art. He took the introductory montage written to establish Janet and me in the border-town setting, and made what's been called the greatest boom shot in the history of the movies. Here's how it goes:

Close-up on hands holding a bomb, setting timer; ticking starts on sound track, continuing behind as the camera booms up over building, follows a scurrying figure down alley, dropping closer as man opens trunk of a parked car, drops bomb inside, and runs off as laughing couple comes from bar, climbs in, and drives off. Camera follows, holding car in full shot, picking up Heston and Leigh walking arm in arm, dialogue establishing their recent marriage. We pick up car going through border checkpoint, drunken girl complaining of ticking in her head. Car drives off, Heston and Leigh pass checkpoint, dialogue with guard conveys Heston's Mexican government status. Newlywed banter, Heston kisses her as bomb explodes offscreen.

It was technically an all but impossible shot, depending on precise timing, not only from Janet and me, the couple in the car, and the passing extras, but most critically of all, from the boom grip (the man running the boom) and the camera operator. Today, a remote-controlled camera on the end of a Python boom would make the shot far easier to prepare and not nearly as hard to shoot. Then, it was a wonder.

They started lighting in mid-afternoon and had it ready to rehearse when darkness came. We shot on it all night, with various things going wrong, most often due to the actor playing the U.S. guard at the border crossing. He had only a line or two, but it must have been terrifying for him to see the whole company bearing down on him from a block away. When we got to him, he'd flub his lines. At last, as dawn began to lighten in the east, Orson said to him patiently, "All right, let's do it once more. This time, if you aren't sure of your line, just move your lips . . . we can dub it in later. But whatever you do, please God *don't* say, 'I'm sorry, Mr. Welles.' " That's the take that's in the movie.

More than half the picture was shot at night in the alleys, canals, and crumbling corners, interior and exterior, of Venice, built in the 1920s by Abbot Kinney as a curious homage to the Italian original. Parts of it look like a Salvador Dalí landscape.

One night, preparing a showdown scene in a hotel lobby between my character as the crusading Mexican prosecutor and

Orson's corrupt cop, he was fuming at the slowness of the lumbering elevator. Suddenly, he stopped, transfixed. You could almost see the cartoon light bulb glow over his head. "Chuck," he said, as the elevator finally sank to lobby level, "would you see if you can run up the stairs to the third floor before this thing gets up there?" I did. (It was a really slow elevator.)

Orson then laid out the scene with me arguing with him in the lobby, he bundling his cronies into the elevator, shutting the door in my face and starting up, talking all the way, only to find me waiting at the top. Again, not tough to do today, with battery-powered sound and camera, but a real killer shot in 1957, with light and sound cables hanging three stories down the elevator shaft.

Later that same night, Orson and I were peeing into a drain down in the basement of the hotel. He looked at the dank cellar clutter around us and said, "Wouldn't this be a great place to do that scene in the file room with you and Joe Calleia?"

"It sure would," I said, zipping up. "But isn't that scheduled for Friday, back in the studio? They'll have the set built by now. Besides, Joe isn't even called tonight. It's two A.M.; he'll be dead asleep. We've got three more pages to shoot up on the third floor anyway. That'll take the rest of the night."

"Nonsense!" said Orson, his eyes gleaming. "I can wrap that scene in two setups. It'll take them that long to get Joe down here anyway. He'll be better if he's confused. That's what the scene's about."

He was right. He finished the upstairs scene before Joe got down to Venice, muzzy with sleep. He stumbled through the scene, with Orson harrying him. It played wonderfully well. So did the cellar.

Orson was also very good about sharpening your focus on the scene you were doing that day, or the shot you were doing that moment. Even with a great part, you're not likely to have more than three or four really great scenes, which you get to work on for maybe ten days of the whole shoot. A lot of the time you're getting on and off horses, or in and out of cars, or doing someone else's good scenes. Orson could somehow persuade you that this next setup happened to be one of the key shots in the whole movie.

Though I don't think he was a great actor, he could give you an actor's insight into the process. He told me something very casually once that's been permanently valuable to me. "You know, Chuck," he said as we finished looking at several reels of dailies, "you should work on your tenor range. All of us with these deep bass voices tend to rumble along like organs. You've got to use the high end, too. The tenor range has a knife edge. Your bass is a velvet hammer. Use them both." I've tried to do that ever since.

We finished the film early on April Fool's Day, killing Orson on the junk-littered bank of a Venice canal, just before the sun rose. We were one night over our thirty-day schedule and $31,000 over our $900,000 budget. Orson and I celebrated over ham and eggs in an all-night coffee shop, with a bottle of Lanson champagne he had in his trailer.

I lifted my glass to him. "I think it'll be a hell of a picture, Orson. You did waste some time, and a little film, trying to conceal the fact that you had the best part. I knew that. The movie is about the fall of Captain Quinlan." He looked at me quizzically for a moment, then rumbled with laughter.

"You're quite right, my boy. That was stupid of me." He burst out in a happy roar, "Well, now I don't have to worry about it in the cutting room."

That morning was the high point in our relationship. We spent many meetings over many years on different continents trying to find another film, but it never came together again. Orson actually shooting a film was a different man from Orson between films, or, indeed, finishing one. *Badge of Evil,* now retitled *Touch of Evil*, was a long way from finished.

MEANWHILE, IN THE REAL WORLD, or what passes in Hollywood for the real world, MCA, in the person of Herman Citron, was busy securing my future employment. It wasn't till years later that I discovered that Herman's nickname throughout the industry was "the Iceman." To me he was a mild-mannered, avuncular Clark Kent; to the studios, he was a ruthless shark. Fortunately, he was my shark, absolutely determined to see that I got more than my share of the good parts, and that I was compensated beyond my dreams, a point I'd already passed long since. Our arrangement was simple: I chose the scripts, he made the deals. On balance, he did a lot better than I did.

Herman must've been particularly pleased when Jack War-

My mother and me, at maybe three months. (She looks very *Wuthering Heights* here.)

Portrait of the author as a very young man. Am I looking for eggs, or chickens?

With my Dad, about 1930, after I decided not to run away from home after all (note the hobo bindle).

The Aleutians in World War II.
Another day in paradise.

"Letter from Cairo" was another live
"Studio One." I can't remember what
it was about, but I remember Anne
Bancroft was good. (I had a good
trench coat.)

As Mark Antony, mourning the murdered Caesar in David Bradley's
16mm film.

With Cornell Wilde in my second film, *The Greatest Show on Earth*. That's Jimmy Stewart in the clown makeup.

In *The Savage* (1952) with Joan Taylor. "Good Lord, here comes Kevin Costner."

One of my early *Macbeth*s, with Judith Evelyn on "Studio One," directed by Frank Schaffner.

With Lydia in *The Traitor* by Herman Wouk. I played a spy for the Soviets.

With Jack Palance as the scariest Indian I ever saw on the screen.

The Private War of Major Benson, my only successful film comedy. Is there a lesson here, or were Jack Lemmon and Walter Matthau just too good?

OPPOSITE:
Moses in *The Ten Commandments.*

Maybe the best play written about World War II: *Mister Roberts.* The title role is surely the best part in all the fiction of that war.

LYDIA CLARKE HESTON

Mr. DeMille giving me a statuette of Andrew Jackson, marking my second shot at the part.

With Janet Leigh in Orson Welles's *Touch of Evil,* in one of the few quiet moments in the movie.

With Greg Peck in *The Big Country.* East meets west, with no love lost between them.

During the ten months we worked on *Ben-Hur,* Lydia and I spent a lot of time on Sundays showing our very young Roman soldier some very old Roman ruins.

"Then Silver turned and said, 'Who be you, George Merry? Mebbe you thought *you* wuz Cap'n here, p'raps.'"

Ben-Hur (1959). Yes, it was a very tough shoot.

With Glen Randall, one of the guys who trained those white horses.

In the chariot with Willy Wyler, who made it what it was.

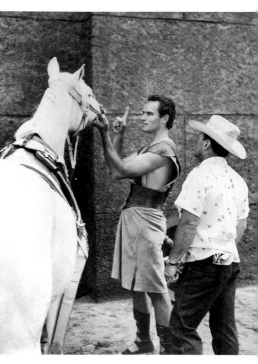

With Jack Hawkins and the smallest soldier in the legions.

With Steve Boyd and Willy.

OVERLEAF:
In the arena.

St. Helen, Michigan, with my dad.

"Hey, Daddy, who is this guy?"

Dying in Sophia's
arms in *El Cid*.

Going home through Spain after *El Cid*.

Besieging Valencia. The armor is eleventh century now, and the soldier's a little taller than in Rome.

Standing up for civil rights. I'm proud I was there early.

Father and son. One of my favorite of Lydia's shots of the two of us.

At home with Holly, 1961. Sons are wonderful, but daughters are special.

FOUR PHOTOS: LYDIA CLARKE HESTON

ZINN ARTHUR

A day off from *The Agony and the Ecstasy.*

Relaxing on the ridge.

Explaining the wonders of the Sistine ceiling to Fray.

. . . and working with Carol Reed, trying to find Michelangelo.

ner decided he had to have me for a World War II film they were
planning called *Darby's Rangers*. As I said earlier, after barring MCA
from his studio the day after I hit town because they'd allowed me
to sign with Hal Wallis instead of Warner, Jack had had to back
down from this rash position. He'd never, however, offered me a
picture. Still, he was a man given to caprice as well as angry impulse. Some years earlier, he'd put Errol Flynn on suspension, no
doubt for good and sufficient reason—to Jack, anyway. "I never
want to see that son of a bitch on this lot again!" he'd announced.
"Unless we absolutely need him." Now, for *Darby's Rangers,* he felt
he absolutely needed me. Herman was in heaven. He negotiated a
deal compensating me with a percentage of Warner Bros.' gross
income from the first dollar. It was one of the first gross deals made
in films. From Jack's point of view, it was a mistake. A dumb mistake.

There are parts for which you must have a certain actor.
Selznick *had* to have Clark Gable for Rhett Butler. To borrow him
from MGM, it was worth letting them distribute *Gone With the
Wind.* Jack didn't *have* to have me for *Darby.* There were a dozen
actors who could've done it just as well and a lot cheaper. *Darby*
was not worth breaking an industry-wide position against gross
deals.

I'm not sure whether Jack simply failed to understand the
deal he'd okayed, or whether he understood its ramifications full
well, and planned to weasel out of it somehow. Anyway, the contract
they sent did not outline a gross deal, but appended all sorts of
deductions, cost of production, cost of prints and advertising, interest, overhead, distribution fee, the whole litany. Of course we sent
the contract back, of course they threatened breach of contract,
whereupon we sued.

We were not then as litigious a nation as we are now; law-
suits were rarer. This was my first (and, come to think of it, my last
. . . so far). I was called to the offices of the Warner attorneys, sworn
and questioned for some two hours, with my lawyer present, but
largely silent. This was Leo Ziffren, there to make sure they didn't
beat me with rubber hoses, I suppose, also to bail me out if I talked
myself into trouble. (Leo was then the lean young partner of his
brother Paul, a gifted gray eminence of towering character in California law and Democratic politics. Paul's gone now, Leo's himself
a gifted gray eminence, also of towering character. He's kept my

family largely free of the problems that beset actors . . . and even real people.)

I thought I handled my deposition superbly. I'd played lawyers before, most recently for Orson in *Touch of Evil*. I felt quite at home threading my way through the complex questions. As we were leaving, I asked Leo what he thought of my performance. He looked at me quizzically. "You did all right, Chuck, but another time, remember it's often best to answer questions with a simple 'Yes' or 'No.'"

When it was Jack Warner's turn to be questioned, Leo asked him some question about fairness. Jack exploded. *"Fair?* My God —those goddamn actors deserve anything lousy happens to 'em, anyway!" Leo closed his legal pad carefully. "Thank you, Mr. Warner. I don't think we need trouble you any further." And that was the end of that. Warner settled for more than my gross piece of the film would have brought me and Jimmy Garner did the picture instead, launching his splendid career. Everyone was happy except Jack Warner, and even he didn't seem to mind that much.

I ran into Jack Warner a month or so later at some industry function and he slapped me on the shoulder. "Hey, Chuck! How ya doin'?" he said jovially. This is a strange town.

ORSON AND I were still struggling to find another script that attracted both of us. One morning he burst over the phone with an idea to film *Don Quixote* in Mexico on a three-week schedule, with some blocked U.S. dollars he'd located somewhere. It seemed a very precarious project to me, but that's a part you can't turn down, so I read the book and sketched makeups till the plan collapsed.

Meanwhile, he was still editing *Touch of Evil*. I'd spent a little time with DeMille's editor, Annie Bauchens, during *Ten Commandments,* but I really didn't understand the process then. Orson let me into his editing room. He actually taught me something about cutting a picture. I've always been grateful for that.

Editing is the most arcane of all the myriad skills and talents required to make a film. I remember Phil Gramm, a distinguished professor of economics before he became a U.S. senator, saying, "Nobody knows anything about economics except economists, and a lot of them don't know much, either." I wouldn't say that about film editors, but some producers and directors are a little shaky

about editing. In the closing decade of the millennium, with film as
the dominant art of our time, there's a trend toward trick editing,
jump cuts, double cuts, five-frame cuts, designed to call attention to
the process . . . the medium instead of the meaning. Now it's precariously easy to smother a movie in style, at the expense of substance.

(Another paragraph on How Movies Are Really Made. The
main difference between film and theater is that when the curtain
goes up on the opening night of a play, it's all there. When shooting
finishes on a film, the actors all go home, but there is no movie.
Only those hundreds of rolls of film on the cutting room racks,
waiting for the director and the editor and the producer to make
the movie. Computer editing, now almost universal, multiplies the
infinite spectrum of choice available, eliminating the exhausting
search that plagued us all: "Goddamn it, I *know* there's a cut where
she looks down before he leaves the frame. I printed it for that. It
must be somewhere in the trims. *Find* it!" That's what it amounts
to, in the end . . . finding the right frames.)

While waiting for a film to appear, I accepted another biographical role—for television, this time. I played the colonel who
prosecuted the commandant of Andersonville prison after the Civil
War in *The Andersonville Trial,* on "Playhouse 90." Considering the
part I was to undertake some months later, I probably should've
played the president of the court-martial, General Lew Wallace, who
later wrote *Ben-Hur.* (The colonel was the better part, though.)

ABOUT THEN, I got an offer from William Wyler. "It's a Western,"
Herman said, "with Greg Peck. This is a very classy project, Chuck."
That was clear, and the script confirmed it. The only problem was
my part. Greg had the lead, of course, but my guy was only about
the fourth role.

There's a great deal of egotistical hoo-hah among actors and
agents about billing—above the title, first position, costar billing,
last billing in a separate box, and so on. It's useful as a negotiating
ploy for the studios. ("No, we can't up the price, but we'll give her
star billing, third position above the title.") Otherwise, billing order
is meaningless. Even in the profession, no one remembers from
one year to the next who had first billing in what picture.

I'd been at it long enough to figure that out, but I was still
very preoccupied with the size and centrality of my part. When

you're reading scripts, you learn to ask "Is my role the guy this movie is *about?*" Laurence Olivier was once approached about doing the Chorus in Zeffirelli's film of *Romeo and Juliet.* He listened to a minute or two of fawning blandishment, then cut in: "No, I'm afraid not."

Stunned astonishment. "But, Larry, it would be such a distinguished contribution. Why not?"

"Because," said Olivier, "I'm too fucking grand."

He was right, of course. Olivier was the greatest actor of the century; he could do, or turn down, any part he chose. The rest of us have to consider it differently. Is it better to have a good part in an important film, or the best part in an OK film? I know the answer to that now . . . I didn't then. I called Herman. "Look, I know this is a major movie, and it's a very good script, but my part isn't very good. We're getting a lot of offers now, anyway. I'll pass on this one."

It was not the mild-mannered Herman who answered, but the Iceman. "Kid," he said, "you don't know what the fuck you're talking about. You have an offer to work with Gregory Peck for maybe the best director in film, and you're worrying the *part* isn't good enough for you? Don't you know actors take parts with Wyler without even reading the damn *script?* I'm telling you, you *have* to do this picture!"

So I did. *The Big Country* was among the last of the big-budget Westerns of the period done by a major director. I was damn lucky Herman made me do it. By the seventies, the genre had faded out of fashion with critics and most filmmakers, its core ethic jarred by the Vietnam syndrome that plagued us for so long. Twenty years later, it has enjoyed a startling renaissance, though filmmakers now must deal with the huge cost of any period film, and most directors feel impelled to Political Correctness, ever the enemy of art.

Along with jazz, the Western is the only totally indigenous American art form. Nobody else can do it, and now some of us have lost the touch. That's too bad. More than any other kind of film, the Western cries out for a camera and uses it most gloriously. Indeed, the Western reaches for its basic images many millennia back before the camera to man's first instinctive creative urges in the cave paintings in Lascaux and the Cretan murals: the running horse, the weaponed confrontation, and the steady eye, unfearful. These are the echoes genetics planted in the bones of Man, the territorial carnivore, ten thousand years ago, impassively immune to the shift-ing tides of taste.

The Western is utterly unavailable to the stage, not just be-cause it can't contain the wide Missouri in flood, or a war party of mounted Sioux braves, but because the stage is, finally, the domain of the spoken word. This is its strength and its mystic power. The best writing for the stage comes most alive there. Shakespeare, the Greeks, Shaw, O'Neill *need* live actors, breathing and bloodful, speaking in the magic light, making it happen before you.

Some years later, my daughter, then seven, had seen me on the screen a few times, but was for the first time coming to see me in a play. Over supper before I left for the theater, she asked me, "Now, Daddy, in the play tonight, will that really be *you* there?" I realized she'd somehow struck on the basic difference. On the stage, the actors are really *there,* alive. They and the words they speak *are* the theater, often supported by only the sketchiest indica-tion of time or place.

Film, conversely, is images—light and shadow, moving im-ages as art. Very often, they speak most eloquently without words. A woman's sleeping eye, suddenly alert to an opening door; a wash of running horses splashing through a stream; a limp hand hanging with drops of blood falling from a finger, or wind sweeping over an infinity of wheat field under a roil of cloud. These images often need not, cannot, be acted; the most brilliant dialogue pales beside them. That's why most film scripts are reworked constantly during a shoot, the words honed and sanded down to their strongest bone structure, leaving the director room to look for that crucially elo-quent moment. Sometimes it's even accidental, as art can be, caught by the camera's hungry eye.

Wyler knew all this from his earliest days directing in silent films, along with John Ford and DeMille. Willy was also, I think, the best director of performance in film. Actors working for Wyler have been nominated for Academy Awards more than thirty times, and won a dozen Oscars (one of them for Burl Ives in *The Big Country*), plus countless lesser awards. No other director comes close to this record. Willy was also a brilliant script editor, a function he per-formed tirelessly on *Big Country*. I learned a great deal about this, watching him scrape every fleck of fat off the dialogue in a scene. His basic dogma was right out of Strunk & White's definitive *Elements of Style:* "Omit needless words."

He demonstrated this wonderfully even in the opening footage of the picture, laid behind the credits: a lean montage of running horses and spinning buggy wheels, with Jerry Moross's unforgettable score, probably the best ever composed for a Western. The sequence somehow prefaced the picture and fulfilled its title, *The Big Country,* indeed.

Willy worked his usual magic with the actors. You always start with good ones, if you can. He and Greg had assembled a fine bunch, Jeannie Simmons, Carroll Baker, and Chuck Connors in his first good part and maybe his best performance, and Burl Ives, originally a folk singer. When Willy was through with him, he not only richly deserved the Oscar I just mentioned, but was well-launched on an acting career that left him little time for singing.

I still remember, as I suspect Fray does too, Burl singing "The Blue-Tail Fly" to him one night. Lydia had brought him up to visit our location in the rolling prairie you could still find east of Stockton before they planted it with broccoli—truly big country then. At two, Fray was stunned by the look and feel of it all. For years after, whenever we drove through any landscape that seemed at all plausible, he'd ask me, "Daddy, is dis da *weal* West now?"

I understand that. I think most American men feel a sort of blood-call to that search for the real West. A new world, a last frontier, for our grandparents, or their great-grandparents, it was a new chance. I never knew an actor who didn't like making Westerns. To stand by a wood fire at six in the morning with the sun coming up behind you and look west at real country . . . mountains, prairie, desert, with a cup of coffee in your hand and the sound and smell of horses around you, is to reach back through centuries, beyond our beginnings as a nation.

I realized there were some advantages in, for the first time, not being the main man in the movie. Instead of shooting a twelve-hour day, week after week, there were stretches of days on standby, when I could spend time with my son. Sometimes Lydia would join us, sometimes she'd go off with her increasingly active camera, exploring the "weal West" as eagerly as Fray.

I often had time to sketch, which is impossible when you're

in every scene, with Fray scrawling away happily beside me, or I could leave him digging under a tree while I worked the big pinto stud they'd found for me in the film. He was a beautiful animal but edgy, as studs are, really just short of being more horse than I could handle. Still, Domino looked marvelous on film: high-headed, wonderfully loose-gaited, like a horse in a Delacroix painting.

Fray kept clamoring to ride too, and I took him up in front of me a few times, feeling a little outnumbered by a feisty stud and an equally feisty two-year-old. At least, the first time he had his bottom on a horse's back, it was a good horse.

There was even time for me to enjoy friends visiting the location. If you're playing the lead, shooting and preparing twelve hours a day, you can hardly lift your head to say hello. On *Big Country,* I had some time off. My half-sister, Kay, came up for a week, fresh out of college and lovely. It was fun to have her with us, suddenly grown up and perhaps a little taken with a handsome young stuntman named Chuck Hayward. He was sure Lord taken with her.

Coincidentally, Greg's stunt double was also named Chuck . . . Robeson. Chuck Connors and I took him to dinner one night, making well over six hundred pounds of Chuck at the table before we ate a bite. The script supervisor was the fifth Chuck on the company, confusing everybody when one of us was called on the bullhorns. They finally numbered us one through five. "Chuck One!" (me) "To the camera, please."

Willy worked, as I was to find he always did, with fiercely focused concentration and little small talk. Off the set, he was a warm and delightful man; we remained friends till his death more than twenty years later. Shooting a film, he was very different. Not harsh—there was nothing of the cartoon tyrant with a viewfinder writers are so fond of when inventing a film director. He was abstracted, digging inside himself for the scene till he got to the root of it, then giving it to the actors.

I think he found that last part the hardest, getting it through to the actors. He didn't try to charm; he wasn't particularly eloquent in conveying his vision. In fact, I'm pretty sure he had no preconceived idea of the whole film. Again, unlike the stage, there *is* no film till months after the shooting's done. Willy understood this as well as any director I know. He was willing to let the scene, and the movie, become what it would become. Working on both sides of the camera since then, I've tried to remember that.

He'd take what you and the other actors gave him, along with any idea the cameraman might have about how to shoot it, and worry the scene through rehearsal till he decided on a master shot. Then, he'd start on the performances.

People claimed Wyler did fifteen or twenty takes on every setup, a wild exaggeration. He averaged, in my experience, maybe eight or nine (quite a lot, mind you). In fact, he'd shoot till he was convinced neither you nor he could make it any better. I think it never occurred to him that encouragement was a useful part of the process. Early on *Big Country,* Willy was working me through a tough close-up. Finally, after maybe ten takes, he stood thinking a moment, then turned to the first assistant director. "Well," he said, "let's do the two-shot now."

I hurried after him. "Look, Willy," I said, "let's not quit on this now. We'll get it . . . I'm not tired. Tell me what we need here."

He looked at me oddly. "Chuck, if I don't say anything, that means it's OK. All right?" Yes, it was, but it was heavy going sometimes. Working for Wyler was like getting the works in a Turkish bath. You damn near drown . . . but you come out smelling like a rose.

He expected a lot from everyone. His towering reputation, and his track record, with both critics and customers, daunted any challenger to his demanding approach. We were having a tough time with a scene one day; I thought of an extensive dialogue cut I was sure would solve it. "Let me show you what I mean, Willy," I said, looking for my script. His was lying nearby, in one of the leather binders we all use, and I snatched it up. It fell open to the leather flyleaf, where the titles of most of his films were stamped in small letters: *Counsellor-at-Law, Dodsworth, Dead End, Jezebel, Wuthering Heights, The Westerner, The Letter, The Little Foxes, Memphis Belle, The Best Years of Our Lives, The Heiress, Roman Holiday, Friendly Persuasion.* I put the binder down. "Forget it," I said. "I agree with you."

Greg Peck, of course, had an impressive track record, too. Also, as coproducer of the film with Willy, he had not only the right but the responsibility to explore any creative differences with him well beyond what's appropriate as actor to director. As far as I

know, they had only one serious disagreement, but it was a lulu.
When honorable men differ, this is likely to be so.

Looking at the dailies of an important early scene in a buck-board with Carroll Baker, Greg felt he could do a better job on his close-up. He asked Willy to do a retake, not uncommon for an actor of Greg's stature and reputation, even were he not a partner. Willy responded, reasonably enough, "Let me do a rough assembly of the whole scene first. If you're still unhappy with the shot, we'll do it over."

Soooo, in a day or so Greg saw the assembled scene. Still dissatisfied with the shot in question, he asked Willy to schedule the retake, as agreed—and Willy refused. To those of us raised to keep promises, this was a shocking breach of faith; to Willy, the film was an overriding end, justifying any means.

A few years earlier, Willy had had a similar disagreement while making *Best Years of Our Lives,* arguably his finest film. Sam Goldwyn, his employer, ordered him to use a longer version of a close-up of Fredric March instead of the one Willy preferred. There was no question of a retake; filming was finished, the shot was there in the cutting room. Willy went into the film lab at night, ran down the negative reels to the shot in question, clipped out fifteen feet of negative, and destroyed it. He was a man of firm opinions.

So was Greg. To him, I think, it was a question of ethics, not art. I agree—you have to keep your promises. Willy's version of the shot is in *Big Country,* and the two men didn't speak till nearly three years later. Backstage at the Academy Awards, Greg was about to make his entrance as a presenter when Willy walked off with his Oscar for directing *Ben-Hur.* Greg stuck out his hand and said "Congratulations, Willy, you deserve it." Willy grinned, shook hands, and said "Thanks, but I still won't retake that buckboard scene." That was the end of the feud.

During the *Big Country* shoot, relations between Willy and Greg were strained. Still, both men were consummate professionals with a picture to finish. They did it, I think, superbly. Greg's not capable of a bad performance, but he gave one of his better ones as the green Eastern sea captain challenging the grim eye-for-an-eye Western ethic.

As the ranch foreman, I was in fast company, but actors, like tennis players, often do better with a top-ranked opponent. Acting is not a competition, of course, but many, even most, good scenes are confrontations between the characters. Greg and I had one like that. It began as a quarrel and ended in what is still regarded as one of the best bare-knuckle fights on film. We worked through it doggedly, blow by blow in the stifling August heat of the prairie for two endless days. At one point, Willy moved the camera up on a ridge two hundred yards away. I thought I must be hallucinating; I knew enough about lenses by then to see we'd be the size of ants on the screen. This was Willy's point, of course—the insignificance of two tiny figures struggling in the dust of this vast land. In the end, there was no winner. Both of us lay bone-battered, panting in exhaustion. That last, we didn't have to act.

I had another fight scene with Carroll Baker that Willy dealt with very differently. Carroll played Greg's fiancée, a beautiful, spoiled girl for whom my surly foreman nursed a hopeless passion. (My part had been getting better as shooting and the rewrites progressed.) Willy was familiar with Carroll's Actors Studio background. He told her, as our quarrel burned to flash point, to hit me with her riding crop. "Chuck's a big guy, you won't hurt him. Really get mad—let him have it." Then he took me aside and warned me. "You have to get that crop away from her, then hold on to her for the rest of the scene. That's a strong girl."

This is a useful director's ploy, common in acting school: give two actors conflicting goals and turn them loose. It's guaranteed to generate genuine emotions. So it did. Carroll was pale with real fury when she swung at me. I managed to catch the crop, snatch it free, and hold her wrists in one hand (I have long fingers). She literally spat the rest of her lines at me, twisting like a trapped leopard. Her anger was wonderfully real, and a little scary, which made me angry, too, both as the foreman and myself. Jesus, what if she'd caught me in the eye with that damn thing?! There was unmistakable passion in the scene—cut, print.

And that's where the Method collided with Wyler's relentless search for perfection. He wanted another take on the master shot, which actually became several more. For each, he exhorted Carroll to more effort and warned me to contain her attack at any cost. I missed the crop in one take and took a hard one under the ear. The first take committed me to holding her wrists with one hand, for matching in the cover angles, which I did with increasing

desperation, fearful of what she'd do to me if she got loose. Her
angry tears became sobs of pain before Willy got what he wanted.
It *is* a very good scene; I guess only Carroll can say whether it was
worth it.

It certainly was for me. I learned a great deal from Wyler on
Big Country, about acting, and movies, and the need to do it better.
In the end, you can only do this by pushing yourself.

This was September, when Wyler had moved the company
back to L.A. and the Goldwyn sound stages for the interiors. It
made for a more civilized life: shooting a five-day week, instead of
working Saturdays and some Sundays, the rule on location.

Steve Leech, the foreman I was playing, didn't have many
interior scenes, which gave me a little more time for my son and
his mother. We snatched a weekend in Palm Springs, where I put
Fray on a horse again, on the pommel in front of me. He clutched
the mane happily when we ran, reassuring me over his shoulder,
"Don't worry, Daddy, you won't fall off." He also met Walt Disney
that weekend, who, not surprisingly, seemed honestly interested in
what a two-year-old boy thought of *Perri,* one of his nature films
and the only movie Fray had yet seen, albeit four times.

Back in town, I took Fray to Paramount for his first haircut.
"Jimmy Stewart just got out of this chair," said Sam, the studio
barber, proudly, putting a board across the arms for my son to sit
on. When he was properly clipped, we stopped by the DeMille
Building, as he'd requested. After greeting his aging Infant Moses,
DeMille asked me if I'd like to play Andrew Jackson again, as a
cameo in the remake of his 1938 film *The Buccaneer* about pirate
Jean Lafitte and the Battle of New Orleans. Of course I leapt at the
chance.

The big office was awash with set models, costume designs,
and sample props, just as I'd seen it during pre-prod on *The Greatest Show on Earth* and *Ten Commandments,* but DeMille himself
had mellowed. The creative fire was still there, but the blaze had
sunk to banked, glowing embers. The fierce, focused drive I remembered had eased. He no longer paced up and down the room,
imagining his film for you with a few props and sketches. Sitting
behind his desk, his eye often strayed to my small son playing on
the carpet with some model soldiers in the uniforms of the Scottish
regiment that marched against Jackson at New Orleans.

We talked about Jackson and the film I'd done about him at Fox. DeMille's insight into the man was sharp, clear as ever. Of course I was glad to have another shot at Jackson, though he didn't really have to ask me. Paramount had long since bought the last of my five Wallis commitments, now available to DeMille at about a tenth of what I was getting for *Big Country*. I did ask him to lend me again the little statue of Jackson he'd let me borrow during the shoot on *President's Lady*.

"Oh, we can do better than that, Chuck," he said, turning to the shelf where it stood and handing it to me. "Let me give it to you. Not a bonus—just a present." It still stands in my den.

It wasn't till we were leaving that he told me, almost shyly, that he would not be directing *Buccaneer*. In his more than seventy films, for the first time he wouldn't be in the director's chair:

Farewell the plumed troop and the big wars . . .
O farewell. . . . Othello's occupation's gone!

It was about this time that my life began to get complicated. Up in Stockton, I'd had nothing to worry about but pleasing Willy. Now I had another part to prepare, finishing my scenes in *Big Country* at the same time. It was also clear I needed a house. The apartment we lived in was spacious enough, but I wanted room for Fray to run in—what I'd had in the Michigan woods. I found it, a little ridge of less than three acres, only seven minutes from the Beverly Hills Hotel, but surrounded on both sides by eight hundred acres of Water Department land, with deer and hawks and raccoons on it. I could build a house there with a view of Catalina Island from one side and Mt. Jupiter, fifty miles into the desert, from the other. I bought it the day I saw it. (As I write this, Fray, now with a son of his own, is looking for a larger house than the one he has, for the same reasons I had. He said to me the other day, "Dad, I don't want you ever to tell me again how little you paid for that land." I won't, but it was worth it.)

Herman Citron reported large noises from MGM about *Ben-Hur,* then preparing to shoot the following year. They'd already talked to two or three guys about the title role, ranging from interesting (Burt Lancaster) to dead wrong (Rock Hudson), as studios often do. Now, they were starting over, with a firm offer to Wyler to direct, which moved everything back to square one. He'd put off a

final decision till he'd finished shooting *Big Country*. Still, they
were desperate to cast the central role. Would I make a firm deal
to play either Ben-Hur or Messala, Wyler's choice? No. I wouldn't.
Well, how about a deal to do either part, *my* choice? That was really
stupid. If Wyler decided to direct, he'd make his own choice, no
matter what deal was in place. If he didn't do the film, I might not
want to do either part for another director. I said no. I'd wait for
Willy. Not the worst decision I ever made.

Then Universal called. I was back in the boondocks by then,
finishing *Big Country,* living in a grungy motel on the edge of the
Mojave Desert. Universal found me just as I'd turned in early for a
5 A.M. call. They had some problems with the postproduction on
Touch of Evil. Could I get in touch with Orson?

I certainly couldn't do it from the Mojave. Besides, why me?
I'd finished on *Touch of Evil* four months ago. Unless they needed
me for some more loops? (You don't want to know what looping
is, do you? Ohhhkay . . . I see a hand in the back. It's what they do
to clean up technically inadequate sound recording, usually tracks
made on location or with uncontrollable nonproduction sound audible in the background. Or if they want to change the dialogue on
material you can't reshoot.)

No, it wasn't the looping, the Universal guy said. They had
some problems with the director's cut Orson had turned in, and
they couldn't reach him. Would I try? I hadn't heard from him since
I started *Big Country,* which I now had to finish, I pointed out. I'd
be back in L.A. in a week. Wait till then.

Ten days later, I finished filming for Willy in a blaze of well-
staged gunplay and went home, where I struck out reaching Orson.
He could be very elusive on the phone (unless, of course, you were
in the Australian outback and he wanted to talk to *you.* Then you
couldn't get him out of your ear). I gave it a rest and took Fray to
the circus. Thanks to my time with them shooting *The Greatest Show
on Earth,* that meant he got to meet the clowns, pet a tiger, and ride
in my lap on an elephant around the big top during the performance. He got almost as big a kick out of it as I did. I also ran into
a guy from Fox who told me Orson was shooting there, on their
back lot (now Century City). The next day I drove over to talk to
him, feeling miscast in the role of mediator.

In the years since it was released in 1958, *Touch of Evil* has become a cult film, much admired, as it should be. It's certainly not a great film, like *Citizen Kane,* but it is immensely imaginative and provocative—among the finest few films from a hugely gifted filmmaker. *Cahiers du Cinéma* probably got it right when they called it "the best B movie ever made."

So, what happened? Did Orson make a great film to begin with, only to have Universal screw it up? Film buffs have been chewing on this for years; I never do a film seminar without having it come up. I'm a crucial witness partly because I seem to be the only guy who wrote it down. For most of my career, I've kept a daily journal, focused on the work in progress . . . films, plays, in every phase. It's a ship's log, but also an archive. It's been a useful data base for this book and the earlier ones: who did what with whom and when. Even more, it's a check on what I really thought about it all at the time. What about this or that actress, director, script when it happened, compared with what I think I thought, or think now. Memory, I've found, is not a reliable guide. Your life is not entirely the way you remember it.

I'd last worked on *Touch of Evil,* according to my journal, on June 28 at Universal, finishing my looping. Among the many things I learned from Orson on that film was that looping is not just a complicated and vexing chore fixing inadequate sound tracks, but actually a last chance to improve the performance. That's what we did that day, the last time I ever worked for him. He gave me a massive bear hug and went back to his cutting room.

Now, in November, I was hanging around the Fox back lot, waiting for Orson to finish a scene with Paul Newman for a picture he was acting in there, so I could find out what had happened. He was in high good humor, and dismissive of whatever was bothering Universal. They wanted some added shots and he hadn't had time to address the issue.

The next day I ran the picture, then still lacking Henry Mancini's extraordinary score and the final sound mix. It looked in good shape to me, very close to its final form. What was the problem, I asked the Universal people? Not much, I gathered. They needed some shots to clarify the geography of the film—which side of the border we were on in this or that scene. I didn't agree, but it didn't seem important. The film is a little nonlinear, especially for its time. I couldn't imagine Orson making an issue out of it.

Orson *was* the issue, it turned out. For some weeks, they hadn't been able to get in touch with him at all, to discuss anything. I could believe this. Orson was at his best preparing a film and shooting it, riding a cresting wave of creative and physical energy, carrying everyone with him. He addressed the editing with the same enthusiasm. The last stages of postproduction were another thing. Sandpapering the edit, mixing in the sound and music, grading the prints are all painstaking, repetitive chores. I think he got bored.

He'd gone to Mexico, they said, leaving neither phone number nor address. I suppose he was pursuing the *Don Quixote* project he'd talked to me about, and would wrestle with for some years, but this was a bad move. You can't leave a studio holding an unfinished film, surely not without talking to them. Orson had an odd blind spot. He was infinitely charming with his crew and actors, but I've seen him deliberately insult studio heads. Very dumb. Those are the guys with the *money*. If they won't give you any, you don't get to make any *movies*.

I was preoccupied for a few days working out my makeup for Andrew Jackson in *Buccaneer*. Then I got a call from Universal for a day of added shots for *Touch of Evil,* without Orson. This galvanized him into action, of course, producing some forty pages of memo. Yes, he would do the added shots, he would even do them free. Universal was not impressed, even when I said I wouldn't do the filming if Orson didn't direct. No soap; both Herman Citron and Leo Ziffren pointed out that I was contractually required to do added footage when needed.

I spent the weekend mulling this over and finally called the studio on Sunday to say I couldn't in good conscience report for the shooting call the next morning.

Instead I expected to meet with Ed Muhl, who was then the studio head. I would reimburse them for unrecoverable costs for the lost shooting day. (This came to something over eleven thousand dollars. It would be ten times that today.) Of course I should've demanded the meeting two days earlier at no cost to anyone (the unions won't let you cancel Monday crew calls on Sunday), but I was still sorting it out then. My instincts were with Orson, but I could see Universal's point.

Early on Monday I met first with Orson, now all contrition

and eager cooperation, then with my advisors, finally with Muhl. He was reasonable but adamant. Orson had stonewalled too long and Muhl knew neither of us had a legal leg to stand on. He'd decided that Orson was not going to do the added shots; I *must* do them.

The next day, I did. With a studio director, Harry Keller, and Janet Leigh, we did half a dozen setups clarifying some of the geography of the film. I don't know if any of them made the film better, or worse. I've never met anyone who could even pick one out of the final cut—I can only identify one or two of them myself.

I didn't see Orson again for several weeks and I have no idea whether he was allowed any hand in the final mix, though his cutting notes, which I have in my files, are very creative. *Touch of Evil* was released in due course, to only fair business but excellent notices and a couple of festival prizes. I'm very proud of the film and of working for Orson. I'm also proud that I was responsible for his directing the last film he made in this country, or for a major studio. I'd have worked for him again, given a chance. Years later he seemed on the edge of getting financing to film *Lear*. I told him I'd love to play Gloucester for him. He was pleased, but unexcited. Perhaps he knew it would never come to pass.

What do I think of Orson Welles? I think he was the most talented man I ever met, which doesn't mean I think he was the best actor or the best director. I don't. But whatever we mean by "talent"—I suppose it's a label we put on the capacity to create art —Orson had it, in spades.

Maybe he had too much of it. It often seemed so easy for him to come up with a marvelous solution for a scene, almost off the top of his head. Maybe he only used the top of his talent, sometimes, then got bored with the end game. It's been said that Hollywood owed Orson more than they gave him. I think that's true, but perhaps he owed them more, too.

He never lost his spirit, though. In the last year of his life, he was holding court in the Bistro, in Beverly Hills, when an intense young man approached him, almost genuflecting in awe at his work, particularly *Citizen Kane*. "There's one thing, though, I've always w-wondered about," the man stammered, abashed. "In the l-last scene, when Kane's dying and he—he drops the glass ball, you know, and he says 'R-Rosebud'? Ahh, there's n-no-one else in the room. So how—how do they know those're his last w-words?"

Orson looked at him a moment, then put a massive hand on the back of his neck and drew him close. "You must *never,*" he rumbled softly, "repeat one word of what you have just told me to a living soul."

I WENT ALMOST AT ONCE into shooting for *The Buccaneer,* which Tony Quinn was directing. Though I'd never worked with him, I'd admired him for a long time as an actor, but this was his first time behind the camera. I liked what he did there. In the original film, Jackson had not been a large part. For this version, they'd made it a costarring role with Yul Brynner's Jean Lafitte.

We'd had a good screen chemistry in *Ten Commandments,* and Tony got some good stuff out of both of us. He drew more on the Method tradition in which I'd been trained than any director I'd worked with in film. I found it a lot easier than the intense, frame-by-frame scrutiny you got from Wyler. More actor-friendly. (On the other hand, who needs to be friendly to actors? That's kiss-my-ass *star* crap, and doesn't help anybody, least of all the actor.)

My first day of shooting, DeMille invited me to lunch with him. I'd heard he hadn't been near the *Buccaneer* set. He'd have surely been a daunting figure for Tony to see standing in the shadows, so I wasn't surprised when he met me at his table in the studio restaurant. That was where I'd been presented to him, one of the Founding Fathers of film, while I was shooting my first film for Wallis. I'd waved to him then, driving off the lot, and out of that had come the circus picture, and then *Commandments,* and now Welles and Wyler, and here I was.

After lunch, he poured me a glass of Madeira from a bottle dated 1815. "That's the year Jackson fought at New Orleans," he said, lifting his glass. "Along the old Chalmette Road. You know all that, you do your research. You'll be a good Jackson, better now than when you played him at Fox. When was that?"

"Nineteen fifty-two," I said. "I think I've got a better handle on him now."

"Ummm. We all get better. Try to, anyway." He sipped his Madeira. "I understand William Wyler wants you for *Ben-Hur.*"

"So they tell me. But he can't decide which part."

He chuckled. "Well, Ben-Hur's the part, of course. You can always get good actors to play bad men. Heroes are harder. Ramon

Novarro was wrong for it in the silent version, 1926. Dead wrong. You can do that part. I'd call up Mr. Wyler and tell him, but— directors like to make their own choices."

"Willy sure does."

"So he should . . . so he should." The old man mused a moment. "Yes, that'll make quite a picture. High time someone did it. Get it right this time." You could see the fires rise in his eyes, fleetingly. "If I were you, I wouldn't worry." I was due on the set. I thanked him for the lunch; I should've thanked him for my career. I never saw him again.

My Jackson *was* better, this time around. I was more secure as an actor, I found Tony a stimulating and sensitive director, I had a firmer grip on the accent, and then, ten days or so into shooting my scenes, I realized I'd made a terrible mistake.

On the stage, you can correct your mistakes during rehearsals, changing the sets, the writing, the performances, even recasting the actors, if it comes to that. Indeed, this is normal all through the road try-out, right up to the New York opening. Few plays escape fairly radical reworking of this kind.

In films, this is impossible. You correct your mistakes in preproduction and, less easily, in editing. Once shooting starts, almost any major change (except rewriting, which you can do at night) is simply too expensive to contemplate. A decade later, Wyler was directing *How to Steal a Million* with Audrey Hepburn, Peter O'Toole, and George C. Scott. In addition to his enormous talent, Scott had problems at the time and showed up more than three hours late for his first day of shooting. Willy fired him. "It isn't just today," he said. "I can't afford to take a chance with you, George. Your part's too big. Once I shoot two or three days with you, it'll be too expensive to reshoot everything. This is the last day I can fire you, pay off your contract, and recast. That's what I'm doing."

My blunder on *Buccaneer* was not of that order, but it was my mistake and a damn stupid one. What's more, there was no excuse for it. I was supposed to be the resident expert on Andrew Jackson, for God's sake . . . I'd played the part before! At the Battle of New Orleans, Jackson was forty-six years old. In discussing my makeup with Wally Westmore, I'd guided him to an intricate creation with a shock of white hair and latex wrinkles suggesting a Jackson of at least sixty.

Tony was not happy when I told him what I'd done, but there was nothing he could do then but go on as we were. There was no possibility of reshooting all my scenes up to that point. What difference did it make? Who even knew it was wrong? *I* knew, for one. You're supposed to get things like that right. There are too many people making film who not only don't know, they don't even *know* they don't know. Or care, sometimes.

I'm afraid that wasn't the only thing that went wrong with the film. In spite of the fine work Tony did with the actors, including me, the picture simply didn't lift. It was—OK. That's not good enough. I think only Mr. DeMille could make a DeMille picture.

11

Four White Horses

FINALLY, AS DEMILLE had predicted, Willy Wyler announced that I would play Judah Ben-Hur. Much later, he told me he'd decided that while we were still shooting *Big Country,* weeks before he finally agreed to direct the picture. That was very like him; he weighed his creative choices carefully and privately, consulting no one. Casting the role was the easier exercise; directing *Ben-Hur* would be a staggering task—physically, mentally, and emotionally exhausting.

It was also creatively daunting. The epic film is surely the most difficult to make well. When they were still financially feasible, epics were often undertaken, and often crashed disastrously. *Ben-Hur* had a very high profile and an enormous budget, larger than any picture yet produced. If it failed, it would close MGM. Willy was at risk, too: failure with *Ben-Hur,* critically or commercially, would scar even his formidable reputation. I think that's what decided him —the challenge. He'd made significant films in every other genre —Westerns, social dramas, comedies, cop stories, suspense pieces, period classics. Now he had to see if he could bring off *Ben-Hur.* I'm surely glad he did. Whether *I* could bring it off was another question.

180   The last weeks in California ran by like loose horses. Lydia

and I focused on our short list of architects and chose Bill Beckett,
a Frank Lloyd Wright disciple, to design a house for us. He brought
over several dozen issues of *Architectural Digest* one evening for
our comments ("No, I hate that chichi crap! Now *this* . . . stone,
wood, yeah"), then spent a day and a night in a sleeping bag on our
ridge to study the light and the land. Just before we left Los Angeles,
he showed us sketches of exactly the house we'd imagined. "When
you get back next year, you can move right in," he said. Ho, ho.

I had the good sense to discuss the problem with my father,
who knew a great deal about building houses. Though he clearly
considered it a challenge, I think it was basically an act of love that
impelled him to come out for most of the next year and supervise
the building of the house I will never leave. His wife, Velda, was
with him some of the time, but for most of it he was alone. I can
never thank him enough for that.

I also managed to fit in a last appearance on live TV, in
Beauty and the Beast, which turned out to be one of the best things
I ever did on the small screen. It's really one of the great classic
roles, present in the literature of almost every culture, and exqui-
sitely simple. I found it a rich part to work on. Reaching for the
physiology of the Beast behind the fine makeup they designed, I
used a grating bass articulation that seemed to suggest human
speech with animal vocal cords. It took some work to master this,
but it also gave me an extra bass note or two I still have, and often
use.

We decided to let Fray watch it, the first time he'd ever seen
me perform. Almost-three was a little young, maybe, but it was a
fairy tale, after all. Between the voice and the makeup, I don't think
he really recognized me. During a couple of the more vivid scenes,
though, he'd turn on my lap and look up at me oddly. Afterward, I
asked how he'd liked it. "It was *good!*" he said. "But dot Beast
wasn't weally *bad.*" No. Not bad at all.

We relaxed cross-country on the *Super Chief,* visiting family,
then undertook for the first time the truly better way to travel:
crossing the Atlantic on the *United States,* the fastest and one of the
best of the big liners, now gone forever, alas.

Based in London for a couple of weeks, I did wardrobe
fittings and some interviews for Paramount, which was still opening
Commandments in some British cities, as well as even more impor-

tunate interviews for *Ben-Hur,* which wouldn't be in any theater for almost two years. I was beginning to get used to the questions about both films people still ask me, more than thirty years later.

We did the last leg of the journey by train. I guess the great days of the European trains ended with World War II; it was a little scruffy compared to the *Super Chief* out of L.A. Still, the welcome in Rome more than made up for it. Metro's publicity people had somehow assembled a crowd of well over a thousand, waiting for us in the Stazione Termini. The last hundred yards or so as we slowed to a stop, the platform was mobbed with cheering Italians. Fray thought they were welcoming him; waving his cap, he leaned out the window and cheered them back. (He's liked Rome ever since.) We were borne through the station on a wave of feeling as warm as any I can remember, then loaded into the black Caddie limo that, along with a chariot and a slave galley, was to be my sole transportation for the next ten months.

The man who drove it, Ivo Palazzi, was key to this; he began and ended all my days there. I'd like to think MGM took pains to find me the best driver in Rome, which he was, but it's just as likely I lucked out. His first chore was to deliver us from the screaming throng of paparazzi and well-wishers to the villa MGM had rented for us, which he did with ancient Roman skill and modern Italian good humor.

Horti Flaviani was built in the nineteenth century on the site of an ancient Roman villa, around a graveled courtyard with a fountain in the center and formal gardens stretching for an acre or so behind. Modern improvements included a run-down tennis court and an empty pool, neither of which I was likely to have time to use. Nevertheless, the villa with its terraced vistas, marble stairs, fresco-ceilinged bedrooms, and brass-buttoned staff was grander than anything we'd ever lived in. We felt very pampered. That was a new experience on location.

After World War II, European countries, except for Britain, refused to allow money earned by American films to be exported, requiring it to be spent in-country. This impelled the American studios to shoot in countries where they had these blocked funds, usually on action sequences using some local technicians and actors, and of course extras. Still, interior shooting was all done at home in Hollywood, as we did on *Ten Commandments.*

As Hollywood production costs began to inflate markedly, MGM realized they could save several million dollars by shooting the entire film in Italy, and casting almost all the parts with British actors—generally better at non-American roles than we are, anyway. *Ben-Hur* was the first of dozens of major American films to follow this plan, as they still do, though the blocked U.S. dollars have long since been spent.

Horti Flaviani was only a fifteen-minute drive from Cinecittà Studios, less at seven in the morning, when I went in. MGM had rented the whole thing, back lot and all, for the dozens of sound stages, offices, dressing rooms, workshops, wardrobe, makeup, projection and cutting rooms we'd need. It looked very much like an American studio, which is not surprising; Mussolini had sent his son to Hollywood to get an idea of what a studio should be when he'd planned it in the thirties. We had a number of major exterior sets to build on the lot, representing a good deal of Jerusalem: the gate of the city, the entire compound of the House of Hur, the exterior of Pilate's palace, and the Via Dolorosa. Larger than all of these put together was the Great Circus of Antioch, with a practice track off to the side.

That practice track was the reason I'd come to Rome several weeks early: I had to learn to drive the chariot. I'd long since realized the crucial importance of learning any physical skill you need for a part before the play goes into rehearsal or the film starts. It's too late then and the time's too expensive to spend on something you should've learned sooner.

Too often actors solve this by simply claiming a skill they don't have and hoping it'll somehow work out. "Ride? Hell, yes, since I was ten years old." Then you watch where they put their hands to mount up and you know you have a passenger, not a rider. I can't count the weeks I've spent learning to look as though I can do all sorts of things I really can't, from making the initial incision in abdominal surgery to painting the Sistine Chapel ceiling. For *Ben-Hur,* though, I had to do better than just look as though I could drive the chariot. I'd have to do it.

Fortunately, MGM had thought of this. That's what the practice track was for, and the month and a half I had before shooting started. I also had Yakima Canutt. Thank God.

His real name was Enos, but he hated it. When he was a

twenty-year-old kid, he won a saddle bronc event in a rodeo in Yakima, Washington, and appropriated the town's name along with the silver belt buckle. He went on to win a bigger prize in Madison Square Garden as World's Champion Cowboy, then went into the movies.

Yak wasn't a very good actor, so he invented a profession he could be better at than anyone in the world: stuntman. When he hit Hollywood, there was no such thing. If you had a car to wreck, or a cliff to jump a horse off, you gave some cowboy twenty bucks and a bottle of whiskey and let him risk his neck. Yak changed all that. He worked out ways to fall with a horse without risking either the animal or the rider, and invented stunt gear that's still used today. By all accounts, he was the best. Next time you see John Ford's *Stagecoach,* check out the Indian who does a bareback transfer from a running horse to the near lead horse in a six-up stagecoach team, then is shot, falling between the leaders, grabbing the center pole and dragging between the running horses, letting go as team and coach pass over him, then leaping up to do a mane mount on a riderless horse running loose and taking off after the coach again. A lot of good men have been hurt trying that stunt since. None of them's ever brought it off. That was Yak.

When his knees were no longer up to jumping off second stories into the saddle, Yak moved behind the camera and became the best second-unit director in films. (That's the unit assembled to shoot action scenes. The first-unit director shoots most or all the dialogue with principals in these sequences, and briefs the second unit director on the shooting of everything else, often in minute detail. The wise ones, though, like Wyler, leave second-unit directors of Yak's caliber pretty much alone. In recent years, major directors often seem impelled to shoot their own action sequences, perhaps uneasy at the idea that someone else might do it better. Willy had been at it long enough to know Yak could indeed shoot the chariot race better than he could, and a lot faster, too. Willy's contribution was still crucial. He edited the sequence.)

Yak had been in Europe for several months, first in Yugoslavia, buying more than a hundred horses to make up the eight teams, with backups. The crucial teams, of course, were Messala's blacks and Ben-Hur's whites. Yak picked them very carefully, supervised their training, and chose the stuntmen to drive them. He also advised on the design of the track itself, including the sand and the gravel base. His advice on the chariots was also crucial; he designed the harness as well, making it possible to control four horses with two reins. I could never have learned to handle the eight reins the drivers actually held racing in the ancient Roman arenas.

We started working the morning after I reached Rome; from then on I spent at least two hours a day on the track with Yak and one of the four white teams he picked for my chariot. Two of them, in fact, had a prior agenda: one was set for the shot of Ben-Hur's team jumping over a wrecked chariot and was being trained for that stunt by Yak's youngest son, Joe. Until that scene was shot, that team would work on nothing else. A second four, the most beautiful and docile, were being trained to work loose in the scene in the Sheik's tent. The most difficult thing to do with a horse is to get him to work with no harness or rein. Ralph McCutcheon was a master at it, but his pupils, too, did nothing in the race until that scene was shot. Of the other two white teams, one was close to being the fastest team in the entire stable, very useful for shots of Judah's chariot passing other teams. They were also difficult to handle, so I didn't often drive them unless the shot really required it.

The team I used the most was the steadiest, particularly the near horse, who also had to be the strongest. The wheels on a Roman chariot can't be steered laterally to turn. You have to skid the chariot through by reining in the near horse, who runs diagonally to his left as a steadying counterweight, and whipping up the other three, particularly the off horse, always the fastest of the four, leading through the turn. The whole thirty yards or so of skidding turn throws up quite a lot of sand; you have to squint your eyes almost shut to keep the grit out so you can check traffic. The entire maneuver merits your full attention.

It took Yak some time to get me skidding through turns, though I soloed the first day. After an hour or so of riding behind me, coaching, he said, "All right, let 'em run now, a full lap." I slapped them on the rumps with the reins, yelled (more of a falsetto scream, actually), and we thundered off. Chariot teams only have three speeds: walk, trot, and dead run. Once in high, you can't really do much with four horses except steer; they're not programmed for slowing down. I kept asking anxious questions as we roared on, trying to sound confident, but Yak answered not a word. I realized why when I saw him standing on the sand as we came around the last turn; he'd stepped off the back of the chariot just as I'd started.

Over the weeks Yak made me into a modestly competent charioteer. One hot spring day, as we sat in the sand resting the horses (and me), I said, with some embarrassment, "Y'know, Yak, I feel pretty comfortable running this team now, but we're all alone here. We start shooting this sucker in ten days. I'm not so sure I can cut it with seven other teams out there."

Yak looked at me and pushed his cap back on his head. "Chuck, you just make sure y'stay in the chariot. I guarantee yuh gonna win the damn race."

THERE WERE OF COURSE other problems looming through the pre-production weeks, the most important being the script. It was based on the novel by General Lew Wallace, a Civil War hero who turned it out in his spare time while he was Governor of New Mexico. Fabulously successful through numerous editions, it was equally so when dramatized for the stage at the turn of the century and again as a silent film in 1926. For our undertaking, MGM had begun preparing the film nearly two years earlier, long before Wyler had taken the helm. Not surprisingly, he was not happy with the script that had evolved over that time, the work of several hands, some of them quite distinguished. It was written in a style that's come to be labeled "MGM Medieval," though it was common to all studios and all periods. Here's a prime sample from Universal's *The Black Shield of Falworth,* as performed by an actor better suited to modern roles: "Yondah lies duh castle o' my foddah. Gladly wully give us welcome."

It's easy to make fun of the line, and the reading; it's not easy, however, to suggest the speech of another time and another country. By the late fifties, the convention of having non-Anglo characters speak English with the accent they might use in their native language, even in stories set in their native lands, had been largely abandoned. Besides, what accent would first-century Romans or Jews use speaking English?

Anyway, the real problem was not how the dialogue would be spoken, but how to make it sound like actual human speech, accessible to a modern audience, yet still conveying a sense of the distant past and other peoples. When he undertook the film, Willy

insisted the script needed further work. I agreed. There are some
fine actors who can't do period parts . . . also some fine writers.

Once we were in Rome, deep in preproduction, novelist
Gore Vidal was briefly imported for a trial. A tart, embittered man, he
seemed an odd choice, but in a few days he submitted his version
of a key early scene between Ben-Hur and Messala. Wyler had at last
cast that part with a young Irish actor, Stephen Boyd—I believe it
was his first major film role. Willy wanted to get the feel of his work
and also hear how Vidal's dialogue sounded with actors, so he had
Stephen and me read the scene in his office. No dice. It didn't
play. Vidal was dismissed—though Wyler later told me that he, incredibly, insisted that he wrote the entire script up to the chariot race.

Vidal also claims his parting recommendation to Wyler was
that the key to the Judah/Messala friendship was to make it homosexual. His comment is no doubt based on a story (also probably
apocryphal) about Laurence Olivier, playing Iago to Ralph Richardson's Othello, suggesting to director Tyrone Guthrie that it might
be interesting to play Iago as homosexually obsessed with Othello.
"Oh, I suppose you can try it for a bit," said Guthrie. "But for God's
sake don't tell Ralph."

Even before Vidal had gone, Willy had persuaded the English poet/playwright Christopher Fry to come to Rome. Until we
finished shooting eight months later, he was on the set all day every
day, six days a week. His changes were seldom structural, but almost always stylistically crucial, such as changing "You didn't like
the food?" to "The meal did not please you?" (Not a trivial difference; the first is inescapably twentieth century, the second acceptably period.) Every scene he touched was the better for it.

Christopher was the archetypical British intellectual, lean
and modestly mannered, gray-haired and tweed-jacketed (yes, even
the leather elbow patches and the pipe). Though his plays were
widely successful, this was the first film he'd ever worked on, but
he seemed to regard the controlled chaos that is any big film shoot
with the serene detachment of the gentleman he surely was. He'd
sit quietly a little back from the camera setup, seldom commenting
unless consulted. I remember coming on the set early one Monday
well into the shoot, when the work pressures were beginning to
tell on us all, though Christopher looked as steady as ever. Waiting
for the first setup, I greeted him idly. "Have a good day off, Kit?"

"Willy had us to luncheon at his villa," he responded.

"Mmmm. Nice time?"

He sighed. Heavily. "We discussed this film," he said.

FROM THE BEGINNING, we knew it would be a tough shoot. So it by God was; I think the toughest I've ever done. Even the last weeks of preshoot were intense. Willy had finally cast the last principal role, the slave Esther, who becomes a Christian. He found a gifted and beautiful Israeli actress, Haya Harareet.

By this time, I was about as good a charioteer as I was going to be; I knew Yak would keep his promise about my winning the race. Still, I worked one of the teams every day to keep sharp. At the end of each session I also shoveled two big burlap bags full of sand from the practice track and brought them home in the trunk of the Cadillac, gradually filling an overgrown old sandbox I'd discovered behind the last hedge in the formal gardens at the villa. Fray was the perfect age for a sandbox, and this was perfect MGM sand. He was delighted, as he was with everything in Rome. He tagged along with his mother, acquiring an early taste for museums; he rode in the chariot, standing between my knees and yelling happily at the horses; he made friends with the gardener's boy, from whom he learned Italian more quickly than Lydia or I did.

We all three went at the language differently. Lydia had studied languages in high school and college; she took lessons at Berlitz twice a week while running a household staffed with non-English speakers. I picked up my Italian working at Cinecittà, from the stable boys and crew on the sound stages. In two or three months I could slip by at a cocktail party. (Actors often sound more fluent in a language than they are; they usually have an ear for accent and idioms.) That left me speaking stable Italian to marquesas.

Fray had no such problem; he never knew he was learning Italian in the first place. Three-year-olds absorb new words like sponges . . . the Italian he used to his pal Tonino was just more words to Fray. Before long he was rattling away all day long, even using Italian body language, his fingers pursed in Tonino's face. "Aaohh, ragazzo, anda' vai'? Que succede?" I realized he hadn't learned to swear in Italian when I heard him raging at Tonino in English strongly colored with the Grimms' fairy tales I was reading

him at night. "Go throw yourself in the mud, you beast of field or
tree! A giant would eat you!!"

The only shadow I recall on Fray's Roman spring was when
he got lost in the grounds one afternoon. Ivo drove me home from
the studio just as his mother's anxious search brought her to the
villa's private entrance to the catacomb of Santa Domitilla. You
could see from the drive that the iron door, several steps below
ground, was a little ajar. I ran down and heaved it open; there in
the dark at the base of a Roman sarcophagus sat my son, looking a
little anxious himself. "Boy!" he said as I picked him up. "I thought
I'd never see America again."

Ivo was clearly the majordomo of our household by this
time. He not only drove us flawlessly wherever we were going, he
served as interpreter and trouble-shooter as well. Lydia stumped
him once, though. Sitting outside in the garden after dinner, we
were often bothered by mosquitoes; Lydia asked Ivo if he knew
where to get some spray "contre le zingari?"

"*Zingari,* Signora?" he said, puzzled. "But . . . dare are no
zingari in dees region."

"Oh, yes. I was bitten twice last night." Lydia showed him
the welts on her arm.

Ivo was really worried now. "But, Signora . . . dey don' bite!
De *zingari* . . . " His face cleared. "Ahhh, you mean *zanzari* . . . de
leetle bog. De *zingari* . . . dat ees wot you call *Gypsies!*" Ivo thought
my wife was afraid of being bitten by Gypsies in the night.

WE STARTED FILMING on May 20 with the sprawling, complex scene
in the paddock before the race, harnessing the teams and entering
the circus. Willy shot it himself with the first unit, since there was
dialogue. He himself would direct little more of the sequence, but
I think he began with that in order to get a feel for the problems of
shooting in that huge, technically challenging set, before turning it
over to Yak. He doubtless also wanted to direct the first setup on
the film. He stood by my chariot watching the dozen or so assistant
directors scurry around getting the extras in order. "I wonder
which one of those guys'll direct the next remake," he said. Willy
had been one of the A.D.s hired to help with the race sequence in
the silent version, thirty-some years before. (Now, another thirty
years later, no one can afford to do a remake.)

After three days, Willy had, as usual, as close to what he wanted as possible. As in *The Big Country,* he focused relentlessly on every detail of every setup. Still, finishing the sequence early one afternoon, he seized the chance to reshoot one of my close-ups from the *Big Country* fight scene with Greg Peck, renting a VistaVision camera and a reel of 35mm raw stock to do it. (We were shooting *Ben-Hur* in 70mm—useless for the *Big Country* retake.)

The makeup man pasted on the 1885 sideburns I'd worn and I lay on the ground and tried to get back inside the ranch foreman I'd played nine months earlier. It was a simple, silent reaction from the end of the fight. I can't remember now exactly what Willy wanted, a little more than I was giving him, obviously. We did a dozen takes as the shadows lengthened, till finally Bob Surtees, the cameraman, said, "Well, that's a wrap."

Willy snapped a hard look at him. "What are you talking about?"

"We just used up a thousand-foot roll of film," Bob said with a certain "gotcha!" tone. "There's no more VistaVision raw stock in Rome." We wrapped, but I never found out whether Willy used the retake, or kept the shot he'd already cut into the picture.

The next day, Wyler took the first unit on to the sound stages and smaller exteriors, leaving Yak on the back lot to struggle with the vast circus set and the Herculean labor of filming the race. It was to occupy him for more than three months. Both he and Wyler were determined that the entire race be filmed full-scale and live action, no miniatures or process shots. I heard Willy tell Yak, "This has to be the best action sequence ever filmed. You shoot it, I'll cut it."

You could say this put considerable pressure on us all, man and beast. Yak knew more about horses than most people, and certainly more about filming them than anybody. He'd imported four American stuntmen and a Brit; adding three Italians, he had a crew of world-class horsemen who, while training the teams for two months, had become world-class charioteers. (Probably the only ones *in* the world, come to think of it.) I was hardly their equal, but I could drive the team. The shots I couldn't do safely, Yak's son, Joe, would double for me. Steve Boyd, who was to give an absolutely superb performance as Messala, had been cast too late to give him adequate training with the black team, and he had trouble with sand in his contact lenses, but he compensated with Irish guts. He was fine.

Yak was superb. To answer the questions I've heard ever since, no, we didn't kill any men, or horses either. No, there is no red Ferrari parked in the corner past the governor's box, though there may be an extra or two with sunglasses lost in the crowd.

The crowd, of course, is a crucial character in the race. As well as being far less expensive than American extras, the Italians were far better, as the Egyptians had been in *Ten Commandments,* mostly because they cared. MGM hired four thousand locals for several days of long shots, moving them about in the stadium for the various angles. The logistics of handling that many people for filming were of military complexity, aimed at preventing people from reporting for work, then disappearing for the day, or checking in two or three times to try to claim triple pay. A completely enclosed wire-mesh passageway, patrolled by Italian carabinieri, was constructed leading from the main gate of the studio through a wardrobe building to the set. As each extra signed in, he was given a numbered disk (a different color every day), which he turned in at the next window for his wardrobe, in exchange for his own clothes. When correctly costumed, he walked a quarter mile through the passageway to the circus set itself, which was also fenced in. At the end of the day, he reversed the process, turning in his costume to retrieve his own clothes and the disk he needed in order to be paid on the way out.

Once we got them on the set, the system worked pretty well. Our four thousand extras found they had only to watch the race, which they did with the full frenzy of their Roman ancestors, cheering the chariots thundering through the turns. When we did the long shot of Judah cantering through the victory lap, our extras screamed like a Super Bowl crowd as I slowed past Messala lying crumpled on the sand.

Suddenly, with no direction, the crowd began to drop out of the stands and caper after the white team. An Arab snatched up Messala's helmet and pranced, brandishing it like a trophy; a wonderfully spontaneous, golden moment that remains in the film.

As they wrapped that day, the A.D.s announced the extra call would be cut next morning to just the four hundred we'd need for background in the closer angles. Several hundred of our four thousand spent the night waiting outside the studio gate, breaking into something close to a riot when they lined up the next morning. It took an extra detachment of carabinieri to sort out the first-comers for our core crowd.

Yak was getting incredible footage, week after week; what's more, he hadn't killed anybody, mainly because he knew exactly what he was doing. There were only two accidents in the whole shoot (not counting the several staged and flawlessly executed wrecks). For one shot, he buried a camera in a shallow pit in the track and ran a team over it. Instead of the wheels straddling the pit, one wheel hit it dead center, wiping out a couple of hundred thousand dollars' worth of camera and throwing the chariot into the wall. The camera operator climbed out of the pit shaken but untouched, but the near horse had a cracked foreleg, usually a death sentence. This was a lucky horse: they taped his leg and suspended him in a sling in a stall fetlock-deep in mud. He recovered and actually worked again in the race.

Far more serious was the accident with Judah's white team while we were shooting the jump over a wrecked chariot. Yak's son, Joe, had been training the chosen team for weeks, first teaching each horse separately to jump the wreck on a long lead, then in pairs, then in four, then finally pulling the chariot, always empty, over behind them. (Yak was not about to risk a driver till the cameras were turning.) Joe was set for it, though; he was the best driver in the company. For the stunt to work, he had to take the team into the jump running all out and evenly, and aim the chariot for the shallow takeoff ramp Yak had devised. The team could jump easily; chariots don't jump at all. The ramp would kick it high enough to clear the wreck.

The day they shot it, Yak brought over a foot of light chain and nailed it to the front of the chariot. "Joe," he said, "when that chariot hits the ramp, the team'll be coming down th'other side o' that wreck. It'll flip you out, sure as hell. Just hook this to your belt." As Yak walked away, Joe unhooked the chain. I've never asked him why. Maybe he didn't want to be chained to the chariot if the whole thing turned over, or maybe he didn't like to be told how to do his job, even by the holy father of the stunt profession. Or maybe just because.

Joe took the team in beautifully, running flat out, hitting the ramp dead center, clearing the wreck by inches, and flipping himself head over heels a foot above the chariot. I thought he was a dead man. The chariot weighed half a ton, with steel-rimmed wheels sure to cut him in half, or at least cripple him.

Not Joe Canutt. He's one of the best natural athletes I've ever seen, quick and strong as a leopard. He dropped the reins, grabbed the front of the chariot, turned and dropped to a handstand on the tongue behind the running team, then flung himself clear. He did get a small cut over one eyebrow.

I was with Willy when we ran the dailies, which he usually watched with the cool detachment of a brain surgeon. Not when we got to that shot. "Jee-*zuss!*" he choked. "We have to *use* that!!"

"Don't see how y' gonna do that," said Yak. "I promised Chuck he'd win this race. I don't believe he can catch that team on foot."

"No, no . . . we can do it. You put him on the tongue, just behind the horses; he can climb back in the chariot." I wasn't wild about this idea; I'm not sure Yak was, either, but that's what we did. Next day, I crouched on the front of the chariot and, when we got up to speed, scrambled back aboard, in about three blinks of an eye. It's a scary shot—it scared me, anyway.

When Yak was finally done, and Willy finished the fine-cut, I believe they got what they'd gone after. At just over nine minutes, start to finish, the chariot race is the best action sequence ever filmed. Still. Everyone involved deserves credit, from Yak on down, but I think a crucial factor was Willy's insight on how to edit the sequence.

It's an overused word, but the huge Circus of Antioch set was awesome. Full of people and careening chariots, it was . . . staggering is the word. I've worked on just a few sets like that; they can fill you with awe, literally. As a director, you think, "Good God, I have to *get* this." But no matter how marvelously crafted your coverage—high boom shots, zoom lens, and tracking angles—it all ends up as pictures on a screen, for an audience that's seen just about everything you can put on a screen. Wyler knew he had to make this more than just a horse race.

He had to resolve the Messala/Ben-Hur conflict that drives the whole picture. In editing, Wyler resisted the temptation to hold on the overwhelming long shots of the packed circus that brought your heart into your throat when you stood on the sand watching. There are only two cuts of the full set in the whole sequence . . . one forty-some seconds long, the other a little over twenty.

Most of the rest of the sequence is covered in closer angles of individuals, Sheik Ilderim, Pontius Pilate, and the drivers, above all, Messala and Ben-Hur. As Wyler had emphasized the triviality of the fist-fight between Greg Peck and me with extreme long shots in *Big Country,* so he made the race a death struggle between two men with the close angles in *Ben-Hur.* It's quite a piece of film-making.

WHEN I GOT BACK into the sound stages, Willy was ready to shoot the scene Vidal had tried to fix: Judah and Messala meeting for the first time since boyhood. Fry had reworked it by then, and we'd read it through in the office; it seemed right to me (unless ego interferes, actors should have a good sense of that). Shooting it was another matter. We dug away at it for two long days, but when we wrapped late Saturday night, Wyler was clearly not satisfied. I said, "Willy, I just can't figure what else we can find here. This is the scene. I know it."

"You guys have to make *me* know it. I've got to *see* how strong this friendship is," he said. "The audience has to believe in you as friends . . . in the next scene you quarrel, and for the rest of the movie you're trying to kill each other. The audience has to remember this scene. They have to know it's real."

I spent most of my Sunday off writing several hundred words of the back story. Actors often construct a character's history, to put him in some kind of context. I worked hard, inventing the two boys' childhood. I sent the piece over to Willy's villa that evening and went to bed feeling justified. That was a major mistake.

Willy hated it. Not so much what I'd written, but that I'd done it at all. He thought it was pretentious, actory showboating. "They've been writing on this script for two years, most of it no good. What I need you to do is act it, not write about it!"

He was right, of course. Willy, as I was learning in my second year working for him, was the artist as pragmatist. He scoffed at the idea of the director as *auteur.* ("But at least I know how to pronounce it.") Acting is the only part of the filmmaking process that has no material existence, except for the actors themselves. Willy was pretty skeptical about us as dedicated artists. God knows he's not alone in that. Over the decades, actors have given directors a lot of ulcers and a few coronaries.

The way films are made requires the actor to bring a performance to the set every day. What he does in the scheduled scene that day is the performance that will be in the film, however shaped and sanded it is in the editing. Wyler was as good at getting the best out of actors as any director I ever saw, but he was not interested in the creative process itself, or the ways actors arouse it. He'd just push and prod and change until you got it. That's what he did with Steve and me in that scene, and all the rest, too.

After we wrapped for the day, I was about to step into the shower when Willy knocked on my dressing room door. "Sorry to catch you with no pants on," he said when I let him in. "I just wanted to talk to you a minute." I grabbed a towel and poured him a drink. "Chuck," he said abruptly. "I need you to be better in this part."

"OK," I said, carefully pouring myself a drink. "What do you need that I'm not giving you?"

"I don't know. If I did, it'd be easy. I'd tell you and you'd do it, but I don't *know* what it is. All I can say for sure is you've got to be better. I know that's not a lot of help, but I thought I had to tell you." He finished his drink and left. I sat a long time alone in my dressing room with no pants on, finishing mine.

Then I carried my wound home to Lydia, who stopped the bleeding. Still, for one of the few times in my life, I didn't sleep well that night. Nevertheless, I did get better. I don't know whether Willy decided I needed an energizing jolt of adrenaline, or whether he was just honestly telling me what he saw. In the end, acting's all smoke, anyway. Like Willy, I can't explain it, but I know it happened. I was better.

As the weeks ground on, it seemed like a series of different films. I was in almost every scene, but the other actors came and went, in cycles. We began in the Circus with Hugh Griffith, the wild Welsh actor who won an Oscar playing the Arab Sheik, Ilderim. Hugh seized the scene like a raw steak, devoured it, then went back to England and did another picture while waiting for his next scenes with us. Haya Harareet did her first scene as Esther and went back to Israel. When journalists asked, "How's the new Israeli actress?" I could only answer, "I only worked with her a couple of days; I haven't seen her in a month."

Wyler's extraordinary casting instincts served him well; Jack Hawkins was a perfect Roman as Arrius, Finlay Currie couldn't have been better as Balthasar, or Frank Thring as Pilate. A dozen other good Brit actors played the rest of the Romans. The Jewish characters were played by Americans, except for Haya, whose accent was American, and a good British actress he'd cast as my mother, Miriam. The first day of shooting on the family scenes, Willy realized her Mayfair accent spoiled the consistency of his Americans-as-Jews, Brits-as-Romans cast. I suggested Martha Scott, who'd played my mother in *Ten Commandments;* you could say she was at home in the role. Willy went for it. Martha was excellent (and would be excellent replacing another actress in another part with me twenty months later).

Willy's convictions about the actors he wanted and didn't want in even very small roles could have repercussions. The part of the Roman decurion (non-com) leading the slave train that stops in Nazareth on the way to the galleys was a nice bit part, but nothing more; mainly one crucial line: "I said, no water for *him!*" when Christ gives water to an unconscious Ben-Hur. The casting on parts like that is usually undertaken by the first assistant director, who interviews ten or twenty candidates and picks the likeliest four or five for the director to choose from.

The village selected as Nazareth was a cluster of stone huts some sixty miles north of Rome, perfect for the scene, but it was a good ninety-minute drive over bad roads, the kind of location that puts you on the road at 5 A.M. and gets you back home fifteen hours later. No fun at all. Still, we were shooting by seven, long shots of the village, the slave train, the well, the watching villagers. We set up a medium angle of Judah, parched with thirst, reaching for a gourd of water and collapsing when the decurion knocks it aside. Willy lowered his viewfinder. "That's not the guy I cast in this part last week," he said.

"Ahh, no, that's right," said Gus, the first A.D. "But this guy was your second choice, remember?"

"What happened to my first choice?"

"Well, he . . . uh, he was holding us up on the salary," said

Gus in an Oh-God-why-didn't-I-check-with-him tone. "But you remember you did *like* this guy. The setup's all ready to shoot."

"Send back for the first guy," said Willy, picking up his script.

"Oh, gosh . . . they'd have to find him, make a deal, bring
him up from Rome. Could take three, four hours." Gus's voice was
ragged with anxiety.

"We'll wait," said Willy. And we did. Gus had goofed badly,
of course. You don't try to slip something like that past a director,
especially not Wyler, not if you're as good a first A.D. as Gus was.

Willy relented a little; we picked up half a dozen small setups
in other coverage on the scene while we were waiting. Willy was
more than right; his first choice was well worth waiting for.

I have no idea whether the man was an actor at all, but his
harsh, burly ugliness was perfect. Sweating and sullen in the brass
helmet, he was the picture of a Roman legionary. We never see
Christ's face in the scene, but the decurion's brutish, stunned awe
looking into the eye of divinity was indescribable. It's one of the
best moments in the whole film.

The scene also gave us our tag line. On most pictures, especially the long, tough shoots, the company, usually by instant consensus, seizes a line of dialogue as the slogan for the whole shoot.
On *Ben-Hur,* after the Nazareth scene, when anyone screwed up,
someone (often several in chorus) would proclaim, "No water for
him!!"

A couple of months later, we chose another line. As the six-
day weeks of ten- and twelve-hour days ground on into the dank
Roman autumn, we perhaps began to see ourselves as prisoners.
Jack Hawkins' grim warning to Judah, chained to a galley oar, rang
true: "We keep you alive to serve this ship. Row well and live, Forty-
one."

Through the summer, we were the biggest tourist attraction
in Rome. Getting a studio pass was almost on a par with a papal
audience. The rotating platoons of press aside, only VIPs, friends,
and family could watch the first unit work. It was easier to get a
pass to the Antioch set to watch Yak Canutt and the second unit film
the chariots, and more fun, too. If I was shooting there, I'd give the
braver souls an easy lap around the track in front of me . . . Lydia
was an early passenger and Fray a frequent copilot.

We had a steady round of houseguests. The Fields, the Seltzers, the Creedys, my mother, Lydia's aunt, all filled Horti Flaviani's bedrooms in turn, though I was working too hard to spend much time with them. They'd visit the studio once or twice, depending on what was shooting. (My mother didn't care; she loved just being on the set, any set.) Lydia would do the full tour of Rome with them over several days. More often than not I had to go to bed too early to go out for dinner, but if I had a late call the next morning I'd tag along, usually sleeping in the back of the limo while they saw the Forum by moonlight or whatnot. Early morning calls are hell on your nightlife. (Or nightlife is hell on your early morning calls, whichever way you want to play it.)

I remember Katharine Cornell coming to dinner one night, along with the Christopher Frys; she was about to do one of his plays. She looked wonderful still. I was striving for an air of warm, comradely hospitality . . . one star to another, as it were. I couldn't bring it off. It couldn't be ten years since I'd thrown her over my hip eight times a week, wrestling for Cleopatra's dagger. She looked at me with her vast, dark eyes and my throat tightened.

Before she left, I took her upstairs to see my sleeping son. Back-lit from the hall, she glowed like some great fairy queen. She stood looking down at him for a long moment, then bent and kissed his cheek. "Good night, boy," she breathed. There was a lady with a lot of presence.

As we soldiered on through the summer, Wyler remained stubbornly determined to make each sequence as good as possible. Still, he'd learned decades before that film as art was inescapably rooted in the iron reality of schedule and budget, reefs that later sent extravagant pieces like *Cleopatra* and *Ishtar* bubbling to the bottom, taking whole studios with them.

Willy didn't waste time, he didn't waste money. Beyond these crucial essentials, all you need to make movies is talent; he didn't waste that either, though God knows he spent it freely, along with all our energy. Talent and energy, of course, are permanent resources, needing only rest for renewal. Time and money, once spent, are gone. A lot of people have come to grief making movies without figuring that out.

Usually, working on a scene, Wyler directed you meticulously through every nuance, shifting his choices as it progressed,

but not always. One time we were doing a long shot of Judah
coming back to find his family mansion dark and neglected after
his years in the galleys. Bob Surtees had lit the entry hall and
main room in a very low key, moonlight glowing cool through the
windows. I walked in and moved hesitantly through the dusty
rooms, thinking of my lost life . . . the kind of shot actors love to do.
So did I, but Wyler kept doing more takes, without a word of how
to make it better. "Willy," I said finally, "you have to give me a clue
here. I don't know what else I can do with this."

"No, it's OK," he said. "In the first take, though, where the
dolly missed a move, your toe ticked into that broken pot on the
steps. It made a nice little clatter. It was the only sound in the whole
shot, a good accent. I thought it might happen again."

"Willy," I sighed. "I *put* the damn pot there, just to try it. If
you like it, it'll happen again, believe me. That's what you pay me
for." So I did it again. He was a very gifted, very quirky guy.

I guess I can't define Wyler's style as a director; I don't really
think he had one, not as many directors and critics think of it. I
remember telling him about a film I'd enjoyed, "really beautifully
directed," I said.

"Then maybe it wasn't," he pointed out. "If you thought
about the directing, he was calling attention to it. You shouldn't do
that. People should come out thinking what a good picture it was,
not what a good director you are." Yeah.

Certainly, he himself never played the great director. His
manner on set was low-key, almost detached from the process. He
never tried to excite or inspire you; that was your job. He was not
enthusiastic about the on-set discussions of character and emotions
we actors indulge in, either. That was for after the wrap, on private
time. During the shooting day, with the crew waiting and the meter
running, the time that counted was when the cameras were turning.
It's like possession time in football—when you have the ball, move
it. He focused on the scene at hand. What it was for, how to make it
better, truer, simpler.

He worked the same way with the actors also, of course.
Shooting *Memphis Belle* from a B-25 (a very noisy aircraft) in World
War II had left him largely deaf in one ear, but the other one, and
his eye, still gave him an uncannily flawless sense of performance.
He'd sit crouched under the lens, sometimes forgetting to call ei-

ther "Action" or "Cut," wholly concentrated on how to make you better. After every take, he'd have specific bits of direction, sometimes contradicting what he'd said earlier. "But, Willy, you said just ignore her when she opens the letter."

"Yeah, but that was wrong. I shouldn't have said that. Give me something else." He had no ego about his own choices, if they weren't working. There was one tough scene we worked on through a whole morning. Finally we agreed on some changes Christopher Fry could make that would fix it. He went off to do them, whereupon Willy said, "OK. Let's try it again."

"Willy," I said, in some confusion. "Aren't we going to wait for Christopher to come back with the new scene?"

"I'm not going to throw this one out till you get it right," he said. We laughed, but it made odd sense. He had to make certain there was nothing in the scene that could help us before he shot the new version. Why just sit and wait?

THE SUMMER LIGHT shortened into autumn, forcing us into an earlier wrap on exteriors. Nagged by the unshot tag-ends we'd left behind around the lot, Willy scheduled a whole day when he and I bicycled from set to set, picking them up. The theory was to give the first unit a setup, whip over to Yak's unit at the track and give them one; by then the first unit would be ready to shoot, so back and forth it went like that all day: one unit lighting while the other was shooting. It worked OK, but Willy and I got no lunch.

When I got back to my dressing room, one tired actor, there was a thirty-inch Roman centurion waiting for me: Fray, in full armor, plumed brass helmet, cuirass, short sword, red cloak, tunic, and boots, made by the chief armorer as a surprise for us both. I got almost as big a kick out of it as Fray did. For the next year or so, until he grew out of the armor, he played all his soldier games with Romans vs. barbarians, picking up a good bit of history on the side.

We'd added another second unit by then, under Richard Thorpe, to shoot the action in the slave galley. As with the chariots, it was hard to break me loose from the main unit to pull that damned oar for Thorpe. One Saturday Willy arbitrarily wrapped the first unit at lunch and spent the afternoon looking at dailies while I put in my time in chains as Number Forty-one in the galley. About 7 P.M., just after we wrapped, he stuck his head in my dressing room. "How'd it go?" he asked.

"OK, I guess. I tell you though, Willy; I'm anxious to get home, but I never figured on rowing all the way."

Mind you, he was as hard on himself as he was on the rest of us, which was comforting. I remember when we were shooting the desert oasis sequences in Anzio, south of Rome. It's a forest of condominiums now; then, it was one of the only two bits of true desert in Europe. (The other's still available on the south coast of Spain, and I've shot there, too.) No, I won't tell you where. You'd just put a hotel on it.

After a long, hot day in the sand, trying to drink from a gourd in a way that would fit Willy's use of water as a symbol running through the film ("Don't make too much of it, now. No, no, more than *that!* That's terrible"), I retreated exhausted to the bar in the meager hotel we were staying in. There was no one there, which made it seem even more like an empty swimming pool. I was about to go up to my room thirsty, when Willy came in, just as tired, maybe thirstier. He walked behind the bar, opened a couple of beers, and set one in front of me. "Those simple little scenes are always the most trouble," he offered.

"That one today sure was a bitch," I said. I wasn't sore, just a little beat up. The bar was still empty, and darker now. I was seized with the sudden, eerie conviction that Willy and I weren't just the only people in the bar, we were the only people on the location; the rest of the company were figures in our imaginations. (It *had* been a tough day.) I pulled on my beer and thought, "Of course there are people here—just nobody *here*. But us. We've got a five-thirty call tomorrow. There'll be people."

Willy was making rings on the bar with his beer glass. "You know, I'd like to be a nice guy. It's easier to be nice, really."

"Yeah, I know that, Willy."

"You just can't make good pictures that way."

"I know that, too. Don't worry about it. I'm fine. Remember, I'm only an imitation Jew." That made him laugh, and we both went off to bed. I didn't even wait for supper; I was asleep in twenty minutes. It was the only time I ever saw him like that.

•

WE WENT BACK to Rome and an early winter, with an awful lot still to shoot. Roman winters are no fun; they're gloomy and dank, like a bad cold. Yeah, we had those, too. People came to work sniffling, or got sent home if you could shoot around them. My don't-get-sick-while-you're-shooting charm held good, but even Willy went home early one day.

The pace and the pressure was beginning to tell on all of us by this time. Maybe it made us a little more vulnerable, too. Shooting one day, I had a curious purging experience unlike anything I can remember. We were doing the scene where Judah, on his way to the slave galleys, breaks free from his guards in Castle Antonia and runs to confront Messala. (Steve had finished his part by then and gone back to London—that's movies for you.)

We did a tracking shot of the two guards marching me along a corridor, holding a stick thrust through my elbows behind me, my hands tied in front. We covered that, then set up a shot of me shouldering one guard off the stairs, leaping down seven or eight stone steps, and escaping. As they were lighting it, I found myself sweating, oddly shaky. "No, no, none of that," I thought. "No time for the flu."

Then I suddenly saw how strongly the set and the shot brought alive a nightmare I'd endured every eight or ten months as far back as I could remember, when I was a little kid in Michigan, in school, in the war, New York, Hollywood, all my life. It was terrifying, and always the same. I'm climbing circular stone steps inside a tall tower, to rescue a princess. (Yes, of course, the Grimm brothers.) I get to the top, open the chamber door to reveal the princess, only to have a hideous witch leap shrieking out at me, pursuing as I desperately plunge down flight after flight of stone steps till I leap into the nameless dark that ends all nightmares.

The shot was ready; as they called me in, the sweat was running down my chest; the muscles on my shoulders were twitching. Wyler must have sensed something. "You OK, Chuck?" he said. "We've got a pad at the bottom for you to land on."

"No, that's fine," I said. "Let's do it." And we did. There was really nothing dangerous about it, except that my hands were tied. I kept my balance in the jump and ran out of frame, as called for. Oddly, Willy printed the first take, which was all but unprecedented for him. The truly remarkable thing, though, is that I've never had that nightmare again. Not once.

A week later, another anomaly occurred. We'd been shooting for two days on a key scene in Pilate's palace, hoping to finish it Saturday, before the day off. So we did, a little after seven. It was winter now, and raining, a chill, bleak night. Willy and I waited out of the wet, just inside the open door of the sound stage, for our cars to come. His came first. "G'night, Willy," I said absently.

" 'Night, Chuck," he answered, as his driver opened the door. "Good scene today." I looked at him sharply.

"What did you say?"

"You were very good. In the scene."

I was dumbfounded. "Oh. Thanks," I managed, as he closed the door. It was the only time, in two pictures, he'd said anything like that. The scene wasn't even that difficult. I've decided that he felt we Scots thrive in adversity (which is true), and it just slipped out that once because I looked cold and tired. I was, too.

Not long after that, on another rainy night, our producer, Sam Zimbalist, stopped by the set. Sam was a large, affable man who'd borne the burdens of *Ben-Hur* for two years, long before Willy and I were on it. In a sense, the pressure on him was greater once preproduction was finished and shooting began; there was little he could do then but try and make the rough way smooth, keeping the logistics working, MGM out of Wyler's hair, and his fingers crossed. He did this best from his office, but he came by the set almost every day, usually just before we wrapped.

About six, when people in the real world have quit for the day, he came up to where I sat waiting for Wyler to finish a shot I wasn't in. "Look like another late one, Chuck?"

"Yeah, I'd say so. He's got this close-up with the girl; that'll take some time. Then a setup with me. An hour sure, maybe more."

"Well, I don't want to bother him while he's shooting. Just tell him I stopped in, nothing important." Sam clapped me on the shoulder and was gone.

It wasn't twenty minutes later; Willy had just printed on the close-up and was picking an angle for my shot when a call came for me. (The phones on sound stages don't ring when the camera's turning.) It was Sam's assistant. "Chuck, you have to tell Willy . . . I can't. Sam's dead."

"You're crazy," I said. "I was talking to him here on the set, just now. Call his villa, he's gone home."

"No, I'm telling you. It's true. They called me. He dropped dead in his driveway ten minutes ago." I hung up the phone, walked over to the camera, and told Willy. He closed his script and sat silent for a moment.

"Dear God . . . you pay the price, don't you? You pay the price." He stood up. "That's a wrap. Same call tomorrow. Let's go see Sam's wife."

There was a proper Orthodox service we went to the next evening, with a kaddish, but I was more moved by the single minute of silence on the set that morning, when all of us doing the work Sam had died trying to finish stood and thought of him. I'd settle for that myself.

Only days later, Tyrone Power died in Spain. He was shooting a film about Solomon and Sheba, and collapsed after several takes carrying Gina Lollobrigida up a long flight of stone steps. I didn't know him well, had never worked with him, but his death hung in my mind, resonating with my own mortality.

They were only ten days or so into their shoot; Yul Brynner took over the role and they started again. We'd been shooting more than seven months; if I died before we finished, they couldn't possibly go back and do it over. There would be no picture, after all our work—or maybe they *would* recast and go back and do it over, which deepened my gloom.

I was running on my Scot's blood by then. Counting learning the chariot, I'd been working well over thirty weeks, six days a week, sometimes shooting on two units simultaneously, bicycling back and forth. Fatigue was settling in my bones like frost. Even my reflexes were slowing. Shooting the scene where Judah tries to give water to Christ carrying His cross, a soldier knocked the gourd from my hand and threw me back. I took the fall wrong and slammed my hip into the well-curb. It hurt like hell, not least because it was my own fault.

The scenes we had left were dark scenes, too. Judah walking heedless past Jesus preaching the Sermon on the Mount, searching for his mother and sister in the leper caves (shot in the old quarry where Caesar Augustus got the slabs to make Rome a city of marble), then back to the Jerusalem we'd made on the Cinecittà back lot to film Jesus dragging the cross up the Via Dolorosa. Then at last, the Crucifixion. It was wonderfully rich material to work on, but very tough to film, under Willy's demanding eye.

I found myself musing on the way to and from the shoot each day, half-dozing in the back of the limo. "If we get the master shot on this scene today, they could certainly use a double for the cover angles if I died, shoot from behind, and dub the voice. You *could* finish the film *without* the scene next week, but there's no way to shoot the Crucifixion without me. Have to have the close angles, and you can't cut it, either." Oh, I tell you, I was in a great state of mind.

Still, the cowboy maxim holds—keep on keepin' on. We did get Christmas off, and the Romans celebrate the Feast of Stephen the next day too, so we got two days in a row—the first two-day break for me since we'd come to Italy. That much time with Lydia, Fray, and the Christmas spirit was potent medicine for me, a wonderful, private holiday. I gave Lydia a beautiful Italian robe which looked all the better on her; Fray and I got robes, too. They were identical (except for size), cut from the blue wool of the cloak I'd worn in the parade before the start of the race. I still use mine; Fray grew out of his at five.

Walter and Mickey Seltzer came for a few days with their daughter, Michael, the last of our houseguests that year. I even stayed up to celebrate New Year's Eve in Rome with them.

Inevitably, we came finally to the last scene of the shoot. For three days, we explored the terrible mechanics of crucifixion. A good German actor, Claude Heater, played Christ. In the film, his face is never seen, his voice never heard, but he had moved me more than once, working with him.

The last setup we made was a close angle on me, looking at the crucified Christ. I'd made a strong case to Willy that I should play it without visible emotion. Judah had seen many men die, in the galleys, in the arena. Christ was simply a criminal condemned to the cross, a common punishment, though usually reserved for slaves. When the camera turned, though, it got away from me; I wept. This can happen more often in film than on the stage. The created surroundings of a place like Golgotha, the cultural weight of an event like the Crucifixion, can move the actor beyond his creative control. (This is beginning to sound pretty ponderous.

Actors talk like that. As people say to us all the time, "Come on, it's only a movie.") I guess what I'm trying to say is that the scene worked, and I think it more or less played itself.

And that was a wrap—on the scene, the set, and the shoot. There was no wrap party, no company jackets or T-shirts. That would get you sent to movie jail today, but all the other principals had finished by then, anyway. Willy walked over to me and shook my hand. "Thanks, Chuck. Next time I'll try to give you a better part."

12

Gary, Larry, and Oscar

TWO HOURS AFTER we wrapped *Ben-Hur,* Willy and I were on a plane for London for the world premiere of *The Big Country.* There wasn't even time to say good-bye to our wives, both buried in packing. Along with my overnight bag, Fray sent his favorite toy rifle and cowboy hat with Ivo in the limo for me to take along, as a loan. "Weoh, it's a cowboy movie, iznit?" he said when I called from the airport to thank him.

Big Country played very well at the premiere and opened strongly the next day. Willy and I did our interviews and flew back to Italy, landing in Rome some forty hours after we'd left. Both villas were a welter of packing cases, so we had dinner in Rome with the Wylers on the roof of the Hotel Cesare Agosto for one last look at the city. Looking down at the Janiculum Hill under a full moon, Lydia said to Talli Wyler, "I can't imagine why Chuck's so anxious to get home. This has been such a marvelous time. I could spend another ten months here."

"So could I," said Talli. "But Chuck and Willy haven't had ten months in Rome. They've had ten months at Cinecittà Studios." As we turned to leave, I realized Fray had slipped off his chair and was dancing to the dinner music, turning in solitary almost-four gravity in the middle of the dance floor. That's my last and one of my best memories of the *Ben-Hur* shoot.

Twelve hours later, Ivo drove us out through the gates of Horti Flaviani for the last time, followed by a van full of baggage. The important baggage was in our memories, of course, where it still lives. The next afternoon, we sailed from Naples for New York on the *Independence*. As we went below to check out the suite, we passed a carved wooden bust of an American Indian chief. I felt at home instantly. Then when we went back topside to watch the huge liner cast off, the tugs nudging her out into the ebb tide, we saw Ivo clinging to a bollard on the end of the pier, waving to us passionately. That was our Roman farewell. It was a passionate time.

The first two or three nights on board, I dreamt of studio messengers calling me back to the sets to shoot scenes we'd somehow overlooked; still, I rested relentlessly as we moved through the Mediterranean and across the Atlantic. Of course I caught the cold that had been patiently waiting its turn for ten months, but I didn't mind much; I wasn't using the equipment that week anyway.

Days later in the Gulf Stream, my cold conquered, I took Fray topside, aft of the forward stack to watch the sun wheel above us as the ship turned north for New York. Looking up from inside the empty dome of sea and sky, it's the sun that seems to be moving, not the ship. Fray was enchanted. "Do it again, Daddy!" he crowed, touchingly confident that I could.

We were going below when Lydia met me with a radiogram: Cecil B. DeMille had died. We shared the news at lunch with Martha Scott, our shipmate on the voyage home. We drank a toast in good wine to him. He'd helped invent the movies and died at seventy-six, his best work finished.

To all things there is a season. I thought again of Ty Power and Sam Zimbalist, and the sense of mortality their deaths had triggered in me. Not to see the work through to the end, yes, that would be very bad. DeMille had done his work. No man can ask more. We came through the Narrows before dawn, with a full moon setting over the shoulder of the Statue of Liberty. To see her so for the first time was indescribably moving, just as everyone's been saying since they first put the lady out there. We checked into the East River penthouse and spent a week or so seeing old friends and new plays, then picked up new cars in Detroit and drove west in convoy, I in my first Corvette, Lydia in her T-Bird, Fray a happy passenger, touching base with our families and more friends on the way. I was in a mood to see something of the country I'd been away from for so long.

Back in L.A., we stopped first on the ridge at the top of Coldwater Canyon where we were very, ver-ry slowly building our house. By then, two months after we'd wrapped *Ben-Hur,* I was ready to work again. (In my experience, actors get edgy with idleness almost as soon as they finish a part—certainly this one does.)

There were some offers waiting. My old Air Corps pal, Bill Darrid (who'd pointed us to our cold-water walk-up in Manhattan at the beginning and was now a producer), wanted me to do a play in London and film it later; I had an offer to do *Macbeth* at a Shakespeare festival in Michigan, and another for a film with Gary Cooper.

Clearly, the Cooper film would be the most lucrative, and would also fulfill a one-picture commitment I'd made to MGM as part of the *Ben-Hur* deal. Besides, I'd been a fan of Cooper's since I was ten years old—the thought of acting with him was a little staggering.

On the other hand, Macbeth is one of the great parts of the world. I'd done it in school and again for live TV on "Studio One," but only once since then. You can't begin on those Shakespearean monsters too early, and you can't play them too often, as long as you have the energy. They eat actors' energy the way Formula 1 cars eat fuel. They take more out of you and they give more. There are no parts like them.

No, I thought, I can't pass it up. So I passed on the Cooper film instead, which upset Herman the Iceman more than a little. A few days later, he came back with startling news: MGM would accommodate their shooting schedule on *The Wreck of the Mary Deare* to allow me to do *Macbeth,* if I'd settle for a limited run and a shortened rehearsal schedule. (Obviously, my value to MGM had been greatly enhanced by *Ben-Hur;* they also gave me my first piece of the gross for *Mary Deare,* almost unheard of then.)

Delighted to have both pieces of cake, I hurried off to Ann Arbor to wolf down my fourth *Macbeth.* I'm afraid that's about all I managed to do with it, too. I hadn't been on stage since the Broadway revival of *Mister Roberts* more than two years earlier, and I hadn't done Shakespeare since my last shot at *Macbeth* three years before that.

That was in Bermuda. There, too, I'd seized a chance to do the play, jamming a short run in between pictures (I think I made three films that year). We staged it in the courtyard and battlements of a fort built in 1605, about the time *Macbeth* was written. Burgess Meredith directed a very spirited redaction of the play we worked out together. It had a spare and vigorous text, real horses in the witches scene, real fire in the battles, the real Atlantic smashing against the castle walls, and a marvelously icy Nancy Marchand (later famous as Ed Asner's publisher in his TV series "Lou Grant") as the blood-stained Lady. Did it have a real Macbeth? Good question.

I was good in Bermuda . . . maybe even very good, here and there . . . but you have to understand, in Shakespeare, good and very good won't cut it. The parts are so mammoth, marked by four centuries of memorials to the actors who've made them theirs, that the very minimum you can squeak by with, doing any of them, is "marvelous."

Still, I was content with what I'd done with the part in Bermuda. Not so in Ann Arbor. I had a good director and a good cast; I should've been able to move deeper into the part, even with a short rehearsal. You've got to do that with these guys, every time. They're tests that demand the very best that's in you . . . the Olympic model again: "Stronger, Faster, Higher." Except that acting is not a competition with other actors; you compete only with yourself, and with the great parts.

Maybe I was still bone-drained from the long ordeal with Wyler on *Ben-Hur,* maybe I hadn't gotten back into condition for Shakespeare, but I wasn't more than an adequate, maybe physically interesting Macbeth that spring. At least I'd done the part again.

Then, it was back to MGM. Sensing they had in *Ben-Hur* the most successful film since *Gone With the Wind,* the studio was blooming with confidence. They didn't stint on *Wreck of the Mary Deare.*

It was a sea story; they were shooting in the English Channel, at Long Beach (doubling for Southampton), and in the enormous Stage 30 at Culver City, which is among the larger sound stages in the world and the only one whose floor covers a tank which could

be flooded to make a huge marine shooting stage, built for the
Esther Williams water musicals of the forties.

They'd begun shooting with Cooper on some scenes I wasn't in while I was still wrestling Shakespeare's bloody Scot; now they did some sequences without him of me on a tugboat, boarding a derelict tramp steamer in a storm. In the tank on Stage 30, they built the starboard side of the ship and all of the bow, full-scale on rockers to make it roll realistically in the storm they created. Then they launched an ocean-going tug in the tank, from which I'd grab a trailing line from the steamer, and climb up the hull and over the rail on board. I'd practiced rope-climbing daily for weeks in the Paramount gym, but it was a little tougher climbing a wet rope off a rolling tug, even in a studio storm. Something unpleasant happened to my shoulder ten feet below the deck; I scrambled aboard whining unheroically. As I lay moaning in the scupper, the director, Michael Anderson, yelled on the bullhorn. "That's marvelous, Chuck!" (They always begin with that.) "Could you do one more, please?"

"You'd better print, Michael!" I said. "I'm afraid that's all there is." I didn't miss any shooting time, but I never did give them another take on the rope climb, or climbed a rope anywhere, for that matter. There are a few things you learn to do for movies that you never want to do again.

Then there was Gary Cooper. He became a star with his first feature film at the end of the silent era and became even more dominant with the coming of sound. He was, and remained till his death, a movie star when that meant a lot more than it does now— principally, that your name on a marquee more or less guaranteed a success.

There's a great deal to be said about Coop. For one thing, he was a far better actor than he was given credit for, with a deft comic touch and an understated impact in serious roles. Within his range (defined in part by his size and formidable presence), he was a riveting actor. When young, he'd been incredibly handsome, with a face born for the camera; as he aged, that face became a map of America. Indeed, along with Jimmy Stewart and Hank Fonda, he was an iconic image of the American male. If this wasn't what the American man was, it was what he was supposed to be.

On screen, you couldn't take your eyes off Coop; he listened as well as any actor I've worked with. Looking at daily footage every evening, when I was supposed to be checking out my own performance, I found myself watching him instead. (Any film actor will tell you that's most unusual.) About that time, I used to joke in interviews that I could play cowboys better than Laurence Olivier and Shakespeare better than Gary Cooper. This speaks more to my insecurities than their talents.

We were scheduled to wrap the *Mary Deare* shoot with two weeks in London, mostly exteriors. For such a short location time, Lydia stayed home, as did Coop's wife, Rocky. We found ourselves camping out in neighboring bachelor suites at the Savoy.

Making a film, or a play, forces a fierce, focused intimacy on everyone involved. You all need each other healthy and stable to get it done, like a combat air crew, or an infantry platoon. They're often men and women you've never met before, but you're all married to each other till the shoot's finished or the play closes. After that, you often hardly keep in touch, until the next time.

I don't make friends easily anyway; those closest to me are mostly people I've known for decades. Coop was twenty-some years older than I; he must've looked on me as a young stud actor coming up. In addition, he was a rather shy man, as I am myself. Still, unlikely as it seems, we became friends.

We didn't talk much about acting. In school, you talk about nothing else—passionate acolytes searching for the Holy Grail. Once it becomes your life, that search is usually internal and private.

Coop was marvelously funny about Hollywood, though, in film's Golden Age in the thirties and forties, the era fueled by the big studios and shaped by Thalberg and DeMille, Goldwyn and Selznick. I was amused by his description of the normal workday on a film he'd made with Marion Davies, the mistress of William Randolph Hearst, who then owned MGM. "Marion'd show up about ten, do two or three setups, and then retire to her dressing room for lunch, pretty wet and pretty long. After a nap, we'd do two or three more shots, then high tea, which was martinis, then Marion was off home. Helluva way to make a movie." He was very circumspect in his comments about Dietrich and Goddard and Kelly and the other sex goddesses he'd loved on- and possibly offscreen. Even

in today's fiercely feminist climate, I doubt any of them would claim
sexual harassment, though maybe Coop could.

I was witness to another sort of harassment, which Coop
handled with a cool ease that amazed me. We'd had dinner at an
excellent steak house off Berkeley Square. Leaving, we passed a
table of young mods and rockers, the London equivalent of today's
punk rock kids, with special wardrobe and haircuts. As Coop
walked by, one of them said, "Oh, there goes the big cowboy star."

Coop stopped, turned in his tracks, and looked steadily at
the young man. "When you say that, smile," he said softly. The kid
couldn't have realized that was a line from Cooper's first hit film,
The Virginian, but it didn't matter. Suddenly, he wasn't in a cozy
London restaurant anymore, but standing all alone on a dusty Western street, with a chill wind on the back of his neck. No one at the
table moved or looked up. Coop stood there for fully thirty seconds,
cold-eyed, then smiled lightly, turned on his heel, and walked out.
As I joined him in the back of his Rolls, I said, "You read that line
very well, Coop."

He grinned and straightened the crease in his Savile Row
trousers. "Well," he said, "I've had lots of practice." I don't know
another actor who'd have dared even to try that, let alone make it
stick.

Coop did not attend the great Nikita Khrushchev lunch at
Fox. He could do as he chose, but most of the rest of us felt obliged
to turn up, some convinced they were thus advancing the cause
of peace in the world. Khrushchev was one of Gorbachev's more
notorious predecessors as overlord of the evil empire . . . a less
smooth performer, but just as wily. Reaching California on his U.S.
tour, he announced that his heart's desire was a visit to Disneyland.
Denied this delight on security grounds, he settled for a tour of Fox
Studios, climaxed with a lunch shared by the major *menschen und
mädchen* of our little workforce.

Given my known skepticism regarding the Soviets, I was
surprised to find Madam Khrushchev as my luncheon partner. She
was a pleasant, motherly lady, but we could exchange nothing more
than tentative smiles, since her minders had not provided her with
an interpreter, perhaps reasoning the less said, the better.

They need not have worried; her husband carried the day.

After an appropriately grand but brisk lunch (grand luncheons are shorter than grand dinners, with less booze and fewer speeches), our host, Spyros Skouras, proposed the ritual toast, which he then followed with a gross blunder. "I was poor boy from Greece," he announced, glass lifted. "I came to America with nothing. Now I am head of Twentieth Century–Fox."

Well, you didn't even need the translator. Khrushchev rose grinning, and said, "I was poor boy from Caucasus. I came to Moscow with nothing. Now I am premier of Soviet Union."

Mary Deare finished on schedule and turned out to be quite a good film, though MGM, with inscrutable thick-headedness, insisted on releasing it in the fall just weeks ahead of both *Ben-Hur* and a major film of Cooper's, *They Came to Cordura*. The audience predictably waited for those films and largely ignored our joint effort. (You're right, actors have all sorts of ingenious explanations for the failure of a film.) Never mind; I'm pleased with the picture and proud that I worked with Gary Cooper.

I spent the next few months watching my son and my house grow, the boy faster than the building. The builders had broken ground well over a year ago but the stone walls were rising very slowly. Only the chimney and fireplace were complete. We used to go up on Sundays and grill hamburgers in what would be our living room. It was perfect for Fray as it was: lots of sand piles and good sticks to play with.

As would also prove true for his sister, Holly, in a few years, his international childhood both enlightened and matured him. True, it was about this time, on a trip to London, that Fray was expelled from the Grill of the Dorchester Hotel for standing on his chair and singing. On the other hand, the next day he made a sufficiently persuasive apology to the maître d' which got him readmitted. To the best of my knowledge, he has never sung since in the Dorchester Grill.

LYDIA HADN'T ACTED on stage or screen in more than two years, so she happily accepted an offer to do a short run in a beautiful Spanish colonial theater in Santa Barbara. I joined her in the political comedy *State of the Union*. I'd directed her in it, but had not acted myself, in Asheville, so I relished playing opposite her again. She was better than I was, but the woman's role is the best part, as

Katharine Hepburn proved when she played it with Tracy in the
film version.

Actually, we both had a marvelous time. In the preceding three years, I'd followed Henry Fonda on stage in the role of his career, then acted for Orson Welles, Willy Wyler, C. B. DeMille, then Wyler again in a film that had MGM's survival riding on it, winding up with *Macbeth* and the film with Gary Cooper. Wonderful career opportunities, every one of them, but fraught, as they say, with pressures and pitfalls. It was nice—no, damn it, it was *lovely*—to do something just for the fun of it.

For Lydia, the play was more than that. She was dealing with a choice every working woman faces with motherhood: Which comes first, the career or the child? For Lydia, that was easy; till Fray was weaned, she was available to him ahead of her agent, or anybody else. By that autumn, his need for his mother wasn't nearly so total, but he was even more fun to be with.

I remember coming back to the house we'd rented in Santa Barbara after a matinee, Fray running to greet us. As she hugged him, Lydia said, "Oh, Bunny, your fly's open. You have to remember to keep that zipped." He looked at her with keen interest.

"Why?" he said. "What wiw get in dere?" Smart kid, for four.

By this time, the preparatory publicity barrage on *Ben-Hur* had rumbled into high gear. It had never really stopped, since Wyler had completed his casting almost two years earlier. You have to understand: the game was very different then. There were a dozen national magazines and scores of foreign publications in which studios could plant double truck color spreads and covers, as well as stories. Newspapers were even more abundant. Outside the Communist bloc, every major city in the world had at least two newspapers, some as many as ten, with Sunday magazine sections and daily movie columnists. Literally hundreds of U.S. and foreign media people made pilgrimages to the set. I'd given chariot rides to at least a dozen I knew while we were shooting the race. (Oddly, none of them seemed to want to help me pull an oar in the slave galley sequence.) From the time we started shooting, there was some sort of press break at least every week.

MGM's publicity people, then considered as skilled as any in the world, handled it all superbly. During the seven months of editing and postproduction, when nothing publicly visible happened on the film at all, they gradually increased the tempo of publicity, building audience expectation as though we were preparing for the Second Coming.

Mind you, this was all done in free space. Films weren't advertised on TV then, though we did the obligatory TV and radio talk shows. Now, films are advertised primarily in tightly orchestrated TV campaigns a few weeks ahead of the opening, at a cost at least equal to that of making the entire film, often scores of millions of dollars. Consequently, most films that don't hit big the first weekend are jettisoned because the cost of further TV ads is too great a risk. MGM had planned a series of premieres; they don't do those anymore, either, except for an occasional fund-raiser in Hollywood. Actually, they were kind of fun, if you remembered that all the attendant press hoopla wasn't because you were such a marvelous fella, but to sell the movie. It's surprising how many actors miss this obvious point.

Lydia had turned down a script she didn't like, so she was free to come with me to the world premiere in New York. When she told Fray about the trip, he disagreed. Strongly. "You're *stupid!*"

"Ah, Bunny," she said. "I know you don't mean that . . . but other people wouldn't understand."

He thought, then leaned to her and said, sotto voce, "But dere's nobody here to *lissen!*"

I'm very glad she came. Maggie Field's mother, when we called on her in New York, insisted on lending Lydia several hundred thousand dollars' worth of emeralds. They looked absolutely smashing against a white satin gown, with my girl equally smashing inside it. Of course Lydia spent the evening crossing herself—earring, earring, necklace, bracelet—to check their security. If we hadn't seen the film at the studio the week before, I doubt she'd have known who won the chariot race. Yes, it was an enormous hit, with great notices. It ran almost two years at the same theater in New York, as it did in most other cities. Lydia went back to the Coast and I undertook a number of other openings, pumping each one up with as much media hoopla as we could manage.

I'd learned to do interviews well by then, not an easy skill for me. (Look at most presidential candidates; it's a lot harder than you think.) As with presidents, so with public actors: on-the-job training helps a lot. I'd had nearly ten years of practice by that time;

really ample time to learn, if you apply yourself. I had. (Another how-it-really-is-in-movies note: young actors with a year of a successful TV sitcom under their belts often come to regard public relations as a dirty job that decent people really shouldn't do, as a matter of principle. It can indeed be a somewhat tiresome chore, but I've done harder work in my life. It needs to be done, and only actors are useful at it. So do it. Well.)

As soon as I'd finished most of the big domestic premieres, I came back home to enjoy my family and my growing house (most of the rock walls were in by this time) and read scripts. Lydia had been offered one she liked, a Western. She asked me to read it, and I liked it, too. "Do it," I said. "It's a good part for you, the location's in Arizona; I can come down to be with Fray and work on my tennis."

So she okayed the film, just about the same day MGM called to announce they'd managed to get a Royal premiere for the London opening of *Ben-Hur*. We would go, of course?

I had to go, and Lydia was mightily tempted. Still, she hadn't done a film in a long while, so she called her agent to discuss it. He was quite upset. "Honey," he said firmly. "You better decide whether you want to make movies or go to Chuck's premieres."

Well, I could have told him. That is not the line to take with the girl I married. "I'll tell you one thing," she said firmly. "I'm damn well going to this premiere." And she did.

About this time, I turned down a film myself, though my choice was easier than Lydia's (or, for that matter, my own the previous winter, when I had to choose between *Macbeth* and Gary Cooper and ended up with both). Fox wanted me to do a movie, *Let's Make Love,* with Marilyn Monroe, then and still one of the iconic legends of Hollywood. She was perhaps the last of the stars created, then grossly abused, by the studio system. After Garbo, there's probably never been a woman the camera loved more than Marilyn, not only for her stunning sexual beauty, but for the oddly innocent carnality she projected.

By this time, though, the years when Fox made millions while making her the world's favorite sex goddess had ravaged her ... from the inside out. She still looked marvelous, but whatever demons of anxiety lurked in her head had all but crippled her professionally.

I knew her casually, but had never worked with her. That had become a formidable task by then. Like many very beautiful actresses, she was deeply insecure about her acting; she was convinced her survival as a star depended on looking perfect in every setup. She'd become almost impossible to coax out of her dressing room onto the set. There were horror stories from the *Misfits* shoot of her keeping Clark Gable (something of an icon himself) waiting literally all day for her to appear at the cameras. At dinner with the Wylers, Laurence Olivier told me that acting with and directing her in *The Prince and the Showgirl* had been the worst experience of his career.

Still, by Hollywood standards, *Let's Make Love* was an attractive proposition—but not for me. I passed. The French actor Yves Montand eventually made the film, and came out of it, I'm told, a scarred but wiser man.

Besides, I'd had a better offer, creatively, if not commercially. Olivier asked me to do a play for him. I'd have killed for that opportunity; instead, I'd be paid for it. Not the gross percentage Fox offered me to wait for Miss Monroe, but I knew I'd be richly compensated in other terms. So I was.

I'd met him some months before, soon after we got home from the *Ben-Hur* shoot, while Olivier was still toiling in *Spartacus*. Wyler, who'd directed him memorably in *Wuthering Heights,* gave a small dinner for him. There were eight or ten people there, but Olivier was the center of the evening, a burden he bore with grace and charm. He told any number of very funny stories very well. They all had a crucial element in common: *he was the butt of the joke in every story he told.* It's a rule I've tried to follow ever since. Actors are likely to have the spotlight in a social situation. When that happens, never tell stories about what a great guy you are.

Olivier was then at the peak of his extraordinary powers, widely regarded as the best actor of his time, perhaps of the century. He did all the great parts, on stage and screen, leaving performances that remain benchmarks for other actors to be measured against: *Wuthering Heights, Henry V, Hamlet, Richard III, Othello.* I'd been in awe of him since high school. I'd turned down two offers to do *Henry V,* an obvious part for me, pointing out that "I've seen his film of it so many times I know all the line readings . . . I

couldn't resist them and I don't want to give you a rough copy of
his performance." To work with Olivier was a shining chance.

The play was called *The Tumbler*. The playwright, Benn Levy, a likable and scholarly man, told me the title referred to my role, though he never was able to explain why. Over the weeks I did begin to understand the play itself (a perception I confess is lost in memory now). It was a difficult piece, written in a sort of free verse I found hard to speak, for exactly the reason Shakespeare is so lucid: once you see the way he says something, there's simply no other way to say it.

I played a morose, intermittently witty, and eventually suicidal outsider, the kind of character (minus the free verse) that has since become standard in the works of John Osborne, Sam Shepard, and David Mamet. There were only three other characters in the piece, principally a wandering girl, also a familiar figure in modern drama, but in our play enlivened by the incandescent Rosemary Harris. I'm sorry I've not had a chance to work with her since (so far).

It wasn't an easy time for me to do a play, in fact. We hear a good deal about how hard it is for a woman to fulfill her responsibilities to both career and family . . . but this is true for men, too. I'd just seen Lydia struggle with such a choice; now I was faced with a similar dilemma.

I wanted desperately to work with Olivier, even in a high-risk play of uncertain commercial appeal. Maybe *especially* in such a play; the longer the odds, the greater the credit. On the other hand, our house was still not finished. We'd been promised we could move in before Thanksgiving, then surely before Christmas. We finally first slept on our ridge on January 4, with not quite all the carpeting down. I was scheduled to leave for rehearsals in New York on the seventh, and on the fifth Fray's pediatrician decided his nagging sore throat needed an immediate tonsillectomy.

We put him in the hospital that evening and stayed with him that night, but the next morning I had to go to some damn meeting at Metro before they took him down to surgery. It was Lydia who was with him in the elevator when he looked up from the gurney, clutching his stuffed yellow Dog, and said wanly, "Tell me a quick cowboy story."

Yes, it was routine surgery; I was there that afternoon, and brought him home the next day. As I carried him up to his new but still bare bedroom before leaving for my plane, he said, "I'n so weak you might as well th'ow me out . . . I wouldn' care."

I flew east examining my priorities over some of TWA's free scotch. Certainly I wanted to work with Olivier, certainly I wanted to renew my stage credentials in New York; this was the time and the play to do that. Still, to leave Lydia to finish moving into the house with one hand while nursing Fray through his tonsillectomy with the other grated on my sense of responsibility.

But I had no choice. I had Olivier and a company waiting for me. I *had* to be there. Acting, taken to the highest level, requires a fierce, total focus of your time and energy, at the cost of just about everything else. I often fall short of that draconian demand.

The Tumbler, of course, swallowed me two hours after we touched down in New York. Olivier met me at our apartment and we read through the play, he doing the other three parts, then sat dissecting it while looking out over the East River till two the next morning.

No, I didn't call him Sir Laurence. "Larry," he insisted. I've always been a little amused by our preoccupation with first names ("I'm Larry; I'll be your waiter tonight"), but Olivier was sensitive to American usage. I think Americans are also rather taken with the chance to use a title. When Bob Mulligan was directing Olivier in something and told to "Call me Larry," he responded, "Do I have to?"

Rehearsals on *Tumbler* were very intensive. I was delighted to find that Olivier felt as I do: you find your way into a script by getting the actors on their feet and moving them around. Larry shared my actor's instinct that you solve the mysteries of meaning, motivation, and movement best by doing the scenes, not sitting around talking about them. From the start we were on our feet, digging.

In this case (as indeed with most scripts), there was also the text to wrestle with. It was very long and the verse was very intricate. It needed a lot of cutting, which meant wrestling with Benn Levy. I diplomatically left most of that to Olivier, since we saw more or less eye to eye on what the cuts should be. Again, actors tend to have good instincts on this.

I soon learned that the disarray in which I'd left my small family was as nothing compared to Olivier's. He canceled an extra-curricular Saturday rehearsal he'd planned with me to fly home to London, getting back Sunday in time for a session at my apartment. He seemed distracted as we discussed the script, so I poured him a second scotch and said, "And how was London?"

"Ghastly," he said. "Bloody . . . fucking . . . ghastly." He stood up abruptly. "I don't think I'm up to working on the suicide scene tonight, after all. Bit close to the bone. Bright and early tomorrow, eh, Laddie?" And he left.

He was still married to Vivien Leigh, though by then some-what precariously. Their tempestuous romance, subsequent marriage, and enthronement as the first couple of the world has been exhaustively chronicled. Its dissolution, unhappily, was explored with at least equal enthusiasm, and less taste.

I know little about it. I didn't know Olivier very well. (Ralph Richardson, who did, almost all his life, was asked once what Larry was really like. After some thought, he said, "I'm afraid I have no idea.") I met Vivien Leigh only twice, and recall primarily being stunned by her beauty. Whether her problems, like Monroe's, were rooted in pills and alcohol and the general insecurities of being an actress, or whether she had more serious mental disturbances, as was hinted at the time, I can't say.

It surely must've been an enormous pressure for her to play, as she largely did after their marriage, opposite an actor of such protean gifts as Olivier's. I saw them do both Shaw's *Caesar and Cleopatra* and Shakespeare's *Antony and Cleopatra* on successive nights. She was very good as the child Cleopatra to his underplayed and doddering Caesar, but completely inadequate as the mature queen of the Nile, even with Olivier playing Antony as flatly as possible, to give her some space to soar. This seemed to me a loving and husbandly thing to do, when you consider he was then establishing himself as the actor of his time, if not the century.

He had no such recourse available to him while we were rehearsing *Tumbler* and she was several thousand miles away "trembling on the edge of a cliff . . . even when she's sitting quietly in her own drawing room," as he put it once. No, he did not unburden himself to me, nor did I press him. Fragments like that would burst out of him at odd moments, over a drink after rehearsal, or in the middle of a walk to a restaurant during lunch break.

He made two more of those overnight trips to London, the second only days before our Boston opening. He came back exhausted and gloomy, with no hint that things were going better with his marriage, or what was left of it. He surely seemed to be trying, though.

Meantime, back in the theater, *Tumbler* had its own problems. Were they compounded by Olivier's crumbled marriage? I don't know; I thought he was doing his best with a very full plate. I was doing my best to concentrate on the play. Our main difficulty was my wife . . . no, no, in the *play!*

Hermione Baddeley had been a significant actress in London for a long time, mostly in comic roles. My harridan wife in *Tumbler* was without humor, and also seemed to call for a younger actress. It wouldn't have occurred to me to cast Toti (as Olivier called her) in *Tumbler,* but I found her to be a good lady, on time, prepared, easy to work with, gamely doing her best with the wrong part.

I was having my troubles with my own part, for that matter. "Don't try to be *liked,*" Olivier told me. "Never play the audience's opinion of your character, or the writer's, either. You have to be on the side of the man you play . . . totally and always." A marvelous piece of direction; it's helped me many times since. This was a hard one for me, though.

Possibly Olivier himself could've brought it off, twenty years earlier. I was struggling just to find the part. I'd never before (or since) felt how *hard* acting can be. With the great parts, Macbeth, Othello, you always fall short a little, but there are also those orgasmic highs where you come to a climax that's in the part, waiting for you. My suicidal Tumbler was all work.

I did finally make the suicide scene play. It was probably my prime contribution to the production. *The Tumbler* ended with a long monologue (yes, in free verse) where I walked around in a barn discussing life with a doctor, whose main structural function in the play was to listen to the people with long parts talk. And talk.

Then the doctor leaves, and my character, Kell, talks some more, to himself and an unseen entity he calls Little Bow-Wow. Neither the script nor its author was clear on who this was . . . God, the Devil, or Death, I decided. Anyway, I talk to Little Bow-Wow for

five minutes or so (maybe it was less, it seemed even longer). Then
I go over and take a coil of rope from a nail, and look speculatively
up at an overhead beam. Curtain.

"Larry," I said, "this'll never play. Something has to *happen*.
The rope has to be planted sooner. Let me use it somewhere." So I
did. At the beginning of the scene, I lowered a bale on a pulley (I
think this was where Rosie Harris left me), then tossed the rope
down while I talked to the doctor, and Little Bow-Wow, and myself.
When the doctor left, I took the rope and began building a hang-
man's noose. (Yes, that's another of the odd skills I've picked up,
pursuing my trade.) Having fashioned the noose and finished the
speech, I looked up, said "Here, Bow-Wow, *fetch!*" and tossed the
noose over the beam, leaving it swinging as the curtain fell. Yes, it
played.

The Boston opening wasn't bad. The critics there are used
to plays opening out-of-town shakedown cruises in their town, and
tend to cover such events as what the nonprofit theaters now call
"works in progress," which is certainly what we were. Lydia had
come east for it, bringing Fray, though he couldn't see the play and
I couldn't see much of him, because I was performing at night and
rehearsing the changes all day. We got to wrestle a bit in the suite
every morning, and I could read to him. On Sunday we built a
snowman in the Boston Common.

We'd planned Fray's fifth birthday carefully around my afternoon of rehearsal, but Olivier phoned me at 7 A.M. (On a film, that's
routine; with a play on the road, it's obscenely early.) I put on a
shirt and pants and went up to his suite barefoot, where I spent
the next seven hours with him and the producer, Alfred DeLiagre,
thrashing out the replacement of Hermione Baddeley.

This happens fairly often in a play, almost always on the
road, when you're reworking the script and the staging almost every
day. Actors are rarely fired on a film, because you must not only
replace the actor, but the work he's already done. This can be
horrendously costly.

On stage or screen, it's one of the nastier parts of the director's job; I was glad I only had to concur with the decision, along
with DeLiagre. Olivier was black with guilt: "Christ, what a bloody
fucking business this is! I acted with Toti when I was twenty. It's my
fault. I should've known." So he should have, no doubt. But we all

knew we had to recast, that day, if we could. We spent an hour or so discussing who was available, right for the part, and the best actress. Of a short list of maybe five on these counts, Martha Scott seemed clearly the cream. I'd worked with her before (she'd even played my wife before, as well as taking over on short notice as my mother on *Ben-Hur*). I could vouch for her absolutely, both as actress and pro. I did. We couldn't afford another mistake. "That's it, then," said Larry. "Call her agent."

Arrrghh!! "She's pregnant." Impossible, then. No, wait a minute, how pregnant? "Pregnant is pregnant, Laddie. Surely you've heard: she can't be a tiny bit pregnant." Well, of course she could, for our purposes. Lydia had played till she was four months pregnant with Fraser, part of the time on a national tour. We needed Martha in Boston that week, and opening in New York two weeks after that. After that could wait.

We got her. Trouper that she is, she was on the afternoon train from New York and sitting in the audience at 8 P.M. The hard part of that performance was after it was over. Olivier had the toughest chore: telling Toti she was fired. He did this in her dressing room, over a brandy he needed more than she did, he told me. I held Rosie and the doctor on stage after the curtain call and told them. They took it with the sad stoicism of the profession. Again, the military analogy holds: if the platoon takes casualties in a fire fight, you bind your wounds, regroup, and move on.

Ah, there was another actor on stage that night, though not for much longer. This is a small story, but this is the place for it. Toti Baddeley was a good actress who did her best in the wrong role. This young man played a postman, with a line or so. His real job was understudying me, the same job I'd had, ten years before, understudying another good actor in the wrong part, where I'd replaced him, also in Boston. Understudy is a crappy job, but the responsibility is enormous. If they need you, they *really* need you.

I hardly saw him. I supposed he was where he was paid to be: in the fifth row at every rehearsal, watching me, listening to everything Olivier said; in the audience every performance, memorizing my part and the way I did it. That's what I'd done, when I understudied, and what Martha was doing from the afternoon she got there. Till she learned it, we had no rehearsals, except for her solo sessions with Olivier. Toti soldiered on, playing several performances, until Martha was ready.

A day or so into this, with more free time than I'd had since I came east, I stopped by the theater to check my mail. Seeing that the stage manager had seized the empty stage to schedule an understudy rehearsal, I slipped into the back of the house to watch. I was horrified to see my understudy still carrying his script, six weeks into his job. I beckoned to the stage manager and said, "You finish your rehearsal for the other actors, if you like, but that young man is through in this company. I'll tell him myself, at half hour tonight. I'll tell Sir Laurence, too."

Olivier of course concurred, and as the director he wanted to handle it himself. "Larry, I have to do it," I said. "You'll scare the shit out of him, just by talking to him. I want to let him know what he's done." I tried to do that at the theater that night.

"You know how hard it is to get a job acting," I said to him. "I want you to know why you lost this one. You've been taking money under false pretenses for six weeks. They paid you to be ready to play this part if I get hit by a truck. You aren't ready, so you're of no use to us. I just did you a favor. I hope someday you'll figure that out."

I hope he has, whatever he's doing.

One week after she saw *The Tumbler* for the first time, Martha went on as my wife—an enormous feat of concentration and sheer hard work. What's more remarkable, she was damn good in it, and more right for the part, as well, which lifted the whole play. Olivier had worked intensively with her all week, of course, leaving Rosie and me on our own. Rosie was fine. I felt I was still . . . not treading water, but searching for bottom in a dark pool I'd never measured. Even now, thirty years and God knows how many parts later, I've never played a man I found so elusive.

After one of our last performances in Boston, Olivier appeared in my dressing room, bearing a bottle of thirty-year-old single malt. "This is not whiskey," he said. "This is the sword in the stone. Excalibur. Draw the cork when you have this part by the throat. You'll know." (I remember something Ken Tynan wrote years later about Olivier. "He played each of the great parts," he said, "until he won.")

That night in Boston, I remembered what Wyler had said to me twenty months earlier when he appeared in my dressing room when I was having trouble with Judah Ben-Hur: "You have to be better." I'd managed it then; I wasn't so sure with Kell in *Tumbler*. Olivier and I walked back across the Common to the hotel, talking technical trivialities about rehearsal schedules and so forth. When I got off the elevator at my floor, he held the door open. "I'm sure you can be a great actor, the only American in my time. You have the equipment. Don't give up on it." I don't know whether any of that is true. I never did give up.

And of course this paragraph should describe our triumph on Broadway a week later. It didn't happen. Martha was very good, so was Rosie; we even managed to cut some more of the text. There's no question: every aspect of the production was better. As Garson Kanin once observed in similar circumstances, though, "Better is not necessarily good." I never pulled the sword from the stone.

An hour into the opening night party on the second floor of Sardi's, our press agent took the phone call with *The New York Times* review: "Jesus, he said *that?* Ohh boy . . . no kidding. That bad, huh?" It was like pouring a bottle of ink into a bathtub—the party was down the drain in twenty minutes. I found myself sitting at a table with Olivier and a bottle of brandy in a more or less empty room. Striving for a note of detached nonchalance (I was still pretty green), I said, "Well, I suppose you learn to forget the bad notices." Larry leaned over and gripped my elbow, hard. "What's much harder, Laddie, and far more important: learn to forget the good ones." He was right, too. Dead right.

Doing your best the last few performances in a Broadway flop after your closing notice has been posted is not any actor's favorite experience, but it's a good moral exercise. Actually, it was interesting to explore that part a few more times with the pressure off and the dice already thrown. We played to fair-sized audiences, no doubt partly because *Ben-Hur* was selling out a three-thousand-seat theater twice a day four blocks away. Some of the people who came to see *The Tumbler* those last nights had never seen a play in their lives. (Of course, we may have persuaded them never to see one again, but still, it was a nice feeling.)

As the smoke cleared those last days, I began to focus on the rest of the world again. Herman the Iceman phoned from Los Angeles to announce that the Academy had nominated r... as Best Actor for my performance in *Ben-Hur* (good), and that he had to turn down an offer for me to costar in a film with Ca... ...rant "because of that play with Olivier" (bad).

227

In the Arena

Herman invariably viewed my stage undertakings ...concealed skepticism, on the firm ground that they didn't... much as movies, and weren't seen by as many people. He'd ... his teeth when I passed on the Monroe picture; I never tr... explain why, even as a failure, *Tumbler* was crucial for me. ... though it had never been possible, I was frustrated at missing ... turned out to be the only chance I ever had to work with ... Grant.

We should talk about the great male stars of the studio ... (No, I'm not forgetting the women, but there were fewer of the ... they had fewer good parts, and it worked differently.) The stud ... system that nourished them all was finished when I began making films, but the men all flourished as long as they lived, or chose to make movies. Gable, Cooper, Stewart, Tracy, Fonda, Astaire, Cagney, Bogart. Each man was unique, though each overlapped a little into the others' special ranges.

Of these, Cary Grant surely stood high among equals, among the most particularly admired of the great stars. One summer many years after he retired, I was doing a play in London, and thus invited to the dinner celebrating the two hundredth anniversary of the British-American alliance, at the American ambassador's residence, along with thirty or forty other identifiable citizens of both countries. As we gathered for coffee on the lawn afterward, I boasted to my wife that my dinner partner had been Prime Minister Margaret Thatcher. Lydia sniffed. "Hah! I sat next to Cary Grant." That says it all.

Grant explored adventure and suspense several times in movies like *Gunga Din* and *North by Northwest,* but he was without peer in films where he stood around in beautiful rooms wearing beautiful clothes and saying beautiful things to beautiful women. Had I been free, I'd have leapt at the chance to sweep up after him in *The Grass Is Greener*. Instead, whatever minor god presides over trivial agenda like actors' careers continued to push me into more onerous undertakings: painting ceilings for popes and running for

leading men on dubious and dangerous errands in every
rom before Christ to the twenty-fifth, often getting killed
rocess and seldom getting the girl . . . or losing her if I did.
uys have all the luck.

So This was certainly the time to do another film. I hadn't been
ont of a camera since *The Wreck of the Mary Deare* wrapped,
months before. I'd renewed my passport on the stage, in the
st possible company; now I was ready for a movie. (I'd have been
ad of the money, too, especially with my price jacked up by my
Academy nomination—I had a new house to pay for.) Unfortunately, the Screen Actors Guild had just declared the first strike in
its history, effectively shutting down production in the U.S. About
this time I got a firm offer to direct a film in Europe, a challenge I
wasn't quite ready for. I did have Herman send over the certified
check they'd offered as bona fide, just so I could hold it in my hand.
Two million dollars isn't much money as film salaries go these days,
but it was a real eye-catcher then.

So we stayed in New York for a week or two, enjoying the
town, something that's a lot harder to do there now. I took my girl
to the theater and to lunch, got in a little tennis and a lot of interviews on *Ben-Hur*.

I also gave Fray his first taste of Shakespeare (on a real stage,
I mean—I'd done some of the good bits boys like—"Once more
unto the breach, dear friends! Once more!!"—when we played
knights and castles). There was a highly regarded production of
Henry IV, Part 1 playing off-Broadway; I figured funny fat knights
and tavern brawls were just about right for a five-year-old.

Easing him into live theater, we did the first half one Saturday matinee, the second the following week. Fray loved it. "I like
dat fat Jack Fawstaff!" he proclaimed, after going backstage to meet
him. We played tavern brawls daily for a while, rolling around on
the floor shouting Elizabethan epithets at each other. I sometimes
failed to do this with proper gusto. "You hafta lift me *up* dere,
Daddy!" he admonished one day. "UP!! Y-R-O-P-D, *UP!* I say dat
because I can't spell, of course."

We went home to L.A. then, because I wanted to be home,
and also because MGM desperately wanted me to attend yet another
Ben-Hur premiere, in Tokyo. God knows the picture was well and

truly launched; my presence at the Tokyo opening was hardly crucial.

Except, it turned out, for the protocol of the thing. The
emperor of Japan was coming, with the empress and the crown
prince. This, apparently, had galvanized everyone in Japan. The
emperor, literally a god to his people until their surrender in World
War II, had never before attended an event outside the palace, or
one that was open to the general public. He had never even set foot
on the Ginza, Tokyo's Broadway. Lydia and I *had* to be there. We
were happy to go along with that.

It was quite an experience. The Japanese are extremely good
at public relations; no detail of the trip was overlooked. The great
Japanese actor Toshiro Mifune, though we had never met, hosted a
small geisha party for me. (We've exchanged Christmas cards ever
since.) Photographers in regimental strength trailed me everywhere
but the toilet; we were feted, interviewed, and honored on a more
or less hourly basis.

I also learned to treasure the Japanese film fan. Perhaps
more courteous than those of any other nation, they write fervent
notes, often in English, and present gilt-edged, foot-square card-
boards for your signature at every turn. Easiest way to sign autographs I ever found. They also go to movies—a lot, especially mine,
I'm relieved to say.

The premiere itself was meticulously planned. The theater
had been redecorated, inside and out, new projectors had been
installed for the 70mm print of the film, the ushers had been specially drilled. Oddly, I could get no protocol instructions for meeting the emperor. "No foreign artist has ever been introduced to
him before," they said. "Just follow his lead."

The imperial party arrived in a black Rolls, driving up a
shallow flight of steps to the theater entrance. When they'd entered
the lobby, a palace official presented us. Still clueless as to protocol,
Lydia and I stepped forward and bowed, whereupon the emperor
nodded, then, to a constellation of flashbulbs, shook hands.

The rest of the audience was already in place; I escorted the
royals to their seats and went to the back of the theater. By this
time, having attended maybe a dozen openings of the film, I'd take
part in whatever opening ceremonies were scheduled, move to the

back of the house as the lights went down, watch the first reel to read the audience reaction, then slip out for dinner, coming back in time for whatever was planned after the film.

The imperial premiere went a little differently. The film broke three times in the first ten minutes. The audience remained silent, doubtless following the emperor's example. He sat impassive, never stirring while the film was spliced and rethreaded.

Jim Castle, head of MGM distribution for the Far East, was not impassive. On the third break, white with fury, he charged upstairs toward the projection booth, clearly bent on murder (at least). I followed, anxious to avoid an international incident, but Jim paused in mid-stride as the projection booth door opened and the Japanese projectionist staggered out, corpse-pale. "Nuthin' I can say to him will make him feel worse than he already does," Jim observed bleakly.

The rest of the screening was flawless. The projectionist, awed by the physical presence of Hirohito, the God-Emperor, had over-tightened the tension on the take-up reel. The next day, the presidents of the projectionists' union and of the company owning the theater, and MGM's top Japanese official, visited the palace to present their personal apologies to the emperor. I was told that in prewar days, they would all have felt bound to commit hari-kari. Happily, no blood was shed over our Japanese premiere.

We got back to Los Angeles just in time for the Academy Awards, neatly avoiding most of the pre-Oscar interviews. "Well, Chuck, how do you rate your chances for Best Actor?" What are you supposed to say? "Actually, I didn't really like what I did with the part; I hope no one votes for me." Or "Mine is so clearly the best performance I'm surprised they sent out the ballots."

We need a How It Really Is in the Movies note here about the Academy Awards. The Academy itself, one of the oldest organizations in Hollywood, functioning superbly over a wide agenda for most of the century in its devotion to film as an art form, is known to the public at large only as the guys who put on the Oscars.

A billion and some people around the world tune in the Awards annually. It's the most widely watched event on earth, eclipsing space missions, small wars, and off-year elections. (Lydia and I were flown to Buenos Aires a few years ago to present a relatively minor Oscar in a beautiful nineteenth-century opera

house there. Our time on the worldwide telecast was about four
minutes. Nevertheless, the elite of Buenos Aires filled three thousand seats in full dress over lobster and vintage champagne to watch
us do it.)

Given all this, it's not surprising that the media film mavens
devote acres of newsprint and weeks of TV and radio time pre-
dicting and post-morteming the event. Their coverage is laced with
irritated disdain, stemming from their deep conviction that they
should be running it. In their hearts, they believe that the dozens
of critic's awards and film festival anointings of political correctness
should somehow be collated into the world seal of approval the
Academy Awards have become.

Mind you, no serious filmmaker suggests that the Academy
choices actually represent some abstract standard of excellence, or
that the winners gave the best performance, wrote the best screenplay, made the best film. There are too many irrelevant factors
involved.

As random examples of things that shouldn't count, but do,
films are seldom nominated unless they've had considerable commercial success. Obviously, failed films don't stay in theaters long
enough to be seen by Academy members (though in recent years
members are sent dozens of videos of possible nominees). November and December releases are considered to have better chances
of nominations; comedies and musicals (the latter an almost extinct
film form anyway) seldom get the nod. Hugely successful filmmakers are often snubbed; witness Spielberg in this era, DeMille in the
studio era, each finally recognized. Then, as now, exceptions can
be found. Nonetheless, Academy voters tend to be drawn to the
medium-sized, meticulously crafted film with an appropriate social
message and at least one outstanding performance.

On an individual level (performers, directors, writers, not
technicians), other personal factors sometimes come into play: political correctness counts again, so does voter perception that someone was inappropriately denied an award a year or so previously,
even if the current work is not of comparable quality.

For actors, the record shows that playing someone who's
handicapped, physically or mentally, gives you an enormous advantage with Academy voters. Since 1932, when Fredric March won
Best Actor for his performance as the psychotic Jekyll/Hyde, and

was later nominated for his role as an alcoholic film star in *A Star Is Born* (as was James Mason later in the very same part), some fifty performers have been nominated for playing handicapped people, often winning.

If the performer is disabled in real life, the advantage is definitive. Of the several so nominated, beginning with Harold Russell in *The Best Years of Our Lives,* all have won.

If there's a lesson there, I guess it's that actors should keep an eye out for those parts—crazies, dummies, and drunks in particular. A certain sympathy vote can also be earned by, in real life, recovering from or continuing to fight a serious illness. Dying is no good—that eliminates you from consideration.

All this having been said, the Academy choices almost always go to very good work. The votes are cast by filmmakers, obviously better qualified to judge film than anyone else, just as NFL players can choose a better All Pro team than sportswriters. As has been said before, the nominations are by themselves the most reliable mark of good work. They are voted only by those members in the same branch of the Academy. Only actors nominate actors, only cameramen vote on Best Cinematography, only directors on Best Directing. The approval of your peers is what we all value most. If you're nominated for Best Actor, that means other actors liked what you did. All of us would rather have that opinion than the best notice or festival prize ever crafted.

Another of not many problems with the Awards is the show itself. It is a very long night. If you're presenting, you can whip downtown in time for your segment, then slip out again (though I almost failed to arrive on time one embarrassing year, when Clint Eastwood actually began my speech, with me leaping on behind him barely in time to take over). If nominated, you have to climb into black tie in the afternoon and show up in broad daylight for the fans in the bleachers and the walk-in interviews, then sit for some five hours to find out if you've won or lost. In addition, as well as long, the show is not really very good, as critics point out annually. It can't be, with dozens of categories to work through.

That's why I once turned down the Academy's offer to produce the show. "You can't make it a good *show,*" I said. "That's not why people watch it. It's like the Kentucky Derby. People watch to see who wins." Nonetheless, they surely do watch.

One of my warmest memories of Oscar night 1960 is Jimmy Stewart. He was nominated for Best Actor as well, for one of his better performances, in *Anatomy of a Murder*. As it happened, we both arrived in the lobby at the same time. The media were delighted to have two nominees at once. We had to pose together, congratulating one another and so on and so on. As the flashbulbs finally petered out and we turned to go in to our seats, Jimmy took my arm. "I hope you win, Chuck," he said. "I really mean that." He did, too. I don't know another actor alive who would've said such a thing. He's an extraordinary man.

Several hours later, as Susan Hayward reached for the envelope announcing the Best Actor award, I had an odd experience. I glanced to my left, at a chandelier on the other side of the hall, and felt an almost audible click. I've won, I thought, then sat with perfect equanimity until Susan read my name. I kissed Lydia and strode to the podium.

My speech was mercifully brief. I thanked William Wyler and Christopher Fry, infuriating the Writers Guild, since they had refused to allow MGM to give Fry any screen credit whatsoever for his sterling work on the script all through the shoot. The Writers' Branch of the Academy had voted a nomination for Best Screenplay to Karl Tunberg, who'd done the first script, before Wyler ever came on the picture. This made twelve nominations for *Ben-Hur*. The picture and those who made it actually won eleven awards— more than any other film has earned. The Academy voters, aware that the Writers Guild had unfairly denied any credit for Christopher Fry, refused to give the Best Screenplay award to *Ben-Hur*. Still, eleven out of twelve's not bad . . . more than any film has ever won, or is likely to again.

Of course we celebrated, moving from party to party all night long. Though I drank, I'm afraid, more or less steadily till we got home at dawn and sat on the front steps to savor the *L.A. Times'* front page, I was stone cold sober. Somewhere in the evening, I'd shared congratulations with Wyler, holding the fourth Oscar of his career. "I guess this is pretty old hat to you, Willy," I said. He grinned at me. "Chuck," he said, "this never gets old."

13

Star

Twinkle, twinkle, little star
How I wonder what you are.

"STAR" IS A PRETTY WORD, but I don't like the label, though it's been my job description for most of my life. "Superstar" is even worse. In the beginning, what I had in mind was "working actor." Yeah, I know—it got out of hand.

Look, I have no complaints. It built my house, put my kids through school, and gave me the key choices in my work, usually what part I play and with whom. Often I'm part of the project from the start, always I have a lot of control over how it's done. It's just about exactly what any actor could want.

So what itch am I trying to scratch here? Guilt over the privilege that cushions my life? Hell, no. The corporations I work for earn hundreds of times the money they pay me; my piece of their gross income is a toy boat bobbing in the wake of their flood tides. But I get to *do* the work.

I can focus on that because other people—very good people —lay out the complicated logistics of my life: tickets, reservations, schedules, names and numbers. When I climb in the car at 6 A.M., I may not know where we're going, but I don't get there late, or get sick, or blow lines. I'm supposed to know more about the piece I'm acting or directing than anyone else, *and* be there earlier and longer . . . just because I'm supposed to.

By the sixties, I'd learned the ground rules of celebrity. (Wait
a minute . . . if there's one trade with no rules, it's celebrity. Even
skipping the subgroup of those well-known simply for being well-
known, there are A-list celebrities who are certified monsters and a
lot more who are public nincompoops. So forget rules.) I guess
what I meant is that I'd learned the rules according to me.

I'm not crazy about a lot of it, mind you. The ego massage is
nice, also the plane tickets and restaurant tables and theater passes.
Free stuff is good, especially if you were raised in the Depression.

Even better, sometimes people say and write things that
make you know they understand what you're trying to do with a
part. The casual one-on-one contacts in the street in Youngstown or
Barcelona can also be truly touching (though I could do without
those bloody little instant cameras—I cringe when I think of the
millions of lousy photographs of me curling in bureau drawers all
over the world).

I would be glad to have a little more elbow room. For an
actor, that's hard to find. But an artist needs time alone. Creating
art, like creating life, is essentially a private experience. Making
films or plays is inescapably a collective undertaking, and many of
the people who do it are designated public property. Still, you need
time alone, all by yourself. As a guy brought up in the Michigan
woods, I *really* need it.

No, I'm not bitching, but that's why I love my ridge so much.
There are a couple of hundred acres of canyon around me still
close to the way God made them. Most of the people I want to see,
the things I want to do, happen right here. Pool, tennis court, Ja-
cuzzi, gym, library, screening room—I've done TV interviews by
satellite from here, linking me to London, live. The only time I
really have to leave is for a very serious meeting (that's with New
York lawyers included, when you have to wear a suit and tie to
show what a significant fellow you are), or when you're actually
doing the work . . . a film or a play. I like that.

I said just now that I learned early how to be a celebrity.
True enough, but I don't think I've ever been a really satisfactory
movie star, the persona that, unavoidably, has defined my life and
most of my work. I never travel with an entourage, and I'm not
much on parties (of course, I go to the fund-raisers that stud everyone's calendar out here—that's part of the work). I'm too square

for Hollywood and I don't display enough public anguish, or proper care for political correctness. Fortunately, people go to my films and plays in sufficient numbers to keep the franchise valid, even though I keep changing nationalities and centuries. I have no complaints; I'm grateful they keep coming.

All that aside, I'm inadequately equipped as a genuine, chrome-plated *STAR*. For that, you must be willing to put up a bigger stake, launch into hyperspace, leap into the maelstrom, even, finally, crash in flames. You offer not only your talent, you have to risk *yourself*. There's a dark side to the public's love for the famously gifted . . . an unsigned contract you may find yourself bound by. The great Spanish matador Manolete said it: "In the end, they will only be satisfied when I am killed." And they killed him. Yes, the bulls did that, not the public . . . but the contract was drawn up long before. In a curious way, his death did satisfy them.

They can make you a living god, but they may ask your life in return. While you dance on the edge of the abyss, they'll forgive you anything, applaud your worst excess, laugh at your most obscene folly. Like Babe Ruth, James Dean, Judy Garland, Janis Joplin, Elvis Presley, Marilyn Monroe, Muhammad Ali, you can do *anything*, but in the end, the unspoken bargain is that you have to pay the bill. You will lie naked and broken in the rainy mud, while they stand on the bank, survivors, looking down at you.

No, I hadn't figured all this out by the spring of 1960, but it was beginning to sink in. After *Ben-Hur* won all the Oscars, I did understand that my situation had altered, radically. I could now not only pick my shots, to a large extent I could control them.

But not just then. The Screen Actors Guild was still on strike, so nobody was going to make any pictures for a while. SAG is all but unique among labor unions. Though by big labor standards we're a tiny union, we can shut down an industry without mounting a picket line. On the rare occasions when we've struck, we've always picketed a studio or two, but it's just for theatrical effect. If the actors don't show up, you don't make movies.

Since I wasn't allowed to make any movies, I was glad to accept SAG's offer to join their board. I was already a member, as I was required to be, of three performing unions, and had helped found a fourth, which represented actors in live TV, and was

promptly absorbed by one of the older groups. Besides, my early
success as an actor imposed, I felt, a certain duty on me.

In those days, the SAG Board was largely made up of very
well-known actors, who were invulnerable to studio pressures in
negotiation. Since then, it's become almost impossible to persuade
stars to be active in Guild affairs; why, I have no idea. In 1960, there
were several. President Ronald Reagan (only of the Guild, then, not
the U.S.) had led SAG longer than anyone else, and was about to
resign and devote his time to larger issues.

He had agreed, however, to lead us through the first strike
in our history. He appointed me to the Negotiating Committee
responsible for winning a new contract from the studios, under the
pressure of a union's strongest weapon: withholding services.

Public service—pursuing a group agenda for a common
goal—was a new experience for me, unless you count World War II.
I did my best. I was certainly used to being a public man by then,
and I wasn't a bad debater. I began to realize, though, that grinding
the other side down in argument isn't really the best tactic, though
a lot of union negotiations are still carried on that way. The old
Marxist dialectic of the employer as the enemy is painfully out of
date. What you want is the common good. For that, you have to find
common ground.

Reagan was very good at that. He could rally the members
in the board meetings wonderfully, but his real skills were in the
actual negotiations. He was patient, persistent, moderate, and above
all, good-humored, even at three in the morning, going back into
caucus to review the same ground yet again.

The dark part of the night is a naked time. Unshaven, no coat
or tie, stocking feet up on a desk, keeping awake with cold coffee
while you wait for the other side to come back in the room; you
get a pretty clear view of a guy. I saw Ronald Reagan clear in those
hours. I remember coming home past four one morning, Lydia
waking as I fell into bed. "How did it go?" she asked.

"Pretty slow work," I answered. "But I do believe we've got
a leader."

We did, indeed. In the end, we won what we wanted, what
the membership desperately needed. In that one negotiation, we
established pension and medical plans funded by the studios, then

a new concept in union contracts, as well as fees to be paid to actors when their work was rerun on TV. It broke new ground in labor negotiation, setting models sought by other unions to this day. In plain fact, it remains the best contract SAG ever negotiated. I'm very proud to have played a small role in getting it.

For the past generation, SAG's leadership has leaned increasingly leftward. They've radically revised the Guild's history, most particularly Reagan's presidency. No one, of course, questions the landmark importance of the 1960 contract, just how it happened. I was there. The contract would not have been possible if Reagan hadn't been Guild president.

AFTER PLAYING A BIT PART in getting us all to where we could make movies again, I thought it would be nice to make one myself. I hadn't faced a camera, or walked a stage either, for five months; my acting genes were beginning to itch. Not to mention my work ethic. Post-Oscar is about as hot as an actor can get; scripts had been piling up on my reading stack even during the SAG strike, though none had excited me much. Now it was time to pick one.

I'd spent several frustrating weeks dancing with Orson Welles, who'd called me at the Guild late one night in the midst of negotiations. "Chuck!" he boomed, with the infectious enthusiasm he could summon so readily. "Have you brought the bastards to their knees yet?!"

"Not quite," I said guardedly. "To the table is more like it."

"Well, finish it up and get back to the work God made you for. CBS wants me to film *Julius Caesar* for them. Which part do you want to play?"

He knew his man, of course. I'll listen to anyone who wants me to play Shakespeare. "Antony, who else? It's the best part."

"Also the easiest, you coward. Can't I persuade you to try Brutus?" No, he couldn't, but I was happy to come on board the project. Over the next month or so we went through a tortuous chronology. Richard Burton was supposed to play Brutus, a dazzling list of good actors were reported as committed; some no doubt in fact were. Lydia was to play Portia, we were going to shoot in Rome, no, in London, no, probably New York. In all this time, I never actually saw Orson, though he phoned me from several continents. Herman the Iceman remained highly skeptical of all this, as he

tended to be of such undertakings, though he negotiated my deal
with CBS, as instructed.

In the end, Herman was right. I have no idea what brought
it down; perhaps Orson's penchant for maneuvering each project
to suit his instinct of the moment, or his need. Anyway, CBS finally
threw in their hand, which was the one with the money in it, of
course.

Meantime, the new scripts on my stack included one based
on a man I'd barely heard of: Rodrigo Diaz de Bivar, the Cid, the
medieval Spanish hero who had fought against the Moors. The
script itself wasn't good, ranging from minimally OK to crappy. But
it was about a remarkable man. Rodrigo of Bivar had actually lived,
and made a mark in his time that had lasted a thousand years. I've
always been attracted to films about real people. I saw an opportunity here, not least because whatever film I made, I'd have a lot to
say about how we made it.

The creative opinions of any actor of reputation and experience should be useful; God knows they're heard. To establish this
as a contractual right is a stickier business. Herman the Iceman was
superb at defining and achieving this. It meant, at the very least,
approval of the script and the casting of the major roles. If the
director's not been set, you have de facto approval there, too. If he
is set, and you have misgivings, you can pass on the project. In all
of this, the ambivalent language of contracts points out "approval
may not be unreasonably withheld."

The catch, of course, is defining "unreasonably." I know
what it means, and so does Steven Spielberg and most everybody
else, but a twenty-year-old actor coming off one hit film can think it
"reasonable" to fire a cameraman who's won four Academy Awards
because he was insufficiently deferential. In reality, the only total
creative control is vested finally in the guys who put up the money.
They own the movie. Still, to have a strong hand in the creative
choices in the work you do is crucial.

I began to learn how to do this in the summer of 1960.
Samuel Bronston had appeared on the scene with that rarest of all
things, a new idea. Why not finance the production of films by
getting advance commitments from the theater chains around the
world that would then release them? It was a valid concept and
carried him triumphantly through a number of films. It did depend

on two crucial elements: first, he had to offer distributors movies they would commit money to before a foot of film was shot, and second, each movie had to succeed, to justify investment in the next.

I was intrigued by Sam's daring, if not by his script. He persuaded me to fly to Madrid, where he was headquartered, to discuss *El Cid*. Somewhat dubiously, I agreed. It was a little like a hot high-school quarterback visiting a university campus to be persuaded what a great place it was to play football, except that I was a lot older and a little wiser—I hoped.

When I landed at Barajas Airport, Sam was standing on the tarmac at the foot of the jetstair, an impressively silver-haired, beautifully tailored figure. Equally impressive was the immigration and customs clearance he'd arranged. (It was a little easier in those days.) My bags were off-loaded directly into the trunk of his Rolls, and we whirled away to the best suite in one of Madrid's grandest hotels.

Sam's agenda was to make him, his company, Spain, and, above all, *El Cid* so attractive I couldn't resist. The easy part was the country itself. It was my first visit there; it seemed to me, and still does, just as Hemingway described it so tellingly. The Spanish are wonderful—vividly alive, vibrantly proud, with a steely sense of responsibility. They make rock-solid friends and, I suspect, awesome enemies, though I've yet to explore that particular relationship.

Sam himself was a very likable man, well equipped with the arcane skills that make a successful studio head. He was not himself a filmmaker, but he seemed honestly committed to making good films, which he was to find as hard to bring off as everyone else does. He'd spread an awesome amount of money around hiring people he thought could do this.

Among these was Phil Yordan, with respectable credits as both writer and producer. He was an extraordinary storyteller, which meant he was a master of "The Pitch." This is a crucial element in making films, since many of the decision-makers in the industry don't actually *read* scripts. (Some are suspected of being in fact unable to read, but I doubt this is true.)

The pitch is what the filmmaker with a project tells the people who have the money to persuade them to give him some to make his movie. Nowadays, studios are drawn to what they call "high-concept films," which are films that can be described in one sentence, like "Arnold Schwarzenegger and Danny DeVito are twin brothers." This method appeals to busy executives, of course. The pitcher stands before the pitchee, leans over, looks him in the eye, and says, "Macaulay Culkin is married to Julia Roberts."

Phil Yordan, pitching to me, did very well. He agreed with my misgivings about the *El Cid* script, and proceeded to improvise a far better one (which of course had not been written yet). There were rumors that Phil kept a couple of young writers chained to the radiator in his office, typing away ten hours a day, but I never believed that.

Sam had another ace to play: his production designers, Colasanti and Moore. As far as I know, they were the only design team in films who did both sets and costumes—clearly a good idea. They showed me their costume designs and the sketches for the eleventh-century interiors planned (the exteriors, of course, would be the real castles of Spain). It all looked impressive, as indeed it proved to be in the film.

I met the director, Tony Mann, who was tough and experienced, with some excellent credits, including a couple of Jimmy Stewart's best Westerns. He'd never undertaken anything on the complex historical canvas *El Cid* required, but he seemed perfectly confident. When I asked him who would handle the second unit for the battle scenes, he played his ace: "Yakima Canutt. This'll be the first picture he's accepted since *Ben-Hur*." That made one thing certain—the action scenes would be world-class. The rest of the film remained an open question. I thanked Sam for his elaborate hospitality, but made him no promises—except to read the new script.

Still, I climbed on the jet back to L.A. leaving part of my mind still in Spain, looking for the eleventh century. When I got home, a formidable carton of books was waiting on the floor of my den. Sam had found out about my penchant for period research and provided me with plenty of food for thought. This was clever of him, since the new script would take some weeks of work. Meantime, I could try to find the Cid, and his century.

I'd liked history in school, but always slid through to the easy B, not digging at it. When I first undertook real research, preparing parts, I began to realize what I'm now convinced is true: history is not only the most important subject; in the end it may be the only subject.

For Rodrigo de Bivar, the principal source material is *El Cantor del Mio Cid,* written two centuries after his death. Though it doesn't survive in complete form, it's marvelous; one of the masterpieces of the Middle Ages, the finest piece of Spanish writing until Cervantes.

In it I found the man I was looking for, a man I felt I could play. Some modern historians, trying to clear the cloud of Arthurian legend that obscures him, have cast the Cid simply as a ruthless mercenary. Certainly they were endemic in Europe a few centuries later, the Italian *condotieri,* the Spanish *conquistadores* who conquered South America. However politically correct that may be, I don't think it's a realistic view of the Cid.

Even if we strip away a thousand years of mythic excess, history still gives us a battered, striving man, stubbornly loyal to the king who exiled him and imprisoned his wife and daughters. I came to see Rodrigo as a biblical Job figure, defiant and enduring.

Phil Yordan sent forty pages of rewrite. They were an improvement over the first draft I'd read, but I remembered Gar Kanin's iron maxim: "Better is not necessarily good." On the other hand, unlike a painter or a novelist, an actor can only work if someone offers him a part. Of the several dozen submissions I'd read, the only other one I liked at all was about the assassination of Trotsky, and the financing on that looked shaky. (Richard Burton did it a decade later, without much success.)

I was the one who'd insisted on the rewrite. I wasn't going to get it sitting on my ass in California, Achilles sulking in his tent. I told Herman to close the deal so I could suit up for the game. Two weeks later, we sailed from New York on the *Leonardo da Vinci.*

For a man looking at six months of hard work, all of which might end in failure, there's nothing like a week at sea in one of the old transatlantic liners. Knowing the physical demands *El Cid* would make on me, I spent a lot of time in the ship's gym, and a lot more working on the script. I wrote in my journal, "It's sometimes very reviving to live exactly the same day, several times over. It feels as if the world's on hold, waiting for me to catch up."

Fray was alert to all this. One day out, after an exhilarating half-hour going down the water slide in the ship's pool, he endorsed the voyage. "I *like* dis ship, Daddy. You have no phone calls here, an' no rehearsals . . . jus' da captain's cocktail party!" There are complications to being five, though. Lying on my chest one evening on the boat deck, watching the sun set over the wake astern, he observed comfortably, "You wouldn' give me up for alla gold inna world, would you?" Reassured on this point, he thought a moment. "Boy . . . sometimes I'd sell *you* for a hunnert dollars." (Not a bad price, actually.)

Mischa Waszynski, Sam Bronston's Number Two, met the ship at Gibraltar, dispatched our considerable luggage north to Madrid by van, and escorted us by car. Mike was a man of infinite charm and exotic background, a great deal of it invented by himself. He was Polish, of noble blood (he claimed), and a considerable talent, primarily for survival. To have lived through the war in Poland and achieved a respectable list of European film credits afterward speaks to that.

We stopped overnight in Granada on our way to Madrid. We were planning to shoot there, and I wanted a look at the Moorish roots in a city that had been significant to the Cid's world. I saw the Alhambra and, to my surprise, Orson Welles. We had a fine evening; as it happened, so did Fray. He stayed in the suite in the company of Orson's daughter, a striking child with whom Fray instantly fell in love. It was reported that he expressed his passion by chasing her around the furniture with a toy cutlass and eventually cornering her in a closet and kissing her. Perhaps it was his early exposure to the wicked ways of Hollywood, or the beauty of Beatrice Welles.

Once in Madrid, my soft time ended. We checked into the Castellana Hilton while they looked for a place for us to live. (On a long shoot, even the most commodious hotel suite becomes claustrophobic. Still, my journal records that they gave us this suite for $38 U.S., a day. Does that boggle your mind?) They soon found a large, comfortable apartment twenty minutes from Chamartin Studio, where we'd be doing our interiors.

The next weeks, before shooting began, were more crucial to the success of *El Cid* than the actual filming. The rewrite on the script I'd insisted on had to be done before the cameras turned.

(You keep fine-tuning all through production, but it gets dicey once you have film in the can.) At least as important, we had to set the major casting, primarily the Cid's wife, Chimene.

From the beginning, Sophia Loren was the first, perhaps in retrospect the only choice. That's what Sam said on my summer trip to Spain when he was wooing me. Her best work was still ahead of her, but she'd already become an international star. That's a small constellation, consisting almost entirely of Americans and Brits. Especially for a woman, it's a tough club to crack, double-tough if English is not your native language.

Not the least of Sophia's qualifications was her spectacular beauty, blended with a rich, Italianate sensuality. Never having met her, I ran some of her recent films, all shot in English. Her chemistry was undeniably world-class, and essentially European; the camera loved her, no question. Besides, she would be playing a titled Spanish lady; the learned, faintly accented precision of her English would be appropriate. Many fine American actresses can't comfortably inhabit another nationality, let alone the eleventh century. I endorsed the casting absolutely.

Casting the other male roles was easy; we chose English actors for almost every role. It's hard to go wrong doing that. Pound for pound, English actors seem to be the best at playing anything but Americans, and some of them can do that, too, as they show us from time to time. In film, we have our Brandos and De Niros, but they are balanced, surely, by the British knights and their heirs. Further down the casting scale, you can choose among half a dozen fine Brits for almost any part. So we did in *El Cid,* with great success.

The excellent Italian actor Raf Vallone was a notable exception to that rule. Orson was also approached to play the fierce leader of the Muslim host, Ben Yussef, whose face is veiled in all but his last shot. Orson was amenable, but his thought was to let a double do the on-camera performance, while he provided the dialogue later, in postproduction. I was drawn to the idea—Orson could do a great deal with just his voice—but Sam would have none of it.

The only other woman in the film, the icy Princess/Queen Urraca, was a key casting. I looked at tests of three or four actresses of various capacities, but the final choice was undeniable: the

French actress Genevieve Page. She proved superb in the part;
wonderfully gifted and a fine woman to boot.

Our mid-November start date was closing in, and we still
didn't have a script I was happy with. Neither was Sophia, which
meant we didn't have her, either. I was working on the script in
Madrid with Tony Mann, Phil Yordan, and a new writer he'd
brought on, Ben Barsman. The revised scenes were flown to Sophia, waiting in Italy, where she had still another writer translate
them into Italian. From time to time, Phil would go himself, to
reassure her that the changes were indeed improvements. They
were. Undeniably, the script was coming together.

Working on any period script, you have to do your homework, as I'd learned long before. If you're playing an actual historical figure, you should know more about him than anyone else on
the film. (It also gives you a clear edge in script meetings.) Undertaking some rudimentary research in California, I'd found that the
outstanding authority on the Cid, Juan Menendez Pidal, was living
in Madrid. I asked Sam's people to arrange a meeting.

The response was an invitation to lunch at his home. Dr.
Pidal was then in his nineties, but he clearly realized that our film
would provide the permanent public impression of the man to
whom he had devoted much of his life. He knew the power of
film; he wanted to do his best to make sure we got it right. That
suited me.

Dr. Pidal lived in a very small house in the suburbs of Madrid, near the University. I got out of the car half a block away and
walked to the house, anxious to avoid the Hollywood image. The
door was jerked open by a stooped old man in a stained black
jacket who looked at me sourly and said *"Venga!"*, turning away. I
followed, bracing for a difficult meeting, and was vastly relieved
when Dr. Pidal stepped out of his study and I realized I'd been met
by his houseman, probably grumpy at having to prepare lunch for
two.

It's surprising how often people are well cast for their roles
in life. Dr. Pidal was exactly as I would have wished him to be. A
trimmed white beard, clear black eyes, and a blazingly vigorous
mind. I don't remember what we had for lunch, but I'll never forget
the fervor with which he led me through his subject. My Spanish is

not very good, and he had little English. Fortunately, he spoke in the accent of Valladolid, which is very clear and easy for foreigners to follow. Happily, he also accepted the handle I'd chosen to play the Cid . . . as a biblical Job, resisting, enduring.

Pidal was also a wonderfully typical scholar in that his tiny house was bursting with books. I mean that every flat surface I saw, including the end of the table we lunched at, was filled with books. When I went upstairs to his bathroom before I left, the treads of the stair had books on either end, as did the tank of the toilet. When I left, he gave me, of course, several books. It was a rich afternoon.

Meanwhile, Yakima Canutt was spending the same kind of energy trying to cast Babieca, the Cid's legendary horse, a task almost as complex as casting actors, though much cheaper. We really needed two horses, so they could be rotated through the long workdays. (Why don't they ever do that for actors?) Yak finally found two nearly identical white studs in Portugal. They were duly imported and housed at the large stable by the Manzanares River where Yak was preparing his second unit. I worked with them daily, riding along the river past the Gypsy camps. They were wonderful animals, with a sensual male beauty matched only by naked women and sleeping babies. Fractious, of course, but soft-mouthed, for studs; a delight to ride, once we'd come to terms with each other. (Yak reminded me, "Any horse is stronger'n any man. Thing is, they don't know that. Y'can't ever let 'em find out.")

I think, with me on their backs, both Babiecas suspected that truth. Still, some of my happiest memories of that whole shoot were riding them along the river with the November mists still curling on the water, too early in the morning for there to be anything else I should be doing.

Then we began working on the mounted broadsword combat laced throughout the script, first simply getting the horses used to having swords swung past their heads. This is not an easy task. Horses are creatures of small brain and deep anxieties about anything new. This includes sharp objects, particularly with stallions, who tend to have passionate reactions to almost everything.

Babiecas I and II gradually came to accept my galloping them back and forth through milling horsemen yelling and slashing around with swords, as long as *they* weren't hit with anything, especially by me. The available record indicates that when cavalry was a

prime weapon of war, the horses actually enjoyed battle; by the
time we filmed, my two white studs certainly relished movie war,
which was my position, too.

In the weeks I spent honing my horsebacking, I picked up
another gem of equestrian wisdom from Yak. We were to have the
use of a full regiment of Spanish cavalry and two or three hundred
mounted police for the big battle at the end of the film; Yak had
also imported some world-class American and English stuntmen to
do the tough stuff, including his son, Joe, from *Ben-Hur.* One morning Yak was choosing twenty or thirty horsemen to be used as
background riders, out of a crowd of more than a hundred applicants.

Each man was to mount, gallop around the large corral, and
dismount. I watched this audition while I was waiting for Babieca II
to be saddled. Yak was his usual laconic self, saying little, but often
crossing off a name seconds after the rider had started. "I suppose
you can tell how well they ride before they've gone very far," I said.

Yak spat tobacco juice in the dust. "I c'n tell if they can ride
a'tall by the time they put a toe in the stirrup." I don't doubt he
could.

I usually rode in the morning, sometimes bringing Fray
along. (Five-year-old boys get up early, too.) He seemed very happy
sitting on a fence rail watching me practice swordplay with one of
the studs for half an hour, then climbing in front of me on the
saddle for a light canter along the Manzanares, with the Gypsy
women looking up from their laundry in the shallows, watching us
ghosting by on that lovely horse, my boy's head against my chest. I
remember it well . . . "The smell of my son is as the smell of a field
which the Lord hath planted." The Gypsies are gone now.

If I had interviews or a session on the script scheduled, I'd
drop off at the studio while the car took Fray home. If not, he'd tag
along for my daily fencing workout, preparing for the sword combat in the film. I'd fenced a little at Northwestern, but Yak was
aiming for the ultimate. As with the chariot race in *Ben-Hur,* he was
determined to make the combat scenes in *El Cid* the best that had
ever been filmed. He came pretty close.

At least I wasn't starting from ground zero, as when I'd
learned to drive a chariot. For the sword work in *El Cid,* Yak had
engaged another man of formidable abilities: Enzo Musemuci

Greco. Enzo's record as an Olympic fencer and his experience training actors for make-believe combats was awesome. He was a quiet man of modest demeanor, but with the legs of a leopard and a forged-steel wrist. Parrying his sword-thrust was like deflecting a train.

I put in a solid hour a day with Enzo in one of the training rooms of the soccer team Real Madrid, then world champions. Their stadium was a gigantic facility dwarfing any in America, only a block or two from our apartment. I could jog home and into a hot bath afterward before the sweat dried.

As with the *Ben-Hur* chariot, I had to crowd in as much training as I could; once shooting starts there's no time for practice. Enzo drove me mercilessly in the weeks we had, working on my shabby technique, drilling me on the fight choreographies he and Yak had designed. My fencing improved markedly and I lost six pounds I'd put on doing the *Ben-Hur* premieres. Both of these are important for an actor; fencing is a useful skill, and a flat gut counts too.

On November 12, Sophia flew in from Rome, in a very public arrival. Hank Werba, Bronston's canny publicity chief, saw to that. Sophia was first off the plane, looking absolutely magnificent; I waited with flowers at the foot of the jetstair as she descended. Though we'd never met, we embraced, and the large Spanish crowd screamed a welcome. There was no band, but with Sophia, we didn't need one. We had our lady; we were ready.

Two days later we began. Officially, that is. The scheduled scene was the first in the script between Sophia and me, in a marvelous circular-columned hall John Moore had designed. His partner, Veniero Colasanti, had done equally well with Sophia's gown, except that it wasn't finished, so she couldn't be photographed. Nonetheless, she was engagingly present to celebrate the start of production, an obligatory opening gun for any big film by then, though two glasses of champagne isn't really a good way to start work. (Of course, the champagne was superb.) So was our cameraman, Bob Krasker, who obligingly used up several hours lighting a single shot of me walking into the hall to meet my love. It was the only film we exposed that day.

We had Sophia for twelve weeks only, so her scenes would be shot first, of course. They were almost all with me; when she was filming those I wasn't in, I went off to the second unit to swing swords and ride horses for Yak.

Looking back, I didn't handle all this as well as I should have. If I was going to be the engine on the film, I had to understand what that entailed. After ten years at it, working with some formidably gifted people, I still was a little green. I didn't really get it.

Sophia was crucial to our project. The more secure she felt, the better she would be. Actresses have a harder time than actors, star actresses even more so, for a lot of reasons that have nothing to do with male chauvinism. There are more of them, there aren't as many good parts, the more beautiful among them tend to be regarded more for their looks than their talent—all of that, and more.

Learning English to do so, Sophia was one of maybe half a dozen women who'd become honest-to-God international stars. It was an extraordinary achievement, and she was determined to protect it. Of course she was concerned that the new script might not serve her well, that Bob Krasker's low-key lighting might not show her face to best advantage. She was wildly wrong about that—I don't think it's possible to photograph Sophia badly—but I understand her anxiety.

Now I understand it. At the time, I found it baffling. She was unfailingly good-humored, though often late on the set. Many actresses are; they have longer makeup, hair, and wardrobe calls, and patchup in between. There's not a lot you can do about it, except wait. This I did, but with a certain amount of Scots dour, for which I'm sorry.

She was coming across wonderfully on film, which is where it counted. Filming French hours—roughly noon to 8 P.M.—I could check the dailies either before or after shooting. Sophia's footage was remarkable. She filled the frame . . . luminously.

An advantage of starting with her scenes was that we could focus totally on the Rodrigo/Chimene relationship. Not in sequence, of course (that's almost never logistically possible), but at least as a whole. I think it helped.

Still, even after our complete rewrite, the scenes tended to be over-written. I think this is the most common flaw in any film script; the screenwriter often tells you things the camera can show you, better and quicker. Also, writers working on period stories often use elaborate syntax to suggest another time. (You'll understand I speak from some experience here.) Thinning out the underbrush helped the scenes and Sophia as well.

It was December by then, especially cold in the Guadarramas where Yak was shooting some of his second-unit skirmishes. I can't adequately describe the pain of settling into a cold saddle in chain mail in the Spanish winter. Fray had a fine time, of course, bouncing around on the rocks in the miniature Cid armor I'd had made for his Christmas gift. My mother had come over for a visit, and she was often there as well, sitting near the heat of an arc light, watching happily.

Sophia did some work in the high country, too. We went out with the first unit one cold dawn for a scene of the Cid and his wife, reunited in exile, coming out of a shepherd's hut where they'd sought shelter to find a host of loyal knights waiting for him to lead them.

I mean, it was *cold*. While they were lighting the shot two riders simply toppled off their horses, chilled to numbness. Sophia was wearing only a thin woolen dress as she watched me ride off to war again. Between takes I held her wrapped in my cloak; she was literally shaking with cold—and we still had a three-page love scene to play inside the stone hut.

"This is insane," I said to Tony. "I was raised in weather like this, but Sophia's from Naples, for God's sake. We can't expect her to act out here in this igloo . . . let's shoot it back on a sound stage. Bob can light it better there anyway." That's what we did, in the end, but Sophia gutted it out in the cold all that morning.

Lydia could adjust her schedule to the weather a lot easier than the shooting company could. If the weather was good, she took Fraser "ruin running," as he came to call it later. If not, there was always the Prado, or the Museo de las Armas. (Only last year, when Fray was discussing the George Lucas TV series "The Young Indiana Jones" with some fellow filmmakers, he said, "You know, that was my boyhood, too . . . climbing pyramids and old temples, being tutored in hotel suites all around the world."

"You mean you're Indiana Jones?" a friend asked. Fray grinned. "No. My mom is.")

And so she is. By the early sixties, she had shifted her creative energies almost entirely to photography, in part because she

found the overriding agenda of motherhood extremely difficult to
fit into an acting career. As a photographer, she was her own mistress, working when and on what she chose.

She sometimes lets her camera lead her where she would
otherwise be disinclined to go. She's always been an unenthusiastic
flyer (after God knows how many hundred thousand miles), but
she once piled both our children, then still small, into a canvas biplane to side-slip through the fog cover and land on a rocky beach
in New Zealand to get pictures of Milford Sound. But it was in
Spain, during the *El Cid* shoot, that she made the photographs for
her first exhibition.

Shooting the crucial sword fight in which I killed Sophia's
father, I had a narrow escape that nevertheless paid a useful divi-
dend. Enzo was doubling Andrew Cruikshank, the English actor
playing the role, whose fencing was not as good as his acting.
Falling back across a table, I rolled the wrong way, right under a
full-armed overhand head cut. Enzo's iron wrist held back the blow,
but the blade's edge actually touched my forehead, right between
the eyes.

When I stopped trembling, I suddenly realized this was the
solution to my makeup for the second half of the film, which was
set ten years later. I wanted my Job/Rodrigo to show the marks of
suffering; the gray-flecked beard I'd already thought of wasn't
enough. A sword scar slashed across my nose would be perfect. It
was, too, but I wish the idea had struck me less traumatically. Talk
about having to get hit on the head . . .

The scar did exactly what I hoped, revealing in the first shot
in Part II the defiant, weary Job figure I'd been reaching for, all
without a word of dialogue.

Sophia, of course, would have nothing to do with any suggestions for aging her makeup in Part II. Perhaps she was right. In
every scene she was in, her glowing image was an enormous asset
to the film. Still, she could've made something of Chimene's suffering, too. The Sophia who made *Two Women* a year later might have
chosen differently. If Willy Wyler had directed *El Cid,* he'd have
made sure we saw not only the beautiful Chimene, but Job's wife
in the second half of the story.

Sophia came down with the flu just after New Year's, and
her stop date was the last Friday in January, which made for a tense

four weeks. The few days she was bedridden I spent with Yak and the second unit up in the Guadarramas, shooting some unusual combat footage in the snow there, while Tony laid out the shots on Sophia's last few scenes, so they could be lit more quickly when she came back.

Sophia's last scene was one of the most important in the film —the death of the Cid. (I'd already come to a violent end in a couple of films, but this was the first in which I died in bed.) It was one of the best-written scenes in the whole script, but quite long, with some complicated camera moves. By the end of the first day, we just got to my entrance (carried unconscious, with an arrow in my chest, I was marvelous). We shot for two days more; John Fraser was excellent as the king, Sophia was deeply moving . . . but at the end of her last day of work, we still had not gotten to my close-up.

There's a clear understanding among actors; you stand out of the shot and play the scene as well as you can for all the coverage in which you're not on camera. Even if it's a bit player, you do the scene for him off-camera. Still, this was unusual. Sophia had finished her work in the film.

"I'll come back in the morning, before I leave for the airport, and do the off-camera for you, Chuck," she said. I was quite touched by her offer, though I could of course do it alone. In fact, that's what I had to do. Three hours after she left the studio, she fell down a flight of stairs in her hotel suite and broke her shoulder.

"What would we have done if I'd fallen last week?" she asked, when I went to see her the next morning, her arm in a sling. The answer is, we would have managed, somehow. We were very lucky to have her, though, even if I did have to do the most important close-up I had in the film while imagining her kneeling beside me. Nevertheless, it's a very good scene.

We'd filmed almost half the picture, but the frantic rush to finish Sophia on schedule had left a loose scatter of shots behind that we had to go back and clean up. We did this over the next few days, simultaneously packing the company for the move to Peñíscola, on the Mediterranean coast north of Valencia. We were to be based there for the rest of the shoot.

One evening we even went out to dinner, somehow having finished shooting before eight o'clock. George Marshall was in town, directing Rita Hayworth and Rex Harrison in a film about an art heist from the Prado. He'd directed me in a Western several years earlier; his daughter, Geri, and son-in-law, Frank Baur, are among our oldest friends. We were delighted to go to dinner with him.

When Lydia and I got to the restaurant, we were pleased to see that George had brought along his stars, neither of whom we'd met. (I'd been offered the male lead with Hayworth in a film version of *Rain* a year or so before, and would work with Harrison some time later in *The Agony and the Ecstasy,* which shows you how small the film community is.) It looked like an interesting evening.

It turned into the single most embarrassing evening of my life. Rita Hayworth was then married (why, I cannot imagine) to a producer named James Hill, who began the evening by relentlessly heaping obscene abuse on her. She was rapidly reduced to a helpless flood of tears, her face buried in her hands; the rest of us simply sat stunned, witnesses to a marital massacre. I didn't know either of them, but I was strongly tempted to slug him anyway. If he hits her, I thought, that's it. Looking back, I really wish I hadn't waited. As it was, when Lydia stood up, almost in tears herself, I took her home, leaving George to sort it out. I'm ashamed of walking away from Miss Hayworth's humiliation. I never saw her again.

Peñíscola was crucial to *El Cid*. It doubled for Valencia in the film because it was the only walled city in Spain (in the world, for all I know) that hadn't yet extended outside the stone walls its medieval defenders built to protect it. The real Valencia is a major modern city, looking not at all as it had in the eleventh century.

Peñíscola did. It was on the sea, with miles of sand beaches for the cavalry battles and amphibious landings that would fill our days and nights. Part II was the strongest part of the script, highlighted with the clash of arms and running horses, the dark betrayals and foul murders, the desperate escapes and savage assaults that marked the Middle Ages and, indeed, all man's time on earth.

Our move to the Mediterranean was simpler than the company's, of course. We settled in a modest hotel in Castellón de la Plana, an easy drive from Peñíscola. Everything we were shooting there was in Part II, so I had an early makeup call, but I'd long since learned to sleep in the back of the limo and then in the makeup chair while I was transformed into the scarred and graying Job figure I was reaching for.

The weather, though milder on the coast than on the Castilian plateau, was not cooperative. It was still winter; our beaches were often obscured by morning fog, sometimes rain. The fog was useful for some of our tag scene, with the dead Cid strapped to his horse, riding into legend, but we had a good bit of down time, sweating out the weather. (At a hundred thousand dollars a day, "sweat" is the right word.)

I did have a chance to celebrate my son's sixth birthday. Bob and Bea Sellmer, new friends we'd met during the Madrid shoot, joined us at Sagunto, along with their two boys, Peter and Mike, for a picnic. Fray was glad to see his new pals again, and the day was brilliant. Sagunto is the site of a major Roman battle that occurred in Caesar's time. Walking the battlefield with the boys, explaining how what happened there shaped the world we live in, I found myself moved close to tears, thinking of the young men charging up that harsh slope, spending their blood to lay the ground stones of the Western world. Along with the Brits in their brightest centuries and our own miraculous experiment in liberty, I admire the Romans. Without the stable world they made, we could still be without good roads, central heating, and running water, as indeed many people outside the Western world remain.

The long standbys while we waited for shooting weather gave me time to improve my still uneasy relationship with the two Babiecas. The ocean, which neither horse had ever seen before, terrified them both. I would have to control one or the other through a tricky shot where the Cid is mortally wounded by an arrow in the chest while riding through the shallows, but I couldn't get either horse within ten feet of the water, though I literally bent a spur trying.

Joe Canutt watched me argue this issue one rainy morning with Babieca I. "Just step down a minute, will you, Chuck?" he said. He swung into the saddle with the panther grace of a true horseman and in forty seconds forced that stud chest-deep into the surf, trembling but docile. I've never seen anything quite like it. With nothing but his will and his skill, Joe imposed physical dominance on a thousand pounds of rebellious stallion, turning him into a well-broke saddle horse. In the Madrid shoot, Babieca I had really been all but too much horse for me; from that day on he never gave me a moment's trouble. A week later I took him through fire, which horses fear, for a scene; he never flinched.

Nevertheless, I chose Babieca II for another chore on my Sunday off a couple of weeks later. The mayor of Castellón had invited Lydia, Fray, and me to the opening of the Plaza de Toros. I was to lead the parade around the arena, with much attendant media coverage. (We were a very hot item that year, thanks to Hank Werba's tireless diligence.)

I knew that Babieca II had had some high-schooling in various equestrian show steps, which was more than I could claim. While refreshing the horse's skills, I could learn the simple cues that controlled him, knee pressures and tapping his flank with the spurs in certain rhythms, not really very difficult. This I managed to do between takes on our still rain-sodden beach.

On the day of the parade, the frosting on the cake was Fraser, who entered the ring parading with the matadors, dressed in a formal gray-and-black *traje de campo* like mine. Babieca II had a marvelous time, side-stepping to the music and my spur cues, then I leaned down and lifted Fray to the saddle in front of me as we galloped out to wild applause. Oh, we were the cat's pajamas.

The weather settled down toward spring about the time my twenty-week guarantee ran out. Of course there was no stop date in my case, as we'd had with Sophia, but I was paid for the run-over weeks, in addition to the gross percentage. I was earning it.

We had most of the major interior scenes in the can by this time, leaving us largely focused on several varieties and sizes of battle scenes, principally the Cid's conquest of Valencia and his subsequent defense against the invading Moors.

We filmed his entry into Valencia as bloodless, following Menendez Pidal's account. The citizens welcomed him in preference to the weak King Alfonso as the abler soldier they needed against the Moors, offering him the crown of Valencia. The Cid, stubbornly unwilling to displace the king who had exiled him and imprisoned his wife and children, refused the crown, surely one of the outstanding examples of loyalty in history.

It was also a key moment in the movie; I thought a lot about how to play it. As sometimes happens in film, that wasn't necessary. It played itself. I led a mounted troop to the gates of the city, real iron gates set in the real stone walls of a medieval city. The sun and the sea were as they'd been a thousand years ago. The gates swung open, two thousand people screamed welcome. I rode through,

Babieca dancing under my hand, both of us aroused by the roar: "Cid! *Cid! CID!!*" I swung off the horse, down into the welling sound, and climbed the steep time-worn stone steps set in the wall. At the top, I turned, the sea behind me, the city and the people lying below, reaching, entreating, warm and open as a woman. "Cid! *Cid! CID!!*"

You don't have to act that. You can't act it. I was there. It happened to me. I know, in my bones and blood, what it is to take a city. Yes, of course it's like sex. It *is* sex . . . to the power of ten.

We then undertook the battle for Valencia, for which we were well equipped. As well as a duplicate medieval Valencia, we had a couple of thousand local extras, a regiment of Spanish cavalry, a squadron of mounted police, and half a dozen world-class stunt-men. We also had Yakima Canutt. And Tony Mann, directing. The battle was really about who would shoot it.

Yak had been hired to shoot the action sequences, but Tony, as director, had to decide which scenes he would delegate. During the difficult Madrid shoot, when Tony had had to concentrate on getting Sophia's scenes, he'd been glad to have Yak shoot anything she wasn't in. With Sophia's role in the can and the major action of the film still to shoot, he was reluctant to turn the company over to Yak, as Wyler had done with the chariot race on *Ben-Hur,* while he himself directed other scenes. For one thing, there weren't many such scenes left to shoot in *El Cid.* Besides, Tony really wanted to shoot the big battle himself.

I think this was the wrong choice. While Tony was perfectly competent to shoot the battle, no one could do it as well as Yak, let alone as efficiently. Tony spent days and days integrating the principal actors into battle coverage that simultaneously included thousands of armed men and horses. Increasingly frustrated at the time he was losing, not to mention the cost of the American stuntmen, who did falls only on a piece-work basis, at several hundred dollars each, he decided to send them all home.

This was a huge mistake. The very next morning, Tony set up a low camera in a pit, to catch a Moorish rider falling six feet from the lens. He spent three hours on the shot without coming close. The horse wouldn't fall, the rider would miss the mark, then finally ran over the camera, breaking a lens and the operator's wrist.

Finally, in desperation, Tony sent a frantic message to get Joe back before he left for the States.

They stopped him just as he was getting on the plane. He came down to the beach outside the walls still wearing a suit. He checked the setup through the camera, took off his jacket and tie, pulled on a Moorish robe, and swung into the saddle, still wearing his Sunday shoes. "Just put a paper cup in the sand there, where you want him to land." He ran the horse out of the city gate and off the edge of a sandbank, landing exactly on the mark on the first take. I loved it. A just man, vindicated.

By then, we'd lost so much time we had to simplify the battle footage. The delay also did me out of a marvelous acting opportunity. While we were fighting for Valencia (both on and off screen), Larry Olivier phoned me. He'd opened triumphantly on Broadway some weeks before, playing the title role in *Becket,* with Tony Quinn in the showy part of the king. As Olivier said to me, "I cannot describe to you the black depression that seized me on the second day of rehearsal when I realized I had chosen the wrong role."

Now Quinn was leaving to do a film. Would I join the company and alternate with Olivier in both roles, switching every performance? Well, of course I would . . . what actor wouldn't? Olivier would no doubt outshine me in both parts, but it would teach me a great deal, and get me back on Broadway in a hit play.

Except that I couldn't do it. I would have to be in New York to go into rehearsal five days before I could possibly finish in *El Cid.* I hated missing the chance, but I had to pass on the offer. I've never yet done the play.

The last sequence we filmed was the tournament. While it's a major action sequence, its position early in the film means it must also make major plot points and set crucial character relationships. For the combat itself, Tony gave the shooting unit back to Yak, and got one of the very best such scenes ever shot.

One night, after a fairly easy day, we took some of the actors to a small local restaurant for dinner. As we finished our meal, I noticed the entire barroom was jammed with people looking through the door at us. "Now, there's true Spanish courtesy for you," I pointed out. "Anywhere else, they'd be all over us by now.

Here, they wait till we finish eating." I paid the check and said to our party, "You guys go on out and get in the cars. I really have to sign autographs for these people." I rose and turned to meet the Spanish crowd flowing into the room. Of course they ignored me completely, settling down to watch soccer on the TV the owner had just turned on. Ah, fame!

A week before we were to wrap the location, Lydia went back to Madrid to pack for the trip home (an experience I've learned over the years to avoid as I would brain surgery). I'm proud to say she left Fray in my care, the first time in his short life he'd been entirely free of female supervision. This meant he spent his waking hours in the company of Spanish horse-wranglers and American stuntmen, drivers and makeup men, prop masters and special effects riggers, and mostly, of course, with me. Horses and swords and sun all day, a walk in the woods before dinner, then a chapter out of whatever book we were reading before we both turned in for an early call. This suited us very well, no matter what Gloria Steinem says about fathers.

We could at last see light at the end of a long and difficult shoot; we'd picked up some of the time we'd lost earlier. I'd seen almost no rough cut and only about half the dailies, but opinion on it ran high.

I'd learned by then to strive for skepticism at this stage. Sam Bronston, however, was euphoric, doubtless because the rough footage he'd been able to show exhibitors had gotten him the release deals he needed to supplement his Allied Artists release in the U.S. and Rank release in Britain.

According to Sam, everyone was great, especially me. This was my first exposure to the kind of treatment *stars* (as in the title of this chapter) get. For doing the work I'd been well paid for, to be additionally compensated by a piece of every dollar the film grossed anywhere forever, I was all but voted into Valhalla, along with the other gods. As a bonus, Sam was going to give me a Jaguar XKE (he did, too). He also urged us to take a week's vacation in Rome, on him, as an extra bonus.

"That's very nice, Sam, but I don't think so. We've been here seven months already, I've done the best I could on the film. That's where it really counts. I'd really just like to go home with my family."

Oddly, that didn't do it. I got a call from Sam's Number Two,
Mike Waszynski, playing Mischa the Fixer. "Dearest Chock! I hef
joost toked to Sem. He is surrounded by eed-yots. Dey felled to mek
clear to you *ee-manse eemportance* uf dis grand reception dey plen
for you in Rome. I know how ri-sponsif you are to de neets of
publicity. As fehvorh to Sem, ulso to me, shorely you ken come?"

"Mike," I said, "I've done at least a hundred interviews and
a dozen receptions since we started this film. When you open it, I'll
do several hundred more. You can't tell me there's suddenly one
party in Rome that has to be done now." Mike, ever the European,
then came clean. Sam had made a coproduction deal with an Italian
company, earning him favored nation status for the film's release
there. He was shooting a scene there, as required, but I was not in
it. Put simply, I had to at least *appear* in Rome (I said this was a
European anecdote) to validate everything.

So I did, of course. Making movies is a curious business.
Lydia welcomed the extra packing time. I flew to Rome the next
day, did the party and the crucial press gefuffle, and caught the
early plane to Madrid the next morning, getting back to the apartment just as Lydia was supervising the loading of the car. We made
it to Burgos by dark, where of course the mayor and another press
gefuffle awaited us.

We spent some days driving north to Cherbourg to catch the
Queen Mary home, absorbing some history en route. Of the châ-
teaux of the Loire, Fray's favorite was Blois, because the Duc de
Guise had been murdered there with unusual savagery some centuries before. Fray repeated the guide's account of this butchery in
bloody detail that evening, somewhat diminishing his mother's
pleasure in the four-star meal laid before us. He also responded
to the Lascaux caves, both their ten-thousand-year-old paintings of
hunters and hunted, and the "stactites an' stagmites" around them.

Our tour ended, appropriately, on the beaches of Normandy. It's hard to explain the D-Day landings to a little boy, but
Fray seemed to get some idea of how it was to struggle ashore that
morning, and why those men did it anyway, in their thousands. "Dat
would be scary," he said, looking up at the rusted gun emplace-
ments. Yes.

14

Riding the Tiger

Tiger, Tiger, burning bright
In the forests of the night.

— WILLIAM BLAKE

WE GOT HOME in the early months of John Kennedy's presidency. Lydia and I had met him in L.A. the previous summer at the Democratic convention, where we came to support Adlai Stevenson, for whom I'd campaigned before. I realized Kennedy's assets as a candidate would likely win him the nomination; when they did, I planned to work for his election. *El Cid* made that impossible; already deep in the tough prep for our even tougher Spanish shoot, I cast my absentee ballot for him in Spain.

Now, many months later, I was home. Just as I was trying to keep my balance riding the *star* tiger, our new president was struggling with an infinitely more significant task: finding his way with Congress and the Russians, both proving resistant to his charm. Civil rights was by then becoming a major public issue, though since President Eisenhower had put troops into Little Rock, Arkansas, to force the integration of their schools, neither Kennedy nor Congress had taken any action. Black protest was growing, but there was little white response, let alone support, which would be crucial.

While we were shooting in Spain, my old friend Jolly West appeared in the pages of the *International Herald-Tribune*. The head of the Department of Psychiatry at the University of Oklahoma, he was the youngest man to head a medical department in any

American university. What got him in the paper, though, was his involvement in a civil rights demonstration in Oklahoma, long before that was appropriate behavior for distinguished academics (or undistinguished, for that matter). I dropped him a note enclosing the clipping and asked if there was anything I could do. "Let me know when you're back in the States," he wrote. "We'll think of something."

I hadn't been in New York three days when he called. "How would you like to come here on your way home and raise a little hell with me?" I thought it was a fine idea. Jolly had already recruited Chet Pierce, a formidably gifted black Harvard man on his faculty, to join us in front of several Oklahoma City restaurants that still refused to serve blacks.

There was some concern that our little action, two large white guys and one large black guy, might provoke a hostile, even violent confrontation. By the time I got to Oklahoma City, there were calls waiting from MGM, who still had *Ben-Hur* in release, and Allied Artists, who would be releasing *El Cid*. They both pointed out the danger of "alienating moviegoers."

"Come on, guys," I said. *"El Cid* isn't going to be in theaters for another six months. *Ben-Hur*'s been playing since 1959; everyone's seen it already anyway. Are you telling me people won't go back for a second look because I picket a couple of restaurants?"

There was no confrontation. We marched peacefully, even happily, attended by TV cameras and eager journalists. I carried a sign quoting Thomas Jefferson, Chet's quoted Jesus, and Jolly's pointed out that racism helped Communism. As Jolly had predicted, my public face got us a lot of ink and airtime. Once openly addressed, civil rights had far more support than people expected. "There is no power on earth like that of an idea whose time has come."

The restaurants we'd demonstrated against soon quietly began to admit blacks, but our little foray made no more than a ripple in the wider world. The Kennedy Administration and Congress still stood pat; Martin Luther King still struggled on, heroically. I was glad I'd stopped off in Oklahoma, though.

I suppose this small civil rights activism, before it got popular, was a significant milestone for me. A certain Scots contrariness and a tendency to shoot my mouth off were to involve me in a good many more public-sector issues. It was also part of my expanded persona, riding the tiger. Back in L.A., I was happy to settle on our beautiful ridge in the house we'd hardly had time to live in and read scripts, but the Screen Actors Guild appointed me to fill a vacancy as vice president. (About a year later, I found myself president of SAG, a commitment that turned out to have many ramifications.)

Then the State Department asked me to be the U.S. delegate to the Berlin Film Festival. I'd turned down (and still do) all offers to serve on festival juries; I don't like deciding which filmmaker gets honored at which festival. But State's request that I represent the U.S. in Berlin seemed something else, perhaps a small signal from the Kennedy White House. Besides, I'd get to wear white tie and tails, by then obsolete in ordinary society. (Unlike most men, I sort of enjoy dressing up. Actors do that, at least if you play the kind of roles I do . . . I've gone a year at a time without playing a part where I got to wear pants.)

So, we went to Berlin, a city at flash point in that long, hot summer of the Cold War. Actually, I went first; Lydia stayed home to give Fray a few days more of Mom-time and joined me toward the end. (Let me give you what Ernest Hemingway used to call "the true gen" on film festivals. Originally conceived as just that, festivals celebrating film as the art form of the century and presenting filmmakers with prizes honoring their work, they have become trade fairs, marketplaces where various projects are promoted for backing and finished films are sold to distributors.

The market has become the dominant element in film festivals. The awards are valued, of course, though only the Academy Awards have real commercial utility in a film's release. Still, we're all happy to pick up a prize at one of the European festivals, not least because it's hard for an American film to win one. There's a certain bias against the Yanks for having preempted the world film market. Also, as with the Nobel Prize, festival honors tend to be distributed on geographically and politically correct terms. As a result, except for films critical of the U.S., American companies often withhold their major releases from festival competition, avoiding the embarrassment of being passed over in favor of a film from Brazil or Bangladesh.)

Berlin was still under siege behind the Iron Curtain, which

was why the State Department focused on that city's festival. I made
my appearances at all the major parties, striving to sound significant
about American film in dozens of interviews, and hosted the U.S.
gala.

On the Fourth of July, we attended the party given by the
general commanding the American zone, in effect the proconsul of
Berlin. His residence was set amid thick fir trees, a handsome building dating back to the Weimar Republic, with walnut paneling still
studded with bullet holes from the fighting in World War II. They
also sent us on a tour of the Soviet zone of the city, with firm
instructions. "You'll cross through Checkpoint Charlie in a car with
diplomatic plates and the flag on the fenders. The Russians are not
allowed to hinder you; your driver will not stop in any circumstances." He didn't, either, barely slowing as we swept through,
earning us nothing more than a stony look from the Soviet sentries.

East Berlin was as bleak as an untended graveyard, which in
a way it was. We saw the official sights, but the naked face of Communism on the downcast East Berliners shuffling along the littered
streets withered my soul. We flew home the next morning, and a
few days later the Soviets began to build the Berlin Wall. One heavy
truck could've punched through it the first day, but we didn't send
it, leaving half the city sealed off like a suppurating sore. It was to
drain for nearly thirty years.

When we got home, I was disappointed to have to give up
my diplomatic passport. (Those suckers are really useful . . . first off
the plane, baggage too, no immigration or customs; when I consider how many hours [*days!*] of my life I've spent looking at baggage carousels while tourists take pictures of me . . . on that ground
alone, being ambassador to a small, quiet country would almost be
worth the time it would take, just to avoid the hassle.)

Having done my duty to the State Department, Lydia and I
were anxious to attend to our own priority, set not long after Fraser
was born: a girl baby to complete our family. To ensure that, adoption seemed the obvious choice; we'd applied to the best adoption
agency we could find two years before. Not long after we returned
from Berlin, the word came. We brought Holly home on the second
day of her life; she was instantly and forever ours.

A father loves his son partly responding to a chromosome
identity. You want your son to *be* you—also himself, and better. But

I think a man loves his daughter with a kind of helpless male devotion. I think Holly began to understand that when she was about four days old.

Fraser's response to her was a little more complicated; it's tough for a six-year-old to accept a sibling readily. Perhaps he felt our love for him was somehow threatened by this exquisite female creature, who was now part of our lives. "We could sell her," he proposed ingeniously one day.

The delights of our completed family and the ridge where we would raise our children deepened my determination to make it all secure. (My Scot's blood again.) In the twelfth century, that meant keeping the swords sharp and the horses fed. In the middle of the twentieth, for me it meant reading a lot of scripts. In the earlier years, Herman the Iceman had overridden my instincts a couple of times, most notably on *The Big Country,* when he'd been absolutely right to insist I do the film. Now, our agreement was firmer. I chose the projects, he made the deals.

It looked like an easy summer. I'd put in a tennis court, so, all on our ridge, I could work on my backhand, read scripts, cradle my new daughter, and watch Lydia teach Fray how to dive. (She'd been a competition swimmer in school.) Even the PR demands were minimal: the full-court press on *El Cid* was some months away, and finally winding down on *Ben-Hur.* On that film, almost two years after its release, God knows I'd already done about every possible interview in the mortal world.

While I was doing my State Department chores in Berlin, Mike Waszynski threw a party for *El Cid.* Actually, he really wanted to pitch me Sam Bronston's next film, *The Fall of the Roman Empire.* Of course he could've done this over lunch, or even a beer, and saved Sam the $20,000 or so the party cost him, but that's the way they do things in movies (today that party would run over $100,000 . . . and they'd still give it).

So I went to Mike's party, which was very grand and, in fact, probably useful to *El Cid* in the end, and talked to him about *Roman Empire.* I read what they'd written of the script on the plane back home. I was not impressed.

What they had in mind, of course, was what they always have in mind: a film as close as possible to the huge success you've just had. Nowadays they've simplified it; they make exactly the same

film, even to the title, *Terminator* I and II, *Home Alone* I and II,
Rocky I through V. In the sixties, Sam smelled a hit with *El Cid* and
wanted to use the unprecedented success of *Ben-Hur* to duplicate
both films in one: *El Hur,* or possibly *Ben-Cid.* (Not bad titles,
actually.)

Their source material was impeccable: Gibbon's *Decline
and Fall of the Roman Empire.* This side of Shakespeare or the
Bible, you can't get classier than that. They hadn't, by a long shot.
What's more, Sam had only an idea—no script.

"Don't worry about the script," they always say. "First, we
have to set our stars." In this case, Chuck and Sophia, together
again, before they even found out how we'd be together for the
first time. Sam was a gambler, though. He smelled an awful lot of
money in *Cid;* he wanted to pick it up and run with it.

Still, when I asked to see the script, they sent an outline,
studded with quotes from Gibbon to impress me. It wasn't much. I
said so, and passed. So much for that, I thought.

What I really wanted was something different from what I'd
just done. (In retrospect, this may have been a career mistake on
my part, but I still lean to that choice.) I'd been in the most ac-
claimed and successful film of the postwar era, done a flop play
with the leading actor of the century, an OK film with one of the
iconic figures of Hollywood, and now what looked like another
success with one of the half-dozen women in the world who were
undeniable international stars.

So I was looking for a comedy, of course. I'd had a success
a few years before with *The Private War of Major Benson;* now
Paramount had a much more prestigious project. Mel Shavelson,
with a fine track record as a writer and, more recently, director,
had a comedy ready called *Easter Dinner.* (Yeah, I know. I said,
"Look, if we stick with this title with me in it, they'll think it's a joke
version of the Last Supper.")

I liked *Americans, Go Home!,* but they went with *The Pigeon
That Took Rome,* which is not bad, but a mouthful. Still, it was a
funny script, set in Italy at the end of the war. The original thought
for the girl had been Sophia, who'd done a very successful comedy
for Mel with Cary Grant (well, of course, who can't do a successful
comedy with Cary Grant?). In any case, as we got down to the short
strokes of the deal, Sophia was not on. Maybe they felt they couldn't

afford us both. At one point, Mel toyed with the idea of switching the locale to France and using Maurice Chevalier and a French actress with me.

I had to go to Italy right about then anyway, to accept the David di Donatello award as best actor for *Ben-Hur*—the Italian version of the Academy Award. Aside from the pleasure of getting it, the prize is distinguished by being one of the few award statues I've ever seen that has any artistic merit in itself. Most of them look like bowling trophies. The Italian award is a foot-high gold replica of Donatello's statue of *David*. (Actually, Michelangelo's version is better, but this one's pretty classy.) I worked on my Italian, which had rusted a bit since the *Ben-Hur* shoot, and avoided disgracing myself in my speech. Fourteen hours later, I was in London, looping on *El Cid.*

To my horror, Mike Waszynski said, in a European "ees no prawblem" tone, that we'd have to re-voice some 70 percent of the sound track, due to fluctuations in the Spanish electrical current when we'd been shooting. (Over the years, as the technology has improved, filmmakers have become more and more vulnerable to these aberrant glitches. Almost the same thing happened on a shoot I did in Israel only last year.) Anyway, I managed to re-voice two-thirds of my dialogue in *El Cid* in three days, making some of it better, as Orson Welles had taught me. In that sort of crisis, you just have to put your head down and do it, in ten- and twelve-hour chunks.

Still, I went to the fancy midnight supper Sam's people laid on at the Dorchester not much inclined to have a good time, which was a little snotty of me. I certainly didn't want to talk about *Roman Empire* again, especially since they still didn't have a finished script. I agreed to read whatever they'd have in a month, got five hours of sleep, and caught the morning plane to New York, where I kept my date with the Allied Artists guys to talk about the PR work on *El Cid* in the fall, when I finished *Pigeon.* I still got back to L.A. the same night, in time to take my son to his first day of school the next morning. It seemed to me he'd grown taller in just the few days I'd been gone, and lean as a trout. Not quite a small boy anymore. He was finished with that part of his life, though I wasn't.

I hadn't had enough time with my baby daughter, either, though at two months our prime communication was the flower

petals of her fingers closing on mine, and her wide eyes giving me
a glimpse of her feminine soul. I needed this, and the life we had,
centered on our ridge.

Yet I needed the work, too, not just for the money to make
us financially secure, but for the *doing* of it, as good as sex, the best
drug in the world. Fray put it right, a few weeks into his first school
year, when he had to stand in turn with his classmates and tell them
what his father did for a living. "My daddy," he said with remarkable
insight, "pretends to *be* people."

So I do, but I hadn't yet really hooked into being the U.S.
infantry captain in Mel Shavelson's script. I've just now figured this
out, going over my work journal from that film. Of course you can't
plan every project in terms of its potential for greatness . . . you
don't get many shots at that. But, looking back on this time, I realize
I was as much concerned with making the film fit my convenience
as with making it as good as it could be.

Paramount had scheduled a twelve-week shoot in Rome,
reasonable for a modern story with neither huge crowds nor huge
action sequences. I noted that only three or four weeks of this were
exterior locations in Italy; the rest were interiors. "Let's just shoot
the locations in Rome," I said. "We can do the interiors better here
at Paramount." Well, you couldn't, of course. You could do them as
well, for a lot more money. It's always been cheaper to shoot outside the U.S., though on the average American crews are more
efficient. The cost disparity has grown in recent years, due in part
to the fringe benefits I helped negotiate for the Screen Actors Guild
thirty years ago, which were later copied by the technical unions.
Shooting the *Pigeon* interiors at Paramount probably added about
a million dollars to the overall negative cost (today, multiply that by
three or four).

I was the six-hundred-pound gorilla here, wearing my *star*
hat. Having agreed to do the picture, I should have accepted the fiscal logic of shooting it all in Rome. Instead, I forced a compromise
on the studio. It makes me uncomfortable to say that. (Only a little.)

We're not talking about mindless excess here, though Hollywood often provides plenty of that. I wasn't insisting that Chasen's
chili be flown daily to Rome, or that my stand-in, dresser, and five
chief pals be maintained on a distant location. But the *star* syndrome inescapably distorts reality.

Every two or three years some studio commits tens of millions of dollars to a film that has almost no chance of breaking even, let alone recouping the multiplying millions poured into it. I won't embarrass some pals by naming names, you know who you are. Let's skip back beyond *Ishtar* and *Howard the Duck,* which almost brought down major companies, and *Heaven's Gate,* which actually did.

Neither of the major disasters of the sixties were doomed from the moment of conception, like the above films. *Mutiny on the Bounty,* with Gable and Laughton, had been and remains one of MGM's proudest projects from the prewar era. By 1961, it was reasonably time to remake it, especially with Marlon Brando, arguably the most naturally gifted actor in American film.

A year or so earlier, Fox had launched an equally promising remake, on an even grander scale: *Cleopatra,* with Elizabeth Taylor, who was at the apogee of her extraordinary beauty and approaching the peak of her considerable talent as an actress.

Neither *Bounty* nor *Cleopatra* is by any measure a terrible film; both have many virtues, not least the performances of their leading players. Both, however, were beset by horrendous cost overruns and internal problems so staggering that the films became exercises in disaster control for the two studios. They were also, God knows, *star*-crossed.

I had nothing to do with either project, of course, but I did have glancing encounters with each one that gave me some insights. When I was in L.A. in the spring, sometime between my civil rights foray into Oklahoma and showing the flag for the State Department in Berlin, Willy Wyler invited Lydia and me to a small dinner he was giving for Sir Carol Reed, who was about to fly to the South Pacific to direct *Mutiny on the Bounty.* After the flawless meal for which the Wylers were noted, I wandered into the bar for a splash of brandy to put in my coffee. Willy was engrossed in intense conversation with Carol, whom I'd met only that evening. (He was to direct me later in *The Agony and the Ecstasy.*) Suddenly, out of the corner of my eye, I saw Willy lean forward and grip Carol's elbow. "Don't do it, Carol," he said. "You have to get out of it. Believe me, it will be a disaster!"

Of course I eased back out of the room and a conversation I had no right to overhear. But later, after Reed did indeed toss in

the towel and resign after weeks of deadlock with Marlon on script,
performance, and showing up for work, I've always wondered...
how did Willy *know?*

It's true that he had an uncanny instinct about actors and
how to handle them. A few years later, after he'd directed Barbra
Streisand to half an Academy Award in her first film, *Funny Girl*
(she tied with Katharine Hepburn), I asked him, "How did it go
with Streisand, Willy? The word in town is that you had a lot of
problems."

"Nah, not really," he said. "Considering it's the first film she
ever directed."

The fall I went to Rome to shoot our little three-week location on *Pigeon,* Fox's *Cleopatra* was on its second year. They'd not
only changed directors but moved the entire shoot from London,
junking their sets there and recasting all the actors except for Elizabeth Taylor. They'd built new and even larger sets on every sound
stage in Rome, including all those we'd used for *Ben-Hur*.

Joe Mankiewicz was directing now, having reshot from the
top, working through the summer and now facing several months
more in the Roman winter. The studio was throwing a birthday
party for him in the Excelsior Hotel. Everyone in Rome with a
public face was invited, including me. I was staying in the hotel, so
I dropped by, though I didn't know Joe well.

I was wandering through the happy throng, feeling more or
less out of place, as I usually do at big parties, especially by myself.
I saw the guest of honor sitting at one end of an empty table, and
moved to greet him. "Hey, Joe," I said, striving for a light note,
"got any work for chariot drivers?" He looked up at me like a man
peering out of a deep well.

"Only for losers, Chuck," he said. "Only for losers." In that
instant, I understood what he'd gone through. Directing any big
picture is like leading a parachute battalion jumping into Normandy
on D-Day. Directing *Cleopatra* must have been like having your
chute fail.

I guess the paratroop analogy occurred to me because of
another offer that came along then. Darryl F. Zanuck, who had
guided Twentieth Century–Fox successfully through the studio era,
finally had been ousted by Spyros Skouras, who now seemed about
to destroy the studio with his excesses on *Cleopatra*.

Zanuck, meanwhile, was personally producing what would be his last film, *The Longest Day,* based on Cornelius Ryan's excellent book on the Normandy landings, a series of vignettes about the experiences of some fifty different men on that first day. Cannily, Zanuck realized that the only way to keep these characters, most of them in identical uniforms, sorted out for the audience was to cast known actors in every role. For Zanuck, it worked well, though George Stevens was to fail with the same approach the next year, of which more later.

I'd been approached about the project a couple of times (each vignette had its own separate shooting schedule), but the part I liked was a paratroop colonel commanding a regiment that had been dropped in occupied France before the landing. He broke his leg in the jump and had to lead his men from a wheelbarrow. I was prepared to arm-wrestle Mel Shavelson for the few days off it would've taken me to shoot the role for Zanuck. (Do you note the six-hundred-pound gorilla again here?)

In the end, John Wayne decided he liked the part, too. The Duke was the *thousand*-pound gorilla, if ever there was one; Zanuck snapped him up at once, so I didn't have to nag Mel Shavelson for time off after all. I did owe him my best in *Pigeon,* which I truly tried to give him.

All that said, the shooting went quite smoothly. Mel was handling the shoot well, with a sure instinct for comedy honed over some years as he wrote for the likes of Bob Hope and Cary Grant. A truism in the trade is that, maybe this side of *King Lear,* comedy is the hardest genre to do well, with the caveat that a pretty good *Lear* is still watchable. A pretty good comedy is not. One of the great comics (there's much argument about whether it was Jack Benny, or Buster Keaton, or maybe even someone farther back in history) said on his deathbed to those there lamenting his passing, "No, no. Dying is easy. *Comedy* is hard." Too true.

The film we made was good enough, but that's never quite good enough, if you follow me. Mel was a good director; his script was solid, too. I thought we did well, getting what we needed in Rome, and the studio shoot back at Paramount gave us plausibly Italian interiors, which is not as easy as you might think.

Reluctantly, I have to say I was probably the guy who fell short here. If we'd shot the whole picture in Rome, it might have

jelled more excitingly. It certainly would have been cheaper, giving
us something more than the extremely modest success we ended
up with. I was the gorilla who brought us home for the studio work.
True, movies are the greatest permanent floating crap game in the
breathing world, as everyone who makes them knows. We might
as easily have ended up with the surprise comedy smash of the
year, as we had a few years earlier with *The Private War of Major
Benson*.

The last weeks of 1961 were complicated for me. I had to go
to Washington to testify for the Screen Actors Guild before Congress, to London for the world premiere of *El Cid*, back again to
finish the studio shoot on *Pigeon*, then to Madrid for *Cid*'s Spanish
premiere. *El Cid* was a huge success, playing in reserved-seat theaters for months around the world, though not into a second year,
as *Ben-Hur* had. (No picture would do that again.) Nor did it receive
as much critical acclaim, a judgment with which I'd agree.

Visually, *Cid* is a marvelous film, impeccably designed and
superbly photographed. Yak Canutt's action sequences were comparable to what he'd done in *Ben-Hur*. (Though he couldn't quite
match the chariot race, still probably the best action sequence ever
filmed.) Miklos Rozsa's Oscar-nominated music was perhaps even
better than the score that had won him the award for *Ben-Hur*.

The script, though, is less than what we tried so hard to
make it. (We could've used Christopher Fry again.) Perhaps more
crucial, not many of the performances are as good as most of them
were in *Ben-Hur*, including mine. (We could've used Willy Wyler
again.) No, we had good actors, again as in *Ben* using a solid core
of British talent. They all gave good performances, some much
better than that, but not many were up to the standard Willy drew
out of everyone in *Ben-Hur*.

Please understand me: Tony Mann was a good director, often
more than that. ". . . inside this tough technician is an artist, struggling to get out," I wrote in my journal during the *Cid* shoot. His
record is not diminished by pointing out that he was not Willy
Wyler.

I muse sometimes on a pet private fantasy. If I'd known
ahead how both films would come out, and had the power to make
it happen, I'd have had Tony Mann direct *Ben-Hur*, and Wyler *El
Cid*. In Tony's hands, *Ben-Hur* might have been a somewhat lesser

film creatively, but I think it would've done nearly as well commercially as Wyler's did in reality.

Cid is a better story, about real people; if Willy had directed, and exercised the kind of draconian creative controls he always imposed on every aspect of production, particularly on the actors, I think *El Cid* would have been far and away the best epic film ever made. I know, it's a silly idea; I asked Willy what he thought of it once. He didn't respond warmly. Still, I think of what might have been. Actors dream up the damnedest things; our fantasies can be just as exciting as sex dreams.

Somewhere in the midst of all this to-and-froing, I realized I had to disentangle myself from Sam Bronston's *Fall of the Roman Empire*. I should have done it earlier. That's one of my character flaws. If respectable filmmakers are involved, particularly people I've worked with, I hate to say no. Conversely, I often accept an offer without examining it as stringently as my advisors tell me I should. I should have been more honest, sooner, with Sam on that film.

When I was in Madrid for the *El Cid* premiere there, Mike Waszynski took me out to a hundred acres or so of beautiful open country near Madrid. It was called Las Matas (a significant battleground in the Spanish Civil War), where Sam's people were erecting the awesome sets Colasanti and Moore had designed for *The Fall of the Roman Empire*.

"Eee-mahgine, Chock," Mike said, "wot eet woll be like, to ride down dese striits. De *glory* dat wos Rome . . ."

I bit the bullet. "They're wonderful sets, Mike," I said. "I don't think I've ever seen any more impressive. But you have to understand—I'm not going to do the picture. I'm sorry."

Mike was very good; he never turned a hair. "Woll, off cawrse ef iss not *right* for you . . ." He was consoling me. "Neffer mind, my dear. Ve woll find someting ellse."

Getting on the jet back to L.A. the next day, I was amazed to find Phil Yordan seated next to me, with Nick Ray across the aisle. Phil I knew well as the driving creative force in Sam's company; Nick was a director of very good reputation, who'd already made a film for Bronston. They had another idea to pitch to me, instead of *Roman Empire:* a film about the Boxer Rebellion.

A transoceanic flight is the perfect setting for a film pitch.

The pitchee not only has nowhere to go, he has nothing much to do either, thus is likely to be in a mood to listen to your story. Phil was matchless in this situation; he outlined the history of the attack on the foreign legations in Peking by a bizarre bunch of Chinese fanatics, secretly supported by the Dowager Empress, the last woman in history to hold absolute dictatorial power in any government.

I listened in growing fascination as Phil sketched the story for a film which of course had no script yet, lulled a bit by the bottle of thirty-year-old single malt they'd brought along, disdaining airline alcohol. No, I wasn't drunk; I was interested. It was a marvelous story. Nineteen hundred is a period seldom explored in film. The Boxer Rebellion really happened; it did require the unified defense of the foreign embassies by a mixed bag of European and American troops. Somewhere over Greenland, I said, "This really sounds very promising. Look, let me give you a tentative approval, subject to your making a deal with Herman and my reading the script. When you finish *Roman Empire,* let's get into it."

Phil poured me another dollop of ancient single malt. "Chuck . . . we've put *Roman Empire* on hold. Our next picture is *Fifty-five Days at Peking*. We want you to star in it. We *need* you to star in it."

"But the Roman sets—you've got them half-built already," I said, confused.

"They started tearing them down before we took off this morning," Phil said, "except for the structural steel. Colasanti and Moore have already started on the designs for the Great Wall of China and the legation compound for *Peking*. We want to move on this right now, for a summer shoot."

I was stunned, impressed, and flattered, in about equal measure. They'd planned to start shooting *Roman Empire* that winter, to catch the snows; that Bronston would abandon a major production that far along simply because I wasn't going to be in it staggered me.

Naturally, that's what Phil had in mind. (I don't think they'd *really* started dismantling the Roman sets; they surely waited to see how Phil played his hand, high over Iceland.) He wanted to show me how much they needed me, valued me, and to what lengths they would go to get me.

That tiger I was riding seemed to be moving a little too fast for me. I wasn't quite the green Michigan kid who'd come out to make movies a decade before, but I still felt guilty, somehow. (Exactly how Phil wanted me to feel, of course.) I think I even apologized for putting them in this fix. (I could've used the Iceman at this point.)

Before we landed, I'd made a semicommitment to do *55 Days at Peking* that summer, pending my approval of script and casting. It's been observed in Hollywood that a semicommitment is about as reliable as a semierection, but I've sometimes proceeded on both.

They did indeed tear down the Roman sets, though they made *The Fall of the Roman Empire* a couple of years later, with Sophia from *El Cid* and Stephen Boyd from *Ben-Hur,* along with some formidable Brits—Alec Guinness for one, not to mention Yak Canutt to do the action.

Meantime, Phil set about getting a script for *Peking,* while I went off to do a film in Hawaii. *Diamond Head,* it was called, about a rich planter with a Eurasian mistress and a possessive attitude toward his younger sister. Columbia had developed it for Clark Gable, who'd given them a go on it just before he died. I suppose every studio in town had projects waiting for Gable. Had he lived to do the film, he would have been a widower and the kid sister his daughter, but the adjusted script worked just as well, though the King's shoes were a loose fit for me.

First, I set my own shoe- and handprints in wet cement at Grauman's Chinese Theatre, an ancient Hollywood tradition. There I was, right on top of Marilyn Monroe and Jane Russell. How many men can say that? The next day I flew to Washington to lobby for the film unions. Over the years, my public face has made me useful at that; I spoke with President Kennedy, Vice President Johnson, the Speaker of the House, and a dozen or so senators, all while someone, I presume, was minding the store.

The historical consensus is that Jack Kennedy was enormously good with people, one on one. I'll sign that. He stepped into the Oval Office while I was getting a privileged peek at it and he was supposed to be in a Cabinet meeting. I wasn't scheduled to see him, so he can't have been briefed, but he had appropriate comments on my work, even referring to an article on the historical

background of *El Cid* in some magazine. That's awesome. (A few
months later, I was rebuked by a prominent Palm Beach hostess
who told me she'd been trapped by protocol in the garden of the
Kennedy compound there one unseasonably chilly night while the
President, warmly wrapped in blankets to protect his bad back,
watched *El Cid* for the third time. "Ah lak t'froze to death," she
insisted.)

Before I went off on location, Fray celebrated his seventh
birthday. I'd turned my back for a minute and the baby who'd
lifted my soul the morning he was born had disappeared inside a
gangling, gap-toothed boy with a grin.

I took his party guests over to Goldwyn Studios and ran *The
Big Country* for them. The film played well, but I was disappointed
in my performance. I've almost never been content with what I've
done in any film. My heart's desire would be to do them all over
again (and not do a half-dozen of them at all).

The *Diamond Head* shoot went smoothly, more than most.
We had a very good English director, Guy Green. He'd just done an
admirable small film, *Light in the Piazza,* with a strikingly beautiful
girl, Yvette Mimieux, whom I was happy to approve in the role of
my kid sister. Hawaii is a pleasant place to work; I've filmed there
since a few more times, though I confess to finding it a little boring
over a long schedule. Our producer, Jerry Bresler, was intelligent
and efficient. (I do remember Guy Green musing, "I wonder that a
man would choose to boast of making a film called *Gidget Goes
Hawaiian.*")

Of course we all (almost all) prefer a smooth-running shoot.
It's miles above the snarling catfights that some directors and rather
more actors and (God knows) actresses impose on their fellows.
Personally, I abhor that kind of ego-driven crap (and it *is* ego,
mostly). It's hard enough to make a good picture when everyone
shows up on time ready to work, resolving differences on script,
performance, and the length of your bloody Winnebago outside the
shooting day.

(Ahh . . . we have to have a How Movies Are Really Made note
here. You guys know about Winnebagos, right? Those forty-foot
buses [well, they come smaller, but you'd better not give one to
anybody with a bankable name] we all have now to change our
clothes and sulk in? Here's a pearl of true wisdom, contributed by

Vanessa Redgrave, possibly the greatest actress alive. She was making a picture laid in the Arctic for a friend of mine, Peter Snell, most of which they wisely shot on the northern coast of British Columbia, some degrees south of the Arctic Circle. The second unit was shooting real Arctic footage a hundred miles north, on a glacier. Vanessa had a day off on the main unit, so they choppered her up to the glacier to get some tie-in shots of her on a snowmobile and the like.

Whereupon a blizzard struck, trapping them on the glacier for some twenty hours. Vanessa spent most of that time huddled in a survival tent half-buried in snow, with two crew members and the second-unit director. They'd long since stopped trying to talk over the wind screaming outside and simply slumped inside their parkas, staring at the flame of the tiny Sterno burner that heated their tea. At last Vanessa lifted her head and spoke in her rich, clear voice, "I shall never complain . . . about my Winnebago . . . again.")

OK, back to Hawaii. Both good and successful films (not necessarily the same thing) have come out of wildly contentious, miserably unhappy and costly shoots, rife with drunken directors, sulking actors, and weeping actresses, though not often.

Diamond Head had none of these obstructions. Our people were good, they worked well. The film turned out to be outrageously successful; I still get checks. I haven't seen it in a number of years; I'm not sure how good I thought it really was, though it did serve to show again that I could carry a film alone.

Riding the tiger, though, you should do more than that. Good isn't enough—you have to try for *better*. My role wasn't hard to reach, but my journal for the shoot has entries like "The stable scene went well. I might've done more." Yes, indeed.

I have no excuses, at least no good ones. A year-and-a-half of two back-to-back films with Wyler had led me to rely on being pressed, if not driven, to the sharpest edge of performance. Lord knows I was working hard on *Diamond Head;* we all were, fitting our exterior scenes in between the drifting rain showers endemic to Hawaii, particularly in Kauai, where we were shooting most of our location.

Choosing that island served us right. It's very beautiful, but has the highest levels of annual rainfall in the world. The locals still intoned the mantra I've heard on film locations from Kauai to

Kyrgyzstan in Central Asia and from Scotland to the south of Spain:
"I can't understand it—it *never* rains here this time of year."

The shooting days we were losing made me worry about our schedule, which was wrong. When I direct, I should worry about that . . . as an actor, it's not my problem, except to be sure I come on time (which trickles down to the other actors). I still worry —a lot. (A few years later, Walter Mirisch, an old friend and gifted producer for whom I've worked several times, said to me on a shoot, "You know, Chuck, you're one of the finest actors in film, but we sure lost a great first assistant director when you took up acting." I suppose it tells you something to know that I consider that a compliment.)

Lydia eased my itching angst by flying out for our anniversary. We had a wonderful reunion with the rain spattering down outside. (It's raining violets?) It was still raining rain the next morning, so we began our nineteenth year of marriage in bed instead of on location, with champagne and pearls for my girl.

A week or so later, we wrapped the Kauai shoot and moved to Honolulu and the short end of the location. They put me into a fine suite in the Royal Hawaiian Hotel, which had once been the only hotel on Oahu. (The last time I was there, three other hotels stood crowded next to the Royal on what had been its surrounding grounds.)

It wasn't hard to persuade Lydia to come visit again. At six months, Holly was a little young for the trip, but Fray came along, insisting on maturity. When I took Lydia out to dinner the first night we were there, he indignantly refused the nurse we'd engaged to keep an eye on him. "I don't need any sitter! I'm not a baby anymore." He had me there.

He also had a little time on the big white stud they'd found in California and flown out for me to ride in the picture. He was as fine a piece of horseflesh as the two Babiecas in *El Cid,* but with a softer mouth and disposition, a better-broke horse altogether. At seven, Fray was no horseman yet, of course, but he was comfortable in the saddle. He'd started at three; I wish I had.

I did take advantage of what down time I had to work with the horse; the more time I put in, the better I'd look in the film. Of all the physical skills actors may need in the movies, horsebacking is the most likely. When I've worn the director's hat, I've found it's pointless to ask actors if they can ride. Absolutely without exception, they said, "Oh, sure, all my life."

Having horsebacked a fair bit, on- and offscreen, I ride well, as actors go. But measuring me against a real horseman is like checking the difference between a good player in your tennis foursome and Pete Sampras. Still, I've always enjoyed it. In Hawaii that spring, I tried polo again, quickly realizing that was yet another sport I'd waited too long to learn.

We came back to California for the interiors and wrapped the picture by the middle of May. Columbia seemed delighted with it, and its eventual success was gratifying. I never have figured out why I feel that I fell short on that film. Looking back on what I've written about it here, I notice I had a lot to say about my family coming to visit and the quality of the horse. No, that's not a crack about the people who made the film, but maybe I was focusing on the wrong agenda when we shot *Diamond Head*.

Meantime, the tiger was pacing up and down while I prepared for *55 Days at Peking*. I was not content with the rewrite Phil Yordan's writers had produced. True, film scripts go through endless reworkings during the shoot, then again in the editing room. But we were to start shooting in six weeks, and the principal roles had not even been cast. They wanted David Niven to play the British ambassador, a wonderful choice, and Ava Gardner for the White Russian countess, not so wonderful a choice, I thought. I decided I'd better go to Madrid to get it all worked out.

It was about this time in my career that I began to feel I was carving a trail in the sky on the transpolar jets, a tiger trail, I suppose. Fortunately, I've always slept well in airplanes, even during the war in B-25s—a very noisy, drafty aircraft indeed. I say this is because my heart is pure, though Lydia, who does *not* sleep well in airplanes, takes a dim view of this position.

The Bronston camp, as always, was in a highly energized state. So were the redoubtable Colasanti and Moore, who had their production design well in hand. They were a very gifted pair. The senior partner, Veniero Colasanti, had a very intense, Italianate manner, while John Moore, perhaps the balance wheel of the team, operated at a slightly lower temperature. It was never clear to me

which of the two designed the costumes and which the sets. They
insisted it was a joint undertaking.

Their task on *Peking* was more challenging than on *El Cid,*
where they'd had the advantage of choosing their castle exteriors
from the dozens of genuine eleventh-century castles that stud the
Spanish landscape. For *Peking,* first having torn down the half-
completed *Roman Empire* sets, they'd then had to build a plausible
Peking, including a good part of the Imperial Palace, the foreign
legations compound, canals, streets, bridges, and a formidable
section of the Great Wall of China. They'd largely accomplished
this by then, on the same ground where I'd inspected the Roman
sets.

The costumes, too, rivaled the splendid work they'd done
for *Cid,* though the turn of the nineteenth century didn't offer quite
the same opportunity, except in the wardrobe for the Chinese imperial court. For my role as the U.S. Marine major commanding the
embassy guard, I wore only dress blues in two scenes, and a field
uniform in which I was to spend most of the next five months. (I
did find a wonderfully battered campaign hat. As DeMille had taught
me, hats are important.)

This was all very well, but meantime we still had to complete
both the script and the cast, above all the role of the Russian countess. The primary problem with wringing an actual work of art out
of film, the art form of our time, is the sheer enormity of doing the
damn thing at all. Michelangelo had no problem carving the *David,*
or the *Moses;* his defeats were rooted in the frustrating distractions
of getting someone to buy him the bloody block of marble in the
first place.

As I was just beginning to understand from my vantage point
on the tiger's back, filmmaking is inescapably driven by the tens of
millions of dollars (now inflated to hundreds of millions) that can
be made or lost in the process. Once you've started drawing down
on your money, you're bound by the iron economics of cash flow,
commitments, contracts. The fight between art and commerce gets
very bitter. As someone observed, "If Hitler's still alive, I hope he's
making a big film on location somewhere."

That's why I went back to Madrid, to thrash out the casting
of our Russian countess. There were then no major American film

actresses who could plausibly play non-American roles. For me, that limited the field to Europeans, of whom only two or three had international star stature. I thought Jeanne Moreau could be wonderful as a dubiously titled Russian (was she really a countess?) barely past the best bloom of her beauty, stranded in Peking in the boiling political turmoil of the time.

The Bronston camp disagreed. They insisted the best choice was Ava Gardner. She was a formidable international star of world-class beauty and an adequate actress whose real-life image echoed our countess's troubled background.

I argued for Moreau because she was plausibly Russian and a better actress. Still, I dutifully flew to Rome to look at some rough-cut footage on a film Ava had just finished. Back the next day for a final, passionately argued meeting, I was the lone Moreau holdout, but I was also the one with casting approval. (As Abraham Lincoln sometimes said in cabinet meetings, "Well, it's six to one against me, so I reckon my vote carries.")

So we agreed Moreau was our lady, with fulsome assurances of confidence and goodwill all round. Brimming with bonhomie, Sam insisted I lunch with him at the Ritz the next day before catching my jet to L.A. It seemed a nice idea; the Ritz is one of the great hotels in the world, then still one of several where actors, if identified, were denied lodging. Only that summer, Jimmy Stewart, who'd remained in the Air Force Reserves after his sterling service in World War II, came to Madrid to do his annual month of active duty at Torrejon Air Base. He'd reserved a suite at the Ritz, where they had no idea this J. Stewart was *the* J. Stewart. As he signed the register, the manager sidled over, discombobulated. "Ahh, Señor Stewart . . . I am honored to meet you, but . . . ah, you are an actor, of course. We . . . ah . . . do not, ah . . . cater to actors, you see."

Jimmy looked at him coolly. "'Zat so? Waal, lemme tell ya. For the next four weeks, I'm Brigadier General James Stewart, United States Air Force." He picked up the keys and turned to the elevator.

Anyway, the next day the maître d' directed me courteously (only for lunch, after all) to Sam's table in the garden. I was happy to have him order for us both. I'd just lifted a glass of a superb Meursault when he launched into a panegyric to Ava Gardner, which lasted through the chilled gazpacho and well into the grilled

merluza. "Sam," I said at last, "didn't we do this yesterday afternoon
... all afternoon? I thought we'd all agreed on Jeanne Moreau."

This only inspired him to further flights of rhetoric, increasingly intense. He had to make me understand . . . the future of the film . . . of the studio, both our careers . . . if not peace in the world, at least tranquillity in Spain. I *must* see he was speaking the truth, on the lives of his children.

I said almost nothing, stunned by the windstorm of words. Suddenly Sam stopped in mid-sentence, his face white. He reached out a hand to touch my shoulder and burst into great heaving sobs, tears dropping on his lapels. "Sam, for God's sake," I said in helpless embarrassment, but he only cried the harder, his head in his hands. I offered him my napkin, knocking his wineglass into his lap.

The waiters clustered round with cold towels while I knelt beside him, patting his back. At this point, the concierge joined us. The driver insisted I must leave at once, or miss my plane. I said my good-byes to Sam, he kissed my hand, and I ran through the garden to the car. As Sam's Rolls accelerated, I leaned back against the leather cushions, and ruefully realized I had just OK'd Ava Gardner for *Peking*. How wise of the Ritz to ban actors.

I went home not only to savor the last two weeks I'd have to myself for the rest of the year, but to explore a couple of interesting projects that had come up. The first was a play I'd been offered for Broadway: *The Lovers*. I didn't think it would work for the stage (it didn't), but might as a film (it did). It was the first property I ever bought, thus dear to my heart.

Walter Seltzer, who'd chaperoned me through the early days with Hal Wallis, had just survived the interesting challenge of running Marlon Brando's independent production company. After some months of total inactivity, Walter urged Brando to pick one of the several projects the studio had optioned for him, so they could put it into production. "You know, Marlon," he pointed out, "Paramount's been spending a lot of money on this operation for a long time. They'll make anything you want. We really owe them a movie."

Marlon was in a humanitarian mood. "How can you talk about making a *movie,*" he intoned, "when we got eight hundred thousand people starving in India?"

George Glass, Walter's partner in the company, responded. "Well, we got two middle-aged Jews sitting here doing nothing. Doesn't that grab you a little?"

When Marlon's company died of inertia, Walter was happy to produce a film someone really wanted to make. We hired John Collier, a fine English writer, to adapt the play for the screen. The pages were slow in coming, but they looked good. Very good.

Herman the Iceman also had an offer for me from George Stevens. "This is a very big picture, Chuck," he said. *"The Greatest Story Ever Told.* He wants you to play John the Baptist. It's the lead."

"Herman," I said, "trust me on this: John the Baptist is *not* the lead in any picture called *The Greatest Story Ever Told.* But you tell Mr. Stevens I'll talk to him about any part he wants me to play."

So I had him over for lunch. George's plans sounded very exciting. Unfortunately, he planned to start in the late summer, when I'd still be shooting *Peking.* Fortunately, he very much wanted me to play the Baptist; I very much wanted to do it. We agreed to try to dovetail the two schedules and left it at that.

It was time to move my family to Spain for the summer, but we laid over at the penthouse in New York for a day or so. I had some odds and ends to clean up before I left the country, among them meeting with my publicist, Bill Blowitz, a lovely, wry man who was superb at his job. (He was killed by a New York taxi not long after . . . I miss him—still.)

Bill was an old Hollywood hand; I valued his opinions. Over lunch, I discussed our problems on *Peking,* but said I was looking forward to working with Nick Ray. I didn't really know him, but I'd admired his direction on a couple of films. Bill looked at me oddly. "I know Nick pretty well," he said. "We used to play poker almost every week. Let me tell you something, Chuck. He's a gifted guy— but he's a loser." That proved to be a prescient observation.

By mid-June, we were well settled in Madrid in a pleasant villa not far from the studio where we'd do most of the interiors. (Sam was actually building another studio, but it wouldn't be ready by our scheduled start date.) The sets planned for both studios were eclipsed by the exteriors duplicating much of Peking, by then all but completed on the beautiful landscape at Las Matas.

Drawing on some experience with sets of this kind, I'd have to say that though single sets—the Great Circus at Antioch for the

Ben-Hur chariot sequence, the walls and gates of the city of Per Rameses for *Ten Commandments*—were more individually impressive, Colasanti and Moore's rendition of whole areas of Peking was the most variegated complex of period exteriors I've worked on, offering a wider spectrum of cinematic opportunities than any I've seen. The contest is over, of course—no one can afford to build sets like that now (though I'm told we'll soon be able to paint them on glass and somehow project the actors inside them. When they figure out how to paint the actors in too, my profession is in trouble.)

Succumbing to the edifice complex, our gifted design team had provided us with more set than could possibly be shot, let alone filled with Chinese. A running joke that summer was that you couldn't get a good Chinese dinner or your shirt washed anywhere in Europe because all the Chinese were in Spain fighting the Boxer Rebellion.

The sets were incredibly good, the casting was falling into place. The script, however, remained a stubborn problem, as scripts often do. I was doing *55 Days at Peking* because the Bronston people had expected and prepared for me to do *The Fall of the Roman Empire*. When I had finally passed on this, later than I should have, Phil Yordan had improvised the idea of *55 Days at Peking* more or less out of thin air on the polar jet.

The idea of a film about the Boxer Rebellion is a very good one. Whether I should've felt morally obligated to undertake it is another question. I didn't; I liked the idea. The rebellion actually happened, in an exotic and cinematic country little explored in film. There surely was a picture in there; the question was how to find it. *El Cid* had been about a real man, a key figure at the center of eleventh-century Spanish history. In *Peking* our fictional Marine major ends up sharing command with an also fictional British ambassador, defending the foreign compound. Add a stranded Russian countess and you have only to knit these principals into the Boxer Rebellion. Simple, huh?

It wasn't. With the Cid, history told me why he was there, why he did what he did, where he stood in the context of his time. In *Peking,* only the Dowager Empress was etched in history; we had to make up the other people. This was easy enough with my Marine major and David Niven's ambassador, both committed career men, serving where they're sent and stoically accepting the likelihood of dying where the dice put them. But what about Ava's Russian countess—now that it would certainly have to be Ava's—how would she see the lady, and what would she be able to do with her?

I'd never met Ava Gardner until she reported to Madrid, a week or so before shooting began. She was a major star, perhaps as perfect an example of classical beauty as Hollywood had found since Garbo, the first star created by MGM when they were inventing the process. Ava Gardner was among the best of the last, at the peak of the studio's luminous trajectory.

I'd come into films after the studio system was breaking down, but I understood how it functioned: very efficiently, but with not much care for its people. Ava had not been treated well, I think —not by the studio that made her, or the several famous men who married her as a trophy wife, nor the larger number who used and abused her as a star-fuck. That's an ugly word, but nakedly honest. For filmmakers, it underscores the value of the old maxim: Don't fuck the talent—it's very distracting and even more counterproductive. It's also true that, for both men and women, sex establishes a certain power. There's an old maxim there, too: "Get hold of a man's balls, and his heart and mind will surely follow."

I have no idea what Ava thought about all this, let alone her opinions on her role. Over a drink in her suite, we talked of other things. She came across as softer and simpler than I'd expected; you could see the Carolina girl in there. "I'm still a Tarheel," she said proudly. It occurred to me this vulnerability she displayed could be useful in the role, but I didn't venture to suggest that to her.

A day or two later, she attended a meeting on the script at Nick Ray's house. She seemed very edgy, saying little until her second vodka tonic, when she launched on a diatribe trashing the entire project and just about everything she had to do in it. This may have been Ava's first experience of a full-court-press script conference; in her time at MGM, actors didn't sit in on script meetings. Nevertheless, she was an instinctive mistress of the slash-and-burn technique: destroy everything in sight, wait till they sweep away the ashes and rescue the children, then start again.

I really hate this approach to the fine art of film, though it's a popular tactic, God knows. I slipped outside for a break from the yelling and suddenly remembered Bill Blowitz's comment about Nick losing at poker. I looked back at the hot, harsh scene inside, tossed my wineglass into the pool, and walked home over the ridge through the Spanish summer twilight.

I got there in time to help Lydia sort out a squabble between Fray and his baby sister. It seemed more soluble and just as important as the screaming that still echoed over the ridge. I know, I should've stayed. Call me coward.

We began shooting only a few days behind schedule, on some easy nuts-and-bolts stuff, the kind of scene you start with because it presents no problems. Then I had a few days off while Nick explored the Chinese imperial court, with David Niven as the outpost of empire against Flora Robson as the Dowager Empress. She was damn good. (Flora, I mean. The real Dowager Empress was close to being insane.)

Robert Helpmann played her prime minister. Bobby had been a great ballet star; when his legs went, he shifted into acting, with some success. Transformed by a wonderful Chinese makeup, he was very effective as the sly heavy in *Peking*. We had no scenes together, but I'll be forever grateful to him: he taught me to do a court waltz with Ava, a key stroke in establishing our relationship and also the centerpiece of a major ball sequence.

Unfortunately, neither Ava nor I was prepared for it. My boyhood in the Michigan woods had not included dancing lessons; I guess Ava had been similarly deprived in North Carolina. Nowadays, they'd call us "choreographically challenged." The fact was, we couldn't dance.

After some hours of intense instruction from Bobby, we could. With a master dancer's heroic carriage, he led Ava through wondrously whirling combinations. Partnered with me, he was transformed, melting in my arms, light as a leaf, all supple grace. Suddenly dancing was terribly easy, and wonderful fun.

Together, Ava and I weren't as good. By a long shot. When the big day of the ball scene came, we avoided disgracing Bobby's teaching, but only barely. I have to say though, with Helpmann, I cut a mean court waltz.

So we settled in for the long summer shoot. Jolly and Kay West, in Europe on some arcane academic chores, dropped in for a visit. That's one of the more pleasant perks of working on an attractive location; you have a nice pad with lots of room for pals. Fray took riding lessons, getting some grounding in the formal Spanish riding school; if you gut it out, it's guaranteed to give you a good seat on a horse. Holly visited the set from time to time, but was happiest with Lydia at the villa, romping in the lush garden and falling in love with our big shepherd, Drago.

(I've owned dogs all my life, mostly shepherds. Of all the animals that came with Adam when God threw him out of Eden, the dog seems to have joined the family of man most joyously. Genetically, dogs are pack animals; millennia of domestication can't erase that. To a dog, the head human around the place is simply the top dog . . . Alpha dog, in animal behavior lingo.

Since Fray fed him and Drago slept by his bed, he saw Fray as the Beta dog. They had a very special relationship. Holly wasn't a toddler, stretching toward little girl, she was a puppy, to be indulged and guarded.

His full name was Arthur Pendragon, and he was surely a kingly animal, somehow always able to establish his presence wherever he found himself. He'd emerged unruffled, from the indignity of flying the Atlantic in a crate, accepting Spain and establishing his territory there with perfect equanimity. He was surely the best of the many dogs that have lived on our ridge, enriching our lives all the years we had with him. We miss him still; the Sainted Drago.)

We were in full production by then, but very carefully, like hunters closing in on a treed bear. After two weeks, we were still shooting from an unfinished script. Incredible? I agree. You rewrite routinely throughout production, but you need a finished script to do that. We were shooting peripheral scenes, avoiding the core of the story, which still wasn't right.

The new sound stage was finished, but after the first day working on it, they realized it would have to be air-conditioned in order to shoot elaborately lit interiors there, with the actors wearing period costumes in the Spanish summer. Ava looked absolutely marvelous, even with sweat curving down her Edwardian décolletage. Nick directed her first scene with the thinnest of kid gloves. She was . . . still edgy, but amiable. Like many very beautiful actresses (and there were none more beautiful than Ava), she was very insecure about her acting, though she was in fact perfectly capable. As a director, Nick was good with actors, but in shaping her performance, he seemed insecure too.

Ahh, what the hell am I doing here? *"Nil nisi mortuis bonum,"* they say. "Of the dead, speak only good." Fair enough, and that last paragraph is true, but it's not really the way it was. Ava's security trembled on the rim of a vodka glass, into which she often slipped. Maybe Nick did, too . . . I don't know.

She was most reliable in the morning, aside from the half-hour-late-on-the-set routinely conceded star actresses. (I think that's now been expanded to an hour for actresses billed above the title.) But we were shooting French hours, eleven in the morning to eight in the evening, to let people sleep in and also leave us the long summer twilights for low-key exteriors. Unfortunately, after four in the afternoon, you couldn't really count on Ava to do lines. We decided the only solution was to kill her. (No, *no!!* . . . I mean her *character.*) It made sense structurally, and Phil wrote a plausible death scene: Ava, felled by Boxer shrapnel while nursing the wounded, has a last few moments to resolve our failed affair. All actors love death scenes; Ava was enthusiastic about this one.

"Schedule it first shot in the morning," I said. "She'll be up for it then." So she was, buoyant and bright, in high good spirits. We ran through the scene once or twice in her dressing room; I thought she was fine. Unfortunately the previous day's scene had slopped over; Nick didn't wrap the other set till midafternoon.

By the time he had Ava's death scene lit, she couldn't do it. The staging was no problem—she was lying in a hospital bed—but she couldn't manage the lines. Paul Lukas, a Best Actor Oscar–winner in 1943 for *Watch on the Rhine,* was playing the surgeon, with little to do in this scene. "Let Paul do her lines," I said. And, with surprisingly little rewriting, he did. I'm still amazed we got away with this, but the dialogue worked quite well, largely because of Paul's skill.

Nick was badly at fault here. Given Ava's problem, he should've shot her death scene as scheduled, when she was ready for it. If she remembered it, to lie listening to another actor play her own death scene must've been an unspeakable humiliation.

I found myself thinking more and more about Bill's measure of Nick as a loser. He was a sensitive and intelligent man. When he was talking about a scene, or an acting problem, you saw a quick, creative mind at work. *Shooting* the scene, you saw something quite different. He wasn't so much directing as acting the role of director. He was surely not a good captain. Whatever his talents, a director must, *must* be a captain.

Nick played a part in his own fall, but it was still a sad, terrible thing. We'd moved to the huge exterior set of the city of Peking at Las Matas, shooting a scene with Ava talking to me while hundreds of refugees streamed in through the looming gates behind us. For the actors, it was an easy scene; technically, it was very complicated, establishing in one setup the chaos of the peasants fleeing to safety inside the city.

It was a lovely, mild day. The several hundred Chinese extras were not experienced, but they were doing well enough . . . until one of them took a picture of Ava. She had a firm rule about that. Aside from assigned and credentialed professionals, no one was supposed to take her picture, certainly not on the set.

She insisted that the offender be found, fired, and stripped of his film. I'm surprised she didn't have him skinned as well. As a rule, Ava was sweet-tempered, but in her fury, she made the Dowager Empress of China seem like your favorite aunt.

Her passion spent, Ava retired to her dressing room to compose herself. This took more than four hours. When it became clear that we were in for a considerable wait, I went to my dressing room, pulled off my boots, and got through three chapters of a very good history of the Spanish Civil War. There was really no alternative; Nick had laid out, lit, and rehearsed a tricky crane shot booming over the extras to Ava and me talking. I'd worked on sets with more people in them, but not when you couldn't turn a camera.

Finally, of course, Ava reappeared, looking marvelous. There was a great noisy bustle of preparation, then silence, waiting for the call to turn over—when Ava heard another camera click. At least she insisted she had, though this time none could be found. She disappeared in a white rage and Nick wrapped the company for the day.

They set an early call for the next morning, while it was still cool. I got to the set even earlier, to discuss with Nick what else we could shoot if we had more trouble. We did indeed. Nick suddenly dropped unconscious, felled by a massive coronary. As the ambulance roared off to the hospital with him, I had the unhappy task of

"Ruin running," the kids used to call it.

With Holly and Lydia on Hadrian's Wall. (Fray's over the hill, looking for the Roman legions.)

Conducting Beethoven.

Revealing my shaky backhand to a paying audience. "Step *into* the ball, dummy. Take it on the rise."

On the *Will Penny* shoot, with Holly at a shining time.

And with Holly and Fray, ridin' old Paint.

Planet of the Apes with Kim Hunter and Roddy McDowall. Homo sapiens on trial.

OPPOSITE:
Directed by Franklin Schaffner again in *Planet of the Apes*.

Waiting for the sun, Glen Canyon, Arizona.

The father as the keeper of the gate.

Julius Caesar (1970). "And the winner by a nose... John Gielgud!"

Looking for Cleopatra with Hildegard Neil (Jane Lapotaire below).

Where an older but no wiser Antony throws away a third of the Western world for a woman.

Another *Macbeth* with Vanessa Redgrave. "I dare do all that may become a man . . .

OPPOSITE:
As Cardinal Richelieu.

With Deborah Kerr and one of the few laughs in Mr. O'Neill's dark master-piece, *Long Day's Journey into Night*.

It's tough to be the captain of a nuclear sub... especially on the bottom.

Dying again: Henry VIII.

THREE PHOTOS: LYDIA CLARKE HESTON

With Holly, eye to eye with the pyramids.

On *The Mountain Men*. Fray's not *that* much taller than I am.

THREE PHOTOS: LYDIA CLARKE HESTON

Shooting a documentary on the Soviet war in Afghanistan.

Wearing the Fraser tartan.

OPPOSITE:
. . . and the heroic Sir Thomas More.

Second trip to Vietnam, near Danang.

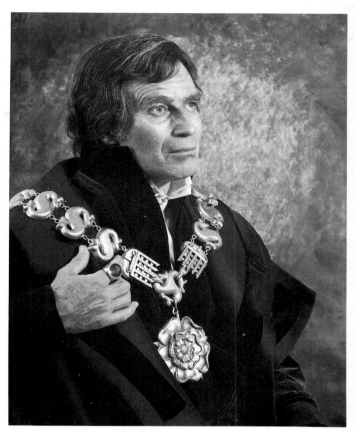

As the murderous Long John Silver . . .

. . . the infamous Captain Queeg.

and Sherlock Holmes.

Also Holmes, disguised as an ancient Chinese opium dealer.

And in *True Lies* (1993), intimidating Arnold.

Touring the Los Alamos nuclear facility.

telling Ava, which I did as simply as I could, conveying no blame. At my urging, she went back to the hotel; without Nick, the only scenes we could shoot were second-unit battle stuff, which we did for two days. It was a bleak and difficult time.

I went to see Nick in the hospital, where he lay gray-faced and frail. Though we talked of his imminent return, it was clear to me that he couldn't possibly finish the film. (In fact, he never directed a feature again.) This presented a major problem. Ava's role was almost completed, but David Niven and I had a great deal yet to do. Worse, we both had firm stop dates; David was due to start a film in Italy and I was supposed to report to George Stevens in Arizona on November 4 to play John the Baptist for him. (I used the slack time while we were figuring out how to shoot the rest of *55 Days at Peking* to work out my Baptist makeup and filming tests.) Still, *Peking* was now six weeks behind schedule.

The prime problem was getting a director for the two or three major scenes Ava still had, all with me. I suggested Guy Green, who'd directed *Diamond Head* successfully a few months earlier, getting a very good performance from Yvette Mimieux. Guy accepted, flew over, reworked the scenes, and served as the white knight to the rescue. We probably would've been wise to have him on the film from the beginning. As is customary, though Guy was of course well-paid for his work, he took no screen credit, following an unspoken tradition when one director replaces a colleague who cannot finish his film.

Ava was shaken by Nick's collapse; I think she even accepted some responsibility for it. Actually, I'm not persuaded she should have. Directing a picture is the toughest job in film; Harry Truman's advice applies here: If you can't stand the heat, get out of the kitchen. I felt sorry for Nick, but I'm afraid Bill Blowitz had been right. Nick was a loser.

You're right—that's harsh. It was a harsh experience—one of the toughest shoots I've ever had, in more than sixty films. Ava was as difficult as any actress I've worked with . . . after four in the afternoon. I also remember a desperate and lonely woman, too.

I was lonely too, by then. Lydia had to get Fray back to school, so she'd flown home with the kids, the dog, and seventeen pieces of luggage. I closed up the villa and moved into the Castellana Hilton.

Ava worked better with Guy; either she'd pulled herself together, or he better understood how to work with her. For one thing, he made sure that her coverage on a scene never included more than a speech or two in a given setup. She was more relaxed, even more sober. We even shot late her last day of work, wrapping after 8 P.M.

We were still six weeks behind, which threatened both my stop date and David Niven's, but Sam Bronston threw a birthday party for Mike Waszynski. A must for me, of course, but I didn't mind. Sam gave good parties and Mike was a nice guy. It was the last I saw of Ava, though (on that film). She attended, looking quite marvelous in white satin, with appropriate and obviously genuine emeralds.

Of course we were seated at Mike's table, with David and the few principal actors still on the film. I was having as good a time as I expect to have at a big party, until people got up to dance. That was my cue to take a turn with Ava, but I didn't feel up to it without Bobby Helpmann there to coach me, so we sat chatting idly, while I sketched in the pad I often carry. After a bit, I started to excuse myself. She gripped my wrist. "You can't leave now," she said, fiercely.

"Ava, I'm just going to the john," I protested. "I'll be right back, I promise. Look, here's my sketchbook. I'll leave it with you." She let me go and took the book, while I made a running trip to the men's room. When I got back, a photographer from *Paris Match* was shooting her, perfectly composed.

He missed a great shot, though. I left the party not long after she did, thinking of my early morning call. Standing at the curb waiting for my driver, I saw Ava, gleaming in her white gown in the middle of the Avenida Generalisimo, performing very creditable matador's passes with her red evening cape on the taxis going by. It was unforgettable, my most vivid memory of that extraordinary lady. I think she'd settle for that.

I have to tell you a story about Bronston Films. I think Sam was a decent man, but not all his people were. My driver, Ricardo Perez, was also a decent man—and a good driver. The main reason to have a driver on location is to let you think about your scene when you're going to work in the morning, and get some sleep

when you're heading home at night. We didn't talk much, except
sometimes so I could practice my Spanish if I'd had an easy day.

One evening after looking at dailies, I greeted Ricardo as I
slid into the back and put my legs up on the jump seat, "Cóme va,
viejo? Todo en orden?" He closed the door and got behind the
wheel.

"Well enough, Señor, except that I have not been paid for
five weeks."

"Five *weeks!!?*" I said, stunned. "You should've told me
sooner. Hold the car . . . I'll go tell Señor Prades." I went inside, to
Jaime Prades' office. Sam's comptroller was an affable, fat South
American with a pencil-thin mustache. He took pains each week to
give me my expense allowance personally, always in mint-fresh
thousand-peseta notes sealed in a thick envelope. When I told him
Ric's story, he was outraged. He pressed the intercom and chewed
somebody out in a torrent of profane Spanish too fast for me to
follow fully.

"A thousand apologies, my dear Chuck," he said, clasping my
hand. "Please tell your driver he will be paid tomorrow morning."
I went back to my car, reassured Ric, and slept on the way to the
hotel, feeling virtuous.

Buried in our various production problems, I finally thought
some days later to check on Ric's situation. "Your back pay all
caught up now?" I asked one morning as we drove to the studio.

"Oh, no, Señor. No one will speak to me about it. It is now
more than six weeks." Now I was angry as well as appalled.

"Jaime, what the hell is going on here?" I said, striding into
his office. "You're spending however many million it is by now on
this film, and stiffing a poor driver working for forty bucks a week?!"

I have to say Prades was spectacular. He leapt to his feet and
screamed "*Federico!* Venga . . . en seguida!" In seconds his head
accountant ran in and stood trembling. For fully two minutes Jaime
stripped the skin off him, switching to English toward the end to
make sure I was following. "You have betrayed the company that
employs you, wounded my honor, and criminally distracted Señor
Heston from the film on which we all depend!"

He scared *me,* and I wasn't the guy he was mad at. As the
accountant scuttled out, the smoke clearing, I said, "Jesus, Jaime, I

don't want you to burn down your office. Just make them give Ric his money, for God's sake. See to it personally, *please.*" Elaborately reassured on this point, I passed the message on to Ric and spent the next ten hours pretending to defend Peking.

At the end of the day, ready for a bath and a beer, I remembered to check with Ric. No, he had still not been paid. I walked in on Jaime still in my uniform, battle-stained and pissed off. He stood, amazed. "Chuck!! Please, please do not tell me your poor Ric does not yet have his money!"

"No, Jaime," I said. "Ric's been paid. By me. Through this week and one month's advance. Now you don't owe him. You owe *me*. I'd like the money right away, please." Prades never turned a hair. He pulled open a drawer in his desk crammed full of neat stacks of thousand-peseta notes, peeled off a dozen or so, and passed them over. "Thank you," I said, unable to think of anything better.

We had larger problems, ones not so easily settled. We were still six weeks behind, slopping beyond David's and my stop dates. If your work on one film prevents you from reporting as agreed to on another, there are serious consequences on both sides.

True, the toughest part of the film was behind us. We'd finished Ava's role, vastly improved by Guy Green's direction. But we still had to shoot the bulk of the action, studded with what Phil Yordan called "little actor's canapes," short cameo scenes highlighting the roles of the various national contingents defending the city.

David and I didn't really see many "canapes" in the several weeks of difficult scenes we faced, with both day and night work, almost all on huge exterior sets involving principals, hundreds of stuntmen and extras, all at the mercy of Spain's autumn weather.

Also, we had no director. Guy had finished what he'd signed on for and there was no possibility of Nick's returning. We did have two very good men directing our two second units, Andrew "Bundy" Marton, who'd worked with Yak on the *Ben-Hur* race, and Noel Brown. Luckily, the actors who still had work to do were all dependable talents, like Johnny Ireland and some reliable Brits. We also had David.

David Niven is my happiest memory of that whole shoot. He was that increasingly rara avis, a true gentleman, funny as only Brits can be, a flawless professional and best of all, a superb actor. When he'd won his Best Actor Oscar for *Separate Tables,* he stumbled going up the steps to the stage. Improvising a thin gag about falling because he was loaded with so many good luck pieces he was top- heavy, he said, "The reason I fell is that I was loaded . . . " and was drowned in the largest laugh in the history of Academy acceptances (admittedly not a rich mine of wit).

No matter what Phil Yordan said about actors' canapes, much of the dialogue was more like pudding. Concentrating on David's scenes because he had the earlier stop date, the two of us managed to turn the speeches into something closer to smoked salmon, if not quite caviar. Like any good actor, David had an ear for the structure of a speech; so do I. We'd rework the scene the night before it was to be shot, or even on set if it was a complicated first setup. If I wasn't in the scene he was scheduled for, I'd go over to the other unit and do battle shots.

Of course Bundy and Noel directed their units, both of them now first units, since both were doing dialogue scenes. David and I were able to help by coming to work with the acting bits a little more rehearsed than usual. We concentrated on getting all of David's angles, often leaving some of the action cuts to be picked up later.

It worked. We finished David a day ahead of his stop date, also picking up four days on the schedule overall. There weren't enough actors left on the film to have a wrap party so I took him out to dinner at Horcher's. We ate well and sat late, over good wine. We talked of acting, and love, and war.

I knew David had an outstanding war record. Though his career was well established in Hollywood when Britain went to war in 1939, he'd squirmed, bullied, and connived his way back to England to take up the reserve commission he still held in one of the Guards regiments. He ended up with probably the best combat record of any actor in the war on either side. I also knew he wouldn't talk about it.

He did tell me a marvelous story about his meeting with Winston Churchill. As a Churchill fan, I relished it. It seems his public face (as David put it) and his combat service (as I suspect) had, toward the end of the war, earned him an invitation for a weekend at Chequers, the Prime Ministerial country manor. There were of course a dozen or so other guests, far grander than David, but he had his moment with the great man. Pacing the graveled paths with him Sunday morning, Churchill said, "Well, Niven. I've been told of the difficulties you surmounted to come back from Hollywood and take up arms again in the service of your country. That's admirable, Niven. Admirable."

"Thank you, Prime Minister," David murmured modestly. "Mind you," Churchill said sharply, "anything less would have been despicable." I do like that story. I liked David, too.

Now my family was gone, my costars were gone, both directors were gone. I'd have been glad if even my dog had stayed behind. But there was just me, and the rest of the movie. I was in every scene that was left, and there were still an awful lot of them. There was also George Stevens, expecting me on November 4 in Arizona.

Then I had my brilliant idea. I've been much praised for it, but a lot of things we "do for others" we really do for ourselves. "Enlightened self-interest," they call it. I was bored rattling around in that big suite at the Hilton; I really had nothing I wanted to do except finish the film, and that looked more and more likely to screw up my next film.

"Look," I said. "You've already got two units shooting the battle stuff. Let me work both of them, half and half, day and night, and sleep on the location." Doesn't that sound noble? Trust me, it wasn't. They'd already built me a little wooden dressing room on the location. I just had them put in a good bed, a good reading light, and a hot shower, and moved in.

I'd get up about nine in the morning, have a quiet breakfast on my little front porch reading the *International Herald-Tribune,* then climb into the dirty uniform I wore throughout the siege and stroll over to the day unit (which of course had already been shooting battle stuff I wasn't in for three hours), work with them till about 3 P.M., when I'd leave them to it and go back to my bungalow for a steak and a half bottle of Marques de Riscal, sketch or read, then nap till 8 or 9 P.M., when they'd awaken me for the first shot with the night unit.

I'd only shoot with them till 1 or 2 A.M., then go back to bed till the day unit was ready for me the next morning. I wore no

makeup; given the siege we were supposed to be enduring, I didn't
even have to shave, just trim the stubble every few days.

I really didn't find the double shift very tough, though everyone kept anxiously asking how I was. I no longer had to waste time commuting back and forth from Madrid every day; I was getting plenty of rest and working only an hour or so longer than a normal shooting day anyway. Plus, I was a hero.

On top of which, I didn't have to do interviews, and the busy Madrid social calendar was cut to zero.

One October evening I was busy fighting a brisk skirmish on top of a couple of hundred yards of the Great Wall when, at midnight, an unscripted salvo of rocket fire arched over us, accompanied by mortar explosions. It was the earliest and noisiest birthday I've ever celebrated. Bea Sellmer, our good friend from the *El Cid* shoot, appeared with Lydia's gift, a fine period sword. I used it to cut the cake, but it also seemed a good symbol for the rest of my life: do what you have to do, and cut through the crap.

Our system worked even better than when Wyler had bicycled me from first to second unit on *Ben-Hur.* On *Peking,* we were shooting two first units, one for day, one for night, fitting me in where they needed to have me. We were gaining spectacularly on the time we'd lost.

I even got some loopholes of down-time, aside from sleeping and eating and all that. They gave me an evening off from night-shooting so I could attend the Madrid opening of *El Cid,* after which Orson Welles bought me a world-class dinner at Horcher's. We ate in one of the exquisite little private rooms, designed in the nineteenth century for discreet evenings with horny noblemen and ambitious women.

Orson had a superb idea for a film—the conquest of Mexico: Hernán Cortés, with four hundred men and fifteen horses conquering the Aztec empire of Moctezuma, absolute ruler of the most advanced civilization in the New World. The tragic confrontation between the two men was an awesome story.

The definitive epic film of all time? Not today. When *Home Alone 2* costs more than *Lawrence of Arabia,* those films are impossible. But in 1962 $15 million could have bought you a hell of a movie, with the right people. Actually, I'm not sure Orson was the right man. There was no film his imagination and creative vision couldn't encompass, but *Cortés* was the kind of project he might have gone aground on. Certainly it was the sort of film he never did.

Besides, he didn't have the fifteen million, or any script, only his own enormously persuasive persona. That night, in Spain, it fell short. "Orson," I said to him at the end of the evening, over a superb brandy, "I've been making movies since last January; I'm about finished here, and I'm a little tired. I feel like a woman after an orgiastic week screwing in Capri. I just don't want to climb into bed again right now."

Feeling a little guilty about turning Orson down, I did my best the next day to persuade Sam to let him make a film on the acres of our marvelous Peking set we would never shoot. "Give Orson two million bucks and the run of the Las Matas location," I urged, "and he'll improvise the damnedest spy thriller you ever saw." He would've, too.

OK . . . I'm proud of wrapping principal photography on *Peking* on schedule. I guess Walter Mirisch was right: I should've been a first assistant director. At least I didn't have to fly directly to Arizona and step straight inside my Christian prophet for George Stevens. Thanks to the two crews who made the last weeks of our *Peking* shoot go like oil on glass, I had time to go home, cuddle my daughter, drive my son to school, and sleep with my wife.

I was even happier to be on my ridge with my family the next afternoon when Jack Kennedy announced the blockade of Cuba, since marked in history as the Cuban missile crisis. He'd failed to take a stand against the Soviets the previous spring when they'd put up the Berlin Wall; this time he was better advised. Or perhaps he remembered the stirring language of his own inaugural address: "We shall pay any price, bear any burden, meet any hardship, support any friend, oppose any foe to assure the survival and the success of liberty." It was a significant responsibility as a father to sit in front of our TV and explain to my son at seven the possibility of war and the reasons for it.

THE LAST WORK I did in that busy year was for George Stevens, fulfilling an actor's dream. He remains a permanent name in the pantheon of great film directors. John the Baptist was the shortest role I'd played in any film, but the chance to work for George was irresistible. (Besides, the Baptist is a marvelous part.)

By the sixties, riding the tiger, I was usually involved in the genesis of most of the films I did, but certainly not with *The Greatest Story Ever Told.* George had been preparing this film for several years, first at Fox, then at United Artists, always with the free hand his reputation had earned him. He surely intended it as the signature work of his brilliant career. It was also beyond question the most difficult.

The life of Christ has often been explored by filmmakers, from DeMille in the silent era onward, because it probably *is* the greatest story ever told. Directors of various persuasions have tried different versions, including rock opera. None of them has quite brought it off.

None was better equipped for the task than George, I think. Aside from the firm backing of United Artists, he had his own talents and reputation, as well as a deep Christian conviction. All of these were ferociously tested in the months ahead.

His single most crucial creative choice was also his most successful: he cast Max von Sydow as Christ. Max had already established his reputation in Ingmar Bergman's films; his work in *Greatest Story* would launch him on an international career still flourishing today. There is no European actor so highly regarded as Max.

There is also no part harder to play than Christ. The great Shakespearean monsters—Lear, Hamlet, Macbeth—are minefields of technical and philosophical complexity. They also carry the historical imprint of the great actors who have played them, against which each of us who follow in those roles must be measured.

The actor who plays Christ faces an even more formidable problem: the expectations of all of Western civilization. More blood and ink has been spilled over this man since they nailed him to the cross than any other human in history. Secular historians, atheists, theologians, and the faithful of three of the great religions of the world have passionately held fiercely conflicting beliefs about him. (Whether that pronoun should be "Him," just for starters.) Max was more than equal to the challenge.

Carl Sandburg worked for some months on the script, though I'm not persuaded he was able to give more than his formidable name to the undertaking. Someone wisely decided to use the King James Version as often as possible. It enlivened every sequence where we did this. George chose to start his shoot with John the Baptist's apocalyptic forecast. Just me and that superb King James jeremiad, echoing through the Arizona canyons.

It was a big scene for me; starting with it was definitely jumping into the deep end of the pool. Stevens plunged right in. I like that approach. Maybe George knew his man:

> Every valley shall be filled, and every mountain and hill shall be brought low. The crooked shall become straight and the rough way smooth . . . and all men shall see the salvation of God!

Given the King James Bible, Stevens didn't really need Sandburg, I think. That first sequence behind us, he turned to the Baptism, my only other scene in that awesome Arizona location. (Critics who didn't like the film also didn't like this choice, but I think George was right. Having thoroughly scouted locations in the Holy Land, he decided that two thousand years of wear had considerably reduced their photogenic potential. The Arizona Rockies, geologically much younger, arguably looked more like the ground Jesus walked on . . . when he walked there.)

So I baptized Max in an estuary of the Colorado River, in Glen Canyon. There was a spooky aspect to this. The U.S. Army Corps of Engineers had just completed damming Glen Canyon. George had been late starting his shoot; the Engineers finished on time.

They'd agreed to wait for us before closing the dam and filling several thousand acres of canyon with water, which put the Engineers in the place of God. What if they changed their minds? I sometimes woke in my tent around dawn thinking of the verse in Genesis:

> All the fountains of the great deep were opened up, and the flood was upon the earth. All the high hills under heaven were covered . . . and the waters prevailed.

Somehow I doubt I'd have thought of that if we'd been doing a Western. All those sets Stevens built in Glen Canyon stand there still, four hundred feet under the water that serves the Southwest.

The spot George had chosen was perfect—superb angles from every side, and easy access for equipment and facilities. The weather was clear and bright. It was November, though. The tem- perature of the Colorado that week was in the forties, Fahrenheit. I spent several days waist-deep in the river in a bearskin, baptizing eager extras.

You don't look for acting from extras, though you often get better work from amateurs than from professional extras. They're more interested. Every day we had several hundred locals lined up on the bank, waiting eagerly to wade in the Jordan and be baptized. We only managed sixty or so a day. The real Baptist doubtless did better.

Still, we couldn't have hoped for better reactions as they stepped down into the frigid Colorado, their eyes widening in shock. They'd stumble toward me in the current, I'd take their shoulders and press them under, then lift them out of the water. As they came up, gasping and wild-eyed, the cameras conveyed pure, heartfelt epiphany.

On the last day, of course, I was to baptize Max. I stood in the water that morning, warming my hands on a mug of very hot coffee, while Stevens laid out his shot. My head was down, focused on the warmth rising from the mug, when he called from the bank. "How ya doin', Chuck?"

"I'm OK, George," I replied. "But I'll tell you this: if the Jordan had been as cold as the Colorado, Christianity never would've gotten off the ground."

While I was busy baptizing Jews for George in Arizona, Fray, already exercising a tendency toward exposure sports that still attracts him as a man, had fallen from the top of a jungle gym at school and broken his arm.

I flew back to L.A. in the film plane from location that night, to be with him before going back to work the next morning. He was in bed, mildly sedated, when I got home. "How you doing, Tiger?" I said, kneeling by his bed. "Does it hurt a lot?"

"No . . . not so much," he replied ruefully, looking at his cast. "It just makes me sad not to be perfect any more." That's about it, isn't it? From a state of grace and innocence, life brings us gradually to an awareness of our imperfection.

(This seems the place for a funny thing that happened last

winter, as I write. Almost exactly thirty years after *Greatest Story,* Fray has grown into a writer-director of appropriately increasing reputation. He was in Vancouver, directing a film for Castle Rock based on a Stephen King novel, *Needful Things,* in which he'd cast Max von Sydow as the devil. [Bloody good he was, too.] I visited the set and stood chatting with another actor in the film, who knew that Fray had played the Infant Moses in *Ten Commandments.* As we stood on the sidelines watching Fray talking intensely to Max, thirty feet away, the actor observed wryly, "Now you don't see that often: there's Moses, telling Christ how to play the Devil.")

I had a respite then, while George finished the Glen Canyon location. I welcomed some time on our ridge, where I'd seldom slept since we'd built there, with Lydia and our children, of whom I'd seen too little since they'd left Spain. Holly, at sixteen months, was still struggling out of babyhood, though with vast determination. I don't know how time works for babies. When I was there, she was delighted, as she was with her mother, her brother, the noble Drago, and the rest of her world when I wasn't. She could still make my heart turn with a small rosebud of a smile.

With a few days at home to catch my breath, I looked back (perhaps, like Satchel Paige, to see whether something might be gaining on me). I'd made five films in a little over two years, been aced out of a cameo in a sixth by Duke Wayne and out of a chance to do another play with Olivier by the schedule. On top of this, I'd picketed for civil rights, done my duty by the State Department in Berlin, and been elected president of the Screen Actors Guild. It suddenly seemed time to slide off the tiger's back, at least for a while.

Of course I couldn't do that just then. I still had to finish with John the Baptist, I had to go to London to do postproduction sound on *55 Days at Peking,* and, more immediately, I'd promised Columbia I'd go to Japan and help launch *Diamond Head* there. But I'd be home for Christmas, I promised myself.

By this time it had been noted, both by me and the various studios, that my films invariably did well in the Far East. Films that flopped elsewhere did fairly well there; those that were hits elsewhere were smashes in Japan. The fact that this pattern has continued unchanged accounts in no small degree for my continued viability in films. Whenever I do a tour for one of my movies, I

try to include one or two stops in the Far East. I've never had any
firm explanation for my continuing popularity with Asian audiences, but I heard a very flattering one from a journalist in Taiwan
not long ago. "Oh, that's very simple," he said. "Audiences in this
part of the world go to your films because you represent the Confu-
cian virtues: responsibility, justice, courage, and moderation." (On
the Spago circuit, of course, that adds up to square.)

I went to Japan, where *Diamond Head* proved to be the
huge success Columbia expected. I was given a really superb seventeenth-century samurai sword by an aged Japanese lady in Osaka
who was the last surviving member of an ancient samurai family
because, she told my interpreter, I embodied the essence of samurai honor. I value that. The sword she gave me is the jewel of my
sword collection, most of them prop swords I've used in various
roles. Her gift is the real thing.

Yes, I did get home in time to take my family for Christmas
in Michigan, where, indeed,

> The woods are lovely, dark, and deep
> But I have promises to keep,
> And miles to go before I sleep,
> And miles to go before I sleep.

(I started reading Frost to Fray when he was about three. He used
to call this one "Stopping by Woods on a Snowy Evening Day by
Robert Frosting.")

Christmas behind us and my family back home, I followed
Santa's reindeer tracks over the Pole (or so I told the kids) to
London to rerecord the *Peking* sound tracks where needed. That
happens to be something I do very well, possibly as well as any
actor. (Would I could say the same for every aspect of the game.) I
did eighty-five sound loops and fifteen voice-over tracks in five
hours, saving them a second scheduled day of dubbing time. With
the free time I'd earned, I accepted Orson Welles' invitation to see
Paul Scofield's *King Lear*.

At supper afterward, I expected another seduction on the
Cortés film. Neither memory nor my journal records anything but
Orson's outrage at Scofield's performance as Lear. His fury echoed
through the restaurant.

True, Scofield's strongest work was not in Shakespeare; his

Lear was low-keyed, very conversational. But he *was* one of the major Brits; it seemed to me he was entitled to a shot at the part the way he saw it, though I wasn't wild about it.

Orson was. Wildly furious. He'd played Lear himself a few years before; we're all sensitive to other actors' assaults on great roles we've played too. *King Lear* is arguably the greatest play ever written; of all the Shakespearean monsters, Lear is surely the most difficult. In the four centuries since it was written, no actor has ever been regarded as great in the part, though most great actors have tried it. (Just to have done the role is regarded in the trade as a badge of honor.) Orson simply couldn't stomach Scofield's *idea* of the part. "He thinks he's still playing Sir Thomas More, for God's sake . . . a Lear for All Seasons! What crap." (This story has no moral; it just demonstrates that actors take all this more seriously than the rest of you do.)

I came back home and went to work again for George, finishing off the Baptist. Stevens had brought his company back from Arizona, where they shot straight through Christmas, with the actors sweeping snow off the rocks at one point so they could match what they'd already shot.

George had many months of work still ahead of him, but my Baptist had only to be arrested, tried, and executed. Roughly in reverse order, as it turned out. In *The Greatest Story Ever Told,* we don't see John get his head cut off, though I'd tried to argue for that with George.

I've died on stage and screen many times, usually violently, almost always to the advantage of the story structure. Death is a powerful cinematic tool, though it's too often spectacularized, and thus trivialized, by exploding boats, blood bags, and futuristic weaponry.

I was looking forward to the beheading of John the Baptist, surely one of the more significant executions in history, followed by Salome's dancing erotically with his head, intercut with artfully framed angles of my real head, for verisimilitude. George heard me out patiently, then observed, "You know, Chuck, the film is really not about John the Baptist, is it?"

He had me there. He played out the Baptist's story in a very good scene with José Ferrer, much of it with the point of a Roman

short sword in the hollow of my throat, at the end of which I was
dragged off in chains to the block.

I didn't really work very long with George Stevens, only a
few weeks, overall. Yet, of the three major directors of the period I
worked for, DeMille, Wyler, and Stevens, I perhaps felt the closest
creative rapport with George. With the first two, I was the green
kid, of course. Both DeMille and Wyler were at the peak of their
creative energy, with a very sure concept of what they wanted. I've
always worked best with a strong director who will push me hard.
George was also such a man. I was riding the tiger, indeed, but
George was pointing us where he wanted to go.

He shared with both the other men a relentless capacity for
detail, a luxury a director can only indulge if he has the track record
the three of them had in common. I remember the first shot I did
back in Culver City on a sound stage, beginning the scene of the
Baptist in Herod's dungeon, awaiting judgment. The cameraman
was Loyal Griggs, much honored over a long career (including *The
Greatest Show on Earth* and *Ten Commandments*).

"Loyal," said George, "I want to start on an extreme close-
up of Chuck chained to the wall. But give me a black screen at the
start. I don't want to see a damn thing till Chuck opens his eyes, we
catch a gleam in the pupils, and pull back, revealing the cell."

Loyal worked some time lighting the shot, but when George
came in to rehearse it, he looked at the setup and said, "Too much
light, Loyal. Kill that light, and that one, and bring the inky on
Chuck's eye down two points." The point is, George could say that
with absolute certainty not because he was a great director, but
because he'd begun as a cameraman. As neither DeMille nor Wyler
could, nor any director who hadn't begun on camera, he could tell
without even looking through the lens that Griggs hadn't given him
what he asked for. He gave me a great deal as a director, too,
exploring ideas in the script, as well as in my head.

He also gave me an unusual gift the last day I worked for
him: an opportunity. We were shooting the capture of the Baptist,
with a troop of Sanhedrin soldiery subduing him in the river (not
the Colorado now, but a back-lot tank, dressed to match). We had a
first-class stuntman to leap from his horse on the riverbank and
drive me underwater. I was trying to persuade George to let me do

the shot instead of a double, when he said, "No, Chuck. Let the double do the stunt. I have to go direct another scene on Stage Five anyway. I want you to direct this scene."

I was stunned. He was going to let me direct a scene in the most important film he'd ever made? There it was, *Carpe diem,* seize the day. "OK, George," I said. "What do you want me to do with it?"

"Whatever you want, Chuck," he said. "Shoot it the way you think it should be." So I did. I think I slid off the tiger's back then. I also didn't make another picture for a year.

15

Public Faces, Public Places

> Democracy is the worst system of government in the world
> . . . except for all the others.
>
> — WINSTON CHURCHILL

IN THE GOLDEN AGE of the great Hollywood studios, from the coming of sound through the all-time peak of American movie attendance in World War II, everyone who made films was under contract. Actors, directors, and writers were all indentured to the studio that employed them and strongly discouraged from speaking out on public issues.

The moguls who ran the studios perhaps perceived that actors and writers are often passionate and volatile people (directors and producers maybe less so). In any case, whatever the ideology of the filmmakers, the movies they made were, except for a mild populist leaning, devoid of political content. Even the Civil War was a touchy subject. *Gone With the Wind* all but ignores that watershed in American history: it contains no battle scenes, and neither secession, states' rights, nor emancipation is mentioned.

When the Spanish Civil War erupted in 1936, most of the Western countries sympathized with the government, since the rebels were openly supported by the increasingly monstrous Fascist governments of Germany and Italy. Soviet support for the Communist Loyalists was more discreet, and Communism, still wearing its human face, had many honest and well-meaning friends in the West. (Stalin called them "useful idiots.") Hemingway and Orwell have written better than I can about this, in *For Whom the Bell Tolls* and *Animal Farm*. The West largely ignored the rising totalitarian tide in both Germany and Russia.

Director Elia Kazan has pointed out (undeniably, since he was himself among them) that there were some honest-to-God Communists in the New York theater in the thirties. Several of them soon found themselves in the movies.

The Hollywood Left did some fund-raising for the Loyalists, though I think none of them went off to Spain to pick up a rifle. The film community has always raised money, often quite a lot, for a wide spectrum of causes, most of them worthwhile.

Not long afterward, in World War II, Hitler's idiotic decision to break his pact with Stalin and invade Russia made the Soviets our allies for the duration of the war. The increasingly clear conflict in our beliefs was ignored (by some unrecognized) like a guest's bad breath, until we won the war and came home.

The climate turned cold very quickly. The Soviet theft of atomic secrets, the convictions of Fuchs and Alger Hiss, the execution of the Rosenbergs, Stalin's dropping the Iron Curtain all left a number of decent people in Hollywood standing in the snow in their underwear.

I don't mean to trivialize this, nor offer any profundities. The seeds were scattered when I was in grade school, the bitter fruit ripened during my first days in film.

The House Un-American Activities Committee's exploration of Communist influence in Hollywood was an appalling exploitation of many public reputations. Then, as now, Washington comes to Hollywood to raise money—or hell. Filmmakers are easy marks, either way. The HUAC hearings abused the democratic process and provided nothing useful to the country's confrontation with the Soviets, an agenda that would drive America's foreign policy for the next forty years.

Several dozen writers, actors, and directors were subpoenaed. According to their conscience and courage, they either fled or testified, as friendly or unfriendly witnesses. Very few survived the experience unscathed; several were blacklisted for years.

A group of writers and directors, quickly labeled The Unfriendly Ten, steadfastly clung to their Fifth Amendment rights and refused to testify on sensitive questions, earning prison terms for

contempt of Congress. (Writer-director Billy Wilder observed sardonically, "Of course, only two of them are talented. The rest are
just unfriendly.") Be that as it may, the HUAC hearings were an
unsavory page in our history, demonstrating what we've seen
proved many times since: a Congressional committee hearing is
unlikely to provide either truth or justice.

(A few years ago, I sat, as president, in a meeting of the board
of the American Film Institute which had been called principally to
choose the recipient of the AFI's Life Achievement Award, given for
the sum of an entire career. As the award has become more prestigious, the field has thinned. The popular choices, even among filmmakers on the board, turn too often to actors. A producer or a
writer has never been chosen, a director only eight times.

This time there were two or three directors on the short list.
Significant among them was Elia Kazan. His films were extraordinary, earning him many awards, a lot of money, and his credentials
as a major director.

I neither nominated nor seconded any of the candidates, but
Kazan surely seemed a likely choice. As debate began, a woman
producer [thirty-something, going on fifteen-something?] attending
her first board meeting spoke up. "I know Kazan's a great director,
but we can't give this award to a man who named names!"

She was referring to the Congressional hearings more than
forty years earlier exploring Communist influence in Hollywood.
Kazan, subpoenaed to testify, had admitted his Party activities and
identified some of his colleagues. At the time, feeling ran high in
the film community, on both Right and Left, as it did in the country
at large. Still, this had not only happened long before the angry
young woman was born, it had absolutely nothing to do with the
criteria by which we were to choose whom to honor. Big Brother's
ugly head hung grinning across the table.

I was stunned and outraged, but challenged her within the
bounds of civility, to an approving murmur from the assembled
board. Two or three of them spoke up endorsing my rebuke. Nevertheless, on the final ballot, Kazan was not chosen. [Nor, I suspect,
will he ever be, now.] Political Correctness has been fouling the
waters in American schools and universities for some years; this is
the strongest manifestation of it I've seen in Hollywood. So far.)

The sad, black irony is that all of the passion, pain, and

polemics were in the end meaningless. Of course there were Communists in Hollywood, some of them no doubt politically educated. But none of these people were positioned to channel crucial intelligence to the Soviets, like the moles in the State Department and the Pentagon. These were artists seduced by the Marxist dream. I can't think of one film made during that time that could be described as politically radical, let alone anti-American.

Lenin observed in the 1920s, when film was in its infancy, "The moving picture is the most powerful tool ever devised to shape the mind of man." (One prescient son of a bitch, wasn't he?) But America took the art form of the twentieth century and made it the American art form, essentially without politicizing it.

Throughout the period we're talking about, Hollywood filmmakers simply didn't express their politics in their movies. Even after war broke out in Europe in 1939 and the Nazis were certifiable bad guys, the politics of film were still careful. Willy Wyler's *Mrs. Miniver* celebrated the bravery of English civilians. *Casablanca,* too, focused on civilians, not soldiers.

Pearl Harbor changed the climate, but even then, the best films on World War II—*Patton, Bridge on the River Kwai, The Longest Day*—were made a generation and more later.

By the time I came to Hollywood in 1950, a huge sea change was looming. The big studios were about to lose the total contractual control they'd always held over the people who made their movies. The Supreme Court had already taken away the studios' theater chains, then men had come back from the war expecting some choice in how their careers were handled, which is why Hal Wallis had given me an independent contract. This unavoidably included the right to shoot your mouth off, though it wasn't spelled out in the fine print.

By 1963, armed with a first-dollar percentage of the gross of my films, a fair degree of creative control, and some fortunate choices, I had more options than I could responsibly sort out, some of them political.

Not the least of these was the Screen Actors Guild. By this time I'd been elected president, a post, I confess, I was proud to hold. SAG had been created in 1933, by the efforts of several courageous actors such as Jimmy Cagney, Leon Ames, and Eddie Cantor who didn't themselves need a guild, but knew their fellow actors did. In the beginning, most of the SAG board were stars and well-known actors, immune to pressure from the studios.

When I joined SAG for my first film in 1950, I already belonged to Actors Equity (for stage performers) and AFRA (for radio). I also helped found a fledgling union for live television actors, TVAA (Television Actors of America, if you care). Almost at once, both SAG and AFRA discerned the future bearing down on them and launched a fierce jurisdictional battle, ending up sharing TVAA's dismembered corpse. Since then, my work as a director has required me also to join SSDC (for stage directors).

I can't explain why all these overlapping organizations have been formed to represent the interests of many tens of thousands of actors, only several hundreds of whom can be employed in a given year. What seems the obvious answer—merging them all into one union—has been passionately debated and earnestly studied for the past thirty years. All studies indicate that it would cost more to run a merged union than what most of us pay to support several separate ones. Who called economics "the dismal science"?

I was recruited for the SAG board in 1960 during Ronald Reagan's last term as president, when he led us through the crucial and difficult strike, which I mentioned earlier. Not long after that, I succeeded him as SAG president. I can hardly claim to have replaced him.

I was proud to have the job and anxious to do it well. Even by the sixties, the membership had grown beyond the number of actors that conceivably could be employed. It seemed to me every couple of months some board member would suggest we institute an Admissions Committee to determine the qualifications of new applicants to join SAG so they could *be* actors. "Like the bar exam," they'd explain.

"The law can be written down," I'd point out. "You can't write acting down. Who's going to sit on this committee, deciding who acts well enough to join SAG? Not me, I'll tell you that."

(Now, thirty years later, the Guild has fallen on parlous times. A decision made some years ago to attract more initiation fees by making it easier to join SAG has swelled our ranks to 93,000 members. No conceivable combination of moving image technologies could provide jobs for more than a fraction of that total. In 1993, 76 percent of the membership made less than $2,500 in our jurisdiction, many a lot less.)

In the sixties, when I served as SAG's president for six terms (longer than anyone else, so far), my worldwide public identity made me an ambassador as well. That dual role's been useful in other chores, too.

In the long run, I'm proudest of the small part I played under Reagan's guidance in negotiating residual TV payments to actors, and, while I was president, the negotiations that gave SAG a pension and welfare plan second to none in the industry and a medical plan that is surpassed in all of organized labor only by the NFL and the NBA.

While I was tending to SAG business, I was of course still plying my trade—or trying to. By the winter of 1963, I'd finished shooting on two major films, *55 Days at Peking* and *The Greatest Story Ever Told,* though there were still months of postproduction on both. While this left me time to settle into the SAG presidency, I was trying to figure out what film I'd make next. A number of scripts came by. I remember a rather moribund piece called *Morituri* which Marlon later accepted. He should've passed on it, too.

I also turned down a cameo in a film that Paul Newman then did. This doesn't mean that Paul was second choice, just that they were trolling through the likely actors, looking for one who had a window in his schedule, was intrigued with the part, and hadn't done too many films in the last year. Too often, we're inclined to take or turn down a part more or less on whim. You shouldn't do that.

The outstanding example of that in my career came a few years later, when I'd just done two or three films almost back to back, only one of which seemed to me very good (*Midway,* and even that hadn't given me a very challenging part). The day after I finished filming, I was offered a script called *The Omen.* It seemed well-written, but I was tired and disenchanted with the idea of three months filming in Eastern Europe, so I passed.

Greg Peck did it. It was the hit of the next summer season, along with *Midway.* I remember being irritated with myself for not being in both of the summer smashes, which was not only greedy

but foolish of me. Greg was much better than I would've been in
Omen. The role was a U.S. ambassador, and he rolled a ten-strike
with it, as he often did. I'd have been unlikely to come near the
success he had with the part. Besides, one smash a summer is as
much as any of us deserves.

The film I really wanted to make then was based on the play
I'd optioned, Leslie Stevens' *The Lovers*. By then, on Broadway, in
live television and film, I'd spent a large part of my career outside
the twentieth century, as indeed I've continued to do till this day.
I've undoubtedly played men in more different periods, ranging
from 3000 B.C. to 2500 A.D., than any living actor, at least a dozen of
them specific historical figures.

There are several problems in playing great men. First,
they're more complicated guys than the rest of us; the most diligent
study will not always tell you what made them tick, or how they
could do what they did. Then it's up to the actor to make the
audience believe it without entirely understanding why. You can do
that.

Far harder is explaining to an audience who the man is and
why they should be interested in a movie about him. This requires
a lot of explaining; if you don't do this in the first reel, you're in
trouble. Certainly there were directors who could handle this—
DeMille, Lean. I'd struggled with the problem often enough at least
to understand it.

That was one of the things that attracted me to *The Lovers*. It
was a *small* story, set in the eleventh century in what was then the
northern marshes of Normandy (now Holland). It wasn't about the
fall of Rome, or the then-imminent Norman Conquest of Britain.
There were no teeming thousands of extras sacking cities, no kings
or dukes, or any man who lived on in history in the story; only a
penniless, landless knight who's spent half a lifetime in hard service
to the Duke of Normandy. "Twenty years I've lived with that cold
wife," he says of his sword. "Twenty *years!*"

He's been sent with twenty men-at-arms, his faithful sergeant, his miscreant brother, and a dotty priest to hold a watchtower
in the marshes on the edge of the duke's domain against a possible
attack by Frisian raiders from the north. There's a sodden village of
some sixty souls, one of them a comely peasant girl who happens

to catch his war-weary eye. They're drawn together by sexual scent-sign, feudal custom, and Druidic spell, but separated by rank, and then finally bound in blood and steel.

Walter Seltzer had signed on to produce the film script we'd fashioned from *The Lovers,* which was now called *The War Lord,* a much more useful title. Unhappily, we had no financing, and no release for the film. This is a limbo in which many filmmakers spend months and months of their lives, even years. You go from studio to studio, peddling your project, which is weighed according to the flavor of the month and the judgment of those making the choices—that month.

They call it "Development Hell" and it can indeed last, or seem to, for eternity. Whether you survive it to actually make the film has little to do with the quality of the script, or the reputation or bankability of the people involved. Kirk Douglas, at the height of his popularity and leverage as actor/producer, bought a "novel" called *One Flew Over the Cuckoo's Nest.* He spent fourteen frustrating years trying to get a studio to back it. When he at last succeeded, he was himself too old for the part. Jack Nicholson played it, Kirk's son produced it, and it was a great success—fourteen years late.

John Huston spent most of his career trying to get someone to fund his film of Kipling's *The Man Who Would Be King.* When he first submitted it, his stars were Gable and Tracy, perhaps the most potent pairing in film history. No dice. When he finally made it, more than a quarter of a century later, he used Sean Connery and Michael Caine.

Walter and I did the Development Dance with *War Lord* on both sides of the Atlantic for some weeks that winter of 1963. Coming up empty, we fell back and regrouped to fight another day. I did score a significant research point in the British Museum, on my way home. If we ever got to make *War Lord,* I wanted to use chain mail, because it looked good on film and was easy to work in. Nooo, said all the experts. Chain mail wasn't developed until after the Norman Conquest. Look at the Bayeux Tapestry, only ring mail. I take historical accuracy very seriously, but I was sure the experts were wrong. I was thus delighted, while examining the newly discovered Sutton Hoo treasure displayed in the Museum, to see an undeniable chain-mail shirt, rusted into a solid bar, that had been buried there before the Conquest.

I found myself back in Europe before long, wearing my SAG hat. As president, I was to preside over an international conference of performing unions in Amsterdam. Our guild was more or less the bellwether group in Western labor negotiations in entertainment, since we had negotiated far better contracts than any European performers' union.

The Soviets had the largest delegation, since it included not only actors in film, but performers in every medium, from circus to ballet, as well as technicians, writers, and journalists. Although it called itself a union, the Soviet group was in fact no such thing. It was simply a dues-paying organization, with no say whatever in wages or working conditions, though it had a very loud voice in controlling its members.

I did have an interesting exchange with a Soviet government official who was clearly the de facto head of the organization. Over lunch, he was explaining to me the highly organized system through which story ideas at Moskva Film were processed steadily into finished movies. "Who makes the decision as to which story ideas will be actually developed?" I asked him.

"Oh, we never abandon a story idea," he said. "Once a film has been approved, it is made." (Just a couple of years ago, I made a film in the new nation of Kyrgyzstan, formerly a province of the USSR. They actually had a small film studio, where they had made films under the Soviets. While they had a small cadre of more or less trained technicians, it soon became clear that they had no concept of working on a schedule. The idea was to be making a film. The longer it took, the longer everyone would have a job. An interesting idea.)

When our conference had worked through its considerable agenda, our only positive achievement was a very useful (so we were told) seminar which instructed foreign performing unions on how we had negotiated so successfully in the American entertainment industry. Aside from that, everything we did for five days was mostly ceremonial. I've since come to realize that's true of any large conference, most particularly on an international level. (In essence, you act out a predetermined script, whose prime purpose is to make everyone there feel important. They do feed you well.)

Before I left, I spent two hours in the Rijksmuseum. It restored some of my faith in mankind, somewhat eroded by the futil-

ity of the union conference, and my own efforts to mount *War Lord*.
I'd never seen so many Rembrandts in one place before.

When I got home, I found three scripts waiting for me, all of
them attractive: *The Agony and the Ecstasy, Khartoum,* and *Major
Dundee,* each from different studios. Each studio had danced with
us on *War Lord* with varying degrees of enthusiasm, each clearly
preferred I make the picture *they* wanted to make instead of the
one I wanted to make. Well, of course. In the end, I would do all
three studio films, and mine as well, but that was later.

Meantime, the civil rights movement was looming larger and
larger on the political horizon. The Kennedy Administration was
walking a scrupulously neutral line on this issue, perceiving it as a
fight they didn't want to get into. I'd already gotten into it two years
earlier, so I was glad to accept a breakfast date with Dr. King to
discuss the absence of blacks in the Hollywood technical unions.

Many men who knew him better than I have written about
Martin Luther King. I can't match their eloquence; I can confirm
what they've written: he was a special man, put on earth, I do
believe, to be a twentieth-century Moses for his people. Over coffee
and toast in his hotel, he was very quiet. Passionately quiet.

"You tell me, Mr. Heston, that there are *no* blacks on Hollywood film crews. As president of the Screen Actors Guild, what can
you do about that?"

"I'm afraid not much, sir," I said. "Our guild has always
welcomed black actors, but I must tell you the technical unions not
only won't accept black members, they wouldn't accept me, or
anyone who isn't the son of a member. I'm glad to speak for SAG at
the interguild conference you've called with the studios, but I don't
believe you have much of a chance with IATSE."

I was dead wrong. At the conference that afternoon, Dr. King
talked them around. They agreed to eliminate the family rule and
accept black apprentices. Amazingly, they also began to take in non-
family whites and women, which wasn't even on Dr. King's agenda.
He was an awesomely persuasive man, even unintentionally.

He was already planning his March on Washington for the
end of August, almost two months later. Although Dr. King and his
main men were organizing the event, along with the NAACP and
the Urban League and some other black groups, the March would
be open to everyone.

Some of us in the film community decided to organize a group from the arts. Our original thought was to include stage people and writers and painters as well, though I don't recall that we got many volunteers there. For that matter, we didn't get as many film people as I'd expected. I was voted honcho of our little band, probably because the SAG presidency gave me some official status (though I was careful every time I spoke publicly about civil rights to make clear I was speaking for myself, not for the entire Guild).

We had a good group: Burt Lancaster, Jim Garner, Marlon Brando, Paul Newman, and several others. Sidney Poitier and Harry Belafonte signed on, but we had no other prominent black performers. You can figure out for yourself who should have been there and wasn't. For that matter, I arm-wrestled more than a couple of prominent white actors and directors who opted out—some of the town's most prominent liberals, too. Well, it's been a long time now; I'd just as soon let it rest.

Anyway, Marlon provided passion enough for us all. At our last planning session at my house, he was eloquent on the potential for confrontation. "We should chain ourselves to the Lincoln Memorial," he said. "We'll lie down in front of the White House and block Pennsylvania Avenue."

"No, we won't," I said. "We live in a country where we get to demonstrate peaceably, and that's the way we're gonna do it, or I ain't going." More important, that was the way Dr. King wanted it. That's the way it was.

As history has recorded, the March was an enormous success. Before it happened, though, there were faint hearts on every side. Gloomy predictions of civil disorder were common. President Kennedy had invited the leaders of the various groups involved to a reception at the White House afterward; this was scaled down to a somewhat furtive meeting between President Kennedy and Dr. King.

Our little group came in the night before, most of us, for a tactical meeting. (I keep saying "our little group," just to make clear how small a part we were of the two hundred thousand Dr. King drew together there that day. We were twenty or thirty at most, counting some New York people who came down.) Per capita, of course, we had more public faces than anyone this side of Dr. King.

Our job was to get as much ink and TV time as possible. Each of the better known actors had a different media statement. I was to speak to the press as we welcomed the last of our New York bunch at National Airport. They asked me if it was OK for James Baldwin to write my statement; he was a famous black writer, he'd flown over from Paris to join us, and he wanted to make a contribution.

I wasn't crazy about the idea, as a matter of fact. Anything that goes out with my name on it, I write. I always have. Besides, Jimmy Baldwin was on the left fringe of the civil rights movement. *The Fire Next Time* was the title of his best-known book. I don't know how Dr. King felt about his being there. But the point is, he *was* there. When an awful lot of good parlor liberals didn't show in case things turned nasty, Jimmy did.

What's more, as a good writer, the speech he wrote for me wasn't what *he* would've written, but instead very close to what I wanted to say. My only encounter with Jimmy Baldwin was that one meeting, which lasted those few hours. We'd both traveled some little distance to come together, though, as so many hundreds of thousands of people did that day. He died years later in self-imposed exile in Paris. God rest him.

For the rest of that shining time, we walked behind Dr. King, and stood on the steps of the Lincoln Memorial to hear him say, yet again, "I have a dream . . ." We were essentially extras in the event that validated that dream, but we were there. In a long life of activism in support of some good causes, I'm proudest of having stood in the sun behind that man, that morning.

I do think Lydia had a truer experience of the March than we did, with our escort of TV cameras. She'd come to Washington with me, simply to be there, though she wasn't credentialed to walk with us behind Dr. King. His personal security was paramount, of course, and guaranteed. Both the White House and the FBI had advised Lydia against joining the main body. "We don't know how this will turn out," they said. "You stay in the hotel and watch it on TV." Well, I could have told them. My girl doesn't take easily to that kind of instruction. After photographing the crowd from the balcony of our hotel room as they moved singing up the Mall, Lydia ran downstairs with her camera and joined the March, walking beside an old black man with broken shoes. "I'll bet we had a better time than you big dogs did up in front," she told me afterward. I'll bet she did, too.

WHAT WITH ONE THING and another, I'd spent two-thirds of the year without acting a lick. Now, with the smoke clearing on the Washington March and the various SAG chores I'd undertaken, I was delighted to get a shot at playing Thomas Jefferson on live TV, in Sidney Kingsley's *The Patriots,* with John Fraser, who'd been so good as the king in *El Cid,* as Alexander Hamilton. I didn't catch old Tom, but it was a learning experience trying. It's hard to play a genius; Jefferson was the only one ever to occupy the White House. As Jack Kennedy said when he hosted a dozen or so Nobel laureates at luncheon in the East Room, "Surely there's never been so much brain power gathered together in this room since Tom Jefferson dined here alone."

As one of Jefferson's biographers put it, "He could break a horse, tie an artery, and dance a minuet. He also wrote the Declaration of Independence." He was one of the greatest Americans who ever lived . . . one of the most significant of those wise old dead white guys who invented this country. I'd like another shot at him; men like that are too complicated to get right the first time around. That's my excuse, anyway.

Still, I hadn't been in front of a movie camera for more than eight months, since I'd finished my Baptist for George Stevens. It was time to choose a film. One that appealed to me, though the script was only two-thirds written, was called *Major Dundee.* There was a lot wrong with it, but the title character was interesting, and the possibility of at last making a film about the Civil War was enormously attractive. I made a deal with Columbia to do it, pending a rewrite. (Never close a deal on a film without a complete script. Most scripts need rewriting, but to jump off on a film without even a complete script puts you, as they say in the military, in a very fluid situation. As for *Dundee,* stay tuned.)

About the same time, Universal decided they wanted to make *The War Lord.* They wanted a rewrite, too, and I can't blame them. John Collier had delivered a script nearly four hundred pages long. Franklin Schaffner, for whom I hadn't worked since *Macbeth* on "Studio One," came on board as director, Walter set up offices for us at Universal, and we undertook cutting our script down to shootable length, budgeting, all that preproduction stuff.

So, I settled down into a familiar role, riding the tiger, but more important, preparing a picture I really wanted very much to do. We were a long way from shooting; I would certainly do *Dundee* first, but I wanted to keep my hand on *War Lord* all the way through. I didn't put in any twelve-hour days—for the actor, that comes when you're shooting. One November morning I checked in for a meeting with Walter and Frank but whatever it was we were scheduled to talk about it was erased from my memory when one of the secretaries ran in and said, "You should turn on the TV—they're saying the President's been shot."

I don't know how many million words have been written about that day, and those that followed; let me not add greatly to their number. We all felt an enormous sense of loss and outrage, of promise denied. History has since given us a different perspective. Most of us now feel John Kennedy was not the man we thought he was. "Johnny, we hardly knew ye . . ." Indeed.

Nonetheless, it was very different then. The death, let alone the murder, of any president in office is an assault on the sense of national comity which in part defines America. As a people, we were shaken. I was one of a lucky few in those first numb days of national shock to be given something specific to do. CBS asked me to fly to New York and take part in the memorial program they were planning for network TV. After thumbing through Shakespeare for most of the flight, I met with the producers and agreed on good choices: I redacted the Twenty-third Psalm, along with the Ninetieth, the Ninety-first, and the One hundred twenty-first, into one whole, and also read some Robert Frost, including "Stopping by Woods on a Snowy Evening," which I knew Jack Kennedy had liked. "And miles to go before I sleep." Yes. Miles to go . . .

A day or so later, waiting for the limo to take me to Idlewild (they hadn't changed the name to JFK yet), I stood in the living room of our apartment, watching the boats on the East River twenty stories below, when the TV suddenly blurted out news of yet another public murder, of Kennedy's assassin, the hapless Marxist misfit, Oswald.

As we flew west, ahead of the sun, I thought of the slain

president and the land he'd led, well or ill, but strongly. I honor
him still for that.

Our Thanksgiving was subdued, but not downcast. We had
friends at our table, our family was intact. So was the nation. Before
we ate, I read a passage from Thomas Wolfe's novel *Of Time and
the River* that I wish I'd chosen for the television memorial. I've
often read it publicly since; it's a wonderful evocation of the spirit
of this country: "Where we believe in love, and victory, and think
that we . . . can never die."

The next day, I took my son riding through the canyons in
the far reaches of the San Fernando Valley (there were no housing
developments there then). We had a fine time, winding up through
the rock-rough trails, ducking under the golden branches of the
cottonwoods, fall's only trademark in California. We talked a little,
too, the way you can, walking a horse down an easy slope. Happily,
Holly was still serene in the cocoon of babyhood.

UNIVERSAL WAS CONTENT to let us do the rewrite on *War Lord* at
our own pace, which meant till we got it right. Columbia was more
importunate on *Major Dundee*. They wanted us shooting early in
the new year. Since we didn't have a director, this seemed impossible, but producer Jerry Bresler, who'd produced *Diamond Head*
successfully with me, called me one day at Universal. "Chuck, come
on down to Columbia, will you? I want you to look at a film." I did.
It was a low-budget Western MGM had made and then essentially
abandoned—*Ride the High Country,* directed by a guy I'd never
heard of, Sam Peckinpah.

In retrospect, *High Country* is not a marvelous film—I
looked at it again a couple of years ago with the thought of re-
making it. But it was directed by a talented man—you could see
that in the first reel. I said as much to Jerry Bresler, who got Sam
on the phone so I could tell *him,* and we hired him to direct
Dundee. (There are a few undiluted pleasures in the frustrating
business of making movies. One of them is giving somebody a job.
Director, cameraman, actress, it just feels good to say "We want
you.") From that moment on, *Dundee* became more complicated.
Much more. I'm very glad I made the film and I'm glad Sam directed
it. I'd go back and do it again, with him . . . but I'd go about it
differently.

We set up shop at Columbia. They were still on Gower Street then, in Hollywood—"Gower Gulch," they called it in the silent days, when the cowboys gathered there for extra calls. Real cowboys.

Meantime, Walter Seltzer and Frank Schaffner were plugging away in our offices at Universal, reworking John Collier's *War Lord* script with a new writer, Millard Kaufman. The new pages seemed very good to me as they came through, though I was increasingly preoccupied with *Dundee,* and Sam.

Sam Peckinpah was . . . an unusual fella. He's been described as a genius, which is probably an overstatement. I've only worked for one other director who's had that burdensome label tacked on him: Orson Welles. I think they both found it an encumbrance. Also, they both had complicated and devious personalities, though Orson was much better than Sam at dealing with actors and technicians. He made them all love him; Sam tended to quarrel with the actors and fire the technicians.

I also worked for each man at opposite ends of his career. *Touch of Evil* was the last film Orson directed for a Hollywood studio (though he made the superb *Chimes at Midnight* in Europe later); *Dundee* was Sam's first film to have a major studio release. They were both mavericks, inclined to disdain the studio and ignore the producer. This got them in a lot of trouble. I've already said a lot about Orson; let me tell you about Sam and *Dundee.*

Columbia put us in the same office (which may have been prophetic; we were all but married to each other for the next few months). My main contribution till the cameras turned would be my input on the script, casting, and production design. Sam was superb on casting. He had an instinct for lesser known actors like Ben Johnson and Warren Oates, as well as rising stars like Jim Coburn. The costarring role of Captain Tyreen was crucial; we were weighing a couple of choices.

Sam had also volunteered to finish the unwritten last third of the script, which we really, *really* needed, not least so the film could be properly scheduled and budgeted, then rewritten. Surely, Sam had bitten off a lot in accepting this chore. He was a good writer, though. He could do it. To do it while preparing his first major film as a director was another question.

The office we shared was huge; it must've belonged to a major figure at Columbia in the old studio days. There was plenty of room for separate desks for Sam and me in the main room, with the usual secretarial anterooms adjoining.

Nevertheless we had a space problem. All my life, both as actor and director, I tend to think on my feet, walking around in random circles. (One of my main problems in writing this book is that I have to sit down to write, but I have to get up and walk around to think.) There was plenty of room for me to do this in that huge room where the studio had stored us, except that Sam was a pacer, too. We kept intersecting each other as we talked.

One morning I checked into the office to find a two-inch-wide strip of silver gaffer's tape bisecting the room. Sam said, "OK, now you pace on that side, I'll pace on this side." It worked fine.

On both sides of the tape, we achieved our key casting for *Dundee:* Richard Harris as the flamboyant Irish Confederate cavalry captain. Richard's star was rising; though we considered other guys for the part, he seemed clearly the best. Let me illustrate here why people trying to break into the film business believe that there are only two hundred people working in all of Hollywood. Richard's very first film job had been for Walter Seltzer (who was producing *War Lord* for me) some years before with James Cagney, *Shake Hands with the Devil,* directed by Michael Anderson. Richard had then done a very good heavy with Gary Cooper and me in *The Wreck of the Mary Deare,* again directed by Michael Anderson, whose son, Michael Junior, would play a key role in *Dundee.* None of this was planned, though of course you tend to stay with actors and prop masters and cameramen you've worked well with. We were damn lucky to get Richard for Tyreen.

I took a little break at the holidays, while Sam worked on the *Dundee* script and Millard Kaufman worked on *War Lord.* Unbelievably, my agent Herman Citron also closed what was by then our standard first-dollar gross deal for me to do *The Agony and the Ecstasy* for Fox, in between *Dundee* and *War Lord.* It was a fine script, and the chance to work with both Carol Reed and Rex Harrison was irresistible, though I'd never before undertaken to prepare three projects simultaneously. I don't recommend it. I might've done better work in all three parts with a little more breathing room between them. (Naah. I don't really believe it. *Carpe diem!* If you don't take the part, someone else will. Do it! Learn! Be better!)

We had Christmas at home for only the second time since we'd built the house, establishing a tradition we've maintained ever since. Unless I'm away on a location (and I try not to be), we have a tree (ten feet or so cut from the top of a mature blue spruce ready for felling) sent from the Michigan woods.

Aside from being better than any tree I could buy off a Los Angeles parking lot, this annual visitor resonates with the woods where it, and I, have roots. I have no close kin in Michigan now, but the land I own matters to me. A lot. A couple of years ago I was flying across Michigan in a little charter jet from one speaking engagement to another. We were about an hour ahead of schedule, so I asked the pilot to divert north a hundred miles or so. We couldn't land at St. Helen, since there's still no strip in the open pasture where I stood awestruck so many years ago and watched that fragile biplane bump down to a landing. We made a low pass over it, though, and the house I used to live in, and the forest acreage I own now, with a lake in the middle and a hunting lodge . . . and a tall dead tree where a pair of golden eagles nested for a long time.

The Michigan tree is the centerpiece of our Christmas Eve party, one of only two big parties we give each year (yes, the other one is on the Fourth of July). Many friends have been coming for more than thirty years, with their children, who of course bring children of their own now. Everyone, from six months to eighty-plus, must put at least one ornament on the tree, which grows through the evening into a Christmas wonder. I savor it best when all the guests have gone and I've turned off all the lights but those on the tree, standing alone, waiting for Christmas. We have a grandson now, Fray's boy, Jack. A child at Christmas is a joy we haven't had since our kids grew up.

Over New Year's, Bill and Clori Isaac, our only neighbors on the ridge our house crosses, invited us with half a dozen other couples to Las Vegas. In 1964, he'd not yet built all the hotels in Vegas he has now, but he'd made a good start at it. He also made a generous and open-hearted host.

In the sixties, Vegas had not yet figured out that the way to *really* make money was to create Disneyland with slot machines;

they still catered to the big player. You could lose your money, eat and drink more than was good for you, do more or less what you wanted, and go back home satiated—being careful not to look back, lest you be turned into a pillar of salt.

All this was fine, except that I don't gamble. That's not a moral position, it's Scots common sense. You don't build an entire city based on gambling and allow the customer to win. All the other men in our group were fairly vigorous players, however. None of the women were, women tending to have more common sense than men. (We *are* pretty, though.)

This imposed a rather unusual social structure on our group, which prevailed for the several years when we'd enjoy an annual weekend of Billy's hospitality. The men would get up about eight-thirty, early for Vegas, and play tennis, then have breakfast, by which time the women would be up, assembled and polished. There would then be much to-and-froing among the adjacent suites, and plans for shopping and museum-visiting (they have some there), but nothing much seemed to come of it. I have a theory that Vegas has somehow legislated the bulk of the daytime out of existence. What with calling the studio or having your hair cut or a bit of a lie-down, night has suddenly fallen and you're meeting for drinks again.

We would all go to some very grand and very good place for dinner. When we'd finished, besotted with Mouton Rothschild '47, Meursault '58, and the like, the other men would go off to lose their money, leaving me in command of what we called the Squab Squad. (Sorry, Ms. Friedan, but there it is. We were *such* a primitive bunch of slobs then.)

I did try to do my best, moving my female band, jeweled, coiffed, gowned, and furred to whichever hotel whose early show we were to watch. You need two cabs (about the only thing I ever got to pay for on those trips) and an eagle eye. There are always stops at the ladies' and bags left in the bar. Every man knows these problems with one woman. Try it with six some time.

Having watched Frank Sinatra or Noël Coward and made the appropriate backstage visits (all performers like to have people come backstage—just don't stay long), we would adjourn to the bar of the hotel where we were to meet the gamblin' men for the midnight show. This meant another squad movement, sometimes on foot if the next hotel was near. All these moves, wheeled or walking, were fraught with complication. I took my responsibility very seriously, and I can boast that, over several years of duty, I never lost a wife. When you think how many wives have been lost in Vegas, this is no mean achievement.

I'd say to the captain in the lounge bar, "We'll need a table for fourteen."

"But you are, ah, seven, sir. With the ladies."

"Fourteen. Take my word for it, and the drink order." As for the maîtres d' in the various hotels, they were all aware of the notoriously insatiable sexual appetites of film stars. They may have thought a fresh shift of six girls was coming to take over for the early morning hours. I think I performed a useful function, guarding my squad from the evils of gambling.

We went back to L.A. and I plunged deep into *Major Dundee.* I wouldn't come up for air again till we finished the shoot. We had a ten-week schedule, tight but doable; what we did not have was a finished script. The extant two-thirds of the original "needed a lot of work," as they say. (I can't resist pointing out that it had been written by a man named Fink. I will resist the obvious joke, but he had let us down badly.) As well as wading through the swamp of preproduction, Sam was working on the script while simultaneously preparing his shoot. I don't recommend this plan.

They pushed our start date back; Richard Harris was working in a film in Italy for Antonioni, who was behind schedule. Sam got a little more time on the script. I got a chance to meet with Carol Reed, who would direct me in *The Agony and the Ecstasy,* and also to read some useful rewrite on *War Lord.* That would be my last contact with those two projects for some months.

I had a chance to choose the horse I'd use (a handsome sorrel stud) and to work him a bit in the valley canyons, taking Fray with me. (The horses ridden by the principal actors in a film mostly come from L.A. ranches specializing in stock broken to work around cameras, ridden by actors with uncertain hands and seats. The ones we picked would then have to be trucked to Mexico, where we were shooting.) Remembering my experience in Spain with *El Cid,* I took some pains to get my stud accustomed to having a sword swung past his head. I also had the special pleasure of

watching a boy I'd helped create trot a horse beside me along a
ridge, and slide down a steep grade.

Six weeks earlier I'd begun cultivating the beard I thought
was right for my Union cavalry major. I've worn more varieties of
hair, fake and homegrown, than any other actor I know. The real
article is better, though a well-made beard may look better. The
problem is that it takes even a world-class makeup man a minimum
of twenty minutes to put one on, and it needs endless attention
during the working day. (Also, it itches.)

Thus, just as my beard had rounded into good shape, I was
irritated when Sam said he thought Dundee should start clean-
shaven, and grow a beard during his harsh incursion into Mexico,
as a metaphor for his internal unraveling. While this made a certain
amount of sense, I wished he'd thought of it earlier, before I'd
started to grow the damn thing.

(On the other hand, it showed that Sam was a director with
firm ideas. I was at a point in my career where I discerned that I was
being given an unhealthy degree of directorial deference, which is
bad for everybody. Only a few years later, on this exact same point,
I was preparing *Gray Lady Down,* in which I played the commander
of a nuclear submarine. Researching that profession, I found that
submariners, alone among U.S. Navy personnel, are allowed to
wear beards. Since I had the time, I proposed to the director that I
grow one. "You're a superstar," he responded, "you can do what
you like." I found this chilling, though I know many actors prefer
to do only what they like.)

By this time, Sam had more or less finished the script,
though it still needed work. Almost every script does; it's common
to make the changes you need during the shoot. I was content to
go on that assumption.

Then Sam decided to rehearse the film at the studio during
our last days in L.A. I've rehearsed film scripts in advance usefully a
few times, but I was dubious about this, though I'm always glad of
any chance to actually say the words with other actors. It works best
with people who've worked on the stage; I don't think Sam had
ever done a play, nor had most of his actors, Richard Harris and Jim
Coburn aside. We just sat around a table reading the script. Ninety-
five percent of the scenes were exteriors anyway; how they were
staged would depend on where the camera was put. Neither our

first A.D. nor our cameraman was present; Sam made no attempt to stage the scenes. The read-throughs were a little like masturbation —pleasant enough, but not much use.

On February 5, my family came along in the limo to see me off on the charter flight to Mexico: Holly in her little blue coat, Fray longer and leaner every month, his hair like wheat, and Lydia as always, most beautiful when I leave her. As we lifted off out of Burbank for Durango, I thought of Bette Davis's line in *All About Eve:* "Fasten your seat belts, it's going to be a bumpy night." So it proved.

Major Dundee had a lot of problems. One of the most crucial, though none of us realized it at the time, was that Columbia, Sam, and I all really had different pictures in mind. Columbia, reasonably enough, wanted a cavalry/Indians film as much like Jack Ford's best as possible. I wanted to be the first to make a film that really explored the Civil War. Sam, though he never said anything like this, really wanted to make *The Wild Bunch.* That's the movie that was steaming in his psyche. Lucky man, he actually got to do it, a few years later. Not many directors get two shots at the same film.

A lot of things went wrong with *Dundee;* Sam was responsible for most of them. A lot of things went right with it; Sam was responsible for most of those, too. He was, as I've suggested, a difficult but very talented man. I think he was a lot like the gifted mavericks who invented the movies in the first place, when a film cost only a few thousand dollars and you were more or less on your own. I also caught Sam at the beginning of his career, when his energy and talent were brightest, before the various excesses to which he was vulnerable began to bring him down.

Even then, he was eccentrically unreliable. He's the only director I've ever worked for who came late to work—often. The director should *never* be late; he must be first on the set in the morning and last off at night, or why would anyone else come on time?

Besides, the job's so bloody hard you need every scrap of every day to keep even with all you have to do. Sam would often show up twenty minutes, even half an hour late, rumpled, unshaven, in desperate need of a cup of coffee, then pull himself together and attack the scene at hand. Somehow his mordant black wit and clear intelligence would bring him up to speed on the work, which is what counts in the end.

I'm not usually good at this kind of thing, but I somehow sensed that I had to be Sam's pal here. Two weeks into the Durango shoot, he'd already alienated the producer and the cameraman; if he lost me or I lost him, we had no chance.

Actually, Sam was a good companion, even when somewhat taken in drink. We even found time to discuss the film, walking from one squalid bar to another, often ending up in some dirt-floored brothel staffed with fifteen-year-olds. Renting a semen receptacle has never appealed to me; I'd sit in what passed for the parlor with a Dos Equis beer, then make certain Sam got home by 1 A.M.

(Sorry, I don't know whether the current Politically Correct position on prostitutes is applause for their entrepreneurial independence or outrage at their exploitation. At the time, they struck me as sad children.) I will say staying up late is overrated. When you're a little kid with a set bedtime, it seems the epitome of personal freedom; in reality, almost anything doable, from planning a dawn attack on a fortified position to seducing the Queen of the Universe (about the same thing, really), can be done before midnight. In the best of times, I'm not much of a carouser. (I told you I make an unsatisfactory movie star.)

Still, for that shoot, I became a carouser (though the carousing you can do in rural Mexico is limited). I had to forge some sort of working bond with Sam. You have to be able to trust your director, he has to be able to trust you. This was harder for Sam than for me; as an actor, I look to the director for guidance and stability. Sam had a streak of paranoia in him. (As has been observed, though, even paranoids have enemies. Sam surely did, most of them in suits, with corporate titles.)

The story line we'd hammered out was very dark. Toward the end of the film, Amos Dundee, my character, scrapes bottom in a kind of purgatory. I'd played flawed men before: Shakespeare's Mark Antony, Macbeth, and Moses are all brought down by their own tragic flaws. Dundee survives, to lead his men back across the river. Still, he was an unusual exploration for me.

For an unspecified tactical error in the field at Gettysburg,

Dundee had been put in charge of a prison camp in Texas, denied any chance at a combat command in the last year of the war. When raiding Apache burn out a ranch and steal two children before fleeing into Mexico, Dundee detaches a small force from his prison garrison, augmented by civilian scouts and some volunteers from the Confederate prisoners—led by Richard Harris's Captain Tyreen —who gives his word to lead his men under Dundee's command "Until the Apache is taken or destroyed."

The incursion into Mexico in pursuit of the renegade Apache is illegal, and Dundee's professional zeal leads him into excess in other ways. Tyreen, a friend and comrade-in-arms before the war that split them apart as it did the country, is as much opponent as ally. At the nadir of his descent into Hell, Dundee is wounded, drunk, and abandoned in a ditch. As an actor, I found it a challenging journey.

I haven't seen the film in some time, but I remember the good things in it, as well as the bitter acrimony of its shooting and editing. The parallel with Orson comes to mind, but Orson kept firm control of his shoot, and came in very close to schedule and budget. For whatever reasons, Sam failed to do this.

Midway through the schedule, he'd fallen some ten days behind, thus setting off alarms back in Gower Gulch. Small delegations of studio executives descended on us. We were shooting in many different locations, working out of two or three different base camps, sometimes driving more than an hour over bad roads to the site of the day's shoot. (Sam had been imprudent here; you're wise to pick locations reasonably close to your base, to preserve the company's energy. More than two hours a day of driving time uses up a lot of that.)

Our visiting brass had no such problem, of course. They'd come out to our desert set for lunch well-rested, shaven, picking their way over the rocks in their Italian suits. After delicately discussing our problems and watching a little shooting, they'd go back to the hotel for a nap. When we got back around 7 P.M., we'd watch dailies together, then meet in the bar for a drink and more discussion. This would go on, very politely, for three hours more, more drinks, much more discussion. I would cut out by ten, since I had a five o'clock call.

We were glad to see them depart for L.A., but I was shocked

to hear the next day that they were firing Sam. True, we were by
then something like a quarter of a million over budget. (Today,
that's like four or five million.) True, Sam's basic pugnacity had not
endeared him to the studio brass. Still, to replace him at that late
date was a terrible idea, and I told them so, citing his talent and the
adage about changing horses in midstream.

Contractually, I had no vote here. *Dundee* was being made
under an old Hal Wallis commitment that had somehow ended up
at Columbia. It provided me with none of the creative controls I
normally exercised by 1964. Nevertheless, the leading actor on a
film has just about all the muscle he chooses to use.

Ethically, I deplore this kind of thing, I'm contemptuous of
star actors who do it, but I was convinced our only chance with
Dundee lay in Sam's finishing it. I made this point, as moderately
as I could, and they got the message. Sam would finish the film. I
never told Sam what I'd done, but he knew. It didn't help our
relationship. I can understand that. (God, I sound so saintly you
want to puke, right?)

Overwhelmed with guilt at having flouted my own standards
of professional behavior, I called the head of the studio the next
day: "Look, Mike, I feel bad about bullying you guys on this. I know
we're facing a considerable overrun on the film. I'd like to offer
you my salary to reduce that." (I wasn't getting my gross points on
this old deal, only a flat sum.)

"Oh, nonsense, Chuck, don't be silly. We're happy with the
way things are going. Thank you, but no thanks."

Feeling very pleased with myself for my selfless and cost-
free gesture, I called Herman. He snorted in disgust. "Chuck, when
are you going to learn this business? They'll take the money." And
of course they did, the next day. A wire-service reporter called me
to ask portentously, "So, tell me, Mr. Heston: Do you feel your
action may start a trend with other actors?"

"Trend, hell!" I said. "It won't even start a trend with me!"

I don't mean to give the impression that the shoot was an
unmitigated disaster. Sam was a gifted director and he'd cast some
fine talent. It's a joy to explore a scene with actors like Jim Coburn
and Richard Harris.

Let me make amends here to Richard. At the time, I wrote in
my published journal "He's more professional Irishman than Irish

professional." In fact, *all* Irishmen, particularly the actors, are very good at being Irish. The best of them are superb.

Richard is one of these. He's both witty and funny. (What's the difference? I'd say wit is a matter of brains, funny is attitude.) He also had a fine native gift, which he's honed consistently ever since he began, in a wide variety of roles, in film and on stage—the best test of all. I've seen him on stage; this guy is an actor.

I never said otherwise, of course. But my dour Scots instinct —come on time, be ready, just bloody *do* it—made me wary of Richard's more laid-back style. Especially in the frenetic chaos the *Dundee* shoot had by then become.

Richard was under some pressure, too. He'd never done a Western before, perhaps had never even been on a horse. He was in the saddle in most of his scenes in *Dundee,* but he never complained. He also gave a hell of a performance, on foot and horseback.

Sam was afraid of horses, which seems odd for a man who made so many Westerns. He did his best to stay clear of them, not easy on a film location where the horses outnumbered the cast and crew combined. Nevertheless, I damn near rode him down—the only time I've ever physically threatened anyone on a film set.

"HESTON JAILED IN MEXICO! DIRECTOR TRAMPLED ON FILM LOCATION!" The headlines would've been a refreshing change from my straight-arrow public image, at the least.

Toward the end of a long, tough day some thirty miles out of Cuautla, Sam hurried over to me. "Chuck, mount up and take the troop up along that ridge. We just have time to get a magic-hour shot of you leading them down." (Magic hour is a shot made either at dawn or sunset, when the sun's low. Properly set up, it can be breathtaking, with dark shadows and rich, ruddy highlights across the screen.)

You do have to move fast, though: that kind of late light is only shootable for about twenty minutes. We all knew that; the crew got the big Chapman boom in place down below in nearly nothing flat. As I swung into the saddle and headed up the ridge, I called back to Sam, "Do you want me to bring 'em down at a trot or a canter?"

"A trot is fine!" Sam yelled. "Just get 'em the fuck up the ridge so we can turn over. The light's perfect!" It was, too. I got the

column in line and pointed down the ridge, silhouetted against
the sinking sun disk, just as "Action!" boomed out of the bullhorn.
We came down at a brisk trot, like real horse soldiers, the sun red
on the dust as we moved under the rising camera boom. It felt
perfect to me.

"Cut! No good, no damn good," Sam snapped. "Run 'em
back up; we've just got light for one more. You gotta be a lot faster
than that."

"OK, but you said trot," I said, moving back up the slope.

"The fuck I did. I said canter, you stupid prick!" he yelled. I
was seventy yards away by then. I wrenched the sorrel around. Not
just the sky, but the whole ridge was red. Blood red. Irrationally, a
line I'd read in some Civil War memoir leaped into my mind: "So I
lifted my saber and stood in my stirrups and shouted, 'Kill 'em,
goddamn 'em . . . *ride 'em down!!'* " That's what I did. I spurred the
horse into a dead run at Sam, my saber high.

Sam stood transfixed for two seconds, then jumped into the
operator's chair on the boom. "Take it up, *take it up!!*" he screamed
to the boom grip. It was a forty-foot boom, which moved very
slowly, but it lifted Sam out of my reach just as I thundered under
him. I slid to a stop and turned the horse. He'd done all the work,
but I was panting as if I'd run the seventy yards myself.

I can't believe I would have actually ridden Sam down, let
alone sabered him, but I was as angry as I can remember being in
my life. I don't really know why. A lot of things had piled up, I
guess. As the blood fell back behind my eyes, I looked up at Sam
and slid the saber into its scabbard.

"You want one more . . . at a canter," I said carefully.

"Yeah, that's right," he said *very* carefully, peering down
from the boom. So that's what we did. Sam printed it, and neither
of us ever spoke of it to the other after, in our lives.

The *Dundee* shoot was not wall-to-wall miserable. Lydia
brought both Holly and Fray down to Mexico; it was Holly's first
location, which she survived very well. Lydia whipped off to Yucatán
to photograph an archaeological dig she had her eye on, then took
Holly home. Fray, by then a veteran of film locations, stayed behind
for a few more days of Dad-time, including riding lessons from Ben
Johnson, World Champion Cowboy, whose career as a character
actor was blooming.

Joe Canutt was on the film, too, after a stint in the Navy as a hard-hat diver, doubling me in the shots I couldn't do myself. Actually, there weren't many of these in *Dundee.* After ten or fifteen films in the saddle in chaps, armor, or cavalry boots, if I had a strong, soft-mouthed horse and a chance to rehearse him through the hard parts, I could pass as a horseman in most scenes.

We were shooting on the Rio Mescala by then, the climactic battle with the French lancers, horses, and men thrashing around belly-deep in the river. Joe rigged my saddle for a Cossack drag (where you slide down along the horse's flank, using his body for cover). I talked Joe into letting me do the shot, so Sam could get a closer angle on it.

It really wasn't that hard, except that when I flung my 210 pounds out of the saddle, I pulled the horse over on top of me, in three feet of water. It could've been terminally nasty if Joe, playing mother hen in a cavalry uniform, hadn't leaned down and pulled me clear, with the easy grace real horsemen always show in the saddle.

It was April and already very hot in Mescala. It had been a long, tough shoot, laced with contention. In a sense, this helped my exploration of Dundee himself. He faced death and disgrace. At worst, I faced only a failed film. Still, I felt I could use some of this. I slept in modest but clean lodgings every night; now, with my family gone, I began going three and four days without a shower, just to get a feel for the reality of Dundee's quixotic foray.

The location food helped. It was appalling. I suffered it until one lunch break after a grueling morning wrestling through a scene with Sam. As I sat slumped on the riverbank in what shade I could find, chewing absently on a particularly gristly piece of meat, I realized I was trying to eat the hide and hair of whatever animal they were feeding us. For the rest of the shoot, I spent lunch lying on the riverbank with my boots in the water, sleeping.

I also had a stunning experience of the kind of total reality a film can provide, as when I rode through the gates of Valencia in *El Cid* and climbed a true medieval tower to accept the surrender of the city while thousands shouted *"Cid! Cid!"* While the immensity of the experience moved me as an actor, everyone understood it was a movie. In Mexico, I found something closer to reality.

We were working in very remote country, south of Durango.

The sequence was finished, except for some shots Sam wanted with extras. "We'll be moving the company in less than an hour," he said. "You guys all have horses. Why don't you take the troop and ride over that ridge to the village we're shooting in next? It's only a couple of miles."

That suited most of us very well. I wanted to see the village, for one thing. Tlayacapan, reputed to have been there before the Spanish came four hundred years ago, was still basically unchanged, lacking radio, electricity, and any awareness of the twentieth century.

As we topped the last ridge and walked the horses down, I understood how true this was. It was a dusty little pueblo of a dozen or so adobes huddled around the trail running through it. We rode in, a dirty, ragged troop of horsemen coming out of the desert with sidearms and sabers, just as so many marauders had done over the centuries. A few impassive Indian faces looked up at us, as some shutters closed quietly here and there. I knew what they were thinking: "Oh, God, here they come again. More bad ones."

When we reached the last adobe and turned the horses, the small domestic sounds in the village had stopped. It was empty by then, though I saw a girl in a red dress running up a hill a hundred yards away.

I realized that, for them, this was real. We were only actors, but till the trucks brought in the twentieth century half an hour later, we were a plausible simulacrum of other times buried in the race memory of the people of Tlayacapan. As an actor, I had to use this.

I walked the sorrel back to the center of the pueblo and sat scanning the surrounding terrain with a glass as Dundee would've done, occupying a probably hostile but not dangerous village. I didn't speak to any of the few men standing back in the shadowed doorways. I was trying to tap into the reality of their reaction.

Besides in *El Cid,* I'd seen this happen twice before, when elements of a filmed scene impose an undeniable reality. In *Ben-Hur,* the five thousand extras reacted spontaneously to Judah's victory in the chariot race because it was fun, but you couldn't begin to direct the reality of what they did. In the Exodus sequence in *Ten Commandments,* most of the eight thousand people there had never seen a movie. Still they recognized the Levite robe I wore and followed me, half-believing, just as the people of Tlayacapan drew back in prudent caution as we rode in.

I did learn from experience; I was better in the scenes in the village. I think I did well overall finding Dundee, another in the growing gallery of dark, driven men that seemed increasingly to define the fictional characters I played.

For that matter, it also defines some of the real men I've played since the beginning of my career. Having been plausible in various centuries and nationalities, I was almost automatically offered most biographical films about non-Americans, especially if the cost of the film required an American name. Nowadays, of course, the Political Correctness Police would deny me some of those roles, on the grounds of flawed ethnicity.

It only occurred to me while writing these paragraphs that those towering figures I've tried to pull from the pages of history have a great deal in common with the men invented for me by screenwriters, playwrights, and novelists. I've always been proud of the chance I've had to play genuinely great men—Mark Antony, Richelieu, Gordon, Jackson, Michelangelo, Thomas More—trying to find each one, and somehow stay true to him.

I realize, though, that many of the fictional men I've played, though moving on a smaller canvas, pursuing lesser goals with less extraordinary gifts than the giants I've named, still have much in common with them. My cops and quarterbacks, conductors, cowboys, attorneys and astronauts all show something of the remote, obsessed drive that motivates most of the great men I've played. Will Penny, an illiterate cowhand, is a shy man with a rock-hard commitment to doing his best and keeping his promises. So was the real General Gordon of Khartoum, who died doing that. The two films I made about those men could otherwise hardly be more different, but that parallel is there. (They're also widely considered to be among the best films I've ever made.)

On April 29 I finished the *Dundee* location. I swung out of the saddle already unbuttoning my tunic, changed into civilian clothes standing in the dust and was in the car taking me to the airport in five minutes. My ridge and my family never looked better.

I didn't have long to savor the pleasures of home. In exactly one month, I was due in Rome, where Twentieth Century–Fox and Michelangelo Buonarroti were waiting. I drove my son to school,

played with my daughter, opened the screening room we'd built at
the end of the tennis court, and generally unwound.

I had few professional responsibilities. The beard I'd ended
up with on *Dundee* would serve perfectly for Michelangelo, but
we'd have to do something about his nose, which was even more
badly broken than mine. Ben Nye, head of makeup at Fox, finally
devised a little rubber washer to go in one nostril. With a little
paint, it bent my nose even further than that high school football
player had done long ago.

Sam was already in trouble at Columbia, striving for his first
cut on *Dundee*. I went over for a conference or two, where I got
the feeling producer Jerry Bresler was so angry at Sam he was
almost willing to have the film fail, if only to clarify Sam's shortcomings.

In the end, like most films, *Major Dundee* was neither a
disaster nor a smash; it was disappointing. Since I'd been foolish
enough to contribute my salary, I don't get periodic statements, but
I suspect Columbia's edged into minimal profit by now. It certainly
set no stars in anyone's crown. Sam's best films were ahead of him.
So were some of mine.

I ran *Dundee* not long ago. There are many good things in
it, mostly performances. Best of all, the troop looks like cavalrymen.
Every one of us. Real horse soldiers. I'll settle for that.

16

Off on the Road to Damascus

The best government is the least government.
— THOMAS JEFFERSON

THE SIXTIES were a time of change for many of us, as the decade ripened; certainly for me. I think I grew up then, perhaps a little late in life. You can argue that actors, preoccupied with being all of the other guys they're paid to present to you, really have no idea who they really are. The reverse is plausible, too: actors spend so much time scraping around inside the heads of all sorts of people that they're better qualified than your average . . . naah, that won't fly. Actors get drunk, into debt, fights, and the wrong beds too often to be taken very seriously.

Nevertheless, I'd sorted myself out, I thought. While I'd been off chasing Sam Peckinpah's Apaches, Congress had passed the Civil Rights Bill, largely, it was conceded, in response to our August march behind Dr. King. I remain very proud of the small part I played in that historic event, though not of the tangle of entitlements and reverse discrimination the bill has spawned over the years.

Meanwhile, Fox had a plateful waiting for me in Rome. Michelangelo would surely rank with Mozart and only a step below Shakespeare among the sublime creative talents in the history of all the arts. He's also among the most elusive. There's a biography by a man who knew him, Vasari, written not long after his death, as

336

well as several hundred letters, mostly to his family, to whom he
gave money throughout his life—largely, I think, because he didn't
know what else to do with it. Certainly the letters reveal no affection
for them. Or for anyone else, either, or anything else . . . except
carving marble.

Irving Stone's massively successful novel about Michelangelo, *The Agony and the Ecstasy*,. was the basis for our film. (It
would also be the second of Stone's novels I'd filmed, after my first
exploration of Andrew Jackson in his *The President's Lady*.) Irving's
novel covered most of Michelangelo's life; our film would focus
only on the four agonizing years he spent painting his sublime
frescoes on the ceiling of the Sistine Chapel. In any exploration of
this thorny, misanthropic genius, it's important to know that he
hated painting ("Painting is good to the extent that it resembles
sculpture; sculpture is bad to the extent that it resembles painting").
And still he created two of the great paintings of the world, in his
only two times at bat as a reluctant painter, the other being the *Last
Judgment,* painted some years later.

Michelangelo was one of two geniuses I've played. Thomas
Jefferson was the other. You can hardly imagine two men more
different, but they both spent much of their lives doing something
they didn't want to do. Jefferson hated public service, longed only
to live at Monticello, yet he served his country superbly, just as
Michelangelo served several popes, because he had to do what no
one else could.

I landed in Rome the last day of May. After two long Italian
shoots, I felt at home there, glad to spend time again in one of the
great and special cities of the world. I was no longer a stranger, but
still unavoidably foreign. Fox had rented me a very grand house on
the Appia Antica, far more opulent than the rather austere nineteenth-century villa we'd lived in for the *Ben-Hur* shoot. This one
made me feel like Elizabeth Taylor (well, not very much, I guess,
but you follow me).

Till Fray's school let out, when Lydia would bring the kids
over, I rattled around in fifteen rooms and an acre of gardens, with
a staff of six. We'd need them when summer brought friends to fill
the bedrooms; till then I only needed a meal when I was there, a
turned-down bed at night, and wheels to go to work. I had a lot of
reading to do.

Actually, I'm comfortable being alone, perhaps not least be-cause I've been a public man most of my life. There are three kinds of public people: politicians, who must always inhabit their public identity; athletes, who experience this largely in a common team identity; and entertainers, who are probably more often scarred, even destroyed by celebrity. Performers, most often rock musicians and comics, frequently travel through their careers cocooned in a web of agents, PR people, girls, gofers, good buddies, and body servants.

I've always disliked that. When I'm not on my ridge with my family, just give me a dry place to sleep and my creature comforts and let me do the work. (I confess, by the sixties, my understanding of "creature comforts" readily included a villa on the Appian Way.)

Before we started shooting, I had to find Michelangelo, one of the most elusive men I've ever played, this side of the Shake-spearean monsters. There was a plethora of sound biographical material about him, but in all those pages he never really spoke to me. I couldn't get my hands on him.

I needed to spend some time with Carol Reed before we started shooting. I'd admired him as a director since his superb *Fallen Idol* and *The Third Man,* but had only met him casually a couple of times at Willy Wyler's house. I made it a point to go along with Carol on several days of location scouts—not normally on my agenda as an actor—but it gave me a chance to trawl through Carol's mind, looking for our man. We both had the same problem: Michelangelo Buonarroti was hard to find. That's not surprising: certifiable, undeniable genius doesn't turn up more than a couple of times a century.

I began to find, as I often had before, that being on the ground where my man had walked gave me a valuable look inside his head that all of the material written about him could never provide. Todi was a good example.

It was a small town north of Rome where we were building the set for St. Peter's Square, which Michelangelo had designed. To walk those streets somehow put me usefully back in the sixteenth century, as did the Carrara marble quarries, near Florence. To stand there on the spot where he chose the block of marble for his *Moses* told me something about what it was like to *be* that angry, driven man.

I finally touched him, I think, when I went back to the Sistine for the first time in years. Thanks to the Vatican and Fox, I saw it not as I had before, in a wash of tourists, but high on a scaffold, alone with the incredible miracle Michelangelo had wrought there over the four years he was nailed to that ceiling. Surely no work of art was ever torn out of so much anguish, against such odds. The physical obstacles against painting anything there at all are overwhelming. To see what one man, driven by his searing need to spend his talent, did here rebukes all of us who call ourselves artists. We can only dream of his infinite talent, but standing there within arm's length of what he'd done, I was seized by the sudden conviction that the glory of the ceiling sprang equally from his will —something all men share. His talent rejected it, aching for marble to carve, but his will and the pope's command drove him to make this among the best paintings a man ever created. Will. I'd found my key to Michelangelo.

I spent some more time with Carol in the last few days before the shoot began. I found him a very available director; he'd surely done his homework on Michelangelo, which surprised me a bit. My goal is always to know more about a biographical character I play than anyone else on the film. Carol was up to speed. On the other hand, I didn't think he was going to push me as hard as Wyler had. I think most actors do best if they're pushed. I know I do.

I also had a large amount of PR to do. Fox had flown over a planeload of press people, 140 of them—more at one time than I recall on any film. This made the chore a lot easier for me, of course, because the interviews were quasi press conferences spread over a couple of days, with a scale model of the Sistine Chapel I could take apart for them.

There was a British journalist who noted the disparity between my six feet three and Michelangelo's five feet eight. "Don't you feel you're a bit *large* for the part?" he asked sardonically.

"No," I said. "I think I'm a bit small."

The whole business of performers' heights is widely misunderstood by the public. The film frame is an oblong; everything and everybody photographed within it are composed in attractive balance by the cameraman and the director: chairs, tables are routinely raised or lowered from shot to shot . . . even automobiles can be driven onto thick planks so a tall actor can lean his elbow on the window and be appropriately balanced with an actress sitting in the car. (Horses are almost impossible to raise at will. They don't like it.)

Women average, what . . . five feet four and a bit, men a hair under five feet ten? This presents no problems, obviously. A woman can in fact be almost any height. Vanessa Redgrave is the tallest woman I've worked with; she must be five feet ten (and every inch of it actress). Working with shorter actors, it's not hard to balance . . . slippers for her, a two-inch board or lifts for the guy.

Height is really only sensitive for actors and, for most of them, only in shots with women. Let's deal only with dead actors, to avoid irritations. Jimmy Cagney, Humphrey Bogart, Valentino, Alan Ladd were very short; Gable, Ty Power, and Robert Taylor were not tall. Spencer Tracy, probably the best of all American screen actors, was short, but he handled it easily.

When he was introduced to the tall Katharine Hepburn for the first of many films they did together, she said to him, "I hope I'm not too tall for you, Mr. Tracy."

"Don't worry, honey," he replied. "I'll cut you down to size."

We began shooting on June 9 in the Carrara quarries. In that vast marble mountain there are a few places marked with signs pointing out that the marble for this or that work of Michelangelo came from this spot. No other sculptor's choices are so indicated. A little testimonial to genius.

The shooting itself was nothing. Carol, as do most directors, chose to ease into it with silent shots of Michelangelo on the mountain. It was also a highly photogenic location, of course, which accommodated the still huge press contingent very usefully.

Darryl F. Zanuck then descended upon us. He had founded Twentieth Century–Fox, run it brilliantly for many years, been forced out, and then regained control. He was among the best of the few men who were up to the awesome task of running a film studio.

He was also unhappy with the first day's rushes—mostly with me. He didn't like my beard, or the way they'd twisted my nose, though all this was based on portraits of Michelangelo; he was especially distressed with the headcloth I wore, copied from

what marble-cutters in the quarry had worn at the time. "I dunno
. . . you look like Othello, or some damn thing, for God's sake!"

Neither Carol nor I had any answer to this harsh public
rebuke, delivered in a restaurant full of journalists. I've found a
respectful silence is often the best response to unhappy studio
heads. So it proved in this case. Zanuck never mentioned beard,
nose, or turban again.

Then Rex Harrison arrived in Rome to play Julius II, known
as the Warrior Pope. In his brief papacy, he extended the temporal
power of the Vatican significantly and, perhaps even more significant, commanded Michelangelo to paint a mural on the ceiling of
the Sistine Chapel, which at that time was a vast expanse of blue
plaster with a scatter of gold stars. The role of Julius was central to
the whole film; the usual "Who's right for it, who's best for it, can
we get him, if not, who?" had gone on endlessly. We settled on
Olivier, on the grounds that he would give a fascinating performance in almost any role; of course, he wasn't free when we
needed him.

I forget who suggested Rex, and my journal offers no clue.
It may well have been Zanuck; he was very good on casting. Though
I was disappointed by the Olivier misfire, the idea of Harrison in
the part intrigued me. He'd had a successful career since the early
thirties, almost invariably in light comedies, until he found the role
of his life in *My Fair Lady*. With that he created a matchless Professor Higgins on stage for some years, followed by an equally impeccable performance in the film, for which he'd won the Academy
Award as Best Actor only two months before he arrived in Rome.

Rex had never played anything remotely like a pope, but the
acerbic edge the role needed was a color he'd used as Higgins and
he was, after all, a very good actor. From the first day, he was
marvelous as Pope Julius.

(As I was writing that paragraph, I thought of an uncanny
parallel between Rex and another actor I played opposite: Yul Brynner, who was my antagonist in *Ten Commandments,* as Rex was in
Agony and the Ecstasy. Yul created the title role in *The King and I,*
though he'd never done a musical before [nor had Rex]. Like Rex,
he did it for two years, then triumphed in the film version, as Rex
did in *My Fair Lady*. Both men won Best Actor awards for their films

[the only actors ever to win for a musical performance]; neither man ever did another stage musical. A final note: the novel on which *King and I* was based was first filmed in the forties by Fox. Who played the King of Siam? Rex Harrison.)

Both Yul and Rex were also alike in being complex, unpredictable men. Both were always polite to me, but you could describe them as . . . OK, difficult. Yul's disdainful arrogance was exactly right for Pharaoh. All our scenes together were confrontations; perhaps he was using that. It certainly worked for the film, which is what counts. We both came on time, knew our words, hit our marks.

Rex was a little stickier. For one thing, he was going through a difficult marriage. He'd tried several wives and never did seem to get it right. The summer we worked together, he was married to actress Rachel Roberts; they seemed always to be simmering just below boiling point. I remember a couple of explosions in restaurants (always worse for the people not involved in the fight), and a small Fourth of July party we gave at our villa when they arrived two hours late, but which Rex salvaged with wonderful British grace and wit.

On set, he was like a racehorse, snorting, rearing, kicking at the starting gate. He flatly refused to wear the papal crown, and picked petulantly at small points, for indiscernible reasons. "What am I to do with this silly *stick,* for God's sake?"

Carol was wonderfully patient with him. "That's a copy of an ivory pointer Julius had in his study. It might be a good prop when you talk to Chuck about the sketches for the ceiling. Let's run the scene and see if it works for you."

We attacked the scene, in which I had little to do but be humble and patient. Rex was neither. "This stupid stick is putting me off!"

"Then don't use it, Rex. We'll work it out." In the end, of course, he broke it across my back, as the script indicated, as the real Julius had done to the real Michelangelo, and indeed as Rex knew perfectly well all along. He was fine in the scene, as he was throughout with the part. I can't imagine a better performance; not Olivier, not anybody.

On June 15 my family arrived, the delicious Holly first down

the steps, burbling happily, then Fray rubbing sleep away, and my
girl, splendid in a white turban. Then, specially unloaded on the
tarmac and into the van along with the baggage, our big shepherd,
Drago, desperate to convey his distress at flying the Atlantic yet
again, along with his joy at seeing me. He's long gone now, but I
know I'll never love a dog again as I loved him.

The Appian villa came alive with my family in it, and got
busier over the next months as different contingents of friends
came to visit. My mother, the Fields, the Isaacs, the Wests, Bea
Sellmer, plus a varying population of offspring. I don't recall how
long anyone stayed, though my memory is that people came and
went, then came again, which is precisely how a house like that is
supposed to work.

I didn't get to play host very often, which worked out just as
it had in Rome and Madrid before. If people wanted to watch the
shooting, I'd lay on lunch at the studio and a tour of the set (though
this time I could give them no chariot rides). Rome itself has more
to offer than you can absorb in a year. If the evening had some late-
night wonder planned—opera at the Baths of Caracalla, the gardens
of Tivoli or the Forum by moonlight—having often seen these
wonders before, I'd have Ivo run me home early to bed, or nap in
the car while Lydia walked our friends over the ancient stones.

What suited me best was a very fine Florentine restaurant
just the other side of the Appia, maybe a third of a mile from the
villa. We'd walk single-file down the path in the late Roman twilight,
Fray in the lead with Drago pacing magisterially by his knee, Holly
usually in my arms ("Daddy, I need a pickering-up"), with my wife,
my friends, and a day's work behind me, now a meal, a night's
sleep, and another day ahead. That's hard to beat.

By the mid-sixties, sound and lighting equipment had improved enormously. Generators were quieter and more efficient,
also smaller, along with the lamps and cables, mikes and wiring.
This meant it was more feasible to shoot in real interiors, rather
than undertake the cost of building sets. We did this in several
nearby locations in Monterano, and Bracciano, where we re-
dressed the interior of the Orsini castle as the papal apartments. It
reminded me of the men's room at the old Roxy in New York,
which was just right; that theater was designed in High Renaissance

style. Rex seemed quite happy in it and the scenes went well. There's something to be said for acting in a real room, not a set made of flats on a sound stage.

We were still falling behind our schedule, principally, I was convinced, because of our cameraman. Leon Shamroy was high on the list of the great studio cinematographers. He'd photographed almost all of Fox's major films since the early forties; he was now the only technician at the studio (maybe in the industry) still under exclusive, year-round contract.

He was very good. Also very, very slow and an irascible crank to boot. Whenever Carol gave him a setup with any kind of camera movement in it, he'd say, "OK. Come back after lunch." It would be damn well after lunch before he'd turn over the set to Carol and the actors.

You're an actor; that's not really your problem, you might say. You might, but I wouldn't. Anything that makes the film less good or more costly is my problem. If the film doesn't turn out well, it's for damn sure my problem.

Of course the cameraman needs time—as much as he needs to light the setup. There are great cameramen who are slow, and others who are fast. Some of them, Bob Surtees and Russ Metty, were incredibly quick. Some of the great ones—Bob Krasker, certainly Leon Shamroy—were very slow.

As recorded in my journal, Shamroy and his crew had the set more than two-thirds of the time on every shooting day. That won't stand. The director and the actors need their share, too. It was a source of constant tension on *Agony,* and cost us both money and quality.

There are enough things you can't help that go wrong with films. Even actors with gross percentiles and creative approvals usually don't make choices on cameramen; directors have men they like to work with, and it's best to leave them to it. In fact, Fox had imposed Shamroy on Carol because he was good, and had a long-term contract. I was determined not to make this particular mistake again.

(Of course I did, only three years later, on *Planet of the Apes.* We were at Fox again, but with Frank Schaffner directing, a harder man than Carol. I told him about our problems with Shamroy on *Agony,* and we determined to make a stand on the issue. Darryl

Zanuck was no longer running the studio by then; he'd been re-placed by his son, Richard. He worked at a slightly lower key than his dad, but he understood perhaps a little better how to deal with filmmakers with creative controls.

He approached the problem head-on: "No, I want to use Shamroy. He's very good; he's been here too long to dump. I'll talk to him. I guarantee he'll give you guys the set more than half the time." I was dubious about this, remembering how cranky Leon had been in Italy, but Dick did it. Leon was just as good as ever, but a little quicker. He turned into a nice guy as well; not vital on a film set, but it makes it all a little easier. As it happened, I never worked with him again after *Apes,* but I would've done so happily.)

We'd about finished the away locations for *Agony* by then. Much of the rest of the film would be shot at Cinecittà, where we'd shot on *Ben-Hur* for so long. It was strange to go back. The grass had grown green over the track where we'd run the race, the doors swung empty on the stables where a hundred horses had stayed. Even the smell of them was gone. We were roughly halfway through the *Agony* shoot; I told myself the rest of it couldn't possibly be as tough as *Ben-Hur* had been. I was right, it wasn't. Not as good, either.

I was pleased with the set they'd put up for Michelangelo's studio, just a big shed with some sleeping room attached. It felt right, except that they had a full-scale, half-finished cast of Michelangelo's magnificent *Moses* in a corner. The figure is seated, but still more than seven feet tall. That's all very well; it gave a touch of the marble that drove his life . . . except that he didn't start work on the *Moses* till nearly thirty years later. Errors happen; everyone makes them. I hate *dumb* errors. (I've made some of those, too.)

By August, we were concentrating on the scenes with Contessina, the woman in the story. There was such a woman in Michelangelo's life. He probably bedded her. She seems to have been one of a very few people with whom he had even casually cordial relations. The homosexual community has long sought to claim Michelangelo as one of their own, but there's even less evidence for this. They miss the point. Michelangelo didn't care about sex, or about much else, except carving marble. That's all he wanted to do.

Still, the studio had decided, probably correctly, that a

woman had to be prominently featured in the story. We were offering little enough sex and violence as it was. Diane Cilento played the part, and very well, too, considering there wasn't a lot to play. (She was then married to Sean Connery, who visited from time to time, between James Bonds.) I could've done more to welcome her into the part, I suppose, but I was striving for the sort of detached amiability it seemed to me Michelangelo must've felt for her in real life.

Our Sistine Chapel set was ready for us at last. It was the crux of the entire film, the reason we were making it. After a great deal of debate, Fox had erected on the largest sound stage in Europe (Di Laurentiis Studios, outside Rome) a full-scale replica of the interior of the Sistine Chapel, which was roughly the size of a tennis court. It was an incredible achievement, certainly one of the most effective sets I've ever worked on . . . or seen.

Originally, the plan had been to shoot in the real Sistine Chapel. The Vatican had been surprisingly cooperative; negotiations had nearly been completed. It then became clear, though, that it would be harmful to the great painting Michelangelo had put there to shoot anywhere near the ceiling's fragile plaster surface. As it was, at close range, you could see cracks in the ceiling wider than your thumb. Also the colors of the panels had darkened terribly in four centuries since Michelangelo had painted his masterpiece.

Even if these problems could've been solved, there would be no way to photograph the painting in progress, or the bare blue, gold-starred ceiling that Michelangelo had covered. This left only one choice: to re-create the entire interior full-scale. Again, the studio's first choice was to have Michelangelo's panels copied by artists—a dozen major Italian painters clamored to have a hand in this, for free. Carol Reed insisted this was a mistake.

"Millions of people in the world will see this film who can never see the real ceiling. We have to show them what Michelangelo put there." He was dead right. The panels were very carefully photographed, printed full-scale, and applied to the arched ceiling of the set, their colors chemically restored to the original tones. Since a movie is in itself a photograph, we then indeed photographed the real ceiling. All the panels were sealed, thus making it possible to cover them with plaster and prepare them in any stage of completion a given scene required. The whole thing was really a staggering achievement, both technically and creatively.

(When the film was released, some said our restored colors were far too bright for Michelangelo's palette, though we'd sought the most expert advice on this point. When at last the real ceiling was restored, twenty-some years later, after even more meticulous research, the colors exactly matched those in the film.)

We began shooting there on the chapel floor, the crowds looking up in wonder at the blazing majesty of the ceiling, finished at last after four years, with Michelangelo standing unnoticed in a corner watching them. I insisted on a simpler jacket than the grand one they'd designed, which Michelangelo would never have worn. By then, as can happen, I felt I'd come to know him very well. I had no lines in the scene, but I knew what he felt.

The scaffolding Michelangelo designed to get within painting distance of the ceiling, seventy feet off the floor, was exactly duplicated for the film; his original plans are still in the Vatican files. When we had a full crew, cameras, and lights on it, it was heavily reinforced. When we shot from the floor and the scaffolding was serving as a set, it remained as Michelangelo designed it. Frankly, it was a shockingly rickety structure for an architect of his talent (he'd designed St. Peter's Square, for example). I felt I might need a stunt double to climb the shaking ladders to the top (though I finally got used to it). I'm good with horses, wild animals, fire and flood, shot and shell, not so good with high places or spiders.

Almost everything we had left to shoot by then had me wrestling with that ceiling through the four years he spent painting it. In winter wrapped in scarves, in summer with sweat mingling with the paint clotting my shirt and face. My makeup consisted of five minutes curling my hair and beard, putting in my nose piece, then lying back in the chair while they spattered paint over me.

Holly's third birthday and my mother's last day in Rome were on a Sunday, luckily. Neither lady would've been happy to have me off making a movie on such an occasion. Both of them had a fine day. So did I.

Another Sunday, with just the family, we had a picnic in the piney shade of the splendid ruins Hadrian left of his villa—and his hopes? Though extraordinarily beautiful, it's not a spot crowded with tourists; I was largely unmolested as I lounged against a fallen marble column, sketching an olive tree and watching my children caper through the afternoon. I cherish the memory; I can still smell the trees.

I'm an admirer of the Emperor Hadrian. Of all the thousands of clowns and tyrants, good men and bad, who've governed other men through all the centuries, he seems to have done as well as any, running an empire that stretched from Poland to Portugal and Scotland to the Sudan, maintaining therein the Roman Peace, which lasted longer than any the world has known since. He wrote to a friend the most penetratingly honest comment on the human condition I've ever read from a head of state:

> It is not true that I despise men. If I did, I should have no right, and no reason, to try and govern them. I *know* men. I know them to be vain, ignorant, greedy, cruel, cowardly . . . capable of almost anything for the sake of their own profit, or increasing their own esteem . . . even to themselves . . . or even simply for the avoidance of their own suffering. I know, because I am like them, at least from time to time . . . or might have been.

Never having played Hadrian, I'm afraid I'm not enormously well-read on him, but it occurs to me he was like Michelangelo . . . and Jefferson and Richelieu and several other great men I *have* played, in that he was lonely. It might well be true that such men are usually *separate* men, cut off a little from the rest of us by their capacities and perceptions. (Yeah, I know; that's a *very* Elitist thing to say. The Thought Police'll drag me off any day now. I can't help it, though. I've played a lot of these guys. Believe me, they are *not* like you and me.)

Turning toward the tag end of August, things got a little lonely for me, too, both on and off the set. Our friends had gone back to the States; we had a lot of elbow room in our Appian villa. Lydia took advantage of the chance to take Fray and Holly ruin-running (a phrase coined by Fraser) even more energetically than when the villa had been full of friends.

The set was emptier, too. Almost all our scenes by then had me high on the scaffold, working on that eternal ceiling. There were some terrific exchanges with Michelangelo looking down at an impatient pope on the floor below: "Michelangelo, when will you make an *end?!!*"

"When I am finished."

I also remember one lovely scene when the pope actually climbs the rickety ladders to the scaffold where Michelangelo is painting late into the night. Grudgingly, the painter takes a candle and shows him some of the images. It was one of the very last scenes Rex did in the film, and one of the best.

Back in California, we'd had a great break on *The War Lord*. Frank Schaffner, for whom I hadn't worked since television in "Playhouse 90," had accepted Walter Seltzer's offer to direct. I was delighted. Frank seemed, and soon proved, exactly the right choice. They both flew over for a few days of conference on the script, the casting, the usual kind of preproduction agenda. It looked as though we'd be able to start soon after I got back home.

By then, on *Agony*, we'd finished with the other principals. Like Michelangelo, I had only to finish the ceiling. Alone. It was a curiously spooky feeling, but very useful to me as an actor. Michelangelo had been nailed there for four years. Now I found what it had been like for him, lying on his back for hours on end, day after week after month after year, stroking those glorious figures into the wet plaster, with the paint dripping in his face. Again, I saw his achievement as an act of will as much as talent. Only a genius could conceive it, only a stubborn misanthrope could finish it.

You could smell autumn, and the end of the film by then. Every morning, the beech leaves were yellow, blowing along the paths as I walked to the huge sound stage where I was playing out the climax of the story. Toward the end of a September afternoon, I did the last shot—of Michelangelo putting the very last brush stroke on his ceiling, tossing his brush aside, and surrendering his work to the world—and history. Very seldom does the last shot made on a movie resonate so well with what the scene—in this case, what the film—is about.

The next day, we flew home—well, at least to New York, where we then still kept the East River penthouse. The leaves were yellow there, too, blowing across our terrace, the full moon over the river hung as it had the night before over the crumbled Roman walls on the Appia Antica. I've always found this comforting, criss-crossing the globe. We move, the earth abides, turning in its seasons, the moon waxing and waning in its own eternal cycle.

The next day, we went to the World's Fair, starting with the Italian Pavilion as guests of their embassy. That's surely the best way to do a vast public attraction. (Given my public condition, really the only way.) With PR people scurrying ahead, opening back doors, a car whisking us from site to site, we were cocooned in VIPness. (It was about then that we began adjusting Holly to the rules of public life, as we had with Fray at three, when he'd thought the screaming crowds waiting as our train pulled into Rome for the *Ben-Hur* shoot were welcoming him. My message to her was just about what I'd said to him: "Honey, all this stuff with the people and the cameras and yelling is just about Daddy's work. It doesn't have anything to do with you and me and Mommy and Fray . . . it just means they like some of the work I do. We're glad they do, and we're nice to everybody, and sometimes we get to do fun things and people help us, but the four of us are still the same.")

The highlight of Holly's day at the fair was her delight at a giraffe stretching ten feet of neck to wrap a long black tongue around a banana she offered him while we were lunching in the African Pavilion. Personally, I was stunned, yet again, by my Florentine friend, Michelangelo Buonarroti, more precisely, by his *Pietà.*

No, they didn't ship it over just to photograph me beside it. The *Pietà,* for the first and undoubtedly only time it would leave St. Peter's, had been the hit of the New York World's Fair all summer. Hundreds of people lined up each day to wait patiently for the chance to stand behind a velvet rope and contemplate one of the great statues of the world for thirty seconds or so before giving way to the next in line. The crowds were that big.

Lydia and I had seen it in Rome several times, but Fray hadn't. I was grateful that they shut the line down for a few minutes and gave us a longer chance to absorb what genius can create. As any of the millions who've seen it can testify, the *Pietà* is an enormously powerful work. Unlike Michelangelo's *Moses* or his *David,* there is sentiment in the *Pietà,* but how could you carve the mourning mother of Christ cradling the dead body of her Son without it? I was pleased to see that Fray, at nine, understood some of this. "Boy," he said. "That is . . . something, isn't it?" Yes.

Two days later, we were back on the ridge, where *War Lord* was waiting. After our conferences in Rome, Walter and Frank had largely concentrated on the script; we now had a draft from Millard Kaufman that pleased us and Universal. (The suits in the front of- fices always want to find a script they can finalize: "OK, we're all agreed, then. This is it; we can lock it up." They stamp FINAL SHOOT-ING SCRIPT on the cover in letters as big as those on the tablets I brought down from Sinai.)

This really changes nothing; you can't carve scripts on stone tablets. (Well, I suppose God could . . . I certainly wouldn't want to be in a script conference with Him.) Of course these guys know all this, really. It's just that as long as the script exists only on paper, with a clean copy on all the important desks, they control it. It's different when you're on the set, shooting it. Even more if you're on a distant location.

(I think that's the main reason Universal nixed our plan to shoot in England. The story was laid in the tidal marshes of what is now Holland. England has many such marshes on its east coast, as well as a matchless talent pool of good actors. The studio was nevertheless happier having us a little closer to home.) I think they'd heard of some of our misadventures in Mexico on *Major Dundee;* Frank Schaffner was an entirely different sort of director from Sam Peckinpah, but Universal was still edgy.

Frank and Walter and I flew up to Sacramento for a day and found some fine marshes near Marysville (not far from where we'd shot much of *The Big Country* a few years before). I liked the look of the area, and wasn't wild about the idea of another long shoot across the ocean anyway. More important, Frank was content. I still saw a problem in finding good American actors who could plausibly play men from different countries and distant times (as I'd been doing long before I came to Hollywood). I need not have worried.

We imported the fine English actor Maurice Evans to play our dotty priest, and used a local Brit, Harry Wilcoxon, who'd starred for DeMille as a Viking chief, plus two excellent American actors for the other principal roles: Richard Boone as my body servant/father figure, Bors, and Guy Stockwell as my dangerously unstable brother, Draco, along with James Farentino as a young peasant. There was no problem; right down to the smallest parts, we found good performers who made fine eleventh-century Norman men-at-arms, especially with those soup-bowl haircuts with the shaved neck and sides. (A lot like what the kids were wearing a year or so ago.)

The crucial casting was still to be done: the girl. Thus it was, thus it has ever been and will remain: "Who do we get for the girl?" (Yeah, yeah, I know . . . "girl" is *very* Politically Incorrect. I believe any female over twelve must now be referred to as a "pre-woman." So shoot me.)

This role *was* a girl, in fact, seventeen or so. We'd long since decided not to go for a name; the part was not really very long, and she said little in the scenes she was in. The whole story turned on the character, but a name actress could've shattered its chemistry. What we needed was a true innocent, a girl who had no idea of anything in the world beyond the peasant huts huddled round the stone tower the Duke of Normandy had built to guard his borders.

We cast as wide a net as possible, looking at hundreds of photos and résumés, interviewing dozens of actresses and testing five on film, in a scene from the script, on a proper set, playing with me. Some actors won't play in screen tests themselves, either feeling it beneath them, or boring. I've always done it, on the theory it gives me a far better idea of the performer I'm acting with than any amount of chit-chat. It's something useful I can do; besides, I like acting.

We did find an actress we liked very much: Rosemary Forsyth. She hadn't done a great deal, but she had exactly the quality of true innocence that we wanted. We tested her in the girl's first scene: her meeting with the knight who's been sent to guard the duke's northern border. She was very good. When we looked at the dailies, we cast her in the part.

In the few weeks left before shooting began, I tried to pick up a few loose ends, doing some chores at the Screen Actors Guild, also attending a couple of fruitless meetings with Sam Peckinpah and the Columbia brass on *Major Dundee.* On some of these things, you don't really expect to win, but you have to try.

I also turned down a couple of film offers, partly to clear my mind for *War Lord,* but mostly because they didn't work for me. Dick Zanuck lunched with me about a film on General Custer. I like doing films with horses and this also seemed a chance to

explore a tragic figure. When I read the historic record and the
biographies on Custer, though, I saw there was really nobody there.
I said to Dick, "Aside from screwing up at the Little Big Horn, it
seems to me George Custer's primary achievement was being the
best horseman in the U.S. Army. I don't think you can make a movie
about that." Dick must've agreed with me: they never did do it.

Walter Mirisch wanted me to be in his film of James Michener's *Hawaii,* though my journal isn't clear as to which part I was
to play. The record failing here, memory doesn't serve either. I
know the casting Walter eventually arrived at was ideal. Max von
Sydow played the driven Protestant missionary, Richard Harris the
roistering Yankee skipper. Though I could've played either part
plausibly, I couldn't have come close to what they did. Walter was
lucky I passed; he ended up with a massive success.

Happily, I had another chance, with both Mirisch and Michener. A couple of years later, I played Richard Harris's grandson in
The Hawaiians, the film based on the second half of Michener's
generational novel. I recall Richard's being represented in that film
by a fine portrait of him hanging in one of the sets. We'll get to that.

In that election autumn of 1964, the Democrats wanted to
include me in the campaign to elect President Johnson to what
would be his first full term of office after he'd shouldered that
burden when John Kennedy was killed. Actors make useful foot
soldiers in political campaigns. Had I not been filming, I'd surely
have joined them, though it seemed the President would need no
help. Still, I was glad to have some weeks of location filming ahead
of me, when I could put the election out of my mind and plunge
into the eleventh century.

We worked very long six-day weeks out of Marysville, almost
all of it in chain mail, sloshing around in the salt marshes on horseback. Each day began and ended with the long commute from the
location to the motel. That was then empty country, with only one
major highway intersection on the route. There was a large billboard, featuring a portrait head of Barry Goldwater on a field of
blue. There were only seven words of copy: "IN YOUR HEART, YOU
KNOW HE'S RIGHT."

Senator Goldwater had been nominated as the Republican
candidate to run against President Johnson more or less as a sacri-

ficial lamb, the general feeling being that the successor to the slain president would be anointed by the citizenry, as indeed proved to be the case.

I'd believed very deeply in President Kennedy's capacity to lead the country, even after the Bay of Pigs and his careful distancing from Dr. King on the Washington March. It seemed to me that President Johnson was the best man to carry out his agenda.

Nevertheless, it made me uneasy to drive by that billboard every day: "IN YOUR HEART, YOU KNOW HE'S RIGHT." I'd try not to look, or at least not to think about it. But one morning there was a convoy of trucks coming through the crossroad. As we waited, I experienced a true revelation, almost an epiphany, like St. Paul on the road to Damascus. I looked at that photograph of Goldwater and said softly, "Son of a bitch . . . he *is* right!" And I knew he was.

It's ironic that President Johnson, who won the '64 election in an overwhelming mandate, saw his popularity erode over the next years to the point where he chose not to run again, while Barry Goldwater's reputation has grown to towering status, even in retirement.

People say to me "You had a political change of heart, didn't you?" No, I don't think I did. I think the Democratic Party had a change of heart. To my mind, the Democrats I voted for and worked for couldn't be nominated by their party today, including Jack Kennedy.

WE SPENT the rest of the year and most of January shooting *War Lord,* the bulk of it back at Universal, in some quite marvelous interior sets, and a fine tower which we moved about on the back lot, part of it even down to the beach at Malibu for different exterior effects. We worked for several nights, attacking and defending the tower, often observed by a determined young man who kept infiltrating the set, only to be ejected again. Frank finally surrendered to his persistence and let him watch. His name was Steven Spielberg.

I put on my SAG hat then and went to Washington to lobby on the Hill for some legislation deemed important to the industry. I've done that kind of chore so often that it's hard to sort out exactly what I did on this particular trip. Some good, I hope.

From Washington I went on to Nigeria, on an assignment from the State Department, spreading culture. This was a holdover

from the Kennedy regime. We thought we were doing good, and
maybe we were, here and there.

It was a very exciting time to be in Africa; the European powers were granting independence to the colonies they'd ruled for more than a century. The continent's incredibly rich natural resources, which had proved so profitable under European control, would surely create even greater prosperity for the new black nations.

In retrospect, there are many reasons why this didn't happen. I think timing was part of it. Most of black Africa gained independence in the sixties, the apogee of Marxist popularity, and most of these new nations chose the Socialist road. They suffered accordingly, quickly collapsing into intertribal warfare and, often, the tyrannical dictatorships Marxism tends to spawn.

Nigeria was one of the promising few that seemed likely to avoid this fate. Newly freed of British rule, they had an educated cadre of black bureaucrats trained by the Brits (who'd seen this must be done, though the French and Belgians refused to do the same with their colonies). With this advantage, plus immense wealth in oil and other natural resources, Nigeria then looked like the star in the crown of the new black Africa, a prosperous and vibrant nation, pointing to a bright future.

It was also, I have to say, really hot. No, that doesn't say it. This was the heat of equatorial Africa, like the moist, hot breath of a horse on the back of your neck. The fecund air was pregnant with growth—if you held your hand up to the breeze from the jungle, you felt green things would sprout in your palm.

I had a very tightly planned schedule, with good people from our embassy in charge. I was based in Lagos, but during my five-day visit I would see most of the country. Of course there was a grand premiere of *Ben-Hur* in Lagos. (Over the years, I do believe I've been to more premieres and grand fund-raisers featuring that film than MGM staged when they first opened the picture.) Then they choppered and drove me into the remoter parts of the country, Enugu and, at the end, Ibadan, in the southwest.

Among the reasons the people at State had chosen Nigeria for this tour was that, along with a trained corps of native Nigerians who could shepherd the country into independence, the Brits had left them with the most valuable tool of all: the English language. It was spoken throughout the country, even in the tribal regions in the north.

Only Lagos had TV in 1965: a BBC feed from London a few hours a day, with intermittent local programming. I did interviews, of course, many more on radio, and read at schools and the university. Dickens, Shelley, a dollop of Shakespeare, and some Kipling (he was a bit out of fashion in the sixties, but he was a big hit in Nigeria).

I had a marvelous time, seeing a part of Africa I'd never visited, at a time of optimism and transition, persuading myself I might be actually doing some good. I did worry now and then about my passport. (State had given me a diplomatic passport for the trip, a privilege I'd enjoyed once or twice before.)

When I landed in Lagos, the passport whisked me and my bags off the plane and into our embassy's limo in nanoseconds. En route to the hotel, I gave it to a Nigerian Foreign Office man for registration. Somehow, as the days passed, it didn't surface. Not to worry, my U.S. Embassy escort assured me, "Things move slowly here. It'll turn up."

By the last day, it hadn't. My official schedule ended with a lunch at the Statehouse with President Aziwiki. It was the ceremonial full-drill: photos, toasts, speeches, exchange of gifts. In the course of this, I ventured to mention the passport, deferentially, to the president himself. The result was rewarding: shouted orders, secretaries scurrying, and motorcycles roaring out of the driveway, spurting gravel. The passport priority had moved from "It'll turn up" to *"Do it!!"*

I could leave Nigeria without a passport, but I knew I'd never get past British Immigration at Heathrow undocumented, famous face or no. As we got out of the limo at Lagos Airport, a motorcycle skidded to the curb with a handwritten note to Her Britannic Majesty, requesting my admission to her realm, signed by President Aziwiki.

It got me into London without a hitch. (Originally, all passports were handwritten, a formal request for safe passage in foreign countries for the bearer.) I may be the last American citizen to use one. I've kept it ever since, though President Aziwiki was assassinated not long after my visit by rival tribesmen from the north, and Nigeria's bright promise darkened. I hope not forever.

In addition to getting a new passport, I spent a day in London
meeting on a script I'd just accepted called *Khartoum*, brilliantly
written by Robert Ardrey. It was in fact one of the two or three best
scripts I've ever read, as I'd told producer Julian Blaustein when he
first pitched it to me. I don't recall any significant rewrites (that in
itself is almost unheard of). In the end, it earned a well-deserved
Academy nomination.

Khartoum was about the last months in the life of the nineteenth-century British General Charles "Chinese" Gordon. He'd
earned the nickname as a field officer on loan to the Chinese government for his spectacular success in putting down a rebellion,
where he more or less invented the modern concept of guerrilla
warfare. He was a very strange bird indeed, one of a line of eccen-
tric military geniuses the Brits seem to produce as required. He put
down the slave trade in Egypt and was sent to the Sudan as governor, where he was slaughtered when the capital fell to the invading
forces of the Mahdi. He was, as I read the biographies, a hero,
martyr, and a little mad. Also a great part.

Playing Gordon presented another problem. None of the
several non-Americans I'd played was English; the films had been
made in English because that's the language of international film. I
used the neutral accent, centered about halfway across the Atlantic,
that I learned at Northwestern. Gordon, though, was a specific Victorian Englishman who spoke with the accent of his time and his
profession as a British officer. All the other actors would be English;
it was up to me to blend in. While we were trying to choose a
director, I began working up my Victorian military accent.

(It's time to acknowledge here the unique contribution to
film made by Robert Easton. There is no shortage of gifted actors,
directors, or writers in this town; indeed, it's hard to find employment for most of them. There's only one Bob Easton. As literally
hundreds of actors and directors will tell you, he can teach any
diligent and attentive performer to do just about any accent in the
world . . . flawlessly, if you're truly diligent.

The only trouble is, there's only one of him. He never stops
working; I've conferred with him by phone on a Mandarin Chinese
accent when he was in Poland teaching an English actor to sound
like an American. If we could clone anybody in the industry, it
should be Bob. In addition to polishing my English accent, he's

taught me first-generation Irish/American, a Scots accent I've used twice, a Russian accent, a Southern accent specific to Georgia, the Mandarin accent I mentioned, and a Devon accent for Long John Silver. As Long John would put it, "Haandsomer than thaat, ye coodn't look t'foind.")

When I got back home, in addition to working on my Victorian accent, I had to come up to speed at the Screen Actors Guild, and be briefed on what had happened while I was in Africa, and where we'd be pointing for the next negotiation. We were also pressing to find the right director for *Khartoum.* Frank Schaffner was still involved in editing *War Lord,* where he was in trouble, too, wrestling with Universal on the final cut. Where are the good directors when you need them? Still, for a script as good as *Khartoum,* I was certain we'd find the right guy. There were several weeks open before I had to be in England to start the film, and I hadn't done a play in several years. Providentially (the poet Thespis being in a good mood), I had an offer to do *A Man for All Seasons* in Chicago for a limited run. Robert Bolt's exploration of the heroic resistance and tragic fall of Sir Thomas More was the best new play I'd seen in years. Now, thirty years later, I've done the play five times and filmed it once; I *still* don't know of any play written in that period that's as good. I was delighted to take my first crack at it before I left for *Khartoum.*

More's wife, Alice, shrewish, illiterate but magnificent ("Why, it's a lion I married . . . a lion!" says More on his way to the block) offered Lydia a large challenge. She'd stuck firmly to the Mommy track since Fray's birth. He no longer needed hourly supervision, but Holly would for some time yet. Still, playing in Chicago meant we could live in the rambling house in Wilmette my mother had kept after my stepfather's death a few years before. She doted on both Fray and Holly, as grandmothers will, and was delighted at the idea. I think she had even more fun than they did.

Rehearsals went very well, as is often the case with a very good play. The material itself is so strong that it carries you through the hard searches for the insides of the characters. We did have many problems with the theater, which was being refurbished for the production. In fact, the play was ready before the theater was. We couldn't get in till the day of the opening, and when we arrived to run the sound and light cues at noon, the sound system shorted out. By the time all this was fixed, the audience was filtering in,

stepping gingerly past the Wet Paint signs still in the lobby. It was the first (and I devoutly hope the last) time I've ever opened a play without either a technical or a dress rehearsal. As often happens, though, the audience, aware of our problems, was wildly enthusiastic. That, as we're fond of saying in my profession, is "the business."

Nonetheless, we had what Mr. Shakespeare calls "a hit, a very palpable hit." Mr. Bolt's play and the actors got lovely notices; our limited run was sold out, setting an all-time Chicago record for a non-musical. Lydia was an excellent Alice, very happy to have trod a board again, and I felt the fulfillment I always relish when I go back to the stage, in the end the actor's medium. I had a *marvelous* time exploring Sir Thomas, and looked forward to a closer acquaintance. Though I came to do the part better in later productions, it was then and since a revelation to see how audiences respond to this densely textured, richly written piece. Thomas and I have had a rewarding time together, over the years.

We sailed for England on the *Queen Mary,* without doubt the best way to travel. It was our last such trip, and Holly's only one. If I'd known that, we wouldn't have enjoyed it nearly as much; as it was, we had a fine crossing. All those great liners are now either scrapped or converted to tourist ferries. The poor old *Queen* is a museum sunk in cement in Long Beach Harbor. I often fly over her eastbound out of LAX, but it would break my heart to visit her.

We landed at Southampton and drove up through the rich green of the English hedgerows. London was what it's always remained for me, the greatest city in the world, as Rome was centuries ago and New York has somehow never quite become. I've shuttled around the world so much by now that all the great cities seem like bus stops where I get off to work, except for London. Even if I'm there for only a day or so, as I sometimes am, I look at the Thames as we slant down to Heathrow with a smile of pleasure I otherwise feel only at home.

The Dorchester's surely one of the great hotels, as well. They put us up in a lovely corner suite overlooking Hyde Park, with rooms for the kids and, for a week or so, my father and his wife, Velda, who were over on his first trip to Europe since his naval service in World War I. I treasure the days they spent with us; it was to be the last good time we had together. Barely more than a year later, he was dead. As it was, I got to show him something of London, and the shooting at Pinewood (my favorite film studio in the world).

By the time we got settled in, the pieces of *Khartoum* had come together. We had Laurence Olivier to play the Mahdi, and Ralph Richardson for Prime Minister Gladstone, along with a fine young English actor, Richard Johnson, as my aide, Colonel Stewart.

I picked up my new Jag XKE and timorously piloted it through London traffic, afraid not so much of losing my way as forgetting to drive on the left. I got safely out to Pinewood, however, and did some makeup tests (how gray the hair, how long the side-burns, how thick the mustache), as well as a test with a good black actor we in fact used as Gordon's Sudanese orderly. I found my way back to London with little trouble, in time for some doubles on the wooden indoor courts at Queen's Club. A good balanced day—work and play; XKEs and spirit gum, tennis and close-ups.

The next day began very badly at 7 A.M. when I phoned the garage to have my car brought up. "But, sir, you never brought it back last night." Like most actors working on a film, I rarely went out at night, a fact that must've been noted beforehand by the scoundrel who'd conned the hotel into giving him my car.

The men from Scotland Yard were most meticulous, but not hopeful that I'd get my car back. A gambling club around the corner in Curzon Street had been knocked off a little after midnight; the robbers would've needed a high performance car to get away from the police.

While the afternoon papers made much of the event—"BEN-HUR'S CHARIOT STOLEN"—we celebrated Holly's fourth birthday with a small party in the suite. She looked enchanting and had a great time, unaware of my loss, which I put firmly out of my mind. As firmly as I could.

The next day was long, as we continued to struggle with the Gordon makeup. As I was leaving the studio, Scotland Yard called with heartening news: they'd found my E-type under a plane tree down in Brighton, undamaged, with only 120 extra miles on the clock. It had indeed been used for the high-speed getaway from the gambling club robbery.

I don't usually share the admiration many people feel for the dashing bandit, but I had to admire the cool self-possession of

the man who stole my car. He'd strolled into the Dorchester lobby
in faultless evening clothes about 10 P.M. and called the garage on
the housephone in an impeccable Mayfair accent, "Would you
please bring Mr. Heston's car 'round?" When they did, he said to
the doorman, "Put my case in the boot, will you?", tipped him
generously, and drove off. As an actor, I had to applaud his performance, especially since they caught him two weeks later.

Having got my Jag back, I abandoned the studio's Rolls and
drove myself to Pinewood every day, just for the joy of it. (At the
time film actors go to work, the traffic's light.) Early one morning,
just as I pulled into my parking space at the studio, I realized that
the man parking the Bentley fifty feet away was Sir Ralph Richardson, one of the great actors of our time. I'd seen his Falstaff and
most of his films; now I'd be working with him.

Still, never having met him, I didn't feel I could just walk up
and introduce myself. I stood silent, watching while he took out his
briefcase and locked his car. Starting toward the sound stage, he
paused a moment, turned, and patted the fender. "Good-bye, old
girl. Back in a while." I treasure the memory of one of the great
actors of the century talking to his car.

We began the shoot at Pinewood, concentrating on Richardson's scenes as Prime Minister Gladstone, since he was going into
rehearsal for a play in the fall. Conversely, since Olivier wouldn't
be available till December, we planned his scenes back at Pinewood
then, after ten weeks of location in Egypt. Believe me, those two
actors were worth twisting a schedule for.

I had only one scene with Richardson, a secret midnight
meeting at a tiny suburban railway station where Gladstone gives
Gordon his orders to the Sudan. There is no existing record that
this meeting ever took place, but something like it, somewhere,
probably did. Trains make great film props, full of portent and
departures, both photogenic and dramatic. We found a Victorian
railway station west of London, complete with a Victorian train that
they keep for precisely such purposes. (We used it again just a few
years ago in a film I did about Sherlock Holmes, *Crucifer of Blood.*)

It was a long scene; we worked hard through most of the
night on it. Richardson was superb to work with, as he was in the
part. It was a lesson in acting for me. When we finally wrapped
about four in the morning, Ralph spilled coffee on his shirt as he

was changing to go home. I had an extra shirt in my trailer and pressed him to let me lend it to him. Two days later the shirt was delivered to the Dorchester, freshly laundered, with a note:

> And when he put on the shirt of the prophet, he found
> that he was stronger than he had been.

Joshua 17:22   Gratefully, Ralph

Ralph was finished with his role and Olivier was not yet available for his, so we pressed on at Pinewood with the other interiors. There were several scenes with Richard Johnson, including one where we sat impassive in the palace of the Khedive of Egypt, watching a wonderfully sexy belly dancer. Since there was no dialogue, it made for an easy day. The lady was literally the only woman visible in the entire film.

The point of the scene, aside from demonstrating Gordon's impervious dismissal of her charms, was to show his tunic, which had been copied from an extant photograph of him wearing it. Designed to impress on the Egyptians the power of Empire, the whole front of the coat was solid with bullion gold braid, adding at least six pounds to its weight. I complimented the tailor from Berman's, the oldest and best costume and uniform house in the world, on their skill at copying the tunic so accurately from a single faded photograph. "Oh, it wasn't difficult, sir," he said. "We made the original, you see. We still have the patterns." He was quite an old man . . . I was suddenly seized with the eerie conviction that he'd worked on the first jacket as well, a century before. Naah, couldn't be.

The last scene we did in Pinewood that summer was of Gordon's death. Gladstone sent him to the Sudan for much the same reasons our presidents send troops to Africa to deal with tragic slaughters. Gordon's military achievements in the field and his success in stamping out the slave trade, as well as his flawless personal integrity, were so impressive that Gladstone felt his solitary presence as governor of the Sudan would stabilize the situation, without troops.

Gladstone was unaware that the Mahdi, Mohammed Achmed, was at least as charismatic a leader in the Muslim world as

Gordon, with even more far-reaching plans: "Ah, Gordon Pasha, do you not know that the streets of Khartoum must run with blood? Also the streets of Cairo, and the streets of Damascus, and of Con- stantinople. This is the will of Allah, whose servant I am."

Gladstone also misread Gordon's nature, assuming he could simply recall him if the situation in the Sudan became untenable. When it did, Gordon ignored the orders to leave Khartoum to its fate and remained in the city, preparing to defend it with the ill-trained Sudanese troops he had at hand against the growing forces the Mahdi was bringing up the Nile.

This put Gladstone in an impossible position. Gordon was perhaps England's greatest living hero; he could not be abandoned. A British relief column was sent to raise the siege of Khartoum, led by Major (later Lord) Kitchener, who arrived two days too late.

We would do the attack on the Governor's Palace in Egypt, of course; the London shoot would cover only the mob bursting into the palace and up the staircase, stopping dead at the sight of Gordon standing at the top, armed only with the bamboo crop that had been his sole weapon in the Chinese wars.

Contemporary witnesses (all Mahdists, of course; everyone else in the city was killed) agree that there was dead silence for perhaps half a minute, then Gordon began to walk slowly down the stairs, with the front rank falling back, till a warrior on the floor below flung his spear, catching Gordon in the chest. He took hold of the haft, smiled slightly, and pitched off the side of the stair to fall under the knives below.

All actors love to play death scenes; God knows I've had more practice than my fellows. This was one of the most effective deaths, even though I had no lines (actors also love dying speeches), perhaps because Gordon faced his death with smiling equanimity.

They weren't quite ready to start the Egyptian location (the logistics were enormous), so Lydia and I and the children toured the Scottish border for a few days. Hadrian's Wall is one of the most impressive Roman remains in the world, surely the most memorable in England. Walking a good part of its length, built to keep my blue-painted savage Scots ancestors out of Roman Britain to the south, I thought of the four centuries the legions had guarded civilization there—twice the time our young republic has existed. It was raining and cold, a fit climate for the lean ghosts of those brave men.

The Cairo shoot still wasn't all in place, but we were ready for a little Egyptian sun. Besides, I was the only one in the family who'd been there before. While I'd been talking with God and leading Israel out of bondage for Mr. DeMille, Lydia had been back in California waiting for Fray, and Holly had been a few years further down the road.

Egypt is one of the few places in the world that is unique— there's no other place remotely like it. We did all the things you do there: climbed the pyramid of Cheops (even my mother, who'd joined us for a few days, came about a third of the way up and waited in the shade of a massive stone block, writing poetry). We rode a Hungarian train down to Luxor and sailed the Nile in a felucca exactly like the ones painted on the walls of the tombs.

I had my family with me, so I wasn't quite as restive waiting for things to come together as I usually am on a long foreign location that isn't proceeding well. Of course, eleven years after the *Ten Commandments* shoot, Egypt had changed, though perhaps only barely on the scale of their more than four thousand years of history. I'd changed, too: I was better at what I'm paid so much money to do, and I better understood the complex logistics and technologies that now and then combine with the even more complex creative elements and deliver a good picture.

We had a British crew for the English shoot, of course; we took the department heads to Egypt, along with the prime Number Twos, filling out the crew with Egyptian technicians. This slows you down, but still makes irrefutable sense on the bottom line of the budget, which is crucial to every film made. Third World countries tend toward a different view of the Anglo-Saxon work ethic. They understand the theory, but they can't quite embrace it, culturally. Mind you, it doesn't always prevail in Western countries, either.

Fortunately, almost everything we were shooting in Egypt was exterior, which is not as complicated to light and dress as interior sets. We did shoot one crucial scene in a tiny jewel box of a nineteenth-century palace, Al Minyal. The interiors took an eternity to light, it seemed to me. While we were waiting we got coverage of Gordon driving up to the palace. Holly, who had been

reluctant to ride a camel, was delighted to sit beside me in an open
barouche pulled by a beautiful pair of black horses through the
several rehearsals needed before the camera was ready.

A day or two later, I loaded them on the plane home. As I
carried my daughter up the stairs into the cabin, she patted my
cheek and said "Poor Daddy, has to stay here alone." (Lydia wrote
me that she wept inconsolably all the way to Athens.) Well, in her
fourth year, she'd seen the Sistine ceiling and Hadrian's villa, as
well as the wall he'd built in Scotland; she'd also sailed the Nile and
climbed the Great Pyramid (if only a few feet up). Not bad for a
little girl.

The shooting was beginning to fall into place. The battle
scenes were of course a significant element in the film; Yak Canutt
was directing those. After *Ben-Hur* and *El Cid,* his reputation as the
master of action sequences was clear to all. He was doing fine,
though his son, Joe, now on about his sixth or seventh film with
me, reported the quality of the horses was not very high.

The location shoot went reasonably smoothly, though we
had an unusual problem with a steam yacht we shot on for a few
days. She was a beautiful little craft. (Well, not so little, really, a
good hundred feet long, extravagantly appointed and luxuriously
comfortable.) She was the former property of Farouk, the last king
of Egypt, and served us very well. But one morning when we arrived at the dock, there was no yacht. I've waited endless hours for
weather, the right light, actresses and other recalcitrant animals, but
the half day we spent waiting for that steamer shines in my memory
as the only time in my film career when the *set* didn't show up.

Speaking of recalcitrant animals, I'd like to say a few words
about the camel. *Khartoum* was the third film in which I had to
work with them, though *Ten Commandments* and *Ben-Hur* had
required little actual contact. In *Khartoum,* since Gordon often rode
camels, I had to as well.

In time, I learned to handle a camel with modest competence, but consistent distaste. I know they have a place among God's
creatures, but I don't care if I never see a camel again, let alone
ride one. They're extraordinarily ugly and very bad-tempered. They
complain incessantly, in a kind of gargling grumble, they can spit a
foul yellow saliva with some accuracy, and, on a whim, reach
around while you're sitting in the saddle and bite you on the knee.

Conversely, I like horses and feel comfortable on them. We only had one sequence where I rode a horse, though, defending a herd of cattle destined for the Khartoum garrison from cattle raiders. Yak Canutt was directing the scene, but Joe had picked a neat gray gelding for me, perhaps a bit small for someone my size. When I pointed this out to Joe, who was usually infallible in these areas, he grinned and said, "Take your left foot out of the stirrup and tap him in the ribs with your boot." When I did, the gray knelt in the sand and rolled on his side as I stepped off. It worked very well in the scene, the horse serving as a bulwark against enemy fire.

Aside from the battle scenes, the most important sequence we had to shoot in Egypt was Gordon's arrival in Khartoum. The real Khartoum was a more or less modern city by 1965, and much too far up the Nile in any event. Masghouna was closer and smaller; we dressed it for 1885 Khartoum, and I disembarked from our pretty little steamer, as Gordon had, with his aide and a staff of six or so, to be greeted by an ecstatic crowd of hundreds, welcoming me as the savior of the city.

Our PR people claimed that there were people in that crowd whose grandfathers had known Gordon. I don't know if that's true, though I talked to one old Sudanese who claimed to remember his grandfather's description: "Ohh, yes, Gordoon Pasha had ver-ry blue eyes. Blue like the sky. When he looked at you, you felt that you could not tell a lie." I can't vouch for the grandfather, but the biographies do speak of Gordon's very quiet, awesome demeanor.

Certainly the crowd remembered Gordon. As our steamer approached the dock, they began an ululating Arab cry, interspersed with shouts of "Gor-doon! *Gor-doon!*" As I moved up the street, people pressed round me, still crying out. I picked up a beautiful little Sudanese child, who seemed content to be carried by this large stranger. I found tears running down my cheeks.

Once again, as when I'd led the Exodus for Mr. DeMille and later entered Valencia as the Cid, the crowd's emotion was palpable, and irresistible. The scene played itself.

By the end of October, we'd finished the Egyptian location and I flew to London for the scenes with Olivier. As I'd felt about Richardson, I'd been looking forward to acting with Olivier from the beginning. I hadn't been able to finish the *El Cid* shoot in time to take turns with him in the two main roles in *Becket* on stage a few years earlier, and of course on *Tumbler* we'd been actor/director. (Surviving a disaster is a bonding experience.) We hadn't worked together since.

Athletes will tell you they do better playing against the best. I know working with a fine actor lifts you, though acting isn't a competition. (True, there's an odious minority of actors, some of them household names, who devise pathetic little plots to spoil the other guy's scene. Olivier was above all that.)

We had two long scenes together, wonderfully balanced confrontations, duets for two voices. Olivier was a joy to work with, meticulously professional and totally prepared. (Of course, in reality Gordon and the Mahdi never met. When this point was raised with the current Mahdi, great-grandson of the man whose tribesmen had killed Gordon, he said, "Ahh, but they *should* have!" I agree. Life often fails to live up to dramatic imperatives.)

Still, the two scenes served the film, not least because the two of us sparked off one another well. There aren't many film scenes I've done better—or as well. Thank you, Larry, once again.

When *Khartoum* opened with a Royal Premiere in London a few months later, it got excellent notices and did equally excellent business in the U.K. and Japan, good in Europe, and not as well in the U.S., where it was clear my star power did not extend to a film with no women about a famous Brit largely unknown to American audiences. (At least I earned a place in Tussaud's Wax Museum in London, where they refurbished one of their big attractions, Gordon's Death, by substituting a figure of me as Gordon into the group. I was very flattered.)

The film is, in the opinion of several people whose judgment I trust in these matters, one of my two or three best. I'm sorry it wasn't more widely seen in this country. It's also the only film of mine I like that I don't think is very well directed. This hardly seems possible, but there it is. We had a superb script, a very high-powered cast, and a dedicated and intelligent producer, but the director, Basil Dearden, though he had some decent credits under his belt, did only a routine job on the shoot, contributing little to the performances. With Olivier and Richardson, he perhaps felt safest simply leaving them alone.

That the film should still have turned out so well challenges the given wisdom about the crucial significance of the director on a film. I have no explanation at all for this.

A further aberration: though the acting notices overall were excellent for everybody, a few critics suggested that I had eclipsed Olivier's performance because his Mahdi was too reminiscent of the *Othello* he'd just finished doing on stage in London for several months.

This is a ludicrous criticism. The two roles had a good deal in common; both were passionate Muslim generals. How many different ways could any black or Moorish actor play them? In fact, Olivier's Mahdi was markedly different from his Othello, which I saw. Though historically guilty of horrendous mass slaughter far eclipsing Othello's murder of his wife, Olivier's Mahdi was a far more controlled, even engaging man.

Olivier's Othello was widely regarded, not only as the best Othello in living memory, but perhaps of all time. I'll sign that. It was also a performance of archival significance as the last Othello by a Caucasian actor. Black actors had intermittently played Othello over the past two centuries, most notably perhaps Paul Robeson in the 1940s. But for some years before Olivier played it, Othello had been a designated black role, setting a challenge for the many fine black actors who have undertaken one of the four or five greatest roles in all dramatic literature.

Given this, it was daring of Olivier to undertake the part; even more that he was determined to achieve a black African Othello. He was no longer a young man, but he worked himself into sufficiently athletic condition to allow him to play the part in loose robes, his body stained from head to toe, then polished with a cloth to give it a fleshy sheen. The soles of his feet, his palms, and the inside of his mouth were colored, his nails painted a faint blue. His Othello was a black panther, padding across the stage with a rose in his teeth, awesomely persuasive and nothing like the Arabic Mahdi he created to face me in *Khartoum*. No other actor alive could have come near his Othello. No other white actor, even then, would've dared to try.

He worked for six months with a voice coach to bring his normal baritone voice down a full octave into the bass range he wanted for the Othello he was reaching for. (I'd added a few notes at the bottom end of my normal bass range for *Beauty and the*

Beast, and managed to train up into a falsetto I could maintain for a
ten-minute scene as an aged Oriental opium dealer in another film.
This is trivial compared to Larry's using a new voice throughout
one of the most difficult roles in the world.)

His Othello was . . . great. That adjective has worn out its
value; we now use it to praise a good haircut. Olivier's Othello was
really great. Of hundreds of panegyrics to his performance, here's
Franco Zeffirelli's: "an anthology of everything that's been discovered about acting in the last three centuries." I saw him do the part;
I'll sign that, too.

Here's one more Olivier story: in the several months of its
run, his Othello came to be regarded as not only the best in living
memory, but maybe the best performance by any actor in any part
—ever. That covers a lot of ground; I've seen a few great actors and
many very good ones give unforgettable performances, on stage
and screen. I've never seen anything that could match Larry's
Othello.

But then there came a night when his performance somehow transcended itself. Running through what he had always done,
he found an extra dimension. As Larry had said to me when we
were working on *Tumbler,* "Sometimes the gods blow in your ear
and you can do no wrong." This surely happened to him that night.
I'd love to have been there.

Especially as a play settles into its run, actors don't linger in
the wings when their scenes are done; they go back to their dressing rooms and put their feet up. This night, so I'm told, the entire
cast hovered offstage watching the extra magic "Sir" was working.

When the play ended, it got the standing ovation it had
gotten since opening night; Olivier was reported to have given
the performance of his life and so he had. But Maggie Smith, his
Desdemona, knew how far beyond this he'd carried everyone that
night, including his fellow actors; she had to make sure he knew
what had happened.

She went to his dressing room; his man admitted her and
nodded to the inner room. Olivier sat slumped in a chair, sweat
running through the ebony makeup, a whiskey in his hand. "Larry,"
she said softly. "You do know how good that was?"

He looked up at her, haunted and bereft. "Yes," he said. "But
I don't know how I did it."

When I tell that story to civilians, they laugh. Actors shut their eyes in anguish. To come, as he must finally have done, to accept the given wisdom that he was the finest actor alive, and that this was his finest performance, then suddenly to transcend all he had ever done in the part—yet realize he had no idea how to reach that level again—must have chilled the depths of his soul. Acting is a hard mistress.

Khartoum finished, I plunged into the full PR schedule I'd promised Fox for *The Agony and the Ecstasy,* starting with a Royal Premiere in London, then a couple of the European openings, New York, and so on. I was able to stop in Detroit and see my father. He seemed tired, his energy sapped, but we were glad to see each other.

Another daunting development was the modest reception for *Agony*. Though Rex and I got some good notices, the film was not widely admired by the critics, nor was it the overwhelming box-office success we'd looked for. "Well, whaddya expect, kid?" Herman asked. (I really wasn't a kid by this time, but the Iceman still found me green in judgment.) "Another picture with no dames, about some guy painting a ceiling, f'Chrissake. Y'gotta do a movie people want to *see*." I was all for that, of course, but I'd thought one of the advantages of being me then was that I could do the films that interested me, with parts that offered a challenge. I still like *Agony,* I'm still proud of what I did in it. It's not easy to find your way into a man like Michelangelo. (In the end, according to the statements Fox is required to provide me, reflected still in modest checks, we broke into profit on the film.)

I spent the last few weeks of the year not exactly Achilles sulking in his tent, but reexamining my priorities. I still felt I should do pictures I wanted to do, but perhaps not ignore those scripts that had the sweet smell of success on their pages.

To this end, I listened carefully when Walter Seltzer approached me about doing a remake of *Beau Geste*. It had been done twice before, first as a silent film, then very successfully with Gary Cooper. Walter insisted the part to play was the brutal Sergeant Markoff. Running the Cooper film, it was clear that without him in the title role, Markoff was indeed the best part, but I finally passed on the project, much as I was drawn to doing another film with Walter. Maybe I was sulking in Achilles' tent at that.

Instead, I took Fray down to ride in the desert. It revived my
soul mightily to see my son slide his horse down the side of a
ravine, leaning back loose in the saddle. From biblical times, the
desert has served as refuge, a healing cauldron. If it raised the
spirits of Moses, Jesus, Mohammed, Buddha, and Brigham Young, it
would surely serve me, however modestly. We prophets know
where to turn.

17

Wars,
and Rumors of Wars

> And you shall hear of wars and rumors of wars. See that
> you be not troubled, for all these things must come to pass,
> but the end is not yet.
>
> — Matthew 24:6

MY JOURNALS provide no clue and I honestly can't recall why I decided in 1966 that I should go to Vietnam. I'd volunteered for my own war as we were supposed to do, serving where they sent me in what turned out to be a fairly risk-free posting. I'd also given God heartfelt thanks that two atom bombs had canceled my scheduled inclusion in the invasion of the main islands of Japan, with a projected cost of a million American lives and twice as many Japanese.

I'd done three pictures in a little more than a year; I was considering three more, all of which I would eventually do, but none was then close to being a "go" project. Herman had a couple of firm offers for the kind of films he'd been pushing on me consistently, but I didn't see a good reason to do something I wasn't wild about.

I don't mean to paint Herman Citron as the bad guy here. He was an agent of the very first rank, superb in negotiation and frighteningly ruthless in pursuing my best interests. (I remember early in my career when an accountant I'd retained had been late in filing some tax returns. I was shocked to discover this, but even more stunned to sit in a meeting with Herman when he literally reduced the man to tears, so ferocious was his denunciation. I've never since seen a grown man with his head in his hands, sobbing.)

Herman's been gone some years now, succeeded by Jack Gilardi of ICM, a formidably gifted and energetic man who represents me as fiercely and vigilantly as ever the Iceman did.

No one could have represented me better. From his perspective, he probably could've done even better if I'd let him pick my films. I'd said at the beginning, though, "You make the deals, Herman; I'll read the scripts."

The trouble was, none of the three projects that interested me *had* scripts. One was being peddled around town by an enormously determined young producer named Arthur Jacobs, who'd acquired the rights to a French novel called *La Planète des Singes,* by Pierre Boulle, about an astronaut stranded on a planet inhabited by intelligent apes.

The novel was singularly uncinematic; there wasn't even a treatment outlining an effective script. Still, I smelled a good film in it. All Arthur had was the rights to the novel and a portfolio of paintings depicting possible scenes. He came up to the house and displayed them, along with what Hollywood calls "The Pitch." When Frank Schaffner came by, he liked it enough to commit as director, but Arthur was a long way from persuading a studio to put up any actual money to make the movie.

He spent the next year and a half in Development Hell, trudging from studio to studio with his paintings and being laughed at. *Star Wars* and the still-enduring cycle of space operas that followed came later; then, the project recalled the Saturday serials of the 1930s. "No kidding, talking monkeys and rocket ships? Buck Rogers and Ming the Merciless, right? Gedouttahere!"

There was also a project at Universal based on a book called, I think, *The General,* set in World War II. No script yet, though one was promised soon; besides, I'd just finished playing a general. There *was* another part in it: a symphonic conductor. I had never played one of those . . .

Flying home over the Pole from some errand or other, I was struck by a photograph filling the back page of *Life* magazine: it showed Y. A. Tittle, a great NFL quarterback rounding out a superb career with the San Francisco 49ers. He was on his hands and knees, head hanging, his helmet knocked off and blood running out of his ears after having been taken out by a vicious blindside tackle. He never played another down of football. Lord! I thought, What a marvelous last shot for a movie. It was, too, but it took me a long time to get there.

In short, the movies I wanted to do weren't doable; the movies deemed doable, I didn't want to do. Lydia's and my success on stage in Chicago the year before with *Man for All Seasons* had brought us a couple of standing offers to do the play elsewhere. That was attractive, but not right then, somehow. Maybe I was just all acted out for once, something I can hardly recall happening in my life. So then what?

Golf doesn't move me. I know, it's a great game, but it takes too long and you get no exercise, just a lot of frustration. (Who was the golfer who said "Y'know why they call it 'golf'? Because 'shit' was already taken.") I was working as hard as my life allowed on my tennis, but the dubious pleasures of pro-celebrity tournaments were beginning to pall.

Cruise ships and famous resorts are exercises in public relations for me; I've filmed in such places long enough to have used up all the pleasure of being there. What then? Suddenly, I knew. I should go to Vietnam.

Entertainers have visited U.S. troops in foreign wars since World War I. It's not true that Bob Hope was in the Argonne in 1918 with General Pershing and the First Marines, but he was in every theater of war where Americans served in World War II (though he never made the Aleutian air base where I spent most of that conflict). Many American performers toured the fronts, often placing themselves in some danger—Glenn Miller was killed on such a trip.

Dozens of entertainers visited Vietnam as well, twenty years later—usually a comic, and a singer, with a few musicians and some pretty girls. Bob Hope went there at least a dozen times with larger groups, playing to thousands of GIs at every performance.

None of this helped me, since I don't sing, dance, or do stand-up. Then I realized I had one advantage: I was just one guy. I could go to places where they couldn't send the musical groups with girls and pianos and portable stages. Traveling light, I could hitch rides on any chopper with spare space. I argued this with what connections I had in the military and the USO who would have to arrange my transport to Saigon. Finally, they agreed.

I got all my shots; I had my tiger suit in jungle camouflage (very spiffy, not anything like the fatigues we wore in World War II). I was all set to take off when someone asked, "Now once you get in country, what are you going to *do,* exactly?"

I said, "Get as far back in the boonies as I can, where they'll never see a show troupe. Maybe they'll settle for a friendly face from home." That was about it; no songs, dancing, or snappy patter. It sounds trivial and I guess it was, but I was surprised at how nice the guys were to me. They'd even thank me for coming. "Hey, pal," I answered. "Thank *you* for coming."

I guess that's why I went, really—to thank them. I went back a couple of times in the following years, never for more than two weeks or so, never spending more than a day in one place, almost never in forward positions overnight. Ba To, Pleiku, Danang, Gia Phuoc, Tra Bong, Dong Tre, La Hai, Me Thout, Buon Ea Yang, Tan Rai—as many different commands as I could get to, from tanks and Marine F6s to grunts and riverboats.

I was anxious not to burden the troops. I didn't need a shower or clean underwear, I could crap in the bushes and drop off the skids of a chopper four feet off the ground. (No, I couldn't do that now; my knees aren't up to it. I've even forgotten which color smoke from the LZ meant it was clear to come in.) I did my best not to be more trouble than I was worth, which wasn't a lot.

Early into my first trip to 'Nam, I thought of something useful I *could* do. We were set to visit a MASH unit somewhere near the Cambodian border. ("We" meant me and my escort officer, usually a captain, whose prime task was seeing that I didn't get shot. I never did.)

I've gone to military hospitals all over the world, from the Veterans Hospital in Los Angeles, where there are still some gallant old guys from my father's war, to Beirut and Somalia. It's not easy to do, though I think it's harder for the visited than the visitor. There's not much you can say to a dying man, or a guy who's had his foot blown off. "Thanks for coming, I hope you feel better soon," just won't cut it. (Though that's exactly what you *do* say, cringing at its inadequacy.)

I did say to the guys lying bleeding on the stretchers in the MASH units, "Look, I'll be home in two weeks. If you'd like me to call your wife, or your girl, or your mom, just give me the number; I can tell her I saw you." When I got home, I did that, not just for the wounded, but the other guys, too. Dick Zanuck, by then running Twentieth Century–Fox, gave me an office and some secretaries to place the calls. (He also picked up the phone tab on the whole operation, for which I thank him, underlined in red.)

I'd written the names and numbers down in a little 4 x 7 spiral notebook I took along to sketch in. Some of the numbers were blurred with sweat when I got back home, some of them I'd copied wrong or people had moved. I talked to more than three hundred women, though; they were all glad to get a firsthand message from their men. I did talk to one wife whose husband had died of his wounds since I'd seen him. She'd only heard the news the day before I spoke to her; somehow she still managed to thank me for calling.

I can't say whether my time with the troops was of any use to them; I do know it sent me back home content with what I'd done and reinvigorated with my basic commitment: pretending to be people.

The easiest project to put in place was another shot at *Man for All Seasons* on stage with Lydia. We had a good offer to open a new theater in the Valley; I was all for it. For one thing, we'd be working at home; I hadn't done that for a while.

We had a success once again with *Man,* as you're likely to have with that play, if you know your words and don't fall down. More important, we were both better in it. One of the rich joys of doing a play is that if it's a really fine piece, you know that and have the joy of exploring it night after night. In a film, you seldom really know if it's going to be extraordinary till it's all cut together. (Often the reverse is true: you expect it to be better than it turns out.) Even if you do know, you only get to do the scenes that make it special once. I'm very glad we got to do *Man* again. And again and again.

Unanimous critical raves are rare, on stage or screen; combining them with box-office success is even rarer. Of course, the adjustment you make to absorb bad notices (Ahh, what does *he* know?) means you have to dismiss the good ones, too. You never do. Our opening coincided with a flu epidemic in Los Angeles; my journal notes "I only hope the flu subsides; if so, we'll sell out the whole engagement." My concern for public health here is touching.

After an extended run, we took the production to Florida. That run sold out, too, which was rewarding in more than the obvious sense. As president of SAG, I had a responsibility to touch base with the various proliferating branches. I was glad I could do that with no drain on the union purse. Miami was the headquarters of what was becoming one of our more active branches. Since Florida was among the growing number of right-to-work states, it was attracting more and more production by companies who wanted to avoid excessive union regulation.

The local SAG board threw a coffee-and-cookies reception. I fielded questions ranging from where did I study and who was my favorite leading lady to how to get an agent and/or a part (in either order). I couldn't give very good answers to any of these questions, skipping as always the one about leading ladies. Answer that one and you make one friend and fifty-seven enemies. (Yes, I know the answer; she's a friend.) I was able, I think, to give some useful insight into the problems of working actors. God knows I'd been at it long enough by then.

We had a good time in Miami. It was hot, but pleasant, like a woman breathing gently in your ear. We had a good bit of down time to unwind in. One of the advantages of doing a play over a film is that the work week is short and all of it except the matinees takes place at night. Normally, a lot of what you do at night is likely to be illegal, immoral, or fattening; doing a play fills your evenings in a healthy and creative undertaking, for which you get paid. It also gives you a good reason to avoid wine at dinner and the hard stuff after. You then have the whole day to improve both mind and body (and do interviews).

I spent a good part of my days hitting tennis balls with my son and teaching my daughter to build drip castles on the tide line. Every kid can learn to do it, at about three, and it's an early triumph for them. We all need early triumphs.

All four of us went back to California. While I was in 'Nam, Fox had expressed interest in seeing a treatment on the French piece about the talking apes, as well as one on the football picture. Universal still had the project about the German general and the American conductor, but they had no script on it.

There were two or three other scripts, but none that rang a bell for me. The Iceman kept leaning on me, but I reminded him, "If I'm going to make a mistake, let it be *my* mistake, on a film I want to do, instead of yours, on one you talk me into." (Let the record show, if "mistake" means a film that didn't make a ton of money, Herman was right far more often than I.) On the other hand, following his keenly tuned sense of a hit project would have done me out of some much smaller but more challenging films I'm proud I made.

Herman's point was certainly sound. After an actor has reached a certain eminence, he's supposed to sit in isolated splendor, grandly choosing from the offers humbly left at his door. This doesn't work quite as well if *you're* leaving humble offers at *other* people's doors. Still, if you want to make your projects, the two concepts have to be reconciled. It can be done. Sort of.

Back in L.A., a trip to Southeast Asia I'd more or less promised the State Department I'd do seemed to be growing like a weed. It had originally been planned for Australia and was supposed to be like the Nigeria trip: reading various classy bits of American prose and poetry, keyed to the country visited. (Mark Twain is ideal for this; he went almost everywhere, and wrote about it usefully.) The suits at State now wanted me to add New Zealand, Rangoon, and Bangkok to my itinerary, which whetted Lydia's insatiable appetite for exotic foreign climes. Obviously, it wouldn't do for the taxpayer to pick up the tab for my family as well; United Artists was happy to do so in Australia and New Zealand, since I could do useful interviews in both places for *Khartoum*. Before the South Pacific, I had to lend a hand with the European openings.

Lydia came with me to London for the Royal Premiere and all the attendant press fadiddle. We had, predictably, an enormous success; the critical response was overwhelmingly positive. The audience's reaction is always warmer when they know you're there, but you can still read it. I count toilet traffic and coughs. For the *Khartoum* openings I attended, there were neither.

We flew back to Washington for the premiere there, then Lydia angled off to Wisconsin to see her father, and I stopped off in Detroit to see mine. He seemed diminished a little from when I'd last seen him, but we had an easy, drifting time, lounging in the sunstruck, shadowed summer haze of a Midwestern backyard. I read him some of the poems I was considering for my tour—Frost, Sandburg. When he went inside to nap, my sister Kay drove me to the airport, both of us talking carefully around our father's health.

En route to the Coast, I stopped for openings in Minneapolis

and Denver and a State Department gig in Lincoln, Nebraska, with
Ladybird Johnson, an extraordinary woman. I think I was more
useful to *Khartoum* than to the Administration, but maybe not.

Once home, I could sleep in my own bed, but I had a
heavier PR schedule. (That's always true with the L.A. opening; some
of us forget what's expected in exchange for a piece of the first-
dollar gross.) There are two things only the actor can do: play the
part and do the interviews. It does grind you down a bit, they do
ask the same questions; of course, how could they not? And of
course you give the same answers, but you can frame them better,
more succinctly, more colorfully. Hey, it's better than working in a
steel mill. I tried that when I was fifteen. I didn't like it.

UA went whole hog for the L.A. premiere of *Khartoum*. They
opened in the Cinerama Dome on Sunset, then as now the largest
screen in town. (That's now even more true, when my projection
room at home has a larger screen than many cineplexes. Miramax
reissued a new print of *El Cid* not long ago in the Dome . . . crystal-
sharp, digital sound. Awesome.) UA's party after the *Khartoum*
opening was the last time I recall seeing one-pound cans of caviar
at each table.

Patinaed over with the high life of the PR tour, I took my
family to New Zealand, and had a briefer look than they would
have at that incomparably beautiful country filled with educated,
employed, and contented people, perhaps unique in the world.
Lydia and the kids stayed behind for a few days while I went on to
Australia, another country I admire enormously.

To my chagrin, I've never worked there, though I've often
gone to peddle my films and books, mostly in the eastern half of
the country, Brisbane, Sydney, Melbourne. They seem to me very
English cities, which is not surprising: Cook discovered the continent, and through World War II it remained a bulwark of the British
Empire. On the other hand, the Australians are more like Americans
than any people I know (well, except for maybe the Scots). In this
century, they've fought beside us in almost all our wars. I know, to
count battle as a virtue is very Politically Incorrect, but I warned
you about that some chapters back. I give you Shakespeare:

> For he today that sheds his blood with me
> Shall be my brother; be he ne'er so base.

Over the years, I've gotten to know a fair number of Australians, as well as a couple of New Zealanders, which is close to the same thing. Tennis players, actors, military types, guys you'd be glad to have beside you walking down a dark alley. (Yeah, I know, that's an inappropriate and out-dated criterion too . . . unless you're actually walking down a dark alley.)

The last time I saw U.S. Marines and Aussies on the same errand was three years ago. I was in Somalia briefly, visiting various Marine and Army units deployed there by President Bush to maintain order and put down the bad guys. Later they were withdrawn in some disorder by President Clinton when that goal was judged as either inappropriate or undoable, your pick.

My first and last days in country were spent in Mogadishu, where I felt my visits to Ambassador Oakley and the CIC of U.S. forces, Lieutenant General Robert Johnston, USMC, took more of their time and required more security than whatever small value my being there was worth. Three Humvees to move outside the compound, Kevlar vest and helmet for all hands, all weapons loaded and locked. The rules of engagement were clearly very strict, primarily to make sure that none of our guys shot at anybody first.

In our New Age of Enlightenment, war is widely condemned as a major, permanent no-no, though grudgingly conceded as gaining us our independence in the Revolution, preserving the Union in the Civil War, and Western democracy in World Wars I and II. It also deserves an A in trauma medicine. Auto accidents kill more people than most wars, but fewer now because of the advances in trauma surgery learned in those wars.

I went into the field for a couple of days, including a visit to a Catholic orphanage where some sixty undernourished kids the nuns had rescued from the tribal thugs that terrorize the country sang me a song, then I visited a unit of the Royal Australian Regiment, in Bardera. They gave me an OK lunch (we were out in the deep boonies, after all) and a fine welcome. I talked to many of the men: they were glad they'd come, but felt it was an undoable operation, given the ground rules. I agree. The Aussies left a month later; our guys hung on till the fall, when we lost a good number of men, disgracefully. Our last image of Somalia was of a slaughtered American soldier being dragged through the street by

the happy Somalis we'd gone to help. That's simply unacceptable—
or should be.

My impressions of Somalia in 1993 were eerily like Vietnam
a generation earlier: in both cases the military found itself increasingly hog-tied by the Administration's micromanagement. In the
sixties, of course, I hadn't figured that out yet. The morale of the
troops in the field was still high.

Obviously the war could be readily won; it required only a
commitment from the White House to do that. Wars are undertaken
by statesmen, but inevitably must be won by soldiers. President
Johnson inherited the incremental involvement in Vietnam that
President Kennedy had begun, after President Eisenhower had rejected it. His soldier's instinct was sounder than that of his succes-
sors, consummate politicians both. They felt we could somehow
finesse our way through Vietnam. Ike could've told them otherwise.
A politician can finesse his way through an election, not a war.

This was becoming clear to the men in the field by 1966—
but not to me, and certainly not to the statesmen who were taking
over the war by then. After I'd carried out my cultural chores in the
major Australian cities (this was where I first read publicly the final
chapter of *Moby Dick,* which I've done often since and recorded
for Caedmon, with some success), I was called abruptly to the
American Embassy in Canberra, where I was graciously received by
our ambassador. I read Melville to his guests, and slept in the star
guest room just vacated by Secretary of State Dean Rusk, who was
en route, of course, to Vietnam to manage the war.

I was also asked to undertake a small chore requiring neither skill nor daring on my part, only a close mouth. I was glad to
accept, as I've done from time to time since then, confident I was
serving the good of the Republic. Just about all the people I knew
in this line of work are dead or retired by now; we have a different
bunch of bad guys, and the current administration has revoked my
security clearance anyway, so this is all irrelevant, but I'm proud of
what little I did. Or may have done—those people don't give you
progress reports.

In Brisbane I met my family, who had come in from New
Zealand along with the Isaacs and two of their kids, Mark and
Shauna. We were about to undertake something rare for me: almost
two weeks of actual vacation. I'd finished my chores for United

Artists and the State Department (the Asian stops were canceled). There were a couple of scripts cooking at home, but nothing that would heat up overnight. I could claim some down time.

Normally, I'd have been off like a shot for home, where I could close the gate, play tennis, read, write, swim, run the films, and see the people I wanted to see; just kick back for a while and forget my role as public actor/public face. The exotic locales people spend months planning and saving to visit are often my workplaces, either acting or being the public me. My ridge is nirvana.

Of course not all performers share my tastes in this area. By the mid-sixties, many of them embraced their public identities in a haze of hormones, chemicals, and excess. Some of the rock stars took as their credo "If it flies, floats, or fucks, charter it!"

Lydia had chartered a plane in New Zealand, a canvas-covered biplane into which she loaded my two children and took off at dawn from a gravel beach in a narrow window of open weather to show them Milford Sound. As Fraser has observed, his mom is in fact Indiana Jones.

With the Isaacs, we'd arranged to spend some time on Australia's Great Barrier Reef, one of the few places on earth that is truly unique—a thousand miles of living coral reef some forty miles off the northeast coast of Australia, rising a few inches out of the sea at low tide and rife with all kinds of exotic plants and sea creatures, all in the middle of the open ocean.

We spent several nights on a motor cruiser over the reef itself, then cruised on a full-rigged three-masted barkentine, the first I'd ever sailed on. It was exactly as it should've been, the water hissing under the bow-wave as the sails filled, dolphins leaping ahead of us, even a green sea snake casting a malevolent eye from the wake behind.

As the sunset darkened I read to the company the last chapter of *Moby Dick,* probably better than I ever have, and surely in the perfect setting. It echoes Homer and Conrad, Stevenson and O'Brian, all the men who've written well about the sea: "The morning of the third day dawned fresh and fair . . ."

I made a damn fool mistake on our last morning. Leaving Lydia to pack in peace, I took Fray half a mile across the bay in a motor dory to a little islet where I'd promised him we could dig for clams. After sandwiches and an hour of struggling with a truly giant clam shell, I realized the dory was hard aground, and the tide ebbing.

It was unlikely we'd be marooned for long, but we did have a plane to catch. When a motor cruiser passed near enough to hail, having no other signal at hand, I took off my red trunks and waved them, cavorting naked on the beach, which got the attention of the crew, all of them women, I realized. Still, they did pick us up.

Changing to the transpacific 747, I had time to take Holly to the Sydney Zoo, where she held a koala as her brother had some years earlier. Seventeen hours later, we were back on the ridge, where my life was folding in around me in familiar patterns.

I don't know which group in Washington asked the Stanford Research Institute to include me among those interviewed on whether there should be an American Film Institute, or what it should do, but they did. For the record, I was in favor of it, and in 1967, Congress went ahead and did it, using tax dollars, of course. It's thrived ever since and I'm glad to be part of it.

Back in town after a considerable absence, I attended to SAG business and also preparation for the Universal project about the German general and the symphonic conductor. Amazingly, though still short of a final script, they were willing to offer me gainful employment as the conductor, which seemed to me the more interesting part. Ralph Nelson, a fine director both Lydia and I had worked for, would take the reins.

The last two days of August I flew to Washington for a cultural event the White House had lined up, as well as another small errand for the good guys.

I was pleased that I could go home via Detroit, a chance to see my father. Though weaker than when I'd last seen him, he seemed in better spirits. I got on the plane home the next morning hoping I could somehow persuade him to come west for Christmas.

When I got out of the limo in our drive, Lydia embraced me gently, different from her usual fervent welcome. "Charlie," she said, "your father died while you were flying home." I squeezed her hand and walked through the house to the end of our ridge, where you can see Catalina on one side and Mt. Jupiter in the northern desert on the other. I wept . . . and wondered if he'd just waited for me to stop and see him. He was ready, I think, but I wasn't. I remember him stronger and taller than I.

The next day I kept the appointments I had to keep, and canceled the rest. I even hit some tennis balls with my son, while I was fitting my father's death into my life. I thought of Thomas Wolfe's "that dark and secret river, full of strange time, forever flowing past us to the sea." The stream still ran in its course, making only a ripple over the rock fallen in the current.

Then we flew to Michigan with Fray, leaving Holly behind, a bit young for a funeral. My stepmother, Velda, was, I think, prepared for Russ's death, though we'd never spoken of it. She had her brother, my half-sister, Kay, and a cushion of friends that must surely have sustained her mightily then.

I found the sight of my father lying in a box like a painted wax doll almost unbearable, though I properly endured the parade of people walking by to peer at him. I shook their hands and murmured thanks. I felt better the next day when I chartered a plane to take him north and bury him in the woods my grandfather had helped clear half a century earlier. There was a thin rain falling; our feet slipped on the leaves, as we carried the coffin. (Why does it so often rain on funerals?)

Afterward I walked with Fraser through the woods I'd lived in as a boy, and stood on the shore of our small lake as the sun lowered. "Try and remember your grandpa here, not in that box," I told him. Then we flew home, chasing the sun.

"THE SUN GOETH DOWN, and the sun also rises." So I've found, before and since. I came back to California to find several projects on the back burner bubbling busily: We had a firm go at Universal with the American conductor/German general project, script deeply in work, still titled *The General*. (If I'd played the general, that would've been fine, but you can't call a movie *The Conductor*—people will think it's about a streetcar.) We began with *Battle Horns* and ended up with *Counterpoint*. No, I know, neither title's very good; maybe that was one of our problems.

Universal was also hot on a Western script, the first forty pages of which Walter Seltzer had shown me some weeks before. "Read this. I think it's marvelous."

"If it's marvelous," I said, ever the voice of reason, "why don't we wait for the whole script?"

"Chuck, *read the goddamn forty pages!*" So I did. Walter was
right. It was rich, true writing.

I said to him, "This is one of the best openings I've ever
read. If the rest is anything near as good, we can get anybody we
want to direct—Wyler, Stevens, John Huston . . ."

Walter interrupted. "Chuck, the guy who wrote it wants to
direct."

"Oh? What's he done?"

"Just a couple of TV episodes."

"*Wal*-ter!! Come *on!*"

"Otherwise, he won't sell us the script."

I paused . . . maybe eight seconds. "I just changed my mind."
So Tom Gries came aboard as director as well as writer of *Will
Penny*. The accuracy of his ear for the way Westerners talk was so
true, I expected a younger Yak Canutt with a typewriter, from an
old Wyoming family. When we met for lunch, I was amazed to find
that Tom was from Chicago, the son of a jazz singer. We got on very
well (How could we not? He'd written me one of the great parts of
my life), though it would be a while before we got it in front of the
cameras.

Life on our ridge, public and private, became complicated.
While wading on the Great Barrier Reef with her cameras as the tide
ran out, Lydia had slipped and fallen on the coral. In a desperate
convulsive grab to keep her equipment dry, she'd apparently pulled
a back muscle. It turned out to be a lot more than that, troubling
her for the next twenty years, through three spinal surgeries on
three different continents, the last triumphantly and permanently
successful, healing both our lives.

On a shorter time line, things were not going well. *Will
Penny* had the inside track at several studios, given my status as a
hot fella, but Universal, United Artists, and Fox all passed on what
is still, along with Bob Ardrey's script for *Khartoum,* one of the best
film scripts ever submitted to me. Mind you, I'd just done a film for
UA, I was preparing another for Universal, and would shortly be
offered a third by Fox.

As I've observed, studios don't want to do what you want to
do, they want to do what *they* want to do. Who can blame them? If
I ran a studio, that's what I'd do: pick the projects I liked that I

thought would work and get the best people I could hire to make them. On balance, that's proved the best way to make movies. But they were wrong on *Will Penny.*

Meantime, I had a pressing item on my agenda—I had to learn to simulate a symphonic conductor for *Counterpoint.* Among my many character flaws is a tendency to put off doing unpleasant things: going to the dentist, telling a friend there's really no part for him, signing all the checks before I go off on location, doing the research reading on the Emperor Constantine for a film on the Holy Roman Empire (no, in the end, they never made it).

Fortunately, I learned early on not to procrastinate on the physical preparations an actor so often has to undertake for a role. I started more than two months ahead of our shooting date on what I knew would be a daunting task: learning to pretend to conduct a symphony orchestra. Unlike, say, charioteering, jousting, and fresco painting, where I was at least on familiar ground, this was entirely new territory. Still, work will do wonders. *Poco a poco,* as we musicians say.

This turned out to be the toughest thing I've ever learned for a part. (Oddly enough, one of the most physically exhausting, too. I used to come out of the sessions dripping with sweat. I don't see how Arthur Fiedler did it.) Leo Damiani, a California conductor, spent two months coaching me into a plausible semblance of a symphony conductor for *Counterpoint.* Since I can't read music, he even invented a simplified system of musical notation, so I could memorize the scores.

It was at least as hard as learning to drive a chariot. Also as exhilarating. Walking on stage, crossing to the podium to bow, taking the baton from the first violinist and seeing a hundred musicians lift their instruments for your downbeat has an almost sexual excitement to it. The preparation was miserably difficult, but I loved the doing of it.

In the end, my limited repertoire included the opening thirty bars of the Beethoven Fifth, the last half of the second movement of the Brahms Second, most of the overture to *Tannhäuser,* and the overture to *Swan Lake.* Aside from my daily sessions with Damiani, I had tapes at home and another set for the car. I even rehearsed in the shower and the pool, humming the scores (though of course I couldn't do it on pitch). I learned again what I already knew—the best of the great composers are in the same class as Shakespeare and Michelangelo, which is to say another world.

My preparation time with the orchestra overlapped Halloween, sort of an actor's holiday anyway, especially in our house when the kids were young enough to enjoy trick-or-treating. I got as much fun out of it as they did, providing professional makeups and wardrobe and driving them on their rounds. That year Fray made a marvelous space-suited Martian with a total head makeup in green, with red eyes, pointed ears, and antennae, courtesy of Universal's makeup and wardrobe departments. We had elaborate plans for Holly, too, but she was set on a princess outfit she'd seen advertised on TV. Lydia pointed out that the dress would just make her look like all the other girls. "No it won't! It'll have *me* in it!" Good point.

My part in *Counterpoint* fit well, too, another one of my hero-heels, as Lydia puts it. I played an immensely gifted but arrogant and tyrannical conductor (as many of them are, I came to learn). I based my guy on a combination of Beecham and Toscanini, only taller. Leslie Nielsen, a handsome young actor some years away from his comic triumphs in the *Naked Gun* series, played my first violinist. I seduced his wife, as I recall.

The costar was the wonderful Maximilian Schell as an anti-Nazi German general whose panzer corps captures the orchestra I'm taking on a USO tour when the Germans break through in the Battle of the Bulge. The film is essentially a battle of wills between two very similar men.

At one point I say to him, "As a soldier, you should understand Beethoven better than you do, General. You must conduct his symphonies like battles . . . until you win." In fact, Max was a very accomplished amateur musician. After a shot where he watched me conduct the Brahms one day, he said, "You know, I could play your conductor."

I touched his epaulet with my baton. "I know that, Max. I could play your general, too." Actually, that would've been an interesting idea. Maybe we should have made two films, and released alternate versions. As usual with good actors, Max was a joy to act with; a true pro and a good man.

Oddly, having done my best to seem a competent symphonic conductor, I also had to deal with the reverse: to seem incompetent at something I did know how to do. In the climax of the film, when Max's general has gone to the front to exploit the Ardennes breakthrough, my orchestra is in the dubious care of the Nazi officer left in charge. We break free in the ensuing chaos. I pointed out to Ralph Nelson that, despite my screen experience as a skilled and dauntless warrior, the conductor I was playing would be unlikely to have any skill with firearms. It was an unusual acting challenge, holding ineptly a German machine pistol I had in fact fired on a range. I think I was properly clumsy. We still escaped.

I had plenty to occupy my off-hours during the *Counterpoint* shoot. Walter sold Paramount on *Will Penny*. Aside from me, it wouldn't be a very costly undertaking. The script needed almost no work at all; we turned at once to the casting. We got some very good actors: Bruce Dern in one of his first parts, Donald Pleasence as a crazed wandering preacher/bandit, Ben Johnson, Anthony Zerbe, and Lee Majors before he became the Six Million Dollar Man. All of them were extraordinary, rising to the quality of the writing.

The really hard casting turned out to be for the woman, though it's the best female role I've ever seen in a Western. We offered it to every hot actress of the right age in town. I couldn't believe the turn-downs we got from actresses like Jean Simmons and Eva Marie Saint, as well as a couple I'd have been inclined to veto. I finally figured out the reason why. Tom had written in the character description in her first scene, ". . . she has a determined, somewhat plain face." I suspect most actresses didn't read past that point.

Happily, we found one who did, and recognized the quality of the role. Joan Hackett, who was just beginning to rise in her tragically short career (she died of cancer several years later), was delighted with the part, and absolutely wonderful in it. I cannot imagine another actress who could've done it as well. (How Movies Are Really Made note: For some inscrutable reason, the opinions of those making the choices on who's right for a female role are more sharply divided and more firmly held than with the men's roles. Doubtless Gloria Steinem would detect a sinister reason for this, but I can't.)

Unlike most of my locations, the *Will Penny* shoot wasn't a hemisphere away, only a hundred miles or so. This meant Lydia could come up a couple of times with the kids, Fray more and more

confident in the saddle, and Holly, at five, ready to enjoy exploring
all the interesting things that happen on movie sets, including falling in love with actor Tony Zerbe. I got home once or twice for
long weekends when they were shooting scenes I wasn't in, including putting in an appearance at the Academy Awards in white tie
and Will's three weeks' growth of beard to present a special Oscar
to Yak Canutt, still the only one ever presented to a stuntman. For
directing that chariot race alone, Yak surely deserved it.

We shot in the winter, out of Bishop, where a great many
Westerns have been made over a great many years, though I think
none as good as this one. We even had good luck with the weather:
beautiful most of the time in that high country, then snow just when
we needed it, and a day of rain, improving a scene where Will rides
into a ranch with the body of a cowboy who'd been bucked off and
killed by his horse. Will hopes to get the dead man's job, but is met
with a chorus of opinions on how good a cowboy the dead man
had been . . . "a mighty good hand."

"Wull, that's always the way, isn't it?" says Will, rain running
off his hat. "How was he b'fore he bucked off?"

We were very lucky on the whole film. The part of Joan's
son was a good example. More or less because he was the right age,
I OK'd Tom Gries' casting his son, John. The boy was wonderful in
Will Penny, though I think he acted hardly at all after that film. The
whole question of child actors is worth talking about, though nobody really seems to know much about it.

All children can act, of course. Their pretend games are
acting, an instinctive part of their play life, unless they collapse into
couch potatoes, watching instead of doing. Only a while ago, my
grandson, Jack, at three, came upon the Moses staff standing in the
corner of my den. I told him a bit about who Moses was and what
he'd done, whereupon he found a stick more his size and spent the
afternoon leading his playmates around the front patio with the
mantra "Follow me!"

At eight years old, John Gries shifted very easily from child-
play to performing in a structured film environment, as I've seen
happen with much younger children. A few years ago I did a remake of a fifties film called *The Little Kidnappers,* playing the Scots
grandfather of two very little boys. It was a very good part and my
employers were flatteringly exultant that I'd accepted it. I said to

the producer, Phil Fehrle, "You understand that this all depends on the kids. You could have Laurence Olivier as the grandfather; the picture won't work if the boys aren't good. What's more, with children of five and seven, you can't change them. And you can't really audition kids that young, either, just talk to them. You'll have to wait and see what they give you on the set. That's all you'll get." As it happened, the two little boys were wonderful. So was the film, I think.

As with John Gries, I doubt those enchanting little boys have acted again. Very few child actors have long careers, even if they achieve blazing success. Shirley Temple was the biggest star in the world as a child, but the public seemed unwilling to accept her as an adult. The same was true for Freddie Bartholomew, Margaret O'Brien, Deanna Durbin, and several others. I can think of only a few who successfully made the transition to adult performers. The outstanding examples are of course Mickey Rooney, Judy Garland, and Elizabeth Taylor, whose triumphant adult careers were perhaps earned at considerable personal cost. I know only one child star, Roddy McDowall, who still enjoys a successful career free of personal trauma.

I asked Roddy how child actors go about acting. "When you're a little kid," he said, "it's really just pretend games. If you go on with it as you get older, you have to start over and learn to act. It's not easy to do."

The *Will Penny* shoot went fairly well, though Tom ran into some of the problems a first-time director is likely to encounter, such as when you're doing a scene that includes special effects, like sulphur poured down a cabin chimney. Do it at the end of the day; shoot the acting scene first. Special effects *always* take more time than you've scheduled, leaving the actors exhausted, with their acting still to be done. In another scene, to get Will's reaction to a shot of rotgut moonshine, he had the propman serve me gin laced with lemon juice. I damn near strangled. True, my response was undoubtedly genuine, but I couldn't manage another take, or I'd have been blotto for the rest of the day. To play a good drunk scene, or anything else, you have to be cold sober. I remember the story they tell about Dustin Hoffman and Olivier in *Marathon Man*. Olivier was shocked to see Hoffman come to work one Monday red-eyed

with fatigue, having gone without food or sleep all weekend "because that's my situation in the scene, you see, Larry. How else can
you do it?"

"Acting??" said Olivier gently.

Still, Tommy did a beautiful job with the film. It turned out
to be one of the best I've made, certainly among my best performances. The release date unfortunately came just as a new manage-
ment team had taken over at Paramount. As is common, they more
or less buried the release of films made under the previous regime,
preferring to press forward with their own plans. In recent years,
though, *Will*'s done so well on video, TV, and cable that my gross
percentile brings me checks regularly. The film itself remains my
best satisfaction.

Life in the real world had been moving along in interesting
ways, too. Ronald Reagan won his race as governor of California by
a million votes, a percentage of victory he would maintain for two
terms as governor, then two more as President. I don't believe there
are many men who've done that.

Still, it was Lyndon Johnson who'd appointed me to the
Council on the Arts, in theory the executive body controlling the
grants made by the National Endowment for the Arts. Even then,
the bureaucracy that in practice *was* the NEA was already assuming
control of the grant process. Lydia came along to Washington to
hold the Bible while I was sworn in. I'm not sure what we all swore
to do—probably not waste the taxpayer's money. I'm afraid the
NEA has failed in that task, over the years. In the beginning we had
about a tenth of the money Congress has now voted the Endowment, attracting ten times more critics as well. Somewhere in the
process, the thousands of applicants for grants have gotten the idea
that, since the NEA exists to give money to artists, any artist whose
grant is denied is somehow deprived of his freedom of speech.
Aside from the fact that only a small percentage of those thousands
can be approved in any case, the logic behind their claim is laughably empty. Back in the beginning it all seemed like such a good
idea.

My experience on the SAG board came in handy with the
NEA. In such cases, it's useful to strive for the voice of reason, as
when Lincoln Center in New York turned out to have lost (not

spent, *lost*) over three quarters of a million dollars in one season, common sense demanded that their grant be cut. (It was, but not by much.)

President Johnson gave a reception at the White House for a fair sampling of what's come to be called "the arts community." There were certainly a lot of us wandering around trying to look bored and artistic at the same time. (Personally, I'm honestly awed every time I'm in that house, thinking of the history that's been made there.)

It was then that I met the man who in fact had suggested me to the President for nomination to the NEA Council: Jack Valenti, long since one of my most valued friends. He'd gone to Washington with LBJ that dark day in Dallas, serving him invaluably throughout his White House years, as he has the film industry as president of the Motion Picture Association, in effect, Hollywood's ambassador to the world. Lydia took a wonderful shot of Jack and me standing talking in front of a painting of Lincoln at some reception. She titled the print she gave Jack *The Patriots*. It hangs in his office, and I'm proud I'm in it.

Back in California, we won a victory at SAG I'm proud of too. Since its birth as the century's art form, movies and the people who make them have captivated the world. Every tourist who comes to Hollywood wants to visit a movie studio. When we were shooting the worship of the Golden Calf in *Ten Commandments* on Paramount's enormous Stage 14, still one of the largest in the world, DeMille saw me looking at a timber catwalk some ten feet deep stretching along most of the wall high above the floor, accessible only by stout ladders.

"I put that up in 1922. Everybody wanted to come and watch us shoot. I thought, Why not? We charged fifty cents." (Not a tiny sum then.)

I don't know whether anyone else picked up on it then, but the coming of sound rendered DeMille's idea impractical. When Lydia, touring the West by car with her parents in the thirties, reached Los Angeles, one of their first stops was Paramount Studios. The wrought-iron gates were guarded and impenetrable, but they took pictures through the bars. By the time I got to Hollywood in the fifties, most studios maintained a small office through which VIPs and various muckety-mucks could arrange guided walk-through tours of the back lot. If you knew someone on a film, you could even arrange to watch the shooting, which is often not what it's cracked up to be. I remember when my mother came out for her first visit to California, she wanted to see some filming. I wasn't shooting, but I was preparing a picture at Fox, where I knew Yul Brynner was making *The King and I*. As we drove on the lot, I prepared my mother for disappointment. "You understand, darling, there's no telling whether we'll see any shooting at all. A single setup can take an hour or two to light; when they do shoot, it could just be someone walking downstairs five or ten times. It can be pretty boring."

Just as we reached the heavy door of the stage, the warning light beside it flashed red; they were about to film. I pulled the door open quietly and we slipped in just as the first A.D. said, "Turn over." It was the master shot on the "Shall We Dance?" number, covered by four cameras, swooping and circling back and forth across a wondrous set, each exposing a thousand-foot roll of film. When it finished, the director said "Cut. That's a print; let's break for lunch."

"Well, I didn't think that was boring at *all*, Charlton," said my mother. "It was very nice."

It was some ten years later that Lew Wasserman got two great ideas. Lew gets a lot of those. He made MCA the most important talent agency in film, then bought Universal Studios and turned it into one of the major studios in town—in the world, actually. By the mid-sixties, he'd become the major executive in film, an eminence he retains to this day. It occurred to Lew (perhaps he got the idea from DeMille's experiment forty-some years earlier) to exploit the public hunger for getting on a film set. His vision was larger. He built on the vast Universal back lot a semblance of a movie studio, with star dressing rooms and stunt shows and animal acts, even a small-scale version of the parting of the Red Sea. The Universal Tour has become one of Hollywood's major tourist attractions as well as a financial bonanza, out-grossing many of the studio's films.

His planners stumbled only once. In the beginning, the tour buses would stop by any company that happened to be shooting on the back lot and let the customers watch them actually making a movie. It occurred to us at the Screen Actors Guild that this meant that, in addition to the film performances our members were providing, they were also simultaneously acting live without pay for the tour groups. It was an easy negotiation; Universal eventually conceded the point and the buses have avoided real film shoots ever since. Still, I'm proud of it.

By the time we wrapped *Will Penny,* Dick Zanuck at Fox had finally decided to go forward with *Planet of the Apes.* Dick's an extremely canny and highly motivated man, rich in the arcane skills that make a producer, as well as the even more mysterious capacities that make a good studio head.

Apes was a risky undertaking, the first of the space operas, and dangerously expensive. We all understood this, but Dick perceived another problem. Having read the script, he looked through the several very effective paintings Arthur Jacobs had prepared. "For the apes, you can't use real monkeys, right? They'll be actors in makeup?"

"Well, sure. Actors."

"What if the audience laughs at the makeups? This is not a comedy." He had us there. Frank Schaffner and I looked at each other, at a loss. "I tell you what I'll do," said Dick. "I'll put fifty thousand dollars into developing the makeups; then we'll see." That was a giant first step: at today's prices, that's half a million dollars. Zanuck assigned the task to John Chambers, then one of the best there was on special makeups. They came out wonderfully well. "We'll shoot some makeup tests to show the board back east," Zanuck said. "I want their reaction. If they like it, we'll go."

Frank and I thought we could do better than that. "Let me direct a full-scale test of a real scene from the movie," Frank said, "with proper costumes and a decent set."

"And I'll act in it," I added. So that's what we did. Edward G. Robinson seemed a likely final casting for Zaius, the arrogant orangutan who headed the ape government. He endured the two-and-a-half-hour makeup the role required, and performed wonderfully in the test we shot. Dick Zanuck and his board were delighted; we had our go. Then Eddie opted out of the project. "It's a good part, but that makeup is a bitch. My heart's just about gone to hell as it is; I couldn't stand it."

Maurice Evans, who'd played our dotty priest in *War Lord,* proved a salubrious choice to replace him. (Another How Movies

Are Really Made note: There's some grumbling in the business that producers and directors and stars keep using the same people— cameramen, editors, production designers, makeup men. Well, of course they do, actors too. John Ford had a stock company of actors he used again and again all the way down to bit players. So did DeMille. So did we with Maurice in *Apes.* He was bloody good, too.)

The other principal castings were both chimpanzees, played brilliantly by Roddy McDowall and Kim Hunter. For them, too, the makeups were hell to put on, endure, then painfully take off at the end of a long shooting day. When we ran the finished film for the company months later, as I was going into the screening room I was embraced by a very attractive woman I didn't recognize. "Chuck, it's Kim," she said, seeing my confusion. "Kim Hunter." Over the months we'd worked together I'd seen her only as transformed into a chimpanzee.

For the ape extras, masks were sufficient, but anyone near camera or with speaking parts had to wear articulated molded pieces, each applied separately, so the movement of their facial muscles would translate to the surface of the makeup. Our three principal apes became very skilled at this. "You just have to overact with your face," said Roddy, "and it shows quite subtly on the makeup."

As for me, I had time to grow my own beard and thus wore no makeup at all (and damn near no clothes either, except a loincloth not unlike the one I wore pulling galley oar Number Forty-one in *Ben-Hur*). The primitive, voiceless humans should of course have been naked, but all that frontal male nudity would be a problem in the film even today. Frank wanted me naked for the trial scene, but he shot from the rear. (One of the girls supplying coffee on the set said archly "Mmmm, nice buns." I suppose I could nail her for sexual harassment for that today.)

The shoot was a very tough one. In an effort to keep the budget down on a film that was then testing unknown waters, Fox had cut ten days off our shooting schedule, crowding us badly given the preponderance of location work we had. Still, Dick Zanuck had stepped forward on a film the other studios were leery of; we bit the bullet and conceded the ten days.

Summer in the Arizona desert is no fun. One of my fellow astronauts passed out from the heat on the first day, trudging over the sand dunes. Paddling a life raft ashore from our spacecraft, crashed in the waters of Glen Canyon Dam, I realized that the channel of the Colorado River was four hundred feet below me. Four years earlier I'd stood chest deep in its cold water, baptizing Max von Sydow for *The Greatest Story Ever Told.*

I did get one day off from the desert, finishing early enough on a Saturday to catch the plane carrying the day's film home. I slept with my wife and woke in my own bed, soon joined by Holly in her nightgown, a rumpled angel with tangled gold hair. I had to fly back that afternoon, but I had time to take Fray to watch the pros play tennis, explaining the strokes to him. It would've been worth twice the travel time to spend fifteen hours on my ridge.

Halfway into the shoot, back in California for even more extensive locations on the Fox Ranch (now condominiums and parkland) in the Santa Monica Mountains north of Malibu, I began to discover how rough a film this was for me physically. I was in shape, as my profession requires, whether you're driving a chariot or playing Henry VIII on his deathbed, as I've also done. An actor's body is his crucial tool, like a concert pianist's Steinway. If it's out of tune, you don't do very well.

Still, it was a rough summer for me. Barefoot and all but naked in most of the scenes, I was ridden down by gorillas, whipped, chained, gagged, stoned (even rubber rocks hurt), fire-hosed, and finally trapped in a net and jerked upside down. (Joe Canutt doubled me for the net-trap; when they printed it, he said "Y'know, Chuck, I remember when we used to win all these fights.")

The tough shoot worked to my advantage for one key scene. Having spent an entire day in the mountains being driven around a cage with a fire hose, I dried off, changed, and helicoptered back to L.A. in time to chair a Screen Actors Guild negotiation with the producers. (No, Fox paid the tab, not SAG.) By the next morning, I had a cold, which I never get, *ever,* while I'm working, on stage or screen. Before or after, yes, not during. Until then. The next day, my voice was reduced to a rasping croak. As it happened, I had only one line in the scene, for which that was exactly the voice I needed. Taylor, captured at last after his escape from the apes, speaks his first words after the throat wound that's rendered him mute. A key Trivial Pursuit question, the line's often quoted to me by devotees

of the film: "Take your stinking paws off me, you damn dirty ape!"
Not Shakespeare, certainly, but it works a ton for the scene.

I noted a curious anomaly on the location shoots. At lunch, the ape actors lunched separately, since their makeups limited them to liquid foods taken through a straw. But beyond that, they self-segregated by species: gorillas at one table, chimps at another, and orangutans at still a third. I leave it to the anthropologists to figure this out.

We finished on schedule, a goal I value more than some of my colleagues do. The wrap party (long since mandatory and now often rivaling Nero's banquets) hadn't been invented then, but Frank and I shared a drink in his office after looking at the last dailies. "I smelled a hit in this from the beginning," I said, "but I think maybe we also made a very good movie." So it proved, some months later. It not only grossed enormous numbers, it created a new film genre: the space opera. Fantasies set in outer space had long been a staple of the comic strips and Saturday-morning kiddie TV, but had been disdained by Hollywood. Later, Steven Spielberg and George Lucas were to explore space wonderfully, with far better technology, over a series of films, but *Apes* broke the ground.

Dick Zanuck was the first to perceive the future. Hollywood had done sequels in the thirties, producing low-budget films with the same characters, exploring and re-exploring the same plots and relationships with the Dead End Kids, and Abbott and Costello, much as the networks do now with sitcoms. MGM did the same thing a little more seriously with Andy Hardy and with the Thin Man films. But it never occurred to Louis B. Mayer to make a sequel to *Mutiny on the Bounty*.

It occurred to Dick. When *Apes* was halfway through its triumphant release, with rubber ape masks in the stores and so forth, he called me. "Chuck! *Apes* is showing incredible legs, and I know why. It's a different kind of film, something people haven't seen before. There's a wealth of stories there. We have to do a sequel, maybe two." (In the end, they did four, plus two TV series. The networks picked up on that and gave us "Star Trek," which in turn spawned several features.)

"You're probably right, Dick," I said. "But we've *made* the movie; I think it *is* special. You can't remake the same story. A sequel would just be further adventures among the monkeys."

"Chuck, Fox has to make this film; the opportunity's too big to miss. But I can't do it if you're not in it."

"Look, I see your point, but for me, I'd just be repeating the same part." I'd totally missed the point, of course, a point Arnold and Sly and Harrison and Eddie Murphy grasped instantly, eventually repeating the same parts through some twenty vastly successful films. I'm content, though. I had the best part of them all, if only in one film. The first *Apes* actually has a philosophical point to make. Commander Taylor (we never know his first name) is a cynical misanthrope, so disenchanted with his fellow man that, perhaps unconsciously, he's exiled himself from Earth, launched through time to an unknown future. The crash of his spaceship strands him in a simian civilization where he finds himself the sole defender of Homo sapiens as a superior species.

The half-buried Statue of Liberty shows him at last that he's home on Earth. On his knees, despairing, he condemns his fellow man: "You did it, didn't you . . . you really did it. Goddamn you all to *hell!!*" Given the freedom of screen dialogue now, I have to point out that you couldn't say that in the sixties. "But he's not *swearing,*" I said. "He's literally calling on God to damn the people who destroyed the world." We won that one.

I also solved the sequel problem, I thought. I said to Dick, "Look, I realize you can't do a sequel if I'm not in it. You stepped up to this film when no one else would; I owe you one. I'll do your sequel free, if you kill me off in the first scene. Contribute whatever you think it's worth to Harvard School." (A very fine private school in Los Angeles where Dick had gone and Fray was then enrolled.)

So that's what we did. I had no involvement in the script, of course; Dick asked me if it was OK for me to disappear in the first scene and be killed in the last. I accepted this, still dealing with only a few days of free acting, and thought I'd checkmated the whole process by talking the director into letting me detonate an atom bomb in the last scene, presumably wiping out both the ape civilization and any further sequels.

Wrong. The third film, I'm told, went back to a time *before* the second, and so on and so on. I've seen only the original film, but I understand a couple of the sequels were good. I'm still comfortable with the way we worked it out. My grandson's trust fund would be fatter if I'd taken the path my colleagues did later and done all the sequels myself, but he'll be OK on his own.

As we got to the end of the *Apes* shoot, my family moved out from under me. We'd planned a cruise in the Greek islands for the end of summer with some good pals, Walter and Mickey Seltzer, Bill and Clori Isaac with two of their kids, Mark and Shauna, Bea Sellmer, and my mother. Lydia left a few days early with Holly, stopping off in Germany to visit her brother, Bob, then a U.S. Army major. Fray left two days before me with his friend Jeff Match, the son of the man who'd been trying to teach me tennis for some years. When we wrapped the film, I had a steak and a glass of a good Margaux alone by the pool, content to watch the sun go down as scheduled. Living as much of my life as I do in public, I like being alone now and then.

This was our first trip to Greece, high time to touch the cradle of Western civilization. It was as I imagined it: olive trees, pines, and cicadas clicking in the heat. Gray rock and old stones carved by gifted dead men. On my first night in Delphi, we sat under the waning moon, watching actors trace the patterns of my trade in a stone amphitheater twenty centuries old.

The glory of Greece is a true glory, worth coming so far to see. The ruined marble and the tumbled columns speak eloquently of what is gone. You sense this overwhelmingly in the cave that was once the seat of the Delphic oracle, the voice on earth of the ancient gods. When the Roman emperor Constantine became a Christian, changing the course of Rome and the West forever, he prudently sent an emissary to explore the reaction of the Delphic priestesses. There was only one left, a wrinkled crone sitting alone in the holy cave. Before he spoke, she answered him: "The glorious house is fallen, tell the king; the sacred snake is dead, the spring is quenched, Apollo has no longer any shelter here." Part of the glory is in the fall.

You can't escape the past in Greece, but the little bus we'd rented to take us to Athens reminded us of the present, noisily polluting the air behind us. We stopped for lunch in the garden of a tiny taverna, cheese and wine and fruit, which I ran off for a couple of miles behind the bus through the Greek hills. I felt like the messenger from Marathon.

Walter joined us in Athens, having struck a deal to do the football film with United Artists, and another deal with the NFL to use the New Orleans Saints as our team. We had only a day in Athens, its streets too crowded and its air too polluted even then to make it an attractive city. It still has, however, the Parthenon, one of the places in the world you must see, like the Great Pyramid or the Grand Canyon. We arranged to do this at dawn, for the best light and the fewest people. It was worth the trouble—a magnificent ruin, though eroding steadily in the acid atmosphere of Athens. The faces on the caryatids were all but featureless, even a generation ago. We must be grateful to Lord Elgin for buying major elements of the Parthenon reliefs a century before and preserving them in the British Museum. I take a run by them almost every time I'm in London, along with the Turners at the Tate.

Then we boarded the *Alexandra Lisa,* the sailing yacht we'd chartered, an ocean racer, 110 feet, lean and fast, yet luxurious enough for our bunch of blue-water tourists. I suspect it was that voyage that nudged Fray toward the serious sailor he's become.

There are some experiences in life that fulfill your every expectation; sailing the Greek islands is one of them. Our flurried departure from the hotel, buried in luggage, didn't daunt us, nor did the wait while our food stores found their laggard way dockside. The Aegean Sea is all Homer said . . . wine-dark and unforgettable.

The island of Santorini seems right for the site of lost Atlantis it's held by some to be—the black cliffs looming over the gaping crater that was left when the volcano that drowned Crete blew up. Swimming in the hundred-degree water it still warms, I lost my gold Fraser ring in the depths, a fit offering to Poseidon for the trip, I reckoned.

We cruised the Aegean for two weeks, running on favorable winds down to Rhodes, where we found no sign of the Colossus that once bestrode its harbor. The ancient world seems much closer, sailing these waters. Kos, Patmos . . . we had to choose between the birthplace of Hippocrates and the island where John wrote Revelation. We had a stormy crossing back to the mainland, actually splitting our mainmast, but we dropped anchor safely and on time off Vouliagmeni.

Fray promptly offered to race me to the hotel dock, part of

the ritual passage at arms I think most fathers and sons g̶ through.
You roughhouse with your three-year-old on what he t̶ s to be
even terms, letting him win every time. Every physical̶ est is
resolved like this, also chess matches. As the years pass, t̶ the
boy gets stronger, quicker, smarter, as you concede les̶ ss,
with time tapping gently on your shoulder. This small r̶
dock was the first time Fray bested me, all out. A few y̶
when he was seventeen and spending a summer as ̶
white-water guide on the Middle Fork of the Salmon in
wrestled seriously on a sandbar there. He was taller than
quicker and stronger; he pinned me twice in seconds. ̶
grined, but also pleased. The tiny acorn I'd planted in his̶
womb had grown to an oak too strong for me. Besides,
compensations. Now, when we play tennis, Fray never pu̶
far to my backhand side. (Well, almost never.)

The next day, our group regrouped. Bill and Wal̶
go back to the States on various errands, as did my mot̶
Clori, Bea, and Mickey were determined to see the ruins
then on to Istanbul. That gave me the Squab Squad I'd shep̶
before in Vegas, plus Fray, Holly, Jeff, and Mark and Shauna ̶
From Turkey, I would be off on the road to Mandalay and po̶
beyond, to Southeast Asia again, from the other side. We flew to t̶
Turkish coast, chartered a small bus, and found our way to the
remnants of Homer's Troy. You could imagine the Greek ships
drawn up on the beach below the walls of Ilium . . . perhaps even
the wooden horse.

We left the bus at Bandirma to transfer to a small feeder
airline to Istanbul. The airport consisted of one runway and a single
small building with one man—manager, baggage master, and ticket
agent—and a fourteen-year-old boy porter. Both blanched when
they saw the mountain of bags in the back of our bus. Even I was
traveling a little heavy, with boat clothes and field gear for Vietnam.
The women were even more amply loaded, of course. The agent, a
Turk of anxious demeanor, looked dubiously at the several bundles
of tickets I thrust at him, then at the tumble of luggage the boy was
dragging to his desk. "Iss offer-weight," he said firmly.

"Yes, I know," handing him my charge card.

"Vot iss??" peering at both sides.

"That is an International Air Travel card, good anywhere in

" He put the card carefully in the center of his desk and
ough a catalogue of rules for nearly a minute, searching
leafence. At last he handed me back my charge card.

for Ho-kay." He'd clearly decided the card was some sort of
nent pass, good on any airline. I was tempted to see if he'd
board without surrendering our tickets, but that would've
cheating. I still treasure my one win over the bureaucrats.

Istanbul was memorable, too, the real splendors of St. So-
's Cathedral, now a mosque, and the Blue Mosque and the
e Byzantine splendors of the Presidential Suite, with a bed large
ough for a sultanate harem. Since it was the last good bed I'd
eep in for a couple of weeks, especially with my girl in it, I took
ull advantage of it.

I left my Squab Squad to make their way back home with
bags and offspring and boarded a PanAm jet going east. We landed
in Karachi long enough to see what hot really was (and to talk to a
guy for one minute who could identify me by looking at me—a
public face can be useful in different ways).

Saigon was at least as crowded as it had been almost two
years before, though the number of U.S. troops was much reduced.
Before heading out to the boonies, I did the hospital tour, which is
hard. The lines and lines of beds, with the young faces lying there.
There was a boy who'd been badly hurt by a mine, his body stitched
like quilting, red and seamed. He thanked *me* for coming out. I had
dinner at the Italian Embassy, which served no useful purpose,
though the food was good.

I flew out the next day on the same sort of tour I'd done
before, choppering into various places where they couldn't send
the show troupes. I spent a good part of the first night in the back
of an old C-47, two wars past its time (like me) rigged as a gun ship,
circling over an unnamed target below in the DMZ, tumbling flares
out the side door to illuminate the incredible firepower pouring
down.

We went to some places I'd been before, like Pleiku; other
bases were new to me, the An Khe Valley with the Special Forces,
also Luach, Tanan. I spent a day at a Green Beret base up in the
hills, in the Montagnard country. They were small, wiry men, very
tough fighters, not Orientals but ethnic Aryans. I submitted to a
ritual ceremony involving cutting the throat of a bull-calf, catching

the blood in a cup and drinking it, mixed with rice wine. I was a
little dubious about this, but one of the Beret sergeants said, "Ah,
the blood's OK, but that rice wine'll give you the shits, sure as hell."
It did, too. (Looking back, when I was made a blood brother of the
Miniconjou Sioux, blood was let, but we didn't drink any. Still, both
that and the Montagnard initiation were easier than swallowing that
sheep's eye at the Berber feast in the Sahara.)

Over the years since those first two trips to 'Nam, I've found
myself in a number of odd corners of the world where our guys
were getting shot at (though I take great pains to make sure no
one's shooting at *me*). Sometimes I've had small chores, mostly I
just go where the good guys are. Never doubt they are the good
guys, either; they're the ones who must fulfill the core of every
president's oath: "... to protect and defend the United States of
America." As a group in our society, who serves the nation better
than they do—the government, the schools and universities, the
courts, the church, the arts community ... the *media,* God help us?

When a president commits troops, they serve where they're
sent within the mission parameters. In our recent history, the commitment has sometimes been ill-considered, the mission abandoned under political pressures. This was most spectacularly true in
Vietnam, where a sitting president abandoned his own re-election
because of the political pressures of a war begun by his predeces-
sor, then dragged out until American soldiers coming home were
spat at in airports (at least in towns like San Francisco). Yet we
wrestled on with a war we could've won in a tenth the time we
spent getting out of it, killing fewer people and making fewer enemies, at home and abroad.

In the eighties I went to Ethiopia for the Red Cross, watching
hundreds die daily in the refugee camps in the North. We had no
troops in country, thank God, though there was an aircraft carrier
handy in the Gulf of Aden. (This was when we had enough carriers
to park in useful gulfs.) I spent an interesting evening back in Addis
Ababa with the skeleton staff left in our embassy, being briefed for
a meeting the dictator Mengistu had promised us the next day. He
broke the date, but was overthrown not much later, I'm glad to say.
A bad man, really nasty.

A much happier visit later was to an Afghan camp just inside
Pakistan. No, we certainly had no troops there, either, but we'd just

begun to supply the Afghan mujahideen with Stinger missiles. The Afghans would slip over the border to what was officially a refugee camp. They'd rest a few days, then go back to shoot down Soviet helicopters with the Stingers, eventually driving the Soviets out of Afghanistan.

Two days after Christmas in 1983, I flew to Beirut. The plan was for me to visit several ships of the task force stationed offshore to stabilize the Israeli/Syrian unpleasantness then going on. I'm always happy to make shipboard visits (Navy food tends to be a little better and you get hot showers), but I insisted they also let me go ashore, in spite of (*because* of, for me) the recent terrorist truck-bombing of a Marine barracks, killing 241 men. The dead men didn't care, of course. I left a pathetic little bunch of flowers I'd bought off a kid in the street on the marker they'd put up.

I spent the rest of the day with the First Division Marines dug in near the airport, which was shell-pocked and empty of all but military traffic. It was lousy ground tactically, though they'd dug in deeply, with bunkers and connecting trenches reminiscent of World War I. When I queried the light colonel in charge of me, he said, "Yeah, it's crappy. That ridge up there's fine high ground, but the Israelis are afraid to have us that far out." Politics and war are often intermingled, but they seldom have the same agenda.

A few months ago, Fray and I were invited down to Camp Pendleton to watch the First Marine Division in field exercises and take part in a memorial for the men they'd lost in Somalia. After a moving ceremony, the division commander, Major General Charles Wilhelm, reminded me that we'd met in Somalia, where he'd commanded all the Marine forces in country.

This I recalled. Then the general surprised me. "We met in Vietnam, too. I was a first lieutenant in a difficult position some forty miles out of Danang with nearly half my company gone. You dropped off the skids of a chopper with a major as escort officer. After we shook hands and you turned to talk to some of my marines, the major stepped over and poked me in the chest. 'I got two things to say t'you, Lieutenant. One, I don't know what the fuck we're doing here. Two, if anything happens to him ... it's your ass.'"

I think the major's concern was a little excessive, but I share General Wilhelm's relief that I escaped untouched. I was even happier a few weeks ago to hear that Lieutenant Charley Wilhelm now has a third star.

He deserves it, along with our thanks. So do they all—the commanders and the sergeants and the buck-ass privates in all the wars where they won the country and then kept it for us. God bless them. Bless 'em all—the long and the short and the tall.

On March 31, 1968, in New York, about to take off for a round of *Apes* openings in Europe, I called Lydia from the VIP lounge at Kennedy. She'd heard a rumor that President Johnson had announced he was not running for re-election. Disbelieving, I called Jack Valenti at the White House. Yes, it was true, Jack said, sounding stunned. So was I. "That's bad news, Jack," I said, as they called my flight. "Bad for the country."

So it proved . . . the winter of our discontent, turning into a long hot summer. I hadn't been in London a week when the Academy phoned asking me to wire the network to postpone the Oscar telecast in deference to Martin Luther King's funeral. Only weeks after that Robert Kennedy was murdered. The Democratic convention in Chicago degenerated into street fighting. It was a hard time for the country, but we survived, as we have survived worse.

> For if they do these things in a green time, what shall be done in the dry?
>
> —Luke 23:31

18

Hills and Valleys

Every valley shall be filled
and every mountain brought low.
The crooked shall become straight
and the rough way smooth.

— LUKE 3:5

I'VE HAD MORE than my share of luck in my life . . . stumbling into a great high school, winning a scholarship to a university with a fine theater school where I found the perfect girl my first time at bat, surviving World War II and coming home to a career, children, the brass ring, and the whole damn thing. Still, I never assumed John the Baptist's forecast of the world preparing for the coming of Christ would apply to me. It didn't.

For one thing, my earnest forays into the public sector were beginning to complicate my life more than I'd imagined. Much more. The presidency of the Screen Actors Guild was still a significant responsibility, becoming increasingly complex. I was learning how to do the job better, but our membership was growing steadily, and our branches in other cities were proliferating as well. Since the number of acting jobs remained roughly constant, this aggravated the members' frustration.

I did manage to negotiate one deal that delighted the members, though no actor made a nickel from it. The National Endowment for the Arts had funded the establishment of the American Film Institute (in which I wasn't then involved aside from voting for it on the Council on the Arts). They'd set up a Center for Advanced Film Studies in Hollywood, where they trained a small number of film students, most of them graduates of university film schools like UCLA. These fledgling filmmakers needed actors for their modest films, but acting was not among the disciplines taught at the Center. I helped cut a deal with George Stevens, Jr., then the AFI's director, whereby SAG members could work free in Center films (which couldn't be shown commercially, since they were funded by taxpayers' money). The young directors were delighted to get professional performances free, the actors happy for the chance to practice their craft and borrow the films as audition material. It's not often both sides of a negotiation are equally content.

Too often I found myself on the East Coast, mostly for SAG or NEA business, both on and off Capitol Hill. The red-eye gets you there about dawn; with luck you can finish and catch a plane home the same day, though a little used up.

In my experience, congressional hearings are quite boring, unless they're about to indict you for dreadful wrongdoing, in which case I'm sure Samuel Johnson's observation about a sentence of hanging applies: "it focuses the mind wonderfully."

Then there's the pro bono work most well-known actors do for various worthwhile groups: breakfasts, luncheons, dinners, and receptions; letters, recorded appeals, and instructional materials. For me, these range across the spectrum from the Boy Scouts and libraries to the Pentagon and the Department of Energy. I've done appearances, audios, and videos for just about every Cabinet-level department in the federal government, including, I recall, my very first one: a training film for the Army called *Hill 606: The Infantry Platoon in Attack*. I made it before I'd set foot in Hollywood, and I got paid for it, too, eighty-seven dollars a day. Ever since, all the rest have been freebies.

You're glad to do it, obviously; if you weren't, you wouldn't. Still, it can wear a bit. Take one of the most successful fund-raising tools in the history of charitable giving: the individual posed photo. I think it was invented by a U.S. President, though I don't know which one.

Having charged your guest list whatever the traffic will bear, you lean a little harder on your large donors. They're committed people who care about whatever good cause or undertaking you're supporting. So, for an extra thousand, they get a photograph with whatever grand pooh-bah you've imported to highlight your event.

Everyone seems delighted with it; it's almost automatically included in charitable events of all kinds. It does impose an iron discipline on everyone involved. Since I've done it so often, this falls on me. Say a couple approaches, looking forward to a bit of conversation. I shake the man's hand, reading his name tag, then move it to the back of his coat, so it won't show. "I'm happy to meet you, Mr. Norvant, would you stand on this tape, please? How are you, ma'am, may I hold your purse so it won't be in the shot, I promise I'll give it back, would you let me move you, please? Now turn just a little . . . that's it, look at the camera. *Excellent!* Here's your purse."

I know it sounds superficial; it is. It's also something people want. Properly organized, with good help at each end of the line, you can run three hundred people through in an hour and a half. That's valuable to the people who have to wait in line for the photos and a useful contribution by the guy who has to stand on the tape, smiling. If presidents do it, why can't I?

THE LATE SIXTIES was a time of intense media expansion (with cable still down the road). They needed people to interview, even those with dubious credentials as Public Figures. They'd ask anybody about anything—congressmen, sixteen-year-old tennis players, actors, anybody. It's surprising how readily you can get people to reveal their areas of ignorance, especially on television.

I went to London about this time to do some flacking for *Will Penny,* and meet with British Equity on some SAG matter. I also lunched with a British director, Sandy Mackendrick, about a film Walter Seltzer and I had set up about an American president driven ashore by a hurricane in Cuba, where he's rescued by a reprobate Australian charter boat skipper who happens to be his double, and so on and so on. Actually it was a very good idea, rather more lighthearted than most of my roles (certainly more so than *any* of my other three presidents).

I spent several days doing meetings and interviews on all three of my agenda items and entirely extraneous subjects such as the heating up of the Cold War. I'd boned up enough on that to skate through without making an idiot of myself, ending with an unchallengeable quote from John Kennedy: "In defense, America must be first. I don't mean first 'if,' I don't mean 'first when,' I don't mean 'first, but.' I mean first, period." A very useful observation, even a generation later (though no longer for Democrats).

I woke early my last day in London to find Dickensian snow swirling down Park Lane as the Horse Guards led the remounts back to barracks in the dawn dark. I was on time to Heathrow, but my plane was an hour late, then lost an engine over Scotland and finally landed in Iceland in the polar night. I sat in a chilly VIP lounge until they fixed whatever it was that was broken, playing chess with a stunning Icelandic hostess who was far too good for me (too good at *chess,* that is).

Not long after I got back, CBS, which was then dipping a toe into theatrical films, got cold feet and pulled the plug on our presidential movie, nervous about putting an American president in Castro's clutches. The good news was that they made this decision after they had committed to it, so we got paid an awful lot of money for not doing the film. The bad news was that they dumped the project, which amounted to another setback for me. I'd had enough of those.

Home on my ridge, I unwound readily with a lot of tennis and some enchanting time with Holly. As we approached her seventh birthday, she admonished me, "You know, I don't want to grow up *too* fast, Daddy." Fray was old enough to be serious about his tennis and his shooting, at which he was showing some natural aptitude as we destroyed platoons of empty bottles out in the desert.

Still, there was a darkening swale on the other side of that sunny ridge we lived on. My girl was beginning to be plagued by migraine headaches of shattering intensity, which would trouble her increasingly over the next several years. Blessed with disgusting good health, I tend to be a little inadequate dealing with other people's physical disorders. (Mental complaints I dismiss entirely, siding with Albert, the alligator in the old Pogo comic strip: "The inner me? Naw, got no time fer him. Ah got trouble enough with the me whut's out cheer whar Ah kin get mah hands on 'im. Ez fer the inner me, he goes his way, Ah go mine.")

I hadn't set foot on a stage in a couple of years so I was sorry when my plans to do *Becket* at the Ahmanson Theatre in L.A. fell through. They didn't want to do *Becket,* would I do something else? No, I wouldn't (grumpily).

This daunting rejection was tempered by word from Walter Seltzer. After drifting from studio to studio for several months, our football movie had finally hit at United Artists, who liked the rough-draft screenplay we'd submitted well enough to give us a go on it. They also approved Tommy Gries to direct, on the basis of his fine work in *Will Penny*. We would work with the New Orleans Saints, who were happy to accommodate us.

This altered my year considerably, as often happens in films. We wouldn't shoot till the end of summer, but I'd have to devote most of the next several months to the physical preparation for the film, now titled *Number One*. It proved a gruelingly tough time. I was in physical condition for it, but brought no football skills to the job; my brief struggle with high school ball as a gangly fifteen-year-old receiver had left me nothing useful but my broken nose.

Craig Fertig, who'd been a great quarterback at USC, would coach me, helped by Marv Goux, then a defensive coach there. The QB training was, you could say, arduous. We worked on the football field at Harvard, a fine school five minutes from our house, where Fray was then a student.

Two hours a day, five days a week. The drills were extremely detailed, not surprising, considering the enormity of Craig's task. He defined it the first day: "I can see it doesn't really matter whether you ever actually complete a pass; the camera can do that. I've got to teach you to take the snap, drop back in the pocket, and release as though you've been doing it since you were twelve years old." The whole session the first day was devoted to taking the snap from center and the first step back, with the right toes planted in exactly the same spot every time. We worked hours and hours, days and days on every aspect of what a quarterback does on the field, from running the huddle to scrambling out of the pocket on a busted pass play.

All I could bring to the undertaking was physical condition and determination. As with the symphonic conductor role I'd undertaken the year before, I had no talent whatsoever for what I was trying to learn. I did, however, have Craig. Also Marv, a man whose awesome energy was only matched by the ferocity of his competitive instinct. He spent all of both qualities on being my center. Hundreds of times he snapped the ball up into my flat right palm,

laces turned to my fingers. Neither he nor Craig let up for a minute,
so of course I couldn't either.

Over the weeks, it began to pay off. I was beginning to feel
more confident, even nailing the receiver with a short pass every
so often. One day Walter Seltzer dropped by our practice field.
"How's Chuck doing?" he asked Craig.

"Not bad," Craig opined. "I think he's beginning to develop
delusions of adequacy."

Adequacy was my goal, of course. I knew well by then that I
respond best to demand, not coddling. I pointed this out to Craig,
who said, "I'm pushing you, Chuck, but I can't really turn you into
a pro quarterback."

"I know that, pal. But you've got to make me look like one."
Outside the daily training sessions, I read all the books I could find
on quarterbacking. I ran film, I went down to watch the USC team,
only a level or two below NFL standards. I got better—incremen-
tally, but perceptibly.

We began to cast some of the other roles; Bruce Dern, who'd
been a chilling psychopath in *Will Penny,* came aboard as the wide
receiver who'd helped me take the Saints to victory in the Super
Bowl (a triumph they've never achieved off the screen, though I
root for them yearly); Mike Henry; also Rosey Grier, who'd only
recently retired as a member of the L.A. Rams front four—the "Fearsome Foursome." They joined our daily workouts, along with a
half-dozen or so off-season players who came along just for the fun
of it. This made it possible to send Bruce downfield as a receiver
and mount some semblance of a pass rush, though the drills were
all no-contact, of course. This quarterback would only be sacked
when the cameras were turning.

We ended each workout with a lap around the track that
circles Harvard's football field. Marv Goux was past his playing days
and had the build of a defensive lineman, but I was impressed by
his determination to finish at least abreast of the leaders. (I was
content to be in the top half.) The first day Bruce Dern showed up
for practice, we rigged a joke on Marv. Football players are big on
practical jokes. Bruce was no footballer, but he'd run in school; he
had close to receiver speed. I urged him to join our run; he pre-
tended reluctance. "Naah, I can't run; I hate it." When we shamed

him into it, he loafed in the back for the first fifty yards, then turned it on and began passing everybody. When he went by Marv, Goux was galvanized. He put his head down and pounded after Bruce as though he were cutting off a sure touchdown. When Bruce finished half a lap ahead of everyone, Marv's face was pale, white foam running down his chin. If he'd been able to catch Bruce, he'd've tackled him for sure. It taught me something about the will to win.

I had to take a couple of weeks off from Q-backing then to go to New York for SAG, Washington for the Arts Council, and London for a retrospective the British Film Academy was doing on me. Besides, I was beginning to develop a bone spur in my right heel, stabbing that foot in the ground time after time with the first step back from center. It was a good time to give it a rest.

The NEA meeting was routine, with me once more the hatchet man on the Lincoln Center grant. They had not mended their fiscal inadequacies, so we cut their dollars again.

My chore for SAG in New York was not a happy one. I chaired a disciplinary meeting with John Cassavetes for making one of his often brilliant independent features outside the SAG contract. I was beginning to feel uneasy about how well SAG was serving its working members by then, but I carried the can on this one. Not to my surprise, John was intransigent. "Go ahead and fine me. I think you should." In the end, we didn't. I don't know how many of his subsequent films John made under SAG contracts. This is union heresy, but I think John Cassavetes deserved a little elbow room.

England, on the other hand, was wonderful. Aside from America, Britain is my favorite country, and London my favorite city. We had Fray and Holly with us, both experienced world travelers by this time.

I think the most vivid memory I carry from that trip is the primitive hill fort now called Maiden Castle, where my savage ancestors were finally defeated by the Romans. In the end, I think the right guys won, carrying Western Civilization in their baggage wagons. The spirit of the Second Augusta Legion slogging up that steep, grassy slope into the flying stones still hung almost tangibly in the air centuries later, like the smell of blood. I'm always moved by the mark of the Romans in Britain, the shadow of four centuries of sentry duty.

The retrospective went well, too. The British Film Academy

did me fair, though of course no retrospective rests entirely on your worth, but at least as much on the honoring body's agenda. Still, I was flattered. It's interesting, also useful, to look at your earlier films on a proper theater screen. (I avoid them on video . . . the technical shortcomings of the TV screen are too distracting.) I'm never entirely pleased by my performances, of course, but it's valuable to pick out where you fell short and figure out why, so you don't do it again.

In August, we flew down to New Orleans to get some footage of the Saints in a preseason game. The film we got was largely adequate, and I got in some useful time with the team and a little deeper understanding of what life in the NFL is like. It's a tough way to make a living. Over breakfast a big offensive lineman put it succinctly: "Playing one game is like going out in an alley and having three guys beat the shit out of you."

Once home, I got back into my own workout routine, sticking with it each day till my arm started to ache. Then as I cooled down, my legs would knot with cramps. It was useful; pain was a part of the story. Tommy Gries had done some constructive changes in the script; we now needed to do the crucial casting, the two women. I don't know why, but casting the women's roles is always a complicated process though hardly the most onerous work in the world. Interviewing attractive, talented women and doing test scenes with some of them ranks well above, say, an NFL workout.

We settled soon enough on Jessica Walters as my wife. She's a very good actress and happened to be a member of the SAG Board, though that's not why we cast her. The Other Woman was harder to find. She needed to have the appropriate sexual appeal without coming across as a predator. Diana Muldaur filled both bills wonderfully well. The superb character actor John Randolph turned out to be just about perfect as the coach.

There remained my character. Since I'd conceived the idea of the whole film from one photograph of Yat Tittle on his knees and bleeding after the last play of his career, I felt a strong proprietary interest in my quarterback. I didn't use Tittle himself. I purposely avoided reading about his career, though I was at some pains to study every other great quarterback. Technical skills were common to all, but other qualities defined them. I found the best of them to be highly motivated, strongly disciplined and laser-focused men, superb natural leaders. Not unlike, it occurs to me, some of the presidents, prophets, geniuses, and generals I've played from real life. Like them too, my franchise quarterback, while superb at motivating his teammates, was not very good in his personal relations off the field.

Ron Catlin was the name I chose. "Ron" to his wife, "Big Cat" to the fans, and "Cat" or "Daddy Cat" to his teammates. Matchless on the field, a private man off it, struggling with the imminent end of the career that had driven most of his life. It didn't occur to me till much later that this was a description of many of the men I've played. I'm not sure how closely it describes my own character. Aging athlete, aging actor—there were resonances there I understood better than I could have at twenty-five.

We began filming in St. Louis, where the Saints were playing the Cardinals. Aside from game footage, and my warming up with the team, all we needed was a short scene on the sidelines with a young Cat going in to run the team for the first time. I don't remember ever before doing a scene with men who were really doing what I was pretending to do. That's what I'd be doing for the next month. After a while it got a little easier.

What I couldn't get used to was the *size* of the linemen, in both units. I'd always thought I was a fairly big guy, 6'3", 210. I've never felt so short in my life as I did hanging out with the Saints. When we were suiting up for that first day of filming with them, I was sitting on a bench in the locker room pulling my sock on, one foot on the next bench. Doug Atkins, then the Saints' All Pro defensive tackle, came over to ask me something. He leaned over and put his hand on the bench by my foot. "Excuse me, Doug," I said, and gripped his wrist, then my own ankle. They were the same size —his forearm was as thick as my calf! I felt like Tom Thumb. (For the record, Doug was 6'8" and played at 270 pounds. Like many big men, he was gentle and soft-spoken, though I'm told opposing coaches used to caution their linemen, "Look, play him hard, but whatever you do, *don't make him mad.")* The given wisdom used to be that linemen were big but slow. Believe me, over the distance that separates a quarterback from the defensive line, they can *inhale* you. In fact, that's what they do for a living.

Still, that first day, I wasn't supposed to get inhaled. We were shooting various angles of the invincible Cat Catlin, in his MVP glory days, dropping coolly back in the pocket and launching bull's-eyes to the open receiver. After the first setup, one of the Saints, Monte Stickles, said, "Y'know, Chuck, it would be good if you could get the pass as far as the line of scrimmage." Well, I was *nervous*.

The next play was a pass up the middle to Danny Abramowicz, then the leading receiver in the NFL. (Now, Danny really *was* a little guy. He was fast, though, and had what Coach Tom Fears, himself an all-time great receiver, called the prime requirement for the position: "a willing disregard for the consequences.") The shot was angled to show me dropping back in the pocket and actually completing the pass to Abramowicz. As we lined up, Danny trotted over to me and said, "Look, man, I'll be right out there in the flat. You get the ball within three yards o'me, I'll catch the sucker, make us both look good. Just look for my number—forty-six."

I took the snap and cross-stepped back, looking for Danny. All I saw was a brown wall ten feet high coming at me, Saint defenders suited up as Cleveland Browns. I threw desperately over them and fell to the ground. Danny trotted back as I got up. "Hey, didn't y'see my number?"

"Number, hell," I said. "I didn't even see any white jerseys."

Of course, as I got a little cooler, it got better. The actor invading the character, I began to feel like the Big Cat of his Super Bowl season. Call the play, out of the huddle, over the center, read the defensive sets, call signals, take the ball, six steps back, look for your receiver and throw, stepping into the pass rush. This worked well until the last shot of the day, when my offensive line opened the gate on me, doubling over with laughter as I disappeared under the entire defensive line.

This was really a sign of approval, for which I was grateful. The next day we moved into the shots where Catlin gets sacked more often, as his personal life grows darker and his skills decline an inch, about all that separates a champion from journeyman failure.

Still, these were controlled sacks. I took sixteen of them in one night of shooting and never really got hurt, though it was no fun, mind you. These guys were all superb athletes; they could control what they did to a fraction. The sacks looked good, the guys were hitting at about three-quarter speed, always catching me exactly where they said they would. Craig said, "Remember, when you absolutely know you're gonna get hit, step into it. It's a cleaner shot that way."

A week later, I really bought my ticket onto the team. We were shooting the tackle that ends Cat's career, and all but ended mine on the film. Three big linemen blitzed in on me, just as we'd planned it, but on the last take the second guy, faking a clothesline, turned me slightly in midair so that Doug Atkins caught me not with his shoulder, which he could roll with, but with his helmet—and all 270 pounds of his brawn, square in my ribs, cracking one.

These guys weren't clowning; they knew better than I did how badly they could hurt me. This was an accident. Still, Doug's response was typical. When he got up and saw me writhing on the ground, he trotted over and patted me on the cheek. "Welcome to the NFL, pal," he said.

It was my great good luck that the schedule called for me to spend the next day in a whirlpool tub, where Cat was nursing an injury. We didn't miss a minute of shooting time.

The next day was Sunday, game day, when we could put our cameras on the sidelines to pick up shots tying me in with the team in a game atmosphere. On this Sunday, they wanted me running on the field as the offense was introduced: "And, at quarterback . . . Ron Catlin!!" The footage we got works for the film, though I have a rather silly grin on my face in many of the shots, not really right for the moody guy I'd invented as the Big Cat. Normally I'd have spent the day in a bed, nursing my cracked rib. However, given the NFL's loose medication policy in the sixties, I felt no pain. On the other hand, I had no idea where I was, either. (Hey, look, you want a drug scandal? Best I can do.)

Behind the cameras, Tommy was having at least as tough a time as I was on the field. He directed with a very light touch, without a lot of conviction, really. This can be OK; he was an easygoing kind of guy, but he was a little casual about the schedule, too. This was not OK. UA had saddled us with a tight schedule, and Tommy was always trembling on the brink of falling dangerously behind on it. He had endless clashes with our production manager, Frank Baur, who was responsible for both the budget and the schedule. I'd known Frank since he was a fourth assistant director for DeMille on *The Greatest Show on Earth*. He was a formidable opponent for Tommy.

This conflict only got us into trouble once. On a day when I was scheduled to finish early, I'd agreed to escort the First Lady, Mrs. Lyndon Johnson, to the ballet. It was a benefit for the NEA, and I guess I was the only Council member within reach.

As the end of the day approached, it was clear I'd never finish the night shots we had to get in time to make the ballet. There was a small window of time when they didn't need me; I had one hour to whip over to the theater, escort Mrs. Johnson down the aisle and introduce her, then race back to the stadium. It has to be the only time anyone ever went to the ballet in dinner jacket, jock-strap, and taped ankles.

We managed to scrape through the location shoot barely on schedule, leaving the far less formidable interiors for Los Angeles. I was glad to be home, sleeping in my own bed, shooting on the familiar Hollywood sound stages, but it was an odd feeling to real-ize I'd never again throw another pass under the stadium lights.

We finished the interiors effectively; Frank Baur stopped snapping at Tommy's heels. We no longer had to worry about film-ing the team on their turf, their time, and their agenda. We were shooting on sets we'd built or chosen, usually with me and one other actor. We wrapped on time, if only just.

We finished *Number One* a few days before Christmas, but for no clear reason it was not a happy holiday for us. Lydia was fighting her migraines with no solution in sight, I was coming down from the physical pressures of pretending to be a great quarterback, combined with the usual demands of making a film. Oddly, the triggering flaw seems to have been our Michigan tree: for the only time in memory, it did not show up. Not a big deal, really, we all had our shopping done, but on the afternoon of Christmas Eve, I suddenly found myself thrashing through a horrendous quarrel with my wife, complete with hurricanes of tears and slamming bedroom doors. Who was the Grinch who stole Christmas? Probably me. I had not yet learned, in any domestic friction, large or small, the saving value of those three little words "I was wrong."

We skipped our usual Christmas parties; I took the kids cruising down Sunset Boulevard late Christmas Eve trying to re-member where the lots with trees were. We found one, with all the good trees gone. From the culls, we went with Holly's choice, a scruffy little spruce, mangy compared to our usual Michigan wonders. "It looks like it needs a home," she insisted.

We brought it home, where it served very well in what turned out to be a happy Christmas after all. A couple of days later I caught the flu, or something like it. I think I was just in a dark mood, Achilles sulking in his tent.

THE NEW YEAR began with a torrential rainstorm that took out half our driveway, all but burying a house in the valley below. I spent a month or so putting in, strongly buttressed, what I'm afraid is now the most expensive driveway in the county.

Happily, I also had two new jobs, the first for Walter Mirisch, a good friend by now, who wanted me to do the sequel to his smash hit based on the early chapters of James Michener's historical novel *Hawaii*. Walter is one of the best producers in film and among the most successful. His films are also amply honored, not necessarily the same thing. I was happy to be part of a Mirisch film, with the usual approvals. The script needed a bit of work, and Walter and I agreed Tommy Gries would be an appropriate director.

I also had another offer to film *Julius Caesar* (no, not from Orson again, but from a young Canadian named Peter Snell). Peter actually had his backing in place, and was prepared to go almost at once, which meant I could make the film before *The Hawaiians*. Of course I accepted. I can't imagine an actor turning down a chance to film Shakespeare.

Peter must then have been in his late twenties, but he looked about nineteen. We've done several films since, in deepening friendship, but even though he's grayed a little, I still think of him as "the boy producer."

"Boy wonder" would be more apt. To get a Shakespearean film mounted at all is a feat of entrepreneurial dexterity almost beyond measure. Peter had done it with nothing more substantial than a verbal commitment from me.

Peter had also gotten Sir John Gielgud on board as Caesar. John had played all the other major roles in the play already, as well as those in most of the other plays in the canon; he must've found the casting irresistible. We also had Richard Johnson as Cassius, Richard Chamberlain as Octavius, and Diana Rigg as Portia.

I would play Mark Antony, as I had before. It's the shortest
of the great parts, and the easiest—every scene is gold. If you can't
play Antony in this play, don't do Shakespeare.

We still had to cast Brutus, the central role in the play. The
part has been described as a rough sketch for Hamlet, though not
as interesting a role. Jason Robards is among America's best actors.
I'd seen him give a superb performance as the elder son in Eugene
O'Neill's last and greatest play, *Long Day's Journey into Night,* a
season or so before in support of Fredric March. O'Neill is our
greatest playwright, but his roles are not actor-friendly. If you can
play O'Neill, you can play anything. Or so I thought.

Casting Jason as Brutus turned out to be a crippling mistake.
Let me be clear; Jason Robards is a very fine actor. Nevertheless, I
still must say that I have never seen a good actor so bad in a good
part as Jason was as Brutus. It's true that our director, Stuart Burge,
had more experience on stage than in film, and it's also true that
Jason was going through a bad time in his life. His marriage to
Lauren Bacall was coming to an end; he had other problems as
well. Also, Brutus is a knotty kind of role, in which no actor has
ever really triumphed . . . but a good actor must be at least good in
it. You have to *be* there, make the scenes *work.* Jason was . . . terrible
is the only word.

We began with a week of rehearsals in London. Rehearsals
in film are not common, nor often useful. Most film people are not
really comfortable rehearsing a whole script in advance of the
shoot. Still, for Shakespeare, I think it's essential, just to get the
actors in form, and remind them of who they're dealing with. The
Old Gentleman of Stratford is an awesome partner; you have to
take care he doesn't leave you bleeding in the dust.

Our rehearsals went OK. The one day Sir John's scenes were
scheduled, he appeared precisely on time and showed us how easy
it is for a great actor to be great. Jason missed a day or so, which
was too bad, because he had the longest part and needed the rehearsal. I think he was the only principal actor in the film who'd
never done the play before. The rest of us were easing into it well
enough. I was a bit edgy about Stuart Burge's experience in film,
but we were moving ahead.

One of our problems was that I'd been tied up with *Number*
One, with no proper preparation time for *Caesar.* I like to think a

lot of things would've been better if I'd been there earlier. The costumes, for one.

We had a very talented designer, Julia Trevelyan Oman, with whom I've worked since. She chose to design the costumes in the baroque style that had been developed by eighteenth-century painters to suggest ancient times, though it bore no relation to anything actually worn in Republican Rome (or anywhere else, for that matter). Aside from being anachronistic and ugly, they were impossible to wear, especially the armor, particularly on a horse. When I pointed this out to one of Julia's minions at an early fitting, he responded, pouting, "Well, you certainly see this kind of thing all the time in the opera." I turned on him, I'm afraid, rather tigerishly. "Opera costumes are made to stand and sing in. This is a movie. I have to *move* in this stuff; I also have to do battle scenes in it— cavalry battles. I was getting on horses in armor when you were designing wedding gowns in a bloody trade school. Don't argue with me, *listen* to me." They did, and we at last arrived at armor I could mount a horse in, but it was among the worst flaws in a flawed film. Of all wardrobe, armor must be totally subject to function.

By the end of May, spottily rehearsed, we left for our Spanish location. I'd managed to avoid the Cannes Film Festival until then, hoping I might get through an entire career without attending it, but Commonwealth United was determined to show us off and insisted the company stop off en route to Spain for a grand party. I suppose the party was of some publicity value, but the fifty thousand dollars it cost could have given us an extra shooting day, too.

Still, the next day we went to Madrid in appropriate style. I was ensconced in the same suite at the Castellana Hilton I'd stayed in after Lydia took the kids back home to school at the end of the *55 Days at Peking* shoot seven years earlier. The problems Ava had posed then still glowed dull red in memory. Unhappily, Jason seemed likely to do much the same on our *Caesar* shoot. He declined to go to the stables and pick a horse, on the reasonable ground that he was not being paid to ride horses. (I found a very handsome sorrel with a soft mouth and a theatrical gait.)

Our first day's shooting in fact required Jason's presence on a horse, but only sitting on its back, unmoving, which he did carefully but adequately. The scene is the only one between Antony,

Brutus, and Cassius in the entire play. Playing it mounted is of course impossible on the stage; the horses served us very well in the Spanish Guadarramas, where I'd shot so much of *El Cid*. A running horse is one of the most beautiful things on earth; even standing still, a horse has an air of portent about it.

We had very little location shooting to do in Spain—the suicides of Brutus and Cassius, Antony's eulogy over the dead body of Brutus, and of course, the battle of Philippi, where the armies of the conspirators are defeated. Joe Canutt joined us to direct the battle; I think this was the first time Joe had sole control of a second unit. He did a wonderful job, though in this film he was making bricks without straw. Here, we were not attacking Valencia with Sam Bronston's thousands; we could give Joe only about five hundred foot soldiers and maybe a hundred cavalry, shifting from army to army as the shots demanded. One sequence had Antony leading a cavalry charge down a steep hill to scatter a column of Brutus's infantry. The horsemen, almost all of them stuntmen, handled the charge well enough. The infantry, though, were mostly just local farm boys; they were not inclined to deal with a cavalry charge. As soon as we got within thirty yards of the column, they broke and ran—no sign of the iron discipline of the Roman legions here. It was no use having the redoubtable Joe show them individually how to face a charging horse till the last second, side-stepping and cutting at the rider as he thundered past. Joe had to settle for using the master shot only as long as his infantry held their ground. When they broke for cover, he intercut the clash with closer angles using stuntmen and, indeed, some of the braver farmers. It was a short location, and modestly successful.

The London interiors were easier to shoot, though somewhat more demanding in acting terms. Lydia flew over to join me, making the familiar suite at the Dorchester a much happier place, though she was more and more troubled by the migraines that marred our lives then.

We shot our interiors at Pinewood, my favorite studio in the world, where they'd put up excellent sets. I'd persuaded them that the scene after Caesar's murder where Antony and Octavius tick off a list of which of his assassins must be killed should be set in a Roman bath. It played with chilling detachment, the two men lounging naked and sweating, wreathed in steam, checking off names on a hit list while nubile slave girls filled their wine cups. A meeting of Mafia capos, really, with Antony as godfather.

A curious thing about Antony, surely one of the choicest of all the Shakespearean roles: he has the best scenes, yet almost none with the other principals. The best (indeed, the play's best) is the oration over Caesar's dead body on the steps of the capitol, which he plays to a mob of anonymous citizens.

Brutus speaks first, the crowd responding enthusiastically, then Antony counters with what may be the finest single speech in all of drama. Almost every schoolboy can quote at least the first words, "Friends, Romans, countrymen! Lend me your ears."

Jason didn't show up for the first day's shooting on the funeral scene, so we began with my oration. I knew it well, having done the play twice before. We covered the master angles first, mostly long shots as Antony strode back and forth across the vast marble steps, inflaming the crowd.

Then we moved tighter to a close angle where Antony reveals the bloody body of the slain Caesar. Sir John lay, waxen-faced and immobile, while I whipped the blood-stained, dagger-torn toga off him. That done, I knew we planned no other angles close enough so the camera could recognize Gielgud, so I thanked him for the pleasure of doing the scene with him, even playing a corpse. Ever the professional, he said, "Oh, Chuck, I'm happy to be here off-camera for you during the rest of the scene." While the rule in film is that you do off-camera reactions and dialogue for the other actors, he had no lines and I wouldn't be able to see him anyway. I only needed a body to play to; an extra under the toga would do fine. Gielgud still felt his professional duty was involved.

"John," I said finally, "the last thing I need is to have one of the world's great actors lie under a sheet for the rest of the afternoon listening to me play one of the world's great scenes." He smiled gently and left me alone to arouse the mob to murderous frenzy, then send them to the streets in bloody riot. I was very good. It's hard not to be very good in this scene; it's an awesome piece.

Jason did appear the next day for his part in the scene, where I wasn't needed. We did a cast photo on the steps of the capitol, all of us looking very impressive and as Roman as those damn costumes would allow. I took advantage of the short day to watch

Pancho Gonzalez beat Charlie Pasarell at Wimbledon in one of the
great matches of that glorious tournament.

The next morning, the Fourth of July, I took my girl and flew home. Fray rode the limo out to meet us, while Holly stayed home "in charge of the decorations." We had a fine quiet family evening, the sparklers and Roman candles reflecting in the pool, darkening as the sun went down.

I had time for more reflections, also fairly dark, over the next few days. Walter Seltzer and I met with the UA suits. They were now doubtful about the European release of *Number One,* on the theory that audiences there neither knew nor cared much about American football. (This was some years before NFL teams were routinely filling overseas stadiums for exhibition games from Moscow to Mexico City and Tokyo to London.) I insisted that our film wasn't *about* football, but about a man who *played* football. I did not prevail; in the end, UA did not release *Number One* overseas, a serious handicap.

Before leaving for Hawaii, I was also trying to sort out my impressions of the *Caesar* shoot. I'd be filming for Walter Mirisch, half a world away from London where Peter was editing. We talked endlessly on the phone; Peter was optimistic about the progress of the first cut on the picture, while I was less sanguine.

I'd seen some rough-cut footage so I knew there were some fine performances. Gielgud, of course, was superb, so was Richard Johnson as Cassius; Diana Rigg did well in the difficult one-scene role as Brutus's wife, Portia. It was simply too early to tell. To paraphrase Forrest Gump, "Makin' a movie's like a box of choklits . . . y'never know whut y'gonna git."

IT WAS TIME to open another box, *The Hawaiians,* for Walter Mirisch. The script was in good shape by then, carved out of the third quarter of Michener's epic novel. At one point, Walter had considered a very long film that covered roughly the middle of the novel and several generations of two or three families through most of the nineteenth century. This proved too daunting (and expensive), so he'd made *Hawaii,* which was set in the 1840s, with Max von Sydow, Julie Andrews, and Richard Harris—a huge success. In *The Hawaiians,* set in the last half of the century, I would play Richard's grandson. (I've kidded him about that ever since.)

Flying to the islands, I left *Caesar* behind me. Peter would handle the editing of the film with Stuart; I couldn't take part in the process, and shouldn't try to. I owed Walter Mirisch my best shot at *Hawaiians.*

While I'd been wrestling Mr. Shakespeare in Europe, Walter had prepared his film with the meticulous attention I was to find characteristic of him. (We've done two more films together—so far.) The script was tightened, its joints now seamless, which must have been hard to do considering the story covered several decades.

The main problem in the film had occurred to me earlier. "This is a good script, and a good part for me, Walter," I said. "I think I can give you this guy. The fact is, though, the movie's not really *about* Whip Hoxworth. It's about Nyuk Tsin, the Chinese girl, and her husband and her children and grandchildren. You can't change that, you shouldn't try. I'm happy to play Hoxworth. But for Nyuk Tsin, you really need an internationally famous Oriental actress who can carry the picture—because that's what she has to do."

Amazingly, that's just about what Walter did, except for the international star bit. He found a stunningly beautiful Chinese girl —a medical technician who had never acted before named Tina Chen, who *became* Nyuk Tsin, with an almost flawless performance marked by her serene energy. The fine actor Mako played her husband; together, they put a spine in the film that my part didn't allow me to provide.

We had other good actors in the film: Alec McCowan, Geraldine Chaplin as my deranged wife. For a scene with my twelve-year-old son, it was suggested that Fraser might do the role. He was already on the location and a veteran performer, having played the infant Moses at the age of three months. I can't recall why we decided against it, or even whether I explored his opinion on the matter, as I should have done. He's since suggested to me that he felt I didn't want him to be an actor, which isn't really true. I didn't want him to be an unsuccessful actor.

Happily, he's grown up to be a successful writer-director, displaying a fine camera eye, a good captain's sense of how to handle a company, a very true actor's ear for how a line should be written (and read), and total recall of all the dialogue in a script.

His close pal on the *Hawaiians* shoot was a schoolmate, Martin
Shafer, who grew up to be president of Castle Rock Pictures. Maybe
there are good filmmaking chemicals in the Maui water.

Settling in for the long haul, we had two months of shooting
on Maui and Kauai, then several more weeks of work at home.
For the Maui location, we had an appropriate suite, with adjoining
bedrooms and a lanai opening on the ocean. We would need the
space: our superb British housekeeper, Muriel Ashby, had come
with us, for the first vacation she'd taken in years. My mother would
join us, as would my stepmother (not at the same time), my sister
Kay, her husband and son, Chad, and Martin's parents, Joe and
Marie.

The shoot began well, for such a big, physically complex
story. Tom Gries worked diligently, perhaps more focused than
he'd been on *Number One.* I tried my best to dismiss my anxieties
about Whip Hoxworth's structural function in the film. Maybe this
blunted the swordblade edge an actor should bring to any role. If
that's so, I have no excuse for it.

Still, it was a pleasant location, a lot more comfortable than
the Spanish Guadarramas in winter, or the Sahara in summer, both
of which still quiver in memory. We began with a scene that was
scheduled for four days of shooting aboard a square-rigged barkentine featured in the story. It took us more than a week. (How Movies
Are Really Made note: For any scenes taking place on or in water,
schedule as much time as you think needed, double it, and you
will *still* run over. Prime example: Universal's *Waterworld,* several
months over schedule, and hovering at $160 million.) The only
happy people on the ship were Fray and Martin. They came out
with us every day and had a marvelous time climbing the rigging
and watching the shoot, when we could shoot. I presume they also
learned something they could use later in life when they had to
make choices about filming on the water themselves.

Digging in a bluff near the beach, the boys also unearthed
some bones from an eighteenth-century Hawaiian burial ground
and got their pictures in the local paper. Far more memorable were
the pictures beamed down from the moon, where man set foot for
the first time, as we sat transfixed to the TV in the lanai, with the
sea crashing on the sand behind us. "... one giant step for mankind." So it was.

From shooting on a ship, we moved to shooting from a chopper, which also has its problems. It can give you wonderfully acrobatic shots, not possible before the quantum leap in helicopter design provided by the Vietnam War, but it's almost as tricky as filming on the water. What looked like a fairly simple shot—throwing a dead leper from a cliff into the sea off the leper island of Molokai (no, we used a dummy)—was vastly complicated by the chopper's problems. We spent half a day on it.

I still got to the hotel in time to help celebrate my daughter's eighth birthday. She suddenly seemed more than a year older than seven. I think girls give that birthday a special weight boys can't understand. Perhaps they know something we don't. I also noticed, standing in the shallows with her as the sun set, that the foam sliding around our ankles was actually violet. I've never seen that elsewhere.

Only a few mornings later, Lydia's back went into spasm as she was brushing her teeth. I had a late call, giving me time to take her to the hospital, where she spent several days of undiagnosed but gradually decreasing pain. I'd stop by on my way to and from location. I remember getting back to the hotel one night to find Sam Peckinpah sitting in my lanai, fresh from his triumph with *The Wild Bunch* (really the picture he'd somehow had in mind when we wrestled *Major Dundee*). We sat drinking single malt for an hour while he fulminated about life and work and the world, all of which he viewed sourly, even as he rode the crest of his greatest success. I went to bed too late, feeling fairly black-hearted myself. Sam and too much scotch could do that to you.

By late August, we were several days behind, but finished on Maui. The company was moving to Kauai for the rest of the location, beginning with a couple of days' work on scenes I wasn't in. That gave me time to drop the kids off in California and go on to New Orleans with Lydia for the premiere of *Number One*. I can't imagine how many premieres and openings I'd done by then, but New Orleans is a good town for them. In addition to the usual press hoo-ha, there was a lot of promotional stuff of dubious value (though you have to leave those choices to the PR people, really).

Still, we were very lucky. If the premiere had been half an hour later, we'd all have been caught in the cloudburst that soaked the city just about the time everyone was seated. Yes, it's true that my experience with the Red Sea gives me a certain control over the weather, but that didn't prevent the Roosevelt Hotel where we were staying from catching fire just as the film began. When we got back after the film, I managed to con my way past the firemen and police in the lobby up the stairs to our penthouse suite, which I found undamaged by fire, but flooded with water and smelling pretty smoky.

I crammed most of our stuff into the two largest suitcases and dragged them down seven floors to the lobby, where I turned them over to the bell captain and went across the street to the premiere party. I presided over that in reasonably good form, smelling of smoke, till we retired to a local motel for four hours of sleep before taking off for L.A., along with our damp baggage. Public life and a public face equip you for that kind of evening.

Lydia was vastly distressed when she realized we'd have to fly home at 8 A.M. in full-drill evening dress; I found it pretty funny. "Honey, we can't fly in wet clothes. Who cares, anyway? My God, before long you'll see guys flying from New Orleans to L.A. with rings in their noses." (I was sure Lord right on that, wasn't I?)

Back on the ridge, I showered, changed, and caught my afternoon flight to Kauai to finish the location, starting with a full day of PR for the foreign press. You always get a good turnout for press junkets to Hawaii. I wonder why that is?

The shoot pressed on, but slowly. There were a number of sequences I wasn't in, so I had time to run back home for a few days with my family, which refreshed me mightily. Walter Seltzer had moderately cheering news about the *Number One* grosses. This encouraged us to try and get United Artists to let us release the film overseas ourselves, but they wanted no part of that. If we had a hit with an independent release, UA would've been revealed in an embarrassing mistake. Studios hate that.

In its U.S. release, *Number One* eventually proved a modest success, bolstered later on with cable revenue, but it certainly left no stars in my crown. It's perhaps a darker film than I'd realized while we were exploring "Cat" Catlin's fall from grace and glory to the last shot of him lying unconscious and bleeding on the torn turf as the camera booms up high over the stadium.

Still, every pro player I've talked to who's seen the film (and there are a lot of them) says the same thing: "Hey, man, you got it right. That's the way it *is!*" Balanced with the general audience, that's a small constituency, but I'm proud we pleased the guys who know.

Not for the first time (or the last), I'd made a film as close to the way I wanted it to be as we could get, and ended up with a movie not a huge audience wanted to see. A lot of people said the same about *Will Penny.* "That's maybe the best movie you ever made, Chuck, but if you'd taken the girl with you at the end, it would've made a ton of money, too."

Maybe so. Maybe not. It still seemed to me I should only make the movies I wanted to make. Otherwise, what's the point? I had all the money I needed to keep my family. I still had the girl, the brass ring . . . and the whole damn thing? Not yet, for sure. So what then? *Carpe diem!* The Olympic motto echoed again: *Citius, Altius, Fortius*—faster, higher, stronger. Do another Shakespeare, but a harder, much better play than *Caesar.* Why not film *Antony and Cleopatra?*

I'd been hooked on the play since high school, seen it, acted in it; I'd worked on it even longer than on *Caesar,* where Antony's also a driving force. I had more experience in Shakespeare, on both stage and screen, than any American filmmaker I could think of. I was alone on the Kauai location now; given the scenes I wasn't in and the modest pace of the shoot, I had a lot of time I could spend on the screenplay for *Antony.* I would need every minute of it.

While I was cutting Shakespeare in my downtime, Walter Mirisch was cutting our *Hawaiians* script, with input from Tommy Gries and me. I do believe this is something actors usually are, and certainly should be, good at. I don't mean the final, crucial assembly that makes the film: that takes months, and is mostly the job of the director and the editor, with supervisory input from the producer and random comments from the Alpha dog actor, depending on his inclination and his contract. Walter also made some purely budgetary cuts, which can be useful as long as you make them before you shoot them.

We did proceed with the burning of Honolulu (naahh, just a few blocks of a reconstruction of the city in 1900). Very spectacular, even with a night or so of that cut, too. That wrapped the three and a half months of the island location on my birthday, which I was delighted to celebrate at thirty thousand feet, homebound. It's

amazing how often I start or finish a filming stint on my birthday.
I've either made too many movies or had too many birthdays. A bit
of both, I expect.

I sank into my ridge like a child settling in his crib. At home
everything is easier, also nicer—and private. We still had weeks of
shooting to do on *Hawaiians,* but it would be on the sound stages
at Goldwyn and the MGM back lot, familiar, focused workplaces.

Please understand, the public me is the same as the private
me, except that he's a mote in the public eye. On a location, being
a public man is part of my job, serving the movie, or play, or
whatever we're doing; I think I've learned to do it well. But it's still
work.

My real work, the performance which is my passion and my
life, is in the theaters, sound stages, rehearsal halls, recording studios, screening rooms, and cutting rooms on the several continents
where it happens. I've been working in these places for nearly half
a century; they're as familiar as the path from my side of the bed
to my bathroom. (Yet even today, in Melbourne or Milwaukee,
Manhattan, Milan, or Manchester, when I go to a TV studio for a live
interview, I'm met by a comely young woman who, as we move
through the dark toward the lighted set, invariably whispers in
warning, "Be very careful—there are cables on the floor." I can't
help smiling, but I always whisper back, "Oh, I will. I've heard
about them.")

Halloween brought the usual small crisis about Holly's costume. At first, she was delighted with the hula girl's outfit I'd borrowed from the *Hawaiians* wardrobe department. It turned out to
be a chilly night, though, so she vetoed that choice. "It'll be too
cold, and besides, I don't want to show my tummy." That was that;
she went trick-or-treating as a Gypsy, all veils and head scarves and
brass bracelets. I was delighted just to have the time with her—
there hadn't been enough of it on the various locations over that
year.

For the same reasons, I took Fray scuba diving the next
Sunday, or maybe he took me. I'd learned scuba in a crash course
for *The Wreck of the Mary Deare* a decade earlier, and had done a
little spearfishing here and there since, a couple of times with Gary
Cooper (I just dropped that name to class up the paragraph).

Fray had taken to it, and gotten proper training, ending with the certification then required of minors. My memory is that, at fourteen, he was the youngest qualified diver in the county. Lord knows he was better than I was. We dove off Anacapa Island on a clear day, calm water, not more than fifty feet down. I was quite pleased with how well I was doing till I realized Fray was hovering over my head like a mother hen watching her chicks, every second I was on the bottom. I found this very touching. I still do.

Happily, based at home, with much of my time waiting on standby till they got to my scenes for *Hawaiians,* I was able to finish my screenplay of *Antony and Cleopatra.* It went more easily than it should have, really. I'd never written a screenplay before, though I'd read hundreds of them over the previous twenty years and wrestled with at least forty trying to get them on the screen. Besides, I knew this play so well I was sure I could capture its passionate glories and usefully address its complications. *Antony and Cleopatra* is one of the two or three greatest of Shakespeare's plays, thus one of the finest in the world, yet it's rarely done. As far as I know, it's not had a major production in the U.S. since Katharine Cornell undertook it in 1947, in what became the longest run, both on Broadway and out of town, the play has had in its history. It had also marked my Broadway debut, in very remote support of Miss Cornell, as those of you who've been paying attention will recall.

Since then, I'd often thought about Antony, and worked on it too, if only in using some of the best speeches in my daily vocal workouts in the pool. (There's nothing better than Shakespeare to exercise your vocal cords. The technical challenge is formidable, and the speeches are so good they excite you every day.)

Over the years I'd come to understand why Antony is not done often. Aside from the enormous difficulty of Cleopatra as a role, the play itself is a sprawling odyssey. Most of the great plays happen within clearly defined boundaries: *Macbeth* in Scotland, with one scene in England; *Lear* in England; *Hamlet* in Denmark and inside Hamlet's head.

But *Antony and Cleopatra* not only happens in Rome and Sicily and Athens and Egypt and on the seas that separate them, it is about the differences and the distances between those countries. You can't just put it on a bare stage and have Egyptian and Roman pillars alternate on turntables, with Antony's men in red and Caesar's in blue and neat yellow kilts for the Egyptians.

The play, in fact, cries out for a camera. William Shakespeare,
I truly and deeply believe, was the first screenwriter. He would
have been enchanted with making movies.

Once I realized this, the screenplay all but wrote itself. I was
very proud of what Old Will and I had wrought together. Once I
had it typed, though, I put it aside to finish shooting *Hawaiians*.

Walter Mirisch may have thought it was about time, though
he never said so. Giving everything you've got to a film involves a
lot more than staying healthy, and showing up on time, lines
learned and ready to go, though God knows you need all of these.
You also need to fall in love with the guy you're playing, to marry
his story. I'd done this readily working for DeMille and Wyler and
Stevens and Welles—even with the quirky, doom-driven Sam Peckinpah on *Major Dundee*. I'd certainly done it with Tommy Gries
on *Will Penny* and *Number One,* but we somehow fell short on
Hawaiians.

Tommy's long gone now, dying too young without having
reached what he and many of us expected of him. He was a gifted,
mercurial, oddly unpredictable and somewhat childlike man. Not a
good captain, which a great director must be, but with the right
material, he was very good. I thank him for one of my very best
films, *Will Penny*.

We wrapped the *Hawaiians* shoot in mid-November, reasonably close to budget and schedule. I'd been a hired gun on the
film and properly had no hand in the postproduction, leaving it to
Walter and Tommy. Ralph Winters, who'd won one of *Ben-Hur*'s
record eleven Oscars for editing, was in the cutting room. They'd
surely make the best of what we'd given them.

I owed the Screen Actors Guild some focused time, having
been elected to a fifth term as president. We had some meetings
with the technical unions, exploring the idea of establishing lower
pay-scales for a category of low-budget films, to encourage increased production and create more jobs for actors. The idea was
good and there was a lot of hoo-ha about it, but production costs
were already beginning to explode through the roof; in the end, it
came to nothing. I think I know something about this, but I have
never understood the enormous increase in production costs over
the last twenty years. I'm not persuaded the studio heads do either.

Then I climbed on yet another aircraft, furrowing even

deeper the transatlantic jet-trail I keep cutting in the sky. I was taking my script for *Antony* to London, along with my expectations for *Julius Caesar,* which I'd not yet seen.

Peter Snell and Stuart Burge had finished the director's cut by then, so the film was about as good as it was going to be. Gielgud was matchlessly marvelous in a short part, and Richard Johnson gave us a superb, angry Cassius. My Antony was good, but in that part, "good" is only barely enough. Diana Rigg was fine as Portia, a part in which it's hard to be good. Jason was . . . well, I've said about all I want to say about that. Since he had the leading role in the film, his shortfall was deeply damaging. A film can often work very well with a bad performance in a major part, but not in the leading role. Still, *Julius Caesar* has always been a popular piece, driven by the story more than the characters. In a few months, the audience would render the final verdict.

(If you're biting your nails in suspense, I'll tip you off: six months later the audience failed to flock to the theaters to see our *Caesar,* another valley in a time in my career when there were several of those.)

I'd shot three films back to back in a little more than a year. Only on the first, *Number One,* had I spent adequate preparation time. With a proper prep on *Caesar,* we could've avoided some of our more grievous errors in design and casting. When I finished that shoot, I rushed back for the (again) insufficient prep for *Hawaiians.* That shoot, in turn, had been crowded by the time I spent on the *Number One* premiere and adapting a screenplay from *Antony and Cleopatra.* I was beginning to look like a large dog chasing his own tail, or an actor still riding the tiger. Looking back, it occurs to me that when you can do anything you want, your instinct is to try and do everything you want, all at once.

In London, I got very good reactions to my *Antony* script. Peter Snell was high on it, and Commonwealth United, who'd financed *Caesar,* were willing to plunge in again on *Antony and Cleopatra.* We made some early explorations on the crucial casting for any production of that play: who would be our Cleopatra? Also, almost as difficult, who would direct?

After some useful if inconclusive talks exploring these problems, I hopped the polar trolley for home. Somewhere over Hudson Bay I reached a couple of useful decisions: I would try to go

ahead with a project Walter Seltzer and I had been mulling over,
based on a novel I'd stumbled across, *I Am Legend*. I would also talk
to my wife about having been approached by a group of prominent
Democrats to run for the U.S. Senate.

This query about a Senate bid was not the first, nor would it
be the last. Actually, it comes up all the time; any interview of
more than ten minutes—print, TV, or radio—is sure to produce
the question, "Mr. Heston, the time you've given to a wide spectrum
of public sector issues over the years suggests you might consider
a run for public office at some point. What about it?"

"I've already been President of the United States three
times," I reply, getting my laugh and moving on to the next topic.
The men who talked to me in 1969 dismissed my joke answer. They
were not kidding, and were relaxed about raising the millions of
dollars such an undertaking required; the least I could do was think
about it. I'd do that, I said, and decide when I got back from London.

First, I talked to friends who knew the dimensions of the
challenge and my interior measurements as well: Bill Buckley, one
of the Founding Fathers of the conservative movement; Jolly West,
my oldest and one of my wisest friends; Paul Ziffren, the gray eminence of the law firm that represented me, and former chairman of
the California Democratic Party; Jack Valenti, now head of the Motion Picture Association after his crucial service to President Johnson. They all supported the idea, Republicans and Democrats alike.
Their reasons were similar: service to the nation, the significance
of the U.S. Senate as a uniquely crucial body in world affairs—all
that good stuff.

So the night I got home, I talked to Lydia, who's known me
longer and better than anyone alive. She heard me out, then said,
"What do *you* want, Charlie?" My poor mind cleared. I knew what
I'd been chewing on all along. Never mind the talk of service,
challenge, rewards. I didn't want to do it.

I couldn't bear the idea of never acting again. Never to have
one more shot at Macbeth, never to stand in the shining dark offstage, waiting for my entrance cue, never to find one more great
film role, or slide a good horse down a grade in a Western one
more time, and smell the morning. No, it wasn't possible. I told
them so the next day.

I then made the rare choice of taking a week's vacation, at a small hotel in one of the more remote Florida Keys where it seemed likely I'd be anonymous. We flew down with the kids, of course, and Fray's friend Martin. The idea was fishing, tennis, diving, and photography, in any order.

It worked out very well. I had as quiet a time as I'm likely to get anywhere away from home; if not unrecognized, at least I was left alone. The boys took full advantage of all activities, I joined them for diving and tennis, we all fished a bit; Holly pattered about barefoot (a state, I swear, in which, outside of school, she passed most of her girlhood). Lydia took a lot of photographs.

I didn't read one single script, indeed, I'd brought none down with me. I spent the last day of the decade being towed across a quiet lagoon holding onto the dorsal fin of a porpoise. That gentle mammal gave me a much easier ride than the tiger I'd been clinging to for so long.

Back in L.A., the *I Am Legend* project with Walter Seltzer seemed promising. I'd read the novel on one of my polar runs (ten hours, an ideal reading period. Even if it seems likely movie material, though, if you haven't finished the book by the time you land, it'll need considerable cutting to make a film).

There was surely a film in *Legend*. It rested on a familiar but evergreen concept, a universal fantasy that seems to have invaded everyone's imagination and launched a thousand speculations: What would you do if you were the last man on earth? It's the dark side of the Genesis story of the creation of Adam, the first man— the end instead of the beginning.

We got strong early interest from Warner Bros., almost simultaneously with word that an Italian company had already filmed the novel. They hadn't released their film in the U.S., but if we announced I was doing it, they'd certainly try to sell their version here. We got hold of a print; fortunately for us, though it starred my friend Vincent Price, it was a pretty torpid piece.

Walter and I felt we needed a different approach to the script, anyway. How do you get to be the last man on earth? Of the classic four horsemen of the Apocalypse prophesied to end man's span on the planet, we picked War and Pestilence. In the treatment we cobbled together and sold Warners on, the Chinese had launched a deadly bacteriological war which infected the entire

world. (Students of the film community will not be surprised to
hear that the only part of the entire world seen in the film is Los
Angeles.)

Among the survivors is a U.S. Air Force colonel, airborne at
the time of the attack, who's been injected with an experimental
serum that renders him immune to the dread virus that's wiped out
just about everyone else. Everyone except a few scattered covens of
infected survivors who have become so light-sensitive that they
must stay indoors in darkness during daylight hours, like vampires.
(I know, it sounds strange, but it played very well.)

We hired a good young writer, Bill Corrington, to start flesh-
ing out the treatment into a script. This he did, with skill and dispatch. I liked his ideas on *Legend* (perhaps not least because he
responded so creatively to my suggestions).

Still, the first months of 1970 were not happy ones for me.
God knows there was plenty to do, a whole list of public chores I'd
somehow acquired over the years: the Screen Actors Guild, the
National Endowment for the Arts, small errands here and there in
aid of useful groups. Of course what I really wanted, and spent all
the time I could trying to find, was backing and a release for *Antony
and Cleopatra.*

There had been what they call "warm expressions of interest" from a couple of the majors, though Dick Zanuck jumped
back from the script like a scalded cat, doubtless remembering the
disaster Fox had gone through making the same story, with Elizabeth Taylor but lacking Mr. Shakespeare. When *Julius Caesar,*
which opened quite promisingly, proved to have no legs, Warners
and Universal lost interest too. Commonwealth United, who'd financed *Caesar* and promised to do the same with *Antony,* was
about to close its doors (no doubt in part due to their laudable
willingness to undertake difficult projects); it was no longer an
option for us. We would have to raise the money independently, an
agonizing and often humiliating process.

Peter Snell undertook this task with infinite resourcefulness
and indomitable determination. My job, whenever Peter had located a potential backer, was to meet with him, being as charismat-
ically starry as possible, and at the same time persuade him that our
film had enormous potential, which I in fact believed with all my

heart. I still do. I went through this over the next few months more times than I care to remember. I seemed to be drifting in limbo . . . waiting.

Interspersed with all this transcontinental/transatlantic commuting (the Japanese were not buying up American studios then, or I'd have been on the L.A./Tokyo run too), I fitted in meetings on stuff for SAG and the NEA, wearing my other hats.

I recall Jack Valenti phoning me for an urgent meeting in Washington with Senator McClellan on the CATV copyright problem (that's what it says in my journal, but I'm damned if I can remember what the CATV was, or why it had a problem. I trust I understood it at the time). I red-eyed east, spent the day in hearings on it (the senator, I do remember, turned out not to be quite the fierce old son of a bitch he was reputed to be). Jack gave a small dinner with some useful guys, then my late flight to St. Louis for an NEA meeting was canceled, so I couldn't get there till the next noon, having missed half the meeting. I did get a motorcycle escort from the airport, the only fun I had on the whole trip. The rest of the meeting was not pleasant.

One of the advisory panels had submitted a grant request for a hundred thousand dollars to the sculptor Noguchi, for an outdoor piece to be erected in Seattle. I was one of several on the Council who objected to this ferociously on the ground that Noguchi was a well-known artist who didn't need taxpayers' funding. It made for a bloody afternoon, but the damage was done . . . Noguchi already had the money. I trust he eventually supplied a sculpture.

I left the meeting in a black mood, wonderfully soothed by a solitary walk to dinner through a street of leafing maples, with ripe mulberries dropping and staining the sidewalks. The broad Midwestern lawns stretched back to the solid, cut-stone houses standing for the time they were built . . . when we would live and thrive forever.

When I got home Peter called from London (he uses a transatlantic phone like an intercom to the kitchen) and spent about two hours running through the status of our various options for funding *Antony and Cleopatra.* None of them added up to any chance to shoot, or even prepare, in 1970. For one thing, we hadn't found a director I was wild about, nor an actress in whom I could smell Cleopatra.

This was a bitter pill, with nothing to wash it down. The arena was a bleak and dusty place just then. I turned down a couple of scripts that were probably not really as bad as my dark mood made them seem (well, yes, they *were* that bad, actually). As always, my ridge was a healing place, though I wasn't exactly Charlie Charm for a while. Lydia was hit by another migraine attack; when I asked "How's your migraine, honey?", she cried "It's not *mine,* goddamn it! I don't want it. Let it go to hell!" I'm afraid neither of us was a lot of help to the other just then.

A day or so later, I met Fray at Burbank Airport, back from a trip in the bush, and found his pack had somehow gone to LAX. We drove out and got it, I dropped him off at a tennis tournament, then whipped over to SAG to gavel a meeting with the Chicano committee (ethnic quota casting was becoming an issue about then . . . I'd have been damn sorry to have been denied the Mexican cop I played for Orson Welles a dozen years earlier). It turned into a real hair-raiser, the closest I've ever come to losing control of a meeting. At one point I found myself standing up, white with anger. I managed to keep my voice down (don't ever yell, talk *under* them) and kept it in hand. We finally came to some actual communication at the end. It was worth it, but not a lot of fun.

Then of course I had to go up to San Francisco to the state AFL-CIO convention, largely to lunch with George Meany, then national president, and host a reception. SAG is of course a tiny union, but we had a lot of public faces on the board then, which gave us a certain utility in the echelons of Big Labor. I'd neglected to tell Lydia I had to make the trip, which did not please her, which did not please me—you get the idea. It made for a chilly evening on the ridge when I got home.

I do believe that the comity between men and women crucial to the survival of the race has been vastly confused by the feminist rhetoric holding that men and women are the same, except that women are smarter. (That last bit may well be true.) A long life has shown me that no man can fully understand any woman. True, I'm dealing with a small sample personally; I don't really know many women, most of those are related, and I know only one really well, but I've known her for more than fifty years. Among the meager list of things I'm sure of is that she's got a better brain than mine.

Not for everything, mind you. Maybe not for carrying a scared old man down a fire ladder, or flying an F-14. But I do know this: the *difference* between the sexes is the whole idea. Whoever designed it, that was the plan. If you really understand that when you deal with each other, you can work through anything. We did.

So did my daughter, at eight (maybe sooner, but she didn't tell me). She's never been a morning person, though we shared breakfast on school days. By the time she came down, I'd have had my swim and read the paper, which was just as well, because she didn't like me to read it at the table. Nor did she like to converse that early (all her synapses were not yet operative). Ten minutes later, though, driving down the canyon, she'd often reach over and pat my hand on the wheel, with a smile that stroked my heart. Who was the writer who spoke of "that purity of spirit, pure as sunlight, that suffuses little girls just before they enter adolescence"? That's a crucial part of the difference, too.

By autumn, Bill Corrington had finished a good strong draft of *I Am Legend* (with enough input from his wife, Joyce, to earn her a joint screen credit). Walter Seltzer made a crucial contribution: he changed the title to *The Omega Man,* which pleased everyone, including the many who didn't know omega is the last letter in the Greek alphabet. (I know, *The Last Man* is a good title, too, but *The Omega Man* is sexier.)

We also cast the other two major roles in the piece: a very good and quite stunning black actress named Rosalind Cash (against Warners' urging that we go with Diahann Carroll), and Tony Zerbe, who'd been so fine in *Will Penny.* The main *Omega* casting done, I went to Chicago for a meeting of the SAG branch there, had dinner with my mother, and caught the last flight back to L.A. to get into the *Antony* problems. There I was again, trying to prepare two pictures at the same time.

I hoped to find a director who was at home in both film and Shakespeare. That's a pretty short list; it then consisted of Orson Welles and Laurence Olivier. I met with Orson, he'd read the script, spoke most warmly about it, "Really well-done. You're quite right, it should be a film—the geography is crucial to the play. You can't put that on a stage, but you can film it. Old Will would have loved the movies." I warmed at his words. "Now, do you have a great Cleopatra?"

"We don't have *any* yet," I replied. "You direct it, we'll pick an actress and you'll make her great."

"Not with that part, dear boy," Orson rumbled. "Believe me, if you don't have a great Cleopatra, you can't do this play." Orson was very perceptive. He'd never done the play, but he put his finger instantly on its central problem: finding Cleopatra.

Fortuitously, Olivier was in Los Angeles for a few days, doing publicity for an upcoming visit by the National Theatre of Britain, which he then headed. As I knew, this meant he couldn't possibly direct *Antony* (though he could fit in a short film role as an actor now and then; he'd done that with me in *Khartoum* a few years before). But the year it takes to prepare, direct, and cut a film was out of the question.

Still, I wanted to pick his brain; he'd directed and acted in what still remain the three best Shakespearean films I know of. We had a drink at his hotel, where he gave me both encouragement and advice. "It's a wonderful part for you, Chuck. With Macbeth and Othello, it's the only one of the great roles which absolutely requires a real physical presence. You don't have to act that."

He hadn't seen the script, but I showed him a few pages, pointing out several small parts I'd melded into two or three pretty good ones, as well as some quite radical transpositions of scenes I'd made. "I suppose I'll get some flak from the critics for that."

He snorted derisively. "Ahh, do what you like, laddie. They none of them fucking know!"

Much heartened, I packed for England, where I hoped to get a Cleopatra. On my way, I stopped in Boston for a day of PR on *Julius Caesar,* which was just opening. I'd been there often with both plays and movies since my anonymous appearance with Katharine Cornell a quarter of a century before.

A firm feature of PR visits to Boston as long as I was doing them (you do satellite interviews from Hollywood now) was the ritual luncheon for the trade press, well laid on and very wet, often ending in a quarrel between two rival women columnists. I never saw that done in any other city . . . the lunch, not the quarrels.

Boston still had four or five newspapers then, with critics worth quoting in the national ads. Elliot Norton, then with the Boston *Record,* was especially well-regarded, not least by me; he often had very good things to say about my work, as indeed he did about my Antony. Again, that's a part where good notices should be almost automatic. Anyway, even Norton's notice didn't give us anything more than modest business in Boston.

After surveying the field and the problems of the part, I'd come to feel that our Cleopatra should be played by an actress for whom English was a native language, and who'd played at least one Shakespearean lead either on Broadway or London's West End. Arbitrary? It made sense to me.

Shakespeare is at the same time the easiest and the most difficult writer to play. Easy because there's so much in all the parts that's pure gold and they are, after all, the best roles ever written ... dauntingly difficult simply because they *are* the great roles; every actor who dares to try any one of them knows he's stepping into the shadow of the great actors who've preceded him, over four centuries. Now he must somehow not only reach beyond his own personal best, but see it measured against the giants of the past, now gold-plated with legend.

Many of the parts are not only psychologically complex; they're also pretty tough technically. Simply to get your voice in shape to give you the breath to get through the yards of iambic pentameter is an awesome task, as Jason had discovered with Brutus.

Cleopatra has all these problems ... and more. As I'd learned when I was a green kid watching Miss Cornell assault the part, she is all but unreachable. The several women contained within her range from slut to schoolgirl, wise queen to willful tyrant, lost lover to vengeful virago, wily politician to, at the last, tragic heroine. That's a hell of a stretch for any actress; to manage it under the exploratory eye of the camera expands the problem exponentially. I interviewed several and tested three.

The night before the tests, I had dinner with Frank Schaffner, then in London preparing his *Nicholas and Alexandra*. I'd worked for Frank many times, beginning with the old live TV days when I did *Macbeth* for him. "I'm going to direct these tests myself," I said. "Depending on how things develop, I may direct the film."

"Why not?" he said off-handedly. "Nothing to it." Armed with that encouragement, with a short lecture on lenses thrown in, I dove into it next morning. My first setup was complicated, but it set up the relationship between the royal lovers in one shot, as the

camera can. We open focus very tightly on a woman's hand holding
a makeup pot, dipping a small brush into it as we pull back to
reveal Cleopatra about to paint the lips of the Emperor Antony,
sweating in postcoital and half-drunken slumber.

The shot really worked very well. When we had it rehearsed,
since I obviously couldn't watch it and act at the same time, I said
to the operator, "Let me see the opening mark through the finder
. . . I want to be sure we're getting it right." He unlatched the finder
from the side of the Mitchell we were using and handed it to me. I
looked through it in growing irritation, unable to focus an image.
At last he leaned over and whispered, "Guv'nor, yer lookin' through
the wrong end." I survived this embarrassment, and we shot a hard
day of tests without further mishaps, though I acted the scene more
confidently than I directed it.

When we saw the film, I liked one of the tests very much: a
South African actress, Hildegard Neil, whom I'd seen a month or so
earlier as Lady Macbeth. She had the right kind of beauty, with a
classical face and a contralto voice. The camera liked her, I'd found
her directable in the scenes we did. There was another possibility:
the Greek actress Irene Pappas. Her English was fluent, but faintly
accented. You could justify this: the real Cleopatra had been an
Alexandrian Greek. On the other hand . . . In the end, we went with
Hildegard. Over lunch the next day, we had the pleasure of telling
her, and I caught the afternoon polar trolley home.

The day I got in, I ran most of the *Woodstock* concert film,
which is pretty dull stuff, really, but we were picking shots from it
to use in a scene for *Omega Man* where the lone remaining man
on earth sits alone in a movie theater running the scenes with
thousands of people crowded together. It worked well for our
movie.

We began filming *Omega Man* in downtown L.A. the following Sunday morning, when the streets would be deserted. The first
setup also happened to be the opening shot in the script and, like
the setup I'd designed for *Antony,* established the story with filmic
economy. It's a moving shot, closing on me in an open convertible,
casually well-dressed, carefree on a sunny morning. Glancing up, I
suddenly slam to a stop, lift an automatic weapon, and fire a long
burst at a second-story window. The glass shatters, the curtains
sway, but nothing more. I put the car in gear and drive on. It's a

wonderfully provocative opening. There's something to be said for starting with a shot you know is going to work—it's like a quarterback completing a long pass on the first play of the game.

The whole *Omega* shoot went very smoothly, in fact, especially since we had a tight schedule. Of course I was the only actor in many of the scenes, which simplified each day's shot list. We also had Russ Metty as cameraman. Russ had photographed me in several films, starting with Orson's *Touch of Evil*. He was very, very good, also very, very fast, which is true of very, very few of the very, very good cameramen, if you follow me.

In fact, Russ made a game of his skill (aside from his talent). When the director and the actors started to block a scene, he'd go sit in his oversized leather chair, seemingly listening to the small radio mounted on it. When the blocking was set, the director would call "OK, Russ, it's all yours," and turn away to consider his next setup while Russ lit the shot, a process routinely requiring anywhere from twenty minutes to three hours, depending.

With Russ, sometimes before you'd gotten twenty steps away from the camera, he'd call "Ready!" without having moved from his chair. His gaffer had been setting lights at his direction for twenty years; Russ could give him hand signals from his chair about where to set the key lights, the fill, and thus silently light the shot while the director and the actors were still blocking it.

From the beginning, our director, Boris Sagal, was at odds with Russ, though it was hard to see why. Certainly we were getting fine footage, and no one could fault Russ's pace. Perhaps Boris felt threatened by his cameraman's large reputation.

In truth, Boris had a volatile disposition, given to spectacular displays of anger when roused. This is a bad idea. Everyone gets angry, but the higher up the chain you are, the less you should show it. The director, never. You can correct, rebuke, reprimand, even excoriate, but you should never raise your voice. It diminishes the control of the company a director needs. Boris didn't understand this.

Some years later Boris was coming back from a day's helicopter shooting on his current film. They landed while he was angrily reviewing the day's work with his cameraman. Boris stepped down from the chopper, turned brusquely away—and walked into the tail rotor blade. As far as I know, he's the only member of the Directors Guild ever killed in the line of duty.

Boris did a good job for us on *Omega Man,* particularly with Rosalind Cash. This was, I think, only her second film, and she was understandably a little edgy about beginning her first leading role in a love scene with me.

It was in the seventies that I realized a generation of actors had grown up who saw me in terms of the iconic roles they remembered from their childhoods. "It's a spooky feeling," she told me, "to screw Moses."

Ros rose to that challenge, though I remember another scene where she had to hit very precise marks countering the moving camera, ending with me falling into the shot. We did several takes to her increasing distress about how many falls I'd had to do when she missed her mark. "Honey," I said, "don't worry about it. In *Ben-Hur,* Willy Wyler had me do twenty-one takes of a Roman soldier knocking me down a flight of stone steps. I'd rather fall down with you any day."

Aside from having to ride a motorcycle for the first time in my life (driving a chariot is harder), my challenge in *Omega Man* was to inhabit my colonel's unimaginable situation. What would it be like to be always alone, day after day, yet threatened every night by murderously dangerous creatures maniacally intent on killing you?

You'd talk to yourself a lot, I decided, which worked out to some interesting soliloquies in my fortified apartment, decorated with some Renaissance paintings taken from the L.A. County Museum (surely one of my first acts, were I really in such a fix). The Getty was the source of the superb marble head of Caesar Augustus with whom I played chess, making his moves for him, of course.

A subliminal theme that appeared more or less accidentally during the shoot proved valuable in the film. In the script, my colonel is immunized against the virus that has all but wiped out the population of the world, leaving only tiny pockets of deranged, fatally infected night creatures, as well as an even smaller group of mostly very young people who are still healthy and living in hiding.

He finds that his blood, injected into the veins of one of these innocents, can give them life too. The analogy to Christ as

Savior is inescapable, though there's no such reference in the script, and we didn't plan the shoot in those terms. Still, there were irresistible spins I added in performance.

I'm killed in the last scene by a thrown spear and fall into a fountain, arms outspread, my blood staining the flowing water. The innocent young people leave, carrying a flask of the blood that will redeem them, as the inheritors of mankind.

These were largely improvised bits imposed in the shooting; it wasn't till a rough cut was assembled that we realized how strongly it played. At this point, Warners got a little edgy, anxious that we were screwing up what they saw as a high-class horror film. They asked us to cut a very short, silent scene I was sorry to lose: a ten-year-old girl bicycles up during the safe daylight hours to the fortified building where I live, leaves on the doorstep an offering of a few wilted flowers and some fruit, and pedals quickly away. Even with the scene gone, I'm surprised at how often people mention the Christ analogy in the film.

We finished the *Omega* shoot on schedule; I was content to have what looked like a strong commercial movie to sustain me while I dragged *Antony and Cleopatra,* kicking and screaming, to the screen. Some months later, *Omega* proved a large hit in the theaters. It was high bloody time; of the four films I'd made in the previous two years, none had been huge at the box office.

I still had to get *Antony* made.

19

Looking for Cleopatra

Antony: O, whither hast thou led me, Egypt?
. . . Thou knew'st
My heart was to thy rudder tied
And thou shouldst tow me after.

Cleopatra: I dreamt there was an Emperor Antony.

— W. SHAKESPEARE

CLEOPATRA SPEAKS after Antony has driven his sword into his own vitals, black with shame at his self-willed defeat, driven by his obsession with what must have been one of the most extraordinary women in the ancient world (or the modern one, by all accounts). By 1971, I realized that I was obsessed by her, too.

One way or another, I had to film *Antony and Cleopatra.* Happily, Lydia understood this. "Whatever it takes, whatever you need to do, Charlie," she told me, reinforcing my opinion of her as one of the superwomen of the world.

Peter Snell had by then found a major Spanish distributor, Izaro Films, whose chief, José Maria Rezobal, was willing to finance half the production cost in return for distribution rights in Spain. Peter planned to follow Sam Bronston's example and presell different markets to raise the rest of the money for the film, though Shakespeare proved a harder sell than *El Cid* or *55 Days at Peking,* particularly in advance. Of course my own bank was quite happy to guarantee any shortfalls, though Herman Citron took a very dim view of one of his clients putting any of his own money at risk. Happily, not very deep into production, the Rank Organization picked up the film for release in the U.K., giving us a certain cachet and removing the financial pressure as well.

Before this, I had to tidy up at home; I'd be gone six months. First there was the Screen Actors Guild: I was in my sixth term as president, longer than anyone else had held the office; you could make a clear case that it was time for me to step down.

I was proud of what I'd done in the office, though certainly not everyone agreed. I was the last of the highly visible public actors to serve as SAG president; a useful face in the service of the members, I felt. When I spoke for the Guild, it usually got on TV, always in the trade press; I could argue for us in congressional hearings; when they needed a public voice, I was better able to provide it than anyone else on the board.

Nevertheless, the first vice president, John Gavin, was waiting in the wings. He made only the most gentle suggestion that this was the perfect time for me to go. I was counting on the strong presidency I knew "Black Jack" would give us, but I waffled ("When it's time, I'll know"). Not long after I was in Spain, buried in *Antony,* they nominated Jack in my place, and a damn good thing, too. He ran SAG with a slightly tauter hand than I had.

The following year, when I was back in L.A. for a good stretch of time, Jack persuaded me to come back on the board, without office, the idea being that I might contribute some senior wisdom. I was dubious, but sufficiently flattered to accept. "OK . . . but I'll sit off to one side, not at the big table. I want to keep a very low profile."

At the first meeting I attended, I was comfortable in my modest corner . . . until some thorny issue came up. (It was probably merger with AFTRA; we've been wrestling with that for thirty years at least.) I raised my hand, was duly recognized, and launched into a five-minute polemic I thought worthy of Tom Paine.

When I finished, the distinguished Walter Pidgeon cleared his throat and said, "Well . . . there goes the low profile."

Before I went off to make *Antony,* I picked up another public-sector chore. Greg Peck asked me to join the board of the American Film Institute, which he was chairing, and which I'd helped create when I was on the Council of the National Endowment for the Arts.

I could put the AFI board slot on hold, but I also had to pass on a very good part in what turned out to be a very good film: *Deliverance.* Burt Reynolds did the role very well. It was his first major film, impelling him into an impressive career. Yes, I'd like to have played it . . . but not instead of Mark Antony. I spent some weeks that winter in Spain, nailing down our coproduction deal and scouting locations. Frank Schaffner was shooting *Nicholas and Alexandra* there by then; we had a pleasant dinner or two, he very encouraging on my decision to direct *Antony,* and most useful in giving me a copy of his glossary of technical film terms in Spanish. My Spanish was adequate for cocktail parties and interviews by that time, but a director needs to be able to give specific technical instructions to crewmen, most of whom have little English.

Spain, as I knew very well by then, has fantastic locations of all kinds. I realized that Mediterranean architecture has altered little since ancient times. The red-tile roofs are still properly Roman; the squat white buildings are right for both Rome and Egypt (you just have to be sure to miss the TV aerials).

Frank also gave me the location of the only sand dune left in Europe, now that the one near Anzio we used in *Ben-Hur* is all villas. "It's a peanut dune, really," said Frank. "You'll think you don't have enough room to shoot, but you do. Barely." He was right. Barely.

I flew back to L.A. for a few weeks then, partly just to be on my ridge with my family, partly to look at the first director's cut on *The Omega Man.* I also had Robert Shaw, whom I knew only slightly, up to lunch, after he'd said to me at a cocktail party that he might be willing to play Pompey in the film. We played tennis and I managed to lose a set to put him in a receptive mood, but the role was never a realistic option. His career was far too hot at that point to do a smallish part. He did give me a marvelous idea I used for the role: to have Pompey, drunk at Antony's party, do a scurrilous imitation of his host. It worked very well.

By April I was back in London, casting the rest of the parts and audiotaping the scenes of the four Spanish actors I'd hired to qualify us for Spanish nationality, so they could work on their English. One of them was the fine Spanish actor Fernando Rey, who gave us an extraordinary Lepidus, though I knew from the beginning we'd have to re-voice all the Spanish actors in postproduction.

In a few days of interviews and readings I was able to cast the remaining roles very strongly. I'm always amazed at how deep the talent pool is in London. For any part, in a day or two of readings, you'll get two or three actors good enough to be almost interchangeable. It must be something in the water . . . or the weather.

The most important of the English castings was Enobarbus, by far the best of the dozens of wise, cynical old sergeants in all of drama (but Shakespeare thought of it first). Eric Porter's triumph as Soames in the BBC's *The Forsyte Saga* was still ahead of him, but his Enobarbus was superb.

So was John Castle's Octavius Caesar. He perfectly rendered both Shakespeare's and the historic Caesar: a cool and ruthless political tactician, aware he couldn't out-fight Antony in battle, but he could out-think him. Jane Lapotaire was perfect as Charmian, Cleopatra's bawdy chief lady-in-waiting.

In a sense, though, the most crucial casting of all these parts was Proculeius. I'd played it with Miss Cornell in 1947, another of those tantalizingly short parts in Shakespeare that can easily be melded with a couple of others and made into something very good. I'd done that in my screenplay with some care, feeling somehow responsible to Proculeius.

To play him, I cast a fine young English actor, Julian Glover, the first time I heard him read. I knew he'd give me a good Proculeius, but he could clearly do more than that.

Both Orson and Olivier had said essentially the same thing: "If you're directing this and also playing Antony, you have to find a very good actor to play the part while you're setting up the shots and directing the other actors in the scenes you're in." Julian did this superbly, not merely reading the lines in rehearsal, but acting every scene. What's more, he took care to watch my performance very carefully, before I stepped behind the camera. Then, through the technical rehearsals, Julian meticulously gave me back *my* interpretation of Antony rather than his own (which he later offered on the London stage with Vanessa Redgrave). It was an awesomely selfless feat, for which I can't praise him enough.

Then I had two days of rehearsal with Hildegard Neil, reading through her scenes and talking about the mountainous terrain she had to travel to find Cleopatra, without daunting her with the difficulties of the journey.

On my last night in London, I had dinner at Peter Snell's house and taped the role of each of the Spanish actors, to be sent so they could practice. Yes, we'd be re-voicing them, but I wanted the best English I could get in performance.

I had to go home to do the looping on *Omega Man* and to soak up enough of the joys of my ridge to last me a few months. I also won an important small victory: though MGM had initially turned us down flat, Kirk Kerkorian, who then owned the studio, had agreed as a personal favor to let me buy a few hundred feet of outtakes of the war galleys in action in *Ben-Hur* to enhance our footage for the battle of Actium. In the finished film, it did just that.

The last week in May, I left for London to begin rehearsals. Lydia, of course, couldn't come till school was out, but she was torn at the time with a horrifying cycle of migraines which complicated our parting. On top of that, our polar run was grounded in Gander to fix an oil leak, which meant Joe Canutt missed his connection to Madrid, where he was to start shooting at once on the second unit he was directing for us.

The next day we began in a rehearsal hall in Covent Garden. As my cab swung through Leicester Square, I swear the statue of Shakespeare lifted his head from his book and said "Don't fuck up, now." We didn't, at least not at first. We got most of the interiors blocked loosely the first day; that evening I went to see Olivier's Shylock at the National—a daringly original interpretation. I went back to his dressing room afterward, where he gave me some good single malt and some better advice, on both directing and Antony.

Our budget allowed only a week of rehearsals, but it brought us about as far as we could go before moving to Almería, on the south coast of Spain, where we'd shoot most of our exteriors. I checked into the tiny apartment we'd live in (about a tenth the size of the grand villa we had in Rome on *Ben-Hur,* but our budget was about a tenth the size of *Ben*'s as well). I checked the costumes and Hildegard's Grecian wig, which made her look very much like the Alexandrian Greek history gives us. The second day my actors arrived and, more or less simultaneously, my family. All together, I had everything I needed to do the film I wanted to do more than any I remember in my life.

We began with a crucial scene among the triumvirate that then ruled most of the known world—Mark Antony, Octavius Caesar, and Lepidus, the hapless third wheel of empire. The scene is early in the play, setting up the Byzantine politics of the time, ending in Antony's grudging agreement that he abandon his Egyptian dalliance and marry Caesar's sister. There's so much background information crammed in that the scene is pretty . . . boring is the word.

It's usually staged around a table with bowls of fake fruit. Still boring. I set it in the training arena for a gladiatorial school. (Roman big dogs of the time often kept a stable of professional gladiators, just as their modern counterparts own an NFL team.)

I opened the scene down in the sanded arena, close on a sweating pair of gladiators in fierce combat, widening to Antony and Caesar in political confrontation in the owner's box, now and then glancing at the fight below, much as Mr. diBartolo might look up from an angry argument on his cellular phone to watch Steve Young complete a pass in the Super Bowl. Joe Canutt chose and trained the gladiators and staged the fight, which was an immense contribution to the scene, as was everything he shot in the film.

Later, editing the film, I cross-cut the civilized exchanges between Antony and Octavius with angles of the bloody, sweating gladiators, straining for advantage in the damp sand of the arena. The gladiators were fighting for their lives; Octavius and Antony were wrestling for the future of the world. (In the long view of history, though I'm drawn to Antony, I have to say the right guy won. The foundations of modern civilization that Octavius, as Augustus Caesar, put in place created a stable environment for almost everything that's happened since.)

We gained a day of shooting on that sequence, then promptly lost it the next day when Carmen Sevilla, the Spanish star I'd cast as Caesar's sister, was a day late getting back from an Argentine location. In the end, I shot the scene without her, saving her coverage for whenever I could get it.

We finished the Almería exteriors in three weeks, including land battles, sea fights, and helicopter shots, mostly because I turned those sequences entirely over to Joe (as Wyler had turned the chariot race over to Joe's dad, Yak Canutt). This freed me to direct other sequences, shuttling to Joe's second unit when I was needed there. Fray, at sixteen, had his first film job since he played the baby Moses, as Joe's second assistant, where he was just about run into the ground.

What did I learn as a director? That there's almost no mishap

that you can't shoot around, or adapt. We finished the Almería shoot
a day behind because I'd forgotten to factor in the short nights in
those latitudes in June. You really only get about seven hours of
darkness then. I learned, as every director must, that there is never
enough time, never enough pains taken. You can always make it
better.

Still, we did well, wonderfully well on some sequences. We
solved one of the play's perennial problems when Joe devised a
kind of instant stairway of shields to allow Julian Glover's Proculeius
to invade Cleopatra's pyramid tomb in seconds and disarm her
before she can stab herself. As usually staged, it's ridiculous. As we
shot the scene, it served both Shakespeare and the camera perfectly.

What did I learn as an actor? An awful lot, as you do every
time you attack one of these monster parts. I'd been wrestling Mark
Antony, in both the plays he's in, since I was a kid in high school.
Of all the great parts, as Olivier said, this was the one I was best
equipped for; of all the great plays, this was also the one that cried
out for the special magic of the camera. I was better prepared to act
this role then, in probably the only film that will ever be made of
the play, than I've ever been for any part. (I know; you can always
be better.)

I did Antony's suicide well, both as actor and director. The
Soothsayer (appearing in the play as a quasi-comic character in an
early scene with Cleopatra and her women) had become both oracle and sorcerer in our script, appearing to Antony after he's fallen
on his sword with the dark news that Cleopatra is not dead: "Your
star is fallen, sir. You may not live."

As June became July, when we were due back in Madrid, we
were two days behind, and I was shuttling between units, trying to
catch up. I scheduled Joe's second unit to a Sunday shoot, so I could
join them to fight the land battle where Antony's troops are betrayed by a planned Egyptian desertion. No, it's not specified in the
play, since Shakespeare's stage couldn't accommodate such a scene,
but he would've loved it: "Think, when we speak of horses, that you
see them/printing their hooves in the receiving earth!" For Antony's
escape down a steep hill, Joe gave me one of the most spectacular
horse falls I've ever seen. (No, I did not do the shot myself.)

Of course the unit had to wait two hours for me. I'd had my
driver pick me up at 5 A.M. to get me on location for the maximum

shooting time. I fell instantly asleep in the back. (Always sleep both to and from locations; it's a good time to catch up.) I woke forty-five minutes later on the seacoast where we'd shot the day before, now entirely deserted. The driver had taken me to the wrong location. We were another hour away from where Joe was waiting with the second unit.

Yes, I was really mad, but my Spanish wasn't equal to the task. (Though it's a great language to swear in. You could say words failed me.) Still, we got our scene, if a little late.

We moved back to Madrid for the rest of the shoot, most of it in very good sets. Interiors are usually easier to shoot: you don't have as much travel time, you're not dependent on the weather, both crew and actors are a little better rested (except for the director, of course, especially if he's acting in the film as well, especially a part like Antony. Still, I was doing exactly what I wanted to be doing).

My body, usually docilely obedient, almost let me down once, though. I woke at five, as usual, got up—and promptly threw up, copiously. I was more outraged than anything else. This couldn't happen, not on this film, not after all the years of showing up on time every day, everywhere. Lydia knew me well enough not even to mention staying in bed. She got me cleaned up, into a shirt, pants, and the back of the car, where she rode with me to the studio.

The doctor was waiting to stick me with something or other while the makeup man covered my white face as I dozed. I had one card to play: the director gets to sit down. There were a couple of pages in the scene between Enobarbus and Cleopatra before Antony entered. I knew the scene, of course, and the list of shots I'd worked out the day before. I gave the cameraman a slightly more complicated master shot than I'd planned, knowing it would take an hour or more to light. This gave me time to lie down and let my insides pull themselves together and join the team.

This they did, though for the first few setups I was glad I could sit down. I had good actors who knew what they were doing, though I hope they didn't know what *I* was about. By the time I got to my angles, I was able to get up and be Antony. (I kept thinking about Godfrey Tearle in the same part twenty years earlier—getting up off a cot in the wings, wiping the vomit off his mouth, and going onstage to play Antony through the flu. The whole part, not just one

scene.)

In the play, when Antony agrees to marry Caesar's sister, it gets a little confused, even flat. No matter how much you cut, you have to go to Sicily and Rome and Athens, and back and forth to Egypt, and you have to explain where you are and what's going on. A camera can make this clear with a couple of shortcuts. Oddly, in the play we never see Antony decide to go back to Cleopatra, nor see the lovers reunited. (I can imagine Richard Burbage nagging at old Will: "I'll be damned if I'm going to do another love scene with that pimply boy you have doing Cleopatra. He's got breath like a hog. And I still think I should have Enobarbus' speech about her. It's the best bloody thing in the play, for God's sake!")

I shot it in a handsome villa outside Madrid we'd chosen as Antony's palace in Athens. He endures the cold and frustrating scene with his new Roman wife, wanders through the gardens to hear the Soothsayer's chilling warning, then through the open window hears Enobarbus describing Cleopatra to an entranced fellow officer, who asks, "Now Antony must leave her utterly?"

"Never. He will not. Age cannot wither her, nor custom stale/ Her infinite variety . . ." and so on for twenty lines or so of the best writing in the language. Eric Porter did it so well I found it hard to find places to cut away from him to Antony listening, heartsick with longing, outside in the garden. But when he hurls his wine goblet against the wall and we cut to a shot of the chill Octavia at her dressing table turning her head at the sound, you know the next cut will be Antony standing in the prow of his ship, his cloak blowing back, then the bronze doors of Cleopatra's palace smashing open to show her standing stunned. "Oh, thou day of the world," he says, and she runs like a girl to leap into her lover's arms, tears streaming down her cheeks.

Rereading my journal entries for the *Antony* shoot, as well as some of the sounder critical essays on the play (Kittredge, Granville-Barker), I've come to realize that, while the play is routinely included with *Lear, Macbeth, Hamlet,* and *Othello* as one of the great Shakespearean tragedies, thus high among the greatest plays of all time, it deserves to be ranked even higher. I think *Antony and Cleopatra* is the finest of all his plays, which translates to just about the finest of the world.

It's the last of the great tragedies, written not long before his retirement, and shows in almost every scene the mature flowering of Shakespeare's talent. None of the other plays can match the glories of the poetry, nor the rich development of every character. (As I've said, Cleopatra is the best woman's part in all of drama, and the hardest to play.)

Even the comedy, rare in tragedy and even more rarely funny, is beautifully done. The comic turns of the drunken Porter in *Macbeth* and the First Gravedigger in *Hamlet* are clearly stuck in to give the Globe's resident clown something to do. ("Yes, Will, this is good stuff. Tom'll make 'em laugh, right enough.") But the hapless messenger who brings Cleopatra news of Antony's marriage, then comes back later with a description of Octavia, is really funny, not just clown-funny, yet heart-touching too. When the poor fellow escapes her fury, she says to her handmaiden, Charmian, "In praising Antony, I have dispraised Caesar?"

"Many times, madam," answers the girl.

"I am paid for it now." You can't write a leaner line than that, or a more touching one. It's assumed that Shakespeare writes long and complex speeches. Not true. Some are long, almost none is complex. As Shakespeare matured, his language got leaner and deeper, never more than in *Antony and Cleopatra*. When Antony, his fortunes failing, sends a challenge to Octavius to meet him in single combat, sword against sword, Octavius smiles and says, "Let the old ruffian know I have better ways to die."

After the battle of Actium, which Cleopatra has lost for Antony by fleeing with her ships, she's pacing up and down in her empty throne room, wringing her hands. "What shall we do, Enobarbus?" she asks desperately.

"Think, and die," is his answer. Neither Shaw, nor Ibsen, nor Chekhov, nor O'Neill could write a line like that. Modern playwrights would spend a page making the same point.

We spent the first days of August on the last scenes in the film, inside Cleopatra's monument. Antony's death is brief, in the arms of the queen for whom he's thrown away a third of the known world. Still, we see again the special genius of the mature Shakespeare. His greatest tragedies are all towering works, mountains in the history of drama, yet in four of them, the protagonists don't die eloquently. Hamlet has a self-pitying speech wishing he had more time to talk, Macbeth simply plunges into combat, Othello points out that he loved well, if not wisely, and Lear mourns his daughter.

Alone among the tragic heroes, Antony understands what has happened. His last words illuminate the play: "No one but Antony has conquered Antony." That's a hard line to screw up. I didn't.

Being dead as Antony, I could concentrate on Cleopatra's end. It begins with another master stroke from the author. Octavius Caesar climbs into the tomb chamber with a couple of aides to find Cleopatra standing in regal splendor between her women, the embodiment of the legend that has spread through the Roman world. He looks at her casually and turns to Proculeius: "Which is the Queen of Egypt?" With six words, he's beaten her. She sinks to her knees, no choice left but suicide.

"I wish you all joy of the worm," says the eunuch Mardian when he brings her a basket of asps. When DeMille directed Claudette Colbert in his (non-Shakespearean) film of the story, she made it clear to him before shooting began that she was horrified of snakes and would have nothing to do with them in the suicide scene. As he told me the story twenty years later, on the day, he said he walked on the set with a six-foot python coiled around one arm. "Get that monster off this set!" she screamed, whereupon he extended the garter snake he'd held behind his back.

"What about this fellow, then, Claudette?"

"Oh, that little thing," she said, taking the snake in her hand.

I'd told that story to Hildegard; she said she could handle the snake, as long as it wasn't a real asp. I'd checked out some real ones, just to see what they looked like. Nasty buggers, though small. Hildegard's performance in the tomb scenes was her best work in the film. (The final scene is certainly the perfect place for your best acting.) She did the eulogy to her dead paramour wonderfully well.

> I dreamt there was an Emperor Antony.
> O, such another sleep, that I might see
> But such another man. . . .
> His legs bestrid the ocean: his reared arm
> Crested the world . . .

I don't think Hildegard was acting when she trembled (like, I'm sure, the real lady) before reaching into the basket of fig leaves,

clutching the snake and pressing it to her naked bosom. "See, see
. . . my baby at my breast." Unlike the Bible's Eve and the serpent,
Old Will makes sure in Cleopatra's death that the snake doesn't
have the best part.

And that was the end of the shoot. I poured a small company
party that night, appropriate to our budget. Wrap parties, they call
them now, six-figure extravaganzas with laser shows and rock
bands. Actors will accept food and drink of any kind.

The next day I went back to the studio to review the numbers with Peter, and took the time to walk through the tomb set
once more before they tore it down. An actor spends his life closing
in plays, finishing films. Circumstances alter cases (I did my last
shot in *Major Dundee* and changed out of my uniform in the limo
rushing me to the airport), and how you feel about the project
determines how you say good-bye. The tough ones are like coming
out of combat: "My God, I did it—we got through." That's what I
felt like at the end of the *Antony* shoot.

Shutting up shop the following day, it appeared that, though
I'd finished on schedule, we'd somehow gone $194,000 over bud-
get. Remembering the old days with Sam Bronston, I was sure we
were the victims of creative bookkeeping, endemic even with the
big American studios. It could've been worse.

Two days later, we flew to New York, where I'd scheduled a
full day of PR for *Omega Man,* about to open there. I hadn't seen
the film since the rough cut some months earlier. I was very happy
with what Walter Seltzer had done with it since, and even happier
to discover that we had a hit. It's become something of a cult film
since, still pumping in checks every so often. I think we'd had a
chance to make a really fine film of *Omega,* but I was quite willing
to settle for a merely successful one at the time.

Back on my ridge, I prepared to cut *Antony.* Peter realized
it would be cheaper to import my editor and set up a cutting room
in my screening room on the ridge than to maintain me in London
and cut at the studio. It was perfect for me, of course. We'd bring
over Eric Boyd-Perkins, who'd cut *Julius Caesar* for us, and move
him into a nearby motel down the hill in the Valley.

I'd get up in the morning, do my swim and my workout,
while our housekeeper, Muriel, gave Eric and his assistant breakfast,

then we'd go out past the tennis court and settle down to the scene
set for the day. Eric would show me his assembly of the day's scene,
I'd give him my notes and then go back in the house and do other
work, or even fit in a set of tennis while Eric and his man cut and
spliced what we'd discussed.

About this time, I had lunch with Frank Schaffner, returned
from filming *Nicholas and Alexandra*. I recounted my travails, as
well as the rich pleasure of fitting the scenes together according to
my vision. Frank looked at me quizzically. "Let me tell you something, friend. When you've finally got your first cut put together and
run it, you . . . will . . . hate it." He was right, too.

Of course, editing has changed enormously since my first
directorial effort, changed probably more than any single element
of filmmaking. Then, you sat over a Moviola and planned your next
few edits, which had to be pulled out of the racks where they sat
filed with hundreds of the printed takes of all the setups in your
movie. What took you and your editor a half hour or so to plan,
creating a scene, would then require half the day for him to put in
place.

Only a few years ago, as has happened in so many other
areas of our lives, the computer revolutionized film editing. Now
all printed takes on a film are transferred to a single computer disc
where they're permanently stored in memory, instantly available.
The director sits before a fair-sized video screen, where his computer editor selects one of, say, four different takes you printed of
a setup and instantly cuts it into your scene, runs it, and goes back
to the original or tries another version, in no more time than it
takes to run the footage. (I recently spent some time in Fraser's
cutting room on his last film; it was awesome.)

But the thing I've come to like best about editing film is that,
aside from writing the screenplay, it's the closest to individual,
private effort you have in making a movie. Yes, there is an editor,
and the producer drops in now and then. But as a director, assembling your film, you're alone. That's rare in movies.

While I was waiting for Eric to come to L.A. with his rough
assembly, which would be our work base, I took my new seat on the
board of the American Film Institute. Halfway through a meeting I
went to the men's room and came back to find myself chairman.

That was the only time my dad's old adage "Never miss a chance to pee" led me astray. I stayed in the job ten years, with George Stevens, Jr., as executive secretary. "The Chuck and George Show," they called us.

Also, the National Council on the Arts was still on my plate, though the meetings were less frequent. I was beginning to have some doubts about the Endowment for the Arts by then. It seemed to me that we spent too large a share of our comparatively meager funds (then some $14 million a year, now over $170 million) on projects of primarily social merit which were perhaps more appropriate to the Department of Health, Education and Welfare, which boasted a budget of billions. This opinion wasn't popular in the seventies, however, and I was pooh-poohed down.

I spoke at one meeting as passionately as I could about the gradual dilution of the arts program with political grants of various kinds. The instinct of any bureaucracy to become bigger, combined with the Council's knee-jerk instinct to approve any grant application that could be described as socially useful, defeated my best efforts—though they were endorsed by my friend Greg Peck, one of Hollywood's more vigorous and intelligent liberals.

Then, just about the time Eric and my rough assembly arrived so I could start really editing *Antony,* I got another job. The sweet smell of *Omega Man*'s success was like cologne in our armpits; Walter and I were suddenly hot commodities. Walter had found a likely novel, and MGM snapped at it. It was the first of the disaster films, really. It was called *Skyjacked,* about a nut with a grievance who hijacks an airplane to get it to the Soviet Union. (Though not all those with grievances are nuts, most nuts have grievances.) For that matter, MGM had a grievance on this film. They were reluctant to pay me my then standard percentile of first-dollar gross. (And after all I did for them on *Ben-Hur,* too!) After a little arm-wrestle with the redoubtable Iceman, they gave in, and Walter proceeded with preproduction.

Meanwhile, sixty-eight cans of film were still on the racks along the walls in the screening room, with my movie in there somewhere, waiting for me. In the old studio days when everyone was under contract and everything was a lot cheaper, they used to shoot a film, assemble it in rough cut, then go back and reshoot the mistakes. That's what Irving Thalberg did in making himself the only genius who ever ran a studio—but it became impossibly expensive, abandoned long ago.

The tightness of our shooting schedule had limited the coverage I could shoot, thus limiting also what flexibility I had in editing. I'd have given an arm (well, a little finger) for a few hundred feet of intercut to fix what I had failed to shoot and what I had shot that didn't work. I finally ran my second cut, now down to two hours and twenty-four minutes, and sent the film back to England so the sound editor could work on it for a while. I wouldn't see it again till I went over to supervise the looping and do the final mix.

Having, to my surprise, some actual free time on my hands, I'd thought to go along with Fray for a few days in the high and lonely, but it was a really bad time for my girl, who by then was losing more than half her time to migraines. I really felt I couldn't leave her overnight, so I stayed home and took my daughter to the movies instead, which gave me equal pleasure. Before I had to take off for London, Fray and I did go up above Santa Barbara to Joe Canutt's ranch, where we got in some boar hunting. (Very ugly beasts, but tasty.) It was a perfect California fall day, the hills like fat yellow cows in the sun.

Then it was back to London for the looping and sound mix. Richard Johnson, who'd been so good in both *Julius Caesar* and *Khartoum,* most generously gave us his talents in re-voicing our three Spanish principal actors into spoken Shakespearean English. Remarkably, he managed to supply a different voice for each of them, God bless him. Unhappily, our Spanish composer had not finished his score for the film, and what he had was not promising. We replaced him with a young English composer, John Scott, who turned in a brilliant score on very short notice. It remains one of the strengths of the film.

I spent a Sunday at Cambridge, where I'd been asked to do a seminar on *Antony and Cleopatra* (the play, though I inevitably spoke of the film). It was a marvelous day, spent with a dozen or so really bright young men, though they couldn't resist the impulse to see the play in terms of their own values and prejudices instead of Shakespeare's. The most beautiful thing I saw there was the Wren Library, with the late light glowing through the windows. The most impressive was the crooked stairway at Jesus College, where for four centuries students have been climbing to their cramped quarters to study. Christopher Marlowe carved his initials on one of the newels.

I rerecorded those bits of my own dialogue in the film that were inadequate for one reason or another, and directed our Brit actors in the same chore. Oddly, though I long ago became skilled at ADR (Additional Dialogue Replacement) and early learned from Orson Welles the creative opportunity to improve what you have irrevocably filmed, it's such concentrated, demanding work that there's no kick in it. Directing other actors in the same chore, though, I found quite interesting. I also had to put in time on the battle sequences, where production sound is never adequate and hardly even attempted; you can do it so much better and more easily in the final mix. You do record the actual dialogue, of course, knowing you'll likely redo it in postprod. I'd planned to spend two or three days with Hildegard, fine-tuning some of her earlier scenes, but I didn't *have* two or three days, so I decided to leave that to Eric and Peter. I spent the morning before I caught my plane home guiding six young actors through the battle cries, warning shouts, and odd grunts and groans. Even a death scream has a lot of possibilities: "All right now. Each man give me three deaths—two long, one short. In turn, if you please."

Peter and a couple of the marketing guns from Rank rode along in the limo to Heathrow to show me some of the designs for the ads. Some were very promising (you only need one really good ad for a film), but then they showed me a layout for the title card in the opening screen credits:

CHARLTON HESTON'S
Film of
Antony and Cleopatra,
by William Shakespeare

I shot that down, instantly and absolutely. "On this movie, no one's name comes ahead of Mr. Shakespeare's."

"Mmm, yes," said one of the Brits. "It does verge on hubris a bit, doesn't it?"

"It wallows in it," I said. In Hollywood they call it chutzpah, as when Louis B. Mayer insisted that the writing credit on MGM's film of *Romeo and Juliet* read

By William Shakespeare
with additional dialogue
by Samuel Taylor

Preserving Old Will's credit intact was the last work I did on *Antony and Cleopatra,* though of course I'd do the PR for the openings in the New Year. In the few weeks before Christmas, I had some slack time, which God knows I had earned.

WE HAD TO FINISH CASTING *Skyjacked,* since Walter Seltzer had gotten the script itself in pretty good shape. (We weren't dealing with Shakespeare here, after all.) I played (of course) the pilot of the hijacked 707; we cast James Brolin as the psychotic hijacker. Yvette Mimieux, who'd played my kid sister a decade before in *Diamond Head,* played the chief hostess very well (and looked absolutely stunning).

I remember a scene with Yvette that gave me the easiest day's work I've ever had on a film, the kind of shooting day people imagine leading men have all the time. "We start with scene 121 tomorrow, Chuck," the first A.D. told me. "We're shooting in that park down the canyon below your house. If you're there at eight, we'll be in good shape." (You understand, above-the-line actors are given their calls in deferential tones, besides which he knew I'm never late.)

Next morning I drove down the back road to the set, five minutes from the house. Unlike some of those historical guys I've done, this pilot required no makeup or elaborate costume. I changed my shirt and pants and stood around with a cup of coffee till they were ready, which wasn't long.

It was a dream sequence, flashing back to our love affair, now ended. "OK, Chuck, we start in a long shot and dolly in on you pushing Yvette in this swing. On about the third time, catch her in your arms as she swings back, then hold her." Nothing to it; indeed delightful. Another take for insurance, then a close-up when I kiss her. Two more takes of that (double insurance), and the director called, "Cut, print. Thanks very much, Chuck . . . that's a wrap for you today. See you tomorrow." I was away from my house for an hour and a half. (Boy, these actors have it easy.)

I did have one more thing to learn for this role: how to fly a

707. Well, not really; how to *seem* to fly it, as with the quarterbacking in *Number One* and the conducting in *Counterpoint.* (Of course, as is well known, I actually *did* part the Red Sea for Mr. DeMille.)

Compared to quarterbacking and conducting, plausibly flying a 707 for the cameras was relatively easy, requiring only a few days in a simulator out at LAX. Those are wonderfully sophisticated machines, exactly duplicating what happens in a real aircraft in flight, on landing, and on takeoff. They're designed to take you in and out of most of the major airports in the world, in a variety of weather conditions which they can simulate. They can also throw you into an emergency situation in seconds—the loss of an engine, a fire—without any real physical risk, of course. It can be scary, though. If they set up a landing at La Guardia at night in fog and you undershoot the approach and land in the bay, the most god-awful cacophony of bells and whistles you ever heard explodes around you. Very embarrassing.

We went back to Chicago the day after Christmas for a few days with my mother and sister. For me, it turned out to be one day. Walter phoned to say they'd decided to include me in some of the air-to-air filming they were doing out of Albuquerque; I had to be there in twenty-four hours. Mother was the prime loser, of course; the rest of the family would join me in Yellowstone to see in the New Year.

My charter jet landed in Albuquerque with our 707 waiting on the taxiway, the number one engine already turning. I boarded through the belly hatch, put on my pilot's uniform and (more or less) my pilot's identity for a long day of air-to-air shots of Soviet MIGs intercepting my aircraft as it entered Russian airspace.

We were using National Guard F-100s, painted with Soviet insignia. They were no longer frontline American aircraft, of course, but they approximated MIGs well enough. I'd had some experience in World War II of the closing rate of fighters on a convergence course with bombers flying slower. Those were piston aircraft. Even with both the F-100s and the 707 flying at reduced speed to allow for more precise camera work, the closing speed was incredibly fast. In my war, you had several seconds to identify an approaching plane. From the pilot's seat in the 707 that day, even knowing where the fighters were coming from—dead ahead at twelve o'clock, fo-

cusing intently to pick them up—the windows of perception were
incredibly short. Horizon clear, no aircraft—distant dots closing,
yes, that's them—then almost instantly a dark swipe of blurred
shapes blowing by on either side twenty yards away, rocking our
aircraft with jet-wash. It was a memorable experience, and gave us
some useful footage as well, establishing me undeniably flying the
plane.

I connected with my family the next day, in Yellowstone
Park, where we could be pretty much by ourselves. The company
had moved back to MGM to film, but I wasn't shooting for a few
more days, down time I could surely use.

At almost seventeen, Fray was already a more experienced
outdoorsman than I, and differently committed. For me, the outback was simply the kind of country I grew up in, where I was at
home and did things I enjoyed. For him, it was more than that, sort
of a testing crucible where he could find out things about himself.
Diving, windsurfing, sailing, hunting, mountain climbing, fishing,
skiing, whitewater rafting—these were all different edges of the
envelope, whose outside he was determined to push.

I left Fray to his higher slopes and took Holly and Lydia off
to see Yellowstone's geysers, which performed on schedule. Back
at the lodge, we waited for the New Year, which also appeared on
time. We were all together and glad to be.

It's been my experience that New Year's Eve seldom lives up
to its billing. The mood is almost always contemplative, the cele-
brant joy laced with melancholy, mourning all the songs you might
have sung, the year passing, not used as well as you'd planned.

It was clear to me that the movie really didn't offer much in
the way of acting scenes. This was a film about an event, of the same
sort as the excellent film *Speed* (about the bus with the bomb on
it). It's a genre they were just beginning to explore in the seventies,
now a cinema staple in the nineties. The actors, depending on their
roles, are required largely to register fear and determination, in
various mixes (for the leading man, make that concern and determination). For the heavy, of course, determination often reads as
monomaniacal obsession, Dennis Hopper sharing the current copyright with James Woods. That means the actor can do anything because he's crazy, which is why those roles are so popular with
performers.

Making such a movie, character being secondary, the central threat of your plot must work with overpowering effect. We felt we did that very well in *Skyjacked,* using real aircraft and a forced landing in Alaska to refuel, the ultimate destruction of the aircraft never in fact happening.

Given the evolving skill of the special effects men and the heightened expectation of the audience, you have to give them a lot more than that now. In *Speed* (the title implies the film), an elevator is destroyed in the first minutes of the movie, followed in rapidly climaxing succession with several houses exploding, to mocking laughter from Dennis Hopper.

In *Skyjacked,* we had to rely on the audience's interest in what *might* happen, then just barely didn't. It worked very well then; I'm not so sure it would now.

My primary concern with the script was not really in contention. Remember, we were just emerging from the *Jonathan Livingston Seagull* sixties. I said to all and sundry when we were putting the final polish on the script: "This heavy is a no-kidding-crazy who richly deserves the sorry fate meted out to him at the end. Let's not forget that." We didn't. We weren't doing *Rebel Without a Cause,* nor surely not, a generation before its time, *Natural Born Killers.*

If the acting challenges in *Skyjacked* were modest, shooting the film was a monstrous technical problem. Almost 90 percent of the movie took place inside a 707. (Yeah, I know, Hitchcock shot all of *Lifeboat* in a lifeboat, but at least the *camera* didn't have to be inside it.)

Walter chose his director wisely. John Guillermin was just about perfect for this film. He was an imaginative and skillful director, very strong on the use of his cameras. (Harry Stradling, Jr., was his cameraman, one of the early examples of second-generation technicians following in the distinguished footsteps of their fathers.)

Both men dealt superbly with our major problem: finding ways to use the camera creatively when most of the scenes took place on the flight deck of a 707, where there's barely room for the three-man flight crew, let alone several hundred pounds of camera and sound equipment, plus film crew and lights. Having done this, they managed to resolve the problem variously for every scene, so that each setup is different.

Given all this, it must also be said that John Guillermin had an irascible streak. This is not unknown among directors, from some of the worst to some of the best. Hank Fonda, who'd made some of his best films for John Ford, once said to me, "He was a great director. He was also a cruel son of a bitch."

Only John Ford would embarrass a leading actor, as he did routinely to Fonda, Jimmy Stewart, and Duke Wayne. I was never the target of Mr. Guillermin's ire, but one day he ruthlessly reamed out the actor playing my copilot. When the shot was finished, I sent for Walter Seltzer. "Please tell John I don't want to humiliate him as he did Mike. But if he does that to another actor on this film, I'll leave the sound stage." He never did.

I never have walked off a set, though occasionally much provoked. The image I turn to in such moments is Clark Gable, wardrobed and ready to work on the set of *The Misfits,* the film that killed him, sitting waiting patiently day after day in case Marilyn Monroe might appear from her trailer. If the King could do it, so by God can I.

Actually, John Guillermin was a very effective director. Our cast worked out well, Yvette's chemistry making more of her role than was in it. Jimmy Brolin was excellent as our mad bomber, not least because he gave us such a straight-arrow image in the first half of the film.

Halfway through the shoot, the MGM brass found they liked our dailies enough to slot us for a Memorial Day opening. This was of course the jump-off for the summer season, but it meant a very tight postproduction schedule and, even harder, a quicker finish on the shoot itself. John was equal to it. We were cruising along, exactly on schedule, when he tightened it up a notch, designing a mobile scaffold that could move to any position against the 707 and shoot close interior shots through camera portholes cut in the fuselage. We finished the film three days ahead of schedule.

Happily, *Skyjacked* had been the kind of shoot where the production sound track was very good. Nonetheless, I had to crowd in some just-in-case ADR before the film was finally cut so I could leave for London and the premiere of *Antony*. I had no hand at all in the *Skyjacked* edit.

THE RANK PEOPLE laid on the full drill for our London *Antony and Cleopatra* premiere—the Odeon in Leicester Square, black tie, no effort spared. The film played very well, if we use the no-coughs-no-toilet-traffic guideline as the sure monitor of audience response. We left the theater and met a gratifyingly large crowd of (as always) courteous English fans. Bea Sellmer had come up from Madrid for the premiere, and our New Zealand friends, the John McDonalds, were there as well.

As the crowd around me thickened, I said to Lydia, "You guys go ahead and get in the car. Tell the driver to start the engine, but don't get out to hold the door for me. I'll get in myself; when I say 'Go!', pull away slowly."

I'd done this many times before; it really works very well. I worked my way through the crowd, head down, signing busily as I neared the car, a black Austin Princess, like most of the limos in London. "No, it's OK, take it easy, you're welcome. OK, just let me open the door here; OK, you're welcome. One more; I have to close the door now, watch your fingers. OK. *GO!*" As I sank back, an impeccably dressed stranger said, "Look here, sir, what are you doing in my car?" Very embarrassing.

Not nearly as embarrassing as the notices next morning. With a few exceptions from critics who liked what I'd done, on either side of the camera, the reviews were lousy. Filmmakers are very resourceful at dismissing bad notices, most often falling back on that classic standby, "That idiot knows absolutely nothing about movies." It is true that a film's success or failure often has little relation to critical opinion. I have no idea why this is so. Having had my share of both good and bad notices, I can say for sure: good is better.

Why did most of the London critics, usually so generous to me, come down so hard on us? Did they resent the idea of a Yank, especially as a first-time director, invading the special British preserve of the greatest writer of them all? I don't think so; most of the critics had good things to say about my Antony, and I was the only American in the movie.

I'm sure I took the right line with the part. In recent years, there's been a trend to play the great tragic heroes as less than great, thus less than tragic. I've seen Antony played as a sex-besotted drunk. If you don't have the great commander and charismatic leader brought down by his obsession with the Egyptian queen that both Plutarch and Shakespeare give us, you have nothing.

True, most of the critics found Hildegard Neil an inadequate Cleopatra, but no actress has ever fulfilled the part. Maybe Orson was right: "If you don't have a great Cleopatra, you can't do that play."

If Orson or Olivier had directed her, would she have been better? Almost certainly. Did I press her too hard, or not hard enough? I don't know, but I think she got a very large part of the infinitely complex lady Will wrote. If she fell seriously short, I have to take most of the blame.

In the next few weeks, the film did modestly well in England (I could, as they say, open a picture). But me in armor couldn't carry Shakespeare very far without great notices, and we sure Lord didn't have those. We went on to Tokyo, always one of my strongest markets and also an audience fond of Shakespeare. Our Japanese distributor, Shochiku Films, had laid on a very full release. As always, the Japanese media is an overwhelming presence, very useful to us. Our notices there were very good, they told me—but of course I don't read Japanese.

Back home, the modest English response had dampened any chance of a wide U.S. opening, though we had a small independent release. The sum of it was that the film I cared more about than any I've ever made was a failure. I believe that's about all I have to say about that.

In the remaining months of 1972, I would act in a hugely successful film that I like a great deal, do a very successful stage production of Arthur Miller's *The Crucible,* and make the worst film of my career.

20

The World's a Stage

. . . and all the men and women merely players.

— W. SHAKESPEARE

NO, OLD WILL wasn't being bitter about life, but noting that it goes by, and things don't always turn out the way we thought they would. Well, of course. We all know that; he just says it better, also briefer.

That's what I'd like to try to do with the rest of this book— give you my life in broader swatches. I don't want to go through the genesis, birth pangs, and postmortems of thirty-some more plays and movies, as well as exploring all the commitments on behalf of any number of public causes, and who did what and said what and to whom. I've been at this for most of my life; the book is going to be big enough to knock someone down with as it is.

First, let me tell you how this ridge works. Our house has been running well throughout the twenty-seven years Muriel Ashby's been keeping it. Lydia has two fine women with her, Grace Sampson in her studio and darkroom (where much of their effort is now in digital images, computer-printed) and Helene Bean as longtime secretary.

For the first twenty years of my career, however, I had a secretary who just about drove me crazy. Martha (not her name— I've changed it to protect the guilty) was modestly competent in her duties, but maddeningly difficult to be around. No, she didn't smell, except of cigarette smoke and, late in the day, gin. She did com-

468

plain, incessantly, of everything and everyone around her (except me, of course). In consequence, I set her up in an office in the studio and spent as little time there as possible. That meant, outside of acting, my life wasn't very well organized, but I simply couldn't bring myself to let her go, especially as her years of service lengthened. But "at last there came a morning . . . ," to quote Exodus.

We were on a London shoot. (No, she didn't like London, but she hadn't thought much of the other foreign locations where she'd joined us either.) I gave her a ride every morning to Pinewood Studios, discouraging conversation, which was hard to do with Martha. She was whining away about how inadequate her hotel was compared to the Dorchester (she had me there), and how poorly the first A.D. was handling the company. That did it. "Martha," I said, "you don't know the least goddamn thing about running a company." As she opened her mouth to retort, I said "Don't speak. If you say one more word between here and the studio, I'll send you home."

The next few minutes were blissfully silent, but as we pulled up outside my dressing room, she said primly, "Well, we all have a right to our opinions, surely."

"Have the driver take you to the production office. Tell them I said to put you on a plane for L.A. this afternoon. I'll see you there." I felt as though a sack of rocks had fallen from my shoulders. When we got home at the end of the shoot, she was not only better behaved, but told me she'd be taking retirement at the end of the year. I almost kissed her; instead, I gave her a pension.

If I were a little surer of God's good opinion of me, I'd think He felt I deserved a break and delivered Carol Lanning. No, I'm not implying Divine Intervention; Carol has a lawyer husband, kids, and grandkids; she was not suddenly made manifest on my doorstep. She has surely, though, taken over the nuts and bolts of my life.

When I go on a location, the script, along with my notes for revisions, is in my briefcase. So are memos on stuff I may have to deal with during the shoot, and all the phone numbers on a card. Muriel Ashby does the packing, but Carol makes sure our regular driver, Harold Jones, picks me up. I don't have to ask if he knows where we're going and how to get there; of course he does, he's an ex-marine. All I need to think about, or want to, is the work I have to do when I'm there.

It's not true that Carol pins a note to my coat in case I get lost. It is true that she runs my public life with awesome efficiency, but unvarying good humor. I've yet to hear anyone speak ill of her, though she denies people daily. Her opinion, when sought, is cool and considered, shaped not only by what is right for me, but what is right. One of my few regrets at not trying for the U.S. Senate is that I'd love to have seen Carol Lanning run a senatorial office.

She is, in every sense of the word, a good woman. I humbly submit that, after Martha, I deserve her.

LET'S DO THE DISASTER FILMS now; they loomed very large on the movie landscape for most of the seventies, but I don't think they've been much examined as a major genre, which they were, as surely as the Western, though they surely didn't last as long. I don't think they've even been properly defined.

A more specific label would be "multiple jeopardy film." The basic situation always involves a disparate group of people, most of them strangers to each other, thrown suddenly into a life-threatening situation, usually (not invariably) a natural disaster. The movie explores the disaster as spectacularly as possible, and traces the reaction of the various characters to the common danger. The story structure requires as many as a dozen or so substantial roles in the film, though in two hours' running time, none of them can be very long.

This imposes an iron mandate on the casting. With such a crowd of characters, you absolutely have to cast stars in the three or four best parts, and identifiable names and faces in the others. The first reel must be spent introducing them all. Each can have only a short introductory scene, then might not be seen again for another fifteen minutes. You have to be sure the audience can keep them all in mind as you move from story line to story line: "There's Paul Newman again; who's the guy in the helmet?"

"That's Steve McQueen, dummy. He's the fire chief. Newman is the architect. I forget who Bill Holden is. Shut up and watch!"

Making these films meant, of course, that most of the major actors were playing smaller parts than they had in years, though still getting their standard salaries. Those of us compensated in first-dollar gross percentiles worked no more than a few days for seven-figure paychecks. Some of the films were quite good, even more of them were wildly successful. Just about all of us did at least one.

In my first, I played an architect (no, no . . . Paul's architect was in *The Towering Inferno,* mine was in *Earthquake*). Both films were megahits. None of us, I think, imagined we were involved in very significant creative endeavors; we were all hugely compensated to fill out what were in essence cameo roles, with about twenty minutes of screen time to work in. After the blood and sweat (no tears) I'd spent on *Antony,* I felt I'd earned it.

Guess who Universal wanted to cast as my wife? *Riiighht!* Ava Gardner. Actually, her casting was not the issue with me it had been in *55 Days at Peking.* There, she'd had to play a Russian aristocrat at the turn of the century, suggesting another time and background. In *Earthquake,* she could play herself in a modern context. Also, it was a much shorter part, in which she didn't have to face the cameras every day. In fact, she gave us no trouble whatever.

She did seem, since *Peking,* to have lost some of the fiery core that had been so much a part of her persona. Watching her work through a longish and modestly complex speech one day, I learned something useful to me as a director. Mark Robson had the helm on *Earthquake;* he'd done maybe a dozen takes in which Ava had been adequate, but not much more. She was also growing a little restive. Mark talked to her quietly and did one more take. "Cut! Print! That's very good, Ava. Much better. We won't need you now till the dolly shot."

As she left the stage, he noted my quizzical look. "Sometimes," he said quietly, "you have to know when you've gotten all there is." I don't know if that's the answer, but it's surely the question.

I did have one considerable arm-wrestle with the studio. In the early drafts of the script, our really very spectacular earthquake killed off several characters, including Ava as my wife, swept away in a flooded storm drain. In the classic tradition of male stars, I survived. Having considerable experience in dying usefully for the cameras, I held out for doing so yet again while trying to save my wife (I did have script approval).

"Naahh, Chuck, for God's sake! The audience will want you to live. The last shot has to be you embracing Genevieve Bujold from the chopper as it pulls up and away to show the city you're going to rebuild."

"And they'll be way ahead of you on every cut!" I said. "Here you've got me playing this genius architect who knew all along they were wrong about the building codes, then there's this great earthquake that levels Los Angeles and kills his dumb father-in-law and his bitchy wife, leaving him with his nice girlfriend to screw while he rebuilds Los Angeles. All he does in the movie is prove he was right in the first place. Let's surprise them for a change. Let him die trying to help someone . . . *especially* his bitchy wife."

Well, they agreed because they had to, but they took one more crack at it in a scene where George Kennedy (he played a cop who did survive in the end) and I lead some people to safety barely before the roof collapses. That done, they set up a shot where George didn't make it, crushed under several tons of concrete. "What's this?" I said. "We need George alive at the end."

"No, no, Chuck, don't worry," said Mark. "This is just cover footage. When we get to shooting the scene in the sewer where you're swept away, we'll do a quick alternate shot of you surviving, just in case we change the ending so you live, not George."

I sighed wearily. "Mark," I said, "let's be realistic. I have script approval, I don't have final cut. You're the director, you have a shot set up to kill George. I don't want to embarrass you. If you want to shoot this, I'll do it, of course. What I will *not* shoot, I promise you, is a scene where I survive. That's not in the script I approved."

Our death scene was one of my more spectacular screen demises. Ava slipped and fell from the iron ladder leading up from the sewer to safety; I turned and dove after her, struggled with her in the rushing torrent till we were both sucked under. The ending did what I predicted: it stunned the audience into shocked silence. *Earthquake* was a monster success. I know, for other reasons too, but my sacrificial death worked. Every time another check from the film crosses my desk (I don't get to keep them, you know . . . just watch them go by), I think with some relish of what I hope wasn't the only time where I was right and they were wrong.

The success of both *Towering Inferno* and *Earthquake* just spurred everyone on, of course. Burt Lancaster did a disaster film, so did Jack Lemmon, and I don't remember who all. For several years, filmgoers seemed to have an insatiable appetite for films with a fistful of stars in deep poop.

At last, Universal set up yet another, which they predicted would be the blockbuster disaster film of them all. It was about a crazy who shoots up a Super Bowl, creating a massive panic at the same time. We shot it in the Los Angeles Coliseum; I played a lieutenant of detectives.

Two-Minute Warning was actually a pretty good film; Universal was positive it would out-gross *Earthquake.* It was a flop. We had struck a nerve; the public didn't want anything to do with terror in a Super Bowl.

WHILE EXPLORING DISASTER, we can't overlook a film I alluded to in the last chapter: the worst movie I ever made. I'd match it against Paul Newman's *The Silver Chalice* for lousy any day. Besides, Paul has an excuse—he doesn't do period parts. This was a perfect part for me, based on a novel by a great American writer, and it's perfect screen material: Jack London's *The Call of the Wild.*

How can you possibly screw up that story? You may well ask. I asked the same thing myself, while we were in the middle of screwing it up. I didn't come up with many answers, but I've sorted out some good excuses.

The root of our troubles was the producer, a sort of rogue Brit who flickered shadowlike in and out of the country to avoid his various creditors. No, I was not among them. To deal with just such a contingency, Herman the Iceman had long since established a firm policy that my guarantee on any overseas shoot be deposited in a U.S. bank before I left the country. Since Paramount was distributing the film in the States, they were responsible for my domestic gross percentile.

The film should have been shot in the Yukon, where Jack London laid the story. They had dogsled teams and a talent pool of American and Canadian actors and technicians. What they didn't have were distribution arrangements with all the European countries, which was crucial to our producer's plans. What we finally ended with was a joint British/American/Norwegian/German/French/Italian/Spanish coproduction. No kidding. This gave the film nationality in each of those countries for distribution, but also required that both performers and technicians from each country be significantly employed. The United Nations is a good analogy; we were doomed to failure before a camera turned.

The script was acceptable as an OK-this'll-do-to-start-with, we'll-rewrite-as-we-go effort. Some good films have been made from this premise. Our director was Ken Annakin; his wonderful *Those Magnificent Men in Their Flying Machines* a few years earlier had enchanted me.

If you had to shoot in Europe, Norway was the only country with reliable snow. They also had by far the highest level of English language proficiency. Some of the Norwegian actors didn't even need to be re-voiced. The Norwegian dog teams were another thing. They don't really have them in Norway, it turned out.

We imported sleds, dogs, and trainers, at considerable expense and with mixed results. It turns out that sled dogs like to do two things: run, and fight with their teammates. Unless you're a skilled driver (and on this film, there was no time for me to learn this arcane capacity), you spend a lot of time breaking up fights and getting run over by your own team.

I was able to befriend the lead dog, Buck. He was a beautiful animal about the size of a small bear, and just as strong. After my family went back to the States, I moved him into the hotel suite with me, and we came to a useful understanding. Indeed, he gave by far the best performance in the film; would that the rest of us had done as well.

Holly also got close to him. For several days while Fray was off climbing mountains in northern Norway and Lydia was in Holland researching a play she was writing about Juana, an unfortunate Spanish queen, Holly and I had some good Dad-and-Daughter time. I was particularly moved by her concern when we were shooting a scene where I fell through the ice on a frozen lake and Buck rescued me.

It was a real frozen lake; the water was so cold I didn't really feel it at first. When Buck ran to the edge of the hole, right on cue, and started to pull me out by the collar, our combined weight broke the ice and he fell in with me. There was no danger, really; it made a better shot and we struggled out in good time. The wardrobe people rushed in with towels and blankets, scrubbing me dry. I was touched to see Holly running from the sidelines, calling "Daddy! Daddy!"

I swept her up in my arms, comforting her. "Hey, Munchkin,
I'm all right! Don't be upset!"

She squirmed free and ran over to the wardrobe man.
"Don't you have any towels for the *doggie?!*"

Call of the Wild really fell apart, though, because of the
foreign performers cast to fill the quota requirements of the various
European partners. There are many good actors in all these countries whose English is perfectly competent. Our producer did not
hire them. Some of our actors, playing Americans, could hardly
read their lines in English from cue cards.

One who could was Juan Luis Galliardo, who'd played a
small but central part for me in *Antony and Cleopatra*. He was a
handsome young Spanish actor who'd begun to establish a name in
Spanish and South American films. On my recommendation, Ken
Annakin cast him in quite a good part as a half-breed Indian guide.
In his first scenes he was very good, coming through to the camera
with vigor and presence, as he had in *Antony*.

He was, however, very lonely. I didn't realize it until too late,
but I was the only person in the company who spoke Spanish, and
mine was by no means perfect. Most of his scenes were with me; I
translated for him on the set, but there was apparently no other
Spanish speaker in all of Oslo.

Norway in the winter can be a gloomy place, with only six
or seven hours of thin winter light each day. When I realized Juan
Luis' state of mind, I took him out to dinner a couple of times,
but my imperfect Spanish seemed to drive him further back into
himself.

His part wasn't very long, but when he was called to the set
he'd sit in the car, or the makeup trailer, or the chair you put him
in until he was needed in front of the cameras. Each day he worked,
he seemed a little more remote.

Still, none of us realized how far Juan Luis had gone till he
was scheduled for a scene where he and the dog, Buck, rescue me
from a snowslide. I hadn't seen him in some days, but when I
greeted him in Spanish on the location, he simply smiled and
turned away. I made nothing of it; I was planning my part of the
scene.

It wasn't very complicated, certainly not dangerous. I had to
be buried in snow, of course, but there's some air to breathe; it's

not like being buried in sand. Anyway, I'd be dug out in less than a minute.

Except that Juan Luis could really take no part in the scene. He couldn't enter on cue, or move to a mark, or speak a word. Buck could do all of that, except the dialogue. We did any number of takes exploring this problem. My problem, of course, was breathing as shallowly as possible under the snow, hoping they wouldn't forget me while trying to get Juan Luis into the shot.

All the time, of course, Buck performed perfectly: finding me unerringly, digging me out in a shower of snow with fierce canine energy, and accepting my grateful embrace with warm dignity. Finally we had an A.D. stand just off-camera and gently nudge Juan Luis into the shot, where he stood quietly, unaware.

Then they drove him to a hospital in Oslo for tests. I visited him there that night—he was still silent, still smiling. Within a day or so, they flew him back to Spain, where I hope he found himself. I don't know whether he was ever again able to perform. As I'm often reminded, this is a harsh profession.

Call of the Wild was an utterly failed film because it was assembled, not created. It was indeed a United Nations of a movie, using actors according to nationality rather than ability. When Paramount saw it, they refused to release it, to my immense relief. I heard not long ago that it had somehow escaped into syndication on cable. Should you run across it late at night while channel surfing, don't watch it. Please.

I THINK I deserved better luck, and I got it, along with one of the most rewarding acting relationships of my career. While I was getting run over by Norwegian sled dogs, Walter Seltzer had taken a novel I'd wanted to film for a long time and sold MGM on it. (It wasn't hard; after *Skyjacked* hit so big, they'd have probably made even *Call of the Wild.*)

The novel was called *Make Room! Make Room!,* laid in New York in 2022, when the city's population had exploded to 47 million people. Since I strongly believe that overpopulation is by far the gravest problem the world faces, this would be my only message movie. *Make Room! Make Room!* obviously reflects the story; so does the title we finally chose: *Soylent Green.* You haven't seen the film? Soylent was a nutrient cracker, the primary staple food in a starving Manhattan. What was it composed of? Well, as I said in a memorable line often quoted to me, "Soylent Green . . . is people."

I'm very proud of the film and delighted by its success. In a perfect world, all the films we're really proud of would be showered with critical praise and runaway grosses, like *Soylent.* The flops would be the ones we were edgy about from the beginning. We had an original idea with a good script, well directed and well acted. (We got Richard Fleischer, who was crucial to both goals.) Still, I think the central reason why people turned out in such multitudes to see the film was Eddie Robinson. Casting him was my idea; probably my most important contribution to the picture.

I play a worn-down New York cop in a Manhattan crumbling on the edge of chaos. Crime and people so glut the streets that there's little left to steal save food and water. Eddie plays an old man (born about 1950) who earns a meager subsistence and a corner of my two-room flat because he's a "book." He knows how to read and use the long abandoned public library to furnish useful information to the NYPD's fraying thin blue line, still striving to defend society.

You can never tell in advance how casting choices will pan out. I'd worked with Eddie Robinson before; he was Dathan in *Ten Commandments,* and we'd tested him for the orangutan Maurice Evans subsequently played in *Planet of the Apes.* Eddie had pulled out of that one because he felt his bad heart couldn't take the pressures of that difficult makeup. But he was delighted to play old Sol in *Soylent,* though he smiled when MGM, agreeing to his substantial salary request, wanted to defer half of it: "At seventy-nine, I'm not much interested in deferments."

Eddie knew he was dying when he undertook *Soylent,* though none of us did. He sat in a chair on the sound stage all day, seldom going back to his trailer, talking to the other actors, the crew people, Dick and Walter. I think he wanted to feel the banter behind the cameras once more too, not just the work. I remember him listening to a couple of young actors bitching about the boring waits between setups while the shot's laid out and lit.

He grinned, "You know, I've always figured the waiting is what they pay me for. The acting I do free."

The acting was also very fine. His Sol was quirky and wary without falling into the standard oddball old geezer that actors so often use. The chemistry between us also worked. We call it that in the trade because we can't really define it. It doesn't depend on either talent or compatibility, though that helps. When it works, it enlivens a film. Eddie and I had it in *Soylent Green*.

So finally we came to his last scene. Eddie knew it was truly his last scene; he would never again speak a line of dialogue for the turning cameras, the tuned mikes and focused lights. What's more, it was his death scene.

Sol has found life no longer tolerable in the rotting ruin of Manhattan, even protected by Thorne, the jaded cop I played. He's decided to "go home," meaning check into a huge facility where he'll be gently euthanized while he watches film footage of anything he likes, listening to whatever music he loves for the last minutes of his life, after which he will be ground into Soylent Green to feed the teeming tens of millions.

I've bullied and badgered my way through iron security to the glassed chamber where Sol lies on a white couch, surrounded by huge screens filled with flowing images of the world as it was in his youth, now gone forever. Running horses, soaring eagles, leaping dolphins, rivers of fish, and fields of wheat. Thorne is stunned by the look of a world he's never seen, cannot even now comprehend. Sol smiles gently, his eyes glistening. "See," he says. "I told you, didn't I?"

Thorne's like a child in a cathedral. "How could I know? How could I ever . . . imagine?" There are a few lines more, then Sol dies as the images go white. It is a *very* good scene; Eddie is marvelous. As fine an actor as he was, he could hardly have been less, playing that. I was very good too, unconsciously picking up the truth he was exploring. I've never heard of an actor playing a death scene in terms of his own true and imminent death. It was an awesome experience.

We wrapped early, after covering the close angles, and held a little wrap party for Eddie. For us, he was finishing in the film. For Eddie, he was finishing as an actor, standing for the last time on a sound stage, where he'd lived so richly, for so much of his life. Twelve days later he was dead. No actor could ask for a better way to go.

I HADN'T DONE A PLAY in two years, and had yet to play in either of the two houses in L.A.'s new Music Center. The Mark Taper Forum is an absolute jewel of a house, only seven-hundred-and- some seats. I think it's the finest small theater in the country, maybe the world. It's been run since it opened by Gordon Davidson, superbly.

The Ahmanson Theatre, on the other hand, was conceived in chaos and born to trouble. It was a classic example of the Edifice complex, built with no idea of what a theater needs to be as a stage machine. On top of which, the acoustics were terrible. A pal of mine in the Royal Shakespeare Company defined it succinctly when they played an engagement there twenty years ago: "Playing on the Ahmanson stage is like doing Shakespeare on the white cliffs of Dover . . . except the audience is in France."

I speak with such ruthless candor because *we have fixed it.* Actors are the people who *use* a stage, but they never get in on the planning. I was on the Ahmanson/Taper Board when they undertook to remake the Ahmanson; I made sure I was part of that process.

When it was finally ready to open last January, there was a sort of a mini-gala for all the people who'd worked to make it happen. I was the first actor to speak on the new stage (yeah, it was Shakespeare). It's a wonderful house now—no more white-cliffs-of-Dover, the audience is not in France. I've been trying to persuade Tom Selleck to do *Mister Roberts.* I've done it three times; I'd love to direct him in it.

Now cross-fade back to the seventies. I knew they wanted me in the Ahmanson because they thought I could fill it. (It's a big, for-profit house; the Taper is small, nonprofit.) Besides, my old friend Bobby Fryer, who'd given me my first professional audition when I came back from the war, as well as my entry card into live TV, had taken over as artistic director of the Ahmanson. I knew I was in good hands.

"The play," they say, "is the thing." I wanted to do *Becket* (as I'd said about four times before). Bobby thought this was a fine idea, but when I made clear I wanted to take the chance Olivier had offered me a decade earlier and find an actor who could alternate with me in both parts, everyone stepped back a pace.

"Well, who could we get?" "Not every actor can do that kind of double, switching every performance." "It's a hell of a stretch, Chuck . . . we need another star then." "We really can't afford it."

Well, that wasn't it, of course. Any major film actor who does a play is taking a huge pay cut going in from what he'd get in a film. Everyone understands that. It's also true that many actors are edgy about doing a play "all by yourself, from the top, no second take." If you've never worked on the stage, that may be a point. Why take the risk?

But what *is* the risk? "Ahh, I liked her better in that movie with . . . what's his name?" "I thought he was taller." Isn't risk part of it anyway? Several audiences and three critics hated your Hamlet, so you'll never get another movie, when your *Love Zombies of Zion* had the top gross last spring for two weeks? Come onnn!

As for *Becket,* I gave in on that. I will now never get to play the king one night, Becket the next. Well into this century actors did it all the time, in all sorts of plays. Not any more. Never mind; I've had my shot at some wonderful parts.

For my Ahmanson debut, we decided on Arthur Miller's *The Crucible.* I share the widely held opinion that it's his best play, from a rich offering. While I appreciate the universality of *Death of a Salesman, The Crucible* somehow speaks to me more strongly— maybe because I play so many parts where you wear funny clothes.

One of the strengths of Miller's *Crucible* is the way his people sound. Very few writers can plausibly suggest another period— as I've surely had ample opportunity to discover. Miller's characters are inescapably *of* the seventeenth century. I had the temerity to search out Mr. Miller's phone number and ask him about this. He gave me a very generous piece of his time, and told me he'd relied mostly on court records of the testimony from the trial that's the centerpiece of his play. Like many good solutions, it sounds simple.

Crucible is a very powerful piece; Joe Hardy directed, I think we gave it a strong production. Certainly it was very successful by any measure. John Proctor is a rich and challenging part; not a tragic figure, perhaps, but surely a heroic one. In the last scene, when he has signed a confession he knows to be false, then withholds it lest he implicate others, he cries out in desperate explanation, "Because it is my *name!* Because I cannot have another in my

life!" The fiber of what it is to be a man is in that speech, that action.
I felt taller every time I played it.

I did six plays at the Ahmanson over the next twelve years, more than any other actor has done there. It's difficult to fit the three or four months even a limited run of a play takes in between films, but it can be done. I learned something valuable from every one of the plays I did, even though I'd acted in three of them at least once before.

The stage is different from film; different challenges, problems, rewards. "It keep yo' muscles loose, so you don't lose de juice," as Satchel Paige memorably observed. (He wasn't talking about acting.) I recommend it to my colleagues. Strongly.

Let's run through the Ahmanson cycle while we're at it, then we'll switch back to other undertakings, OK? In 1975, Bob Fryer asked what I'd like to do next. (I'd just come back from filming *The Three Musketeers.*) "Let's do *Macbeth*," I said. "No one's done Shakespeare on this stage since the Royal Shakespeare Company was here. It's high time we danced with the Old Gentleman."

So we did. Bobby flew to London and got Vanessa Redgrave to do the Lady and a very fine English director, Peter Wood, to direct. I went over for some meetings. (There's always an elegant lunch in some very grand restaurant, in which mutual compliments and high hopes are exchanged, and then you get down to it.) I flew home very happy with our beginnings.

Peter Wood came over a week later for the rest of the casting, as well as checking out the costume and set designs. I was delighted with the set; I should've paid more attention to the costume designs.

A Shakespearean set can always use a good staircase, for kings going up and down, and fights, and love scenes. In *Macbeth,* it's particularly essential, useful for the drunken Porter and killing Macduff's children. H. R. Poindexter gave us a great swooping stone structure down which I could stumble, half-naked, drenched in blood and horror-struck after killing the king. He also gave us a vast steel disc, extending out over the orchestra pit and bringing us closer to the audience. It was a great set.

I wish I could say the same for the costumes. The real Macbeth lived in the eleventh century—a brutal, bloody time. Our costume designer had come up with some very intricate and fancy clothes. When Peter and I saw them for the first time, he said wryly, "I suspect you had in mind something a little more . . . primitive? Iron and leather?"

"I'll tell you this, Peter," I said, "I'm damned if I play this part looking like the king of clubs in a royal flush at poker." That's exactly what the outfit looked like, too. We fixed the costumes, more or less, in the time we had. A crucial problem is that many costume designers can't draw; I have no idea why. I'd say that should be a requisite to their trade.

Peter and I had larger fish to fry. We spent several days by my pool (the English love pools, not necessarily to swim in, just to sit around), doing a line-by-line on the text. This would be the fourth time I'd done the part; I'd arrived by trial and error at a good many cuts and redactions that I was convinced clarified, even sharpened the text. Peter was more of a textual purist than I, but we compromised amicably enough.

When Vanessa arrived, a few days before rehearsals began, she joined us by the pool. As Peter had predicted, she did not like any of my redactions in her scenes. I wasn't such a fool as to cut any of her lines, of course, but she preferred them arranged exactly as the Old Gentleman wrote them, as was surely her privilege.

Peter, who'd directed her before, soothed me. "It will take her time," he said, "to realize that you have not suggested these changes to improve your own part."

A few days into rehearsal, we were in agreement on the text. Vanessa is a fiercely dedicated actress, born from the genes of the only true acting dynasty I know of. I worked with her father, Sir Michael Redgrave, one of the great actors of our time, and with her sister, Lynn, though not with her mother, Rachel Kempson. Believe me, the bloodline runs true.

We spent a full day wrestling with the banquet scene, dealing with Lady Macbeth and the guests, the ghost of Banquo, the murderers, and me. Our problems in the scene had nothing to do with her part, but Vanessa soldiered on patiently. We were all beat when Peter finally wrapped the rehearsal. Packing his briefcase, he grinned at me. "Well, at least Lady V. doesn't give you any of the standard great actress behavior."

"My experience of great actresses is limited," I said wearily.
"What do they do?"

"Ohh . . ." he mused. "They rehearse with their hats on."

Vanessa never did that, though often with her passion on
her sleeve.

Among the major challenges in staging *Macbeth,* especially
for the guy playing the bloody Scot, are the combats. I'm not talking
about the battles; there are many of those throughout the canon. In
the theater, they take place largely offstage, with men running on
and off telling us how it's going. On film, as Olivier demonstrated
spectacularly in his *Henry V,* and we more modestly in *Julius Caesar* and *Antony and Cleopatra,* you can do what Shakespeare
dreamed of doing: actually show them Agincourt, Philippi, Actium.

In the tragedies, only Hamlet and Macbeth must be killed in
personal combat onstage. The Hamlet fight is easier. In his estimable film of the play, Mel Gibson juiced it up a bit by having them
change outfits in midstream, but it's a formal fencing match with
sporting foils (except that Laertes has poisoned the point of his).
You're still working with light weapons, easy to control through a
choreographed fight.

Macbeth has two fights: the prelim with Young Siward,
whom he must kill brutally and quickly, both to show his warrior's
skill and to save his breath for the main event with Macduff.

That fight must be as ferocious as possible. Audiences used
to seeing men blown through windows and ships explode on the
screen will not settle for two actors carefully clacking swords together for two minutes. (Even half a century ago, an eminent critic
destroyed a famous Macbeth, observing, "His fight with Macduff
looked like two angry boys with butter knives.")

Aside from the necessity of heavy broadswords, you get no
doubles, and no retakes. You have to do it yourself, every night and
twice on matinee days. When I pointed this out to Joe Canutt, whom
I asked to design the fight for me, he shook his head. "Well . . . you
better be damn sure you learn the routine. Someone cuts at you
with one a'those blades an' you miss a parry, you'll be sorry."

I took his words to heart. (I do that with most of what Joe
tells me.) He worked out a brutal slugging match with broadswords
on my tennis court. Richard Jordan, who was playing Macduff, and

I rehearsed it for an hour every day before we went down to rehearse the play. After we opened we had to run through the fight onstage ten minutes before they let the audience in. Every performance. As George Washington said, "Eternal vigilance is the price of not getting hit in the head."

I did, one night, though not because I missed a parry. I made it very neatly, but my sword blade snapped off at the hilt. Richard's stroke was slowed, just grazing my head. Now I had no sword, and blood in my eyes. I grabbed him by the throat. "Cut to the end!" I hissed. "Roll me off the stairs and kill me."

We did it very well, I thought, for an improvisation. Richard wrestled me out of sight, swung his sword up into the lights, chopped the melon we'd planted (it made a great sound), and staggered out holding the bleeding cast of my head aloft.

I was safely out of sight, but I couldn't get offstage till Malcolm was created king of Scotland. His descendant, James I, the first Scottish king of all Britain, saw the original production—so this is not a short scene. Till the curtain fell, I lay panting in the dark under the stairs licking my lips to taste how much of the blood running down my face was real. (The sweat was real, most of the blood was fake.) Old Will would've been delighted.

Any production of *Macbeth* stands or falls on the two central characters and the curious nature of the play itself. As is often said, it's a dark and bloody piece, filled with witches, curses, and murder. The number of night scenes supports the theory that it was first performed indoors, at night, for the king.

Lady Macbeth, of course, is one of the two or three greatest women's roles in the canon; not as transcendent as Cleopatra, perhaps, but more readily encompassed. It's a much shorter part, for one thing, and follows a definable line from gnawing ambition for her husband through homicidal obsession to clinical depression. After her pitiable sleepwalking, she disappears from the play. Her death (suicide, surely) is reported by a messenger; Macbeth hardly reacts to the news.

Most of the actresses equipped for the part have undertaken it; the best of them have often triumphed in it. Vanessa was certainly one of them. She had an icy passion that was at the same time alienating.

Macbeth is a brute of a role, but those man-killers are the

ones you have to play—the rest is Triple A ball. All the great actors in history have done Macbeth; not one has given a career performance in it. We remember Olivier's Othello, Gielgud's Hamlet; we read of Henry Irving's Lear and Edmund Kean's Shylock; they all played Macbeth as well, but not with the success they found in the other roles. There have been two films, both disasters.

This was my fourth shot at the part; I surely knew the ground by then. The good man destroyed by his own ambition, seduced by his wife, who's herself destroyed by the monster she makes of him. Then there are the witches, who confront Macbeth with his future at the beginning of the play and point him down the road he walks.

The actor hardly has room to show us the good man before he starts to crumble. The solution I came to in this production was to have Macbeth embrace the evil he's unleashed with the murder of his king; to lust for it. "I am in blood stepped in so far that I can wade no more . . ." So he plunges on, finding only in his own death a scrap of honor.

We had a hit, nearly selling out the whole run, and got some good notices, but I think Old Will wrestled me down again. I got up, brushed the sand off my knees, and checked to see if any teeth had been loosened, then did a very good and hugely successful film for Walter Mirisch. (I'll fill you in on that in the next chapter, when we get back to the movies.)

After shooting the film, we went to Scotland for some family time. Of course we went to the Fraser country, near Inverness (also Macbeth country) and the island of Iona, where King Duncan is buried. The current Macshimi (chief) of the clan, Simon, Lord Lovat, welcomed us warmly; Fraser and I got to wear our kilts in the country they were made for. He also got to climb Ben Nevis. Lydia and I climbed halfway.

The Scots have good blood in them, back to Roman times when we painted ourselves blue and kept trying to get over Hadrian's Wall and down into Britain. When the Viking raiders pillaged up and down the Highland coast a couple of centuries later, they left some more good blood. It may be one of the more successful genetic mixes in history. I'm proud of it.

Then I accepted an offer to do a two-week cameo as another royal tyrant: Henry VIII, in a film of Mark Twain's *The Prince and the Pauper* (released as *Crossed Swords*).

I look less like Henry than any of the dozen or so historical figures I've played (except for the size; he was even taller than I am), but Ziggy Geike, who was designing all my character makeups by then, made my face into a very plausible Henry.

The film covers the last days of Henry's life, so I tried to show his physical decline by playing the first scene leaning on a staff, another one sitting on his throne fondling a girl, then dying in bed. His last words are among the most mysterious of all deathbed comments: "Monks, monks . . . monks."

The film, unhappily, didn't turn out. We had Richard Fleischer, who'd done such a fine job with *Soylent Green,* directing some very good actors—Rex Harrison, George C. Scott, Oliver Reed. Sadly, Mark Lester, the boy they cast in the dual title roles, as both Henry's son, Prince Edward, and a poor street boy who looks exactly like him, simply wasn't up to either part, though he'd been superb nine years before in *Oliver*. The shelf life of child actors is often very brief. I had a fine time with Henry, though.

OK, BACK to the Ahmanson plays. Peter Wood had finished directing his opera, so we had lunch. "I can see it would be interesting to stage an opera, but how do you go about directing opera singers as actors?" I asked.

"With immense difficulty," he answered, closing his eyes. "In fact, it's almost impossible. I don't know which are more daunting, the sopranos or the tenors." Over coffee, I was speculating as to what play I might do at the Ahmanson the next year. "I know *exactly* what play you should do, dear boy." He paused. *"Long Day's Journey into Night."*

I threw my napkin on the floor. "You son of a bitch! You know perfectly well that play is just about un-actable."

"Quite right. I also know it's the best American play ever written, it's a marvelous part for you, and if you don't do it you won't be able to live with yourself."

"You think I don't know all *that,* too? That's what I'm so pissed off about. Just for that, you can pay for the damn lunch!"

"I will happily pay for lunch. In fact, just because you asked me so charmingly, I will direct the production."

And he did.

Peter was right, of course; *Long Day's Journey* probably *is* the best American play, as Eugene O'Neill is our greatest playwright. He has, however, a very prolix style. His ear is true; unlike many writers, his dialogue sounds like people talking, but he does go on. And on. His characters sometimes signal a line in advance, then say it, and not long after reprise it. They are, as I said to Peter, very difficult to act.

They also throb with life. O'Neill wrote the play from 1939 to 1941, but refused to allow its production in his lifetime, since it explores the shadows in his own family. It is a shatteringly powerful work.

It's also, as Peter pointed out, a very good part for me. Modeled on O'Neill's father, James Tyrone is an actor, a husband, a father, and a rich man who remembers poverty. You could say I knew the ground, though not in the dark dimension of tragedy O'Neill unfolds.

It's curious how you can bring bits and pieces of your work home with you, colors of the character you're trying to find. After a long rehearsal looking for James Tyrone, I came home and stumbled into a furious quarrel with my wife. A run along Mulholland Drive in the dark eased my mind a little, but not nearly as much as when I got back to the ridge and found my sweet daughter bicycling slowly up and down the drive softly singing "When the dog bites, when the bee stings, When I'm feeling sad, I simply remember my favorite things and then I don't feel so bad."

Peter Wood took me a long way toward James Tyrone, a resilient and charming—but totally selfish—man, performing always. Peter quoted Olivier: "One of the reasons I'm so good at acting is that there is nothing so despicable I can't imagine myself doing it." Tyrone is not despicable, but he is hollow; only his love for his poor, drug-ridden wife is real.

Deborah Kerr played Mary. Her considerable reputation had been largely earned playing thoroughly capable women; the haunted, drifting wraith Mary becomes at the end of the play was a stretch for her. She found an elegiac quality in the part that worked, though.

She was resistant to the textual cuts Peter and I felt had to be made, not only to sharpen the impact of the play, but to get the running time under three hours. No matter how much the audience likes your play, those of them who have to drive back to Malibu or the deep Valley will be a little grumpy if they don't get home by midnight.

The *L.A. Times* was a little grumpy too, but we came up with a sold-out run, breaking the house record I'd set with *Macbeth*. Grosses like that with heavyweights like Shakespeare and O'Neill are something to be proud of. I'm also proud of what we did with Mr. O'Neill's masterpiece.

(Speaking of Deborah Kerr, a true story about Alfred Hitchcock: Long ago when they were still holding what used to be called "star-studded premieres," Deborah and Hitch happened to emerge from the theater at the same time. The studio PR guy told the kid with the bullhorn, "OK, call their limos, but remember, her name is pronounced 'Car,' *not* 'Cur.' " The kid dutifully called out "Miss Karr's car!" and then with equal clarity, "Mr. Hitchcar's cock!")

IN 1978 it was my turn at the Ahmanson again, this time in a reexploration of *A Man for All Seasons*. I was delighted to come back to the play, and the part, again. Robert Bolt wrote it in 1960; I still think there's not been a better one written since then. It's deeply touching, witty, and eloquent; so is its protagonist. Sir Thomas More was one of the outstanding men of the sixteenth century, a time filled with men of both capacity and achievement.

I've played a dozen genuinely great men; they all possess enormous energy, will, and focus. More had a quality not common in such men: he was fun to be around. He liked people, had friends all over Europe; loved his family, music, hunting; and genuinely liked the king who cut his head off.

All this is of course at odds with the definitive interpretation of the part by Paul Scofield, who created the role on stage and won innumerable plaudits when he brought it to the screen, all well earned.

Paul Scofield is one of the outstanding actors of his generation. I still suggest that the astringency that colored his Thomas More is perhaps closer to Scofield than to More. Both Bolt's More and the historic Sir Thomas were men of considerable wit. I submit that a man who can make a joke on his way to the block is a man with a sense of humor.

In any case, every actor chooses his own way into a part, inescapably colored by his own nature. In the six times I've played

More I find myself reaching more and more for the man who loved his life, though he chose to give it up.

Jack O'Brien directed the Ahmanson production, brilliantly, I think. For the first time I found myself with the time and elbow room to explore the play, not just get it on. Jack pointed us toward a brighter tone for many of the scenes. The play can easily fall into a sedate, even lugubrious climate. More is a brilliant lawyer with a rich sense of the humor to be found in the darkest situation.

On trial for his life, when his former protégé, Richard Rich, perjures himself with false testimony that will send More to the scaffold, he touches a gold chain of office Rich is wearing. "What's this?" Cromwell replies: "Sir Richard is appointed Attorney General for Wales."

"For Wales?!" says More, smiling. "Why, Richard, it profits a man nothing to give his soul for the whole world. But for *Wales?*"

The laugh that follows the wretched Rich from the courtroom is invariable and full—but also with an angry, bitter tone. I've never heard a laugh like it. They laugh at More's wry joke, and condemn Rich's betrayal.

When the play opened, we got some pretty good notices, also great business. We didn't quite sell out the run, but we didn't miss by a lot. I went almost at once into a film—two films, in fact, that filled out the rest of the year. Four of the actors from *Man for All Seasons* were cast in the first . . . but I'll get into that when we get back to the movies.

I DID TWO MORE PLAYS at the Ahmanson. The first, in 1980, was *The Crucifer of Blood,* an enormously well-crafted play. The detective story is one of the most enduring genres in all fiction. Its prime creator was Sir Arthur Conan Doyle, who also fathered the greatest detective of all time: Sherlock Holmes.

Holmes, along with his friend and colleague, Dr. Watson, are formidable crime solvers; they also share one of the most enduringly sound friendships in fiction. (Watson is sometimes referred to as "bumbling," but never by Doyle or any good actor who's played him.) He's an ex-army doctor of skill and common sense, innate decency, and a full measure of courage. It's a fine part; Jeremy Brett played it wonderfully with me at the Ahmanson, then went on to an equally fine performance as Holmes through several years of a successful BBC TV series. He played Holmes better than I could've played Watson. *The Crucifer of Blood* is based broadly on Doyle's *The Sign of the Four,* though there's enough new work to make it a separate piece entirely. The author is listed as Paul Giovanni, though some theater people held the play was largely, if not entirely, the work of Peter Shaffer, the gifted English playwright, whose companion Paul had been. Whoever wrote it did a fine piece of work, catching exactly—even enhancing—Doyle's style and structure, both in plot and dialogue.

Crucifer begins with a daring difference: a first act in which Sherlock Holmes doesn't appear. Indeed, he cannot even be expected; the scene is laid in India, in the Red Fort at Agra during the Indian Mutiny in 1857, when Holmes would've been a young boy.

When we finally see the lodgings at 221B Baker Street, they are as we expect. The set, the props, and the furniture must be exactly as Doyle described them more than a century ago. Certain things must happen, because they always do in the Holmes stories.

At least once, for example, there must be an extraordinary display of Holmes' incredible deductive faculty, using only logic and whatever meager physical evidence is available. In *Crucifer,* Watson shows Holmes a gold watch which has "come into my possession" and challenges him to describe the habits and character of its previous owner. Holmes of course does so in minute and perfectly accurate detail, whereupon Watson apologizes for his lack of faith in Holmes' "marvelous faculty."

"I'm the slave of my faculty," Holmes replies. "I am a brain, Watson. The rest of me is a mere appendix." I used that line as a key to the sardonic detachment Holmes displays to the world.

Another iron requirement in any Sherlock Holmes piece is that at some point in the story, Holmes must appear in disguise, usually searching out information he feels he can't get in his own identity. The *Crucifer* disguise role poses an enormous challenge, thus an even bigger opportunity. From one of his mysterious connections, Holmes borrows an opium den on the banks of the Thames and disguises himself as its aged Cantonese proprietor, Fung Tching. I had to persuade the audience through a ten-minute scene that Fung Tching was being played by an ancient Chinese a foot shorter than I. I even wrote a program note about the Chinese actor we'd supposedly cast in the part; his background in Beijing,

his escape from Communist China, and his work in London on both
stage and screen. His name (I just checked the program) was Liu
Han T'seng, "... born in the shadow of the Great Wall, descended
from Genghis Khan's chief lieutenant, Wei Tang," etc., etc. A hell of
an actor.

My two problems were the accent and the makeup. Fortunately, the men I turned to for help in both areas were the best in
the world. No kidding. Bob Easton first, for the Cantonese accent:
Bob could readily teach me the accent; the problem was the pitch.
My voice is a medium bass; it would be a dead giveaway if I couldn't
get up into the falsetto common among Cantonese. Fortunately, I
had several weeks before rehearsal began without too much else
to do, so I put my head down and dug at it. I finally was able to do
the whole scene in a range almost an octave higher than my own. I
also learned to play the part with my back and knees bent under a
loose Chinese robe, making me almost a foot shorter. Fung Tching
was a wonderfully sardonic old bugger; I loved doing him every
night.

Ziggy Geike had a harder job with the makeup, but I think
he enjoys challenges. As a young makeup man, he climbed over the
Berlin Wall and escaped to the West without being shot by the
Communists. I described the character to him: "You understand,
Ziggy, this is on the stage. I have to have a complete makeup . . .
bald cap, beard, long fingernails, and I have to put it on myself."

"Yah, yah; ve could do dat."

"And I have to put it all on myself, including wardrobe, in
the interval between the acts: twenty minutes, with only my dresser
to help."

A slight pause: "Yahh . . . ve could do dat."

"And the main thing is, I have to take it off, *onstage,* in full
view of the audience, revealing Sherlock Holmes, in about four
seconds."

Another, longer pause, then, with a sigh, "Yaaahh. I belief ve
can do dat." And he did. It was a blowout scene. (Sure, I know, it
had nothing to do with performance, but I needed it, and Ziggy
gave it to me.)

We had a very successful production, and why not? We had
thunderstorms, pygmies with blowguns crawling up windows. Still,
I was especially pleased when Wayne Rogers, fellow actor and

friend, came back to the dressing room: "You gotta tell me, Chuck. When the Chinese actor bends over the cabinet and you suddenly straighten up and take over as Holmes, how did you make the switch?"

"There is no Chinese actor, Wayne. There's no switch. That's me all the time." He was dumbfounded.

I DON'T KNOW WHETHER Paul Giovanni wrote *Crucifer* or not, but he surely directed it well. I concentrated on films for the next three years, but my number came up at the Ahmanson again in the fall of 1983. I made one more stab at getting them to do *Becket,* but they balked as before on the problem of getting another actor who would and could alternate the two leading roles with me.

"OK, I give up," I said to Bobby. "Let's do *Detective Story.*" This was the play by Sidney Kingsley in which Lydia had played her first leading role on Broadway. It had looked, briefly, as if it would be my second film, but I was a bit young and green for it; Kirk Douglas did a better job than I could have then. Still, I'd built up an itch for the part, somewhat eased by a summer of playing it with Lydia long ago. This was the time to do it.

When Sidney wrote *Detective Story* in 1949, it was the first play to explore the realities of police life. It's a harsh piece, for its time even brutal, the forerunner of the ongoing series of films and TV dramas on the same subject. As the first line of the script tells you: "The entire action of the play takes place in the detective squad room of a New York precinct police station on a hot day in August between 5:30 and 9 P.M."

I play a tough detective, Jim McLeod, determined, obsessed with the idea he can bring to justice all the evildoers in his precinct. He is in fact on the edge of what they hadn't yet learned to call burnout. His desperate and finally suicidal drama plays out against a kaleidoscopic mélange of police life: shoplifters, petty thieves, troubled kids, mafiosi, crazy ladies, journalists . . . and cops. It really works very well. We gave them a worthwhile restaging of a groundbreaking play.

Paul directed *Story* very well, particularly in handling the multitude of characters—there are thirty-four parts in the play (an unacceptably large number for today's production costs, but Bobby Fryer bit the bullet and hired them). It was a formidable job just getting them on- and offstage; moving them about appropriately for their scenes was even more complex.

One of the very best performances (in, appropriately, the second best part in the play) was Keith Carradine's as Charlie, a murderously dangerous burglar, very good at performing as an innocent man. I take pride in the casting because it was my idea. Though this was a few years before his leap to stardom as Will Rogers in the musical, I'd worked with Keith before (and his father, John, before that). I can smell good acting genes.

Keith was wonderfully Italian (even operatic, properly) in protesting his innocence, vicious in turning on his dim-witted partner, and psychotically murderous when he seizes a gun from a careless detective and holds the whole station at bay.

McLeod has by this time broken with his wife, the only person in the world he loves. He sees in Charlie an equally desperate man, perhaps even an honorable end for himself. He stands up:

> "Give me the gun, Charlie."
> "In the gut you'll get it! One step . . . anybody!"
> "Easy, Jim," says his partner as McLeod moves nearer. "He can't get by the desk. Careful . . . he's a four-time loser."
> "Goddamn right," Charlie snarls. "Rot in jail the resta my life?! I'll take five or six a you bastards wit' me."

McLeod smiles. "You evil son of a bitch," he says, and lunges at him. Charlie shoots him three times in the belly and goes down under two or three detectives as McLeod is blown back over a desk. There's a page or two where McLeod comes to some sort of terms with his own flaws and dies before a priest can come to give him last rites. The last line in the play is the lieutenant's, on the phone to Headquarters: "Notify . . . the Commissioner . . . the D.A., the Homicide Squad. Twenty-first Precinct . . . detective shot . . . killed."

It's a very strong ending, but it needs strong and careful staging, particularly the shooting. Fights of all kinds on the stage have largely been treated very carefully in this century, since actors, not stuntmen, have to do them. True, by the time I was at Northwestern, most acting students were getting some training in falls, tumbling, fencing, and so forth. The movies have forced a higher standard in all sorts of stage violence, as I said a few pages back about *Macbeth*.

Stage shootings, though much safer than sword fights or high falls, used to be done with a very small caliber pistol, often a .22 with a quarter load of powder in a blank cartridge fired offstage by the prop man. Today, this will not satisfy an audience which also goes to the movies. Believe me.

Paul, normally a very confident and forthright director, seemed diffident about staging McLeod's death, neglecting even to block it out in the early rehearsals. I finally sensed he was nervous about firearms. "Paul," I said one morning over coffee, "why don't you let me work this out? I've used guns all my life, including many times on stage and in film. So has Keith."

"Well . . . yes, fine," said Paul. "Yes, do that. Just be sure not to look toward the gun when it goes off, and Keith mustn't point it close to you. Maybe he should only fire one shot? Should you wear padding or something?"

"Paul, please don't worry about it. Trust me, nothing will go wrong. We really need this to be a strong scene." It was, too. We used full-charge blanks in a standard .38 service revolver. No vest was necessary, of course. Keith fired three rounds at my belly from about seven feet away; in nearly a hundred performances, he was never off-target. I picked up a planted blood-bag just before I stood up and burst it against my stomach as I took the shots, wearing light elbow pads so I could hit the desk hard and knock off a typewriter. (We used up four typewriters during the run.) It caught the audience's attention, believe me.

We had a hit for my last play at the Ahmanson . . . so far. I also had a very humbling experience in the course of the *Story* run, perhaps the theater gods rebuking me for my hubris about never missing a performance. It stirred one of my true fears. I don't mind water work, or fire, or animals. I'm comfortable on a horse; I can learn to do combats. What I am afraid of is heights and spiders. Go ahead, laugh. There it is. I suppose it's appropriate, therefore, that it was a spider that almost brought me low. By the eighties, audiences were coming to the theater on weekends more and more. We started doing two performances a day both Saturday and Sunday, and going dark on Monday. It worked very well.

One Sunday morning, after a few sets of tennis, I was lounging on our living room floor, leaning against the long stone hearth

that extends outward from the fireplace, drinking a non-beer before showering and shaving for the matinee. Driving down to the Ahmanson, I felt an itch on the back of my left hand, growing to a swelling that smarted a bit. By the time the curtain went up, my hand had swelled to the point where it was very painful if I let it hang normally. If it had been my right hand, I don't know how I could've managed. As it was, I kept the left hooked in my belt or holding my lapel most of the time—it must've looked very odd.

The last half of the second act was worse—I must've looked drunk by then. I was stumbling a bit and my hand was throbbing, with red streaks running up my wrist. I could hardly wait to get shot. (I thought I might be dying anyway.)

Between performances, I fell into a deep sleep and woke feeling faintly better . . . at least no worse. My dresser had just helped me into a clean shirt for the evening show when Bobby Fryer knocked on my dressing room door. "Chuck, I think I'd better put in your understudy tonight. Okay?"

I walked over to him and put my good hand carefully on his shoulder. "Bobby," I said softly, "if you put on my understudy tonight, I will kill you. Do you understand me?" He nodded. "Thank you. This performance will be better . . . I promise you."

It was, too, though pretty shaky. The house doctor came back in the interval, but could offer no useful diagnosis, except that I appeared to have been bitten by something, which couldn't have happened without my noticing. I did let them drive me home afterward, and slept eleven hours.

I called Jolly West the next morning and described my experience. "It sounds to me like you've been bitten by a brown recluse spider. The most dangerous spider in North America, though fairly rare and quite small—no bigger than your thumb nail. Its bite is anesthetic, which is why you didn't feel it. With your constitution, you'll no doubt survive, but you'd better get over here to UCLA and get an antidote. As it is, you'll probably end up with a little pit in your hand where you were bitten." (I did, too. I don't know where Jolly picks up this stuff. He's supposed to be a psychiatrist, for God's sake.)

Lydia had flown to Washington to witness her brother Bob's retirement from the army; she was shaken to phone and find me in bed, where I spent most of the time for the next few days when I wasn't onstage. "For Pete's sake, Charlie, I go away for two days and you almost get yourself killed!" I did improve every day, of course. Every performance was less painful, though it took almost two weeks for the swelling to disappear entirely, and the little pit on the back of my hand is still faintly visible. Yes, I'm still edgy about spiders.

OK, THAT'S the Ahmanson record, but I've changed my mind. I think we ought to do London, too, while we're at it. It's only a couple of plays, but they came off very well and good things flowed from them. About then, Bobby Fryer introduced me to Duncan Weldon. Duncan had by then become the most active independent producer of straight drama in the London theater, as I expect he is still. Only the subsidized government theaters—the National and the Royal Shakespeare—did more plays.

Duncan wanted me to do a play for him, in London. You have to understand that the capital of the English-speaking theater is still London. Every American actor who does theater wants to play there. When the *Antony and Cleopatra* company where I began on Broadway as a kid ended its long run, Godfrey Tearle was going back for a season at Stratford. He'd asked me to join him but, since I was a no-name actor, the British union had turned me down. Now I was welcome at last.

My journal doesn't note, nor can I recall, which of us suggested the play I should do, though it was instantly recognized as the right choice. Herman Wouk's World War II novel, *The Caine Mutiny,* had been a huge success, as has just about every other book he's written. A widely successful, Academy-nominated film was made, flawed only with the difficulties of encompassing a complex novel covering the closing months of the war into two hours of screen time. I think Mr. Wouk understood this beforehand. Before the film opened, he'd composed a play focused on the crucial event of his novel: the court-martial of the executive officer of the destroyer minesweeper USS *Caine* for relieving his captain from duty at the height of a Pacific typhoon.

The Caine Mutiny Court-Martial is a wonderfully crafted but somewhat quirkily disturbing play. The protagonist is a Jewish naval lieutenant, Greenwald, a failed flyer but a good lawyer who hates

his assignment to defend the accused exec. He succeeds in this task
by persuading the court (and the audience) that the real culprit is
the ship's captain, Lieutenant Commander Queeg, whom he reveals
as a petty tyrant, liar, thief, and physical coward.

I flew to Washington to clean up a couple of chores, but
primarily to breakfast with Herman Wouk about my doing his play.
He heartily approved the idea in almost any context: I could do
either or both of the two leading roles, and/or direct, as I chose.
On the noon plane home, I decided to direct (which I'd not done
on stage for some time) and play Captain Queeg.

Queeg is a dream of a part, especially if you're going to
direct as well. He has only two scenes: he's the first witness called
in Act I, when he seems a model officer. In Act II, he's the last
witness; in the course of a riveting cross-examination, Greenwald
breaks through his shell and reveals the quivering paranoia beneath. I don't get many chances to play guys that unravel completely. I was looking forward to it.

Back in California, I managed to negotiate a deal with British
Equity; they allowed us to import a largely American cast. I abhor
the idea of quota casting of any kind. You should use the best actors
you can get for the parts—always. Fray helped me enormously with
the auditions here; we found some very good actors, including a
couple from *Detective Story*.

On the first day of 1985 I left my ridge for what I knew
would be at least half a year, stopping overnight in Chicago to see
my mother. My sister had died not long before; my mother was
only then coming back to an even keel. Having lost her parents and
two husbands, she told me there is no loss like that of a child. I can
well believe it.

We had time for the Art Institute exhibition on Sargent, a
painter we were both fond of, only then edging back into fashion,
and lunch at the Pump Room, and touching base at all the places
you remember, going home. Thomas Wolfe was wrong . . . you can
go home again. It's just hard to do.

In London, I checked into the Dorchester. I've stayed there
since 1952, so it feels pretty much like home to me. It was a good
base for preparing the play. One of my first moves was breakfast
with Ben Cross, fresh off his triumph in *Chariots of Fire*. I was
anxious to use a Brit as Lieutenant Greenwald, and I'd heard that

Ben had a very good American accent. So he did, certainly as good as the English accent I'd used in several parts. All the roles in *Caine* are American naval officers and enlisted men; I managed to recruit an appropriate Yank crew, with a couple of Canadians, resident Americans, and Brits with an ear for accent like Ben's. One of these was a young English actor I cast as Signalman Urban. I decided to make him a Georgia farm boy. An enormous number of Southerners enlisted in that war, and the Southern accent is the easiest American regional accent for Brits to learn. I wrote his entire role out phonetically and taught him myself; he did a wonderful job. There are more than a few laughs in *Caine,* but Urban's scene is the best of them; he usually got an exit hand.

Ten days into rehearsal, with the play well blocked and the actors settling well, I gave the cast Saturday off and took the Concorde back to Washington, D.C., for President Reagan's second inauguration. (The night before I left, I stopped by a reception where I met a British Airways captain who flew the Concorde. When I mentioned I'd be riding her for the first time, he cocked an eyebrow at my height and said, "She's a lovely bird, but she discriminates against two classes: the poor and the tall.") In fact, I can just stand erect in the cabin, and I got to Washington before we took off, given the time change. Besides, my girl was waiting at the gate. So were Fraser and his wife, Marilyn (more on that later); he was on his way up the Amazon to research a script he was writing for Warners.

I was glad to see them, and to congratulate the president on his second term, but it turned out to be the coldest inaugural in the history of the Republic. The swearing-in, scheduled to be witnessed by thousands, had to be moved indoors, though most of the gala performances went off properly. I read Washington's second inaugural address at one of them.

Lydia was of course catching the midnight plane back to London with me. We boarded through the umbilical, feeling an icy wind through the seal, but the cabin was warm enough. After we took off, though, there was a call on the intercom for a doctor. One of the hostesses, standing for twenty minutes in the door welcoming the boarding passengers, actually had frostbitten feet.

About once in ten years, it works perfectly. The plane was on time, the car met us at the stairs, they walked us through Immigration, and our bags were first down the chute. I dropped Lydia off at the Dorch and drove on to the rehearsal hall to reboard the *Caine* and go back to work.

The whole production fell into place with uncanny ease. It's impossible to explain the curious fascination audiences find in courtroom dramas. There can really be no physical action at all: the judge and jury sit in specific seats, the witnesses come and go in turn, sitting in the same chair; only the prosecution and the defense attorneys have any latitude of movement, and that minimal. Still, it's riveting, as we've seen in real life in the trial of O. J. Simpson for murder. Just so, a well-written courtroom drama can hold an audience spellbound. *The Caine Mutiny Court-Martial* did exactly that.

After twenty-three days of rehearsal, fitting the uniforms and checking the set, we trucked the show down to Brighton for the pre–West End tour. We set a record there, also in Bath. Of course I was delighted by our success, but also overwhelmed simply to be working in theaters where the great actors of history had played. The Theatre Royal in Bath is where Edmund Kean, surely one of the greatest of all time, arrived late for an engagement, having eccentrically chosen to walk from the previous stop on his tour. (This is the actor of whom Byron said, "Watching Kean act is like reading Shakespeare by flashes of lightning.") Not a bad notice.

The sweating manager gave Kean his stipulated salary: a hundred guineas in gold in a chamois bag *in his hand* before each performance. "We . . . ahh, have no time for a rehearsal now, Mr. Kean. Do you, umm . . . have any instruction for the other actors?"

"Instruction?! No, by God," said Kean. "Just tell 'em to keep a good arm's length out o' me way."

We then did a week in Manchester, where we played the Palace, a huge 2,200-seat nineteenth-century house that was really a bit large for our play. It was not, happily, too large for our audience. We ended our week with an all-time record gross for a drama in Britain: 123,000 pounds sterling. The record meant more to me than the extra money it earned me.

I had an extraordinary experience on the opening night at the Manchester Palace: I lived out in real life the Actor's Nightmare. (You've never heard of it? That's because you're not an actor. One version goes like this. You're in the theater, ready to perform, and you somehow cannot find your way to the stage. I've never known a professional actor who hasn't experienced some version of this nightmare . . . more than once or twice.)

So: opening night at the Manchester Palace. I was a little anxious about the size of the theater and its acoustics, sight lines, and light angles. *Caine* opens with a six-minute scene in the empty courtroom between defense attorney Greenwald and Lieutenant Maryk, the accused, then the court convenes, and the first witness is called: Captain Queeg, my part. I'd found there was time for me to go out front to the back of the house, leaving off my uniform jacket, and check out the sound-and-light balance. I did this and began to make my way backstage for my own entrance (having turned down an offer of escort, insulted that anyone would imagine I couldn't find my way around a theater). Well, I couldn't, at least not in this Victorian rabbit warren.

Panicked, I burst through a fire door, found myself in the alley, and ran down to the stage door where my dresser was waiting almost in tears with my jacket. I buttoned it three seconds before my cue and stepped into my first scene. Half a minute earlier, running toward the stage door in the rain, I'd almost persuaded myself it was only the nightmare and I'd waken in my own bed any second.

I wonder if other professionals have this burden. Do bank presidents dream of walking into the vault on a routine check and finding it empty, generals of launching a major attack and finding the enemy is on the other flank, surgeons of standing naked in the operating theater with a nail file for a scalpel? I doubt it, somehow. Actors tend to live out their worst fantasies—which may not be entirely bad.

We swept into London on a wave of advance publicity, largely generated by Duncan's people, and a good thing too. The English audiences are among the best in the world; if you can get them to respond, you're home free. So we did, in fact. One or two critics carped a bit about the structure of the play (as someone always does about any play more than ten years old not written by Shakespeare, Shaw, or Ibsen), but by and large we got raves.

We deserved them. Hank Fonda, one of America's best actors, had created the role of Lieutenant Greenwald, but Ben Cross brought a kind of dark saturninity to it that I found useful as a director. John Corey, who'd had a pretty good part in *Detective Story,* had a much better one in *Caine.* He played Maryk, the defendant, with a dogged earnestness that was exactly right. John Schuck had been my partner in *Story;* he was the prosecutor in *Caine* and made a great deal out of a difficult part.

My performance as Captain Queeg was much admired, with all kinds of embarrassing superlatives to put in the ads. (What crap . . . I wasn't embarrassed, I was delighted.) Of course it's an incredibly good part, structured for a triumph.

Mr. Wouk knew exactly what he was about. Queeg gives the first testimony of the trial; he seems the perfect naval officer, composed, informed, at ease, with no hint of the terrified paranoid that lives inside him. He also testifies last, near the end of the play, when Greenwald gradually reduces him to a pitiable wreck pursuing the ghosts of past and present enemies in and out of reality.

It's a wonderfully written scene, lasting twenty-some minutes (even the nine minutes the film version had time to spend on the whole court-martial earned Humphrey Bogart an Academy nomination, not least because he was so right for the part).

I'm not, in fact. Wouk describes Queeg as short and insecure about his height. I simply went at it from the other end; in the first scene I played Queeg as though he were right (as you must always do, of course, whatever kind of man you're playing), and a thoroughly competent officer. On a certain level, the utter collapse of a strong and forthright man is even more shocking.

I had an unusual problem with Queeg's final speech. I have a strong mnemonic faculty; I've always been able to learn lines in the course of rehearsing them, without studying. I couldn't do that with Queeg's final wandering monologue, which runs nearly six minutes. As he progresses toward dementia, the speech becomes less and less logical, without specific connections from one subject to another. For the first time in my life, I had to really study the speech before I got it nailed down.

Settling into a long run of a hit play is a pleasant experience. Once you've opened, you no longer need devote every waking hour to the play: restaging key scenes, soothing anxious actors, sorting out wardrobe and set problems, and doing interviews on which "the success of the play may depend." That's over once you open (though never entirely, of course). Still, you can set up some sort of a life. I was able to play tennis a couple of times a week—indoors, of course. Tennis outdoors in England is often a bad bet, even during Wimbledon, given the amount of rain.

A special pleasure was Holly. She was living in London then, having completed her studies at Pepperdine and a year at the Sorbonne focused on nineteenth-century European painting. She'd gotten an apprenticeship at Christie's in London (though she was later to realize her American passport blocked the road to promotion, whereupon she went to New York, found a better job at Sotheby's and, in due time, an extraordinary husband and an even brighter future).

But in the winter of 1985, she was there, in a tiny flat in South Kensington. Of course she came to the opening; Fray and Marilyn came over for that as well (Fray was wrestling with an Irish film he was interested in). Carol Lanning had been there through most of the rehearsals, making the rough way smooth, as is her wont.

They'd all gone back; we were settling in. I remember I had time to help Holly edit a paper she was doing on John Singer Sargent that would more or less determine her future at Christie's. I'm good at editing text. I should be; it's been a crucial factor in making my living for almost half a century. Still, it was wonderful to see a young mind prodded into exploring the glories of the language to communicate what she knew about the painter (which was a hell of a lot more than I did).

We had a major setback in March, when it became clear that Lydia would have to have her back cut again, the second attempt to repair the damage done long before when she slipped on the coral of the Great Barrier Reef and tried to save her cameras from getting wet. We had the services of one of the major specialists in the field. John O'Brien was Australian, but like all British surgeons, preferred to be called "Mr." O'Brien, not "Dr."

The surgery seemed successful, but the convalescence was long and very painful, for both of us. While she was in the hospital, I could only stop by two or three times a day, on my way to and from performances. It was nearly two months before she was fully mobile again. Our good friend Maggie Field came over from Paris

for a couple of weeks, which helped enormously. And there was
Holly.

Meantime, the play kept charging on, and I had no choice but to serve it. I'd originally agreed to play through April, but we were still selling out then, so I agreed to extend the run two months more. "O, to be in England, now that April's there," seemed like not such a bad idea, with my girl coming back to herself again.

Of course the closing weeks were studded with celebrations almost every Sunday (our day off). Duncan gave a luncheon at his country house near Guilford; I threw a company party; we were invited to a large do given by Charlie Price, the American ambassador.

At the latter affair, I was over-awed to find that my dinner partner was Prime Minister Thatcher, a woman I admire enormously. As we gathered for coffee in the garden afterward, I sought out Lydia and boasted, "Guess who I sat next to . . . Margaret Thatcher!" The love of my life looked at me coolly and said, "Guess who *I* sat next to . . . Cary Grant." Point, game, set, match, obviously.

We closed *Caine* the last Saturday in June to tumultuous applause—hands on almost every scene, multiple curtain calls, flowers, forty minutes' worth of fans waiting outside the stage door. It made me feel we'd truly left a mark there.

Three days later, having packed (a function I've decided is roughly compounded by the square of the weeks you've been away, which means we took eighteen bags of various sizes to Heathrow), we said farewell to England. About twelve hours later, we were back on our ridge, with our Fourth of July party to give the next day. I was happy as a clam at high tide.

I was by no means through with *Caine,* mind you. I filmed till the following winter, then mounted *Caine* again for Los Angeles. The Ahmanson, which I'd come to regard as my private turf, was not available; *The Phantom of the Opera* had taken up residence, and would remain for several years (earning us several millions of dollars to reinvent that theater).

Even the Doolittle, the best medium-sized theater in town, was booked. We ended up at the Henry Fonda, a nice but very small house, which meant we couldn't gross as much. I didn't care, really.

I was very proud of what we'd done with Mr. Wouk's play; I wanted a Los Angeles run.

We had another success. John Schuck had a film to do, so I cast Stephen Macht, who'd been so good in both the Ahmanson *Man for All Seasons* and *Mountain Men*. He had a different tone from Ben's in the role, but he did a heroic job of learning the whole part in a few days so he could fit in with the actors in the cast who'd done the play in London.

It's true that when we got to Washington (yes, Roger Stevens wanted me to bring the play to the Kennedy Center, too), Stephen and John Corey, our Maryk, conceived a dislike for each other. I can't recall what the issue was; I did note that one of the advantages of having the director also in the cast is that he's handy to play Daddy when needed. I tried to do that.

Fortunately, their performances did not suffer. The President and Mrs. Reagan attended and came back afterward to meet every member of our large cast, which I thought was very good of them. At a private dinner later, they had nice things to say, as well. Throughout our Washington run we had a good number of navy people in the audience, better equipped than most to judge the realities in the play.

Amazingly, the greatest challenge *Caine* could offer was still ahead. Meanwhile, I spent a good bit of time in front of the cameras and then accepted another offer from Duncan Weldon to do a part in Britain he knew I couldn't refuse: to take over the title role in a company he had running at the Chichester Festival of *A Man for All Seasons*.

I accepted, of course; I couldn't resist one more shot at Sir Thomas, especially on his own turf. We flew out on October 1, the morning of the Great Whittier Narrows Earthquake. (It wasn't so great, really, unless you lived in Whittier. In Coldwater Canyon, it only disturbed the rhythm of our packing.) Our good friend and neighbor Clori Isaac was alone in their house; I walked up the hill to comfort her a bit, then we caught our polar flight on schedule.

Oddly enough, two weeks later London was visited with the worst windstorm in this century, leveling thousands of hundred-year-old oaks over all of southern Britain.

It didn't level me, however. I'd done the play often over twenty years; I knew More well. But in the city of his birth and

martyrdom, I found him waiting for me just around the corner. The
rest of the company had just closed their run in Chichester; it was
no great task to adjust them to me, and me to them.

They were very good, as was their director, Frank Hauser,
who did with me what I like from a director: he pushed me. In ten
days of rehearsal, I was ready to open. I was looking forward to
playing the Savoy, one of the great West End houses, hard by the
Savoy Hotel. It's historically significant as the first theater in the
world to use electric light. Around the turn of the century, Sir
Arthur Sullivan, then producing his comic operettas with W. S. Gil-
bert at the Savoy, strode to the front of the stage with a small
hammer in one hand and a lighted electric bulb on a trailing wire
in the other. He smashed the bulb, demonstrating the safety of
electricity, and a new age in stage lighting was born.

Sir John Gielgud saw the production, early in its run, and
came back to my dressing room with desultory praise. "Mmm, yes,
very good, Chuck. Well done, indeed. Lovely play." Then, bright-
ening, "Ah, yes, I remember. The star dressing room has no toilet."
He was right.

I expected our business to be dampened by the really horrendous damage the windstorm had done, but we did close to sell-
out business from the first night. *The London Times,* bless their
heart, was particularly generous to me.

I treasured even more Robert Bolt's comment. He'd recently
suffered a devastating stroke, which made it impossible for him to
attend a regular performance, but he struggled up to the front row
of the mezzanine for our last rehearsal. When I went up to talk to
him afterward, he said, with great difficulty but perfect clarity, "I . . .
am . . . oo-ver the . . . *mooon* at . . . what you . . . did." I'll settle for
that.

Our success in London was enhanced on the road, where
we spent several weeks breaking house records in Newcastle, Croy-
don (a very ugly theater, but as Duncan Weldon observed, "Nothing
makes an actor like a theater more than a lack of empty seats"). It
is nice to go in the stage door and see SOLD OUT pasted over the
posters.

We did Brighton and Bath again, as we had with *Caine Mutiny,* then York and Aberdeen, where we sold 107 percent of capacity by putting chairs in some stage boxes they hadn't used in years.

Though both of us loved being in Britain, this was a long way from being Lydia's happiest time there. Not long before we left Los Angeles, she'd undergone her last and permanently healing back surgery. Racketing around England and Scotland in limos and airplanes did not significantly contribute to her recovery, especially in concert with the medication prescribed for her. All in all, not ideal conditions for convalescence from spinal surgery. More than once, we made plans for her to go back to the States and a more sedate recovery, but she is not a lady who gives up easily.

She made a point of attending the performances at least twice in every city to provide the input I've come to rely on from her. She was often in pain, but she was there. There were good times, too. We both loved the Aberdeen engagement, where they housed us in a manor next to a salmon stream. Scotland is far enough north to have pines, like the Michigan woods where I grew up. My girl came out with me one morning in a light snowfall, and we walked along the river as we had beside Lake Michigan a lifetime before at Northwestern, her gloved hand in the crook of my arm and the snow covering it there.

It meant a lot to me to have such a success, in England, with a part that I'd been hacking away at for so long. It meant even more when Fraser opened another door: the chance to film *Man for All Seasons*. But that's for the next chapter . . . on more movies.

THE STAGE had one more really stunning challenge for me. We went back home, back to England for *Man for All Seasons* on film, then home again in June of 1988 for what looked like a quiet summer of editing the movie. It also seemed the ideal time to get a little patchwork done on my plumbing. I checked into the hospital early one morning, lay painlessly under the cutting and stitching for an hour, then back home before lunch and ran some reels with my editor, Eric, in the afternoon (editing a film is a sedentary process, not much running or heavy lifting involved). I had been admonished to refrain from any amatory athletics for a few days, till the stitches came out. I explained this to Lydia. "Actually, the whole thing is going to fall off in a day or so. The good news is, another one will grow back soon, and it will only be seventeen years old."

You can imagine my shock when the dressings came off the

next day and I found the equipment had turned a virulent and multihued purple . . . balls and all. The surgeon assured me it was a temporary and perfectly normal reaction, fading in a few days. I still felt I could only display it to her accompanied by a commemorative verse, which I composed and wrote out in my best calligraphic script,

With Apologies to Gelett Burgess

I've never seen a purple cock.
I never thought there'd be one.
But think of this, to ease the shock:
Be glad it's not a wee one.

She was amused and reassured, though I suppose a tad disappointed when the seventeen-year-old version never materialized.

Instead, almost equally startling, was a call from Jimmy Doolittle. He's one of the most energetic and resourceful producers in California. Would I be interested in directing a play in China?

"That'd be different," I said. "What play?"

The Caine Mutiny Court-Martial. In Chinese."

"Jimmy, you've got my attention. Why me, though? Why this play?"

"The Ministry of Culture knows your work, they know you've done *Caine Mutiny*. They want to give their theater some experience in American realistic drama. This is the play they want to do and they want you to direct it."

I thought about it overnight. *Caine* attempts to define democracy in terms of a justice system the Chinese Communists know little about and care less. Besides, why *me,* a known anti-Communist? Still, next day I called him back. "You're pretty slick, pal. You know damn well this is too special to pass up. I guess I'm your man."

THIS CONSIDERABLY complicated my life. For one thing, I had the film version of *Man for All Seasons* to edit. Well, Fray could take that over, as indeed he did. Would I get paid anything? Nooo, the Chinese Reds don't like to do that. Not even expenses? Well . . . tickets on their airline. (In the end, the Great Wall hotel in Beijing, an American Sheraton, put us in a handsome suite on the cuff as a contribution to our cross-cultural venture, which was damn nice of them.)

By mid-September, we were airborne on a very long flight to Beijing. I tend to go into hibernation on airplanes, but Lydia woke me somewhere east of Japan in really rock-rough air, with hail rattling on the windows, needing to be held. When I did, she murmured what Martha Gellhorn said to Ernest Hemingway when he held her as they were being shelled in a Madrid hotel during the Spanish Civil War: "Living with you is like being in a blizzard—only the snow is warm." I was touched.

We checked into the Great Wall Sheraton about 3 A.M. local time, glad to have a big bed. I slept at once and deeply, then, before going to the theater, I had coffee with Winston Lord, our ambassador here, and his wife, Bette, with whom I'd met in L.A. Both were most warm and forthcoming, though he obviously had a larger agenda than our little undertaking, of which she, I think, was the prime architect. She's also a successful writer of formidable creative and cultural credentials, flawlessly expert in both English and Mandarin. In addition, she's a volcano of energy. I'd need all the help she could give me.

I eased into rehearsals at the People's Art Theater, a large, somewhat dusty complex built in 1955, a theater with many of the design flaws of the Ahmanson. East is East and West is West, but we can both design theaters full of errors.

Ying Ruocheng, one of China's most distinguished actors, was our mentor through all this. Perhaps they were testing him. During the Cultural Revolution of the sixties, he was rendered a "nonperson," to use a Soviet phrase.

Solzhenitsyn describes in *The Gulag Archipelago* the range of indignities, humiliations, abominations, and murders visited on Russians labeled as nonpersons. I had no idea, nor did Ying Ruocheng ever mention, what his punishment was. Many, many thousands of Chinese were simply exiled for years of work, tending pigs or making bricks (without straw, no doubt). Many, many thousands more died. He survived. Toughness counts, I would think.

In 1988, his reputation restored, Ying Ruocheng was Vice Minister of Culture. Approval of our project in general, deciding which American play to do and the invitation to me to direct it, was crucially his. For good measure, Ruocheng personally translated the play into Mandarin.

They set up a very creditable rehearsal set, with doors and stairs and furniture—much more complete than IATSE (our stage-hands' union in the U.S.) would ever let us rehearse in back home.

They showed me a run-through of the play as they'd prepared it to that point. Unbelievably, almost all the actors knew almost all their lines. Even the blocking had been sketched in, an absolute first in my experience as a director (or as an actor, for that matter). ("Blocking" means deciding where the actors stand on the stage, and when and how they get there.)

I'd never before come to the first day of rehearsal not knowing one member of the cast. We stood on tiptoe staring at each other over the language barrier, smiling anxiously. I doubt they'd ever heard my name. ("Who's this big round-eye? Why is he directing us?") I know they'd heard of *Ben-Hur* and *The Ten Commandments,* but no foreign film made since 1949 has ever been shown commercially in China.

Ren Ming, my tall, lean assistant, had done a superb job with the actors. While they had no experience of Western acting, they knew that the traditional Chinese style is somewhat more formal. They understood we were going to explore a looser approach.

The actors seemed keen to start, but it didn't hurt to let that edge build a little. I let them go home and turned to the technicians (often a thorny bunch, anywhere in the world). These seemed OK, though the lighting man had many anxieties, particularly about his equipment. "Some of it is forty years old!"

"My equipment's a hell of a lot older than that," I said. "We'll manage." Even in translation, I got the laugh; it helped break the ice a bit. My main problem, as I knew from the start, was language. I had two interpreters, one a pretty young woman with a dazzling smile who did messages and phone calls, a bilingual gofer, I suppose. Her name was very difficult to pronounce, so we settled on an English approximation that seemed to amuse her: Miss Rainbow. Then there was Mme. Xie (no, that's *not* so hard to pronounce: you just start to say "X" and switch to "Zhee"), an extraordinary lady with wise eyes and lightning facility in switching from English to Mandarin and back. Her composure suggested how she had endured what she went through in the Cultural Revolution (along with millions of her countrymen, of course). Since then, most of her work has been in translating American plays. I was awed by her facility at a press conference at the hotel the morning before the first rehearsal, watching her flick back and forth from Mandarin to French and English. She was a remarkable lady. I could hardly have had a better tongue to reach my actors.

There was the tea, too. On my right was a round low table, decorated with dragons, for my handsomely painted porcelain mug. When I came in the morning, the cup was waiting, a quarter full of dry tea leaves. Someone instantly filled it with very hot water and kept it so all day. I never saw anyone adding either water or fresh leaves, but the tea was always strong, black and *there*. I don't even *like* tea, particularly, but that did the job.

(I didn't notice till some days later that, while all the actors had personal tea mugs, most of them were Nescafé jars insulated with personalized string wrapping. These guys were actors in the most distinguished company in China—and they were bicycling to work and drinking tea out of instant coffee jars. Socialism at work.)

I was amazed at how easy it was—and how useful—just to step into a scene and play it in English, while the other actors played it in Mandarin. "Please watch," I'd say. "Let me be you." (I'd learned how to say this in Mandarin.)

I knew the script almost verbatim, of course, and the scenes were there. It's hard to explain; I'd never have guessed it, but it worked, wonderfully. It also let me leap over the language barrier and reach the actors directly, *doing* for them what I meant, rather than having the estimable Mme. Xie tell them what I meant.

True, I had to do this by acting it with them, unavoidably *giving them readings*. When I was studying at Northwestern (God, we were all so *sure,* then. We were seventeen and we *knew!*), they practically sent you to directing jail for giving an actor a reading. In fact, since I was acting the scene in a different language, what I gave them was not a "reading," but the body temperature of the line, the chemistry of the character.

We had a curious small crisis one day. I resolved it easily enough, but I learned a little about the Chinese and a lot about Communist bureaucracy in the process. There were about a hundred actors permanently employed in the company, on a shamefully small yearly salary, with some of them getting living quarters in the compound as well. When they were actually performing in a play, there was an additional stipend, its size depending solely on the actor's seniority in the company. When *Caine Mutiny* opened, some of the older actors cast as members of the court, who never spoke, were paid more than the actors who played the leading roles.

I found out that an additional stipend was paid to actors who were rehearsing, a flat fifty cents a day. This seemed to me such a revoltingly tiny sum that I felt driven to do something about it. I called Bette Bao Lord at the embassy and made her understand how strongly I felt. It was well enough for me to work free: I could afford it, and they couldn't afford to pay me. But to rehearse eight hours a day for fifty cents? I told Bette I'd like to contribute a few hundred dollars to flesh out our company's rehearsal compensation. She said she'd like to join me but pointed out that the actors would be compelled to throw the money into a common pot, to share with everyone else in the People's Art Theater. "I won't do that, Bette," I said. "I don't believe in that. I want to get the money in the pockets of the people who are doing the work: the actors, the assistants, the interpreters who are helping us raise *Caine.*" Bette agreed and undertook to go to Ying Ruocheng at the Ministry of Culture. He agreed, too, which bore a little more weight, and we gave the money, shared among only the *Caine* company. A done deal.

Not quite. The next morning, as always, I was in the rehearsal room well before nine. Given the language barrier, I couldn't be part of the usual actors' morning banter. We greeted each other in Mandarin (I could do that, but I didn't want to put Mme. Xie to work before I had to). I read the *Herald-Tribune* for ten minutes, then discussed the scenes I wanted to work on with Ren Ming, my assistant. At ten of nine, I got the actors' attention and announced the work schedule for the day, then sat down to finish my tea before the hour ticked over. I suddenly noticed an odd little man in a double-breasted suit and a blue tam standing in the center of the room addressing the company—in Mandarin, of course. I leaned over and asked Mme. Xie what he was saying.

She listened a moment. "More or less what you just told the actors," she said.

I got the pitch. I walked to the center of the room and said,

"I don't know what the custom is in China, but in America no one gives instructions to the actors but the director. When this man has left our rehearsal, we will begin. I don't want to see him in this theater again."

It turned out he had been an executive there during the shambles of the Cultural Revolution, when the current and previous head of the theater had been banished to shoveling pig shit. The little man in the tam had hung on in a minor clerical position, and thought to join our company and thus earn the rehearsal bonus, too.

I had no illusions, of course. He wouldn't set foot in the compound while we were working there, but once the big ugly round-eye had gone, he'd be back, doing whatever it was he did. Full employment . . . among the joys of the welfare state.

An odd thing happened while we were working on Captain Queeg's breakdown scene. You have to be careful in rehearsal to direct your actors as privately as you can, especially when you're asking them to explore very intimate emotions. I went to where Zhu (the actor playing Queeg) was sitting in the witness chair and knelt beside him to make a point. There was a sudden, very audible gasp from every Chinese in the room. Zhu stood up, distressed. Mme. Xie explained to me afterward that I was surrendering face as director by kneeling to an actor. There were cultural complications here.

HERMAN WOUK and his wife, Sarah, flew in from the States for the opening. I was very pleased he wanted to come. Of course, they came to the tech that night, as did Lydia (well-cameraed) and the other people who'd made this happen. This was in theory a technical run-through, but there must've been 150 people in the house, mostly drama students, with some others as well, including, I was startled to find, the critics. This is the custom there; not a terrible idea.

After I'd dismissed the actors, we had what could've been a really serious confrontation. Bette Bao Lord came up to me in the little huddle of technicians sorting through the glitches. "Chuck," she said, "there's a problem." She often said that to me and then proceeded to solve it herself, with the energy and dedication of a tigress. This seemed different. "You said it was OK to have photographers in the front row for the preview tomorrow?"

"That's right. I'm not enchanted with the idea, but you said we've had an awful lot of requests for coverage."

"But there are four photographers who want to shoot on opening night, too."

"Too bad," I said. "They can't." Well, we then had about fifteen minutes on this, increasingly impassioned on the Chinese side (not Bette Lord; she did her extraordinary best to mediate). I saw this was one I had to win, for the play. You don't do that by getting mad, or yelling. Tough counts a lot.

"Please tell me one shot you can get on opening night that you can't get the night before, with the other twenty-seven photographers," I said to the four men in question. Well . . . the shots of the speeches afterward and the presentation of the flowers.

"Fine, you can shoot the flowers. But if one of you takes out a camera during the performance on opening night, I will personally throw you out of the theater. I am able to do that. I *will* do that."

It was clear by then that the only reason these four guys wanted to shoot opening night was to demonstrate that they could shoot when nobody else could. For some curious reason, they are the official government photographers. I sensed a move to postpone it all and somehow slip it through at the opening, when the big broken-nosed round-eye had forgotten about it. The theater manager, a perfectly fine man, cleared his throat and said equably, "Well, we will talk to the board."

"Don't do that," I said. "This discussion is over. On opening night, the play belongs to the actors and the audience. There will be no photographers during the performance." All this was painfully thrown back and forth over the language barrier, which never seemed so high. As I turned to go out to the car, I said to Bette Lord, who could read these things from both sides, "Be sure they understand this, Bette. I've been infinitely flexible on a lot of problems—painting the stage floor, intercoms, better audiotapes—things they can't afford. That's fine. *This* is nothing but vanity. I won't damage the play and distract the actors for that. I just drew a line in the dust. No further. Believe me."

It wasn't really a large problem, of course. If this was our only major difference—and it was—it meant the whole cross-cultural, international undertaking had worked. It had. After I discussed the whole thing with Lydia, she said, as I turned out the light, "Maybe Herman Wouk can help you on this."

"I don't need any help, honey," I said. "We're OK now."

And so we were. We had a truly triumphant opening. After Lydia and I went home, the play ran all through the winter. They took it up north for a successful engagement in Shanghai, then brought it back to Beijing, where it was still running in early June, when the demonstrations began in Tiananmen Square. I learned later that our actors gathered there, wearing the jackets I gave them with the *Caine* logo on the back and carrying a sign that said *The Caine Mutiny Court-Martial*. That evening, the power was cut at the theater, making it impossible to perform. Later still, I got a letter from my stage manager, by then in Singapore, translated into very guarded English. My contacts in the State Department advised against trying to reach any of the Chinese I worked with, for fear it would worsen their situation. I'm still glad I did the play. I'll bet they are, too.

OVER THE LAST FEW YEARS, the only play I've done is Pete Gurney's *Love Letters,* an unusually structured piece consisting entirely of letters between a man and a woman over fifty-some years, starting when they're both eight years old. The period covered by the play (the mid-thirties to the eighties) and the socioeconomic status of the two characters (both are Ivy League WASPs, he from an affluent family, she from a truly wealthy one) would seem to limit its relevance for contemporary audiences.

Not so. Though it consists of two people sitting side by side reading letters, never looking at one another, the play has enchanted audiences just about everywhere in the world. It's been played by couples as young as eighteen, of various races and nationalities.

It probably works best with mature actors; no actor can actually encompass all the ages involved, but I can vividly recall what it was to be fourteen, and thirty, and forty-five. My character, Andy Ladd, at eight, I understood instantly.

I know of very few plays that are as genuinely funny and at the same time as deeply moving as *Love Letters*. I've played it with five actresses in a number of different cities: Jean Simmons, Stephanie Beacham, Alexis Smith, Carol Burnett, and Lydia. Each brought her own strength, her own chemistry to the role of Melissa Gardner. For me, Lydia was the best, not least because she is in fact so like her. Melissa's life is tragically unfulfilled, Lydia's (a few bumps aside) has been a happy one, but many of Melissa's reactions are exactly like my girl's.

The same thing is true for me. Andy Ladd's life is very different from mine, but I've never played a part that was so right for me. I look forward to playing him again . . . with Lydia.

21

Moving Images

All of us who make films should
thank God for the chance we have to get
people to come sit in the dark for two
hours and let us tell them a story.

— FRANK CAPRA

THE SEVENTIES AND EIGHTIES were a busy time for me, shuttling back and forth between stage and film. As is true for any actor who does both, you look to the film work to increase your net worth and maintain your public identity, keeping your eye open for the now-and-then very good film (are there more than one or two great films a decade?). The stage is to keep your muscles stretched and take an occasional shot at the real man-killers.

True, those parts had sometimes left me on my knees in the arena, spitting sand. I still think a good deal of my best work through this time was onstage. Let's flip through the films I did at the same time. Some were forgettable, some were very good. I've always been drawn to the characters, the directors, and the writers I can learn something from.

Still, when Richard Lester phoned from London to ask me to play Athos in his film of *The Three Musketeers,* my immediate reaction was gloomy: Oh, God, I thought. Four or five months in Spain doing sword fights and horsebacking through the Guarradamas, in winter? On the other hand, Lester's a good director . . . OK, read the script.

George MacDonald Fraser had done a fine job. His script was wonderfully tight and witty, with a better sense of period dia-

logue than 90 percent of the scripts I read. I called Dick back and
told him how good I thought it was, but how gloomy the idea of a
long shoot seemed. "I'd really like to work with you, though, and
the script's very good. Why don't you let me play one of the cameo
parts, with a couple of good scenes . . . the Duke of Buckingham,
maybe?"

In the
Arena

I think he knew he had me. "What about Cardinal Richelieu?
He's got about eight good scenes, and he's one of the best villains
in fiction. It's about time you played a bad guy." That got my attention. It *was* about time; in more than half my films I've played tough,
often harsh, authority figures, yet in each the audience was on my
side. Dumas made Richelieu a classic villain: all-wise, all-powerful,
determined to thwart the gallant musketeers at any cost. The more
I thought about it, the more I knew I had to play the cardinal. (True,
it helped that Richard promised to film all my scenes in ten shooting days and pay me an obscene amount of money.)

The more I researched Richelieu, the more I admired him.
He served Dumas as a villain; he was in fact a great man. He more
or less invented France as a modern nation, resourcefully and tirelessly serving a fool of a king. He was indeed ruthless in the service
of his country. I ran across a marvelous quotation that I inserted
into a scene with Christopher Lee, playing my lieutenant: "It must
be difficult, your Eminence," says he, "to have so many enemies."

"I have no enemies," said Richelieu. "France has enemies."
I've never been able to understand why the French persist in re-
vering Napoléon instead, a bloody tyrant who all but destroyed
France.

The prep on the film went very well. Ziggy Geike did me a
fine false nose. (It's very seldom I play a man with a larger nose
than mine, but Richelieu's was.) In the film, I look quite like him.
The crimson cardinal's robe is very dramatic (though you have to
be very careful not to trip going upstairs). To suggest a somewhat
less physically able man than I usually put on the screen, I used a
very slight limp, entirely nonhistorical. Richelieu did suffer from
insomnia, and kept secretaries on duty around the clock so he
could dictate during the dark, sleepless hours.

The company had been shooting for some weeks (yes, in
the snow) when I flew over for my ten-day stint. A bit beat from the
long flight, I checked into the Castellana Hilton (for my fourth film

based there). Turning away from the desk, I heard a shout from the bar: *"Chuck!!"*

It was Oliver Reed, whom Lester had cast as Athos. I could never have done the part as well as he did. Oliver has a dangerously manic quality that was perfect for Athos. He wanted to buy me a drink. I was still drinking then (though no American actor should try to match a Brit in a bar; they have a long tradition, all the way back to Edmund Kean). I can only say that after some time, I proceeded with careful sobriety to my suite to unpack . . . and woke the next morning at seven. No, that's not meant to make you laugh.

The shoot went very well while I was there. I had lunch with Richard at the studio and asked him a crucial question: "This is a swashbuckling romance . . . how much satiric spin do you want me to put on Richelieu?"

He all but leapt out of his chair. "None at all, Chuck, for God's sake! You have to play the part as though we were doing a film about him. I need you to be the solid center of this piece. Cardinal Richelieu is serious, and dangerous. He is not joking."

So that's what I did. Richard was right. I did a cameo for James Cameron a year or so ago in Arnold Schwarzenegger's *True Lies* in which he played an agent and I played the head of the CIA. I asked Cameron what he wanted from me in the part. "I need you," he said, "because you can plausibly intimidate Arnold." I understood him at once; it was the same point Richard Lester had made.

In addition to Oliver, Richard had very good people: Michael York, Richard Chamberlain, Faye Dunaway as a truly dangerous Milady de Winter, and Raquel Welch in perhaps her best performance as a clumsy girl.

Lydia brought Holly over for the last half of my shoot, along with her niece, Elizabeth. We were to go on to Stuttgart to visit Lydia's brother Bob, then an army colonel stationed there, then Wimbledon on the way home. It gave us a nice end to what had been a very happy shoot for me. It turned out to be a very successful film, too, as well as a good one, I think. Certainly the cardinal was one of my more interesting biographical roles.

A curious coincidence near the end of my *Musketeers* stint: we were shooting near Aranjuez, along the banks of a summer-shrunken stream. It seemed oddly familiar, then it struck me. "You

know, Dick," I said, "I shot a scene in *Antony and Cleopatra* on
this exact spot."

"Great!" he said. "Do you remember where you put the
camera?"

THE FOLLOWING YEAR, Walter Mirisch asked me to breakfast with
him in the Polo Lounge of the Beverly Hills Hotel. I'd breakfasted
there at least a hundred times before, often with Walter, to discuss
various film projects. (Press interviews are usually at lunch, because
journalists like a free meal.) He had a very interesting idea: with the
two-hundredth anniversary of the founding of the country ahead,
he wanted to do a film on the Battle of Midway. A couple of mid-
dling movies had been made on Pearl Harbor, and a very good one,
The Longest Day, on the Normandy landings (which my schedule
on *El Cid* had kept me from joining).

Midway was the turning point of the Pacific war. Before that,
Japan had not lost a battle; afterward they never won one. Had we
lost Midway, we'd have been forced to keep our forces tied down
in the Pacific for several years. The battle was crucial; it called for a
film.

Walter's research gave him the tools to make the movie. But
two key factors were both completely unpredictable and utterly
beyond control. We needed a World War II aircraft carrier, and
aerial combat footage from the Pacific War . . . in color.

By the seventies, carriers were very different from those
used during World War II. Indeed, only one carrier from that war
was still in commission and available to us for filming: the USS
Lexington, stationed in the Gulf of Mexico. The Navy allowed us to
shoot on board for a couple of weeks.

In World War II, of all the warring forces, only two services
shot their combat footage in color: the U.S. Navy and the Japanese
Navy. Both services made their footage available to us, and the
studio re-processed it to match the fresh footage we shot. Lacking
either of these elements, we couldn't have made the movie.

After some deliberation, Walter decided on a semi-docu-
mentary approach, presenting the battle as accurately, both tactically and strategically, as possible. Happily, Henry Fonda, who'd
served in the Pacific as a naval officer in the war, liked the idea of

playing Admiral Nimitz, commander in chief of the U.S. Naval forces, though it was not a long part. This opened the door; all sorts of name actors came on board: Bob Mitchum as Admiral Halsey; Hal Holbrook, Jim Coburn, Bob Wagner, Dabney Coleman, Cliff Robertson. With actors like that playing officers who'd actually been a part of the battle, it would be much easier to sort out what happened. I was almost the only one who played a fictional character: a Naval Air Wing commander, beached with wounds after Pearl Harbor. This made it plausible for me to be in scenes both ashore in Pearl before the battle and at sea during the action. I was killed again, my most spectacular screen death, using real footage of a hideous crash aboard the Yorktown, returning from an attack on the Japanese fleet. Structurally, the part worked very well, and we had the leeway in my part to develop a personal story in ways you couldn't use with the real-life participants.

We had another piece of good luck in the casting: Toshiro Mifune, Japan's greatest actor, accepted the role of Yamamoto, the senior Japanese admiral. Along with some good Japanese actors as the six or so significant pilots and commanders on that side, we had a well-balanced cast.

The shoot went well. Planning was crucial during the time we were at sea aboard the *Lexington;* we could only film on the flight deck, the hangar deck, and the bridge at specified and rigidly circumscribed times, but the whole voyage was exciting. I even did several carrier landings and takeoffs. (No, I didn't drive.) Even better, I had a couple of scenes with Hank Fonda to file along with my memories of working with Jimmy Stewart and Gary Cooper. Those three seem to me the most quintessentially American actors. It was a pleasure, gentlemen.

With Jack Smight directing, the shoot went smoothly. One scene we shot aboard the *Lex* with my son wounded and in sick bay almost got out of hand. Eddie Albert, Jr., was playing the part very well, but I substituted Fraser's face on the bloody stretcher, and almost lost it completely. Real emotions can be vital in a scene, but you have to be careful with them.

In the end, *Midway* turned out to be a very good film, probably among the best about the war. Only good luck saved us from an expensive glitch, though. Some months after the shoot was finished, I was at Universal running some footage on a project I was

considering. Coming out of the projection room, I ran into Walter
Mirisch outside the room next door. "Chuck!" he said. "I just finished running the trailer on *Midway;* we're sending off twelve hundred prints to the theaters this morning. Would you like to see it?"
Well of course I would. I hadn't seen the film since a rough-cut,
unmixed print some weeks before. I sat down and watched three
or four minutes of very expertly edited footage showing highlights
from the battle and a fragment between Hank Fonda and me. "So
what do you think?" said Walter.

"It's really a good trailer," I said. "Except that you misspelled
my name in the main credits." I don't know how much it cost to
redo the trailers and get them out a day late, but I can't resist
twitting Walter about it from time to time.

Universal had counted on a success; *Midway* exceeded their
expectations. As always, this simply expanded their PR plans. Of
course we did Washington and the Navy, with some very nice official carryings on. Then they sent me to Japan, where they'd had
some anxieties about the film; it explored a major Japanese defeat,
after all. They need not have worried. The Japanese loved the film.
It's true that my movies have always found favor there, but I think
Midway was successful because it presented an evenhanded picture
of the battle, recognizing the courage and resourcefulness of the
Japanese.

I did Britain, of course, and the major stops on the Continent. There was a large press conference in Berlin, where the
media people are sharp, sometimes a little feisty. A lanky guy with
long hair, stubble, and counterculture clothes stood up and said,
"I'm a Communist. You make this movie about a battle I never
heard of that has nothing to do with me. I hate America. Why should
I give a damn who won?"

"I'll tell you why," I said. "If America had lost this battle,
we couldn't have joined Britain in the Normandy landings, which
would've been postponed indefinitely. If Hitler had won the war,
or a negotiated peace, what do you think would've happened to
you, as a German Communist?" I cherish the memory of his mouth
hanging open, speechless.

My favorite event of the whole tour, though, was in Paris,
where Walter and Pat Mirisch joined me. There was a day or two of
interviews, after which Walter laid on dinner at La Serre, one of the

city's best restaurants. My last visit there had been some years before, when Sam Bronston threw a gala dinner for a hundred or so after the opening of *El Cid,* in the days when they did that kind of thing. "This was in the summer," I explained. "This restaurant has a glass roof they can roll back in good weather. Sam arranged to release a hundred white doves, which flew off into the starry summer sky. Very impressive."

At this point the manager of the restaurant, who'd overheard me, came to the table. "M'sieur Heston, perhaps your friends would like to see the roof opened for a moment?" How nice, all agreed, indeed we would. So he pressed a switch, the roof ground back to reveal a dark winter sky, but you got the idea: appreciative murmurs all 'round.

He pressed the switch again . . . and the roof would not close. Perhaps a fuse. Whereupon it began to rain, a cold winter rain that put out the candles, watered the wine, and spoiled the sauces as well as the ladies' hairdos . . . all over the restaurant, which emptied like magic. So much for kind gestures in a naughty world.

DURING ALL THIS BUSY TIME I spent to-and-froing between good films, some not so good, and good plays, some not so well done, Fraser and Holly were growing up. I boast of how well they did that without claiming much credit. In the end, it seems to me, you become who you will be because of who you are.

The best thing Lydia and I gave our children was our time, which we did not so much out of any feeling that we *must* ("quality time" . . . what an ugly phrase), but because we liked it. Love is, or should be, a given; I *liked* driving Holly to ballet lessons, or lip-synching show tunes with her to records while she cavorted in makeshift costumes, just as Lydia liked teaching both kids to swim, and we both loved reading to them.

From babyhood, they'd come along around the world while I made my living; gone down the Nile and up the pyramids (and some of the slightly smaller ones in Mexico), seen lions in Kenya and moose in Montana, tracked the Romans from Italy to both Spain and Scotland, sailed Homer's wine-dark seas, Ionian and Aegean, as well as rubber-rafting down the Middle Fork of the Salmon. They'd seen the Sistine ceiling up close, heard Mozart in Vienna, and seen Shakespeare in Stratford. They'd gotten a fair overview of a good

deal of Western civilization. I'd say they were the better for it. I
think they would, too.

By the seventies, they'd just about become themselves, though Holly was still in school. Fray, from the time he was twelve, seemed possessed by what Jolly West called the Ulysses Factor: the urge—no, the need—to climb the mountain, cross the river, get to the top of the cliff, the bottom of the gorge. He'd appear after days or weeks in the bush, unshaven, stinking but smiling. He ran the bulls in Pamplona when he was sixteen, was a white-water guide when he was seventeen, and sailed 'round the Horn not many years later. All this, I came to understand, was also to find things to write about, because that's what he wanted to do. Indeed, his first directing job was a scary second unit in Pamplona for *City Slickers.*

He had a couple of short pieces in print, and sold a few scripts that never made it to the screen. Then he wrote one called *Wind River* about the fur trappers in the American West in the 1830s. The producer Martin Ransohoff liked it very much and showed it to Columbia, who were also enthusiastic. They bought it; Ransohoff put the film in preproduction and offered me the lead. I thought it was a wonderful part, in a rich script.

The character in *Wind River,* Bill Tyler, spoke very clearly to me: one of several men I'd played on both stage and screen who recognize that their own time is coming to an end. This was true of my aging quarterback in *Number One,* also of Will Penny, maybe even, on a somewhat more exalted level, of Mark Antony. Tyler's time was special, only a single generation, really, when the popularity of beaver hats drove the demand for beaver pelts to unprecedented heights, until the introduction of the silk hat collapsed the market overnight. The fur trade was controlled by England's Hudson Bay Co., in competition with the American Fur Co. There were always a few men, though, who preferred total independence, never more than a hundred in all, collecting pelts alone or with a single partner.

There was a chance of modest wealth in a single season, if the beaver were plentiful, the Blackfeet absent, and you didn't get killed by a bear or break a leg a thousand miles from help. What motivated the freelance trappers to choose such a harsh life, though, was the chance of absolute freedom. For that short span of years, these men had more freedom than any group in any time in recorded history. As Bill Tyler says to his partner, Henry Frapp, when he questions the roughness of their life and how much freedom they really have:

> "Ye kin walk for a year in any direction with
> jest yer rifle, live good an' easy . . . never have
> t'say sir t'nobody. Yeah . . . I call that free."

Brian Keith gave one of the very best of his gritty, charismatic performances as Frapp—we hadn't worked together since *Arrowhead,* a quarter of a century before. A wonderfully quirky actor, he's a joy to play with. His death scene was enormously effective, and very moving to act with him. Stephen Macht, fresh off his performance as Henry VIII in the Ahmanson *Man for All Seasons,* was a terrifying Blackfoot chief. We shot for some ten weeks in the Tetons, the Absaroka range, and Yellowstone, in both winter and spring.

The elegiac quality I perceived in much of the writing leached through to the film itself in many scenes, I was glad to see. That kind of color, clear on the printed page, is very elusive on screen. Shooting in the big skies of the American Rockies, as beautiful as any country on earth, makes it easier to get some of it on film. We got, I was sure, some wonderful footage, worth all the difficulties of shooting in such difficult locations.

The film we ended up with was very different from the script with which we began. Its theatrical release was disappointing, though it eventually edged into profit in video. What happened to the film itself in postproduction was far more damaging.

A lot of things were done to the film, not all of them bad. *Wind River* is a good title, but also, as we say in the trade, a little soft. *Mountain Men* works much better, and is certainly not untrue to the film. The editing on the film was pretty much slash-and-burn, focusing on the action and the raucous relationship between Tyler and Frapp. The print ads were worse, featuring cartoon drawings of Brian and me running away from some pretty ridiculous Indians. The ads were an appalling surprise, the editing was a shocking violation of assurances Ransohoff had given me. It was my first and to this day the most outrageous encounter in this town with that kind of behavior. *Mountain Men* remains a bitter memory of what could've been a fine film.

THE EIGHTIES BEGAN in high style for us: Fraser got married, to a wonderful Canadian girl he'd met a few years before on, believe it or not, the *Love Boat*. Fray had spent the better part of a year in Alaska, working for an Eskimo entrepreneur and soaking up the country (where, several years later, he's now directing a film). Having squeezed all the juice out of the time there he could, he was ready to come home, but wanted to give us a look at the Brooks Range and some of the country near the Arctic Circle. He invited us up to go moose hunting. With our warm friends the Isaacs, we accepted. I can't honestly say that Lydia and Clori, Holly and Shauna actually enjoyed sneaking off to pee in the bushes, alert for bears while the men tramped around in the boonies looking for moose, but they endured it with good grace.

Homeward bound, cruising down the inland waterway in considerable style, we debarked at Vancouver, where we were catching a plane for the rest of the way home. Marilyn Pernfuss, a stunning blonde, was the Princess Line's expediter there. She seemed taken with Fray, he surely with her, and now, a few years later, there we all were, encamped in Vancouver, celebrating their marriage on a bluff overlooking Vancouver Sound. They both looked beautiful, as did everyone, golden in memory.

There was no filming in Hollywood that summer, though much talk. The Screen Actors Guild was on strike, for the first time, I think, since I left the Board. I was out of sympathy with the leadership by that time, but when they asked me to come back on the board just for the negotiations, I couldn't in conscience refuse. In the end, we got a deal very close to what we could've gotten in the first place, without a strike.

A few weeks later, one of my predecessors as SAG president won a somewhat larger constituency: Ronald Reagan was elected president of the United States. Lydia and I were invited over to the Reagan suite at the Century Plaza to watch the election coverage on TV. I expected a long evening, waiting for the late returns. In fact, President Carter conceded defeat before the West Coast polls closed, while I was driving home from the Ahmanson, where I was rehearsing *The Crucifer of Blood*. We whipped over to the hotel in time to catch the last of Mr. Reagan's response, which had the easy grace and good humor that would be one of his most valuable assets in serving the country, indeed the Western world, for the next eight years. That evening I called him "Sir," though he'd been "Ron" in the old SAG days. After he was sworn in, I always used "Mr. President." I'm more than a little put off by those who flaunt their intimacy with public figures by using their first names—"I was talking to the president at this small luncheon Barbara gave. 'Bill,' I said . . ." Jack Valenti, who's been around more presidents than I have, says he's never heard an incumbent or former president addressed as other than "Mr. President."

In January, we went to the inauguration, where I was asked to read a couple of things at one of the several galas laid on. I perhaps served the evening most usefully when I noticed at the afternoon rehearsal that Dean Martin, who was to sing, was having considerable trouble getting up the steep steps to the top of the pyramid where we were to perform. That night, changing to black tie in the communal dressing room we all shared, I realized Dean was in deeper trouble. He stood swaying in shirt and socks, fumbling with his dress tie. I tried to knot it for him, but he sank into a chair. Clearly, he couldn't get out of the dressing room, let alone sing. I dropped the tie and went into the corridor to look for Frank Sinatra, who was producing the gala. By God's grace, he stood at the foot of the stairs, waiting to welcome the vice president. "Francis," I said. "A problem. Dean Martin is smashed; he can't possibly get onstage, let alone sing."

Sinatra looked at me sharply; we've always been cordial, never particularly close. "You positive?"

"No question."

"He's out." He turned to go, then looked back. "Thanks." So that's how I saved the Reagan inaugural. It would've been on the front page of *The Washington Post:* "Reagan Off on Wrong Note, Singer Stumbles. A Sign of the Future?"

I feel sorry about Dean, though. I always liked the way he sang "That's Amore."

A FEW WEEKS after the inauguration, the President asked me to co-chair with Dr. Hanna Gray, the president of the University of Chicago, a Presidential Task Force on the National Endowments for the Arts and Humanities. Our mandate was to appoint a group (properly unpaid, of course) to explore what both endowments did, how

well they did it, whether it should be done, and whether tax money
should be spent on it. Both bodies, particularly the NEA, had become hot-button issues, though neither cost very much. The first
step was to recruit some capable, high-profile people to serve.

Not long after the wheels began to turn on the Task Force,
President Reagan was shot, with three members of his staff, by
exactly the kind of schizoid nonentity who often undertakes to kill
people in high places.

I think the most extraordinary example of courage (in Ernest
Hemingway's definition as "grace under pressure") I've ever heard
from a public figure was President Reagan's comment when he was
about to go under the knife so they could take the bullets from his
chest: "Gee, Doc . . . I sure hope you're a Republican."

The surgeon's response is fine, too: "Mr. President . . . we're
all Republicans today."

After all the years, I'm now more amused than irritated by
the relentless dismissal of Reagan as a serious political figure because he'd been an actor. Governor Pat Brown, falling behind in
the race against Reagan for that office, had the graceless taste to
remind the voters that it had been an actor who killed Lincoln. (It
didn't help him.)

Nevertheless, liberal pundits and media types kept insisting
throughout his two terms as governor and two more as president
that his skills as a performer were of no use in high office. Anyone
examining even casually the careers of Churchill, de Gaulle, FDR,
Jack Kennedy—even Hitler, for God's sake—can see that political
leadership, especially at the highest levels, is in large part performance.

Churchill, at the nadir of Western hopes in 1940, lifted the
spirits of his countrymen with a speech he wrote himself, memorized, and delivered at least twice, ending, "We shall defend our
island, whatever the cost may be, we shall fight on the beaches, we
shall fight on the landing grounds, we shall fight in the fields and
in the streets, we shall fight in the hills; we shall never surrender."
Does anyone imagine he made that up on the spot? It was performance of the highest order and it went a long way toward saving
his country.

That's what leaders do. They exhort, they inspire, they *lead*.
Reagan was not a great actor—but he understood the *idea* of per-

formance, and its function in the presidency. I did little for him in the 1980 campaign, largely because I was working. In 1984 I did more, mostly in senatorial races. The president clearly felt perfectly able to reelect himself.

I spoke to him hardly at all that campaign summer. (My rule of thumb is, just because you can get an important man on the phone is a very good reason not to do it.) I did talk to Nancy from time to time; we'd known each other a long while. She seemed very anxious about the election; based on the concerns she expressed to me, I began to worry, too, though Mondale didn't seem to me a serious threat.

Reagan had launched and ended every one of his campaigns for office in San Diego; I was asked to take part in a rally there the day before the election—the final rally he would ever attend on his own behalf. It was hardly an exclusive invitation. In addition to the scores of thousands of real people who jammed the vast outdoor amphitheater, there were several dozen public faces appearing on-stage: political eminentos, pundits, and performers in various media. Milling around in the backstage crowd, I ran into Nancy Reagan, who offered me a lift to L.A. in *Air Force One*. I doubt that many people decline that invitation; I certainly didn't.

The program was the appropriate mix of country and western, comics, talk, and fireworks, both black powder and rhetorical. The audience response to the president was volcanic—in comparison, it made the Rolling Stones' audience sound like the polite patter of applause for a harpist at a tea dance.

There had been a new *Air Force One* in the pipeline for some years; a modern 747 to replace the old 707 by then on the verge of obsolescence. Like many government projects, it had languished while they pondered the update on the electronics security and communications it would require. In the end, the current *Air Force One* wasn't turned over to the White House till the middle of the Bush administration. (I did a documentary on the history of the presidential aircraft, all the way back to President Roosevelt's, the first one. It's very good.)

The *Air Force One* I got on that afternoon took off from a military facility (like all presidential flights) and was covered en route by four F-14s. It was full of very tired people, at the end of an exhausting campaign. Meese, Deaver, Baker all looked at the end of their energies. Not President Reagan. He was in high good spirits, glowing with health; I do believe he could've undertaken another campaign the next day.

The next day was the election. Mindful of Nancy's anxieties during the summer, I asked Jim Baker, who'd run the campaign, "Well, what does it look like for tomorrow?"

"Oh, we'll lose the District of Columbia, probably Minnesota, too. We'll take everything else."

I was stunned. "What do you mean, 'everything else'?"

"We'll win all the rest of the United States." And so it proved.

BACK TO 1981 and the NEA. By late May, Hanna Gray and I had recruited our volunteers. A brilliant and engaging woman, Dr. Gray did that better than I; I suppose a university president gets a lot of practice at it. I don't like to ask people to do things for me (unless I'm directing them or arguing for script changes). I did manage to persuade a few people I knew could help, like Frank Schaffner and Bob Fryer, Armand Deutsch and Roger Stevens, Beverly Sills, Daniel Boorstin, Franklin Murphy, and George Roche. Really, a formidable group, for almost any job.

I went to Washington and a tiny room in the White House basement while we were renting space and hiring staff. The first day or so, I kept losing my way looking for the men's room. If you made one wrong turn, a Secret Service agent would materialize out of the woodwork and say, smiling, "Can I help you, sir?" They do not encourage wandering in that building.

Through the summer, we met as a body in a number of different cities in search of informed opinion on the weighty agenda the president had asked us to explore. Not surprisingly, the informed were vastly outnumbered by the uninformed, most of them with media credentials. They had determined before our first session that the president had convened a new Spanish Inquisition. I had been appointed Lord High Executioner with a predetermined mandate to cut off some heads. I spent almost as much time doing interviews denying this as I did chairing meetings.

In the end, we decided, by fairly firm consensus, that there was an appropriate role for government in the arts and humanities, but since taxpayers were footing the bill, the Feds should keep an eye on things. We signed off on this, submitted our report to the president, paid the staff, and shut down the Task Force.

I think that closure may have been our best work. There are dozens of groups in government originally organized for useful goals that still survive, decades beyond their time. I'm sure there are green baize doors hidden in the Capitol behind which sit centenarian clerks in green eye shades and sleeve protectors, diligently writing checks to subsidize the production of buggy whips. We just shut up our shop.

IT WAS TIME I turned back to my own profession, anyway. Fray had been working on a good idea for a film all winter; prodded by Martin Shafer and another friend, Andy Scheinman, they developed an even better screenplay. It was about a young couple who fly into the Canadian bush in search of an undiscovered mother lode for all the gold deposits along the western Canadian coast. *Mother Lode* was undeniable as the title. (Later, when the film was released, there was a gay bar in West Hollywood that stole the title, along with some posters to put in the window.)

They offered me the role of a maniac. Well, that's overstated. Silas McGee was a hermit miner, slightly skewed after years of living alone. He had a dead brother, who might not be real, might not be dead. Might be, in fact, McGee himself.

I didn't plan to play McGee as a maniac, but seriously disturbed characters do give you a lot of elbow room. I looked forward to the part, not least because the incomparable Bob Easton had prepared phonetic cards for me on an Inverness Scot's accent. I worked with them every day, carried them on the trips I took for the Task Force. No, I did not practice my Gaelic glottals in my head while I chaired the meetings (well, maybe once or twice).

We'd been able to keep *Mother Lode*'s preproduction on schedule through the summer. The early priorities, as always, were casting and the never-ending work on the script. I would direct as well as act, Fray would produce. First we had to find some actors.

Aside from me and a one-scene bit at the beginning, there were only three other roles in the whole film. We had a piece of luck on the most crucial. Kim Basinger had done one film, which had almost no release, but Martin Shafer had somehow picked up a clue. We ran most of the film, called her in for an interview, and cast her without a test. Aside from her stunning beauty, there was, even then, a special presence the camera turns to.

For the man, we first thought of James Brolin, who'd made a scary and plausible nut in *Skyjacked*. He rose to the idea in a lunch meeting, but we could never come together. Then we came across a film about a young man caught in the Moonie cult, where an actor named Nick Mancuso gave a telling performance. We decided to go with him, not realizing that he was not acting; the moodily mercurial man on the screen was in fact Nick himself. This misperception proved costly.

Our last casting also had its difficulties, but we got a good performance in the end. The role was a mysterious old Indian. (In the movies, almost all Indians are either mysterious, murderous, or noble. Now, of course, they must also be real Indians.) We went in the opposite direction. I don't know what John Marley's ethnic background was; I've never cared about that much, though it's now become a crucial casting concern. His mane of silver hair and hawk nose gave me the look I wanted, as did his acting, which *is* a prime concern for me.

I'm not sure John had ever worked outdoors before. His best-known role was the film producer whose racehorse's head is put in his bed in *The Godfather*. All his scenes in our film were shot in various remote parts of the Canadian wilderness, the first in a small lake, accessible only by float plane and four-wheel drive.

Lydia came up for the shoot, of course, providing tender loving care and some good still coverage to boot. My sweet Holly visited, albeit briefly. Carol Lanning joined the company as well; with me acting as well as directing on a tight eight-week schedule, we needed her. Peter Snell came aboard as executive producer.

Fray was absolutely crucial. All those years on film sets had given him a better apprenticeship than you can get in any film school. I suspect he had even soaked up something from Wyler on *Ben-Hur* when he was three years old. On *Mother Lode* he was a shadow director, especially in the scenes I was acting in.

I started the second unit shoot a few days early, to get some good flying footage through the mountains during an unexpected burst of good weather. Joe Canutt was running the unit with his usual skill, but when he set up two-camera coverage of the plane angling through the cliffs and landing on the lake, the aircraft caught the tip of one pontoon in the water and cartwheeled upside down.

Neither the pilot nor the stunt girl doubling Kim was hurt; Joe was able to find a canoe on the shore and rescue both of them. He also managed to hook a line on the plane and tow it to shallow water where we could use it as a set, demonstrating yet again why he's the best second-unit director since his old man, Yak.

As Wyler had done when Joe was thrown out of the chariot in *Ben-Hur,* we altered the script to take advantage of our spectacular plane crash with a scene Fray rewrote with Nick diving to retrieve gear from the capsized plane and talking to Marley's old Indian. John had to sit in a motorboat for the scene. I doubled him driving it into the shot, but he was still edgy, especially with the sunken plane before his eyes. He did well, though, with some grumbling about the precarious conditions in which he was forced to act. "How the hell can I remember my lines when this damn boat might tip over, too?"

His last and longest scene was at least on dry ground. Dry, that is, the first day of shooting, when he had little to do. It rained heavily all that night and into the next day. By then the river was rising as well; it was clear the gravel bar we were shooting on would be underwater before long. Our set would be gone, irretrievably. That doesn't happen very often on a film.

Happily, the scene had John, Kim, and Nick sitting around a campfire through some three pages of dialogue. I tarped over the area where they sat. (No, the rain didn't show. If you want to see rain in your shot, you have to enhance it with a hose.) The crew and I were out in the rain, but the actors were warm and dry by the fire, under the tarp. It should have been a fairly easy day, all things considered. Kim and Nick bore up well enough, but John had most of the dialogue. He was unable to get through the scene without stumbling. I kept altering the shot pattern to give him less to say in any one setup, but it didn't help; he blew take after take. I do believe it was simply a new experience for him to act out in the open, where rain and smoke from a fire happen, where you're not cocooned on a sound stage, but in the real outdoors.

To compound my problem, this was John's last contract day on the picture; at its end we'd lose not only the set, but John. There was no alternative; I had to get his lines on film. With each setup, when he blew his lines, I'd say, "That's fine, John. It's going very well, the camera's still turning, just go on from there," and give him the next sentence. It worked. We got all his dialogue on film in bits. As the waters began to lap into our set, I wrapped the company. "Thanks, John," I said. "I think you're going to be very special in this film. I appreciate what you gave us."

"Well, yeah," he said. "Thanks. It's just that I don't like to work this way."

"What way is that, John?"

"Ah, all these fuckin' bits 'n' pieces. I like to do a scene straight through from the top." I really could've drowned him. Right there in the river.

I thought we'd have to scrap the scene, but Eric Boyd-Perkins (editing for me again) somehow assembled the fragments of speeches Marley had given us into a cohesive whole. John comes off very well in the film, demonstrating the value of a good editor.

Tennessee Williams visited Vancouver while we were based there on *Mother Lode*. "When the weathah is cleah," he said to the press, "theah is no lovlieah landscape in the Weste'n Hemispheah than the Bay of Vancouvah." Mr. Williams was right, but the weather is not always cooperative. Still, we had anticipated this resourcefully. We hadn't anticipated that our leading couple would loathe each other.

Interpersonal chemistries are unpredictable and inexplicable. "The heart has its reasons," the poet says. In the real world, people can respond to their feelings as they choose. For actors, it's more complicated. All of us have played love scenes with partners to whom we were not passionately attracted, maybe even disliked. They call it acting.

I have no idea why Kim and Nick found it impossible to act the attraction the script required. Both were at the beginnings of their careers: Kim was just becoming aware of her own potential, Nick was a complex young man whose capacities I may have missed. I don't believe there was any particular personal encounter that created the mutual hostility that colored the shoot.

The director has to deal with this as best he can. I did have one key success. We had a scene where Kim wakens before dawn in her tent and finds Nick gone. Searching for him in the foggy woods, she encounters a shadowy figure and runs in terror . . . into Nick. He comforts her in a warm embrace, nothing more.

Kim simply couldn't/wouldn't do this. Desperate at losing my perfect fog-wreathed forest light, I cleared the set. "OK, everyone back off . . . out of sight. I want to talk to Kim." They went. I took her hand and walked up and down the forest glade we were shooting in. "Look," I said. "I want you to help me get past your feeling about Nick. This scene is not about love, it's not about sex. It's about being scared. You did all that, very well. Now I need you to let him comfort you. Like this." I took her in my arms and held her. "Can you do that?"

"Yes," she said. And she did. Through the rest of the shoot, she was a real trouper. She comes across wonderfully in the film. I like to think we gave her career some crucial early impetus.

Nick's in fact also good in the film. He was dogged by anxieties and personal quirks that complicated his work, and the difficulties with Kim were surely not all his fault. Still, I had only one serious confrontation with him. It was one I couldn't afford to lose, though.

We were shooting in an intricate mine set that was one of the most effective creative elements in the film. Infinitely flexible, entirely controllable, and very claustrophobic, though God knows I've worked in several even more oppressive. Nick, perhaps, had not.

Having worked through a scene between Nick and Kim for several hours, I was marking the moves for the next setup so the cameraman could light it, when Nick said abruptly, "I don't need this crap. Let my stand-in do it!" and pushed past me out of the shot.

I caught him in four steps and took him by the shoulders. "Listen to me, Nick," I said. "You won't like how you feel about yourself if you do this. Come back and let me finish blocking the shot, then go to your trailer till we're ready. That's the way we do it. You know that." Of course he did. He came back.

I liked *Mother Lode* very much, though it didn't achieve the success we'd hoped for. It did give Fray and Martin and Andy some useful experience in what had become their life work.

IT GAVE ME GOOD EXPERIENCE, too—as happens, after all, with every piece of work you do. So it proved again a couple of years later, as the English production of *A Man for All Seasons* was going into its final weeks, after a six-month run. Fraser pointed out that Ted Turner was about to launch a very ambitious new cable network, Turner Network Television (TNT). A new, full-scale film of *Man* would make a very prestigious opening production, for Ted and for us.

Ted Turner is an extraordinary man. He had already reinvented television news coverage with CNN; he was about to break some new ground with made-for-cable movies aimed at a more upscale audience than the networks were reaching for, or than HBO was willing to pay for.

When *Man* closed in Britain, Fray and I stopped off in Atlanta on the way home to meet with Turner. Essentially, we had a go on the film in ten minutes, subject to the inevitable lawyerly back-and-forths. Turner's only condition was that the cast be beefed up a little with star power, for which Turner was prepared to spend extra money.

That suited us exactly; if they hadn't asked for it, we would have. The cast I'd played with for half a year was fine, but none of them had names that would attract an American audience. The wish list was obvious. My first call was to Sir John Gielgud. "John," I said, "I'm filming *Man for All Seasons,* using most of the actors you saw with me at the Savoy last fall, but I need you to play Cardinal Wolsey."

"Oh, goodness, Chuck," said John. "I really don't think so. One does remember Orson Welles in the first film. He was so *large.*"

"John, I suggest to you that your reputation alone is ample enough to fulfill any conceivable dimensions of the role."

"Mmmm. Yes. It *is* a very good part, isn't it?"

"I don't know of a better one-scene part in modern theater."

"Mmm . . . possibly so. Well, yes, then. Very well, I'll do it." I didn't talk to Vanessa Redgrave directly about playing Thomas More's wife, Alice, but we'd worked together before in *Macbeth;* I was hopeful she'd accept our offer. So she did, as did Richard Johnson, when I told him how much I wanted him to play the Duke of Norfolk. So there I was, three for three on our top three choices. That speaks not so much for me as for Robert Bolt's play; any actor would be glad of a chance to do parts like those in a play like that.

I had a little time before I was due back in England to accept another public sector chore. The State Department asked me to attend a UNESCO conference on cultural affairs in Mexico City as a special envoy. There were several hundred delegates, assistants, secretaries, and dogsbodies from two or three dozen countries, funded largely by the U.S., gathered ostensibly to . . . ah . . . discuss culture.

The real agenda was somehow to produce a document that would embarrass the United States and lend some faint moral stature to the French government's policy of excluding as many American films and TV shows as possible from their country. Jack Lang, the French Minister of Culture, made a speech on the first day of the conference searingly vitriolic in condemning the U.S. as "cultural imperialists." Our ambassador in Mexico was John Gavin (whom I recalled from my time with the Screen Actors Guild, where he followed me as president, as "Black Jack"). He was one of the best men we've ever posted to Mexico, tough and resourceful. (He also spoke the best Spanish of any of our ambassadors to that country.) In retaliation, Gavin decided that the U.S. delegation would not attend the reception at the French Embassy that evening. To this day, a dozen years later, this issue is a flash point of contention between the two countries. So much for diplomacy.

My prime utility for our delegation was that I could attract press. There was a large turnout at the press conference we called where Melina Mercouri, the Greek Minister of Culture, was to speak for the European position. She was quite good, denouncing the U.S. and pointing out that artists must defend the "culture of the country." I said, "Surely, Madam Minister, as an artist who has yourself fled from persecution, you recognize that governments who recruit the artist to the service of the state only drive him away, as Hitler did with Thomas Mann, and Brezhnev with Solzhenitsyn." She flushed, and walked out of the room.

A WEEK OR SO LATER, I was in London, where we were ready to roll on *Man for All Seasons.* We were based at Pinewood, my favorite and among the most familiar of studios. We had wonderful sets and an absolutely top-grade crew. Fray was producing again, with Peter Snell as executive producer.

Most important of all, I had a cast that had done the play with me for most of a season, with only three new performers, who were of superb ability and experience. At Fray's insistence, we'd gotten several days of rehearsal, some of it on the actual sets. I'd also spent some time walking the sets to plan the shots.

All this meant we were able to shoot the film in eighteen shooting days, an incredibly fast pace. One day, we shot fifteen and a half pages of a scene with seven characters in it. You could only do that with a cast who knew the play, and actors of the caliber of Gielgud, Redgrave, and Johnson. Robert Bolt came to the set to watch Sir John's Wolsey scene—far and away the best Wolsey I've ever seen.

I've forgotten who it was said, "In the beginning, an actor impresses us with his looks, later his voice enchants us. Over the years his performances enthrall us, but in the end, it is simply what he *is.*" John Gielgud brings that to a part. I'm proud to have acted with him, even prouder to have directed him. Like all the great actors I've seen, he is infinitely directable.

I'd acted with Richard Johnson before and would again—six times, so far. They are all fine performances, but his Norfolk is surely among the best. The bluff, hearty friend, the choleric duke, the stern judge . . . all wonderfully done.

I think Vanessa Redgrave is the finest actress alive. Not simply because of her talent; informed observers could list five or six actresses equally gifted, including her kid sister, Lynn. But I can think of no living actress who has undertaken the range of parts Vanessa has. Not just Shakespeare, the Restoration comedies, and the Greeks, but Ibsen, Shaw, *bad* Tennessee Williams *(Orpheus Descending),* a musical, and, to my great good fortune, a couple of parts with me.

Politically, Vanessa and I could hardly be farther apart. I'm a conservative; her radical beliefs make Jane Fonda sound like Herbert Hoover. I refuse to believe that I've lost parts because of my politics; Vanessa is openly blacklisted because of her anti-Zionist convictions. The film and theater communities should be ashamed of that.

Her performance as Alice More was a wonder. She began with a West Country accent that was historically accurate for the illiterate Alice, but almost unintelligible. When Peter showed her some footage, though, she said, "Oh, no . . . that won't do," and gave us a different voice entirely.

Her true loyalty to the part, though, was in her unrelenting portrayal as the combative shrew we're told Alice was. Only in the very last moments of the prison scene where she bids her husband good-bye did she change. It broke your heart. Her performance did a great deal to make the film.

It really was a fine piece of work. It did very well for Turner, and for us. It's also, I think, one of my best film performances.

FRAY AND I did two more films for Turner, the first as much a labor of love as anything I've ever done. I think Fray would say the same. When he was small, I used to read to him every night, as most fathers do. When he was about four, I decided it was time to read him a real novel: *Treasure Island,* which is not really a kid's book. It's an adult reminiscence of a boyhood experience. I read it to Fray a chapter every night, to his great delight. Finally we finished the last page. I said, "Well, that's the end of the story. Now let's find something to start tomorrow night. What would you like?"

"Let's read dat one again!" said my son. So we did, from the beginning. I think I read him Stevenson's classic four more times. By then he could read it himself. And did. I truly believe *Treasure Island* lay germinating inside him all the years he was apprenticing in film locations around the globe.

The success of *Man* meant Turner wanted another project from us. Fray says he'd carefully crafted his pitch speech to Ted: why we should make *Treasure Island,* why he should direct as well as write the screenplay. He didn't get past the title before Ted said, "Great idea! We already have the ship, too. Let's do it!" That's part of the secret of Ted's success, of course. Like the men who made up the movies in the first place, he's willing to go on his instinct. Very few studio people have the authority, or the guts, to do that. Fray says he'd still like to have finished his speech.

Ted also well knew the importance of a trump card he held: the ship. You can't make *Treasure Island* without a full-rigged ship, of which there are very few in the world. By chance, Ted owned one of the best, the *Bounty.* Built for the disastrous Brando remake

of *Mutiny on the Bounty* in the sixties, it had somehow come into
Ted's possession and was then docked in Florida, at some cost. It
would serve very well, and also earn its keep as the *Hispaniola* in
our film.

Fray and I had discussed *Treasure Island* more than once. It
had been filmed three times: in 1934 by MGM, in 1950 by Disney,
and in 1972 by a British/French/German/Spanish consortium. (This
last was an unwatchable mishmash with Orson Welles, who was
embarrassed in a film to which he could make no useful contribution.)

The first two films were seriously undertaken, but crippled
by their casting. Both Jackie Cooper in the MGM black-and-white
effort and Bobby Driscoll in the Disney film were under twelve
when they played Jim Hawkins. Stevenson's Jim is not a little boy,
but a gritty and resourceful adolescent. If he's a child, then the
pirates can only be "Disney" pirates, the lovable softies that both
Wallace Beery and Robert Newton provided. Long John Silver is
one of the great villains of fiction; one of the prime reasons I was
anxious to play him was to explore the murderous, bloody rogue
Stevenson had in mind.

Fray's script was excellent. (He said, "Hey, I didn't write it,
Robert Louis Stevenson did.") We flew to London to cast the actors
to fulfill it, which was not difficult. As I've observed, Britain is awash
with good actors (especially for a piece like this). In a couple of
days of readings, you're two-deep in actors who could be good in
each part.

Among them was Nick Amer, who gave one of the best auditions I've ever seen. He'd played the Spanish ambassador for us in
the film of *Man,* also in the theatrical run. He had memorized from
the novel the entire scene of Jim's first encounter with Ben Gunn,
the half-mad castaway Silver and his mates have stranded on the
island, and did it for us, playing both roles. Of course he got the
part (and was bloody good in it, too), but I thought again, in contrast, how ill-prepared many actors are in readings.

Of course we had a wish list of actors we didn't have to read,
just persuade. Almost every one of them joined us, which speaks
well for me, or Fray . . . or Mr. Stevenson. Richard Johnson would
be Squire Trelawney (less rank than the Duke of Norfolk, but as

good a part); Julian Glover, who'd been working when we did *Man,* was Dr. Livesey; and his wife, the beauteous Isla Blair, played Jim's mother. Christopher Lee did a scary Blind Pew, and Oliver Reed played a part he was born for, Captain Billy Bones.

As Fray said, "With actors like that, you just stand back out of their way." It comes to a lot more than that, of course. It's odd to think of the problems we had with Nick Mancuso and Kim Basinger and poor John Marley in *Mother Lode,* and how easily it went on *A Man for All Seasons* with Vanessa Redgrave and John Gielgud, and the people who did *Treasure Island* with us. It's true that good actors are secure; they know what they can do and they welcome anything you can give them to make them better. Even so . . .

Fray cast a boy named Christian Bale as Jim. He'd spent a year with Steven Spielberg in *Empire of the Sun,* from whom he'd clearly learned a great deal. His idol, it seems, was Steve McQueen; his acting choices tended toward the impassive. He was very athletic, though, and quite fearless. All the scenes Fray had been prepared to double, Christian did willingly and well—climbing the rigging, dodging sword blades, and diving off the ship. He was in fact very effective, certainly far truer to Stevenson's vision than the children who'd played the part before him.

Fray began shooting on the Devon coast, in Clovelly, a village listed in the *Domesday Book.* It still looks like the eleventh century. I had only one scene in England, at Pinewood on a set for the Spyglass Inn where Jim first meets Long John Silver. I'm ashamed to say that on my very first take in the film, walking out of the shadows on a crutch with one leg strapped up behind me and a parrot on my shoulder, I fell down. Very embarrassing. I got better from there.

Silver is a wonderful part, of course, especially if the boy is old enough so you don't have to be cute with him. The balancing element in the role is his genuine fondness for Jim. "Oi like thaat boy. Oi never seed a bet'ter boy than thaat. He's mower a maan than eny pair o' you bilge rats aboh-erd uv heer." Yet, to gain the treasure, Silver would kill Jim in an instant.

I'd worked hard on the Devon accent (with Bob Easton, of course). I'm very proud of what I did with the part (including not falling down again). Fray had chosen some wonderful Jamaican

locations, exactly what the story needed. Of course the *Bounty* was
itself an incredibly valuable set, both below decks and at sea. Fray
being a sailor himself, I think he was able to use her to the best
advantage for the film. Joe Canutt directed the second unit; every
shot he turned a camera on showed his hand.

All of our location shooting was along, and off, some twenty
miles of the northeast coast of Jamaica, the most unspoiled part
remaining of that exotic island. They put the company up in a hotel
complex with all the appropriate amenities; we had a lovely villa
overhanging the sea itself. It gave me an ideal coast and a good
incentive to swim early every morning.

Holly and her fiancée, Carlton Rochell, came down for a
visit, bringing my mother, for what would be her last visit to one of
my film locations. She was over ninety then, and not as spry as she
had been, but her spirit was the same, as was her unquenchable
interest in every aspect of the island, the shoot itself, and the chance
to watch her grandson direct a film.

She seemed anxious about me after watching a scene where
Silver throws his crutch to fell a loyal sailor, then knifes him.
"Mother," I said, "I can still *do* these fights. I just need a hand up
afterward."

We finished the day in an all but inaccessible narrow ravine.
As the light began to go, Fray had just printed a long, high-angle
master, then displayed considerable directorial courage (otherwise
known as the guts of a burglar) by announcing, "Sorry, I made a
mistake. The scene won't work with Silver on this side of the trail.
He's got most of the lines. We have to re-block and shoot it again."
And we did. I recall Wyler doing the same thing in a tricky scene in
Ben-Hur. That night when we were all at dinner, Mother com-
mented on how imperturbable Fray seemed as a director. "Even
more than you, I think," she said.

"Ah, but he is the real me," I said. "The me you see before
you is a man worn down by the women in his life." I got my
laugh, though I like to think I'm pretty unflappable on the set. The
difference is that Fray's calm goes all the way down to the bone, I
do believe.

He displayed a perhaps more definitive example of directorial cool a week or so later, when we were shooting one of the

most crucial scenes in the novel: where Jim hides in the apple barrel down in the ship's galley and, hearing Silver talking to some of the crew, realizes that they're not simple sailors, but pirates, and Silver is not the ship's cook, but their leader and the most dangerous cutthroat of them all. We were shooting below decks in the real ship's galley, a very cramped space with barely room to set the lights and camera and get the actors in place. As the day wore on, the lights and the tropical sun made it incredibly hot as well. It was a long scene, too: four or five pages. We worked through the afternoon, moving through the master angles to the close coverage of the several actors.

Finally, as the sun was setting, we got to my close-up of the entire scene, the last setup of the day. I like having the last shot, really. You've explored all your options with the scene by then, when the camera's on the other actors. Besides, this finished the sequence, it was the end of the week and the end of shooting below decks on the ship. Also, it was faintly cooler.

The cameraman fine-tuned his lights and we began shooting. I felt good about it. We did three takes from the top and Fray said, "OK, everyone, that's a wrap. Thank you for a good week's work." A bit weary, but pleased with myself, I said to Fray, "Which one of those takes did you print?"

"I didn't print any," he said. "You're tired. I should've done your close-up earlier; it's the key shot in the scene. We'll come back Monday morning; you'll be better." I was better Monday, but the pressure on Fray to settle for less on Saturday must have been considerable. I knew I was in very good hands, though I'd never doubted it.

We finished on schedule; Fray cut the film with conviction and dispatch. (He arrives at his editing choices more quickly than I do . . . the confidence of youth?) We were delighted with the film. For reasons not clear to me, some of the Turner brass didn't want Ted to see it until they'd arm-wrestled us on some changes they wanted. I knew he was in Palm Springs; I called to ask him if he'd like to see it. Of course he did; we flew it down and he was overwhelmed. We stayed with Fray's cut and TNT had a successful run with the film.

Thus encouraged, we made a theatrical release deal with Warners for Europe. It was disappointing, opening in theaters the

weekend of the World Cup soccer final. You could've shot quail in
any film theater on the Continent without harming a soul.

DURING MY DOWN TIME, I played chess with Bobby Fischer. Naah
... not exactly. I do play chess, but not very often, nor very well.
When I was a kid and moved down from Michigan, the only teams
I could make in high school were the rifle team and the chess team.
Then when I was in the Aleutians during the war, I sometimes
played with our crew chief. In fact, the last fistfight of my life (so
far) was over a chess game, on the island of Attu. Very few chess
players do fistfights, which tells you something about my game.
Jolly West, who really can play, says I'm the only instinctive chess
player he's ever seen. (Mind you, he says this in a tone of bemused
wonder. I have never won a game from him.)

Aaanyway, about Bobby Fischer. Some time after we finished
Treasure Island, I agreed to a quick up-and-back to Fresno for a
political fund-raiser—the best kind, where you don't have to overnight or do a banquet, and you sleep in your own bed after five or
six hours' effort for something you believe in.

At Burbank Airport, walking out to the executive jet belonging to the man who was picking up the tab for our evening, I
suddenly realized that the man walking ahead of me had to be
Bobby Fischer. In 1972 he'd defeated the Soviet world champion,
Spassky, in Iceland, becoming the youngest champion since Mor-
phy and making chess an American sport overnight.

Since then, he'd not played competitively, isolating himself
from public view. Yet here he was, walking ahead of me—a hero.
Our host confirmed that it was, indeed, Bobby Fischer. "But please
don't call him by name. He wants to be private." God knows I
understood that. Once we were airborne, he took out a very sophisticated chess computer and began playing, winning a couple of
games in minutes. I was seated across the aisle, a foot or so away. I
couldn't resist.

Avoiding his name as instructed, I asked, "Can any of those
computers beat you?"

He looked at me, darkly. "No. They're just machines. They
can't think, just run through possibilities. You want to try it?" Well,
there was no getting out of it. Fischer demonstrated the electronics
of the board, then watched in growing irritation through my first

ten or twelve moves, when I was down something like a bishop, a knight, and a couple of pawns. "That's terrible ... you'll be mated in about eight moves."

I did have one move left. "Could *you* win from here?" I said. "Well, it's not *that* terrible," Fischer snorted, taking the board back. He played out twenty moves in three minutes, faster than the computer could keep up, till it resigned, beeping forlornly. "It can't play very well," he said, tossing it into his briefcase.

I was much heartened. "Well," I said, "we won, right?"

TREASURE ISLAND was named one of the best cable films of the year; it was time to find another one to do for Turner, before the flowers faded. Without much difficulty, we agreed on *The Crucifer of Blood,* the Sherlock Holmes play I'd done at the Ahmanson. It appealed to me because I find it interesting, also instructive, to do the same piece in both media. You tend to get better, for one thing.

Turner was willing, but wanted Fray to do a screenplay as soon as possible, so we could shoot in the fall. Fray said, "I have to give Paul Giovanni a shot at it first; he wrote the play." Paul was interested, but ill; he'd get back to us.

Some time passed; no word from Paul. "Look, Fray," I said in my most fatherly tone (on which the license was expiring anyway), "why don't you at least *start* on the screenplay? In the end you'll be writing most of it anyway. Paul hasn't gotten back to us; he may not have written the play anyway. Some people think Peter Shaffer did."

Fray was immovable. "I don't care if George Bernard Shaw wrote it. Giovanni's name is on it; I have to find out if he wants to try a screenplay." A week or so later we got word that Paul was too ill to write, but he wished us well. A month or two later he was dead of AIDS. I was pleased, though, to be reminded that, in the black heart of Hollywood, I had managed to raise a son who knew right from wrong.

Fray's screenplay was first-class, as was his prep on the film overall. We were back on familiar ground at Pinewood; most of our shooting was planned there, except for a chase scene on the Thames. We had our regular team behind the camera: this would be the third film on which Tony Woolard would be our production

designer, and Terry Needham first assistant director. It's impossible
to overstate the importance of a good A.D., or to explain this to
civilians. Believe me, it's true. I've made seventy-some films, a number of them very high-stakes undertakings with very demanding
directors. I have never worked with a better A.D. than Terry. He
runs a company like a combination of a friendly uncle and a marine
gunnery sergeant, which is exactly what you need.

I know it's frustrating for qualified people trying to break
into the business, but you unavoidably tend to hire people you
know can do the job, because they've done it before. I'd worked
with Peter Snell for twenty years, for God's sake.

I came over a little ahead of the schedule for the last of the
casting, though much of that, too, was simply finding which of our
old mates were free. To our great good fortune, Richard Johnson
was. We really needed him for Dr. Watson. *Crucifer* is unusual in
several ways, principally in that it's about Watson in love. You need
an actor in the part who's a plausible romantic figure, which Richard surely is.

The woman's role is also a fine part, unusual for Doyle's
women, who are generally drawn rather thinly. This role was created in the original New York production by Glenn Close (whatever
became of her?). A fine young English actress named Susanna
Harker played the part for us, wonderfully well.

We also had John Castle, who'd done such a wonderful Caesar for me in *Antony;* Edward Fox; and Simon Callow, almost as
good as Inspector Lestrade as he was recently in *Four Weddings
and a Funeral*.

I was up to speed on Holmes, of course, and came up to
Fray's standards, I think. He's not an easy director to please. I like
that. We were able to do much more with the makeup where
Holmes disguises himself as the ancient Chinese opium dealer,
Fung Tching. Nick Dudman, who'd just finished the exotic makeups
in *Batman,* took Ziggy Geike's basic design and made it a more
intricate film makeup. It took two hours to put on, but it was
worth it.

Fray's only serious confrontation on the film was not with
me or any of the actors, but with Peter Snell and Tony Woolard, the
production designer. The opening scene of the film is laid in the

Red Fort of Agra, in India, "the only structure in the world with a hundred gates," as Holmes describes it (I've been there, and it's got nothing like a hundred gates, but it's a great line).

We'd toyed with the idea of shooting a short location there, but it was far beyond our means. Instead, Tony built Fray a large exterior section of the fort on a sound stage, with towers and minarets in intricate perspective. Fray looked at it and said, "Fine! All I need to bring it alive is a troop of British lancers riding up the street in the opening shot." No, no—it wouldn't work, the set wouldn't bear it, it would cost too much. "Forty lancers," said Fray, "at full gallop, all good horsemen." Peter and Tony argued back and forth with him, trying to cut down the number of horses, but he stuck to his troop of forty. "Plus one elephant." He got that too. I have to say the shot gives you India.

I DID A FEW other interesting parts in the early nineties ... a hard old Scots grandfather in Disney's remake of *The Little Kidnappers* was perhaps the best of them, not least because the producer on the film was Phil Fehrle, who would figure later in an even more important project.

But the paramount event of 1991, beyond challenge, was the birth of Fray and Marilyn's son, very early in the morning of July 25. We drove down to the hospital, hugged the triumphant parents, viewed the serene little male cub nestling in his dad's arms through the glass. Then we came home and sat on our courtyard steps just as the sun came up, as we hadn't done for thirty years, when I sat there with an Oscar beside me. Believe me, a grandson is better.

I HAD STARTED doing biographical roles very early in my career, so I came to understand the importance of research sooner than I might have otherwise. Surely there was a lot of material on Moses when I started researching him for Mr. DeMille. Sigmund Freud, Breasted; there are dozens of standard works, a good many of which I wrestled with. In the end, the Five Books of Moses in the Old Testament, most particularly in the King James translation, proved the most valuable. This side of Shakespeare, there is no finer writing in the language. DeMille used only fragments of it, as did George Stevens when I played the Baptist for him. By this time, I was captured—not only by the quality of the writing, but by the stories themselves. I began to redact them as performance pieces, for various public occasions. With some success, I had recorded some LPs for Caedmon in the sixties.

In the nineties, I suddenly realized what perfect material this was for a TV series. Not on network television, which had long since abandoned any such programming, but on one of the expanding cable networks, which were absorbing the network audiences anyway. We began peddling it around to "the usual suspects," as Claude Rains had put it.

I have to say—unique in my experience—we never got a flat turndown. Everyone we talked to said, "What a great idea." The catch was, as ever, the money they were willing to put up. Not enough, though the offers kept improving. My original idea had been to position me as sort of an Alistair Cooke, doing our version of *Masterpiece Theatre,* maybe even shooting in my own library, simply telling the stories.

Fray saw it more clearly. "First," he said, "you have to go to the Holy Land. People have been making pilgrimages to these places for thousands of years. You can't do this from your library. Second, we need background commentaries about all the stories . . . how they located the room of the Last Supper, the walls of Jericho. You have to talk about all these places, *in* these places."

I saw his point. "So who's going to write all this commentary?"

"Who else?" Fray said. "You redacted all the stories, as it is. You'll be speaking as yourself in the commentaries. You have to write them."

"Thanks a lot, pal," I said, but of course he was right. We were calling it *Charlton Heston Presents the Bible.* So I wrote the commentaries, too.

The prep was in some ways harder than the shoot. Glenn Jones' cable company, Jones Entertainment, were our prime partners. We sold the first two rounds of cable exposure to Arts and Entertainment, and Good Times Video put up a hefty sum for a share of the video rights. Fray would be doing a film for Castle Rock, and couldn't direct, though he managed to be with us for the shoot as executive producer, along with Phil Fehrle for Jones.

We had an enormous stroke of luck which enhanced the whole project. By this time we'd decided I would tell each story in the location where it was laid, along with my commentary. John Stronach, producer, and Tony Westman, director and cameraman, had gone to the Holy Land to scout locations. While there, they found a recently excavated Roman amphitheater from the first century, called Beit She'an, near the Sea of Galilee. It was the perfect place to stage the stories, with genuine marble columns and arches. It made everything we shot there better.

With our financing in place, our preproduction schedule should've brought us quickly to the shoot. This was not to be. We had planned, of course, to shoot most of the Old Testament commentaries in Egypt, where I'd filmed four times before. Anything you do anywhere in the Middle East, of course, from starting a war to making a movie, is upholstered with endless bureaucratic bumphh. So it was with our Bible series. We were never told we couldn't get a production permit, indeed we were assured on the highest level that we *would* get one, just as soon as this minister or that under-secretary signed off on the project, "in the twinkling of an eye." The Middle Eastern eye can take many months to twinkle.

During our Egyptian eclipse, of course, the world continued to turn, very usefully. Having crushed Iraq, we neglected to eliminate Saddam Hussein. Still, both Mikhail Gorbachev and the Soviet Union collapsed, more or less simultaneously, removing a threat to world peace that had hung over my children's heads all of their lifetimes. Fray's son would doubtless face other problems, but not, it seemed, from the Soviets.

I was also invited by the Prince of Wales to take part in a concert to raise several million pounds to restore the roof of Salisbury Cathedral, a bit worn after six centuries. I was to join Placido Domingo, Jessye Norman, Kenneth Branagh, and the like. (I guess I was a token Yank.) I did a couple of American poems, some of the small parts in Branagh's offering from his *Henry V,* as well as Moses' farewell, which I'd already redacted from Exodus/Deuteronomy as one of the pieces in our Bible series.

The concert went very well, played to an audience of some fourteen thousand, seated outdoors in the cathedral close (God gave us good weather). Afterward at a reception for the performers, HRH paid me a compliment so extravagant that vanity requires me to repeat it: "You know, I've gone to church every Sunday I can

remember in my life," he said. "I must tell you that I wish the
Archbishop of Canterbury could read the Bible as well as you can."

WHEN WE FLEW BACK HOME, we found a crisis waiting, though it's
a story with a happy ending, and a heroine: Holly. For years Holly
had repeatedly urged Lydia to have a mammogram, which, for the
same reasons many women find compelling, she had avoided
doing. That fall, Holly phoned her from New York and said, "Mom,
I'm not going to talk about this anymore. Don't call me, don't write
me. I won't answer your letters, I won't speak to you on the phone
or come to see you, until you tell me that you've had a mammogram. I love you. Good-bye."

That did it—barely in time. The specialists at UCLA found a
malignancy in Lydia's left breast. Without Holly's tough love, it
would've been hopeless. They scheduled the surgery at once. The
night before, we were walking on our terrace. "Isn't it nice," I said,
"that all our lives, we've both had people who love us . . . especially
each other." There was a full moon, covered with clouds. As we
watched, they cleared. We took that as a good omen.

And so it proved. They got all the bad cells out, replaced her
breast with one formed from her own tissue. When they unveiled
it, I said, "Remind me . . . which is the new one?" As the resident
expert on her breasts, I gave them a "ten."

Holly flew out, of course, the one who made it happen; Fray
and Marilyn stood by at the hospital. (Fray and Jolly West gave
blood, mine was the wrong type.) Not long before Lydia came
home, I went out to Simi Valley to help open the Reagan Presidential Library, as I'd promised long before.

There were five presidents there: Nixon, Ford, Carter,
Reagan, and Bush, more than have ever been assembled together
in the history of the country. I was allowed to speak first, everyone
understanding why I must then leave to go back to the hospital.
Five presidents sent their good wishes to my girl.

TWO MONTHS into the New Year, with joy now undiluted, we gathered our friends at the house and christened our grandson, Jack,
even by then becoming his own self. I put a cedar bar stool draped
with white linen in the front patio, and dug out a sterling silver
punch bowl as a font.

God had given us a warm, clear day; a fine Episcopal priest named Peter Kreitler took over from His hands and named our boy "John Alexander Clarke," honoring godfather and grandmother, and no doubt marking the last time he'd be called "John" in his life. He was a "Jack" if ever I saw one.

His role was passive, but he followed events with interest, smiling angelically at the applause, retiring briefly for a meal and wardrobe change, then ending the day sleeping happily in the arms of his great-grandmother. Watching my mother holding him, I thought, as she must have, that she'd held me just so, more than half a century before. My toast at the end of the afternoon was the same I said for Fraser when he was born, from Genesis: "The smell of my son is as the smell of a field which the Lord hath planted."

BY THE SPRING OF 1992, we still did not have our permits from the Egyptian government, though their ambassador had phoned me from Washington to express his delight that I'd be filming there "once again"; a reception must be laid on for my arrival, he said. Meanwhile, John Stronach, back in Egypt again wrestling with the various agencies, was getting absolutely nowhere. Though no one ever denied him, he spent most of his time in his hotel, awaiting word. Fray decided it was time to move the unit to Israel and prepare. If the Egyptian approvals came through, it would be easy to go there from Israel and get the footage we'd planned.

President Bush had invited Lydia and me to a State Dinner for the president of Chile. The fashionable Washingtonian, I believe, looks down on such affairs as rather blah, but we've enjoyed those we've gone to. The White House is a stunning national domicile, the food is good, and the evening always ends on time.

I sat at Mrs. Bush's table—she's a lady I've always admired enormously—and was able to squeak by in Spanish to the Chilean president. Lydia was next to the Secretary of State, Jim Baker. I stopped by his table to pick her up when dinner was over to find that she'd outlined our Egyptian problem to him.

"This shouldn't be difficult," he said. "Seems to me you've got some clerks jerking you around. I'm meeting President Mubarak in Lisbon in two days. I'll ask him." Sounded good to me.

President Bush also asked me to a ceremony in the Rose Garden, where he announced the implementation of the Beck decision handed down by the Supreme Court freeing union members from having their dues spent on political causes with which they disagreed. The ruling was so sweeping and so overwhelming in its impact that the president backed off from it, fearing the wrath of Big Labor.

Labor is no longer the working man with a lunch-bucket; it's fat cats in limousines milking the shrinking union membership to fund the AFL-CIO as a political money-raising machine. The president simply misread the realities on this, I think. Tony Makris, a Deputy Assistant Secretary of Defense under Cap Weinberger, does some political staff work for me. He leaned over and said, halfway through the President's speech, "He won't implement it." And he didn't, unwilling to take on the paper tiger.

The current Secretary of Labor, Robert Reich, has said of unions, "Sometimes you have to put the members' feet to the fire . . . tie them to the mast. . . ." Never mind, Beck will happen. Supreme Court decisions don't go away.

Our little film project seemed relatively trivial in this grand context, but it was important to us. Lydia and I flew to New York for two days, so I could appear at the American Museum of Natural History, where Holly was then working, at a fund-raising banquet she arranged, and have some family time with Holly and Carlton. We took off then to Tel Aviv, where Fray had gone after deciding to abandon the Egyptian shoot. It wasn't the government that had been blocking us, but Muslim fundamentalists who saw our film as a threat to their beliefs. With all due respect, that seems very strange to me. The stories in the Koran are essentially the same stories as those in the Jewish Bible and the Christian Old Testament.

In one sense, our shoot was eased because I was the only performer, thus simplifying the lighting, blocking, and camera moves. I'd worked on the material over some years, redacting the core Bible stories. I chose the ones I liked best; the Creation, Adam and Eve, Cain and Abel, Noah and the Flood, and so on through the Five Books of Moses. The New Testament is easier to redact: the four Gospels each explore the life of Christ, but each with stories found in none of the other Gospels, and stories common to all four. Again, in the Books of Moses, there are stories told more than once, with changes. I dealt with them the only way I knew—as a storyteller.

That's my only credential. I'm an actor; actors tell stories. One of the reasons the Bible stories are so good is that they've been crafted over thousands of years—as stories. Whatever their divine inspiration, the Old Testament stories were passed on in an oral tradition for centuries before the Phoenicians invented the alphabet, told around a campfire by an old guy who had to have an apprentice kid: "Look, I'll protect you from the bullies, I'll see you get food and a tent, but you have to learn the stories, for when I'm dead. Then you have to do them."

And so with the Christian Gospel. Sure, the Romans were literate, so were many Jews, but the men who preached the Gospel of Christ were talking to an illiterate audience. Again, they were telling stories. "Listen to me . . . I was *there*. Let me tell you what He said . . ."

Still, I was stepping out on a pretty thin plank. I recruited three biblical scholars: a rabbi, a Baptist minister, and an Episcopal priest, all with formidable academic credentials to reinforce their standing as theologians. I was surprised by the readiness of their independent consensus. They endorsed my redactions (correcting some of the King James translation textual confusions), accepting my identity as a storyteller, not a theologian.

They were even more helpful in the commentaries I'd written. We began shooting with one of the first of these, at the Temple Mount ruins at the southwest corner of a marble wall. Why? It was held by the ancients to be the center of the world, because it enshrines the Stone of Abraham, and nearby is the church built on the site of the Crucifixion. Since the three religions involved have among them provided the fount of our culture and shaped our ethical principles, I could say that the marble block I put my hand on was the cornerstone of our civilization.

We shot for twenty days, plus religious holidays and travel time, up and down the length of a small country, filming my commentaries in the Negev, in small boats in the Red Sea and the Sea of Galilee, in the ruins of Jericho. I learned something in every location, changed some of the things I said, as well as how I said them. It added enormous weight and significance simply to be there, on the ground where these things happened.

It was exhausting. On one day in Jerusalem, we shot both interiors and exteriors—day, dusk, and night—twenty-seven setups

at seven locations, including five dolly shots and co*ing six pages*
of script. A day like that can also be exhilarating f*n actor. You* *555*
get on a mightily energized creative high, where yo *spurred on*
by the pressure. "Yeah, I know—that was no good. I *this time,* *In the*
let's do it. Now. Turn over." *Arena*

We didn't break for dinner, just had pizza s*
just as I was about to do a major speech. "No, I don*'t came*
let's get a print on this first." By the time we did, the *now,*
gone. Art can be cruel. *is all*

The best part of that long day was the end, th
middle of setting up a shot where I explained why the
were in was probably the site of the Last Supper, one o-
authorities helping us pointed out something I'd not kr
the reputed tomb of King David lay two floors below us.
lap between the two faiths amazed me; I included it in the
tary, adding what seemed to me a key question: "I wond
knew that?"

At every level, the Israelis were enormously su
though half the stories we were filming were Christian. A k
ber of our American team from the beginning was Gwen
rising young independent producer, who ended up as our firs
She was the first woman A.D. I'd ever worked for, but I was
surprised that she succeeded at what is the most requisitely mascu-
line of any job on a film company. I've known her since she was
four years old; my only problem was that her nickname as a child
was "Simsie," a cognomen to which I've long been accorded lifetime rights. My solution was to call her "Sir" on the set at all times.
It worked very well.

Of course the best part of the whole shoot for me was doing
the stories, acting them out in that vast ruined Roman amphitheater,
larger than any stage I've ever seen. It was a wonderfully flexible
acting arena: there were solidly intact Roman arches for palaces,
Pilate's and the Pharaoh's; also tumbled slopes of marble rubble
for roaming in the wilderness, Jesus, Moses, the Baptist. We had a
long table for the Last Supper, and various seats of judgment, a
very useful Roman camp chair, and a fine lectern with a true
seventeenth-century copy of the King James Bible. It was a prop,
really; I knew the stories by then. As an actor, it was pure joy to do
them.

e thing, I got to do all the parts: not just God, but
For f
Adam and ?, and the snake, which is a very good part indeed.
(" 'Ye ss not sssurely *die,*' said the serpent.") Aside from the
qualitye stories themselves, it was a fascinating actor's exercise
to plfe parts—male, female, divine, human. It stretched a lot
of d for me.

cribed course there's the King James translation itself. It's
at work scribed as "the monument of English prose" as well as "the
ire true. at work of art ever created by a committee." Both state-
ork from ire true. Fifty-four scholars worked seven years to produce
nglish. Su ork from the extant texts in Aramaic, Hebrew, Greek, Latin,
iarship, b nglish. Such an undertaking can be expected to produce great
es. iarship, but hardly writing as spare and sublime as the King
es.

I'm persuaded that somewhere in that pack of distinguished
ademics and priests was a humble monk, perhaps a bastard son
f Shakespeare, and the true inheritor of his divine spark. After
ighting through to some consensus on theology, I see one of the
big dogs saying, "Well, that's agreed then. Now, on the language,
let's just run it by Brother William. That lad has a way with words."

The authors of the several boring translations that have followed over the last fifty years mumble that the K.J.V. is "difficult,"
filled with *long words.* Have a look at the difficult long words that
begin the Old Testament, and end the Gospels:

> In the beginning God created the heaven and the earth.
> And the earth was without form, and void; darkness was
> upon the face of the deep.

and

> Now, of the other things which Jesus did, if they should
> be written every one, I suppose the world itself could not
> contain the books that would be written.

Shakespeare aside, there's no comparable writing in the language, as has been observed by wiser men than I. Over the past
several centuries, it's been the single book in most households, an
enormous force in shaping the development of the English language. Carried around the world by missionaries, it provided the
base by which English is about to become the lingua franca of the

world in the next century. Exploring it during this shoot was one
of the most rewarding creative experiences of my life.

The whole Israel shoot went wonderfully well, though I
wouldn't for an instant suggest that Anyone was on our side. A more
tangible presence, lifting all our spirits, was Jack Heston, then not
yet a year old. Marilyn would often bring him out for lunch, a
serene and relaxed tiny boy, not yet quite walking but hungry to
explore the world expanding around him.

He called me "Ba," almost his first word, now his name for
me as long as I live, I guess. When I picked him up, he'd point
imperiously up the hill, "Dere, Ba. Dere!" Now, of course, he can
outrun me. When I pointed this out to him the other day, he looked
speculatively at me and said, "Ba, are you old?"

"Yeah, I'm pretty old, Jack," I said. He walked over and
patted my arm.

"You're strong, doh." Now there's a considerate young man.

One of my last and best memories of the Bible shoot involved Jack. We were doing my commentary on the Baptism of
Jesus, with me standing hip deep in the Jordan (not as big a river
as you would imagine, considering the swath it has cut through
history). Marilyn had brought Jack down, and Lydia was shooting
stills of him, when Fray said, "This is the shot you want here."
Picking his infant son up, he strode to the bank of the Jordan and
dipped Jack's toes into the water. Roll, Jordan, roll.

22

What's It All About, Charlie?

Though the mills of God grind slowly,
yet they grind exceeding small;
Though with patience He stands waiting,
with exactness grinds He all.

— H. W. LONGFELLOW

A YEAR OR SO AGO I got home from a difficult location in what used to be the Soviet Union, where I'd gone to shoot a small but interesting part in a film about Genghis Khan. It had gone very badly; indeed it was never finished. It was a multinational production and they ran out of money. I'm afraid my makeup man, Nick Dudman, and I were the only people in the company who got paid (and that only because my agent, Jack Gilardi, made them put all the money in a U.S. bank before we left the States).

It was a great makeup. Ziggy Geike had designed it here; Nick had created it in London and put it on me in the Caucasus. When I walked on the set as a Mongol Khan, the company didn't recognize me. I didn't have to act the part—I just carried the makeup around. (It occurs to me that I must be the only Anglo actor in America who's still allowed to play other ethnicities: Scots maniacs, Chinese opium dealers, French cardinals. Gilardi must've somehow slipped a grandfather clause in my contracts twenty years ago.)

Anyway, Lydia and I flew home, enriched but deflated. I don't mind the time change, even the fifteen time zones from Russia, though I did sleep very deeply the first night back on my ridge. I woke early and abruptly the next morning to a startlingly vivid

memory of an extraordinary dream, clear in every detail. It was also
linear, as few dreams are, structured with a beginning, middle, and
end.

In the dream (still vivid, even now), Lydia and I were at
Burbank Airport, about to board a borrowed executive jet on some
useful errand. As we stood talking while they took the bags from
the limo to our plane, I saw a World War II B-17 parked fifty yards
away, its crew in flight gear, standing as crews always did when they
were being photographed. I walked over. "Where are you guys
bound?"

"England," said one of the officers. "Eighth Air Force." In
the dream, I was not surprised. "Want a lift?"

"Wish I could," I said, and watched them turn and move to
the plane. At my feet, I noticed a single flight bag left behind. The
stencil on it read S/SGT HESTON, C. 16170644. Suddenly, I understood.
I turned and ran back to Lydia. "Darling!" I said. "I have to go. It
means we get to do it all over again—everything, only better. It
happens for both of us."

"I know, Charlie," she said. "I understand, too." I took her
in my arms and kissed her and she was suddenly eighteen again,
black curls tossing in the wind. "I'll meet you after the war," she
said, smiling. "Fly safe. Write me." She waved as I ran for the plane,
scooping up the flight bag. The number four engine was turning
over as I tossed the bag up into the belly of the plane, waved back
at my girl, and chinned myself up inside.

The crew were all at their stations; the plane began to bump
down the runway. Standing near one of the waist guns was *me* . . .
myself at eighteen, skinny, in uniform. He looked at the older me
speculatively and lifted his hand. "See you later," he said. Then,
suddenly, I was inside him, looking back toward the front of the
plane where I'd just been standing . . . and there was no one there.

Now, I didn't serve in England, I wasn't in the Eighth, nor in
B-17s. I don't believe in dreams as indicators of anything, really.
Still, I have never had such a specifically detailed dream, nor one
which I wrote down the next morning. What does it mean? I have
no idea. (I certainly didn't go back and do the war all over again
out of England in a '17. I would've remembered *that*.)

So, looking back, what would I like to do differently, what
would I like to change? I don't want to change anything; life's been

too good to me as it is. Sure, I'd like to do it all over. I could do it better.

Still, after all these months—years now, trying to remember my life and write it down in some sort of order—I realize I've just finished doing that about as well as I can. This is what happened to me, up to now, and what I thought about it, or remember that I thought.

When I was an arrogant young cock who thought I could do everything because I hadn't done anything, I remember a title I'd read somewhere: *The Girl, The Gold Watch, and the Whole Damn Thing*. I surely have the girl, I guess the gold watch too, by now, but not the whole damn thing. Nobody gets that, and if by any chance you do, it can destroy you. The guy in Ecclesiastes got it right:

> I returned, and saw under the sun, that the race
> is not to the swift, nor the battle to the strong,
> neither yet bread to the wise, nor yet riches to men of
> understanding, nor favor to men of skill;
> but time and chance happeneth to them all.

I'll surely sign that. "There is a tide in the affairs of men, which, taken at the flood, leads on to fortune," said Mr. Shakespeare, with equal insight into the human condition.

THE SHINING TIMES of the last couple of years haven't been this or that film, or the other stage appearance, but family milestones along the way I hardly dreamed of reaching. One of the very best of these was Holly's marriage, two years ago. Fathers have written about this event for several centuries, at least; many deeper and more eloquent men than I. The message is the same: giving a daughter in marriage is different. Your son says, "I've found this wonderful girl, I want to marry her and make children," and they do, and you're happy.

But for a father, a daughter has a private place. Her husband doesn't diminish that place, but he changes it. That's why I was touched that Carlton Rochell chose to fly to California and, over lunch at the Polo Lounge, ask my permission to marry Holly. Aside from sharing with me a similarly cranky first name, subject to all kinds of errors in spelling and pronunciation, Carlton is an ideal

son-in-law. A rising star at Sotheby's, where he's a vice president,
he and all his relatives seem to love Holly. Sounds reasonable to
me. We have acquired a wonderfully compatible set of in-laws.

As with Fray and Marilyn before their marriage, Carlton and
Holly were already "posslqs." (You don't know what that *means?*
It's the only useful word ever created by a government bureaucrat.
At the Census Bureau, it stands for "Persons of Opposite Sex Shar-
ing Living Quarters," a not uncommon arrangement in the closing
decade of the millennium.)

The wedding was a celebration, with guests coming to New
York from everywhere—Spain, France, England, California. It's simpler to list those who couldn't make it: the Wests and Leo Ziffren,
who were working, and my mother, who'd reached a time when
she found travel impossible. Just about everyone else who knew
Holly was there. The service was at St. Thomas's Episcopal Church
on Fifth Avenue; I gave her away and read from the Song of Solomon and, believe it or not, "More I Cannot Wish You" from *Guys
and Dolls:*

Mansions I can wish you, seven footmen all in red
And calling cards upon a silver tray.
But more I cannot wish you than to wish you
    find your love,
Your own true love, this day.

The celebration carried over into the next day, after the
happy couple had gone honeymooning. Fray and I had taken Prince
Jack to the American Museum of Natural History, where Holly
worked at the time. He stood on tiptoe, joyously awestruck under
the great blue whale suspended from the ceiling, his arms stretched
wide, straining to encompass it. That's how I felt about the whole
wedding.

LAST YEAR Lydia and I hit another significant date: our golden wedding anniversary. Fifty years does seem a long time, though looking
back, it's no more than a time-tick back to the day I stood beside
her, a gangly kid in uniform in that Carolina church. We were
willing to settle then for what weeks we had left before I went
overseas; maybe the last we'd ever see of each other. Instead, half a

century and two generations of progeny later, here we were, contrary to the stats, celebrating fifty years together.

Of course we did more than the normal run of TV and radio interviews, dealing with the standard query on how to have a "successful marriage in this town." "Nothing to it," I said. "You need a deep and lasting personal commitment, a lot of flexibility, tolerance, and understanding. But above all, you need a superb husband, and I happen to be a superb husband."

This always got a laugh, but nothing like Lydia's response when a probing talk-show host asked her, "Now, Lydia, seriously: did you never, even briefly, consider divorce?"

"Divorce? Never!" said my girl, with a steely look. "Murder, yes." Actually, I think that defines a successful marriage.

"There are only two ways to celebrate a golden wedding," I said from the first. "We can go out to dinner with Fray and Marilyn, Holly and Carlton, or we can have a little party for two hundred and fifty people. There's no middle ground." We made the right choice, of course. A goodly crowd was gathered at the Nikko Hotel. All available blood kin, of course, including my half-sister, Kay, and Prince Jack, who, after starring in his white suit for the press, wisely retired to an upstairs suite.

Jolly West was master of ceremonies. Mel Tormé, though flying that night to a concert tour in Australia, came and sang "Our Love Is Here to Stay" for us. Any number of wise and witty fellows spoke extravagantly about us—pundits, actors, generals, senators, cabinet secretaries. Fraser and Holly both made us weep, I spoke as well as I could, and Lydia spoke better. My gift was a digital imaging system with which she's prepared her last two photo shows. She said it's the best gift I ever gave her (except, of course, the still-viable me). It couldn't have been a finer evening; we're gearing up now for the seventy-fifth.

MY MOTHER MISSED both Holly's wedding and our fiftieth celebration last year. She was a proud and passionate lady, who'd survived the deaths of a son, a daughter, a beloved sister, and two husbands. She lived her last years alone in the house I'd bought her, strongly supported by the nearby presence of her beloved grandson, Kris, a successful Chicago lawyer, and the visits I was able to make, crisscrossing back and forth around the globe in pursuit of my living.

Throughout this time, she resisted with all her being the inroads of time on her capacities. When I flew to see her the last year or so, I could no longer take her to the opera, nor the Art Institute of Chicago, nor finally even out to dinner. She loved her rose garden, but she'd stopped tending it. Her letters became infrequent.

By this time, I'd engaged a gerontologist to supervise her care, with a rota of nurses to be sure she was comfortable. The last time I saw her, she wasn't interested in the videotapes I'd brought, though I was featured in some of them. We talked, reexploring some of her firm and favorite opinions: Luciano Pavarotti's clear claim over Placido Domingo as the premier tenor of our time; John McEnroe as the best tennis player of them all. She ate little of the Chinese takeout I'd picked up for dinner, though. I read poetry to her for a bit, till she drifted off. The next morning I flew home, then phoned to see how she was doing. "Oh, Charlton," she said. "I'm so tired."

Two weeks later I was in Utah, playing Brigham Young in a film about the Mormons for Ted Turner, when the phone rang at 6 A.M. I was already having breakfast before my 7 A.M. departure for location; this could be a change in my call, but I had an edgy feeling it wasn't. My mother had died in the night, in her sleep, in her own bed, in the house I'd promised her she'd live in all her life. She was ninety-six years old.

She'd had a long, rich life, full of travel, adventure, children, and grandchildren—people she loved. She lived to hold her great-grandson in her lap.

I went to work (the best therapy), and they condensed my last two days of shooting into one, with Fray flying out from L.A. to keep me company, God bless his true and loving heart. It was a very tough, long day, which was just what I needed. There's a laserlike intensity to that kind of shooting that lets you shut out everything else. Night shooting has a pressure of its own, as well. We got my last shot just before 3 A.M.

I thanked the director, the crew, and Tom Berenger, the star of the film, then hugged my son (he was off to interview bear trainers for his next movie), and got back from the location with time for two hours' sleep before catching my plane home.

By the weekend, Lydia and I were in Chicago, where Holly and Fray joined us from opposite directions. Kris, her grandson, had followed my mother's wishes: cremation and no funeral. We met him and the several members of my brother's family on a narrow bridge near the old Maple Street house over a quiet canal flowing into Lake Michigan. I spoke some Tennyson I knew she liked, while Fray and Kris scattered her ashes into the placid, moving waters.

> Sunset and evening star,
> And one clear call for me!
> And may there be no moaning of the bar,
> When I put out to sea,
>
> But such a tide as moving seems asleep,
> Too full for sound and foam,
> It brought my soul from out the boundless deep
> Now turns at last for home.

Then we went back to her house for . . . a Celtic wake, I guess it was, with the families and the dozen or so friends who'd known my mother long and well. An Episcopalian priest, Father Myers, who'd been a great comfort to her in the last years, said a prayer. I reprised Tennyson, and everyone went home, across the continent on diverse journeys, while my mother's ashes drifted into the great inland lake she loved so much.

Lydia and Holly, Fray and I had kept time enough to walk again on the Northwestern campus where I met Lydia and my life began. Fray photographed us on the steps of the Speech School. Then we drove to New Trier, the high school where I'd struggled to fit into a different kind of life. The theater was empty, but the stage door was open; I walked again on the first real stage where I'd ever acted. My work will take me to Chicago now and then, but probably not to the North Shore where I spent my adolescence and, more or less by accident, became myself. We stopped by the church in Wilmette where I'd knelt a month before and prayed for my mother, weeping, "Please, God, take her when you will. She has so much pain and no joy in her life now." And so He did, in His time.

It was a good day, a fine farewell to my mother, and all the places I knew so well, and doubt I'll see again. (About this time,

Lydia's secretary, Helene Bean, lost a four-year fight with cancer.
Mercifully, just as April came, she left us—bereft yet again.)

Not long ago, going through some of my mother's papers, I
ran across a lengthy obituary in the *Chicago Tribune* for my great-grandfather, James Charlton. I hadn't realized he was born in 1832. That was during Andrew Jackson's presidency. His life and my mother's, then, encompassed most of the history of the Republic. Time and the river . . .

I DIDN'T START playing the game till I was in my twenties and that's too late to learn to do it very well, but it's been important to me ever since, so I should tell you about tennis and me. My only boast is that I've undoubtedly played with more great players than any other lousy player in the world. In the course of this exhilarating experience, I've gained some insight into the game. Almost all club players, including some who could beat me easily, imagine there are three levels: themselves, their club pro, and the top ten men in the world. In fact, there are at least five other groups to sandwich in above your basic hacker; a player at any level would have trouble getting a set from anyone the next rung up. Tennis has probably the slowest learning curve of any sport; a beginner can play for a year and hardly be able to hit the ball in the court five times running. But once you get past that, you can play tennis anywhere in the world, day or night, indoors, outdoors, summer or winter. It's a wonderful sport for a workout; if you hit with a pro he can have you on your knees and sweating in an hour (unlike that other sport, where you ride around in a cart for four hours tapping a ball toward a small hole on two-thirds of your shots). Tennis is the only one-on-one major sport in the world. Just you against the other guy (well, boxing too, but that leaves you with bits of brain bumping around in your skull).

I'm not a joiner (as you will have observed by now), but I'm proud of having inexplicably gained membership in the All-England Lawn Tennis and Croquet Club. (For non-tennists, that's the club that annually stages the most important tournament in tennis, better known as Wimbledon.) After several years of underground effort, a few players like Laver and Emerson and Johnny MacDonald, along with some sympathetic board members, sort of smuggled me in as a temporary member. At one point, Rod Laver said, "Tell y'wot,

Blue, p'raps y'better just win the bloody Men's Singles. Then they *have* to tyke ye in." A year or so later, no doubt through some computer error, I was voted a full member. (Unfortunately, a really reliable low backhand volley is not included with the membership card.)

There are a few other Americans in the club, but I think I'm the only actor (both identities are burdens to be borne). Still, they tolerate my shortfalls as a player, and I can see great tennis— some of the best matches ever played on Centre Court (*any* center court), from Laver through Sampras. As a hacker, I do have one advantage: as we get older, we can still get better. I have. John McEnroe will never again play as well as he did four years ago. I'm better now than I was then. It's a joyous, infinitely rewarding part of my life.

I built a tennis court not long after I finished the house, with a gym-spa and pavilion attached later. After my early morning pool workout, if I'm not filming or rehearsing a play, I hit for an hour with a pro. On weekends, we have a loose quorum of doubles both mornings, sometimes stretching into the afternoon. Some of the guys have been coming up since I built the court, a few I played with even before that: Sammy Match, who gave me my first lesson; both Panchos, Gonzales and Segura; Alex Olmedo; Walter Seltzer; Jolly West; Ray Daley; and a fine young Ethiopian pro, Ghebre Gebregziabeher, lean and quick as a whip. (I'm the only guy on my court who can both spell and pronounce his name.) To everyone else, he's Gabby. He's already working with young Jack (now that's the time to take up tennis . . . at three and a half).

I remember sitting on my observation deck watching a doubles match between Laver/Rosewall and Emerson/Hoad when they were all ranked in the world top ten. At that level, the quality of play is awesome: Hoad's booming serves, Emerson's crushing volleys. Laver, uncannily, could turn and chase down a ball lobbed over him and hit an unplayable backhand winner down the line while still running in the opposite direction. Rosewall's service return was perhaps the best in tennis, often followed by a volley winner clipping the line. I suddenly thought: Good Lord . . . in the whole world at this moment, there can be no better tennis being played anywhere than on this court.

●

I'VE HUNTED all my life, but not so much of late, except for an occasional day after quail with Fray and a couple of his pals. The arroyos in the San Gabriel Mountains are fairly heavy country, a little rough on the knees, and you don't like to hold the younger guys up. I do go often with Fray to shoot sporting clays, out in the deep Valley, and for some years I've hosted a Celebrity Shoot (no, we don't shoot celebrities, they shoot clays) down near Dana Point. Every year we get more and more participants, some coming from as far as New York.

There are numbers of gun owners—collectors, hunters, sport shooters—in the film community, plus many more who keep firearms for protection. I suspect, in fact, that there are more film-makers who are closet gun enthusiasts than there are closet homo-sexuals. Steven Spielberg has one of the finest gun collections in California, but never refers to it, and never shoots publicly. Can you imagine the most famous filmmaker in town worried about his reputation?

Still, most people in the film community are unfamiliar with firearms and many oppose them, some quite virulently. During the L.A. riots in 1992, a good many of these folk suffered a change of heart. As smoke from burning buildings smudged the skyline and the TV news showed vivid images of laughing looters smashing windows and carting off boom boxes and booze, I got a few phone calls from firmly antigun friends in clear conflict. "Umm, Chuck, you have quite a few . . . ah, *guns,* don't you?"

"Yes, I do."

"Shotguns and . . . like that?"

"Indeed."

"Could you lend me one for a day or so? I tried to buy one, but they have this waiting period . . ."

"Yeah, I know; I remember you voted for that. Do you know how to use a shotgun?"

"No, I thought maybe you could teach me. This is getting a little scary."

"I noticed. It does that sometimes. I could teach you, but not in an hour. You might shoot yourself instead of the bad guys. The Marines are coming up from Pendleton; that'll end it. When it does, go buy yourself a good shotgun and take some lessons. It doesn't get so scary then."

My friend writer-director John Milius had more calls than I did. His answer was more forthright: "Sorry. They're allll being used."

Public opinion on this issue seems to be shifting in the face of rising violence in the country. No police force can guarantee always to protect all citizens, nor are they legally responsible for failing to do so. Besides, it seems to me ethically questionable to expect a policeman earning $35,000 a year to risk his life to protect you if you accept no responsibility to protect yourself. That's why more and more women are buying guns and being properly trained in their use. Fraser's wife, Marilyn, knows how to use a gun; I'm working on Lydia.

Our only neighbors on our ridge are the Isaacs. Between us, Billy and I must own at least forty firearms of various types (some of them antique weapons a century or so old). We would resist with deadly force any assault on our homes or those who live in them.

UNLIKE SOME PEOPLE, I support the First Amendment as vigorously as I do the Second. Indeed, the whole Bill of Rights is a wonderfully unique instrument. Though in recent years it's been often cited to justify various federal intrusions on individual rights, its original intent and prime purpose was to protect, in every Article, the rights of citizens against the intrusion of their government. There's no other governmental codicil in the world like it. I'm a fan.

Two years ago I won my most significant victory in the public sector since the civil rights marches in the early sixties—and then we were following Dr. King. This was just me vs. Time Warner, the biggest entertainment conglomerate in the world, and they backed down. It didn't involve any of my own professional projects; this was pure pro bono, "for the public good."

I got a call from Tony Makris, my guru on Washington. "Chuck, you ever hear of a rap performer named Ice-T?"

"No, why would I? I remember some rock critic saying 'Rap is made by people who can't sing, can't play an instrument, and can't write lyrics. It's vocal graffiti!' I believe I can sign that."

"I think you ought to hear these lyrics. They've pissed off just about every policeman in the country, but Time Warner's stonewalling them because it's a hit record, and the press is tiptoeing around because the guy's black."

Tony was right. The lyrics (aside from being badly written) were an obscene ode to the killing of policemen. I did a press conference about it, along with some other brave souls, and Warner backed down to the extent of changing the album title from *Cop Killer* to *Body Count,* without removing the song. They also were sending out demo CDs in cute little black body bags. (The corporate counterculture at work.) The press was very cautious on the issue. My civil rights credentials dating back to 1961 protected me from the racist accusations that would otherwise have been hurled. I was told that Ice-T himself threatened to kill me. He didn't, though.

Then we found that Time Warner had a stockholders' meeting scheduled in Beverly Hills. I happened to hold several hundred shares of Time Warner stock (I've since sold it). This meant I could attend the meeting, closed to outsiders and the press. So I did.

There was the usual gaggle of media outside, as well as a large contingent of police, both on- and off-duty, though no violence was expected. Inside the auditorium were perhaps a thousand shareholders. I doubt that any of them had ever heard a rap album, though this material is an enormously profitable cash cow for Time Warner. Of course that was the whole problem. As someone trenchantly observed, "It's not the money . . . it's the *money.*"

By this time President Bush, police across the country, members of Congress, and major religious and media figures had condemned the *Body Count* album. Ice-T had weighed in with the comment, "I ain't never killed no cop . . . I felt like it a lot."

Even at this point, the chairman-CEO of Time Warner, Gerald Levin, could have said—no doubt with perfect honesty—"Look, I don't read rap lyrics. If some clown in the record division screwed up, we can fix it." Instead, he chose to defend the album in terms of the First Amendment, which was ridiculous. Ice-T, in search of his fifteen minutes of fame, certainly could have performed his work publicly—but Warners had no obligation, constitutional or otherwise, to pay him to do so. Their motivation was not the Bill of Rights, but simple corporate greed.

I had the floor for perhaps only eight or ten minutes, but it was enough. I spoke briefly and quietly to the meeting, then simply read, in full, the lyrics of "Cop Killer," which almost no one in the room had heard or seen, they being too offensive for the media to quote. Unhappily, I can't do that here, since Time Warner would almost surely refuse permission, and my editors are also reluctant to print what is basically racist filth. I'll simply say that the lyrics begin with "F—k the police . . ." and go on from there.

"Mr. Levin," I said. "Jews and homosexuals are also sometimes attacked, though of course not as often as police officers. Let me ask you: If this piece were titled 'Fag Killer,' or if the lyrics went 'Die, die, die, kike, die!', would you still peddle it? It's often been said that if Adolf Hitler came back with a dynamite treatment for a film, every studio in town would be after it. Would Warner be among them?"

It was a large room, crowded with nearly a thousand people, but it was death-still. I gave them one more dose, a few lines from another cut on the CD, less notorious but even more disgusting. In this "song," Ice-T fantasizes about sodomizing two twelve-year-old nieces of the next vice president of the United States, again in language Time Warner is surely not proud of and my editors would rather not print. One sanitized line will give you all you want or need to know: "She pushed her butt up against my c—k, — —in her ass." Then more, much more of the same, and worse.

I left the room in an echoing silence, then repeated much of what I'd said inside to the media. One or two journalists said, "You know, we can't run that."

"Yeah, I know," I said. "But Warners is selling it." A week or so later, the company pulled the album, pretending that Ice-T had asked them to. A month after that, they terminated his contract.

I asked the women's organization NOW to join me in condemning the album, in view of the vicious verses about sodomizing little girls. Sliding around me in two or three conversations with a couple of different women honchos, NOW never did. I've never understood why. Perhaps they didn't want to attack a black man.

Still, I'm proud of what I did, though now I'll surely never be offered another film by Warners, nor get a good review from *Time.* On the other hand, I doubt I'll get a traffic ticket very soon.

LOOKING BACK NOW, trying to sum things up, I find it more puzzling than it used to be. "What's it all about, Charlie?", indeed. A generation ago, though we were in a fierce inflationary spiral and the depths of the Cold War, it was unthinkable that a respected and intelligent head of a giant conglomerate would defend the marketing of a record celebrating the sexual abuse of young girls and the murder of policemen. Now the children of that generation have grown up in the ruins of what was once the best system of public education on earth—barely literate, many of them hardly English-capable, too many more raised in fatherless welfare families.

Our borders are awash in immigrants, a large proportion of them illegal, but all nonetheless qualified for the fruits of our welfare state, entitled to generous benefits, including not only voting in our elections on ballots in the language of their choice, but the education of their progeny in that language. This last is the most colossal blunder of the many made in supposed support of the young: to deliberately deny children, at an age when they learn most quickly, access to full command of the language that can best offer them a chance at productive employment anywhere in the world in the twenty-first century can only be described as cruelty to children.

Multiculturalism is not only perceived as a virtue but a goal. I actually heard a young woman at an arts fund-raiser say, "Well, that's the motto on the U.S. currency, isn't it? *'E pluribus unum.'* From one, many."

"Actually, you've got it backward," I said. "The correct translation is 'From many, one.' As in one country."

"No kidding?" she said. "Well, whatever."

A columnist described the childhood of a welfare kid with brutal honesty: "first felony arrest at fourteen, becomes an absent father at sixteen, out of school at seventeen if he gets that far, with a diploma he can't read."

The Senate chaplain, the Reverend Richard Halvorsen, put it somewhat more fully: "We now demand freedom without restraint, rights without responsibility, choice without consequences, pleasure without pain. In our narcissistic, hedonistic, masochistic, value-less preoccupation, we are becoming a people dominated by lust, avarice, and greed." (Isn't it odd that the Congress has a full-time chaplain who opens every session with a prayer—which is forbidden in schools? How did we get to that?)

How did we get, for that matter, to the point where the ethical foundations of Western civilization are now in question? The *L.A. Times* reported not long ago that some geneticists have advanced the possibility that much of what we've understood for thousands of years as failings in the human condition are in fact genetically imprinted in us at birth. Wife-beating, obesity, alcoholism, murder . . . none of these is *our fault.* Just think how that frees us! We are now responsible for *nothing!* There is no good nor evil; man is no longer burdened with free will. Old Tom Jefferson's comment serves here, I think: "Indeed I tremble for my country when I reflect that God is just."

Which brings me to another point. The current Congress, engaged in a massive effort to cut spending, decided to trim school lunches. "ARRGghh!" said the Dems. "That's like melting down the Holy Grail!"

Hey, just a damn minute . . . did I miss something here? What ever happened to peanut butter sandwiches and an apple? I was in school all through the Great Depression. I carried a brown bag lunch through grade school, high school, and what college I had before I joined the Army Air Corps. (Yeah, then the taxpayers bought my meals, most of them not very good, but that was for attending World War II.) So tell me, when was it decided that there *is* a free lunch, after all? I don't believe Mr. Jefferson would've thought much of that—and he was a pretty smart guy.

As the new congressional majority is steering national policy away from the welfare state, the monstrous 1995 bombing in Oklahoma City stains the national psyche. It is inexplicable and unforgivable. Those of us with Old Testament ethics perhaps feel a little more strongly than some on how to deal with those found guilty of such a crime. I can think of no punishment too harsh for the random killing of children, in Israel or Oklahoma.

Violence is once again an issue—happening far too often—in most of our larger cities as we turn toward the new century. That has created a strong focus on violence in films. I must've done at least a hundred interviews on this over the years, most of them in the past decade: "Are films too violent? Are you corrupting our kids?"

"No," I've always answered. "There's been bloody violence in drama since the Greeks and Shakespeare. In two plays alone, *Macbeth* and *A Man for All Seasons,* I've had my head cut off in ten different productions, on stage and film. But I get a pass because those are great plays, while Arnold Schwarzenegger and Bruce Willis have to take the heat for perverting our young. Is that it?"

Actually, far more significantly dangerous violence is available to little kids in the latest generation of interactive video games, where a ten-year-old boy is not simply the awed witness to elaborately staged screen violence, but an actual participant, personally slaughtering the enemy at will in the bloodiest way. Lay off Arnold and Kevin and Sly and Bruce. A lot more kids now spend their money in video arcades than in a movie house. It's not what they see there, but what they *do* there, as surrogate video Rambos, that should concern us.

No, I don't indict Hollywood for excessive screen violence. We *are* guilty of dismantling the American ethic. Over the past quarter-century, too many of our filmmakers have adopted the classic comic-strip artist Walt Kelly's line: "We have met the enemy, and he is us."

Shakespeare's plays all end, no matter how many bodies strew the stage, with the restoration of peace and the hope of a better future. Jimmy Cagney played manic thugs as vicious as any on film, but they were all seen to deserve their violent ends—unlike, say, the warm and caring philosopher-assassins Mr. Tarantino gave us in *Pulp Fiction.* Really swell guys, deep down, weren't they?

When Clint Eastwood did the Dirty Harry films in the seventies, he played a tough maverick, pressing for elbow room to deal with the unequivocal nasties he faced. Harry was not a rogue cop; his superiors were not corrupt. But in 1975, *Three Days of the Condor* gave us Robert Redford as an innocent CIA researcher who finds everyone in his office has been slaughtered by . . . surprise: the CIA honchos, who spend the rest of the film trying to kill him.

By that time, Hollywood had about used up the Nazis as bad guys, and many filmmakers are uncomfortable with using the Soviets. I did a film for Universal then, *Gray Lady Down,* about a sunken nuclear sub, with the Navy desperately trying to find her before the Soviets did. The studio insisted that we cut the Russians as adversaries . . . too provocative. Absent that conflict, the film was a flop. This year's submarine smash, *Crimson Tide,* has the Russians back in the action, but the bad guy is the captain of the U.S. sub.

In a staggering number of Hollywood films of the past twenty years, the villains are authority figures in American society. Lawyers are not widely popular, but in *The Firm* there's a whole company of corrupt lawyers; in the remake of *Cape Fear,* Greg Peck's upstanding country lawyer is transformed into Nick Nolte's moral equivalent of Robert De Niro's paranoid killer.

Policemen have been the bad guys in more movies than you can count, recently in *Speed* (paranoid cop). *Blue Sky* and dozens of other films demonize anyone in the military above the rank of colonel (or anyone in uniform, in films like *Dances with Wolves*). The FBI and the CIA are always fertile fields of film villainy, but the focus has shifted of late to the White House. *Line of Fire* gives us a presidential Chief of Staff as a heavy; in *Dave* it's the president himself, plus a manic Chief of Staff. *Clear and Present Danger* does the same thing, altering Tom Clancy's novel radically. We see the same condemnation of the government in *Legends of the Fall,* also not in the novel. *Panther* made a hero of the murderous thief and revolutionary wannabe, Huey Newton.

Oliver Stone, one of our best directors, has spent his entire career attacking core elements in our society, from *Platoon* and *Born on the Fourth of July* to *JFK* and *Natural Born Killers.* His next film is *Nixon;* he seems unlikely to produce a panegyric to the thirty-seventh president.

Yep, I know the speech . . . given it myself more than once. "It's the artist's *right* to criticize, to challenge, to open doors. More than that, it's his *job* to push the edges of the envelope, to shock people!" (That's the short version; when you're in school, or trying to get your first job, it's much longer.) Stone and Tarantino have different takes on the same theme: "Hey, this is a *movie,*" says one, while the other proclaims, "It's all black comedy. Didn't you *get* it?" (this is a devastating question. Cool people cannot bear *ever* not getting a joke).

Vladimir Ilyich Lenin got the joke, incredibly early. No, this is not a political statement, it's an awestruck appreciation. He must have been a genius. In the course of running the Bolshevik Revolution and creating the Soviet State and a world view that killed some fifty million people, he had time to notice the movies, which had barely been invented. Not long before his death in 1924, he said, "The moving picture is the greatest tool ever devised to shape the mind of man." How did he know that?

The moving image has incalculable power to persuade. Over the last generation, hundreds of films have given us an image of

government, at every level of our society, as villainous. Is it any
wonder a lot of people accept this as reality? If the government is
corrupt, take to the hills and hunker down! I roamed the Michigan
woods with a gun when I was a kid, but I was looking for rabbits
for supper, not federal buildings to blow up. Back then, though, we
were the good guys. I grew up before they started making all those
films.

OF COURSE we've had real-life bad guys in high places, though
surely in neither the numbers nor the degree which some of our
filmmakers insist on. Happily, we also have a system of government
wonderfully designed to absorb the shock of earthquakes, fires,
floods, random riots, and terrorist assaults.

Over time, our government has become bloated. Lincoln
had only a dozen people working for him, even Roosevelt only a
couple of hundred. The White House now has some two thousand
people working there. There are too many federal departments
with too many people exercising too much authority over the individual American citizen. The independence and responsibility of
each of us as Americans was the whole idea in the first place.

Over the past forty years, the nation has gradually fissured
into a jostling tangle of groups seeking separate identity as victims,
entitling each to special status and compensation. The Declaration
of Independence says we're all "created equal" and have inalien-
able rights: "life, liberty and the pursuit of happiness." There are
no other guarantees.

I was there for civil rights, in 1961, through the Washington
March, and until the Civil Rights Act passed in '65. Hubert Humphrey, God rest his soul, stood on the floor of the Senate, held the
bill over his head, and swore to eat it page by page if anyone could
find in it any mention of special preference. That was a shining time
in American history.

Dear God, what a sorry road we've slid down since then.
Affirmative action is a stain on the American soul. To say that anyone
is entitled, not just to an even start but an even finish, defies all
reason. "To make up for past discrimination" is nonsense.

Every group that ever came to this country started off well
behind the field, most of them with a language barrier to boot. My
Scots ancestors were driven off their crofts in the Highlands to

make room for more sheep, for God's sake. The Jews have been discriminated against for several thousand years, slaughtered within living memory in numbers exceeding by millions anything blacks have endured. Even in America, there were negative quotas at many American universities limiting Jewish admissions well into World War II. Enough. This must not stand. It hurts most those it's supposed to help . . . black and Hispanic Americans.

At a recent seminar on film, Richard Dreyfuss, first-class thinker as well as actor, explored this in depth. "American society," he said, "has lost belief in itself. Our artists have become embarrassed to celebrate the extraordinary or the potential for greatness in the nation. And our fears of offending, our pursuit of political correctness, has made our culture bland and timid. This is a road that leads nowhere. It doesn't sustain or give strength, or heighten our collective imagination."

I agree with Dreyfuss, vigorously. Over the last two generations American society has abandoned even the idea of greatness. The media, academe, the creative community, now extol the ordinary, enshrine the victim. The only major film in half a century about one of the Founding Fathers ignores Thomas Jefferson's towering achievements to explore his putative relationship with a slave-girl. The cultural mavens of our society recently dismissed a film about the discovery of the Americas because it honored the man who opened half the world, but failed to give sufficient credit to those who had not yet discovered the wheel.

The only other major gripe I have with my country in the closing years of the millennium is the social charade called "political correctness," or "P.C." George Orwell invented it for his novel *1984*. He called it "Newspeak." It was a seductive tool of the oligarchic tyranny the government had become, which simply altered the meaning of words by decree: "chairperson," "Freedom is slavery," "Ministry of Love" . . . Orwell foresaw the onset of political correctness with chilling prescience. His "Thought Police" are of course our custodians of P.C. May they cringe in shame at what they are doing to our language and our society.

I think this egregious nonsense, in real life, started in the sixties. "Personhole" for "manhole" was one of the first, though that was laughed away quickly. Then academics and activists saw a chance to peddle a sociopolitical line with the scheme, laughably lunatic though it was. When the media joined the band, quickly followed by government bureaucrats, they were on a roll. Now, alone among the nations of the world, the United States has allowed political correctness to creep like crabgrass, clinging to every part of our daily lives.

To justify this ludicrous pomposity, those who impose it on us insist it is morally uplifting and encourages diversity. This, to a country that has thrived by providing an example of common values and common goals. An increasingly cacophonous diversity is one of the main things wrong with us.

"Well," say its visionary defenders, "P.C. language promotes self-esteem." That's oxymoronic to begin with. Self-esteem, in modest proportion, is valuable—but by definition, it can only come from within. Helen Keller didn't become one of the prominent women of her time by being called "visually and aurally challenged." Franklin Roosevelt didn't become president by thinking himself "differently abled."

But the worst excess of P.C. English is hyphenated ethnic labels. I'm proud of both my Scottish and English heritage, but I'm an American, not a Scots-English American. I am also, of course, a native American. On his mother's side, Fraser is a twelfth-generation native American.

Regarded objectively, political correctness has done much to destroy civil discourse in American life. This is not a small thing, in a country widely regarded as a seedbed of democracy. I had a chilling experience of this during the election campaign last fall. I campaigned in fourteen states, on behalf of twenty-four candidates for both the Senate and the House. As a foot soldier in the revolution (if it proves to have been that), I'm proud that in the states we visited, we won nineteen of the seats contested.

In Minnesota, we campaigned for Rod Grams, running an uphill battle for a Senate seat. In a TV interview on the issues, I said, "We have to get back to the values and perceptions of those wise old dead white guys who invented this country." Well, I want to tell you, the opponent's camp erupted, branding me with the familiar P.C. epithets: "racist," "sexist," and "elitist." I was in another state by then, but I taped a response, which the local stations didn't run. (Never mind, Rod Grams won.) "Let's see now," I said, "they were wise, they were old, they're dead, they were white guys, and they invented this country. Which word in that sentence don't you understand?" (I must confess, I love it when they blunder like that.)

I believe America will survive political correctness. We survived the Civil War and the Great Depression, and won World War II, for Pete's sake. I believe we can also survive the current struggle between the two parties for the soul of this country—which of them is best equipped to take us into the twenty-first century, the spenders or the savers? Being neither an economist nor an expert political scientist (if such exists), I'll struggle along with everyone else while we try to figure out who's right. I do recall George Bernard Shaw (also neither economist nor politician, but a very smart man) saying, "A government which robs Peter to pay Paul can always depend on the gratitude of Paul." Americans are basically optimistic. We believe in the power of the future, and that we, as a nation, can do things better.

We do it because we decide it's right. As a country, as a people, we still believe in that . . . in doing right. Doing *good.* Not many nations see the world like that; too many never did. It has been said that the creation of the United States is the greatest single political act in the history of mankind. How did that happen? What brought about that extraordinary confluence of time, place, circumstance, the concerted effort of a people in arms . . . and a few great men??

The American experience. So far, it seems the most successful. To history, the two centuries of our small experiment in freedom are an eye-blink, but we are still here. We may not have been able to make democracy spread, but we have made it prosper. This country is still what we've been from the beginning—an example to the world. Man can live free. In America, democracy works. Not, in these bleak, beleaguered times, as well as we need it to work, but we are still, to the rest of the world, the shining door to freedom.

Why? Why is this? Is it our system? Surely, that's part of it. The American dream? (which is *not* success, but freedom). It's not that alone, though. Other countries have cherished that dream, and lost it. Well, what, then? Are we smarter, more determined? Is it luck, or the grace of God? I truly think it's, in part, the land itself. That broad swell of continent between those shining seas. From the very beginning, before we were Americans as a people, we were captivated by the *land.* "The land was ours before we were the ers, poets have tried to capture this idea for us.

Trying to capture it myself, over the last year or so I put together a clip file, noting what extraordinary Americans have said about this country over the past two centuries and more: bits from books by or about them, anecdotes, retrospective newspaper clips. When I read through them all to find who had best put what I wanted to say, I realized how they all seemed to speak with the same voice, through two centuries. All had vastly different lives in different generations, yet any one of them might have said what another said, fifty years earlier.

I spread out my file cards and fitted them in minutes into a single paragraph, with an ease that stunned me. I can't do better here than to leave you with the words of these Americans: Martin Luther King, Jr., F. Scott Fitzgerald, Tom Paine, Samuel Eliot Morison, William Faulkner, Thomas Wolfe . . . and Abraham Lincoln. Perhaps not many can sort out just who said what, but I think most would agree that these men speak truly, with a common voice about America—one country, one people:

"I have a dream. I refuse to accept the end of man. I believe he will endure. He will prevail. Man is immortal, not because, alone among God's creatures, he has a voice, but because he has a soul . . . a spirit, capable of compassion . . . and sacrifice . . . and endurance. About America, and Americans, this is particularly true. It is a fabulous country. The only fabulous country . . . where miracles not only happen, they happen all the time. As a nation we have, perhaps uniquely, a special willingness of the heart . . . a blithe fearlessness . . . a simple yearning for righteousness and justice that ignited in our revolution a flame of freedom that cannot be stamped out. *That* is the living, fruitful spirit of this country. These are the times that try men's souls. The sunshine patriot and the summer soldier will in this crisis shrink from service. But he that stands and serves his country now will earn the thanks of man and woman. We must bind up the nation's wounds. With firmness in the right as God gives us to see the right, let us finish the work we are in."

I believe that says it all. Thanks. It's been a pleasure.

Index

NURSE

AT THE TRENCHES

By

Agnes Warner

First Published in 1917 as 'My Beloved Poilus' by Barnes & Co. Ltd,
St. John, New Brunswick, Canada.

British Library Cataloguing In Publication Data
A Record of This Publication is available from the British Library

ISBN 0-9515655-6-7

This edition first published April 2005 by Diggory Press, an imprint of
Meadow Books, 35 Stonefield Way, Burgess Hill, West Sussex, RH15 8DW, UK

Email: publish@diggorypress.com
Website: www.diggorypress.com

PUBLISH YOUR BOOK
FOR ONLY £30 OR US$50!
See www.diggorypress.com for details.

We can sell your book worldwide for you too!

These home letters from a Canadian girl, daughter of a retired general of the U.S. Army, giving her trained services, caring for the wounded in France at an Army Ambulance and succoring distress wherever she meets it, were published by her friends without her knowledge, simply and solely to raise money to aid her in her work which began on the 4th of August, 1914.

Every dollar received from the sale of the book, less bare cost of printing and express charges, went to the fund.

PREFACE

When Florence Nightingale began her great work in the hospital wards at Scutari in 1854, she little realised how far-reaching would be the effect of her noble self-sacrificing efforts. Could she today visit the war-stricken countries of Europe she would be astonished at the great developments of the work of caring for the wounded soldiers which she inaugurated so long ago. Her fine example is being emulated today by hundreds of thousands of brave women who are devoting themselves to the wounded, the sick and the dying in countless hospital wards.

All too little is known of what these devoted nurses have done and are doing. Some day the whole story will be given to the world; and the hearts of all will be thrilled by stirring deeds of love and bravery.

In the meantime it is pleasing and comforting to catch fleeting glimpses of a portion of the work as depicted in this sheaf of letters, now issued under the title of 'My Beloved Poilus,' written from the Front by a brave Canadian nurse.

Two outstanding features give special merit to these letters. They were not written for publication, but for an intimate circle of relatives and friends. And because of this they are not artificial, but are free and graceful, with homely touches here and there which add so much to their value.

Amidst the incessant roar of mighty guns; surrounded by the wounded and the dying; shivering at times with cold, and wearied almost to the point of exhaustion, these letters were hurriedly penned. No time had she for finely-turned phrases. Neither were they necessary. The simple statements appeal more to the heart than most eloquent words.

These letters will bring great comfort to many who have loved ones at the Front. They will tell them something of the careful sympathetic treatment the wounded receive. The glimpses given here and there, of the efforts made by surgeons and nurses alike to administer relief, and as far as possible to assuage the suffering of the wounded, should prove most comforting. What efforts are made to cheer the patients, and to brighten their lot, and what personal interest is taken in their welfare, are incidentally revealed in these letters.

For instance, 'The men had a wonderful Christmas Day (1916). They were like a happy lot of children. We decorated the ward with flags, holly and mistletoe, and paper flowers that the men made, and a tree in each ward.'

How these letters bring home to us the terrible tragedy that is going on far across the ocean. And yet mingled with the feeling of sadness is the spirit of inspiration which comes from the thought of those brave men who are offering themselves to maintain the right, and the devoted women who are ministering to their needs. Our heads bow with reverence, and our hearts thrill with pride, when we think of them. But we must do more than think and feel; we must do our part in supporting them and upholding their hands. They have given their all. They can do no more, and dare we do less?

Rev. H. A. Cody. St. John, N. B.,
February 19th, 1917

INTRODUCTION

THE writer of these letters, a graduate of McGill College, and the Presbyterian Hospital, New York, left New York in the Spring of 1914 with a patient, for the Continent, finally locating at Divonne-Les-Bains, France, near the Swiss border, where they were on August 1st when war broke out.

She immediately began giving her assistance in 'Red Cross' work, continuing same until the latter part of November, when she returned with her patient to New York, made a hurried visit to her home in   St. John and after Christmas returned to again take up the work which these letters describe.

MY BELOVED POILUS[*]

Divonne-Les-Bains, France,
August 2, 1914.

Dear Mother

The awful war we have all been dreading is upon us - *France is mobilizing.* At five o'clock yesterday morning the tocsin sounded from the Marie (village hall) and men, women, and children, all flocked to hear the proclamation which the Mayor of the village read. It called upon all of military age - between twenty years and fifty years - to march at once, and inside of twenty-four hours five hundred men had gone, they knew not where. The bravery of these villagers - men and women - is remarkable, and not to be forgotten. No murmuring, no complaining - just, 'Ma Patrie,' tying up the little bundle - so little - and going; none left but old men, women and children.

We have started teaching the women and girls to make bandages, sponges, etc., for the hospital which will be needed here.

Divonne-Les-Bains, France
August 23, 1914.

Your letter came yesterday - twenty days on the way - but I was fortunate to get it at all; so many of these poor people,

---

[*] Editor's note: Poilus was an affectionate term for the unshaven fighting men in the trenches.

9

whose nearest and dearest have gone to fight for their country, have had no word from them since they marched away, and they do not know where they are.

From this little village 500 men left the first day of mobilization; there is not a family who has not some one gone, and from some both fathers and sons have gone, as the age limit is from twenty to fifty years.

I am filled with admiration and respect for these people. The courage of both the men and women is remarkable. There is no hesitation, and no grumbling, and everyone tries to do whatever he or she can to help the cause.

I do not know if I told you, in my last letter, of the poor lady who walked all night through the dark and storm to see her son who was leaving the next morning. All the horses and motors had been taken by the Government for the army, so she started at eleven o'clock at night, all by herself, and got here about five in the morning - her son left at seven, so she had two hours with him. While there are such mothers in France she cannot fall. There are many such stories I might tell you, but I have not the time.

The 'Red Cross' has started a branch hospital here, and I have been helping them to get it in order. It is just about ready now, and we may get soldiers any day.

I have classes every morning and find many of the women very quick to learn the rudiments of nursing. Everyone in the place is making supplies and our sitting room is a sort of depot where they come for work.

If my patient is as well in October as she is now I am going to stay and give my services to the 'Red Cross.' If I have to go home with her I will come back – I would be a coward and deserter if I did not do all I could for these poor brave people.

October 25, 1914.

Another Sunday – but this is cold and rainy – the days slip by so quickly I cannot keep track of them. We have only two soldiers left at the hospital – they tell us every day that others are coming. The country all about is perfectly beautiful with the autumn coloring.

We do not see any of the horrors of the war here. If it were not for the tales that come to us from outside, and for the poor broken men who come back, we would not know it was going on. There are very enthusiastic accounts of the Canadians in all the English papers.

Paris,

about February 15, 1915.

Back safely in Paris after taking my patient to New York and a short visit home, which now seems like a dream.

I have been spending a lot of time at the American Ambulance this week, but have not gone out to stay as yet, as

11

I still have to see some other small hospitals and had to go to the Clearing House to make arrangements for sending supplies, which I brought from home and New York, to different places.

I have seen quite a number of operations, and as X-ray pictures are taken of all the cases there is no time wasted in hunting for a bullet; they get the bullet out in about two minutes. They are using Dr. Criles' anæsthetic - nitrous oxide gas and oxygen - it has no bad effects whatever.

The patients come out of it at once as soon as the mask is taken off, and there is no nausea or illness at all; and most of them go off laughing, for they cannot believe that it is all over - they feel so well; but oh, mother, it is awful to see the sad things that have happened.

In some cases there are only pieces of men left. One young chap, twenty-one years old, has lost both legs. At first he did not want to live, but now he is beginning to take an interest in things and is being fitted for wooden legs.

The dental department have done wonderful work. They build up the frame work of the face and jaws and then the surgeons finish the work by making new noses and lips and eyelids.

I thought I had seen a good many wonderful things, but I did not believe it possible to make anything human out of some of the pieces of faces that were left, and in some of the cases they even get rid of the scars. Photos are taken when they first come in, and then in the various stages of recovery.

One of the worst cases I saw the last day I was out. He has to have one more operation to fill in a small hole in one side of his nose and then he will be all right.

Last Sunday one of the men in Miss B's ward was given the medal for distinguished service. He had saved his officer's life - went right out before the guns and carried him in on his back. He was struck himself just before he got to his own lines and one leg almost torn off.

When they brought him to the American Ambulance, all the doctors, except Dr. B, said his leg would have to come off at once - he refused to do it and saved the leg for the man. It will be stiff, of course, as the knee joint is gone entirely; but will be better than a wooden leg, and the poor man is so pleased.

I must tell you about the wonderful dog that is at the American Ambulance; perhaps you have read about him in some of the papers. His master came from Algeria, and of course did not expect to take his dog with him, but when the ship left the wharf the dog jumped into the sea and swam after it, so they put off a boat and hauled him on board, and he has been with his master all through the war.

He was in the trenches with him, and one day a German shell burst in the trench and killed all of his companions and buried this man in the mud and dirt as well as injuring him terribly. Strange to say the dog was not hurt at all, and the first thing the man remembered was the dog digging the mud off his face. As soon as he realized his master was alive he ran off for help, and when they were brought into the Ambulance together there were not many dry eyes about.

After he was sure his master was being taken care of he consented to go and be fed, and now he is having the time of his life. He is the most important person in the place. He has a beautiful new collar and medal, lives in the diet kitchen, and is taken out to walk by the nurses, and best of all is allowed to see his master every day.

I will send a photo of him to you. His master has lost one leg, the other is terribly crushed, and one hand also, but Doctor B. thinks he can save them.

I think I shall go back to Divonne-Les-Bains - they are urging me so strongly and there seems to be more need there.

February 19, 1915.

Back again in Divonne-Les-Bains. It seems as if I had never been away - I have fallen into the old work so easily. I left Paris Sunday night about eight o'clock and arrived here at two the next day, and had a warm welcome from everybody. One poor man died of tetanus before I got back. I have nine on my floor.

I have thirteen patients, nine in bed all the time, and the others up part of the day. One of the women of the village helps me in the morning, two others help with the cleaning up and

The dog who saved his master's life.

serving meals; everything has to be carried up three flights of
stairs, so you can imagine the work.

I have a very comfortable room at the hotel, go to the
Ambulance at seven in the morning and generally get back at
nine or half past. I do not know how long I shall be here - until

this lot get well or more come.

One of the patients is a chef, and was acting as cook for the regiment when a shell landed in his soup pot; he was not wounded, but his heart was knocked out of place by the shock and his back was twisted when he fell.

February 28, 1915.

The poor man who was so very ill died on the morning of the twenty-third after three weeks of intense suffering - I stayed that night with him. The others are all out of danger with the exception of two who cannot get well - one is paralyzed and the other has tuberculosis.

I went to the village for the first time yesterday and was quite touched by the welcome I received at every little shop and house. The people seemed genuinely glad to have me back. They cannot seem to get over the fact that I have crossed the ocean twice and come back to them. To them the ocean is a thing of terror, especially since the war broke out.

Doctor R has a great many sick people in the country about here to take care of in addition to the soldiers. In one house they had nothing to eat but potatoes, but he is a good deal like our dear old doctor, and feeds and clothes and takes care of them himself.

March 5, 1915.

I can scarcely believe that it is nearly three weeks since I left Paris. I have been so busy, that the days fly by. Some of the men are leaving tomorrow, and most of the others are getting along very well.

Mr. E is indeed kind. He has just sent an order to the village people, who make beautiful lace and embroidery, for $500.00 worth of work. They are so happy about it, for it means food for many of them. One poor woman, who has lost her husband in the war and has a child to take care of, can earn only eighteen francs a month, that is $3.60, and that is all she has to live on.

March 7, 1915.

One of the American doctors from the American Ambulance came to see me yesterday. He was very much interested in what he saw and is coming back in ten days. We have had one or two beautiful days, the pussy-willows are beginning to come out, and primroses everywhere.

Dr. S said that the man who owned the wonderful dog that is at the American Ambulance is really getting well, and they managed to save one leg and the crushed hand.

In Dr. B's service he did not do a single amputation during the months of January and February - a very wonderful record.

Dr. S seems to think there is no hope of my poor paralyzed man getting better, he may live for twenty years but can never walk. I am giving him English lessons every day. He is very quick at learning; it helps pass the time. Poor man, he has already been in bed six months.

March 21, 1915.

This has been the most lovely Spring day. The violets are blooming in the fields, they are smaller than ours but very fragrant; the yellow primroses are beautiful and grow everywhere. There is still lots of snow on the mountains but none in the valley. If it were not for the soldiers who are here we could scarcely believe that terrible fighting is going on so near us.

A lot of our men went off last week, some of them scarcely able to hobble, poor things, but all the hospitals are being cleared out to make room for the freshly wounded. We are expecting a new lot every day, and have prepared ten extra beds.

I will have some letters this week to send to the 'Red Cross' and 'The De Monts' Chapter, I. O. D. E., thanking them for the things they sent back by me; they have been so much appreciated, done so much good and relieved so much distress. I gave some to Mademoiselle de C who sent them to a small hospital in Normandy near their chateau, some to the hospital here, and some to a small hospital not far from here where they are very poor; the doctor who is in charge there nearly wept when he knew the things were for him.

March 26, 1915.

Another beautiful day and the air is soft and balmy as a day in June. The woods and fields are full of spring flowers, there are big soft gray pussies on all the willow trees and the other trees are beginning to show a faint tinge of green. It is certainly a lovely place.

You probably felt much relieved that I was not in Paris at the time of the last air raid when the bombs were dropped. One fell so near the Ambulance at Neuilly that one of the doctors was knocked out of bed by the shock.

I had my paralyzed man out on the balcony today, it is the first time in six months that he has been out. One of the men here, who has lost the use of both hands, told me today that he had six brothers in the army; two have been killed, two wounded and two are still at the front. He was a coachman in a private family, has lost a thumb of one hand and on the other has only the thumb and one finger left. Fortunately his employer is a good man and will take care of him; but think of the poor man - horses are his chief joy, and he will never be able to drive again.

April 2, 1915.

Easter Sunday and still raining. We had a splendid service from Mr. - and a Communion service after. The service is more like the Presbyterian than any other. We have four new soldiers but the large convoy has not yet arrived. There has been awful fighting in Alsace lately, so the wounded must come soon.

Today we had a specially good dinner for the men. Madam B gave them cigars and Easter eggs, and after dinner they sang some of their songs, then gave us three cheers. They are a fine lot of men and so grateful for every thing we do for them.

The story of the dog has gone through the whole country, but it is nice to know that it is really true, and to have seen the dog. Dr. B was able to save the other leg of the dog's master, and after another operation he thinks he will have the use of his hand.

April 10, 1915.

We had a severe snow storm today and yesterday also, and in between the snow storms it poured rain; all the lovely spring weather has disappeared.

Wednesday night they announced the arrival of a train of wounded, for the next morning at half-past five, but did not tell us how many to expect. We all went to the Ambulance at half-past five and got everything ready for dressing and beds prepared for thirty. At seven thirteen arrived – all convalescents, and no dressings at all to do. The last time forty came, and all in a dreadful state of infection, so we never know what to expect.

I am not sorry I came back to Divonne for I feel that I have been able to help more here than in Paris; there they have many to help and here very few.

I am sending you a photo of three of my patients - Chasseurs d' Alpine or 'Blue Devils' as the Germans call them - they are the ones who have done such wonderful work in Alsace.

April 19, 1915.

I have had quite a busy week, for my men have been coming and going. The paralyzed man has been sent to Bourg, the two Chasseurs d' Alpine have gone and I have six new ones - this lot is ill, not wounded. There are three officers among them - one is a cousin of Madam B, the French lady who helped establish this Ambulance. Her husband came on Thursday; he has eight days leave. He is very interesting, for he has been all up through the north of France. He is adjutant to one of the generals and travels from eighty to one hundred miles a day in a motor, carrying despatches. There is a French aviator here, but he has not got his machine, so I am afraid there is no hope for me.

April 25, 1915.

They took down all the stoves in the Ambulance last week, and the day after it snowed; we had to put some of the men to bed to keep them warm. We have been very busy all week, new patients coming every day till now we have forty. Most of them are not wounded. Poor fellows, they are utterly done out; some have pneumonia, others rheumatism, one paralyzed and all sorts of other things.

This is a wonderful place for them to come to and most of them get well very quickly. They are talking of increasing the number of beds in the hospital and of making it a regular military one. In that case they will send a military doctor here and the whole thing will be re-organized. They want me to promise to take charge of it, but I do not think it would be a wise thing, there is so much red tape and so many things about the military organization I do not understand, that I am afraid I would get into hot water at once.

I am sending you a circular of Mademoiselle de Canomonts' lace school. They do lovely work and need all the help and orders that they can get. They will be glad to execute orders by mail for anyone writing them to Divonne-Les-Bains, France.

May 2, 1915.

I have never seen anything as lovely as the country is now, it is like one great garden; how I wish you could be here. I have had a busy day, as one of my patients had to be operated on. Doctor R took a piece of shrapnel out of his arm, and two others have been pretty ill; four leave tomorrow, so the general clearing up will begin again.

My poor old lady who had a stroke of paralysis died yesterday. I have been helping take care of her. The only son is at the front. So many old people are dying this year; when they get ill they don't seem to have any power of resistance; poor things, they have endured so much they cannot stand any more.

There is a poor little woman here who comes from Dinant, that was destroyed by the Germans in the early part of the war. She has lost all trace of her father and mother; her husband and brother have both been killed and their property utterly destroyed. Mr. B, the pastor of the Protestant Church, has not been able to find his mother, who disappeared last August. Every day we hear of something new.

The papers are full of accounts of the gallant fighting of the Canadians, but the losses have been very heavy.

May 9, 1915.

It is just a year today since I sailed from New York, starting on our trip with Mrs. E.. Little did we think of the horrors that have happened since.

Seven more men went off last night, so we have only twenty left. I have ten on my floor, but only four in bed; the others are able to be out all day. Charrel, one of my patients who just left, was one of six brothers, all of whom went off the first days of the war; three have been killed, the other three wounded.

I am going to Lyons on Thursday for a few days to visit some of the hospitals.

The French papers are full of the heroism of the Canadian troops; they have done wonderful work at Ypres, but at what a terrible cost.

I feel so proud every time I see the dressing gowns the DeMonts Chapter sent me - they are the nicest we have.

May 18, 1915.

I left here Thursday at noon with Madam B who went to Paris. Before I left I telegraphed to Madam M , the wife of the soldier who was here such a long time, asking her to get me a room, but when I arrived I found the whole family at the station to meet me and they insisted on my going home to stay with them. They are very simple people, but so kind and hospitable. I think it is quite an event having a stranger stay with them. We ate in the kitchen, and the whole family seemed to sleep in a cupboard opening off of it.

I saw a lot of hospitals and was rather favorably impressed with them. At the Hotel Dieu, they had received seven hundred patients within twenty-four hours. I think the saddest part was the eye ward, there were so many who would never see again and some of them so young. There were some with both legs gone and others both feet, and many with one arm or leg missing.

The boats on the river that were fitted up as hospitals were very interesting, but I fancy would be very hot in the summer and the mosquitoes would be terrible.

Saturday I spent the day with Mademoiselle R, who had been staying at the Hotel at Divonne for a time.

The R's are a wealthy family who have lived in Lyons for generations. Mademoiselle was able to take me to a good many of the hospitals, as they have done a good deal for them. We visited them in the morning, which was much more interesting, as we saw the work going on.

At two of the hospitals wounded were arriving when we left there, so we saw the whole thing. I also saw the dressing being done in one of the large military hospitals. In the afternoon we went to a 'Red Cross' hospital, where she worked in the lingerie; there are fifty beds and the patients are taken care of by the sisters. They seemed to be very cheerful and well looked after.

Sunday morning I got up at 3.30 and took a train at 4.30 for Romans where Mrs. C is working in a military hospital. At eight I arrived at Tourons and had to walk from there to a small village called Tain, where I got a tramway to Romans. I arrived at eleven, had my lunch on the sidewalk before a cafe - a most excellent meal for fifty cents.

I found Mrs. C at the convent, where she is staying; fortunately she had the afternoon off. She has charge of the dressings and all of the infected operations. At the hospital where she is they have forty wounded Germans; they seem very contented and glad to be there. Mrs. C says it is dreadful to do their dressings, for they have no self-control at all; they have a certain dogged courage that makes them fight as they do, in the face of certain death, but when they are wounded they cannot stand the pain. The French, on the contrary, seldom say a word; they will let one do anything, and if the pain is very bad they moan occasionally or say a swear word, but I have never seen one who lost control of himself and screamed.

I had dinner with Mrs. C at the convent, and at 7.15 took the train for Valence where I changed and waited two hours for the train to Lyons, but there was so much going on at the station that the time did not seem long - troops coming and going all the time and a hospital train with three hundred wounded arrived.

Monday morning I left for Divonne and arrived back very tired but well satisfied with my trip. I found two new patients, one with a leg as big as an elephant and the other out of his head. I have twelve now on   my floor.

Just think! Lily of the valley grows wild here, and you can get a bushel in a morning; the whole place is sweet with the perfume.

May 28, 1915

We got twelve more patients Wednesday - six left. I still have fifteen; this lot were all ill. One man is quite a character. The doctor put him on milk diet the first day - but he did not approve, so he went to the village and bought a loaf of bread and some ham.

Between the florist of the village and the wife of one of the soldiers I am kept well supplied with roses. I wish I could share my riches with you.

I am anxiously waiting to hear of the safe arrival of the Twenty-fourth; as we have heard nothing, they must be all right. It is hard to have them go but I cannot understand the attitude of those who will not go or who object to their men and boys going. You are just beginning to feel now what they have been suffering here since August last.

Madam L.H. was called back to Verdun today; she was supposed to have three weeks' holidays, but has only been away ten days. She is not fit to go back but there is no help for it.

There was great excitement here when Italy finally declared war. It is awful to think of the brutes throwing bombs on Venice. I do hope they will not do any harm there.

I must say goodnight, for I am tired. I am up at half-past five every morning and seldom get off duty before nine at night.

June 20, 1915

Yesterday we got five patients - the four worst were consigned to me. One poor chap was shot through the body and the spine was injured; they do not know just what the extent of the injury is, but he is completely paralyzed from the waist down. Fortunately he is very small, so it is not difficult to take care of him; he is the most cheerful soul, and says he has much to be thankful for as he has never suffered at all.

When he was shot he simply had the sensation of his legs disappearing. When he fell he said to a comrade, 'Both my legs have gone,' but he had no pain at all. His comrade assured him that he had not lost his legs, but he said he could not believe it until he got to the hospital. He has received the Médaille Militaire for bravery, and his comrades said he certainly deserved it. He is so glad to get here, where it is real country and quiet. We put him on a chaise longue on the balcony today and he has been out of doors all day long.

It is after ten o'clock, but I am still at the Ambulance. We are waiting for a train that is bringing us fifteen wounded directly from Alsace. Poor souls, they will be glad to get here, for they have been a long time on the way.

No letters this week; regulations are very strict again, and they are holding up all mail for eight or ten days.

June 22, 1915.

I had to stop my letter as the men arrived. We got eighteen instead of fifteen. Such a tired dirty lot they were; they came straight from the battlefield, and had only had one dressing done since they were wounded. Some of them came on stretchers, others were able to walk, as they were wounded in the arms and head.

I drew two from this lot, which brings my number up to seventeen again. One of mine has both bones broken in his leg and the other is wounded in the left side and shoulder. One poor chap had been a prisoner in one of the trenches for four days and they were unable to get any food all that time; most of them have slept ever since they arrived, they were so exhausted.

Today a military doctor came from Besaucon to show us about some special electrical treatment. They are going to increase the beds by fifty to begin with, and later may make it three hundred.

The news is not good today, the Russians seem to be retreating all the time and the losses in the north are terrible.

There seems to be no doubt in the minds of many people that the war will last another year at least; it seems too terrible.

June 27, 1915.

I did not get my letter off today as there was so much to do. We have had inspection all week. They have finally decided to enlarge the hospital very much and make it a semi-military institution of four hundred beds. We are to turn the large dining room into a ward with fifty beds, and the large part of the hotel will hold three hundred more. They want me to take charge. Dr. R will be chief with two assistants.

There will be forty men nurses – convalescent soldiers – and I do not know how many more women nurses. I am very glad it has been so decided, for it is a great pity this place has not been of more use. Our last lot of men are getting on very well now;

but we have had a hard week, for some of them were very ill. The doctor was very much afraid one man would lose his arm, but he has managed to save it.

I have grown to be a sort of official shotsnapper for the Ambulance and village. It is really very interesting and my camera is very good.

Did I send you the snaps of the Bayin baby? She is only nine months old and runs around like a rabbit - is as pretty as a picture. I am so sleepy I can hardly see, so goodnight.

July 4, 1915.

I was glad to get your letter this week; three weeks on the way is a long time to wait.

I have such mixed feelings when I hear that the troops have left St. John. My heart aches for those left behind, but I am so glad to know they are on the way, for they are needed badly and they will get a royal welcome, for Canadians have proved their worth.

When they were in barracks and had nothing to do but drill they were not always angels; but when there was real work to be done their equal was not to be found. The French papers were full of the stories of their bravery. There were some officers who said that while others were splendid fighters the Canadians were marvelous.

It must have been terribly hard for Mrs. to let S go. I wish you would ask her for his address. I will try and get in touch with him and if he should be ill or wounded tell her I will go to him if I have to walk to get there. Get D's address also, so I can look after him. When I hear of them all being over here a wave of homesickness comes over me and I feel that I must go and join them.

There is much to be done on this side now, for the fighting in Alsace has been terrible. The last lot of soldiers that came were Chasseurs d' Alpine, and out of one thousand two hundred who went off only five hundred came back, and the greater number of them wounded.

Fifteen young men from this village have been missing since the terrible battle of three weeks ago, the deaths of a half a dozen have been confirmed but of the others nothing is known.

I am afraid there is no chance of the war finishing before the winter is over.

I wish somebody would organize a 'French Day' or 'Divonne Day' and collect pennies for me; we will need so many things before the winter is over. The general who came the other day said to make the money we have go to the furthest possible point, and then make debts - the soldiers must be taken care of.

July 11, 1915.

We have had arrivals and departures all week. The days are not half long enough to do all that is necessary. My four men who came for electrical treatment are getting on wonderfully well, the big one who was paralyzed and who could not move hand or foot when he came, is now walking without crutches, and feeds himself.

The poor little chasseur who was shot through the body is really better. He is beginning to walk - with a great deal of help, of course. He can make the movements of walking and can put both legs straight out in front of him, and the doctor says there is great hope of a permanent cure. Poor little man, he deserves to get well, for I have never seen such courage and patience. We begin tomorrow to prepare the big dining room for fifty new patients, so we shall have a busy week. I am to have charge of the big ward and keep my floor as well. I will have two military men nurses and some more people from the village to help.

July 17, 1915.

We have had a most terrific rain for the last two days - the people are getting anxious on account of the grain.

There was no celebration in the village on the fourteenth as is usual, but at the Ambulance we had a little feast in honor of the men who were at Metezeral. We have four from the Seventh Chasseurs, whose regiment was decorated for unusual bravery.

My paralyzed man stood up alone last Sunday for the first time and now he walks, pushing a chair before him like a baby. He is the happiest thing you can imagine; for seven months he has had no hope of ever walking again.

Seven left last week and six more go on Monday, so we shall probably get a train load before long.

I have got a small English boy to help me in the mornings. He has been at school in Switzerland and the whole will be entirely cured. Daillet wrote to his mother and told her that he could stand alone and was beginning to walk, but she did not believe it; she thought that he was just trying to cheer her up, so he asked me to take a photo of him standing up so that he could send it to her. He was the proudest, happiest thing you can imagine when he sent it off. Then his aunt came to see him, so the poor mother is finally convinced that it is true, and is coming to see him as soon as the haying is done, but she has to work in the fields now and cannot get away.

It is wonderful the work that the women do here. There are only two old horses left in the whole village, so the women harness themselves into the rakes and waggons and pull them in place of the horses – and they so seldom complain of the hard work. I asked one woman if she did not find it very hard, and she said at first it came very difficult but she got used to it and it was nice to be able to do their part.

We got twenty men from Alsace on Friday – some of them badly wounded. They did not arrive till half-past eleven at night, and it was three in the morning before we got the dressings done and got them to bed. It is the second time that some of them have been wounded. They are all Chasseurs d'Alpines - they are a splendid type. Some of them had both legs and both arms wounded. Yesterday we were rather anxious about several of them, but today they are better. They generally sleep about three days after they arrive, they are so done out.

Mrs. H has had to leave to care for a typhoid patient, so my hands are very full. My English boy is getting trained rapidly; he is only seventeen and not very strong, too young to go to the war but very keen to do something to help.

Do not worry about me, I am as well as possible and as strong as a horse, but as my day begins at half-past five in the morning and ends at half-past nine at night I fall asleep over my letters.

Thanks for the clippings; I would not have known B. if the name had not been there. I do not dare to think of his coming, and yet I would not be proud of him if he did not want to come. I shall try and get up to the north later so as to be nearer him when he comes.

Goodnight, mother; these are sad times, but we must not lose courage. I wish I could see you tonight.

August 1, 1915.

To say that I was delighted will not express my feelings when I got the letter from the Loyalist Chapter, I. O. D. E., enclosing cheque. It was awful good of them to help us here, for I realize the demands for help on every side and it is only natural that they should send to the Canadians first. But O! it is so badly needed and will so do much good here. I had been racking my brain trying to think of a way to scratch up a few pennies, and then this delightful surprise came.

This hospital is called the 'Paradise of the Seventh Region,' for it is so very far ahead of most of the French military hospitals. But while there is a good deal of luxury on one side, such as pleasant airy rooms, comfortable beds, good food and air, on the other hand there is a great lack of what we consider necessities. The first thing I did when I got the letter with the money was to order a foot tub for each floor, slippers for the patients when they are in the house, scissors for the pharmacy and for each floor, and various other small things that I have been longing for and that will save many steps.

Now that the capacity of the hospital has been increased by fifty beds, it is more difficult than ever to get money from the general fund for things of that kind; it really has to be kept for food and heating. We also need instruments and basins, etc., for a table for dressings in the new ward, as we have absolutely nothing.

Then it is so nice to have a fund that we can draw on in case of need. Sometimes the men are terribly poor and cannot afford to get anything for themselves when they leave. Sometimes a ticket for a wife or daughter to come to see them and cheer them up. It is the second time some of these men have been wounded and they have not seen their families for a year.

It is just a year today (August 1st) since mobilization began. At five o'clock in the morning the tocsin sounded and all the village gathered at the Town Hall to read the notice of mobilization. There were many sad and anxious hearts then but many more now, for there is not à family who has not lost someone who is near and dear to them - and still it goes on. I wonder when the end will come.

My prize patient, Daillet, walks down stairs by himself now by holding on to the railing like a child. We are all proud of him. The doctor who sent him here from Besaucon came in the other day to see how he was getting on and he could not believe it when he saw him.

I am almost asleep so I must stop. I made a mistake this morning, got up at half-past four instead of half-past five.

August 15, 1915.

In the face of all the terrible things which are happening one must not worry over little things. I have got to the stage now when I feel as if one should never complain or worry if they have a roof over their heads and enough to eat, and that all one's efforts should be given to helping others.

I feel perfectly overwhelmed with the letters that ought to be written, but cannot find time to do them. I have been up all night and a couple of days. We got thirty new patients last night. They arrived at 3 A. M. and it was half past five before we got them to bed. I did not get any of this lot, as my rooms were full. There were not so many wounded, more sick, rheumatism, bronchitis, etc. One poor man said it was like going directly from hell to heaven; it was the first time he had slept in a bed for a year. Some of them have been wounded for the second time. It is nearly eleven and I must be up early, so goodnight.

August 21, 1915.

Your letter has been long delayed, as they are very strict and holding up the mails again.

We heard this morning that there are French troops guarding the border at Crassier, just half a mile from here. We hear all the Swiss border is to be protected by barbed wire. I do not know what it all means unless it is on account of spies.

We got fifteen more patients last week, one yesterday and one today, but as several went away we have still the same number - eighty-four.

We have had a very busy morning. An inspector arrived just as we were ready to operate, and between the two I did not know whether I was on my head or my heels. Thirty of our men will go off on Monday and we will probably get a train full later in the week.

We have a phonograph with a rasping voice that plays from

morning to night. The soldiers love it; the poor things are so used to noise that they don't seem happy without it, but sometimes I feel as if I could scream.

One of the men got a telegram saying his mother was dying; the doctor gave him forty-eight hours leave - all he could possibly do - so he went home and has just got back; could not stay for the funeral, but was so thankful to have been able to see her. If he had been at the front that would not have been possible - only another sad consequence of the war. Another soldier received the news of the death of his little girl.

Miss Todd took me out in her motor the other day. We had a beautiful run over the mountains; the view was magnificent. We took one of the soldiers with us and he enjoyed himself immensely; it was the first time he had ever been in one.

Sunday, August 29, 1915.

It is pouring rain, it is sad to say, as the soldiers are having a little celebration. A band came from Nejon and the Count de Divonne made a speech, two of the men received their Croix de Guerre, the doctor made such a nice little speech to each of them. It was very touching to see the groups of men, some with arms in slings and others with legs and heads bandaged, and some who could not stand at all, still others were in their beds. The decorations were given in the Grand Salle.

I am not sure if all your letters reach me or not, sometimes

I get two in a week and then again none for three weeks.

Thirty-three men go off tomorrow, some of them cured and back to the front, some who will never be better, and some to go home on convalescence.

Today the florist in the village sent a clothes basket full of roses to the Ambulance for the fete. I thought of you and wished you could have some.

September 5, 1915.

Thanks for the money you sent from a friend in your last letter. I will use it wisely and make it go as far as possible. There will be more suffering this winter than there was last, but they are so brave, these people, they seldom complain of anything.

There is a little woman here whose husband was killed. She makes twenty cents a day selling papers and gets ten cents a day pension. She has three children, the eldest a girl of twelve. I got her a good pair of boots the other day and warm underclothes for the other children. She was so grateful.

Don't worry about me. My expenses are very small, I have not bought any clothes and do not need any this winter.

Today they had a big concert in the hotel, the proceeds go to the Ambulance.

We have had an awful week of rain and cold, but hope for a little more sunshine to thaw us out.

Our good doctor is going to be married next month. I am so

glad, for he lives all alone and needs some one to look after him.

I shall have to go to bed to get warm. There is no heat in this house and when it rains it is like an ice box.

September 11, 1915.

I expect to leave here in two weeks to go to an Ambulance at the front. It is somewhere in the north in Belgium. I think Dr. R is sorry to have me leave, but it will be a much larger field and the kind of a place where there will be much to do. They have all been so nice to me here about helping me get my papers ready to send to the Minister of War, so I do not think there will be any difficulty of my getting through. I go to Paris first, then to Dunkirk, where Mrs. T will meet me, after that my destination is uncertain.

Do not worry if you do not hear from me regularly, for it may be difficult to get mail through. I will write as usual.

I cannot tell you how glad I am to be able to go to the front, for it means a chance to do good work and I shall be so glad to be in the north when B. comes over and nearer the Canadian boys. Even if I cannot see them I shall not feel so far away.

One of my men today got word that his baby, seven months old, had just died and the little girl of two is very ill. He expected to go next week and has been counting the days till he could see them. He has never seen the baby as it was born after the war began - another one of the sad things of this awful war.

Goodnight; I am so glad of the chance of active service.

September 18, 1915.

It was awfully good of Miss W to send the money to me, it is so much needed here. I expect to get off Monday or Tuesday of next week.

September 19, 1915.

My orders came today, and I leave on Tuesday for Paris and on Friday for Dunkirk. I am up to my eyes in work, for there is so much to be done before leaving and new people to break in. Three military nurses arrived yesterday, but it is rather difficult to manage for they know nothing at all about taking care of sick people. They have all been at the front, and wounded too badly to return and sent into an auxiliary service. One is a priest, one a hair dresser and the third a horse dealer; however, they are nice men and are willing to learn, which is a great thing in their favor.

If they are able to raise any money for me I will see that it is wisely spent. There is great need everywhere, and I am proud of the people of St. John, they have done so much.

There is a poor woman who lives in a little village near here. She had two sons - one has been killed in the war, the other a helpless cripple for eighteen years and is not able to move out of his chair. He makes baskets sometimes, but now there is no one to buy the baskets. The mother goes out by the day but can earn so little. I gave him five francs, one of the De Monts dressing gowns and some warm underclothes. He was so grateful, poor boy, and says he will not feel the cold now. His mother is away nearly all day and he sits by the window all alone and depends upon the neighbours coming in to help him from time to time; he is always cheerful and never complains.

The Ws have such a hard time - they get so little of their income since the war began. It has gradually gone down from $3,000.00 per year to $500.00; four of them to live on that amount. So many people are in just the same condition, there is no end to the misery.

I do not know whether it is the French or the English army we are to follow at my new post.

Paris, September 23, 1915.

I am off tomorrow at 7.30 A. M., to Boulogne, then Calais and reach Dunkirk at 9.30 P. M. I have had two very strenuous days and will be glad to rest in the train tomorrow. It took such a time to get my papers in order. The thermometer for the last two days has been about 100.

Mobile NO. 1, France, 1915.

I am really not in France but Belgium. I cannot tell you just where, but it is within ten miles of the firing line, and not far from the place where so many of our boys from home have been sent. I thought when I came here that it would be entirely English, as the lady who gave the hospital is an American married to an Englishman. The English are not far away but they are taken to their own hospitals.

We belong to a little wedge of the French that is in between the English and Belgians. It is a regular field hospital and is composed of a great many portable huts or sheds; some are fitted up as wards, another the operating room, another the pharmacy, another supply room, laundry, nurses' quarters, doctors' quarters, etc. It is a little colony set down in the fields and the streets are wooden sidewalks.

The first night I arrived I did not sleep, for the guns roared all night long, and we could see the flashes from the shells quite plainly; the whole sky was aglow. The French and English guns sounded like a continuous roar of thunder; but when the shells from the German guns landed on this side we could feel a distinct shock, and everything in our little shanty rattled.

Yesterday I saw my first battle in the air between German and French aeroplanes. We could scarcely see the machines, they were so high up in the air, but we could see the flashes from their guns quite distinctly and hear the explosion of the shells. Today a whole fleet of aeroplanes passed over our heads; it was a wonderful sight.

There are about one hundred and fifty beds in all here.

I have been inspected by doctors, captains, generals, and all kinds of people till I am weary. I hope they are satisfied at last, but I cannot go off the hospital grounds until I have two different kinds of passes given to me - one is a permission to go on the roads about here and the other is good as far as Dunkirk.

We have a man in our ward who had a piece of shrapnel the size of an egg in his abdomen; they had to take out about half a yard of intestines, which had been torn to pieces. He was also shot through the shoulder, in the arm and leg. As we got him within two hours after he was wounded there was no infection, and having a clever surgeon he is getting along famously. Another poor chap has lost his right arm and shot through the liver as well as being cut up by piece of shrapnel - he is getting well also. Two have died, and it is a blessing; for to live in darkness the rest of one's life is worse than death. The Germans are using a new kind of gas, bomb that blinds the men.

It is pouring rain tonight and cheerless enough here, but I can only think of the poor men in the trenches.

I got a joyful surprise today - a letter from Mr. Bell enclosing post office order from Mr. Calhoun, of Philadelphia. Nothing gives me so much pleasure as to help these poor people.

It is beginning to get cold. I shall get bed socks for the men, for they have not enough hot water bags to go round and all suffer from cold feet.

I passed Colonel MacLaren's hospital in the train - it is very impressive to see the rows and rows of white tents. I also saw some Canadian nurses in the distance, and did so want to get out and speak to them.

I must go to bed now to get warm. As long as one keeps going the cold is not so apparent but when one sits still it is not pleasant.

There are four English, three American and three French nurses here.

October 3, 1915.

My fund is like the widow's cruse - it never gives out. Somebody is always sending me something. I do hope they all realize how grateful I am and how much good I have been able to do. I have been very careful how I spent it.

A boy of twenty went off today. He had absolutely nothing warm to put on him, so I got him an outfit at Dunkirk. He was almost blown to pieces, poor boy, and he said that one sock was all that was left of his clothes. They provide them with necessary things at the hospital, but sometimes the supply gets a bit low and now it is so cold they need extra underclothing. When he was brought in they put him in a ward by himself because they thought he would not live through the night, he was so terribly wounded. His right arm was gone, he had a bullet in his liver - it is still there - and multiple wounds of head and body. But he made a wonderful recovery and went away very white and weak,

45

but cheerful and confident that he will get something to do that will not require two hands. He has the Médaille Militaire and the Croix de Guerre, and his Lieutenant, Captain and General have all been to see him several times - they say he was a wonderful soldier.

Three of us went to Dunkirk by motor to get various supplies. We saw many interesting things on the way, and in Dunkirk saw the destruction caused by the bombardment. The whole side was out of the church and several houses were simply crushed like a pack of cards. Some of the nurses were in Dunkirk when it was bombarded, and they said the noise was the most terrifying part of it all.

The day we went to Dunkirk we saw a lot of armoured cars. Such curious looking things they are - some are painted with blotches of yellow and green and gray and red and brown so they cannot be distinguished from the landscape. We saw lots of English troops. I looked in vain for Canadians, but they are not far off.

It has been awfully cold so far and rains most of the time. We have decided that we shall just keep putting on clothes like the Italians do in winter and never take anything off.

We get wounded every day, sometimes not more than half a dozen, but as they are almost all seriously wounded we are kept busy.

There have been so many troops moving on lately, that we

thought we would be left without anything to do. We have orders not to do anything that is not absolutely necessary as we may have to move also.

I believe the hospital at Divonne has been taken over by the nuns. I miss the lovely flowers that I had there. I share a small room with two other nurses and there is not much room to spare. We have boxes put up on end for tables and washstands, and there is only one chair. Some of the nurses have tents, two in each. We have had a terrible busy week. All the new ones that came into my ward lived only thirty-six or forty-eight hours - they were too far gone to save. Five went away cured, and they really were cases to be proud of.

I think it was the sweetest thing of little Mary Murray to send me her birthday money for my soldiers. I have been getting them fruit and cigarettes for Sunday. That is the thing that overwhelms me at times - the awful suffering every way one turns.

Last night I could not sleep for the noise of the guns; they must have been bombarding some place near at hand, for the whole earth seemed to shake.

The boys who drive the American ambulance and bring our patients in say this place is a sort of heaven to them they are always glad to get here. Mrs. T does everything she can for them. They are a nice lot of boys and are doing good work.

Some of the poor men who have lost large pieces of their

intestines find the hospital diet a little hard.

Mobile No. 1, November 7, 1915.

Letter writing is done under difficulties here. I have gone to bed in order to keep warm and have a small lantern with a candle in to light the paper.

Thought to be a hopeless case, but everyone must have their chance, three doctors operated at once, amputating leg, an arm and trepanning.
Now as happy as the day is long.

November 15, 1915.

I did not get any further with my letter for the kitty insisted upon playing with the candle and I was afraid we would have a fire, and since then I have been so busy I have not had a minute. We have had three glorious days and have appreciated them, I can tell you. It has been so cold and wet we have all been water-logged.

As for me, I have no word to express my gratitude for all the friends have sent to me. I am quite overwhelmed with all the gifts of money and supplies, but I shall make good use of them and nothing shall be wasted.

The wool which Mrs. S. sent turned up yesterday and I have already given half of it to the women in one of the villages here to knit into socks.

There is a dear old English colonel who has a soup kitchen near the firing line, and he is always looking for socks. He does a great deal of good, for he gets the men when they are carried in from the trenches and gives them hot drinks and hot water bottles, and warm socks when he has them. So many of the men have just straw in their boots and are almost frozen. It makes such a difference if they can get warmed up quickly. Poor souls, they have had a hard time since the heavy rains began. They are brought in here just caked with mud from head to foot.

Oh, how glad I was to get the cheque from the 'Red Cross' Society and the cheque from Miss C. I have written to her and would like to write long letters to every one who is so kind, but there is not time.

This Ambulance was established by an American lady who then gave it to the French government. The expenses of running it are paid by them, but I think Mrs. S pays the nurses and also helps out in the way of extra supplies.

On All Saints Day we went to the little cemetery and decorated the graves of the soldiers who have died in the hospital. There was a special mass and service in the churchyard and the General sent us an invitation. It was pouring rain but I would not have missed it for anything, and I only wish the mothers, wives and sisters could know how beautiful it all was and how tenderly cared for are the last resting-places of their dear ones.

It was a picture I shall never forget. The corner of the little churchyard with the forty new graves so close together, each marked with a small wooden cross and heaped high with flowers – the General standing with a group of officers and soldiers all with bared heads – the nurses and one or two of the doctors from the hospital behind them, and then the village people and refugees – hundreds of them, it seemed to me – and the priest giving his lesson – and all the time the rain coming down in torrents and nobody paying any attention to it. There were no dry eyes and when the General came and shook hands with us afterwards, he could not speak. He is a splendid man, very handsome and a patriot to the backbone – one of the finest types of Frenchmen.

Do not worry about me for I am very well and so glad to be here in spite of the cold and discomforts. Mrs. S's socks and bandages have just come.

November 28, 1915.

It is bitterly cold here, and we feel it more because it is so damp. I can't tell you how thankful I am to be able to get socks and warm things for the men. We can send things to the first dressing station by the ambulances, and from there they go to the trenches at once. Mrs. D's socks came yesterday, and I sent them off to Colonel Noble, who has the soup kitchen at the front. All Mrs. S's have been given away. It was such a good idea to have them white, for they put them on under the others and it often saves the men from being infected by the dye of the stockings.

This morning when I got up my room was like a skating pond, for the moisture had frozen on the floor and the water in the pitcher was solid. The getting up in the morning is the hardest, but after we get started we do not mind the cold.

The patients have plenty of blankets and hot water bottles, so they do not suffer.

Two Zeppelins went over our head yesterday, but fortunately we are too unimportant to be noticed. I suppose that is one of the reasons they will not let us say where we are, for there are so many spies everywhere that can send information.

An English nurse came yesterday; she has had most interesting experiences. She was in Brussels when it was taken by the Germans and was obliged to take care of German soldiers and officers for some time. She said the officers, as a rule, were brutes, but some of the men were very nice and grateful.

For three days and nights the guns have thundered without ceasing. I wonder what it all means?

My kitty keeps all the seventeen dogs that loaf around here in order. Yesterday she chased a big yellow dog, half St. Bernard, down the main sidewalk of the Ambulance. It was a very funny sight, for she was like a little round ball of fury and the poor dog was frightened to death.

December 5, 1915.

Last night we had the most awful wind storm. I thought our little hut would be carried over into the German lines. It rained in torrents and the roof leaked, and I could not get my bed away from the drips, so I put up my umbrella and the kitty and I had quite a comfortable night.

Ben Ali, the poor Arab who was so desperately wounded, was up today for the first time.

I have ordered six dozen pair of socks from Paris. My nice old English Colonel Noble (with the soup kitchen) is always clamoring for them. I think he saves lots of the men from having frozen feet. Madge S's wool is being made into socks by the women of the village.

December 26, 1915.

Christmas is over, and in spite of the under - current of sadness and the suffering the men had a very happy day. In my ward all but one were well enough to enjoy the tree, and they were like a lot of children with their stockings. Christmas Eve one of the orderlies who was on guard helped me decorate the ward and trim the tree, then we hung up their stockings. They had oranges, sweets and cigarettes and some small toys and puzzles and various things of that kind to amuse them.

I had a package for each one in the morning, and, thanks to my good friends at home, was able to give them some nice things. I had a pair of warm socks and gloves for each one, a writing pad and envelopes, pen, pencil, small comb in a case, tooth brush, tooth powder, piece of soap, wash cloth and a small alcohol lamp with solidified alcohol - a thing made especially for the trenches and which delighted them very much - also a small box of sweets, and to several of the very poor ones I gave a small purse with five francs in it. One poor boy said he had never had such a Christmas in his life; he is one of a family of seven, and says that in times of peace it was all they could do to get enough to eat.

Christmas day at four o'clock the tree was lighted, and one of the many priests who act as infirmiers here came round to the different wards and sang carols. He has a very beautiful voice and was much appreciated by the soldiers. Mrs. Turner then came in, followed by an orderly with a huge hamper containing a present for each man. They had a wonderful dinner, soup, raw oysters, (which came from Dunkirk by motor), plum pudding, etc. I could only give my men a bite of pudding to taste it, but they were able to eat the oysters and other things in moderation.

In the other wards, where there were only arms and legs and heads to consider, they had a royal feast. She also gave a grand dinner to all the infirmiers and men on the place - had a tree for them and a present for each one. We also had a good dinner and a present for each. She certainly went to a great deal of trouble and made many people happy.

The next day we divided the things on the trees and each man made a package to send home to his children. They were even more delighted to be able to do this than with their own things.

One poor man in my ward was so ill that I was afraid he would die, so I moved his bed to the end of the ward and put screens around it so that he would not be disturbed and that the others would not be disheartened by seeing him. He was so much better Christmas night that we had great hopes of saving him, but today he died. He was wounded in seven places and one hip was gone. The General came at four o'clock and decorated him. He roused up and saluted and seemed so pleased. In the evening the doctor came to do his dressing and he seemed much better. After the doctor had gone he turned to me and said, 'that Major knows what he is about, he is a corker.'

Ben Ali, my prize Arab, had a wonderful day. He ate too much and had to stay in bed today, but he has been wrapping and unwrapping his presents and having a fine time. He is just like a child, he is so pleased. He has taken a great fancy to me and asked me to visit him after the war is over.

We had midnight mass on Christmas Eve for the infirmiers and personnel of the hospital. One of the empty wards was fitted up as a chapel and a Franciscan monk from Montreal officiated. He is on duty here in the lingerie, and is a splendid man. He is delicate, has some serious heart trouble, so that he need not stay, but he came over to do what he could for his country and his services are invaluable here. His mother was in the north of the country taken by the Germans and he has not been able to get any news of her for more than a year.

We have had orders from headquarters to close all the shutters as soon as the lights are lit, so we feel as if we were shut up in packing cases.

There were a great many aeroplanes flying about today, so I suppose they are expecting an attack of some kind. It is blowing a gale tonight and I feel as if our little shanty would blow over.

It is hard to believe that we are beginning another year. If only it will bring a lasting peace! The boxes have not turned up yet, but they doubtless will one of these days, and we will be all the more glad to see them because we have used up everything else.

I expected to go on night duty immediately after Christmas, but we had such sick people in my ward they did not want to make a change just then.

It is blowing a gale again tonight, and raining in torrents; it seems as if it would never stop raining. The roof of one of the wards was loosened the other night the wind was so strong, so the patients had to be all moved out while it was being mended. Our barracks had to be propped up also, all one side was loose and the rain came in sheets. I frequently go to bed with an umbrella

January 16, 1916.

We have had orders to evacuate all the men who are able to travel, so we got rid of a great many - eighteen went on Tuesday, twenty on Friday and nineteen more are to go next Tuesday.

The roof nearly blew off my ward last night, so my patients had to be moved into the next ward till it is mended. I am going to take advantage of it and have a thorough house cleaning.

Le Roux, the boy who has been here so long and who has

been so terribly ill, died on Tuesday. I had great hopes of him up till the last day. Half an hour after he died the General came to decorate him. I hope they will send the medals to his people, it seems hard that they should have been just too late to give them to him. The next day I went to his funeral – the first soldier's funeral I have seen. I was impressed with the dignity and simplicity of it. The plain deal coffin was covered with a black pall, which had a white cross at the head, the French flag covered the foot and a bunch of purple violets, tied with red, white and blue ribbon, lay between. It was carried in one of the covered military carts.

At three o'clock the little procession started for the cemetery. First came the priest in soldier's uniform, carrying a small wooden cross, on which was written Le Roux's name and the name of his regiment. One of this kind is always put at the head of each grave. Then came three soldiers with guns on their shoulders, then the car bearing the coffin, and on each side three soldiers with arms reversed; directly behind were two infirmiers and three soldiers with guns on their shoulders, we two nurses in our uniforms, then two officers and some more soldiers.

As we went down the road to the little church in R – we passed long lines of soldiers going somewhere, and everyone saluted. A few stray people followed us into the church and afterwards to the graveyard, where we left Le Roux with his comrades who had gone before. I had not been there since All

Saints Day and it was sad to see how many more graves had been added to the line. The ward seems very empty without Le Roux, but I am glad that the poor boy is at rest for he has suffered so long. I am beginning to think that death is the only good thing that can come to many of us.

January 25, 1916.

We have been awfully busy, wounded arriving every night, sometimes nine and sometimes ten, etc. Tonight we have had only six so far, but will probably have some more before eight a.m., they have all been very bad cases. There has been a terrific bombardment every night we have been on duty.

My little tent nearly blew away in the big wind storm, so I had to sleep in the barracks - or rather try to sleep. I did not succeed very well, so today I moved back to the tent. From my bed in the tent I can see the troops passing on the road and aeroplanes in the sky. Today we saw so many we knew it would mean trouble tonight.

The trenches were bombarded, and some of the poor men who were wounded had to lie in the mud and cold for over twelve hours before they could be moved, consequently they arrived here in a pretty bad shape.

One of the men had on a pair of Mrs. D's socks. I had sent them to Colonel Noble and he gave them to the men in the trenches. It has been clear and frosty for two nights, such a relief after all the rain. The hospital is full of very sick men. I am glad to be on night duty for a change.

January 30, 1916.

It has been so cold and damp today that I could not get warm even in bed. I like sleeping out in the little tent and as a rule sleep very well – have a cup of hot tea when they wake us at six o'clock. I wear two pair of socks, beside the rooms are not so frightfully damp since we got up the little stoves; they get dried out once a day, which is a great advantage.

I am sending you some snap shots of my little kitty. We call her 'Antoinette' after the aeroplane, for she makes a noise like the aeroplane when she sings.

When I have a chance I shall go back to Divonne for a rest – it is too far to go home – but there does not seem any chance of it at present. The English nurses who have been here six months will have to go first, and we are more than busy. There are two new nurses coming next week – Canadians, I think. It is very difficult to get nurses up here, there is so much red tape to go through.

You must not worry about me, for I am really very well. The cold and simple life is very healthy, even if it is not always comfortable. I seem to be as strong as an ox and the more I have to do the better I feel.

It is joyful to hear that I am to have some more money. St.

John people certainly have been good. A box came today from Trinity, it had been opened. There is the ambulance, I must run.

February 6, 1916.

We are so busy here that we scarcely know where to turn. It is just a procession of wounded coming and going all the time, for we have to send them off as quickly as possible in order to make room for the new arrivals. Thirty-eight went off last Tuesday and fifteen on Friday, but the beds are filled up again. The last ones we have been getting are so badly wounded that I wonder who can be moved on Tuesday. We have had wild wind and rain for the last week, but today is cold and clear and for the 'first time in weeks it is quiet - the cannonading has been incessant.

Two English aviators were brought in yesterday whose machine fell quite near here; fortunately they are not very badly hurt.

The box from the high school girls came today, and it was like having Christmas all over again - such a nice lot of things there were. I shall have a fine time distributing them.

Here comes the ambulance. One poor man died in the receiving ward and the other two went to the operating room at once. They both have symptoms of gas gangrene, and I am afraid one will lose an arm and the other a leg.

In spite of the cold and wet we keep extraordinarily well.

Four new nurses have come, much to our relief, for the work was getting rather beyond us. Two of them are Canadians from Toronto. They know ever so many people I know. They sailed from St. John at Christmas time and saw so many St. John friends of mine - they said everyone was so good to them. We do not get a minute during the night and some days have been up to lunch time.

February 22, 1916.

There have been two big attacks and we have had our hands full. Since Sunday the cannonading has gone on without ceasing. It seems to be all round us. At night we can see the flashes of the guns quite distinctly, in fact the sky is lit up most of the time. It is like the reflection of a great fire - it would be very beautiful if one could get away from the horror of what it all means.

The aeroplanes were almost as thick as the motors - one came down in a field near the hospital yesterday - the wings were riddled with bullets, but fortunately the aviator was not hurt. We often see Taubes, and Zeppelins have gone over us several times, though I could not recognize them, but the noise was unmistakable. The wounded are nearly all brought in at night so we have our hearts and hands full. The other night twenty-three came in at once so we had to call up the day people to help us; seventeen were operated upon and all are getting well but one.

From the twenty-third July, 1915, until the first January, 1916, seven hundred and fifty patients have been cared for here and sixty six have died. I have had over one hundred wounded come in at night this last month, and as they all come directly from the trenches you can imagine what it means.

Such a fine box came from Mrs. S and F containing bandages, socks, etc., all most welcome.

The ground is white with snow today but it will not stay long.

It is very difficult to get nurses here as a command of the French language is an essential.

The guns are still at it, so there will be much to do tonight.

March 6, 1916.

We have had snow several times this week and it is snowing again today. It is very pretty for a little while but soon melts, and the mud is worse than ever.

I feel that I can never be grateful enough to the people who have enabled me to do so much for these poor men. I am going to order some more pillows, they are things that we need very much. All the lung cases have to sit up in bed and need a great many pillows to make them comfortable. Strange to say we have not lost a lung case and we have had some pretty bad ones. There is one in now who was shot through the lung, and yesterday they took out a long sibber bullet from under his rib;

he will be able to go home next week. When he came in he was in very bad condition and he could not speak for a week. The treatment is to sit them up in bed and give them morphine every day to keep them perfectly quiet, the hemorrhage gradually stops and they get well very quickly. We have had a number of deaths from that awful gas gangrene; there is not much hope when that attacks them.

The bombardments have been so terrible lately that those who are wounded in the morning cannot be taken out of the trenches until night, and then they are in a sad condition.

One day last week, just as I was getting ready to go to bed, some people came out from the village to ask if we could help a poor girl who had been burned. Mrs. Turner and I went at once with all sorts of dressings and found her in a terrible state - her whole body burned - so of course there was no hope. She only lived three days. I went in the mornings to do her dressing and another nurse in the afternoon. She was burned by lighting a fire with oil.

Things are too heavy now for me to get my holiday.

March 19, 1916.

Only ten admissions. All the efforts are being directed against Verdun. The defence has been magnificent, and if only the ammunition holds out there will be no danger of the Germans getting through; but what a terrible waste of good material on both sides.

Mrs. Turner has been obliged to go to Paris and has left me in charge of the hospital. I hope nothing terrible will happen while she is away.

The snow is all gone and we are having rain again.

My kitty is getting very bad and spends all her nights out. She has grown to be just a common ordinary cat now, but she caught a rat the other day, so has become useful instead of ornamental.

March 20, 1916.

I am left in charge of the Ambulance for a time and am a bit nervous, having French, English, American, Canadian and Australian nurses under me.

We had quite an exciting time yesterday watching a German being chased by four French machines. They all disappeared in the clouds so we do not know what happened. Today I counted eleven aeroplanes in the air at once as well as three observation balloons. One aeroplane came so close over the barracks that we could wave to the pilot.

We had a lot of patients out of doors today, some on stretchers, others on chairs, and others had their beds carried out - they enjoyed it so much. We take advantage of all the good weather. It is pouring again tonight and the guns are booming in an ominous manner.

One day last week I went to Poperinghe with Mrs. C. We heard there were some Canadian troops there and I was hoping to find some friends, but the Canadians had been moved; however, we talked with some Tommies, gave them cigarettes and chocolate and had a very interesting time.

March 29, 1916.

Just a week ago a French general was brought in wounded in the leg while he was inspecting the Belgian trenches. We were rather overwhelmed at first, but I arranged a corner of one of the wards and he spent one day and night there while we fixed up an empty ward for him. The next day his wife arrived and she is camping quite contentedly in another corner of the ward.

She, poor woman, has suffered much from the war but is very brave. Her eldest son was killed, her second son is ill at Amiens, and this is the second time the general has been wounded. The first time he was in a hospital for three months. Her nephew, who is like a second son, has also been killed, and his wife, a young woman of twenty-two, taken prisoner by the Germans, and they have had no news of her since September, 1914.

The general's home was in the Aisne district and is, of course, in the hands of the Germans. There is nothing left of the house but the four walls; everything has been packed off to

Germany, all the wood work and metal has been taken for the trenches.

The day the general was brought in, the King of the Belgians came to decorate him, and we were all so disappointed because we did not know about it and only one or two of us saw him. He came in a motor, accompanied only by one officer, and we did not know anything about it until he had gone.

We had another awful storm last night - wind and rain. Windows blew off and doors blew in, and one poor little night nurse was blown off the sidewalk and nearly lost in the mud.

One day last week I was surprised by a visit from two Canadian boys. They were doing some engineering work in this section and when they heard there were Canadians here they came over to see us. One was from Toronto, the other from Fort William. I gave them one of the Christmas cakes and some cigarettes. They went away very happy.

I was hoping to get news of some of our boys, but they did not know any of them personally but expected to see some of the men from the Twenty-sixth in a few days. I told them to tell any who could to come and see us. I have been hoping ever since their visit to see B or S or D walk in some day. It is awful to know that they are so near and not be able to see them.

April 8, 1916.

A cheque came today from the De Monts Chapter, I.O.D.E., which gave me great joy. It touches me to tears to think of the way the St. John people have helped me. I wish they could have a look in here and see how much more I have been able to do on account of the help they have sent me.

There is a soldier who helps here by the name of Baquet; his wife has just taken three orphan children, the oldest six years old, to look after, in addition to her own four, her mother and her mother-in-law. There are no men left to do the work on the farm, and poor Baquet did not know how they could get along. I gave him one hundred francs and told him it was from my friends in Canada. He did not want to take it at first, saying it was sent for the wounded, but I explained to him that it was sent to me to help the soldiers and the soldiers' families. He said it would mean so much to his wife, she works from four in the morning till dark. They are the sort of people who deserve help, and it is such a joy to be able to lighten their burdens a little.

We have only about eighty patients at present, but they keep us busy. The two men who came in last have been so terribly wounded. We have had a number of cases of gas gangrene. They are trying to cure them with a new sort of serum. Two of the men really seem to be getting better. Four cases were brought in yesterday. One poor man died at noon, and I was glad he did not live any longer; another they had to operate on in the afternoon and take his leg off. He was in very bad shape last night but this morning he surprised every one by asking for pen and paper to write to his mother, and says he feels fine.

Our wounded general left today. He could not say enough nice things about the hospital. He said he was so glad he had been brought here, not only on his own account, but he was so glad to see how wonderfully his men were taken care of. The guns have been going incessantly for the past two days, and we hear that the English have taken four trenches. I have also heard that some Canadians have come over lately and our B may be only four or five miles from me. I asked the general if it would be possible for me to find out; he said he would inquire and if B is anywhere in reach he would get me a pass to go and see him. I feel as if I would start out and walk to try and find him; but alas! one cannot get by the sentries without proper papers.

I hope my fur-lined cape has not gone to the bottom. I think I shall still need it in June, for after two wonderful sunshiny days we are again freezing. Sunday and Monday were like days in June and we moved the beds of the patients out in the grass and others were on stretchers. We had the phonograph going, served lemonade, biscuits, sweets and cigarettes. They had a wonderful time and all slept like tops the next night.

I think I shall have to find a new job when the war is over, for I don't think I shall ever do any more nursing.

I am trying to find a lot of straw hats like 'cows' breakfasts' and cheap parasols to protect their heads when they are taking sun baths.

The dressings are taken down and one thickness of gauze only left over the wound, and they are left in the sun from twenty minutes to two hours according to what they can stand.

April 11, 1916.

Yesterday we had quite an interesting time with air crafts. The machine came down so close, that we could see the pilot and his assistant who waved to us that they were going to throw something to us. A package landed, almost in the pond. It turned out to be a letter tied up in a handkerchief with some shot as weight. It was from the English boys who were patients here for a while; they told us they would pay us a visit some day. We could see the machine gun in front of the aeroplane quite distinctly. In the afternoon there was another excitement - a German machine chased by several French. It looked from below as if they had got him, but they all disappeared in the clouds and we did not know the result of the fight.

At nine o'clock there was a terrific explosion as if a bomb had dropped just outside the gate. We all rushed out and could hear the aeroplane distinctly, but could not see it; no damage was done near us. We have just heard that the bomb landed just outside the village doing no damage.

Thanks for the toilet articles, they are a wise selection. What we before considered necessities we now know are luxuries. We have just got off a motor full of convalescents going home on permission. I hope they will get a month, some of them have been in the trenches twenty months.

May 3, 1916.

I got a lot of linen hats and Chinese umbrellas to keep the sun off the patients when they are out of doors.

The two Canadian nurses are a joy to work with, for they have had splendid training and are the kind that will go till they drop. We have a wounded German prisoner who was brought in three days ago. The poor boy had to lose his right arm, and was at first terrified of every one. He expected to be ill - treated, but now that he sees he gets the same treatment as all the other patients he is happy and contented and very glad to be with us.

I thought if I ever saw a German in these regions I would be capable of killing him myself, but one cannot remember their nationality when they are wounded and suffering.

I am sending you a photo of the Queen of the Belgians, who visited us and was very nice; she spoke so highly of the Canadians and of the splendid work they had done.

Paris, May 24, 1916.

I left Dunkirk Thursday morning in time to escape the bombs, and stopped off at Etaples to look up some of our friends at the Canadian hospital. Dr. MacL had left for London but I saw M D, and M P

Etaples is a real city of hospitals now. I saw the St. John Ambulance and the Canadian unit; they are both most interesting, so well organized.

Captain T took me to the station in a motor, for which I was glad, as it is two miles, and the walk over in the sun was as much as I wanted. Arrived at Paris at five the next morning rather weary, had a hot bath, the first in a real tub for eight months, and when I went to bed that night I slept for nearly twenty-four hours.

Divonne-Les-Bains, May 30, 1916.

I did not go to the Grand Hotel for reasons of economy. This is a clean little place and I am quite comfortable but I miss the bathroom and the balcony.

There are no patients at the Ambulance here for the moment. All the fighting is in the north and at Verdun. Poor Verdun - it is terrible there, one hundred days and still no let up - I think there will be no men left in France before long and then the English will have to take their turn. When will it all end?

Divonne is as beautiful as ever, and so quiet and peaceful one would not realize that there was a war if it were not for the fathers and sons who will never come back, and the women who are struggling to make both ends meet.

I have had news of several of my old patients who were here. Daillet, who was paralyzed, is at Vichy and can walk two miles with crutches, two others have been killed and many of the others back in the trenches.

I have not been able to sleep, it is so quiet.

Mobile No. 1, France, June 20, 1916.

Today I went over to Poperinghe to look up Margaret H. She is in charge of the Canadian clearing hospital and is doing a wonderful work. They have been getting all the wounded from this last fight - receive one day, evacuate the next, and the third day clean up and get ready again. It is wonderfully organized; the trains come right up to the hospital and there is a nurse for each car, so the patients are well looked after. Margaret has been mentioned in despatches, I believe. I am so glad, for she certainly deserves it.

June 25, 1916.

I went over for Margaret H in the motor. She went with me to the cemetery near the hospital and I put some roses on the grave of one of our St. John boys. I wish his mother could see how well cared for it is. Margaret came back to tea with us.

Today I have been specializing a man who has developed tetanus. I would almost wish that he would die, for he has no hands, and has a great hole in his chest and back, but strange to say he wants to live, is so patient and so full of courage. When I have cases like this one I am always so grateful to the people who have helped me in my work. If they could see the comforts that can be given by a bottle of cologne or a dozen oranges they would be rewarded.

Our medicine chef was a prisoner in Germany for eleven months. The things that he tells us makes one's blood boil. One cannot imagine human beings as brutal as the Germans are. When they came into the town where he had his hospital, they shot all the wounded that were left and eight of his orderlies who stayed with him. He expected to be shot also, but they needed his services so took him prisoner.

July 16, 1916.

Another rainy day and as cold as the dickens, but we are glad to get through the summer without extreme heat or a pest of flies.

My tetanus case is really getting better.

Last week I went to a concert given at R for the soldiers who are resting. It was one of the nicest I have ever been at. I did not want to go, for I don't feel like any kind of gaiety, but

Mrs. T insisted. There were only three ladies present, the rest of the salle was filled with soldiers just from the trenches. The concert was held in a stable.

Some English and Canadian officers, who are on construction work near here, have been coming to see us. One is Major H, who was on the Courtenay Bay work at St. John.

July 29, 1916.

We are nearly eaten up with the mosquitoes so I have been to Dunkirk to get some mosquito netting.

Mrs. T gave a grand concert to the men on the anniversary of the opening of this hospital. Denries, from the Opera Comique in Paris, and Madame Croiza, from the opera in Paris, sang. The Prince of Teck was here and in my ward, he was so nice to the patients. We had French, English and Belgian generals, colonels and officers of various kinds.

NO. 3 Canadian Casualty Station, July 31, 1916.

I got twenty-four hours permission and came out here to spend the night with nursing Sister Margaret Hare, hoping to get some news of B. I have found out where he is and that he has been on rest and went back to the trenches today. They are usually on duty eight days and off eight, so Margaret is going to send him word when he next comes off to come here and I will come over and meet him.

I do hope we will be able to make connection. It is so hard to be so near and yet not be able to see him. If he is wounded he will have to pass through No. 10 Clearing Station, which is right next to this. I have left my name and address at the office, so if he should be brought in they will telephone to me and I can get over to him in half an hour.

The patients here are so well taken care of. They have had a light day. I helped her a little in the dressing room this morning, saw some of the men who had come in last night, saw three operations. There is a very clever English surgeon here and several McGill men. It is a scorching hot day.

My tetanus patient is quite cured, is beginning to walk about.

Mobile NO. 1, August 14, 1916.

We have had a strenuous and exciting week. It began with a visit from the King of the Belgians, who came to decorate three of my men who had fought in the trenches with conspicuous bravery. He visited all the wards and talked with the soldiers. Like all the royalty I have met so far, he is extraordinarily simple - wore no decorations or distinguishing marks of any kind. We were all presented to him in turn and shook hands with him.

The next day we got twenty gas cases and several badly wounded men - one Canadian from Ontario and two English boys, one was a policeman in London. I asked the Ontario man how he happened to get to our Ambulance, he said, 'he'd be blessed if he knew,' he was working on the lines which run right up to the trenches when the warning for gas was given. He started to put on his helmet and the next thing he knew he was in a 'Red Cross' ambulance on the way to the hospital. He is getting on splendidly but we lost four of the gas cases. It is the worst thing I have seen yet, much worse than the wounded, and the nursing is awfully hard, for they cannot be left a moment until they are out of danger.

August 28, 1916.

I have met our boy B at his rest camp not very far from here. It was a joy to find him looking so well, and big and brown.

September 9, 1916.

Rain, continuous rain. The guns have been roaring without any let-up for three days and nights, and our little barracks are nearly shaken to pieces. We have had several warnings of gas attacks, but fortunately nothing has happened. One of the orderlies kept his mask on all night and everyone was surprised that he was alive next morning, they are the most awful smelling things you can imagine.

We have never seen so many aeroplanes as during this past week. This morning we counted eighteen in a row.

Mrs. T is going to organize another hospital on the Somme

and is going to keep this one as well. She certainly has done a splendid work. We are all hoping that the fighting will be over before Christmas.

Nurse and nephew meeting in France, one serving with the French, the other with the Canadian B.E.F.

October 1, 1916.

The rain has begun, so I suppose we may expect to be under water for the rest of the winter, but things are going well for us, so we must hope on; but oh, how dreadful it all is!

A stationary balloon that is not far from here, used as a Belgian observation post, was struck by a bomb from an aeroplane and we saw it fall in flames. The men who were in it jumped out with parachutes and both escaped without injury.

Broterl, the famous French sniper and poet, came the other day to sing for the soldiers. He is wonderful, and sang all sorts of songs that he had composed in the trenches. The men were enchanted, it does such a lot of good, for it makes them forget for a time.

One of our orderlies has just got word that one of his brothers has been killed at the Somme, another is dangerously wounded in the head, and a third has lost his leg - he has six brothers, all at the front.

One of the men in my ward got word of the death of his brother also. He was a stretcher bearer and was helping a German officer who was wounded. As soon as the German got to a place of safety he shot the poor man who had been helping him.

I am nearly frozen tonight and will have to go to bed.

October 9, 1916.

Our Bayard has come through the Courcelette fight safely, where the New Brunswickers did such wonders; but Oh, at such a terrible cost.

It has been very cold and rainy here. I am afraid the bad weather has set in.

Wish you would send me an aluminum hot water bottle for Christmas, another pair of Indian moccasins, and fill up the corners of the box with malted milk and maple sugar.

I shall never forget the poor little Breton who said when he saw me - as he roused a little when we were taking him from the ambulance, 'maintenant je suis sauvé' (Now I am saved).

I have just received a cheque from the Rothesay Red Cross. Since I began, my fund has never entirely given out, and I have been able to give such a lot of pleasure and comfort to the men.

If any one wants to know what to send me you might suggest Washington coffee like Lady T sent. It was a great success.

I am too cold to write any more, so goodnight.

I wish I had some of Maggie's crullers and squash pie, but the French don't know anything about squash pies.

Our poor man with a broken back has been moved to a hospital near his home so his family can see him. We sent him on a mattress, fixed up with pillows and cushions so that he did not suffer at all on the journey.

When I have any one who is so ill as he was I bless the good people at home who have made it possible for me to give them what they need.

The guns are busy tonight, so I suppose we will be tomorrow.

November 12, 1916.

I have not had any home letters for three weeks. The Twenty-sixth have a great reputation here and St. John can be proud of them.

November 19, 1916.

We have been shaken almost to pieces with vibrations from the guns, these last three days. What must it be close at hand? On Wednesday we had a visit from the Taubes again. I could not sleep for the noise of the machines, so I went out to see what was happening. We could see the bombs dropping all around us, but fortunately none came very near.

November 26, 1916.

How we laughed over your stories. Send us some more when you have them, anything to make us laugh. It is strange how one can laugh in spite of everything. I don't think we could live through it if it were not for the funny and foolish things that happen.

I got a letter from our boy today. It is such a relief to see the dirty little envelopes with the address in pencil. There is never much news, but just to know that he is alive is enough.

December 9, 1916.

We have all been a little worried about Christmas this year, fearing that we should not be able to give the men a really good dinner. We have all been getting contributions and are turning them into the general fund, and now comes this fat cheque from the Canadian Red Cross at St. John for my beloved Poilus. How can I ever thank them enough for their generous gift!

All anxiety on the dinner score is now removed. We have about two hundred and fifty, counting infirmiers and men that work about the hospital - they are soldiers who have been in the trenches for nearly two years, or been disabled through wounds or sickness, or exchanged prisoners from Germany unfit for military service. They call the hospital 'le petit Paradis des blessés' and are so glad to be sent here. A man was brought in here the other day who was wounded for the second time, but he did not mind in the least about his wounds, he was so glad to get back. He is delighted because he will not be well enough to leave before Christmas.

We sent to England for some popcorn, and today the men have been like a lot of happy children stringing the corn for the tree. They had never seen it before and were much interested.

We made quite a successful popper out of a fly screen and a piece of wire netting.

The other night we were talking over the various experiences we have had since the beginning of the war - the terrible things we have seen - the sad stories we have heard, and the strange but very true friendships we have formed - and we all agree that we could never have carried on our work in such a satisfactory way if it had not been for the gifts which have come from time to time from our home friends. The extra food that we have been able to give to the very sick men has made all the difference in the world to their recovery, and then the warm clothing when they go out, and the bit of money to help them over the hard place. You cannot imagine how much it means to them.

I remember so well one poor little man who had reached the limit of endurance, send when I found the sleepless nights were due to worry and not to pain, the whole pitiful little story came out. His wife was ill, his sister-in-law dead and there were six children to be looked after - the eldest a boy of eleven - and no money. As long as his wife had been able to run the farm they had been able to get along, but she had given out. The French soldier only gets five cents a day, so he had nothing to send them.

He cried like a baby when I told him I could help him. We sent off a money order for one hundred francs the next day, and I wish you could have seen the change in that man. That little sum of money put things straight six months ago and now everything is going well. But he will never forget, and both he and his wife have a very warm feeling in their hearts for the good people across the sea who came to their rescue in a time of need. When I begin to talk of my beloved French it is hard to stop.

January 1, 1917.

The men had a wonderful Christmas day. They were like a happy lot of children. We decorated the wards with flags, holly, mistletoe, and paper flowers that the men made, and a tree in each ward. You cannot imagine how pretty they were. Each patient began the day with a sock that was hung to the foot of their bed by the night nurses. In each was an orange, a small bag of sweets, nuts and raisins, a handkerchief, pencil, tooth brush, pocket comb and a small toy that pleased them almost more than anything else, and which they at once passed on to their children. They had a fine dinner: jam, stewed rabbit, peas, plum pudding, fruit, nuts, raisins and sweets. The plum puddings were sent by the sister of one of the nurses.

In the afternoon the trees were lighted and we had the official visit of the medicine chef and all the staff. After the festivities were over we began preparing for the tree for the refugee children. We had thought that we would have enough left over to manage for fifty children, but the list grew to one hundred and twenty-five.

The mayor of the village let us have a large room in his house, as the first place we had chosen was too small. We had the tree on Sunday afternoon and three hundred and thirty-one children arrived. Fortunately we had some extra things so there was enough of something to go around. They had a lovely time, each one got a small toy, a biscuit, and most of them a small bag of sweets and an orange. The oranges and sweets gave out, but there was enough biscuits and toys, but there was nothing left.

We are all dead tired, for we worked like nailers for the past two weeks; but it was worth while, for we were able to make a great many people happy, and now we are sending off packages to the trenches - things that came too late for Christmas.

We expect to move this month. It will be an awful business breaking up here, for all the barracks have to be taken to pieces and moved with us. We have begun to take an inventory, and to pack up, but I do not know just where we will move to, the papers are not in order yet. It is hard to believe that another year of war has begun.

Postscript

Editor's Note from Diggory Press:

We thought that the following item that we came across in our research may be of interest to readers. It comes from the Saint John Globe Newspaper of New Brunswick, Canada, and is dated April 26, 1926.

The Late Miss Agnes Warner

The quiet modesty of Nursing Sister, Agnes Warner, and the high ideal of duty, characteristic of a daughter of General Warner, and which were the constant influences in her whole life made it impossible for Miss Warner to speak of her own achievements during the years of the Great War.

In France when war was declared she gave her services and her knowledge to the little town of Divonne-Les-Bains, close to the Swiss border, and here helped in a way that has been but dimly realized by those who only know war from hearsay.

From the very outset of hostilities Miss Warner was attached to the French War Department, and she had received again and again assurances from France of the deep sense of gratitude that was felt for her untiring efforts on behalf of the soldiers and of the villagers with whom she was associated. Her interest did not confine itself wholly to the soldiers in hospitals for she knew the families of the wounded men, and many a poor French soldier went back to the trenches happier and more able to go on with the grim work of the war because of the money that Miss Warner sent to the poor mother struggling alone with the family, sustained by the indomitable courage and faith of France: many a word of cheer was sent by Miss Warner, herself overworked and worn, to waiting women telling of the husband of the son, the brother, the father from whom no word has gone for long months.

Everybody, said the author of *A Little Green Door* in France was better because of Agnes Warner, who was never discouraged, never unhappy, and who always in the empty depths of purse found the needed centime.

Miss Warner herself has told of the way she herded odds and ends to the amusement of her associates and how often she was able from the pile of apparently useless articles that filled one corner of her apt, to save the situation. For she was not then or ever in a large and well equipped hospital, nor on the highway of communication, but generally in Mobile Hospital

No 1. at Bevereu so close to the French firing lines that the men came to her deep in the mud of the trenches and needing everything in the way of care and comfort. She had but one thought and that was of her men.

At no time had she said a great deal of the life she "endured." Her letters published in part in *My Beloved Poilus* are perhaps her greatest expression of these years in which she gave so unsparingly of herself. France was to her a country apart, the home of brave men and courageous women, a courage and bravery that could scarcely be put into words, but has enriched her life, just as she, all unconsciously has brought into theirs, the knowledge of a fine sweet, woman whose tenderness and sympathy, who knowledge and skill were freely given for them and their cause.

At the Sunday Morning service in Trinity Church, Rev. C. Gordon Lawrence made feeling reference to Miss Warner's death. He spoke of her as a woman of whom Saint John had to be proud. Her book, *My Beloved Poilus* Mr. Lawrence said, had been placed with the war records in the French archives and her service to the French soldiers would never be forgotten. Mr. Lawrence said that to her aged mother and the members of the bereaved family the deepest sympathy of the congregation was extended in their hour of sorrow.

On Sunday afternoon the funeral of Miss Warner took place.

87

A short service was held at her mother's residence early in the afternoon conducted by Rev. C. Gordon Lawrence. The service in the church was at 3 o'clock and there was a very large congregation in attendance. The Red Cross Society was represented by a special delegation.

His Lordship Bishop Richardson read the lesson, and Mrs. (this is what is printed, but it likely should be Mr.) Lawrence conducted the service. The full choir of the church led in the singing of the hymns *Peace, Perfect, Peace* and *O Love That Will Not Let Me Go*. J.S. Ford was at the organ.

The pall-bearers were J. H. A. L. Fairweather, Percy L. Fairweather, Lieut. Colonel Alexander McMillan, S. A. M. Skinner, F. M. Keator and Lieut. Colonel W. H. Harrison, MLA.

Internment was in Fernhill Cemetery and many beautiful flowers were placed on the field of honour plot.

OTHER BOOKS YOU MAY LIKE FROM DIGGORY PRESS

'A War Nurse's Diary: Sketches from a Belgian Field Hospital'
Anon   ISBN 0951565575

'Mademoiselle Miss'
Letters from an American Girl in a French Army Hospital at the Front
Anon, ISBN 1905363109

'FANNY Goes to War'
Pat Beauchamp, ISBN 1905363052

A VAD in France
Olive Dent, ISBN 1905363095

'The Nightingale Sisters, the Making of a Nurse in 1800's America'
Rosalind Franklin, ISBN 0951565583

'The Nurse's Calling: Practical Hints to Nurses in the Early 1900's'
Harriet Camp Lounsbery, RN, ISBN 0951565591

'The Edwardian Baby for Mothers & Nurses'
Mrs. J Langston Hewer (Midwife), ISBN 1905363060

'When The Nightingale Sang: A Nurse's Life in the 1950's & 1960's'
Rosalind Franklin, ISBN 0951565532

'Ambulance No 10: A Driver's Letters from the French Front
Leslie Buswell, ISBN 1905363036

'Only a Dog: A Dog's Devotion to his Master in the First World War'
Bertha Whitridge Smith, ISBN 1905363079

PLUS MANY MORE!

MOST OF THESE TITLES CAN BE ORDERED FROM
ANY GOOD BOOKSTORE AND ARE AVAILABLE ON
BARNES AND NOBLE & AMAZON.COM

THEY CAN ALSO BE ORDERED FROM US DIRECT AT
WWW.DIGGORYPRESS.COM

Printed in the United Kingdom
by Lightning Source UK Ltd.
104893UKS00002B/67-72